OPENGL
SUPERBIBLE

THE COMPLETE GUIDE TO OPENGL PROGRAMMING FOR WINDOWS NT AND WINDOWS 95

Richard S. Wright, Jr.
and Michael Sweet

WAITE GROUP PRESS™

A Division of

Sams Publishing

Corte Madera, CA

PUBLISHER: Mitchell Waite
ASSOCIATE PUBLISHER: Charles Drucker

ACQUISITIONS MANAGER: Jill Pisoni

EDITORIAL DIRECTOR: John Crudo
PROJECT EDITOR: Kurt Stephan
CONTENT EDITOR: Harry Henderson
COPY EDITOR: Carol Henry
TECHNICAL REVIEWER: Jeff Bankston

PRODUCTION DIRECTOR: Julianne Ososke
PRODUCTION MANAGER: Cecile Kaufman
PRODUCTION EDITOR: Aubrey Wallace
COVER DESIGN: Tina Quarequio
INTERIOR DESIGN: Tina Quarequio, Christi Payne Fryday
PRODUCTION: Christi Payne Fryday
ILLUSTRATIONS: Pat Rogondino

Printed in the United States of America
96 97 98 99 • 10 9 8 7 6 5 4 3 2 1

Library of Congress Cataloging-in-Publication Data
    Wright, Richard S, 1965–
        OpenGL superbible / Richard S. Wright, Jr. and Michael Sweet.
            p. cm.
        Includes index.
        ISBN 1-57169-073-5
        1. Computer graphics.   2. OpenGL.   3. Three-dimensional display systems.
I. Sweet, Michael, 1969–   II. Title.
T385.W73 1996
006.6 --dc20

                                                                        96-22645
                                                                        CIP

Dedications

Dedicated to the memory of Richard S. Wright, Sr.
I Thessalonians 4:16

—*Richard S. Wright, Jr.*

To my folks for putting a computer terminal in front
of me at age six, and to my girlfriend, Sandra, for
putting up with me while I worked on this book.

—*Michael Sweet*

Message from the
Publisher

WELCOME TO OUR NERVOUS SYSTEM

Some people say that the World Wide Web is a graphical extension of the information superhighway, just a network of humans and machines sending each other long lists of the equivalent of digital junk mail.

I think it is much more than that. To me, the Web is nothing less than the nervous system of the entire planet—not just a collection of computer brains connected together, but more like a billion silicon neurons entangled and recirculating electro-chemical signals of information and data, each contributing to the birth of another CPU and another Web site.

Think of each person's hard disk connected at once to every other hard disk on earth, driven by human navigators searching like Columbus for the New World. Seen this way, the Web is more of a super entity, a growing, living thing, controlled by the universal human will to expand, to be more. Yet, unlike a purposeful business plan with rigid rules, the Web expands in a nonlinear, unpredictable, creative way that echoes natural evolution.

We created our Web site not just to extend the reach of our computer book products but to be part of this synaptic neural network, to experience, like a nerve in the body, the flow of ideas, and then to pass those ideas up the food chain of the mind. Your mind. Even more, we wanted to pump some of our own creative juices into this rich wine of technology.

TASTE OUR DIGITAL WINE

And so we ask you to taste our wine by visiting the body of our business. Begin by understanding the metaphor we have created for our Web site—a universal learning center, situated in outer space in the form of a space station. A place where you can journey to study any topic from the convenience of your own screen. Right now we are focusing on computer topics, but the stars are the limit on the Web.

If you are interested in discussing this Web site or finding out more about the Waite Group, please send me e-mail with your comments and I will be happy to respond. Being a programmer myself, I love to talk about technology and find out what our readers are looking for.

Sincerely,

Mitchell Waite

Mitchell Waite, C.E.O. and Publisher

200 Tamal Plaza
Corte Madera CA 94925
415-924-2575
415-924-2576 fax

Internet email:
support@waite.com

Website:
http://www.waite.com/waite

CREATING THE HIGHEST QUALITY COMPUTER BOOKS IN THE INDUSTRY

Waite Group Press
Waite Group New Media

About the Authors

Richard S. Wright, Jr. works for Visteon Corporation in Maitland, Florida, developing Windows-based applications for the healthcare industry. Richard first learned to program in the eighth grade in 1978 on a paper terminal. At age 16, his parents let him buy a computer instead of a car, and he sold his first computer program less than a year later. When he graduated from high school, his first job was teaching programming and computer literacy for a local consumer education company. He studied electrical engineering and computer science at the University of Louisville's Speed Scientific School and made it to his senior year before his career got the best of him. A native of Louisville, Kentucky, he now lives with his wife and three children in sunny Lake Mary, Florida. When not programming or dodging hurricanes, Richard is an amateur astronomer, a beach bum, and Sunday School teacher.

Michael Sweet works at the Chesapeake Test Range at Patuxent River, Maryland, and is co-owner of Easy Software Products, a small software firm specializing in computer graphics on Silicon Graphics workstations. He first started using a computer terminal at the age of six and sold his first program at 12. Michael was hired as a consultant doing computer graphics while finishing his bachelors degree in computer science at the SUNY Institute of Technology in Utica/Rome, New York. He moved to Maryland shortly after graduating. When he has free time, he enjoys cycling, photography, and playing the trumpet.

Table of Contents

Contents

Acknowledgments

There are many people who provided inspiration, technical assistance, ideas, and just lots of really strong iced tea when I badly needed it. Most of all, I wish to acknowledge my own family's sacrifice: Thank you to LeeAnne, my wife, who gave up countless nights, weekends, and quiet evenings, not to mention taking on many extra responsibilities at home so her husband could "get famous." Many thanks to my three children (Sara, Stephen, and Alex), who missed not a few bedtime stories, trips to the park, and bike rides, or who just got grumped at for no reason other than that Daddy hadn't slept in a week. No career achievement would have been worth losing them. I know how fortunate I am that at the end of this I can still have my cake and eat it, too.

Many thanks go out to all the people at Waite Group Press, who really brought the book together. Special thanks to John Crudo for getting my foot in the door a few years ago, and for recommending me for my first writing assignment before my first "real" book. Thanks to Harry Henderson for keeping me on track and encouraging me whenever I started feeling sorry for myself. Thank you to Kurt Stephan for seeing me through, and for being flexible but firm with the schedule whenever disaster struck, or when I decided to suddenly change the fabric of the universe (usually over a weekend before a deadline). Lest I forget, thanks to Jill Pisoni and Joanne Miller, who got the book rolling in the first place—Jill for pulling teeth at one particular software company, and Joanne for sticking through four or five title changes, countless proposal revisions, three revisions of a sample chapter, and a hurricane before this thing took off. Finally, thank you to Mitch Waite himself for helping me shape the first "prototype" chapter, not to mention introducing me to the game Mech Warrior 2.

Credit and thanks also go out to Mike Sweet, author of Chapters 11 through 16 and 18, who jumped in at the last minute and bailed me out when my first co-author fell through. Thanks to Jeff Bankston for checking all the samples and for pointing out the important fact that not everyone has a 24-bit graphics card.

I also would like to thank everyone in the OpenGL community at large. I spent a lot of time in the OpenGL newsgroup asking and answering questions, and from there much of the content of the book was shaped. Special thanks to Hock San Lee at Microsoft, who answered many questions on and off line, and provided me with advance material on the new OpenGL features in NT 4.0. John Schimpf at SGI and Robert Weideman at Template graphics were also very helpful.

—*Richard S. Wright, Jr.*

Many thanks to Harry Henderson, Jeff Bankston, and, of course, Kurt Stephan for making this book come together so quickly.

—*Michael Sweet*

Introduction

Welcome to *OpenGL SuperBible*! The first time I ever heard of OpenGL was at the 1992 Win32 Developers Conference in San Francisco. Windows NT 3.1 was in early beta (or late alpha) and many vendors were present, pledging their future support for this exciting new platform. Among them was a company called Silicon Graphics, Inc. (SGI). They were showing off their graphics workstations and playing video demos of special effects from some popular movies. NT was running on MIPS processors—now owned by SGI—but their primary purpose in this booth was to promote a new 3D graphics standard called OpenGL. It was based on SGI's proprietary IRIS GL and was fresh out of the box as a graphics standard. Significantly, Microsoft was pledging future support for OpenGL in Windows NT.

I had to wait until the beta release of NT 3.5 before I got my first personal taste of OpenGL. Those first OpenGL-based screensavers only scratched the surface of what was possible with this graphics API. Like many other people, I struggled through the Microsoft help files and bought a copy of the OpenGL Programming Guide (now called simply "The Red Book" by most). The Red Book avoids platform issues and uses for all its examples the Auxiliary (AUX) library, a platform-independent program framework for OpenGL graphics.

At that time, the Red Book was the only book available for learning OpenGL. Though quite thorough in its coverage of OpenGL functions, it is lacking in two important respects. First, it is not a primer. Whatever the intent of the authors, the book assumes a substantial working knowledge of 3D graphics concepts in general. The Red Book's second drawback is its platform independence. As a Windows developer, I needed answers to some important questions, such as how to use a .BMP file as a texture, how to create an OpenGL-usable palette for an 8-bit display device, and how to use all those "wiggle" functions Microsoft threw in.

OpenGL SuperBible fills in those gaps. I wanted to provide a 3D graphics introduction and an OpenGL tutorial rolled into one. In addition, I approached the whole subject within the context of the single most popular desktop operating system of all time, Microsoft Windows. And I added a Reference Section of thorough function definitions at the end of each chapter, making this book a good complement to the Waite Group line of bible reference books.

Who This Book Is For

This book will suit a wide audience of OpenGL and Windows programmers. Windows programmers wanting to learn about 3D graphics and how to implement them using

OpenGL will find what they need. So will experienced Windows and 3D graphics programmers wanting to learn more about the industry standard OpenGL. This book will also be of value to seasoned OpenGL programmers who have a workstation background but need some assistance porting their applications and experience to the Microsoft Windows platforms.

System Requirements for OpenGL

OpenGL is not available on the 16-bit versions of Microsoft Windows (3.1, 3.11, and so forth) from Microsoft. Microsoft added OpenGL to Windows NT 3.5, and to Windows 95 via a separate distribution of some DLLs. (These DLLs are available via Microsoft's FTP and Web sites and are included on this book's CD, in the \Windows95 subdirectory.)

OpenGL SuperBible does not attempt to cover any third-party OpenGL or OpenGL-like libraries for the 32- or 16-bit environments. Programmatically, OpenGL used under Windows 95 is the same as OpenGL used under Windows NT. The first set of DLLs shipped by Microsoft for Windows NT supports all of the OpenGL 1.0 functions that are also available under Windows NT 3.5 and 3.51. OpenGL 1.1 functions are being added to Windows NT 4.0, and a new set of DLLs should be ready for Windows 95 by the time this book ships. See the readme.txt file on the CD for any late-breaking information.

All of the samples in the book should run fine on a fast 486 (that's a "real" 486, mind you, which means a built-in math coprocessor!) with at least 8MB of RAM. Most programming environments will require at least this much horsepower, anyway. If you're interested, all the code in the book and on the CD was developed and found to run acceptably on a 90MHz Pentium with 32MB of RAM and a 16/24-bit color display card. You will need a display card capable of at least 256 colors (an 8-bit color card). There is significant improvement in OpenGL's speed and appearance when you give it a good color depth to work with. If you can run in a mode that gives you 65,000 or more colors, your results will be even better.

Language

With the exception of two chapters that specifically deal with C++ frameworks, all the source code in this book is written in C. The choice between C and C++ can become an almost religious crusade between two warring camps. It is reasonable to expect that any competent C++ programmer can also follow well-structured C code, but the converse is not always true. There is a popular C++ library for OpenGL called Open Inventor; any attempt here to build a C++ class library around OpenGL would be a duplication of an already fine effort and is beyond the scope and purpose of this book anyway. This brings us to our choice of tools.

Compilers

All of the sample code was originally developed using Microsoft's Visual C++ 4.0. (Yes, you can compile C with it!) With each sample you will find Visual C++ project files.

Since all samples are in C and make no use of vendor-specific libraries, you shouldn't have any trouble building the projects with any other 32-bit compiler. I will assume that you are familiar with your environment of choice and know how to add libraries and header files to your projects.

For programmers who prefer C++ application frameworks such as MFC or OWL, chapters are included that deal with these two in particular. In addition, many of the C samples are also provided in an MFC (Visual C++) version and an OWL (Borland C++) version. These samples can be found in the \MFC and \OWL subdirectories on the CD. Project files for the Borland Compiler are also provided for these samples, prepared using Borland C++ 5.0.

Another special consideration has been made for users of Borland tools: the CD contains a Borland-specific version of the OpenGL Auxiliary library. This library isn't part of the official OpenGL specification, but it is usually implemented on the same various platforms as OpenGL. For reasons unknown, Borland includes a header file for this library but not the library itself, and the version of the AUX library that ships with Microsoft tools is incompatible with Borland C++. For additional notes on using Borland C++ with this book, see the \Borland subdirectory on the CD.

What's in This Book

OpenGL SuperBible is divided into four sections. Part I is an introduction to OpenGL and the fundamentals of using it from within Microsoft Windows. In Part II we cover the basics of programming with OpenGL. This includes primitives, viewing and modeling transformations, lighting, and texture mapping. In Part III we dig into some of the more advanced topics and functionality within OpenGL—the OpenGL State Machine, special visual effects, more detail on the OpenGL buffers, advanced surface generation, and some interactive graphics. For Part IV, we've added supplementary information on using OpenGL from different programming environments (MFC, OWL, and Visual Basic). Finally, there's a discussion of the future of OpenGL under Windows.

Part I: Introduction to OpenGL

Chapter 1 - What Is OpenGL?
In this chapter, we provide you with a working knowledge of what OpenGL is, where it came from, and where it is going. We also discuss at a high level the differences between and compatibilities of OpenGL and the Microsoft Windows graphics system.

Chapter 2 - 3D Graphics Fundamentals
This chapter is for newcomers to 3D graphics. It introduces fundamental concepts and some common vocabulary.

Chapter 3 - Learning OpenGL with the AUX Library
In this chapter, you will begin writing programs that use OpenGL. For starters, we'll make things simple by using the AUX library. This common toolkit library is platform- and windowing system-independent. We also cover OpenGL function and variable

naming conventions, as well as the DLLs and libraries that contain the OpenGL functionality.

Chapter 4 - OpenGL for Windows: OpenGL + Win32 = Wiggle
Here you'll begin writing real Windows (message-based) programs that use OpenGL. You'll learn about Microsoft's "wiggle" functions that glue OpenGL rendering code to Windows device contexts. We'll also talk about which Windows messages should be responded to and how.

Chapter 5 - Errors and Other Message from OpenGL
We'll explore OpenGL's method of reporting errors, and how it provides information about its version and vendor.

Part II: Using OpenGL

Chapter 6 - Drawing in 3D: Lines, Points, and Polygons
Here you'll learn how all 3D objects are created by assembling 2D primitives. All the OpenGL primitives are covered, as well as how to hide surfaces within your scenes.

Chapter 7 - Manipulating 3D Space: Coordinate Transformations
In this chapter you'll learn about moving your objects or view within your scenes. You'll learn how to rotate, translate, and scale. We take a simplified approach to our study of matrix transformations, so you will understand how to use them even if you don't know the first thing about matrices.

Chapter 8 - Color and Shading
Here you'll learn how to liven up your objects by adding color. Shading objects smoothly from one color to another will be child's play after you've completed this chapter. We also show you how and why you need to construct a 3-3-2 palette for OpenGL when your code runs on a 256-color video card.

Chapter 9 - Lighting and Lamps
OpenGL supports up to eight independent light sources per scene. You'll learn how to use these lamps, how to set lighting parameters and properties, and how they interact with reflective material properties that you can assign to your objects.

Chapter 10 - 3D Modeling and Object Composition
For this chapter, we show you how to build complex 3D objects out of smaller, less complex 3D objects. We also introduce OpenGL display lists as a method of breaking down your objects and improving performance, as well.

Chapter 11 - Raster Graphics in OpenGL
In this chapter you'll learn how to manipulate bitmap graphics from within OpenGL. This includes reading in a Windows .BMP file and displaying it in an OpenGL scene.

Chapter 12 - Texture Mapping
Texture mapping is one of the most useful features of any 3D graphics toolkit. You'll learn how to wrap bitmaps onto polygons, and how to use automatic texture coordinate generation.

Chapter 13 - Quadrics: Spheres, Cylinders, and Disks
This chapter covers the OpenGL Utility library (glu) functions for quickly constructing some common shapes.

Part III: Advanced Topics and Special Effects

Chapter 14 - The OpenGL State Machine
Many global OpenGL parameters and settings are maintained via the OpenGL State Machine. In this chapter you'll learn about this mechanism, as well as some generalized functions for setting and accessing the various parameters.

Chapter 15 - Buffers: Not Just for Animation
This chapter goes into more depth about the various OpenGL buffers. As you'll see, they're not just for doing screen flipping.

Chapter 16 - Visual Effects, Blending, and Fog
Some other visual special effects are covered in this chapter. These include alpha blending and fog effects for transparency and depth cues.

Chapter 17 - Curves and Surfaces: What the #%@!&* Are NURBS?
This chapter explores the utility functions that evaluate Bézier and NURBS curves and surfaces. You can use these functions to create complex shapes with a small amount of code.

Chapter 18 - Polygon Tessellation
Here you'll learn how to break down complex or concave polygons into smaller, more manageable pieces.

Chapter 19 - Interactive Graphics
This chapter explains two OpenGL features: selection and feedback. These groups of functions make it possible for the user to interact with objects in the scene. You can also get rendering details about any single object in the scene.

Chapter 20 - OpenGL on the 'Net: VRML
This chapter introduces VRML (Virtual Reality Modeling Language) and its history with OpenGL. Open Inventor is discussed, as well, and its relationship to OpenGL and VRML.

Part IV: OpenGL with...

Chapter 21 - MFC-Based OpenGL Programming
This chapter is for C++ programmers using Microsoft's MFC class library. We'll show you how to use OpenGL from an MFC-based application, and how to add rendering capabilities to any CWnd window.

Chapter 22 - OWL-Based OpenGL Programming
This chapter is for C++ programmers using Borland C++ and the OWL application framework. You'll learn how to add OpenGL rendering capabilities to any OWL TWindow-derived window.

Chapter 23 - OpenGL Programming from Visual Basic and 4GL
In this chapter we give you an OCX that wraps most of the OpenGL functions and commands. This allows easy OpenGL programming from Visual Basic (4.0 or later) or any 32-bit environment that supports OCXs. Examples are given for both Visual Basic 4.0 and Delphi 2.0.

Chapter 24 - The Future of OpenGL and Windows
This chapter looks at the future of 3D graphics and OpenGL in Windows. We discuss the implications of the Microsoft DirectX API, which includes Direct Draw, Direct Sound, Direct Play, Direct Input, and Direct 3D, and will ultimately incorporate the Reality Labs 3D API.

Appendixes

Appendix A - Performance-Tuning OpenGL for Windows
Here we will provide some general-purpose performance-tuning tips for using OpenGL under Windows NT and Windows 95.

Appendix B - Further Reading
A list of additional reading materials is provided for more in-depth research on any of the topics covered by this book.

Appendix C - OpenGL Version 1.1
OpenGL 1.1 was finalized during development of this book. The new functions and capabilities are not covered here, but Appendix C gives you a high-level overview of the new version's additions. The CD also contains more up-to-date and complete documentation on the new functions and capabilities being added for Windows NT 4.0, as well as some example programs.

Appendix D - Glossary
A glossary of common 3D graphics and OpenGL terms.

About the Companion CD

OpenGL SuperBible comes with a CD-ROM that's jam-packed with samples and other OpenGL goodies. A directory called Book, off the root directory of the CD, contains all the source code from the book. In addition, there are many examples demonstrating the concepts presented from each chapter that may not have been described in the text of the book.

Each chapter of the book has its own subdirectory in the Book directory. Within each chapter subdirectory is another subdirectory for each example on the disk. For instance, the bouncing square program from Chapter 3 is located in the X:\Book\Chapt3\bounce subdirectory (where X is your CD-ROM drive).

Some of the chapter directories have a subdirectory called \Tank. This is a roving tank/robot simulation program that we observe as we progress through the book. Though it's not analyzed chapter by chapter, the simulation becomes more complex as we gradually add more of the functions and features of OpenGL. See the readme.txt file for details on the construction of this example program.

Some of the sample programs from each chapter will also be written in C++ using MFC or OWL. These sample programs are under X:\MFC\ or X:\OWL\. Again, within the MFC and OWL subdirectories there is an additional directory for each chapter.

The two final major subdirectories in the CD root are \Borland and \OpenGL11. The \Borland subdirectory contains a Borland-specific version of the AUX library. See the readme.txt file in that directory for details on the library's functionality and use. The \OpenGL11directory contains a document describing the OpenGL 1.1 additions that Microsoft is incorporating for Windows NT 4.0. In addition, you'll also find several example programs that demonstrate these new capabilities.

Be sure to consult the file readme.txt in the root directory for any late-breaking news or additions to the content of the CD. This file also contains a complete listing of all the files and programs on the CD ROM.

Engage!

If you are learning OpenGL or 3D graphics for the first time, then I sincerely envy you. Nothing is more satisfying and just plain fun than learning a new technology or tool for the first time. Although OpenGL has its roots in scientific modeling and simulation, you don't need to be a rocket scientist to master it. The step-by-step approach taken throughout this book will guide you to new levels of programming skill. Learning OpenGL is comparable to learning SQL for database programming. Before I knew SQL, I could not quite imagine the new power I would wield as a database developer. If you have been tinkering with 3D graphics or are just wanting to get started, you are only just beginning to glimpse the new power and capabilities that OpenGL will afford you!

—Richard S. Wright, Jr.

PART I

INTRODUCTION TO OPENGL

INTRODUCTION TO OPENGL

Part I of this book introduces you to 3D graphics and programming with OpenGL. We start with a brief discussion of OpenGL, its background, purpose, and how it works. Then, before getting into any code, we'll talk generally about 3D graphics on computers, including how and why we "think" we see 3D, and how an object's position and orientation in 3D space is specified. You'll get the fundamental background and terminology you need to get the best out of this book.

In Chapter 3 you'll start writing your first OpenGL programs. You'll learn about the various libraries and headers that are needed, and how OpenGL functions and data types are called and named. Initially we'll cover the AUX library, a toolkit for learning OpenGL independently of any particular platform. Then we'll "wiggle" our way into writing programs that use OpenGL under Windows 95 and Windows NT, in Chapter 4. We'll cover the extensions to the Windows GDI (graphical device interface) to support OpenGL under Windows and describe how they must be used.

In Chapter 5 you'll get some essential information on OpenGL's handling and reporting of error conditions. We'll tell you how you can ask the AUX library to identify itself and who makes it, and how to give performance "hints" to the library. With this knowledge in hand, you'll be ready to tackle the meatier issues of OpenGL in Part II, where the examples will get a lot better!

1

WHAT IS OPENGL?

1

WHAT IS OPENGL?

OpenGL is strictly defined as "a software interface to graphics hardware." In essence, it is a 3D graphics and modeling library that is extremely portable and very fast. Using OpenGL, you can create elegant and beautiful 3D graphics with nearly the visual quality of a ray-tracer. The greatest advantage to using OpenGL is that it is orders of magnitude faster than a ray-tracer. It uses algorithms carefully developed and optimized by Silicon Graphics, Inc. (SGI), an acknowledged world leader in computer graphics and animation.

OpenGL is intended for use with computer hardware that is designed and optimized for the display and manipulation of 3D graphics. Software-only, "generic" implementations of OpenGL are also possible, and the Microsoft Windows NT and Windows 95 implementations fall into this category. Soon this may not strictly be the case, because more and more PC graphics hardware vendors are adding 3D acceleration to their products. Although this is mostly driven by the market for 3D games, it closely parallels the evolution of 2D Windows-based graphics accelerators that optimize operations such as line drawing and bitmap filling and manipulation. Just as today no one would consider using an ordinary VGA card to run Windows on a new machine, soon 3D accelerated graphics cards will become commonplace.

The Windows Graphics APIs
First there was GDI (Graphics Device Interface), which made it possible to write hardware-independent graphics—but at the cost of speed. Then graphics card makers began writing optimized GDI drivers to considerably speed up GDI. Then Microsoft introduced WinG to lure game developers. WinG consisted of little more than a few functions that got bitmaps to the display much faster, but it was still too slow. Microsoft next created the Direct Draw API for *really* low-level access to the hardware. This became rolled in with a whole set of DirectX APIs for writing directly to hardware, making games easier to write and improving their performance. Finally, 3DDI (a part of DirectX) gives high-performance 3D games a much needed shot in the arm. In Chapter 24 we talk more about the evolution and relationship of Windows and 3D graphics acceleration.

OpenGL is used for a variety of purposes, from CAD engineering and architectural applications to computer-generated dinosaurs in blockbuster movies. The introduction of an industry standard 3D API to a mass-market operating system such as Microsoft Windows has some exciting repercussions. With hardware acceleration and fast PC microprocessors becoming commonplace, 3D graphics will soon be typical components of consumer and business applications, not just of games and scientific applications.

Who remembers when spreadsheets had only 2D graphics and charting capabilities? If you think adding 3D to ordinary applications is extravagant, take a look at the bottom line of the companies that first exploited this idea. Quattro Pro, one of the first to simplify 3D charting, nearly captured the entire spreadsheet market. Today it takes far more than flat, two-dimensional pie charts to guarantee long-term success for spreadsheet applications.

This isn't to say that everyone will be using OpenGL to do pie and bar charts for business applications. Nevertheless, appearances count for a lot. The success or failure of products with otherwise roughly equivalent features often depends on "sex appeal." And you can add a lot of sex appeal with good 3D graphics!

About OpenGL

Let's take a look at OpenGL's origins, who's "in charge" of OpenGL, and where OpenGL is going. We'll also examine the principles of OpenGL implementation.

A History of OpenGL

OpenGL is a relatively new industry standard that in only a few years has gained an enormous following. The forerunner of OpenGL was GL from Silicon Graphics. "IRIS GL" was the 3D programming API for that company's high-end IRIS graphics workstations. These computers were more than just general-purpose computers; they had specialized hardware optimized for the display of sophisticated graphics. This hardware provided ultrafast matrix transformations (a prerequisite for 3D graphics), hardware support for depth buffering, and other features. When SGI tried porting IRIS GL to other hardware platforms, however, problems occurred.

OpenGL is the result of SGI's efforts to improve IRIS GL's portability. The new language would offer the power of GL but would be "Open," allowing for easier adaptability to other hardware platforms and operating systems. (SGI still maintains IRIS GL, but no enhancements or features other than bug fixes are being made.)

On July 1, 1992, Version 1.0 of the OpenGL specification was introduced. Just five days later, at the very first Win32 developers conference, SGI demonstrated OpenGL running on their IRIS Indigo hardware. Video clips from films such as *Terminator Two: Judgment Day*, and medical imaging applications were popular attractions in the vendor exhibit hall. Already, SGI and Microsoft were working together to bring OpenGL to a future version of Windows NT.

Further Developments in OpenGL

An open standard is not really open if only one vendor controls it. Thus, all enhancements to OpenGL are decided by the OpenGL Architecture Review Board (ARB), whose founding members are SGI, Digital Equipment Corporation, IBM, Intel, and Microsoft. The OpenGL ARB meets twice a year.

These meetings are open to the public, and nonmember companies may participate in discussions (although they can't vote). Permission to attend must be requested in advance, and meetings are kept small to improve productivity. Members of the ARB frequently participate in the Internet newsgroup comp.graphics.api.opengl. Questions and recommendations can also be aired there.

In December 1995 the ARB ratified the final specification for Version 1.1 of OpenGL. Many of the additions and changes from Version 1.0 were for performance reasons and are summarized in Appendix A.

How OpenGL Works

OpenGL is a procedural rather than a descriptive graphics language. Instead of describing the scene and how it should appear, the programmer actually describes the steps necessary to achieve a certain appearance or effect. These "steps" involve calls to a highly portable API that includes approximately 120 commands and functions. These are used to draw graphics primitives such as points, lines, and polygons in three dimensions. In addition, OpenGL supports lighting and shading, texture mapping, animation, and other special effects.

OpenGL does not include any functions for window management, user interaction, or file I/O. Each host environment (such as Microsoft Windows) has its own functions for this purpose and is responsible for implementing some means of handing over to OpenGL the drawing control of a window or bitmap.

OpenGL under Windows

OpenGL made its debut in the release of Windows NT 3.5. A set of DLLs was also made available to add support for OpenGL to Windows 95 shortly after its release. This book, in fact, is specifically about Microsoft's generic implementation of OpenGL. We will guide you, the developer, through the fundamentals of 3D graphics first, and then show you how to compile and link some OpenGL programs under Windows NT or Windows 95. Moving on, we'll cover the "wiggle" functions provided by Microsoft—the glue that enables the OpenGL graphics API to work with Microsoft's GDI. From there we will cover the entire OpenGL API, using the context of Microsoft Windows NT and/or Windows95.

Graphics Architecture: Software versus Hardware

Using OpenGL is not at all like using GDI for drawing in windows. In fact, the current selection of pens, brushes, fonts, and other GDI objects will have no effect on

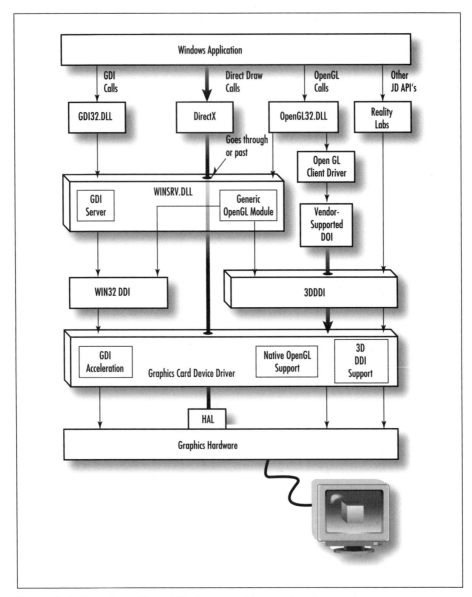

Figure 1-1 Overview of how Windows graphics acceleration works

OpenGL. Just as GDI uses the device context to control drawing in a window, OpenGL uses a rendering context. A rendering context is associated with a device context, which in turn is associated with a window, and voilà—OpenGL is rendering in a window. Chapter 4 discusses all the mechanics associated with this process.

As we said earlier, OpenGL was meant to run on systems with hardware accelera-tion. PC graphics vendors are adding OpenGL support for their cards. Properly written OpenGL applications should not know the difference between hardware accel-erated rendering and the purely software rendering of the generic implementation. The user will notice, however, that performance is significantly enhanced when hardware acceleration is present.

Figure 1-1 illustrates hardware acceleration under Windows, including normal GDI acceleration and Direct Draw acceleration, as well as OpenGL acceleration. On the far left you can see how an application makes normal GDI calls that are routed down through WINSRV.DLL to the Win32 Device Driver Interface. The Win32 DDI then communicates directly with the graphics card device driver, where the GDI accelera-tion is performed.

Direct Draw is optimized for direct access to graphics hardware. It bypasses the GDI completely and talks directly to the graphics hardware with perhaps only a thin hardware abstraction layer in between, and some software emulation for unsupported features. Direct Draw is typically used for games and allows direct manipulation of graphics memory for ultrafast 2D graphics and animation.

On the far right of Figure 1-1 you see OpenGL and other 3D API calls routed through a 3D device driver interface. 3DDI is specifically designed to allow hardware manufacturers to accelerate OpenGL and gaming 3D APIs such as the Reality Labs API. (For a discussion of OpenGL and the Reality Labs API, see Chapter 24. In addi-tion, hardware vendors with specific hardware acceleration for OpenGL (such as the GLINT chipset) may install their own OpenGL client drivers along with specialized device-driver interfaces.

Limitations of the Generic Implementation

Unless specifically supported by hardware, Microsoft's generic implementation of OpenGL has some limitations. There is no direct support for printing OpenGL graph-ics to a monochrome printer or to a color printer with less than 4-bit planes of color (16 colors). Hardware palettes for various windows are not supported. Instead, Windows has a single hardware palette that must be arbitrated among multiple run-ning applications.

Finally, some OpenGL features are not implemented, including stereoscopic images, auxiliary buffers, and alpha bit planes. These features may or may not be implemented in hardware, however. Your application should check for their availability before mak-ing use of them (see Chapter 5).

Future Prospects for OpenGL in Windows

The introduction of OpenGL into the Windows family of operating systems opens up some exciting possibilities. As millions of PCs become OpenGL-enabled, Windows may well become the most popular platform for OpenGL-based applications. Initially this implementation may be for scientific and engineering modeling and visualization applications, but commonplace hardware will make high-performance games and other consumer applications possible before long.

## CHAPTER 1

Even for vendors producing OpenGL based applications on other platforms, Microsoft Windows implementations could prove to be a substantial source of secondary revenue. Windows-based workstations are an attractive alternative to high-cost specialty workstations, with the added bonus of being able to run some of today's best business and productivity applications.

2

3D GRAPHICS FUNDAMENTALS

2

3D GRAPHICS FUNDAMENTALS

What you'll learn in this chapter:

How the eyes perceive three dimensions

How a 2D image can have the appearance of 3D

How Cartesian coordinates specify object positions

What a clipping volume is

How viewports affect image dimensions

How 3D objects are built from 2D primitives

How to work with orthographic and perspective projections

Before getting into the specifics of using OpenGL to create 3D graphics, we'll take some time out to establish some 3D vocabulary. In doing so, we will orient you to the fundamental concepts of 3D graphics and coordinate systems. You'll find out why we can get away with calling 2D images on a flat computer screen 3D graphics. Readers experienced in 3D graphics who are ready to get started using OpenGL may want to just skim this chapter.

3D Perception

"3D computer graphics" are actually two-dimensional images on a flat computer screen that provide an illusion of depth, or a third "dimension." In order to truly see in 3D, you need to actually view the object with both eyes, or supply each eye with

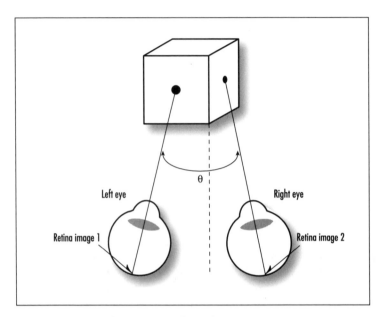

Figure 2-1 How the eyes "see" three dimensions

separate and unique images of the object. Take a look at Figure 2-1. Each eye receives a two-dimensional image that is much like a temporary photograph on the retina (the back part of your eye). These two images are slightly different because they are received at two different angles (your eyes are spaced apart on purpose). The brain then combines these slightly different images to produce a single, composite 3D picture in your head, as shown in Figure 2-1.

In Figure 2-1, the angle θ between the images gets smaller as the object goes farther away. This 3D effect can be amplified by increasing the angle between the two images. Viewmasters (those hand-held stereoscopic viewers you probably had as a kid) and 3D movies capitalize on this effect by placing each of your eyes on a separate lens, or by providing color-filtered glasses that separate two superimposed images. These images are overenhanced for dramatic or cinematic purposes.

So what happens when you cover one eye? You may *think* you are still seeing in 3D, but try this experiment: Place a glass or some other object just out of arm's reach, off to your left side. Cover your right eye with your right hand and reach for the glass. (Maybe you should use an empty plastic one!) Notice that you have a more difficult time estimating how much farther you need to reach (if at all) before you touch the glass. Now uncover your right eye and reach for the glass, and you can easily discern how far you need to lean to reach the glass. This is why people who have lost one eye often have difficulty with distance perception.

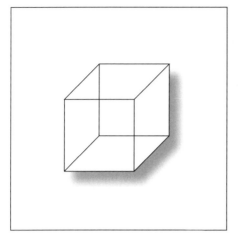

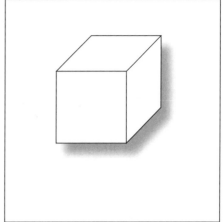

Figure 2-2 This simple wireframe cube demonstrates perspective

Figure 2-3 The cube after hidden lines are removed

2D + Perspective = 3D

The reason the world doesn't become suddenly flat when you cover one eye is that many of a 3D world's effects are also present in a 2D world. This is just enough to trigger your brain's ability to discern depth. The most obvious cue is that nearby objects appear larger than distant objects. This effect is called *perspective*. And perspective plus color changes, textures, lighting, shading, and variations of color intensities (due to lighting) together add up to our perception of a three-dimensional image.

Perspective alone is enough to lend the appearance of three dimensions. Figure 2-2 presents a simple wireframe cube. Even without coloring or shading, the cube still has the appearance of a three-dimensional object. Stare at the cube for long enough, however, and the front and back of the cube will switch places. This is because your brain is confused by the lack of any surface in the drawing.

Hidden Line Removal

Figure 2-2 contains just enough information to lend the appearance of three dimensions, but not enough to let you discern the front of the cube from the back. When viewing a real object, how do you tell the front from the back? Simple—the back is obscured by the front. If the cube in Figure 2-2 were a solid, you wouldn't be able to see the corners in the back of the cube, and thus you wouldn't confuse them for the corners in the front of the cube. Even if the cube were made of wire, parts of the wires in front would obscure parts of the wires in the back. To simulate this in a two-dimensional drawing, lines that would be obscured by surfaces in front of them must be removed. This is called *hidden line removal* and it has been done to the cube in Figure 2-3.

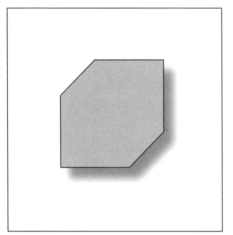

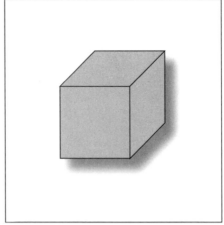

Figure 2-4 The cube with color, but no shading

Figure 2-5 The cube with its visible faces in three different shades

Colors and Shading

Figure 2-3 still doesn't look much like a real-world object. The faces of the cube are exactly the same color as the background, and all you can see are the front edges of the object. A real cube would have some color and/or texture; in a wooden cube, for example, the color and grain of the wood would show. On a computer (or on paper), if all we did was color the cube and draw it in two dimensions, we would have something similar to Figure 2-4.

Now we are back to an object that appears two-dimensional, and unless we specifically draw the edges in a different color, there is no perception of three dimensions at all. In order to regain our perspective of a solid object (without drawing the edges a different color), we need to either make each of the three visible sides a different color, or make them the same color with shading to produce the illusion of lighting. In Figure 2-5, the faces of the cube all have a different color or shade.

Lights and Shadows

One last element we must not neglect is lighting. Lighting has two important effects on objects viewed in three dimensions. First, it causes a surface of a uniform color to appear shaded when viewed or illuminated from an angle. Second, objects that do not transmit light (most solid objects) cast a shadow when they obstruct the path of a ray of light. See Figure 2-6.

Two sources of light can influence our three-dimensional objects. *Ambient* light, which is undirected light, is simply a uniform illumination that can cause shading effects on objects of a solid color; ambient light causes distant edges to appear dimmer. Another source of light is from a light source, called a *lamp*. Lamps can be used to change the shading of solid objects and for shadow effects.

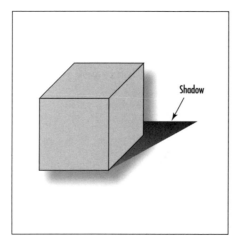

Figure 2-6 A solid cube illuminated by a single light

Coordinate Systems

Now that you know how the eye can perceive three dimensions on a two-dimensional surface (the computer screen), let's consider how to draw these objects on the screen. When you draw points, lines, or other shapes on the computer screen, you usually specify a position in terms of a row and column. For example, on a standard VGA screen there are 640 pixels from left to right, and 480 pixels from top to bottom. To specify a point in the middle of the screen, you specify that a point should be plotted at (320,240)—that is, 320 pixels from the left of the screen and 240 pixels down from the top of the screen.

In OpenGL, when you create a window to draw in, you must also specify the *coordinate system* you wish to use, and how to map the specified coordinates into physical screen pixels. Let's first see how this applies to two-dimensional drawing, and then extend the principle to three dimensions.

2D Cartesian Coordinates

The most common coordinate system for two-dimensional plotting is the *Cartesian* coordinate system. Cartesian coordinates are specified by an x coordinate and a y coordinate. The x coordinate is a measure of position in the horizontal direction and y is a measure of position in the vertical direction.

The *origin* of the Cartesian system is at x=0, y=0. Cartesian coordinates are written as coordinate pairs, in parentheses, with the x coordinate first and the y coordinate second, separated by a comma. For example, the origin would be written as (0,0). Figure 2-7 depicts the Cartesian coordinate system in two dimensions. The x and y lines with tick marks are called the *axes* and can extend from negative to positive

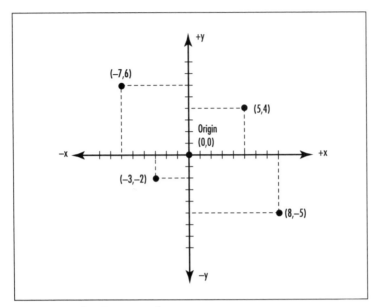

Figure 2-7 The Cartesian plane

infinity. Note that this figure represents the true Cartesian coordinate system pretty much as you used it in grade school. Today, differing Windows mapping modes can cause the coordinates you specify when drawing to be interpreted differently. Later in the book, you'll see how to map this true coordinate space to window coordinates in different ways.

The x-axis and y-axis are *perpendicular* (intersecting at a right angle) and together define the *xy plane*. A plane is, most simply put, a flat surface. In any coordinate system, two axes that intersect at right angles define a plane. In a system with only two axes, there is naturally only one plane to draw on.

Coordinate Clipping

A window is measured physically in terms of pixels. Before you can start plotting points, lines, and shapes in a window, you must tell OpenGL how to translate specified coordinate pairs into screen coordinates. This is done by specifying the region of Cartesian space that occupies the window; this region is known as the *clipping area*. In two-dimensional space, the clipping area is the minimum and maximum x and y values that are inside the window. Another way of looking at this is specifying the origin's location in relation to the window. Figure 2-8 shows two common clipping areas.

In the first example, on the left of Figure 2-8, x coordinates in the window range left to right from 0 to +150, and y coordinates range bottom to top from 0 to +100. A point in the middle of the screen would be represented as (75,50). The second example shows a clipping area with x coordinates ranging left to right from −75 to +75, and

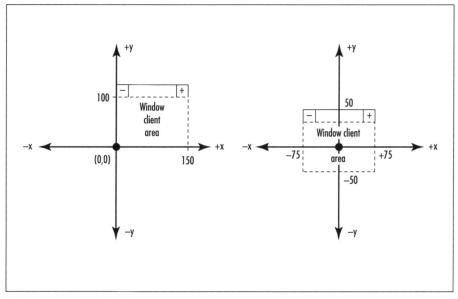

Figure 2-8 Two clipping areas

y coordinates ranging bottom to top from −50 to +50. In this example, a point in the middle of the screen would be at the origin (0,0). It is also possible using OpenGL functions (or ordinary Windows functions for GDI drawing) to turn the coordinate system upside-down or flip it right to left. In fact, the default mapping for Windows windows is for positive y to move down from the top to the bottom of the window. Although useful when drawing text from top to bottom, this default mapping is not as convenient for drawing graphics.

Viewports, Your Window to 3D

Rarely will your clipping area width and height exactly match the width and height of the window in pixels. The coordinate system must therefore be mapped from logical Cartesian coordinates to physical screen pixel coordinates. This mapping is specified by a setting known as the *viewport*. The viewport is the region within the window's client area that will be used for drawing the clipping area . The viewport simply maps the clipping area to a region of the window. Usually the viewport is defined as the entire window, but this is not strictly necessary—for instance, you might only want to draw in the lower half of the window.

Figure 2-9 shows a large window measuring 300 x 200 pixels with the viewport defined as the entire client area. If the clipping area for this window were set to be 0 to 150 along the x-axis and 0 to 100 along the y-axis, then the logical coordinates would be mapped to a larger screen coordinate system in the viewing window. Each increment in the logical coordinate system would be matched by two increments in the physical coordinate system (pixels) of the window.

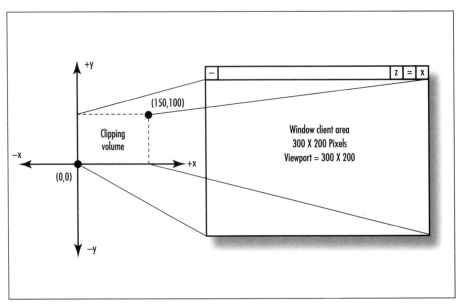

Figure 2-9 A viewport defined as twice the size of the clipping area

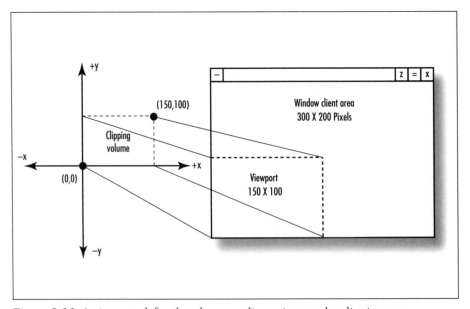

Figure 2-10 A viewport defined as the same dimensions as the clipping area

In contrast, Figure 2-10 shows a viewport that matches the clipping area. The viewing window is still 300 x 200 pixels, however, and this causes the viewing area to occupy the lower-left side of the window.

You can use viewports to shrink or enlarge the image inside the window, and to display only a portion of the clipping area by setting the viewport to be larger than the window's client area.

Drawing Primitives

In both 2D and 3D, when you draw an object you will actually compose it with several smaller shapes called *primitives*. Primitives are two-dimensional surfaces such as points, lines, and polygons (a flat, multisided shape) that are assembled in 3D space to create 3D objects. For example, a three-dimensional cube like the one in Figure 2-5 is made up of six two-dimensional squares, each placed on a separate face. Each corner of the square (or of any primitive) is called a *vertex*. These *vertices* are then specified to occupy a particular coordinate in 2D or 3D space. You'll learn about all the OpenGL primitives and how to use them in Chapter 6.

3D Cartesian Coordinates

Now we'll extend our two-dimensional coordinate system into the third dimension and add a depth component. Figure 2-11 shows the Cartesian coordinate system with a new axis, z. The z-axis is perpendicular to both the x- and y-axes. It represents a line drawn perpendicularly from the center of the screen heading toward the viewer. (We have rotated our view of the coordinate system from Figure 2-7 to the left with respect to the y-axis, and down and back with respect to the x-axis. If we hadn't, the z-axis would come straight out at you and you wouldn't see it.) Now we specify a position in

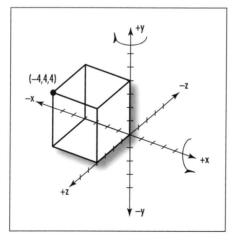

Figure 2-11 Cartesian coordinates in three dimensions

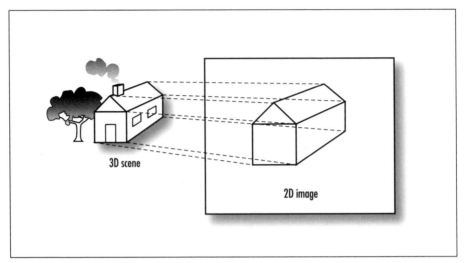

Figure 2-12 A 3D image projected onto a 2D surface

three-dimensional space with three coordinates—x, y, and z. Figure 2-11 shows the point (–4, 4, 4) for clarification.

Projections, The Essence of 3D

You've seen how to specify a position in 3D space using Cartesian coordinates. No matter how we might convince your eye, however, pixels on a screen have only two dimensions. How does OpenGL translate these Cartesian coordinates into two-dimensional coordinates that can be plotted on a screen? The short answer is "trigonometry and simple matrix manipulation." Simple? Well, not really—we could actually go on for many pages and lose most of our readers who didn't take or don't remember their linear algebra from college explaining this "simple" technique. You'll learn more about it in Chapter 7, and for a deeper discussion you can check out the references in Appendix B. Fortunately, you don't need to understand the math in order to use OpenGL to create graphics.

All you really need to understand to get the most from this book is a concept called *projection*. The 3D coordinates are projected onto a 2D surface (the window background). It's like tracing the outlines of some object behind a piece of glass with a black marker. When the object is gone or you move the glass, you can still see the outline of the object with its angular edges. In Figure 2-12 a house in the background is traced onto a flat piece of glass. By specifying the projection, you specify the *clipping volume* (remember clipping areas?) that you want displayed in your window, and how it should be translated.

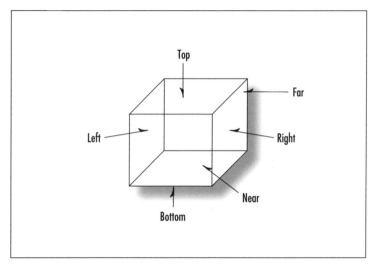

Figure 2-13 The clipping volume for an orthographic projection

Orthographic Projections

You will mostly be concerned with two main types of projections in OpenGL. The first is called an *orthographic* or *parallel projection*. You use this projection by specifying a square or rectangular clipping volume. Anything outside this clipping area is not drawn. Furthermore, all objects that have the same dimensions appear the same size, regardless of whether they are far away or nearby. This type of projection (shown in Figure 2-13) is most often used in architectural design or CAD (computer aided design).

You specify the clipping volume in an orthographic projection by specifying the far, near, left, right, top, and bottom clipping planes. Objects and figures that you place within this viewing volume are then projected (taking into account their orientation) to a 2D image that appears on your screen.

Perspective Projections

A second and more common projection is the *perspective* projection. This projection adds the effect that distant objects appear smaller than nearby objects. The *viewing volume* (Figure 2-14) is something like a pyramid with the top shaved off. This shaved off part is called the *frustum*. Objects nearer to the front of the viewing volume appear close to their original size, while objects near the back of the volume shrink as they are projected to the front of the volume. This type of projection gives the most realism for simulation and 3D animation.

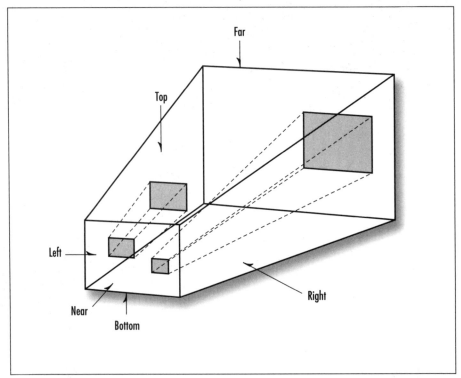

Figure 2-14 The clipping volume for a perspective projection

Summary

In this chapter we have introduced the very basics of 3D graphics. You've seen why you actually need two images of an object from different angles in order to perceive true three-dimensional space. You've also seen the illusion of depth created in a 2D drawing by means of perspective, hidden line removal, and coloring, shading, and lighting techniques. The Cartesian coordinate system was introduced for 2D and 3D drawing, and you learned about two methods used by OpenGL to project three-dimensional drawings onto a two-dimensional screen.

We purposely left out the details of how these effects are actually created by OpenGL. In the chapters that follow, you will find out how to employ these techniques and take maximum advantage of OpenGL's power. On the Companion CD you'll find one program for Chapter 2 (CUBE) that demonstrates the concepts covered in the first section of this chapter. In CUBE, pressing the spacebar will advance you from a wireframe cube to a fully lit cube complete with shadow. You won't understand the code at this point, but it makes a powerful demonstration of what is to come. By the time you finish this book, you will be able to revisit this example and even be able to write it from scratch yourself.

3

LEARNING OPENGL WITH THE AUX LIBRARY

3

LEARNING OPENGL WITH THE AUX LIBRARY

What you'll learn in this chapter:

Which headers and libraries are used with OpenGL

How the AUX library provides basic windowing functions on just about any platform

How to use OpenGL to create a window and draw in it

How to use the OpenGL default coordinate system

How to create composite colors using the RGB (red, green, blue) components

How viewports affect image dimensions

How to scale your drawing to fit any size window

How to perform simple animation using double buffering

How to draw predefined objects

Now that you've been introduced to OpenGL and the principles of 3D graphics, it's time to set our hands to writing some OpenGL code. This chapter starts with an overview of how OpenGL works with your compiler, and you'll learn some conventions for naming variables and functions. If you have already written some OpenGL programs, you may have "discovered" many of these details for yourself. If that is the case, you may just want to skim through the first section and jump right into using the AUX library.

OpenGL: An API, Not a Language

OpenGL is not a programming language; it is an API (Application Programming Interface). Whenever we say that a program is *OpenGL-based* or an *OpenGL application,* we mean that it was written in some programming language (such as C or C++) that makes calls to one or more of the OpenGL libraries. We are not saying that the program uses OpenGL exclusively to do drawing. It may combine the best features of two different graphics packages. Or it may use OpenGL for only a few specific tasks, and environment-specific graphics (such as the Windows GDI) for others.

As an API, the OpenGL library follows the C calling convention. This means programs in C can easily call functions in the API either because the functions are themselves written in C or because a set of intermediate C functions is provided that calls functions written in assembler or some other language. In this book, our programs will be written in either C or C++ and designed to run under Windows NT and Windows95. C++ programs can easily access C functions and APIs in the same manner as C, with only some minor considerations. Other programming languages—such as so-called 4GLs ("fourth-generation languages") like Visual Basic—that can call functions in C libraries can also make use of OpenGL. Chapter 23 discusses this in more detail.

Calling C Functions from C++
Except for the chapters that deal specifically with C++ application frameworks or 4GLs, all of the chapter examples are written in C. On the accompanying CD, many of these samples have also been provided in C++ using two popular application frameworks (MFC and OWL). You can examine these examples and see how we made use of preprocessor macros to keep most of our OpenGL drawing code in C.

The OpenGL Division of Labor

The OpenGL API is divided into three distinct libraries. See Table 3-1 for a breakdown.

■ The first, covered in this chapter, is the Auxiliary or AUX library (sometimes referred to as the "toolkit" library), glaux.lib. The declarations for this library are contained in the file glaux.h. The functions contained in this library are not really a part of the OpenGL specification, but rather a toolkit that provides a platform-independent framework for calling OpenGL functions. If your compiler vendor did not supply these files, they can be obtained from the Microsoft Win32 SDK. All functions from this library begin with the prefix *aux.*

■ The functions that actually define OpenGL as specified by the OpenGL Architecture Review Board are contained in the library opengl32.dll, and its header gl.h. Functions from this library are prefixed with *gl.*

■ Finally, there is an OpenGL utility library glu32.dll and its header glu.h. This library contains utility functions that make everyday tasks easier, such as drawing spheres, disks, and cylinders. The utility library is actually written using OpenGL commands, and thus is guaranteed to be available on all platforms that support the OpenGL specification. These functions are all prefixed with *glu*.

All of the functions in the opengl32.dll and glu32.dll libraries are available for use when using the AUX library for your program's framework, which is what most of this chapter focuses on. Along the way, you'll learn the basics of OpenGL, and a few of the commands from the gl library.

Table 3-1 OpenGL libraries and headers

Library Name	Library Filename	Header File	Function Prefix
Auxiliary or Toolkit	glaux.lib	glaux.h	aux
OpenGL or gl	opengl32.dll	gl.h	gl
Utility library or glu	glu32.dll	glu.h	glu

> **A Note About the Libraries**
> You may have noticed that the AUX library is actually a library that is linked into your application. The other OpenGL libraries, however, are actually implemented as DLLs. The import libraries that you will need to link to are opengl32.lib and glu32.lib. Typically they are provided by your compiler vendor, or you may obtain them via the Win32 SDK from Microsoft. If you are using Borland C++, you will need to build your own import libraries with Borland's implib.exe utility.

OpenGL Data Types

To make it easier to port OpenGL code from one platform to another, OpenGL defines its own data types. These data types map to normal C data types that you can use instead, if desired. The various compilers and environments, however, have their own rules for the size and memory layout of various C variables. By using the OpenGL defined variable types, you can insulate your code from these types of changes.

Table 3-2 lists the OpenGL data types, their corresponding C data types under the 32-bit Windows environments (Win32), and the appropriate suffix for literals. In this book we will use the suffixes for all literal values. You will see later that these suffixes are also used in many OpenGL function names.

Table 3-2 OpenGL variable types and corresponding C data types

OpenGL Data Type	Internal Representation	Defined as C Type	C Literal Suffix
GLbyte	8-bit integer	Signed char	b
GLshort	16-bit integer	Short	s

continued on next page

continued from previous page

OpenGL Data Type	Internal Representation	Defined as C Type	C Literal Suffix
GLint, GLsizei	32-bit integer	Long	l
GLfloat, GLclampf	32-bit floating point	Float	f
GLdouble, GLclampd	64-bit floating point	Double	d
GLubyte, GLboolean	8-bit unsigned integer	Unsigned char	ub
GLushort	16-bit unsigned integer	Unsigned short	us
GLuint, GLenum, GLbitfield	32-bit unsigned integer	Unsigned long	ui

All data types start with a *GL* to denote OpenGL. Most are followed by their corresponding C data types (byte, short, int, float, etc.). Some have a *u* first to denote an unsigned data type, such as ubyte to denote an unsigned byte. For some uses a more descriptive name is given, such as *size* to denote a value of length or depth. For example, GLsizei is an OpenGL variable denoting a size parameter that is represented by an integer. The *clamp* is used for color composition and stands for *color amplitude*. This data type is found with both *f* and *d* suffixes to denote float and double data types. The GLboolean variables are used to indicate True and False conditions, GLenum for enumerated variables, and GLbitfield for variables that contain binary bit fields.

Pointers and arrays are not give any special consideration. An array of ten GLshort variables would simply be declared as

```
GLshort shorts[10];
```

and an array of ten pointers to GLdouble variables would be declared with

```
GLdouble *doubles[10];
```

Some other pointer object types are used for NURBS and Quadrics. They take more explanation and will be covered in later chapters.

Function Naming Conventions

OpenGL functions all follow a naming convention that tells you which library the function is from, and often how many and what type of arguments the function takes. All functions have a root that represents the function's corresponding OpenGL command. For example, the glColor3f() function has the root Color. The gl prefix represents the gl library (see Table 3-1), and the 3f suffix means the function takes three floating point arguments. All OpenGL functions take the following format:

<Library prefix><Root command><Optional argument count><Optional argument type>

Figure 3-1 illustrates the parts of an OpenGL function. This sample function with the suffix 3f takes three floating point arguments. Other variations take three integers (glColor3i()), three doubles (glColor3d()), and so forth. This convention of adding the number and type of arguments (see Table 3-1) to the end of OpenGL functions makes

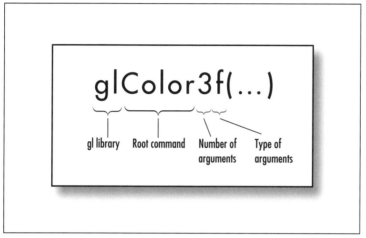

Figure 3-1 Dissected OpenGL function

it very easy to remember the argument list without having to look it up. Some versions of glColor take four arguments to specify an alpha component, as well.

In the reference sections of this book, these "families" of functions are listed by their library prefix and root. Thus all the variations of glColor (glColor3f, glColor4f, glColor3i, etc.) will be listed under a single entry—glColor.

Clean Code

Many C/C++ compilers for Windows assume that any floating-point literal value is of type *double* unless explicitly told otherwise via the suffix mechanism. When using literals for floating point arguments, if you don't specify that these arguments are of type float instead of double, the compiler will issue a warning while compiling because it detects that you are passing a double to a function defined to accept only floats, resulting in a possible loss of precision. As our OpenGL programs grow, these warnings will quickly number in the hundreds and will make it difficult to find any real syntax errors. You can turn these warnings off using the appropriate compiler options—but we advise against this. It's better to write clean, portable code the first time. So clean up those warning messages by cleaning up the code (in this case, by explicitly using the float type)—not by disabling potentially useful warnings.

Additionally, you may be tempted to use the functions that accept double-precision floating point arguments, rather than go to all the bother of specifying your literals as floats. However, OpenGL uses floats internally, and using anything other than the single-precision floating point functions will add a performance bottleneck, as the values are converted to floats anyway before being processed by OpenGL.

The AUX Library

For the remainder of this chapter, you will learn to use the Auxiliary (AUX) library as a way to learn OpenGL. The AUX library was created to facilitate the learning and writing of OpenGL programs without being distracted by the minutiae of your particular environment, be it UNIX, Windows, or whatever. You don't write "final" code when using AUX; it is more of a preliminary staging ground for testing your ideas. A lack of basic GUI features limits the library's use for building useful applications.

A set of core AUX functions is available on nearly every implementation of OpenGL. These functions handle window creation and manipulation, as well as user input. Other functions draw some complete 3D figures as wireframe or solid objects. By using the AUX library to create and manage the window and user interaction, and OpenGL to do the drawing, it is possible to write programs that create fairly complex renderings. You can move these programs to different environments with a recompile.

In addition to the core functions, each environment that implements an AUX library also implements some other helper functions to enable system-specific operations such as buffer swapping and image loading. The more your code relies on these additional AUX library functions, the less portable your code will be. On the other hand, by making full use of these functions you can create fantastic scenes that will amaze your friends and even the family dog—without having to learn all the gritty details of Windows programming.

Unfortunately, it's unlikely that all of the functionality of a useful application will be embodied entirely in the code used to draw in 3D, so you can't rely entirely on the AUX library for everything. Nevertheless, the AUX library excels in its role for learning and demonstration exercises. And for some applications, you may be able to employ the AUX library to iron out your 3D graphics code before integrating it into a complete application.

Platform Independence

OpenGL is a powerful and sophisticated API for creating 3D graphics, with over 300 commands that cover everything from setting material colors and reflective properties to doing rotations and complex coordinate transformations. You may be surprised that OpenGL has not a single function or command relating to window or screen management. In addition, there are no functions for keyboard input or mouse interaction. Consider, however, that one of the primary goals of the OpenGL designers was platform independence. Creating and opening a window is done differently under the various platforms. Even if OpenGL did have a command for opening a window, would you use it or would you use the operating system's own built-in API call?

Another platform issue is the handling of keyboard and mouse input events under the different operating systems and environments. If every environment handled these the same, we would have only one environment to worry about and thus no need for an "open" API. This is not the case, however, and it probably won't be within our brief lifetimes! So OpenGL's platform independence comes at the cost of OS and GUI functions.

AUX = Platform I/O, the Easy Way

The AUX library was initially created as a toolkit to enable learning OpenGL without getting mired in the details of any particular operating system or user interface. To accomplish this, AUX provides rudimentary functions for creating a window and for reading mouse and keyboard activity. Internally, the AUX library makes use of the native environment's APIs for these functions. The functions exposed by the AUX library then remain the same on all platforms.

The AUX library contains only a handful of functions for window management and the handling of input events, but saves you the trouble of managing these in pure C or C++ through the Windows API. The library also contains functions for drawing some relatively simple 3D objects such as a sphere, cube, torus (doughnut), and even a teapot. With very little effort, you can use the AUX library to display a window and perform some OpenGL commands. Though AUX is not really part of the OpenGL specification, it seems to follow that spec around to every platform to which OpenGL is ported. Windows is no exception, and the source code for the AUX library is even included free in the Win32 SDK from Microsoft.

Dissecting a Short OpenGL Program

In order to understand the AUX library better, let's take a look at possibly the world's shortest OpenGL program, which was written using the AUX library. Listing 3-1 presents the shortest.c program. Its output is shown in Figure 3-2.

Listing 3-1 Shortest OpenGL program in the world

```
// shortest.c
// The shortest OpenGL program possible

#include <windows.h>     // Standard Window header required for all programs
#include <conio.h>       // Console I/O functions
#include <gl\gl.h>       // OpenGL functions
#include <gl\glaux.h>    // AUX Library functions

void main(void)
        {
        // These are the AUX functions to set up the window
        auxInitDisplayMode(AUX_SINGLE | AUX_RGBA);
        auxInitPosition(100,100,250,250);
        auxInitWindow("My first OpenGL Program");

        // These are the OpenGL functions that do something in the window
        glClearColor(0.0f, 0.0f, 1.0f, 1.0f);
        glClear(GL_COLOR_BUFFER_BIT);

        glFlush();

        // Stop and wait for a keypress
        cprintf("Press any key to close the Window\n");
        getch();
        }
```

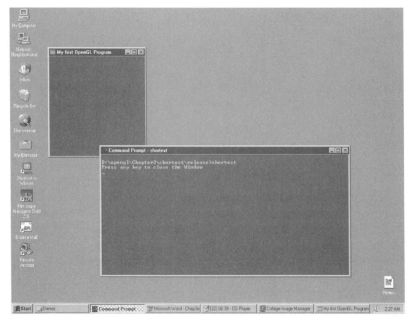

Figure 3-2 Output from shortest.c

Console Modes

A *console-mode application* is a Win32 program that runs in a text mode window. This is very much like running a DOS program under Windows NT or Windows 95, except the program is a true 32-bit application and has access to the entire Win32 API. Console-mode programs are not limited to text mode. They can in fact create GUI windows for auxiliary output (try calling MessageBox() with a NULL window handle from the above program), and GUI-based applications can even create console windows if needed. The AUX library allows you to easily write a console-based program with only a main() function that can create an auxiliary GUI window for OpenGL output.

To build this program, you need to set your compiler and link options to build a Win32 console (or text-based) application. You will need to link to the AUX library glaux.lib and the OpenGL import library opengl32.lib. See your compiler's documentation for individual instructions on building console applications.

The shortest.c program doesn't do very much. When run from the command line, it creates a standard GUI window with the caption "My first OpenGL Program" and a clear blue background. It then prints the message "Press any key to close the window" in the console window. The GUI window will not respond to any mouse or keyboard activity, and the console window waits for you to press a key before terminating (you will have to switch focus back to the console window first to do this). It doesn't even behave very well—you can't move or resize the OpenGL window, and the window doesn't even repaint. If you obscure the window with another window and then uncover it, the client area goes black.

This simple program contains three AUX library functions (prefixed with *aux*) and three "real" OpenGL functions (prefixed with *gl*). Let's examine the program line by line, after which we'll introduce some more functions and substantially improve on our first example.

The Includes

Here are the include files:

```
#include <windows.h>
#include <conio.h>
#include <gl\gl.h>
#include <gl\glaux.h>
```

These includes define the function prototypes used by the program. The windows.h header file is required by all Windows GUI applications; even though this is a console-mode program, the AUX library creates a GUI window to draw in. The file conio.h is for console I/O. It's included because we use cprintf() to print a message, and getch() to terminate the program when a key is pressed. The file gl.h defines the OpenGL functions that are prefixed with gl; and glaux.h contains all the functions necessary for the AUX library.

The Body

Next comes the main body of the program:

```
void main(void)
      {
```

Console mode C and C++ programs always start execution with the function main(). If you are an experienced Windows nerd, you may wonder where WinMain() is in this example. It's not there because we start with a console-mode application, so we don't have to start with window creation and a message loop. It is possible with Win32 to create graphical windows from console applications, just as it is possible to create console windows from GUI applications. These details are buried within the AUX library (remember, the AUX library is designed to hide these platform details).

Display Mode: Single-Buffered

The next line of code

```
auxInitDisplayMode(AUX_SINGLE | AUX_RGBA);
```

tells the AUX library what type of display mode to use when creating the window. The flags here tell it to use a single-buffered window (AUX_SINGLE) and to use RGBA color mode (AUX_RGBA). A single-buffered window means that all drawing commands are performed on the window displayed. An alternative is a double-buffered window, where the drawing commands are actually executed to create a scene off screen, then quickly swapped into view on the window. This is often used to produce animation effects and will be demonstrated later in this chapter. RGBA color mode means that you specify colors by supplying separate intensities of red, green, and blue components (more on color modes in Chapter 8).

Position the Window

After setting the display mode, you need to tell the AUX library where to put the window and how big to make it. The next line of code does this:

```
auxInitPosition(100,100,250,250);
```

The parameters represent the upper-left corner of the window and its width and height. Specifically, this line tells the program to place the upper-left corner at coordinates (100,100), and to make the window 250 pixels wide and 250 pixels high. On a screen of standard VGA resolution (640 x 480), this window will take up a large portion of the display. At SuperVGA resolutions (800 x 600 and above), the window will take less space even though the number of pixels remains the same (250 x 250).

Here is the prototype for this function:

```
auxInitPosition(GLint x, GLint y, GLsizei width, GLsizei height);
```

The GLint and GLsizei data types are defined as integers (as described in the earlier section about data types). The x parameter is the number of screen pixels counted from the left side of the screen, and y is the number of pixels counted down from the top of the screen. This is how Windows converts desktop screen coordinates to a physical location by default. OpenGL's default method for counting the x coordinate is the same; however, it counts the y coordinate *from bottom to top*—just the opposite of Windows. See Figures 3-3 and 3-4.

Porting Note

Although Windows maps desktop coordinates as shown in Figure 3-3, the X Window System maps desktop coordinates the same way that OpenGL does in Figure 3-4. If you are porting an AUX library program from another environment, you may need to change the call to auxInitPosition() to account for this.

Create the OpenGL Window

The last call to the AUX library actually creates the window on the screen. The code

```
auxInitWindow("My first OpenGL Program");
```

creates the window and sets the caption to "My first OpenGL Program." Obviously, the single argument to auxInitWindow is the caption for the window title bar. If you stopped here, the program would create an empty window (black background is the default) with the caption specified, and then terminate, closing the OpenGL window immediately. The addition of our last getch() prevents the window from disappearing, but still nothing of interest happens in the window.

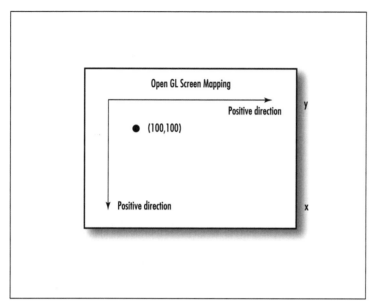

Figure 3-3 Default OpenGL window coordinate mapping

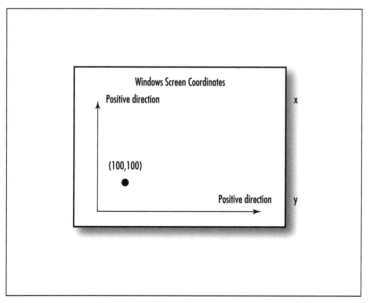

Figure 3-4 Default Windows screen coordinate mapping

Clear a Window (Erase with a Color)

The three lines of code we've looked at so far from the AUX library are sufficient to initialize and create a window that OpenGL will draw in. From this point on, all OpenGL commands and function calls will operate on this window.

The next line of code

```
glClearColor(0.0f, 0.0f, 1.0f, 0.0f);
```

is your first real OpenGL function call. This function sets the color used when clearing the window. The prototype for this function is

```
void glClearColor(GLclampf red, GLclampf green, GLclampf blue, GLclampf alpha);
```

GLclampf is defined as a float under most implementations of OpenGL. In OpenGL, a single color is represented as a mixture of red, green, and blue components. The range for each component can vary from 0.0 to 1.0. This is similar to the Windows specification of colors using the RGB macro to create a COLORREF value. (See the *Windows95 API Bible* from Waite Group Press for details.) The difference is that in Windows each color component in a COLORREF can range from 0 to 255, giving a total of 256 x 256 x 256—or over 16 million colors. With OpenGL, the values for each component can be any valid floating-point value between 0 and 1, thus yielding a theoretically infinite number of potential colors. Practically speaking, OpenGL represents colors internally as 32-bit values, yielding a true maximum of 4,294,967,296 colors (called *true color* on some hardware). Thus the effective range for each component is from 0.0 to 1.0, in steps of approximately .00006.

Naturally, both Windows and OpenGL take this color value and convert it internally to the nearest possible exact match with the available video hardware and palette. We'll explore this more closely in Chapter 8.

Table 3-3 lists some common colors and their component values. These values can be used with any of the OpenGL color-related functions.

Table 3-3 Some common composite colors

Composite Color	Red Component	Green Component	Blue Component
Black	0.0	0.0	0.0
Red	1.0	0.0	0.0
Green	0.0	1.0	0.0
Yellow	1.0	1.0	0.0
Blue	0.0	0.0	1.0
Magenta	1.0	0.0	1.0
Cyan	0.0	1.0	1.0
Dark gray	0.25	0.25	0.25
Light gray	0.75	0.75	0.75
Brown	0.60	0.40	0.12

Composite Color	Red Component	Green Component	Blue Component
Pumpkin orange	0.98	0.625	0.12
Pastel pink	0.98	.04	0.7
Barney purple	0.60	0.40	0.70
White	1.0	1.0	1.0

The last argument to glClearColor() is the *alpha component.* The alpha component is used for blending and special effects such as *translucence.* Translucence refers to an object's ability to allow light to pass through it. Suppose you are representing a piece of red stained glass, but a blue light is shining behind it. The blue light will affect the appearance of the red in the glass (blue + red = purple). You can use the alpha component value to make a blue color that is semitransparent; so it works like a sheet of water—an object behind it shows through. There is more to this type of effect than the alpha value, and in Chapter 16 we will write an example program that demonstrates it; until then you should leave this value as 1.

Actually Clear

Now that we have told OpenGL what color to use for clearing, we need an instruction to do the actual clearing. This accomplished by the line

```
glClear(GL_COLOR_BUFFER_BIT);
```

The glClear() function clears a particular buffer or combination of buffers. A buffer is a storage area for image information. The red, green, and blue components of a drawing actually have separate buffers, but they are usually collectively referred to as the *color buffer.*

Buffers are a powerful feature of OpenGL and will be covered in detail in Chapter 15. For the next several chapters, all you really need to understand is that the color buffer is where the displayed image is stored internally, and that clearing the buffer with glClear removes the drawing from the window.

Flush That Queue

Our final OpenGL function call comes next:

```
glFlush();
```

This line causes any unexecuted OpenGL commands to be executed—we have two at this point: glClearColor() and glClear().

Internally, OpenGL uses a rendering pipeline that processes commands sequentially. OpenGL commands and statements often are queued up until the OpenGL server processes several "requests" at once. This improves performance, especially when constructing complex objects. Drawing is accelerated because the slower graphics hardware is accessed less often for a given set of drawing instructions. (When Win32 was first introduced, this same concept was added to the Windows GDI to improve graphics performance under Windows NT.) In our short program, the glFlush() function simply tells OpenGL that it should proceed with the drawing instructions supplied thus far before waiting for any more drawing commands.

The last bit of code for this example

```
// Stop and wait for a keypress
cprintf("Press any key to close the Window\n");
getch();
}
```

displays a message in the console window and stops the program until you press a key, at which point the program is terminated and the window is destroyed.

It may not be the most interesting OpenGL program in existence, but shortest.c demonstrates the very basics of getting a window up using the AUX library and it shows you how to specify a color and clear the window. Next we want to spruce up our program by adding some more AUX library and OpenGL functions.

Drawing Shapes with OpenGL

The shortest.c program made an empty window with a blue background. Let's do some drawing in the window. In addition, we want to be able to move and resize the window so that it behaves more like a Windows window. We will also dispense with using getch() to determine when to terminate the program. In Listing 3-2 you can see the modifications.

The first change you'll notice is in the headers. The conio.h file is no longer included because we aren't using getch() or cprintf() anymore.

Listing 3-2 A friendlier OpenGL program

```
// friendly.c
// A friendlier OpenGL program

#include <windows.h>      // Standard header for Windows
#include <gl\gl.h>        // OpenGL library
#include <gl\glaux.h>     // AUX library


// Called by AUX library to draw scene
void CALLBACK RenderScene(void)
        {
        // Set clear color to blue
        glClearColor(0.0f, 0.0f, 1.0f, 1.0f);

        // Clear the window
        glClear(GL_COLOR_BUFFER_BIT);

        // Set current drawing color to red
        //            R      G      B
        glColor3f(1.0f, 0.0f, 0.0f);

        // Draw a filled rectangle with current color
```

```
        glRectf(100.0f, 150.0f, 150.0f, 100.0f);

        glFlush();
        }
```

```
void main(void)
        {
        // AUX library window and mode setup
        auxInitDisplayMode(AUX_SINGLE | AUX_RGBA);
        auxInitPosition(100,100,250,250);
        auxInitWindow("My second OpenGL Program");

        // Set function to call when window needs updating
        auxMainLoop(RenderScene);
        }
```

The Rendering Function

Next, you'll see we have created the function RenderScene().

```
// Called by AUX library to draw scene
void CALLBACK RenderScene(void)
        {
        . . .
        . . .
```

This is where we have moved all code that does the actual drawing in the window. The process of drawing with OpenGL is often referred to as *rendering*, so we used that descriptive name. In later examples we'll be putting most of our drawing code in this function.

Make note of the CALLBACK statement in the function declaration. This is required because we're going to tell the AUX library to call this function whenever the window needs updating. Callback functions are simply functions that you write, which the AUX library will be calling in your behalf. You'll see how this works later.

Drawing a Rectangle

Previously, all our program did was clear the screen. We've added the following two lines of drawing code:

```
// Set current drawing color to red
//              R     G     B
glColor3f(1.0f, 0.0f, 0.0f);

// Draw a filled rectangle with current color
glRectf(100.0f, 150.0f, 150.0f, 100.0f);
```

These lines set the color used for future drawing operations (lines and filling) with the call to glColor3f(). Then glRectf() draws a filled rectangle.

The glColor3f() function selects a color in the same manner as glClearColor(), but no alpha translucency component needs to be specified:

```
void glColor3f(GLfloat red, GLfloat green, GLfloat blue);
```

The glRectf() function takes floating point arguments, as denoted by the trailing f. The number of arguments is not used in the function name because all glRect variations take four arguments. The four arguments of glRectf(),

```
void glRectf(GLfloat x1, GLfloat y1, GLfloat x2, GLfloat y2);
```

represent two coordinate pairs—(x1, y1) and (x2, y2). The first pair represents the upper-left corner of the rectangle, and the second pair represents the lower-right corner. See Figure 3-4 if you need a review of OpenGL coordinate mapping.

Initialization

The main body of friendly.c starts the same way as our first example:

```
void main(void)
    {
    // AUX library window and mode setup
    auxInitDisplayMode(AUX_SINGLE | AUX_RGBA);
    auxInitPosition(100,100,250,250);
    auxInitWindow("My second OpenGL Program");

    // Set function to call when window needs updating
    auxMainLoop(RenderScene);
    }
```

As before, the three auxInitxxx calls set up and display the window in which we'll be drawing. In the final line, auxMainLoop() takes the name of the function that does the drawing, RenderScene(). The AUX library's auxMainLoop() function simply keeps the program going until it's terminated by closing the window. This function's single argument is a pointer to another function it should call whenever the window needs updating. This callback function will be called when the window is first displayed, when the window is moved or resized, and when the window is uncovered by some other window.

```
// Called by AUX library to draw scene
void CALLBACK RenderScene(void)
    {
    // Set clear color to Blue
    glClearColor(0.0f, 0.0f, 1.0f, 1.0f);

    // Clear the window
    glClear(GL_COLOR_BUFFER_BIT);

    // Set current drawing color to red
    //                 R    G       B
    glColor3f(1.0f, 0.0f, 0.0f);

    // Draw a filled rectangle with current color
    glRectf(100.0f, 150.0f, 150.0f, 100.0f);

    glFlush();
    }
```

At this point, the program will display a red square in the middle of a blue window, because we used fixed locations for the square. If you make the window larger, the

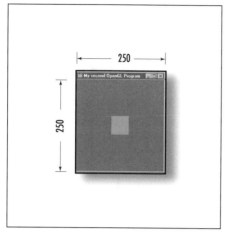 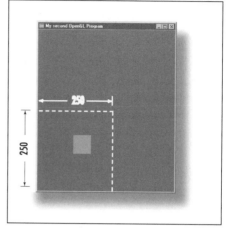

Figure 3-5 Effects of changing window size

square will remain in the lower-left corner of the window. When you make the window smaller, the square may no longer fit in the client area. This is because as you resize the window, the screen extents of the window change; however, the drawing code continues to place the rectangle at (100, 150, 150, 100). In the original window this was directly in the center; in a larger window these coordinates are located in the lower-left corner. See Figure 3-5.

Scaling to the Window

In nearly all windowing environments, the user may at any time change the size and dimensions of the window. When this happens, the window usually responds by redrawing its contents, taking into consideration the window's new dimensions. Sometimes you may wish to simply clip the drawing for smaller windows, or display the entire drawing at its original size in a larger window. For our purposes, we usually will want to scale the drawing to fit within the window, regardless of the size of the drawing or window. Thus a very small window would have a complete but very small drawing, and a larger window would have a similar but larger drawing. You see this in most drawing programs when you stretch a window as opposed to enlarging the drawing. Stretching a window usually doesn't change the drawing size, but magnifying the image will make it grow.

Setting the Viewport and Clipping Volume

In Chapter 2 we discussed how viewports and clipping volumes affect the coordinate range and scaling of 2D and 3D drawings in a 2D window on the computer screen. Now we will examine the setting of viewport and clipping volume coordinates in OpenGL. When we created our window with the function call

```
auxInitPosition(100,100,250,250);
```

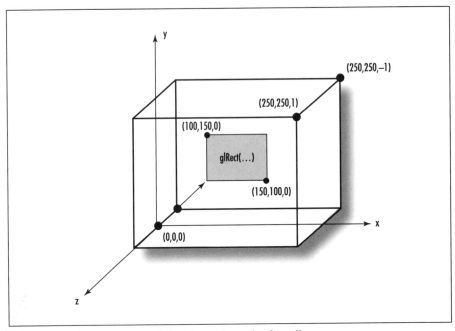

Figure 3-6 The viewport and clipping volume for friendly.c

the AUX library by default created a viewport that matched the window size exactly (0, 0, 250, 250). The clipping volume by default was set to be the first quadrant of Cartesian space, with the x- and y-axis extending the length and height of the window. The z-axis extends perpendicular to the viewer, giving a flat 2D appearance to objects drawn in the xy plane. Figure 3-6 illustrates this graphically.

Although our drawing is a 2D flat rectangle, we are actually drawing in a 3D coordinate space. The glRectf() function draws the rectangle in the xy plane at z = 0. Your perspective is down along the positive z-axis to see the square rectangle at z = 0.

Whenever the window size changes, the viewport and clipping volume must be redefined for the new window dimensions. Otherwise, you'll see the effect shown in Figure 3-5, where the mapping of the coordinate system to screen coordinates stays the same regardless of window size.

Because window size changes are detected and handled differently under various environments, the AUX library provides the function auxReshapeFunc(), which registers a callback that the AUX library will call whenever the window dimensions change. The function you pass to auxReshapeFunc() is prototyped like this:

```
void CALLBACK ChangeSize(GLsizei w, GLsizei h);
```

We have chosen ChangeSize as a descriptive name for this function and will use that name for our future examples.

The ChangeSize() function will receive the new width and height whenever the window size changes. We can use this information to modify the mapping of our desired coordinate system to real screen coordinates, with the help of two OpenGL functions: glViewport() and glOrtho(). Listing 3-3 shows our previous example modified to account for various window sizes and dimensions. Only the changed main() function and our new ChangeSize() function are shown.

Listing 3-3 Scaling in OpenGL

```
// Scale.c
// Scaling an OpenGL Window.

// Called by AUX Library when the window has changed size
void CALLBACK ChangeSize(GLsizei w, GLsizei h)
        {
        // Prevent a divide by zero
        if(h == 0)
                h = 1;

        // Set Viewport to window dimensions
        glViewport(0, 0, w, h);

        // Reset coordinate system
        glLoadIdentity();

        // Establish clipping volume (left, right, bottom, top, near, far)
        if (w <= h)
                glOrtho (0.0f, 250.0f, 0.0f, 250.0f*h/w, 1.0, -1.0);
        else
                glOrtho (0.0f, 250.0f*w/h, 0.0f, 250.0f, 1.0, -1.0);
        }


void main(void)
        {
        // Set up and initialize AUX window
        auxInitDisplayMode(AUX_SINGLE | AUX_RGBA);
        auxInitPosition(100,100,250,250);
        auxInitWindow("Scaling Window");

        // Set function to call when window changes size
        auxReshapeFunc(ChangeSize);

        // Set function to call when window needs updating
        auxMainLoop(RenderScene);
        }
```

Now, when you change the size or dimensions of the window, the square will change size as well. A much larger window will have a much larger square and a much smaller window will have a much smaller square. If you make the window long horizontally, the square will be centered vertically, far left of center. If you make the window tall vertically, the square will be centered horizontally, closer to the bottom of the window. Note that the rectangle always remains square. To see a square scaled as the window resizes, see Figure 3-7a and Figure 3-7b.

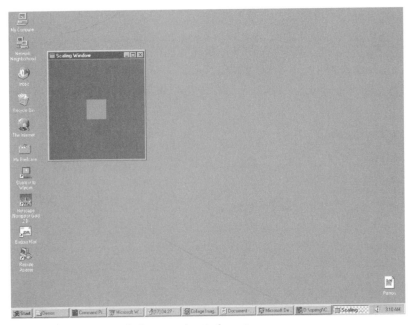

Figure 3-7a Image scaled to match window size

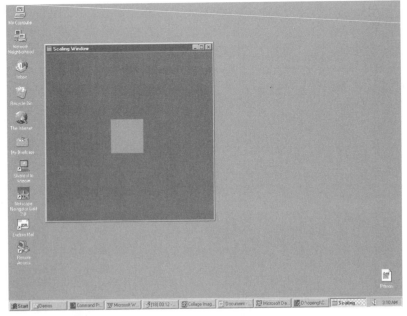

Figure 3-7b Square scaled as the window resizes

Defining the Viewport

To understand how the viewport definition is achieved, let's look more carefully at the ChangeSize() function. It first calls glViewport() with the new width and height of the window. The glViewport function is defined as

```
void glViewport(GLint x, GLint y, GLsizei width, GLsizei height);
```

The x and y parameters specify the lower-right corner of the viewport within the window, and the width and height parameters specify these dimensions in pixels. Usually x and y will both be zero, but you can use viewports to render more than one drawing in different areas of a window. The viewport defines the area within the window in actual screen coordinates that OpenGL can use to draw in (see Figure 3-8). The current clipping volume is then mapped to the new viewport. If you specify a viewport that is smaller than the window coordinates, the rendering will be scaled smaller, as you see in Figure 3-8.

Defining the Clipping Volume

The last requirement of our ChangeSize() function is to redefine the clipping volume so that the aspect ratio remains square. The *aspect ratio* is the ratio of the number of pixels along a unit of length in the vertical direction to the number of pixels along the same unit of length in the horizontal direction. An aspect ratio of 1.0 would define a square aspect ratio. An aspect ratio of 0.5 would specify that for every two pixels in

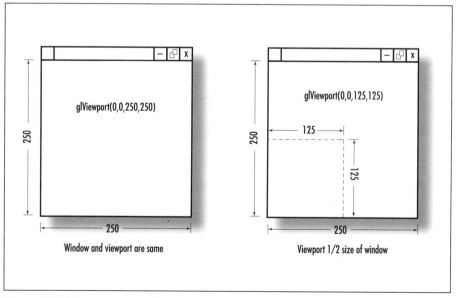

Figure 3-8 Viewport-to-window mapping

the horizontal direction for a unit of length, there is one pixel in the vertical direction for the same unit of length.

If a viewport is specified that is not square and it is mapped to a square clipping volume, that will cause images to be distorted. For example, a viewport matching the window size and dimensions but mapped to a square clipping volume would cause images to appear tall and thin in tall and thin windows, and wide and short in wide and short windows. In this case, our square would only appear square when the window was sized to be a square.

In our example, an orthographic projection is used for the clipping volume (see Chapter 2). The OpenGL command to create this projection is glOrtho():

```
void glOrtho(GLdouble left, GLdouble right, GLdouble bottom, GLdouble top,
                                         GLdouble near, GLdouble far );
```

In 3D Cartesian space, the left and right values specify the minimum and maximum coordinate value displayed along the x-axis; bottom and top are for the y-axis. The near and far parameters are for the z-axis, generally with negative values extending away from the viewer (see Figure 3-9).

Just before the code using glOrtho(), you'll notice a single call to glLoadIdentity(). This is needed because glOrtho() doesn't really establish the clipping volume, but rather modifies the existing clipping volume. It multiplies the matrix that describes the current clipping volume by the matrix that describes the clipping volume described in

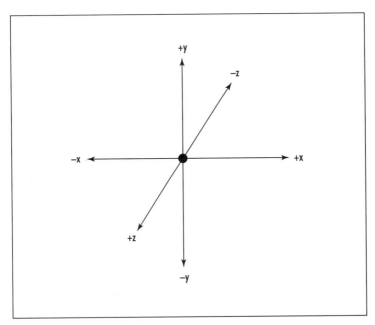

Figure 3-9 Cartesian space

its arguments. The discussion of matrix manipulations and coordinate transformations is in Chapter 7. For now, you just need to know that glLoadIdentity() serves to "reset" the coordinate system to unity before any matrix manipulations are performed. Without this "reset" every time glOrtho() is called, each successive call to glOrtho() could result in a further corruption of our intended clipping volume, which may not even display our rectangle.

Keeping a Square Square

The following code does the actual work of keeping our "square" square.

```
if (w <= h)
        glOrtho (0, 250, 0, 250*h/w, 1.0, -1.0);
else
        glOrtho (0, 250*w/h, 0, 250, 1.0, -1.0);
```

Our clipping volume (visible coordinate space) is modified so that the left-hand side is always at x = 0. The right-hand side extends to 250 unless the window is wider than it is tall. In that case, the right-hand side is extended by the aspect ratio of the window. The bottom is always at y = 0, and extends upward to 250 unless the window is taller than it is wide. In that case the upper coordinate is extended by the aspect ratio. This serves to keep a square coordinate region 250 x 250 available regardless of the shape of the window. Figure 3-10 shows how this works.

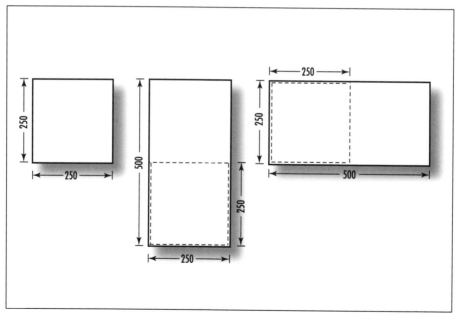

Figure 3-10 Clipping region for three different windows

Animation with AUX

Thus far, we've discussed the basics of using the AUX library for creating a window and using OpenGL commands for the actual drawing. You will often want to move or rotate your images and scenes, creating an animated effect. Let's take the previous example, which draws a square, and make the square bounce off the sides of the window. You could create a loop that continually changes your object's coordinates before calling the RenderScene() function. This would cause the square to appear to move around within the window.

The AUX library provides a function that makes it much easier to set up a simple animated sequence. This function, auxIdleFunc(), takes the name of a function to call continually while your program sits idle. The function to perform your idle processing is prototyped like this:

```
void CALLBACK IdleFunction(void);
```

This function is then called repeatedly by the AUX library unless the window is being moved or resized.

If we change the hard-coded values for the location of our rectangle to variables, and then constantly modify those variables in the IdleFunction(), the rectangle will appear to move across the window. Let's look at an example of this kind of animation. In Listing 3-4, we'll modify Listing 3-3 to bounce the square around off the inside borders of the window. We'll need to keep track of the position and size of the rectangle as we go along, and account for any changes in window size.

Listing 3-4 Animated bouncing square

```
// bounce.c
// Bouncing square

#include <windows.h>      // Standard windows include
#include <gl\gl.h>        // OpenGL library
#include <gl\glaux.h>     // AUX library


// Initial square position and size
GLfloat x1 = 100.0f;
GLfloat y1 = 150.0f;
GLsizei rsize = 50;

// Step size in x and y directions
// (number of pixels to move each time)
GLfloat xstep = 1.0f;
GLfloat ystep = 1.0f;

// Keep track of window's changing width and height
GLfloat windowWidth;
GLfloat windowHeight;


// Called by AUX library when the window has changed size
void CALLBACK ChangeSize(GLsizei w, GLsizei h)
```

```
        {
        // Prevent a divide by zero, when window is too short
        // (you can't make a window of zero width)
        if(h == 0)
                h = 1;

        // Set the viewport to be the entire window
        glViewport(0, 0, w, h);

        // Reset the coordinate system before modifying
        glLoadIdentity();


        // Keep the square square, this time, save calculated
        // width and height for later use
        if (w <= h)
                {
                windowHeight = 250.0f*h/w;
                windowWidth = 250.0f;
                }
   else
                {
                windowWidth = 250.0f*w/h;
                windowHeight = 250.0f;
                }

        // Set the clipping volume
        glOrtho(0.0f, windowWidth, 0.0f, windowHeight, 1.0f, -1.0f);
        }

// Called by AUX library to update window
void CALLBACK RenderScene(void)
        {
        // Set background clearing color to blue
        glClearColor(0.0f, 0.0f, 1.0f, 1.0f);

        // Clear the window with current clearing color
        glClear(GL_COLOR_BUFFER_BIT);

        // Set drawing color to red, and draw rectangle at
        // current position.
        glColor3f(1.0f, 0.0f, 0.0f);
        glRectf(x1, y1, x1+rsize, y1+rsize);

        glFlush();
        }


// Called by AUX library when idle (window not being
// resized or moved)
void CALLBACK IdleFunction(void)
        {
        // Reverse direction when you reach left or right edge
        if(x1 > windowWidth-rsize || x1 < 0)
                xstep = -xstep;

        // Reverse direction when you reach top or bottom edge
        if(y1 > windowHeight-rsize || y1 < 0)
                ystep = -ystep;
```

continued on next page

continued from previous page

```
        // Check bounds.  This is in case the window is made
        // smaller and the rectangle is outside the new
        // clipping volume
        if(x1 > windowWidth-rsize)
                x1 = windowWidth-rsize-1;

        if(y1 > windowHeight-rsize)
                y1 = windowHeight-rsize-1;

        // Actually move the square
        x1 += xstep;
        y1 += ystep;

        // Redraw the scene with new coordinates
        RenderScene();
        }


// Main body of program
void main(void)
        {
        // AUX window setup and initialization
        auxInitDisplayMode(AUX_SINGLE | AUX_RGBA);
        auxInitPosition(100,100,250,250);
        auxInitWindow("Simple 2D Animation");

        // Set function to call when window is resized
        auxReshapeFunc(ChangeSize);

        // Set function to call when program is idle
        auxIdleFunc(IdleFunction);

        // Start main loop
        auxMainLoop(RenderScene);
        }
```

The animation produced by this example is very poor, even on very fast hardware. Because the window is being cleared each time before drawing the square, it flickers the entire time it's moving about, and you can easily see the square actually being drawn as two triangles. To produce smoother animation, you need to employ a feature known as *double buffering*.

Double Buffering

One of the most important features of any graphics packages is support for *double buffering*. This feature allows you to execute your drawing code while rendering to an off-screen buffer. Then a swap command places your drawing on screen instantly.

Double buffering can serve two purposes. The first is that some complex drawings may take a long time to draw and you may not want each step of the image composition to be visible. Using double buffering, you can compose an image and display it only after it is complete. The user never sees a partial image; only after the entire image is ready is it blasted to the screen.

A second use for double buffering is for animation. Each frame is drawn in the off-screen buffer and then swapped quickly to the screen when ready. The AUX library supports double-buffered windows. We need to make only two changes to the bounce.c program to produce a much smoother animation. First, change the line in main() that initializes the display mode to indicate that it should use double buffering:

```
auxInitDisplayMode(AUX_DOUBLE | AUX_RGBA);
```

This will cause all the drawing code to render in an off-screen buffer.

Next, add a single line to the end of the Render() function:

```
auxSwapBuffers();
```

The auxSwapBuffers() function causes the off-screen buffer used for drawing to be swapped to the screen. (The complete code for this is in the BOUNCE2 example on the CD.) This produces a very smooth animation of the red square bouncing around inside the window. See Figure 3-11.

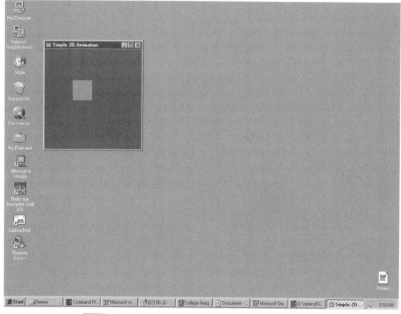

Figure 3-11 Bouncing square

Finally, Some 3D!

Thus far, all our samples have been simple rectangles in the middle of the window; they either scaled to the new window size or bounced around off the walls. By now you may be bouncing off some walls of your own, waiting anxiously to see something in 3D. Wait no more!

As mentioned earlier, we have been drawing in 3D all along, but our view of the rectangle has been perpendicular to the clipping volume. If we could just rotate the clipping volume with respect to the viewer, we might actually see something with a little depth. However, we aren't going to get into coordinate transformations and rotations until Chapter 7. And even if we started that work now, a flat rectangle isn't very interesting, even when viewed from an angle.

To see some depth, we need to draw an object that is not flat. The AUX library contains nearly a dozen 3D objects—from a sphere to a teapot—that can be created with a single function call. These called functions are of the form auxSolidxxxx() or auxWirexxxx(), where xxxx names the solid or wireframe object that is created. For example, the following command draws a wireframe teapot of approximately 50.0 units in diameter:

```
auxWireTeapot(50.0f);
```

If we define a clipping volume that extends from -100 to 100 along all three axes, we'll get the wireframe teapot shown in Figure 3-12. The teapot is probably the best example at this point because the other objects still look two-dimensional when viewed from a parallel projection. The program that produced this image is found in this chapter's subdirectory on the CD in teapot.c.

If you change the wire teapot to a solid teapot with the command

```
auxSolidTeapot(50.0f);
```

you'll see only a red outline of the teapot. In order to see relief in a solid-colored object, you will need to incorporate shading and lighting with other OpenGL commands that you'll learn about in Chapter 9 and later.

For further study of the AUX library objects, see the samples AUXWIRE and AUX-SOLID on the CD in this chapter's subdirectory. These samples make use of the glRotatef() function (explained in Chapter 7), which spins the objects around all three axes of the viewing volume. Some of these objects make use of the utility library, so be sure that you link with glu32.lib when using these objects yourself.

Summary

In this chapter we have introduced the AUX library toolkit and presented the fundamentals of writing a program that uses OpenGL. We have used this library to show the easiest possible way to create a window and draw in it using OpenGL commands. You have learned to use the AUX library to create windows that can be resized, as well as to create simple animation. You have also been introduced to the process of using OpenGL to do drawing—composing and selecting colors, clearing the screen, drawing

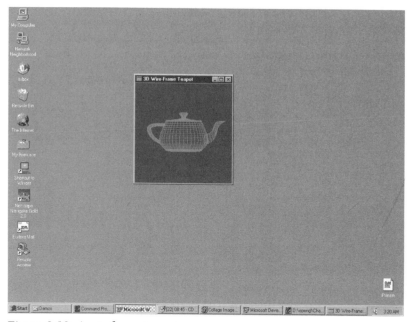

Figure 3-12 A wireframe teapot

a rectangle, and setting the viewport and clipping volume to scale images to match the window size. We've also discussed the various OpenGL data types, and the headers and libraries required to build programs that use OpenGL.

The Auxiliary library contains many other functions to handle keyboard and mouse input as well. Microsoft's implementation of the Aux library contains Windows-specific functions that enable access to window handles and device contexts. You are encouraged to explore the upcoming reference section of this chapter to discover other uses and features of the AUX library. You'll also want to examine and run the other Chapter 3 samples on the CD.

Reference Section

AUXIDLEFUNC

Purpose	Establishes a callback function for idle processing.
Include File	<glaux.h>
Syntax	void auxIdleFunc(AUXIDLEPROC func);
Description	Specifies the idle function func() to be called when no other activity is pending. Typically used for animation. When not busy rendering the cur-

rent scene, the idle function changes some parameters used by the rendering function to produce the next scene.

Parameters	
func	This function is prototyped as
	void CALLBACK IdleFunc(void);
	This is the user-defined function used for idle processing. Passing NULL as this function name will disable idle processing.
Returns	None.
Example	See BOUNCE and BOUNCE2 examples from this chapter.
See Also	auxSwapBuffers, auxMainLoop, auxReshapeFunc

AUXINITDISPLAYMODE

Purpose	Initializes the display mode of the AUX library OpenGL window.
Include File	<glaux.h>
Syntax	void auxInitDisplayMode(GLbitfield mask);
Description	This is the first function that must be called by an AUX library-based program to set up the OpenGL window. This function sets the characteristics of the window that OpenGL will use for drawing operations.
Parameters	
mask	GLbitfield: A mask or bitwise combination of masks from Table 3-4. These mask values may be combined with a bitwise OR. For example, to create a window that uses double buffering and color index mode, call

```
auxInitDisplayMode(AUX_DOUBLE | AUX_INDEX)
```

Returns	None.
Example	See any example program from this chapter.
See Also	auxInitPosition, auxInitWindow

Table 3-4 Mask values for window characteristics

Mask Value	Meaning
AUX_SINGLE	Specifies a single-buffered window
AUX_DOUBLE	Specifies a double-buffered window
AUX_RGBA	Specifies an RGBA-mode window
AUX_INDEX	Specifies a color-index mode window
AUX_DEPTH	Specifies a 32-bit depth buffer
AUX_DEPTH16	Specifies a 16-bit depth buffer
AUX_STENCIL	Specifies a stencil buffer

Mask Value	Meaning
AUX_ACCUM	Specifies an accumulation buffer
AUX_ALPHA	Specifies an ALPHA buffer
AUX_FIXED_332_PAL	Specifies a fixed 3-3-2 palette for the window

AUXINITPOSITION

Purpose	Sets the window position used by auxInitWindow().
Include File	<glaux.h>
Syntax	void auxInitPosition(GLint x, GLint y, GLsizei width, GLsizei height);
Description	This function tells the AUX library where to place the main graphics window when it is created.
Parameters	
x	GLint: The position measured in pixels of the top left corner of the window from the left side of the screen.
y	GLint: The position measured in pixels of the top left corner of the window from the top of the screen.
width	GLsizei: The initial width of the client area of the window in screen pixels.
height	GLsizei: The initial height of the client area of the window in screen pixels.
Returns	None.
Example	See any example from this chapter.
See Also	auxInitDisplayMode, auxInitWindow

AUXINITWINDOW

Purpose	Initializes and displays the OpenGL rendering window.
Include File	<glaux.h>
Syntax	void auxInitWindow(GLBYTE *titleString);
Description	This function opens the window that will be used by OpenGL for drawing operations.
	The window characteristics must first be set by auxInitDisplayMode() and auxInitPosition().
Parameters	
titleString	GLBYTE: A pointer to a character string that will be used for the window caption.
Returns	None.
Example	See any example from this chapter.
See Also	auxInitDisplayMode, auxInitPosition

AUXKEYFUNC

Purpose	Associates a callback function with a particular keystroke.
Include File	<glaux.h>
Syntax	void auxKeyFunc(GLint key, void(*function(void));
Description	Sets a callback function *function* that the AUX library calls when the key indicated by *key* is pressed. The window is also redrawn after the processing of this keystroke.
Parameters	
key	GLint: Specifies the key with which to associate the given function. This can be one of the values in Table 3-5.
function	This callback function is prototyped as
	void CALLBACK KeyFunc(void);
	This function is called by the AUX library when the specified key is pressed. Passing NULL as this parameter disables a previous key function setting.
Returns	None.
Example	See the KEYMOVE supplementary example from this chapter's subdirectory on the CD.
See Also	auxMouseFunc

Table 3-5 Auxiliary Library Key Definitions.

Key Value	Description
AUX_ESCAPE	The Escape key
AUX_SPACE	The Spacebar key
AUX_RETURN	The Return or Enter key
AUX_LEFT	The Left Arrow key
AUX_RIGHT	The Right Arrow key
AUX_UP	The Up Arrow key
AUX_DOWN	The Down Arrow key
AUX_A through AUX_Z	The keys A through Z (uppercase)
AUX_a through AUX_z	The keys a through z (lowercase)
AUX_0 through AUX_9	The number keys 0 through 9

AUXMAINLOOP

Purpose	Specifies the function that should be used to update the OpenGL window.
Include File	<glaux.h>

Syntax	void auxMainLoop(AUXMAINPROC func);
Description	This function is used to specify the function to be called whenever the OpenGL window needs to be refreshed. This function does not return until the OpenGL window is closed.
Parameters	
func	This function is prototyped as
	void CALLBACK MainFunc(void);
	This is the function to be used for updating the window by actually performing the drawing commands.
Returns	None.
Example	See any example from this chapter.
See Also	auxIdleFunc, auxReshapeFunc

AUXMOUSEFUNC

Purpose	Associates callback functions with mouse button activity.
Include File	<glaux.h>
Syntax	void auxMouseFunc(int button, int mode, AUXMOUSEPROC func);
Description	Sets the function *func* to be called when a mouse button is pressed or released. The specified mouse button is set to one of the values listed below. The button action can denote whether the button is pressed or released.
Parameters	
button	int: The button with which to associate the callback function; may be one of the following values: AUX_LEFTBUTTON, AUX_MIDDLEBUTTON, or AUX_RIGHTBUTTON.
mode	int: The action of the button specified above to associate with the callback function. May be either AUX_MOUSEDOWN or AUX_MOUSEUP.
func	The callback function is prototyped as
	void CALLBACK MouseFunc(AUX_EVENTREC *event);
	The event structure contains the mouse position at the time of the event.

```
typedef struct _AUX_EVENTREC {
  GLint event;
  GLint data[4];
} AUX_EVENTREC;
```

    event   GLint: Specifies the event that took place (AUX_MOUSEUP, or AUX_MOUSEDOWN)

data[4] GLint: contains specific data about this event.
data[AUX_MOUSEX] = mouse position in x direction.
data[AUX_MOUSEY] = mouse position in y direction.
data[MOUSE_STATUS] = mouse button (from button).

Returns	None.
Example	See the MBOUNCE supplementary example on the CD subdirectory for this chapter.
See Also	auxKeyFunc

AUXRESHAPEFUNC

Purpose	Establishes a callback function to handle window dimension and size changes.
Include File	<glaux.h>
Syntax	void auxReshapeFunc(AUXRESHAPEPROC func)
Description	This function is called to establish a callback function that the AUX library will call whenever the window size or shape changes. Typically this function modifies the viewport and clipping volume to perform image scaling.
Parameters	
func	This callback function is prototyped as
	void CALLBACK Reshape(GLsizei width, GLsizei height)
	This function receives the new width and height of the window.
Returns	None.
Example	See the SCALE example from this chapter.
See Also	auxIdleFunc, auxMainLoop

AUXSETONECOLOR

Purpose	Sets a single color in the color-index mode color palette.
Include File	<glaux.h>
Syntax	void auxSetOneColor(int index, float red, float green, float blue);
Description	This function is used in color index mode. In this mode, rather than specifying colors with RGB values, a palette of colors is created. Object colors are designated by specifying an index into this palette. This functions sets the RGB values for the color that is represented by a particular palette index.
Parameters	
index	int: The index into the color palette.
red	float: The red component of the desired color.

green	float: The green component of the desired color.
blue	float: The blue component of the desired color.
Returns	None.
Example	See the COLORDX supplementary sample on the CD subdirectory for this chapter. Note that this sample requires operation on a palletized device (most 256-color cards, but not more than 8 bits of color).
See Also	getColorMapSize, auxSetRGBMap

AUXSOLIDBOX

Purpose	Draws a solid box.
Include File	<glaux.h>
Syntax	void auxSolidBox(GLdouble width, GLdouble height, GLdouble depth);
Description	Draws a solid box centered at (0,0,0). An alternative form of auxSolidCube. Generally used for demonstration purposes.
Parameters	
width	The width of the box.
height	The height of the box.
depth	The depth of the box.
Returns	None.
Example	See the AUXSOLID supplementary sample on the CD subdirectory for this chapter. This program exercises all of the AUX library's solid objects.
See Also	auxWireBox, auxSolidCube

AUXSOLIDCONE

Purpose	Draws a solid cone.
Include File	<glaux.h>
Syntax	void auxSolidCone(GLdouble radius, GLdouble height);
Description	Draws a solid cone centered at (0,0,0). Generally used for demonstration purposes.
Parameters	
radius	The radius of the bottom of the cone.
height	The height of the cone.
Returns	None.
Example	See the AUXSOLID supplementary sample on the CD subdirectory for this chapter. This program exercises all of the AUX library's solid objects.
See Also	auxWireCone

AUXSOLIDCUBE

Purpose	Draws a solid cube.
Include File	<glaux.h>
Syntax	void auxSolidCube(GLdouble width);
Description	Draws a solid cube centered at (0,0,0). An alternative form of AuxSolidBox. Generally used for demonstration purposes.
Parameters	
width	The width of the cube.
Returns	None.
Example	See the AUXSOLID supplementary sample on the CD subdirectory for this chapter. This program exercises all of the AUX library's solid objects.
See Also	auxWireCube, auxSolidBox

AUXSOLIDCYLINDER

Purpose	Draws a solid cylinder.
Include File	<glaux.h>
Syntax	void auxSolidCylinder(GLdouble radius, GLdouble height);
Description	Draws a solid cylinder centered at (0,0,0). Generally used for demonstration purposes.
Parameters	
radius	The radius of the cylinder.
height	The height of the cylinder.
Returns	None.
Example	See the AUXSOLID supplementary sample on the CD subdirectory for this chapter. This program exercises all of the AUX library's solid objects.
See Also	auxWireCylinder

AUXSOLIDDODECAHEDRON

Purpose	Draws a solid dodecahedron.
Include File	<glaux.h>
Syntax	void auxSolidDodecahedron(GLdouble radius);
Description	Draws a solid dodecahedron centered at (0,0,0). A dodecahedron is a 12-sided object with pentagon sides. Generally used for demonstration purposes.
Parameters	
radius	The radius of the dodecahedron.

Returns	None.
Example	See the AUXSOLID supplementary sample on the CD subdirectory for this chapter. This program exercises all of the AUX library's solid objects.
See Also	auxWireDodecahedron.

AUXSOLIDICOSAHEDRON

Purpose	Draws a solid icosahedron.
Include File	<glaux.h>
Syntax	void auxSolidIcosahedron(GLdouble radius);
Description	Draws a solid icosahedron centered at (0,0,0). An icosahedron is a 20-sided object with each side a triangle. Generally used for demonstration purposes.
Parameters	
radius	The radius of the icosahedron.
Returns	None.
Example	See the AUXSOLID supplementary sample on the CD subdirectory for this chapter. This program exercises all of the AUX library's solid objects.
See Also	auxWireIcosahedron

AUXSOLIDOCTAHEDRON

Purpose	Draws a solid octahedron.
Include File	<glaux.h>
Syntax	void auxSolidOctahedron(GLdouble radius);
Description	Draws a solid octahedron centered at (0,0,0). An octahedron is an 8-sided object with triangular sides. Generally used for demonstration purposes.
Parameters	
radius	The radius of the octahedron.
Returns	None.
Example	See the AUXSOLID supplementary sample on the CD subdirectory for this chapter. This program exercises all of the AUX library's solid objects.
See Also	auxWireOctahedron

AUXSOLIDSPHERE

Purpose	Draws a solid sphere.
Include File	<glaux.h>

Syntax	void auxSolidSphere(GLdouble radius);
Description	Draws a solid sphere centered at (0,0,0). Generally used for demonstration purposes.
Parameters	
radius	The radius of the sphere.
Returns	None.
Example	See the AUXSOLID supplementary sample on the CD subdirectory for this chapter. This program exercises all of the AUX library's solid objects.
See Also	auxWireSphere

AUXSOLIDTEAPOT

Purpose	Draws a solid teapot.
Include File	<glaux.h>
Syntax	void auxSolidTeapot(GLdouble size);
Description	Draws a solid teapot centered at (0,0,0). Generally used for demonstration purposes.
Parameters	
size	The size of the teapot (approximate diameter).
Returns	None.
Example	See the AUXSOLID supplementary sample on the CD subdirectory for this chapter. This program exercises all of the AUX library's solid objects.
See Also	auxWireTeapot

AUXSOLIDTETRAHEDRON

Purpose	Draws a solid tetrahedron.
Include File	<glaux.h>
Syntax	void auxSolidTetrahedron(GLdouble radius);
Description	Draws a solid tetrahedron centered at (0,0,0). A tetrahedron is a 4-sided object with triangular sides. Generally used for demonstration purposes.
Parameters	
radius	The radius of the tetrahedron.
Returns	None.
Example	See the AUXSOLID supplementary sample on the CD subdirectory for this chapter. This program exercises all of the AUX library's solid objects.
See Also	auxWireTetrahedron

AUXSOLIDTORUS

Purpose	Draws a solid torus (doughnut shape).
Include File	<glaux.h>
Syntax	void auxSolidTorus(GLdouble innerRadius, GLdouble outerRadius);
Description	Draws a solid torus centered at (0,0,0). A torus is a doughnut-shaped object. The inner radius is the radius of the tube and the outer radius is the radius of the center hole. Generally used for demonstration purposes.
Parameters	
innerRadius	The radius of the inside of the torus.
outerRadius	The inner radius of the ring.
Returns	None.
Example	See the AUXSOLID supplementary sample on the CD subdirectory for this chapter. This program exercises all of the AUX library's solid objects.
See Also	auxSolidTorus

AUXSWAPBUFFERS

Purpose	Switches drawing buffer to screen during double-buffered drawing.
Include File	<glaux.h>
Syntax	void auxSwapBuffers(void);
Description	This function is used with doubled-buffered drawing and animation. Calling this function causes the hidden scene to be quickly swapped to screen.
Returns	None.
Example	See the BOUNCE2 example from this chapter.
See Also	auxInitDisplayMode, auxIdleFunc

AUXWIREBOX

Purpose	Draws a wireframe box.
Include File	<glaux.h>
Syntax	void auxWireBox(GLdouble width, GLdouble height, GLdouble depth);
Description	Draws a wireframe box centered at (0,0,0). An alternative form of auxWireCube. Generally used for demonstration purposes.
Parameters	
width	The width of the box.

height	The height of the box.
depth	The depth of the box.
Returns	None.
Example	See the AUXWIRE supplementary sample on the CD subdirectory for this chapter. This program exercises all of the AUX library's wireframe objects.
See Also	auxSolidBox, auxWireCube

AUXWIRECONE

Purpose	Draws a wireframe cone.
Include File	<glaux.h>
Syntax	void auxWireCone(GLdouble radius, GLdouble height);
Description	Draws a wireframe cone centered at (0,0,0). Generally used for demonstration purposes.
Parameters	
radius	The radius of the bottom of the cone.
height	The height of the cone.
Returns	None.
Example	See the AUXWIRE supplementary sample on the CD subdirectory for this chapter. This program exercises all of the AUX library's wireframe objects.
See Also	auxSolidCone

AUXWIRECUBE

Purpose	Draws a wireframe cube.
Include File	<glaux.h>
Syntax	void auxWireCube(GLdouble width);
Description	Draws a wireframe cube centered at (0,0,0). An alternative form of AuxWireCube.Generally used for demonstration purposes.
Parameters	
width	The width of the cube.
Returns	None.
Example	See the AUXWIRE supplementary sample on the CD subdirectory for this chapter. This program exercises all of the AUX library's wireframe objects.
See Also	auxSolidCube, auxWireBox

AUXWIRECYLINDER

Purpose	Draws a wireframe cylinder.
Include File	<glaux.h>

Syntax	void auxWireCylinder(GLdouble radius, GLdouble height);
Description	Draws a wireframe cylinder centered at (0,0,0). Generally used for demonstration purposes.
Parameters	
radius	The radius of the cylinder.
height	The height of the cylinder.
Returns	None.
Example	See the AUXWIRE supplementary sample on the CD subdirectory for this chapter. This program exercises all of the AUX library's wireframe objects.
See Also	auxSolidCylinder

AUXWIREDODECAHEDRON

Purpose	Draws a wireframe dodecahedron.
Include File	<glaux.h>
Syntax	void auxWireDodecahedron(GLdouble radius);
Description	Draws a wireframe dodecahedron centered at (0,0,0). A dodecahedron is a 12-sided object with pentagon sides. Generally used for demonstration purposes.
Parameters	
radius	The radius of the dodecahedron.
Returns	None.
Example	See the AUXWIRE supplementary sample on the CD subdirectory for this chapter. This program exercises all of the AUX library's wireframe objects.
See Also	auxSolidDodecahedron.

AUXWIREICOSAHEDRON

Purpose	Draws a wireframe icosahedron.
Include File	<glaux.h>
Syntax	void auxWireIcosahedron(GLdouble radius);
Description	Draws a wireframe icosahedron centered at (0,0,0). An icosahedron is a 20-sided object with each side a triangle. Generally used for demonstration purposes.
Parameters	
radius	The radius of the icosahedron.
Returns	None.
Example	See the AUXWIRE supplementary sample on the CD subdirectory for this chapter. This program exercises all of the AUX library's wireframe objects.
See Also	auxSolidIcosahedron

AUXWIREOCTAHEDRON

Purpose	Draws a wireframe octahedron.
Include File	<glaux.h>
Syntax	void auxWireOctahedron(GLdouble radius);
Description	Draws a wireframe octahedron centered at (0,0,0). An octahedron is an 8-sided object with triangular sides. Generally used for demonstration purposes.
Parameters	
radius	The radius of the octahedron.
Returns	None.
Example	See the AUXWIRE supplementary sample on the CD subdirectory for this chapter. This program exercises all of the AUX library's wireframe objects.
See Also	auxSolidOctahedron

AUXWIRESPHERE

Purpose	Draws a wireframe sphere.
Include File	<glaux.h>
Syntax	void auxWireSphere(GLdouble radius);
Description	Draws a wireframe sphere centered at (0,0,0). Generally used for demonstration purposes.
Parameters	
radius	The radius of the sphere.
Returns	None.
Example	See the AUXWIRE supplementary sample on the CD subdirectory for this chapter. This program exercises all of the AUX library's wireframe objects.
See Also	auxSolidSphere

AUXWIRETEAPOT

Purpose	Draws a wireframe teapot.
Include File	<glaux.h>
Syntax	void auxWireTeapot(GLdouble size);
Description	Draws a wireframe teapot centered at (0,0,0). Generally used for demonstration purposes.
Parameters	
size	The size of the teapot (approximate diameter).
Returns	None.

Example	See the AUXWIRE supplementary sample on the CD subdirectory for this chapter. This program exercises all of the AUX library's wireframe objects.
See Also	auxSolidTeapot

AUXWIRETETRAHEDRON

Purpose	Draws a wireframe tetrahedron.
Include File	<glaux.h>
Syntax	void auxWireTetrahedron(GLdouble radius);
Description	Draws a wireframe tetrahedron centered at (0,0,0). A tetrahedron is a 4-sided object with triangular sides. Generally used for demonstration purposes.
Parameters	
radius	The radius of the tetrahedron.
Returns	None.
Example	See the AUXWIRE supplementary sample on the CD subdirectory for this chapter. This program exercises all of the AUX library's wireframe objects.
See Also	auxSolidTetrahedron

AUXWIRETORUS

Purpose	Draws a wireframe torus (doughnut shape).
Include File	<glaux.h>
Syntax	void auxWireTorus(GLdouble innerRadius, GLdouble outerRadius);
Description	Draws a wireframe torus centered at (0,0,0). A torus is a doughnut-shaped object. The inner radius is the radius of the tube and the outer radius is the radius of the center hole. Generally used for demonstration purposes.
Parameters	
innerRadius	The radius of the inside of the torus.
outerRadius	The inner radius of the ring.
Returns	None.
Example	See the AUXWIRE supplementary sample on the CD subdirectory for this chapter. This program exercises all of the AUX library's wireframe objects.
See Also	auxSolidTorus

GLCLEARCOLOR

Purpose	Sets the color and alpha values to use for clearing the color buffers.
Include File	<gl.h>

Syntax	void glClearColor(GLclampf red, GLclampf green, GLclampf blue, GLclampf alpha);
Description	Sets the fill values to be used when clearing the red, green, blue, and alpha buffers (jointly called the color buffer). The values specified are clamped to the range [0.0f, 1.0f].
Parameters	
red	GLclampf: The red component of the fill value.
green	GLclampf: The green component of the fill value.
blue	GLclampf: The blue component of the fill value.
alpha	GLclampf: The alpha component of the fill value.
Returns	None.
Example	See the SHORTEST example from this chapter.

GLFLUSH

Purpose	Flushes OpenGL command queues and buffers.
Include File	<gl.h>
Syntax	void glFlush(void);
Description	OpenGL commands are often queued and executed in batches to optimize performance. This can vary among hardware, drivers, and OpenGL implementations. The glFlush command causes any waiting commands to be executed.
Returns	None.
Example	See any example from this chapter.

GLORTHO

Purpose	Sets or modifies the clipping volume extents.
Include File	<gl.h>
Syntax	void glOrtho(GLdouble left, GLdouble right, GLdouble bottom, GLdouble top, GLdouble near, GLdouble far);
Description	This function describes a parallel clipping volume. This projection means that objects far from the viewer do not appear smaller (in contrast to a perspective projection). Think of the clipping volume in terms of 3D Cartesian coordinates, in which case left and right would be the minimum and maximum x values, top and bottom the minimum and maximum y values, and near and far the minimum and maximum z values.
Parameters	
left	GLdouble: The leftmost coordinate of the clipping volume.

right	GLdouble: The rightmost coordinate of the clipping volume.
bottom	GLdouble: The bottommost coordinate of the clipping volume.
top	GLdouble: The topmost coordinate of the clipping volume.
near	GLdouble: The maximum distance from the origin to the viewer.
far	GLdouble: The maximum distance from the origin away from the viewer.
Returns	None.
Example	See the SCALE example from this chapter.
See Also	glViewport

GLVIEWPORT

Purpose	Sets the portion of a window that can be drawn in by OpenGL.
Include File	<gl.h>
Syntax	void glViewport(GLint x, GLint y, GLsizei width, GLsizei height);
Description	Sets the region within a window that is used for mapping the clipping volume coordinates to physical window coordinates.
Parameters	
x	GLint: The number of pixels from the left-hand side of the window to start the viewport.
y	GLint: The number of pixels from the bottom of the window to start the viewport.
width	GLsizei: The width in pixels of the viewport.
height	GLsizei: The height in pixels of the viewport.
Returns	None.
Example	See the SCALE example from this chapter.
See Also	glOrtho

GLRECT

Purpose	Draws a flat rectangle.
Include File	<gl.h>
Variations	void **glRectd**(GLdouble x1, GLdouble y1, GLdouble x2, GLdouble y2);
	void **glRectf**(GLfloat x1, GLfloat y1, GLfloat x2, GLfloat y2);
	void **glRecti**(GLint x1, GLint y1, GLint x2, GLint y2);
	void **glRects**(GLshort x1, GLshort y1, GLshort x1, GLshort y2);
	void **glRectdv**(const GLdouble *v1, const GLdouble *v2);
	void **glRectfv**(const GLfloat *v1, const GLfloat *v2);
	void **glRectiv**(const GLint *v1, const GLint *v2);
	void **glRectsv**(const GLshort *v1, const GLshort *v2);

Description	This function is an efficient method of specifying a rectangle as two corner points. The rectangle is drawn in the xy plane at z = 0.
Parameters	
x1, y1	Specifies the upper-left corner of the rectangle.
x2, y2	Specifies the lower-right corner of the rectangle.
*v1	An array of two values specifying the upper-left corner of the rectangle. Could also be described as v1[2].
*v2	An array of two values specifying the lower-right corner of the rectangle. Could also be described as v2[2].
Returns	None.
Example	See the FRIENDLY sample from this chapter.

4

OPENGL FOR WINDOWS: OPENGL + WIN32 = WIGGLE

4

OPENGL FOR WINDOWS: OPENGL + WIN32 = WIGGLE

What you'll learn in this chapter:

OpenGL Tasks in a Window Without the AUX Library	Functions You'll Use
Create and use rendering contexts	wglCreateContext, wglDeleteContext, wglMakeCurrent
Request and select a pixel format	ChoosePixelFormat, SetPixelFormat
Respond to window messages	WM_PAINT, WM_CREATE, WM_DESTROY, WM_SIZE
Use double buffering in Windows	SwapBuffers

OpenGL is purely a graphics API, with user interaction and the screen/window handled by the host environment. To facilitate this partnership, each environment usually has some extensions that "glue" OpenGL to its own window management and user interface functions. This glue is code that associates OpenGL drawing commands to a particular window. It is also necessary to provide functions for setting buffer modes, color depths, and other drawing characteristics.

For Microsoft Windows, the glue code is embodied in six new *wiggle* functions added to OpenGL (called *wiggle* because they are prefixed with *wgl* rather than *gl*), and five new Win32 functions added to the Windows NT and 95 GDI. These gluing functions are explained in this chapter, where we will dispense with using the AUX library for our OpenGL framework.

In Chapter 3 we used the AUX library as a learning tool to introduce the fundamentals of OpenGL programming in C. You have learned how to draw some 2D and 3D objects and how to specify a coordinate system and viewing perspective, without having to consider Windows programming details. Now it is time to break from our "Windowless" examination of OpenGL and see how it works in the Windows environment. Unless you are content with a single window, no menus, no printing ability, no dialogs, and few of the other features of a modern user interface, you need to learn how to use OpenGL in your Win32 applications.

Starting with this chapter, we will build full-fledged Windows applications that can take advantage of all the operating system's features. You will see what characteristics a Windows window must have in order to support OpenGL graphics. You will learn which messages a well-behaved OpenGL window should handle, and how. The concepts of this chapter are introduced gradually, as we use C to build a model OpenGL program that will provide the initial framework for all future examples.

Thus far in this book, you've needed no prior knowledge of 3D graphics and only a rudimentary knowledge of C programming. From this point on, however, we assume you have at least an *entry-level* knowledge of Windows programming. (Otherwise, we'd have wound up writing a book twice the size of this one, and we'd have had to spend more time on the details of Windows programming and less on OpenGL programming.) If you are new to Windows, or if you cut your teeth on one of the Application Frameworks and aren't all that familiar with Windows procedures, message routing, and so forth, you'll want to check out some of the recommended reading in Appendix B, *Further Reading*, before going too much further in this text.

Drawing in Windows Windows

With the AUX library we had only one window, and OpenGL always knew that we wanted to draw in that window (where else would we go?). Your own Windows applications, however, will often have more than one window. In fact, dialog boxes, controls, and even menus are actually windows at a fundamental level; it's nearly impossible to have a useful program that contains only one window. So how does OpenGL know where to draw when you execute your rendering code? Before we try to answer this question, let's first review how we normally draw in a window without using OpenGL.

GDI Device Contexts

To draw in a window without using OpenGL, you use the Windows GDI (Graphical Device Interface) functions. Each window has a *device context* that actually receives the

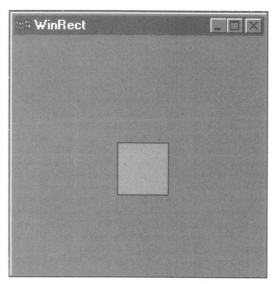

Figure 4-1 Windows version of friendly.c, the OpenGL sample from Chapter 3

graphics output, and each GDI function takes a device context as an argument to indicate which window you want the function to affect. You can have multiple device contexts, but only one for each window.

The example program WINRECT on the Companion CD draws an ordinary window with a blue background and a red square in the center. The output from this program, shown in Figure 4-1, will look familiar to you. This is the same image produced by our second OpenGL program in Chapter 3, friendly.c. Unlike that earlier example, however, the WINRECT program is done entirely with the Windows API. WINRECT's code is pretty generic as far as Windows programming goes. There is a WinMain that gets things started and keeps the message pump going, and a WndProc to handle messages for the main window.

Your familiarity with Windows programming should extend to the details of creating and displaying a window, so we'll cover only the code from this example that is responsible for the drawing of the background and square.

First we must create a blue and a red brush for filling and painting. The handles for these brushes are declared globally.

```
// Handles to GDI brushes we will use for drawing
HBRUSH hBlueBrush,hRedBrush;
```

Then the brushes are created in the WinMain function, using the RGB macro to create solid red and blue brushes.

```
// Create a blue and red brush for drawing and filling
// operations.              // Red, green,  blue
hBlueBrush = CreateSolidBrush(RGB(   0,      0,  255));
hRedBrush = CreateSolidBrush(RGB(  255,      0,   0));
```

When the window style is being specified, the background is set to use the blue brush in the window class structure.

```
wc.hbrBackground         = hBlueBrush; // Use blue brush for background
```

Window size and position (previously set with auxInitPosition) are set when the window is created.

```
// Create the main application window
hWnd = CreateWindow(
                    lpszAppName,
                    lpszAppName,
                    WS_OVERLAPPEDWINDOW,
                    100, 100,                    // Size and dimensions of window
                    250, 250,
                    NULL,
                    NULL,
                    hInstance,
                    NULL);
```

Finally, the actual painting of the window interior is handled by the WM_PAINT message handler in the WndProc function.

```
        case WM_PAINT:
                {
                PAINTSTRUCT ps;
                HBRUSH hOldBrush;

                // Start painting
                BeginPaint(hWnd,&ps);

                // Select and use the red brush
                hOldBrush = SelectObject(ps.hdc,hRedBrush);

                // Draw a rectangle filled with the currently
                // selected brush
                Rectangle(ps.hdc,100,100,150,150);

                // Deselect the brush
                SelectObject(ps.hdc,hOldBrush);

                // End painting
                EndPaint(hWnd,&ps);
                }
                break;
```

The call to BeginPaint prepares the window for painting, and sets the hdc member of the PAINTSTRUCT structure to the device context to be used for drawing in this window. This handle to the device context is used as the first parameter to all GDI functions, identifying which window they should operate on. This code then selects the red brush for painting operations and draws a filled rectangle at the coordinates

(100,100,150,150). Then the brush is deselected, and EndPaint cleans up the painting operation for you.

Before you jump to the conclusion that OpenGL should work in a similar way, remember that the GDI is Windows-specific. Other environments do not have device contexts, window handles, and the like. OpenGL, on the other hand, was designed to be completely portable among environments and hardware platforms. Adding a device context parameter to the OpenGL functions would render your OpenGL code useless in any environment other than Windows.

OpenGL Rendering Contexts

In order to accomplish the portability of the core OpenGL functions, each environment must implement some means of specifying a current rendering window before executing any OpenGL commands. In Windows, the OpenGL environment is embodied in what is known as the *rendering context*. Just as a device context remembers settings about drawing modes and commands for the GDI, the rendering context remembers OpenGL settings and commands.

You may have more than one rendering context in your application—for instance, two windows that are using different drawing modes, perspectives, and so on. However, in order for OpenGL commands to know which window they are operating on, only one rendering context may be *current* at any one time per thread. When a rendering context is made current, it is also associated with a device context and thus with a particular window. Now OpenGL knows which window into which to render. Figure 4-2 illustrates this concept, as OpenGL commands are routed to the window indirectly associated with the current rendering context.

Performance Tip
The OpenGL library is thread-safe, meaning you can have multiple threads rendering their own windows or bitmaps simultaneously. This has obvious performance benefits for multiprocessor systems. Threads can also be beneficial on single-processor systems, as in having one thread render while another thread handles the user interface. You can also have multiple threads rendering objects within the same rendering context. In this chapter's subdirectory on the CD, the supplementary example program GLTHREAD is an example of using threads with OpenGL.

Using the Wiggle Functions

The rendering context is not a strictly OpenGL concept, but rather an addition to the Windows API to support OpenGL. In fact, the new wiggle functions were added to the Win32 API specifically to add windowing support for OpenGL. The three most used functions with regard to the rendering context are

```
HGLRC wglCreateContext(HDC hDC);
BOOL wglDeleteContext(HGLRC hrc);
BOOL wglMakeCurrent(HDC hDC, HGLRC hrc);
```

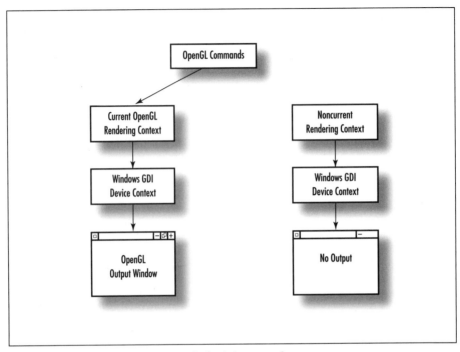

Figure 4-2 How OpenGL commands find their window

Creating and Selecting a Rendering Context

Notice first the new data type HGLRC, which represents a handle to a rendering context. The wglCreateContext function takes a handle to a windows GDI device context and returns a handle to an OpenGL rendering context. Like a GDI device context, a rendering context must be deleted when you are through with it. The wglDeleteContext function does this for you, taking as its only parameter the handle of the rendering context to be deleted.

When a rendering context is created for a given device context, it is said to be *suitable* for drawing on that device context. When the rendering context is made current with wglMakeCurrent, it is not strictly necessary that the device context specified be the one used to create the rendering context in the first place. However, the device context used when a rendering context is made current must have the same characteristics as the device context used to create the rendering context. These characteristics include color depth, buffer definitions, and so forth, and are embodied in what is known as the *pixel format*.

To make a rendering context current for a device context different from that used to create it, they must both have the same pixel format. You may deselect the current rendering context either by making another rendering context current, or by calling wglMakeCurrent with NULL for the rendering context. (Selecting and setting the pixel format for the device context will be covered shortly.)

Painting with OpenGL

If you haven't done much GDI programming, keeping track of both the device context and the rendering context may seem bewildering, but it's actually very simple to do after you've seen it done once. In the old days of 16-bit Windows programming, you needed to retrieve a device context, process it quickly, and release it as soon as you were done with it—because Windows could only remember five device contexts at a time. In the new era of 32-bit Windows, these internal resource limitations are all but gone. This does not give us permission to be careless, but it does mean that there are fewer implications to creating a window with its own private device context (window style WS_OWNDC), getting the window, and hanging on until we are done with it. Furthermore, since most of our examples will be animated, we can avoid repeated (and expensive) calls to GetDC every time we need to make the rendering context current. Another time-saver for us is to make the rendering context current once it is created, and keep it current. If only one window per thread uses OpenGL, this will never be a problem, and it will save the time of repeated calls to wglMakeCurrent.

Only two window messages require any code that handles the creating and deleting of a rendering context: WM_CREATE and WM_DESTROY. Naturally, the rendering context is created in the WM_CREATE message, and it is deleted in the WM_DESTROY message. The following skeleton section from a window procedure of a window that uses OpenGL graphics shows the creation and deleting of a rendering context:

```
LRESULT CALLBACK WndProc(HWND hWnd, ...
        {
        static HGLRC hRC;        // Save the rendering context between calls
        static HDC hDC;          // Save the device context between calls

        switch(msg)
                {
                case WM_CREATE:
                        hDeviceContext = GetDC(hWnd)
                        ...

                        hRenderContext = wglCreateContext(hDC);
                        wglMakeCurrent(hDC,hRC);
                break;

                case WM_DESTROY:
                        wglMakeCurrent(hDC,NULL);
                        wglDeleteContext(hRC);

                        PostQuitMessage(0);
                break;
                }
        }
```

The painting and drawing of the window is still handled by the WM_PAINT message, only now it will contain your OpenGL drawing commands. In this message, you can dispense with the BeginPaint/EndPaint sequence. (These functions cleared the window, hid the caret for drawing operations, and validated the window region after painting.) With OpenGL, you only need to validate the window client area in order to keep a constant stream of WM_PAINT messages from being posted to the window. Here is a skeletal WM_PAINT handler:

```
case WM_PAINT:
        {
        // OpenGL drawing code or your Render function called here.
        RenderScene();

        ValidateRect(hWnd,NULL);
        }
break;
```

> **Programming Trick**
> You can still use the device context with GDI commands to draw in the window after the OpenGL scene is drawn. The Microsoft documentation states that this is fully supported except in double-buffered windows. You can, however, use GDI calls in double-buffered windows—as long as you make your calls after the buffer swap. What's actually not supported are GDI calls to the back buffer of a double-buffered window. It's best to avoid such calls, anyway, since one of the primary reasons for using double buffering is to provide flicker-free and instantaneous screen updates.

Preparing the Window for OpenGL

At this point you may be chomping at the bit to write a quick-and-dirty windows program using the foregoing code and a render function from a previous chapter in the WM_PAINT handler. But don't start cobbling together code just yet. There are still two important preparatory steps we need to take before creating the rendering context.

Window Styles

In order for OpenGL to draw in a window, the window must be created with the WS_CLIPCHILDREN and WS_CLIPSIBLINGS styles set, and it must not contain the CS_PARENTDC style. This is because the rendering context is only suitable for drawing in the window for which it was created (as specified by the device context in the wglCreateContext function), or in a window with exactly the same pixel format. The WS_CLIPCHILDREN and WS_CLIPSIBLINGS styles keep the paint function from trying to update any child windows. CS_PARENTDC (which causes a window to inherit its parent's device context) is forbidden because a rendering context can be associated with only one device context and window. If these styles are not specified you will not be able to set a pixel format for the window—the last detail before we begin our first Windows OpenGL program.

Pixel Formats

Drawing in a window with OpenGL also requires that you select a *pixel format*. Like the rendering context, the pixel format is not really a part of OpenGL per se. It is an extension to the Win32 API (specifically, to the GDI) to support OpenGL functionality. The pixel format sets a device context's OpenGL properties, such as color and buffer depth, and whether the window is double-buffered. You must set the pixel format for a device context before it can be used to create a rendering context. Here are the two functions you will need to use:

```
int ChoosePixelFormat(HDC hDC, PIXELFORMATDESCRIPTOR *ppfd)
BOOL SetPixelFormat(HDC hDC, int iPixelFormat, IXELFORMATDESCRIPTOR  *ppfd)
```

Setting the pixel format is a three-step process. First, you fill out the PIXELFOR-MATDESCRIPTOR structure according to the characteristics and behavior you want the window to possess (we'll examine these fields shortly). You then pass this structure to the ChoosePixelFormat function. The ChoosePixelFormat function returns an integer index to an available pixel format for the specified device context. This index is then passed to the SetPixelFormat function. The sequence looks something like this:

```
PIXELFORMATDESCRIPTOR pixelFormat;
int nFormatIndex;
HDC hDC;

// initialize pixelFormat structure
....
....

nFormatIndex = ChoosePixelFormat(hDC, &pixelFormat);
SetPixelFormat(hDC, nPixelFormat, &pixelFormat);
```

ChoosePixelFormat attempts to match a supported pixel format to the information requested in the PIXELFORMATDESCRIPTOR structure. The returned index is the identifier for this pixel format. For instance, you may request a pixel format that has 16 million colors on screen, but the hardware may only support 256 simultaneous colors. In this case, the returned pixel format will be as close an approximation as possible—for this example, a 256-color pixel format. This index is passed to SetPixelFormat.

You'll find a detailed explanation of the PIXELFORMATDESCRIPTOR structure in the Reference Section under the function DescribePixelFormat. Listing 4-1 shows a function from the GLRECT sample program that establishes the PIXELFORMATDE-SCRIPTOR structure and sets the pixel format for a device context.

Listing 4-1 A high-level function that sets up the pixel format for a device context

```
/ Select the pixel format for a given device context
void SetDCPixelFormat(HDC hDC)
        {
        int nPixelFormat;

        static PIXELFORMATDESCRIPTOR pfd = {
                sizeof(PIXELFORMATDESCRIPTOR),  // Size of this structure
                1,                              // Version of this structure
                PFD_DRAW_TO_WINDOW |            // Draw to window (not bitmap)
                PFD_SUPPORT_OPENGL |            // Support OpenGL calls
                PFD_DOUBLEBUFFER,               // Double-buffered mode
                PFD_TYPE_RGBA,                  // RGBA Color mode
                24,                             // Want 24bit color
                0,0,0,0,0,0,                    // Not used to select mode
```

continued on next page

continued from previous page

```
            0,0,                           // Not used to select mode
            0,0,0,0,0,                     // Not used to select mode
            32,                            // Size of depth buffer
            0,                             // Not used to select mode
            0,                             // Not used to select mode
            PFD_MAIN_PLANE,                // Draw in main plane
            0,                             // Not used to select mode
            0,0,0 };                       // Not used to select mode

    // Choose a pixel format that best matches that described in pfd
    nPixelFormat = ChoosePixelFormat(hDC, &pfd);

    // Set the pixel format for the device context
    SetPixelFormat(hDC, nPixelFormat, &pfd);
    }
```

As you can see in this example, not all the members of the PIXELFORMATDE-SCRIPTOR structure are used when requesting a pixel format. Table 4-1 lists the members that are set in Listing 4-1. The rest of the data elements can be set to zero for now.

Table 4-1 Members of PIXELFORMATDESCRIPTOR used when requesting a pixel format

Member	Description
nSize	The size of the structure, set to sizeof(PIXELFORMATDESCRIPTOR).
nVersion	The version of this data structure, set to 1.
dwFlags	Flags that specify the properties of the pixel buffer, set to (PFD_DRAW_TO_WINDOW | PFD_SUPPORT_OPENGL | PFD_DOUBLEBUFFER). These indicate the device context is not a bitmap context, that OpenGL will be used for drawing, and that the window should be double buffered.
iPixelType	The type of pixel data. Actually, tells OpenGL to use RGBA mode or color index mode. Set to PFD_TYPE_RGBA for RGBA mode.
cColorBits	The number of color bitplanes, in this case 24-bit color. If hardware does not support 24-bit color, the maximum number of color bitplanes supported by the hardware will be selected.
cDepthBits	The depth of the depth (z-axis) buffer. Set to 32 for maximum accuracy, but 16 is often sufficient (see Reference Section).
iLayerType	The type of layer. Only PFD_MAIN_PLANE is valid for the Windows implementation of OpenGL.

Return of the Bouncing Square

At last we have enough information to create a Windows window that uses OpenGL, without using the AUX library. The program shown in Listing 4-2 contains the necessary Windows code along with the rendering function from Chapter 3's BOUNCE2 example program. You can see by the length of this code that the AUX library saves you a lot of effort.

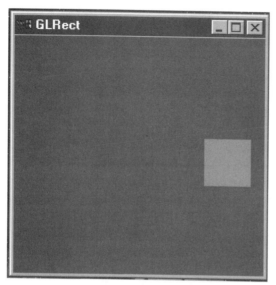

Figure 4-3 Windows version of the bouncing square

The RenderScene, ChangeSize, and IdleFunction functions are virtually unchanged from the Chapter 3 example and are thus omitted here. These functions, along with the function in Listing 4-1, make up the sample program GLRECT. Figure 4-3 shows the familiar bouncing rectangle. Listing 4-2 shows the WinMain function that creates the window and services messages for the program and the WndProc function for the window that handles the individual messages.

Listing 4-2 Animated square program, without the AUX library

```
// Entry point of all Windows programs
int APIENTRY WinMain(   HINSTANCE       hInstance,
                        HINSTANCE       hPrevInstance,
                        LPSTR           lpCmdLine,
                        int             nCmdShow)
        {
        MSG         msg;         // Windows message structure
        WNDCLASS    wc;          // Windows class structure
        HWND        hWnd;        // Storage for window handle


        // Register Window style
        wc.style            = CS_HREDRAW | CS_VREDRAW;
        wc.lpfnWndProc      = (WNDPROC) WndProc;
        wc.cbClsExtra       = 0;
        wc.cbWndExtra       = 0;
```

continued on next page

continued from previous page

```
        wc.hInstance            = hInstance;
        wc.hIcon                = NULL;
        wc.hCursor              = LoadCursor(NULL, IDC_ARROW);

        // No need for background brush for OpenGL window
        wc.hbrBackground        = NULL;

        wc.lpszMenuName         = NULL;
        wc.lpszClassName        = lpszAppName;

        // Register the window class
        if(RegisterClass(&wc) == 0)
                return FALSE;


        // Create the main application window
        hWnd = CreateWindow(
                        lpszAppName,
                        lpszAppName,

                        // OpenGL requires WS_CLIPCHILDREN and WS_CLIPSIBLINGS
                        WS_OVERLAPPEDWINDOW | WS_CLIPCHILDREN | WS_CLIPSIBLINGS,

                        // Window position and size
                        100, 100,
                        250, 250,

                        NULL,
                        NULL,
                        hInstance,
                        NULL);

        // If window was not created, quit
        if(hWnd == NULL)
                return FALSE;


        // Display the window
        ShowWindow(hWnd,SW_SHOW);
        UpdateWindow(hWnd);

        // Process application messages until the application closes
        while( GetMessage(&msg, NULL, 0, 0))
                {
                TranslateMessage(&msg);
                DispatchMessage(&msg);
                }

        return msg.wParam;
        }



// Window procedure, handles all messages for this program
LRESULT CALLBACK WndProc(       HWND    hWnd,
                                UINT    message,
                                WPARAM  wParam,
                                LPARAM  lParam)
```

```
{
static HGLRC hRC;              // Permanent Rendering context
static HDC hDC;                // Private GDI Device context

switch (message)
        {
        // Window creation, setup for OpenGL
        case WM_CREATE:
                // Store the device context
                hDC = GetDC(hWnd);

                // Select the pixel format
                SetDCPixelFormat(hDC);

                // Create the rendering context and make it current
                hRC = wglCreateContext(hDC);
                wglMakeCurrent(hDC, hRC);

                // Create a timer that fires every millisecond
                SetTimer(hWnd,101,1,NULL);
                break;

        // Window is being destroyed, cleanup
        case WM_DESTROY:
                // Kill the timer that we created
                KillTimer(hWnd,101);

                // Deselect the current rendering context and delete it
                wglMakeCurrent(hDC,NULL);
                wglDeleteContext(hRC);

                // Tell the application to terminate after the window
                // is gone.
                PostQuitMessage(0);
                break;

        // Window is resized.
        case WM_SIZE:
                // Call our function which modifies the clipping
                // volume and viewport
                ChangeSize(LOWORD(lParam), HIWORD(lParam));
                break;

        // Timer, moves and bounces the rectangle, simply calls
        // our previous OnIdle function, then invalidates the
        // window so it will be redrawn.
        case WM_TIMER:
                {
                IdleFunction();

                InvalidateRect(hWnd,NULL,FALSE);
                }
                break;

        // The painting function. This message sent by Windows
        // whenever the screen needs updating.
        case WM_PAINT:
```

continued on next page

continued from previous page

```
        {
        // Call OpenGL drawing code
        RenderScene();

        // Call function to swap the buffers
        SwapBuffers(hDC);

        // Validate the newly painted client area
        ValidateRect(hWnd,NULL);
        }
        break;

    default:   // Passes it on if unproccessed
  return (DefWindowProc(hWnd, message, wParam, lParam));

    }

return (0L);
}
```

The code for the Windows version of the bouncing square will be quite under-standable to you if you've been following our discussion. Let's look at a few points that may be of special interest.

Scaling to the Window

In our AUX library-based example in Chapter 3, the AUX library called the registered function ChangeSize whenever the window dimension changed. For our new example, we need to trap the WM_SIZE message sent by Windows when the call to ChangeSize occurs. Now we call ChangeSize ourselves, passing the LOWORD of lParam, which represents the new width of the window, and the HIWORD of lParam, which contains the new height of the window.

```
// Window is resized.
case WM_SIZE:
        // Call our function which modifies the clipping
        // volume and viewport
        ChangeSize(LOWORD(lParam), HIWORD(lParam));
        break;
```

Ticktock, the Idle Clock

Also handled graciously for us by the AUX library was a call to our function IdleFunction. This function was called whenever the program didn't have anything better to do (such as draw the scene). We can easily simulate this activity by setting up a Windows timer for our window. The following code:

```
// Create a timer that fires every millisecond
SetTimer(hWnd,101,1,NULL);
```

which is called when the window is created, sets up a Windows timer for the window. A WM_TIMER message is sent every millisecond by Windows to the OpenGL window. Actually, this happens as often as Windows can send the messages—no less than a millisecond apart—and only when there are no other messages in the applications message queue. (See the *Windows API Bible,* by James L. Conger, published by Waite Group Press for more information on Windows timers.) When the WndProc function receives a WM_TIMER message, this code is executed:

```
case WM_TIMER:
    {
    IdleFunction();

    InvalidateRect(hWnd,NULL,FALSE);
    }
    break;
```

The IdleFunction is identical to the version in BOUNCE2 except that now it doesn't contain a call to RenderScene(). Instead, the window is repainted by calling InvalidateRect, which causes Windows to post a WM_PAINT message.

Lights, Camera, Action!

Everything else is in place, and now it's time for action. The OpenGL code to render the scene is placed within the WM_PAINT message handler. This code calls RenderScene (again, stolen from the BOUNCE2 example), swaps the buffers, and validates the window (to keep further WM_PAINT messages from coming).

```
case WM_PAINT:
        {
        // Call OpenGL drawing code
        RenderScene();

        // Call function to swap the buffers
        SwapBuffers(hDC);

        // Validate the newly painted client area
        ValidateRect(hWnd,NULL);
        }
        break;
```

Here we also find a new function for the Windows GDI, SwapBuffers. This function serves the same purpose the auxSwapBuffers—to move the back buffer of a double-buffered window to the front. The only parameter is the device context. Note that this device context must have a pixel format with the PFD_DOUBLEBUFFER flag set; otherwise, the function fails.

That's it! You now have a code skeleton into which you can drop any OpenGL rendering procedure you want. It will be neatly maintained in a window that has all the usual Windows properties (moving, resizing, and so on). Furthermore, you can of course use this code to create an OpenGL window as part of a full-fledged application that includes other windows, menus, and so on.

Missing Palette Code

If you compare the code from the GLRECT program listing here with the one on the CD, you will notice two other windows messages that are handled by that code but not by the code listed here. These two messages, WM_QUERYNEWPALETTE and WM_PALETTECHANGED, handle Windows palette mapping. Another function, GetOpenGLPalette, creates the palette for us. Palettes are a necessary evil when using a graphics card that supports only 256 or fewer colors. Without this code, we could not get the colors we asked for with glColor, nor even a close approximation when using these particular cards. Palettes and color under Windows constitute a significant topic that is covered in Chapter 8, where we give it the attention it deserves. This is yet another dirty detail that the AUX library hid from us!

Summary

In this chapter you should have gained an appreciation for all the work that goes on behind the scenes when you use the AUX library for your program and window framework. You've seen how the concept of rendering contexts was introduced to the Windows GDI so that OpenGL would know which window into which it was allowed to render. You have also learned how selecting and setting a pixel format prepares the device context before a rendering context can be created for it. In addition, you have seen which Windows messages should be processed to provide the functionality of the AUX library helper functions for window resizing and idle-time animation.

The following Reference Section contains some additional functions not covered in this chapter's discussion because their use requires some concepts and functionality not yet introduced. You'll find examples of these functions on the CD, demonstrating all the functions in our References. You are encouraged to explore and modify these examples.

Reference Section

ChoosePixelFormat

Purpose	Selects the pixel format closest to that specified by the PIXELFORMATDE-SCRIPTOR, and that can be supported by the given device context.
Include File	<wingdi.h>
Syntax	int ChoosePixelFormat(HDC hDC, CONST PIXELFORMATDESCRIPTOR *ppfd);
Description	This function is used to determine the best available pixel format for a given device context based on the desired characteristics described in the PIXELFORMATDESCRIPTOR structure. This returned format index is then used in the SetPixelFormat function.

Parameters

hDC   HDC: The device context for which this function seeks a best-match pixel format.

ppfd   PIXELFORMATDESCRIPTOR: Pointer to a structure that describes the ideal pixel format that is being sought. The entire contents of this structure are not pertinent to its future use. For a complete description of the PIXELFORMATDESCRIPTOR structure, see the DescribePixelFormat function. Here are the relevant members for this function:

nSize	WORD: The size of the structure, usually set to sizeof(PIXELFORMATDESCRIPTOR).
nVersion	WORD: The version number of this structure, set to 1.
dwFlag	DWORD: A set of flags that specify properties of the pixel buffer.
iPixelType	BYTE: The color mode (RGBA or color index) type.
cColorBits	BYTE: The depth of the color buffer.
cAlphaBits	BYTE: The depth of the alpha buffer.
cAccumBits	BYTE: The depth of the accumulation buffer.
cDepthBits	BYTE: The depth of the depth buffer.
cStencilBits	BYTE: The depth of the stencil buffer.
cAuxBuffers	BYTE: The number of auxiliary buffers (not supported by Microsoft).
iLayerType	BYTE: The layer type (not supported by Microsoft).

Returns   The index of the nearest matching pixel format for the logical format specified, or zero if no suitable pixel format can be found.

Example   This code from the GLRECT example code in this chapter demonstrates a pixel format being selected:

```
int nPixelFormat;

static PIXELFORMATDESCRIPTOR pfd = {
        sizeof(PIXELFORMATDESCRIPTOR), // Size of this structure
        1,
        ...
        ...
        };

// Choose a pixel format that best matches that described in pfd
nPixelFormat = ChoosePixelFormat(hDC, &pfd);

// Set the pixel format for the device context
SetPixelFormat(hDC, nPixelFormat, &pfd);
```

See Also   DescribePixelFormat, GetPixelFormat, SetPixelFormat

DescribePixelFormat

Purpose	Obtains detailed information about a pixel format.
Include File	<wingdi.h>
Syntax	int DescribePixelFormat(HDC hDC, int iPixelFormat, UINT nBytes, LPPIXELFORMATDESCRIPTOR ppfd);
Description	This function fills the PIXELFORMATDESCRIPTOR structure with information about the pixel format specified for the given device context. It also returns the maximum available pixel format for the device context. If ppfd is NULL, the function still returns the maximum valid pixel format for the device context. Some fields of the PIXELFORMATDESCRIPTOR are not supported by the Microsoft generic implementation of OpenGL, but these values may be supported by individual hardware manufacturers.

Parameters

hDC	HDC: The device context containing the pixel format of interest.
iPixelFormat	int: The pixel format of interest for the specified device context.
nBytes	UINT: The size of the structure pointed to by ppfd. If this value is zero, no data will be copied to the buffer. This should be set to sizeof(PIXELFORMATDESCRIPTOR).
ppfd	LPPIXELFORMATDESCRIPTOR: A pointer to the PIXELFORMATDESCRIPTOR that on return will contain the detailed information about the pixel format of interest. The PIXELFORMATDESCRIPTOR structure is defined as follows:

```
typedef struct tagPIXELFORMATDESCRIPTOR {
    WORD nSize;
    WORD nVersion;
    DWORD dwFlags;
    BYTE iPixelType;
    BYTE cColorBits;
    BYTE cRedBits;
    BYTE cRedShift;
    BYTE cGreenBits;
    BYTE cGreenShift;
    BYTE cBlueBits;
    BYTE cBlueShift;
    BYTE cAlphaBits;
    BYTE cAlphaShift;
    BYTE cAccumBits;
    BYTE cAccumRedBits;
    BYTE cAccumGreenBits;
    BYTE cAccumBlueBits;
    BYTE cAccumAlphaBits;
    BYTE cDepthBits;
    BYTE cStencilBits;
    BYTE cAuxBuffers;
    BYTE iLayerType;
    BYTE bReserved;
```

```
        DWORD dwLayerMask;
        DWORD dwVisibleMask;
        DWORD dwDamageMask;
}       PIXELFORMATDESCRIPTOR;
```

nSize contains the size of the structure. It should always be set to sizeof(PIXELFORMATDESCRIPTOR).

nVersion holds the version number of this structure. It should always be set to 1.

dwFlags contains a set of bit flags (Table 4-2) that describe properties of the pixel format. Except as noted, these flags are not mutually exclusive.

iPixelType specifies the type of pixel data. More specifically, it specifies the color selection mode. It may be one of the values in Table 4-3.

cColorBits specifies the number of color bitplanes used by the color buffer, excluding the alpha bitplanes in RGBA color mode. In color index mode, it specifies the size of the color buffer.

cRedBits specifies the number of red bitplanes in each RGBA color buffer.

cRedShift specifies the shift count for red bitplanes in each RGBA color buffer. *

cGreenBits specifies the number of green bitplanes in each RGBA color-buffer.

cGreenShift specifies the shift count for green bitplanes in each RGBA color buffer. *

cBlueBits specifies the number of blue bitplanes in each RGBA color buffer.

cBlueShift specifies the shift count for blue bitplanes in each RGBA color buffer. *

cAlphaBits specifies the number of alpha bitplanes in each RGBA color buffer. This is not supported by the Microsoft implementation.

cAlphaShift specifies the shift count for alpha bitplanes in each RGBA color buffer. This is not supported by the Microsoft implementation.

cAccumBits is the total number of bitplanes in the accumulation buffer. See Chapter 15.

cAccumRedBits is the total number of red bitplanes in the accumulation buffer.

cAccumGreenBits is the total number of green bitplanes in the accumulation buffer.

cAccumBlueBits is the total number of blue bitplanes in the accumulation buffer.

cAccumAlphaBits is the total number of alpha bitplanes in the accumulation buffer.

cDepthBits specifies the depth of the depth buffer. See Chapter 15.

cStencilBits specifies the depth of the stencil buffer. See Chapter 15.

cAuxBuffers specifies the number of auxiliary buffers. This is not supported by the Microsoft implementation.

iLayerType specifies the type of layer. Table 4-4 lists the values defined for this member, but only the PFD_MAIN_PLANE value is supported by the Microsoft implementation.

bReserved is reserved and should not be modified.

dwLayerMask is used in conjunction with dwVisibleMask to determine if one layer overlays another. Layers are not supported by the current Microsoft implementation.

dwVisibleMask is used in conjunction with the dwLayerMask to determine if one layer overlays another. Layers are not supported by the current Microsoft implementation.

dwDamageMask indicates when more than one pixel format shares the same frame buffer. If the bitwise AND of the dwDamageMask members of two pixel formats is non-zero, then they share the same frame buffer.

* Chapter 8 explains how this applies to devices with palettes.

Returns
The maximum pixel format supported by the specified device context, or zero on failure.

Example
This example is from the GLRECT sample program on the CD. It queries the pixel format to see if the device context needs a color palette defined.

```
PIXELFORMATDESCRIPTOR pfd;        // Pixel Format Descriptor
int nPixelFormat;                 // Pixel format index

...
...

// Get the pixel format index and retrieve the pixel format description
nPixelFormat = GetPixelFormat(hDC);
DescribePixelFormat(hDC, nPixelFormat, sizeof(PIXELFORMATDESCRIPTOR), &pfd);

// Does this pixel format require a palette? If not, do not create a
// palette and just return NULL
if(!(pfd.dwFlags & PFD_NEED_PALETTE))
        return NULL;

// Go on to create the palette
...
...
```

See Also
ChoosePixelFormat, GetPixelFormat, SetPixelFormat

Table 4-2 Flags for the dwFlags member of PIXELFORMATDESCRIPTOR

Flag	Description
PFD_DRAW_TO_WINDOW	The buffer is used to draw to a window or device surface such as a printer.
PFD_DRAW_TO_BITMAP	The buffer is used to draw to a memory bitmap.
PFD_SUPPORT_GDI	The buffer supporting GDI drawing. This flag is mutually exclusive with PFD_DOUBLEBUFFER.
PFD_SUPPORT_OPENGL	The buffer supporting OpenGL drawing.
PFD_GENERIC_FORMAT	The pixel format is a generic implementation (supported by GDI emulation). If this flag is not set, the pixel format is supported by hardware or a device driver.
PFD_NEED_PALETTE	The pixel format requires the use of logical palettes.
PFD_NEED_SYSTEM_PALETTE	Used for nongeneric implementations that support only one hardware palette. This function forces the hardware palette to a one-to-one mapping to the logical palette.
PFD_DOUBLEBUFFER	The pixel format is double buffered. This flag is mutually exclusive with PFD_SUPPORT_GDI.
PFD_STEREO	The buffer is stereoscopic. This is analogous to front and back buffers in double buffering, only there are left and right buffers. Not supported by Microsoft's generic implementation of OpenGL.
PFD_DOUBLE_BUFFER_DONTCARE	When choosing a pixel format, the format may be either single- or double-buffered, without preference.
PFD_STEREO_DONTCARE	When choosing a pixel format, the view may be either stereoscopic or monoscopic, without preference.

Table 4-3 Flag values for iPixelType

Flag	Description
PFD_TYPE_RGBA	RGBA color mode. Each pixel color is selected by specifiying the red, blue, green, and alpha components.
PFD_TYPE_COLORINDEX	Color index mode. Each pixel color is selected by an index into a palette (color table).

Table 4-4 Flag values for iLayerType

Flag	Description
PFD_MAIN_PLANE	Layer is the main plane.
PFD_OVERLAY_PLANE	Layer is the overlay plane.
PFD_UNDERLAY_PLANE	Layer is the underlay plane.

GETPIXELFORMAT

Purpose	Retrieves the index of the pixel format currently selected for the given device context.
Include File	<wingdi.h>

Syntax	int GetPixelFormat(HDC hDC);
Description	This function retrieves the selected pixel format for the device context specified. The pixel format index is a 1-based positive value.
Parameters	
hDC	HDC: The device context of interest.
Returns	The index of the currently selected pixel format for the given device, or zero on failure.
Example	See the example given for DescribePixelFormat.
See Also	DescribePixelFormat, ChoosePixelFormat, SetPixelFormat

SETPIXELFORMAT

Purpose	Sets a device context's pixel format.
Include File	<wingdi.h>
Syntax	BOOL SetPixelFormat(HDC hDC, int nPixelFormat, CONST PIXELFOR-MATDESCRIPTOR * ppfd);
Description	This function actually sets the pixel format for a device context. Once the pixel format has been selected for a given device, it cannot be changed. This function must be called before creating an OpenGL rendering context for the device.
Parameters	
hDC	HDC: The device context whose pixel format is to be set.
nPixelFormat	int: Index of the pixel format to be set.
ppfd	LPPIXELFORMATDESCRIPTOR: A pointer to a PIXELFORMATDESCRIP-TOR that contains the logical pixel format descriptor. This structure is used internally to record the logical pixel format specification. Its value does not influence the operation of this function.
Returns	True if the specified pixel format was set for the given device context. False if an error occurs.
Example	See the example given for ChoosePixelFormat.
See Also	DescribePixelFormat, GetPixelFormat, ChoosePixelFormat

SWAPBUFFERS

Purpose	Quickly copies the contents of the back buffer of a window to the front buffer (foreground).
Include File	<wingdi.h>
Syntax	BOOL SwapBuffers(HDC hDC);
Description	When a double-buffered pixel format is chosen, a window has a front (dis-played) and back (hidden) image buffer. Drawing commands are sent to

the back buffer. This function is used to copy the contents of the hidden back buffer to the displayed front buffer, to support smooth drawing or animation. Note that the buffers are not really swapped. After this command is executed, the contents of the back buffer are undefined.

Parameters

hDC   HDC: Specifies the device context of the window containing the off-screen and on-screen buffers.

Returns   True if the buffers were swapped.

Example   The following sample shows the typical code for a WM_PAINT message. This is where the rendering code is called, and if in double buffered mode, the back buffer is brought forward. You can see this code in the GLRECT example program from this chapter.

```
// The painting function. This message sent by Windows
// whenever the screen needs updating.
case WM_PAINT:
        {
        // Call OpenGL drawing code
        RenderScene();

        // Call function to swap the buffers
        SwapBuffers(hDC);

        // Validate the newly painted client area
        ValidateRect(hWnd,NULL);
        }
        break;
```

See Also   glDrawBuffer

WGLCREATECONTEXT

Purpose   Creates a rendering context suitable for drawing on the specified device context.

Include File <wingdi.h>

Syntax   HGLRC wglCreateContext(HDC hDC);

Description   Creates an OpenGL rendering context suitable for the given Windows device context. The pixel format for the device context should be set before the creation of the rendering context. When an application is finished with the rendering context, it should call wglDeleteContext.

Parameters

hDC   HDC: The device context that will be drawn on by the new rendering context.

Returns   The handle to the new rendering context, or NULL if an error occurs.

Example   The code below shows the beginning of a WM_CREATE message handler.
Here, the device context is retrieved for the current window, a pixel format
is selected, then the rendering context is created and made current.

```
case WM_CREATE:
        // Store the device context
        hDC = GetDC(hWnd);

        // Select the pixel format
        SetDCPixelFormat(hDC);

        // Create the rendering context and make it current
        hRC = wglCreateContext(hDC);
        wglMakeCurrent(hDC, hRC);
        ...
        ...
```

See Also   wglDeleteContext, wglGetCurrentContext, wglMakeCurrent

WGLDELETECONTEXT

Purpose   Deletes a rendering context after it is no longer needed by the application.

Include File   <wingdi.h>

Syntax   BOOL wglDeleteContext(HGLRC hglrc);

Description   Deletes an OpenGL rendering context. This frees any memory and
resources held by the context.

Parameters

hglrc   HGLRC: The handle of the rendering context to be deleted.

Returns   True if the rendering context is deleted; false if an error occurs. It is an
error for one thread to delete a rendering context that is the current context of another thread.

Example   Example shows the message handler for the destruction of a window.
Assuming the rendering context was created when the window was created, this is where you would delete the rendering context. Before you can
delete the context, it must be made noncurrent.

```
// Window is being destroyed, clean up
case WM_DESTROY:

        // Deselect the current rendering context and delete it
        wglMakeCurrent(hDC,NULL);
        wglDeleteContext(hRC);

        // Tell the application to terminate after the window
        // is gone.
        PostQuitMessage(0);
        break;
```

See Also   wglCreateContext, wglGetCurrentContext, wglMakeCurrent

WGLGETCURRENTCONTEXT

Purpose	Retrieves a handle to the current thread's OpenGL rendering context.
Include File	<wingdi.h>
Syntax	HGLRC wglGetCurrentContext(void);
Description	Each thread of an application can have its own current OpenGL rendering context. This function can be used to determine which rendering context is currently active for the calling thread.
Returns	If the calling thread has a current rendering context, this function returns its handle. If not, the function returns NULL.
Example	See the supplementary example program GLTHREAD in this chapter's sub-directory on the CD.
See Also	wglCreateContext, wglDeleteContext, wglMakeCurrent, wglGetCurrentDC

WGLGETCURRENTDC

Purpose	Gets the Windows device context associated with the current OpenGL rendering context.
Include File	<wingdi.h>
Syntax	HDC wglGetCurrentDC(void);
Description	This function is used to acquire the Windows device context of the window that is associated with the current OpenGL rendering context. Typically used to obtain a Windows device context to combine OpenGL and GDI drawing functions in a single window.
Returns	If the current thread has a current OpenGL rendering context, this function returns the handle to the Windows device context associated with it. Otherwise, the return value is NULL.
Example	See the supplementary example program GLTHREAD in this chapter's sub-directory on the CD.
See Also	wglGetCurrentContext

WGLGETPROCADDRESS

Purpose	Returns the address of an OpenGL extension function for use with the current rendering context.
Include File	<wingdi.h>
Syntax	PROC wglGetProcAddress(LPCSTR lpszProc);
Description	Extension functions are functions that either are not yet part of the OpenGL standard or are proprietary to a specific vendor implementation of OpenGL, usually adding some platform-specific performance feature.

Many extensions are supported by more than one vendor. To use these functions, you must call wglGetProcAddress and specify the name of the extension function exactly. In this way you can also test for the presence of a particular extension. The exact address can vary for different pixel formats, so be careful not to store the address returned and try to use it across rendering contexts, unless you can be certain that the pixel format of both will be the same. You can call glString(GL_EXTENSION) to receive a space-delimited string containing any extensions that may be present (see Chapter 5 for more details).

Parameters

lpszProc   LPCSTR: The name of the extension function. The case and spelling must exactly match that of the desired extension function.

Returns   If the extension function does not exist, the return value is NULL; otherwise, the return is the address of the specified extension function.

Example   The following code segment retrieves the address of the Windows-specific extension function glAddSwapHintRectWIN. This extension allows you to accelerate buffer swapping by telling OpenGL that only certain regions of the window actually need to be copied. This feature is demonstrated in the supplementary example program SWAPHINT in the GL_EXT subdirectory.

```
// Find out if a particular extension is handled
char *szBuffer;
szBuffer = (char *)glString(GL_EXTENSION);

// If it is handled, get the new function's address and call it.
if(strcmp(szBuffer,"GL_WIN_swap_hint") == 0)
        {
        PROC pSwapHint;
        pSwapHint = wglGetCurrentDC("glAddSwapHintRectWIN");

        // Call the function
        pSwapHint(40.0f, 40.0f, 50.0f, 50.2f);
        }
else
        {
        // If not supported, handle some other way...
        ....
        ....
        }
```

See Also   glGetString

WGLMAKECURRENT

Purpose   Makes a given OpenGL rendering context current for the calling thread and associates it with the specified device context.

Include File   <wingdi.h>

Syntax	BOOL wglMakeCurrent(HDC hdc, HGLRC hglrc);
Description	This function makes the specified rendering context the current rendering context for the calling thread. This rendering context is associated with the given Windows device context. The device context need not be the same as that used in the call to wglCreateContext, as long as the pixel format is the same for both and they both exist on the same physical device (not, say, the screen and a printer). Any out-standing OpenGL commands for the previous rendering context are flushed before the new rendering context is made current. This function can also be used to make no rendering context active, by calling it with NULL for the hglrc parameter.
Parameters	
hdc	HDC: The device context that will be used for all OpenGL drawing operations performed by the calling thread.
hglrc	HGLRC: The rendering context to make current for the calling thread.
Returns	True on success, or False if an error occurs. If an error occurs, no rendering context will remain current for the calling thread.
Example	See the example for wglCreateContext.
See Also	wglCreateContext, wglDeleteContext, wglGetCurrentContext, wglGetCurrentDC

WGLSHARELISTS

Purpose	Allows multiple rendering contexts to share display lists.
Include File	<wingdi.h>
Syntax	BOOL wglShareLists(HGLRC hRC1, HGLRC hRC2);
Description	A display list is a list of "precompiled" OpenGL commands and functions (see Chapter 10). Memory is allocated for the storage of display lists within each rendering context. As display lists are created within that rendering context, it has access to its own display list memory. This function allows multiple rendering contexts to share this memory. This is particularly useful when large display lists are used by multiple rendering contexts or threads to save memory. Any number of rendering contexts may share the same memory for display lists. This memory will not be freed until the last rendering context using that space is deleted. When using a shared display list space between threads, display list creation and usage should be synchronized.
Parameters	
hRC1	HGLRC: Specifies the rendering context with which to share display list memory.

hRC2	HGLRC: Specifies the rendering context that will share the display list memory with hRC1. No display lists for hRC2 should be created until after its display list memory is shared.
Returns	True if the display list space is shared; False if they are not.
Example	See the tank/robot simulator directory (\TANK) from Chapter 10's subdirectory on the CD. This program uses multiple windows to produce various views of the same scene simultaneously. To save memory, the rendering contexts for these windows all share the same display list memory space, by using this function.
See Also	glIsList, glNewList, glCallList, glCallLists, glListBase, glDeleteLists, glEndList, glGenLists

wglUseFontBitmaps

Purpose	Creates a set of OpenGL display list bitmaps for the currently selected GDI font.
Include File	<wingdi.h>
Syntax	BOOL wglUseFontBitmaps(HDC hDC, DWORD dwFirst, DWORD dwCount, DWORD dwListBase);
Description	This function takes the font currently selected in the device context specified by hDC, and creates a bitmap display list for each character, starting at dwFirst and running for dwCount characters. The display lists are created in the currently selected rendering context and are identified by numbers starting at dwListBase. Typically this is used to draw text into an OpenGL double-buffered scene, since the Windows GDI will not allow operations to the back buffer of a double-buffered window. This function is also used to label OpenGL objects on screen.
Parameters	
hDC	HDC: The Windows GDI device context from which the font definition is to be derived. The font used can be changed by creating and selecting the desired font into the device context.
dwFirst	DWORD: The ASCII value of the first character in the font to use for building the display lists.
dwCount	DWORD: The consecutive number of characters in the font to use succeeding the character specified by dwFirst.
dwListBase	DWORD: The display list base value to use for the first display list character.
Returns	True if the display lists could be created, False otherwise.
Example	The code below shows how to create a set of display lists for the ASCII character set. It is then used to display the text "OpenGL" at the current raster position.

```
// Create the font outlines based on the font for this device
// context
//
wglUseFontBitmaps(hDC, // Device Context
                  0,    // First character
                  255,  // Last character
                  1000); // Display list base number

...
...


// Draw the string
glListBase(1000);
glPushMatrix();
glCallLists (3, GL_UNSIGNED_BYTE, "OpenGL");
glPopMatrix();
```

See Also   wglUseFontOutlines, glIsList, glNewList, glCallList, glCallLists, glListBase, glDeleteLists, glEndList, glGenLists

WGLUSEFONTOUTLINES

Purpose   Creates a set of OpenGL 3D display lists for the currently selected GDI font.

Include File   <wingdi.h>

Syntax   BOOL wglUseFontOutlines(HDC hdc, DWORD first, DWORD count, DWORD listBase, FLOAT deviation, FLOAT extrusion, int format, LPG-LYPHMETRICSFLOAT lpgmf);

Description   This function takes the TrueType font currently selected into the GDI device context *hDC*, and creates a 3D outline for *count* characters starting at *first*. The display lists are numbered starting at the value *listBase*. The outline may be composed of line segments or polygons as specified by the *format* parameter. The character cell used for the font extends 1.0 unit length along the x- and y-axis. The parameter *extrusion* supplies the length along the negative z-axis on which the character is extruded. The *deviation* is an amount 0 or greater that determines the chordal deviation from the original font outline. This function will only work with TrueType fonts. Additional character data is supplied in the *lpgmf* array of GLYPH-METRICSFLOAT structures.

Parameters

hc   HDC: Device context of the font.

first   DWORD: First character in the font to be turned into a display list.

count   DWORD: Number of characters in the font to be turned into display lists.

listBase   DWORD: The display list base value to use for the first display list character.

deviation	FLOAT: The maximum chordal deviation from the true outlines.
extrusion	FLOAT: Extrusion value in the negative z direction.
format	int: Specifies whether the characters should be composed of line segments or polygons in the display lists. May be one of the following values:

WGL_FONT_LINES	Use line segments to compose character.
WGL_FONT_POLYGONS	Use polygons to compose character.

lpgmf LPGLYPHMETRICSFLOAT: Address of an array to receive glyphs metric data. Each array element is filled with data pertaining to its character's display list. Each is defined as follows:

```
typedef struct _GLYPHMETRICSFLOAT { // gmf
    FLOAT    gmfBlackBoxX;
    FLOAT    gmfBlackBoxY;
    POINTFLOAT gmfptGlyphOrigin;
    FLOAT    gmfCellIncX;
    FLOAT    gmfCellIncY;
} GLYPHMETRICSFLOAT;
```

Members

gmfBlackBoxX	Width of the smallest rectangle that completely encloses the character.
gmfBlackBoxY	Height of the smallest rectangle that completely encloses the character.
gmfptGlyphOrigin	The x and y coordinates of the upper-left corner of the rectangle that completely encloses the character. The POINTFLOAT structure is defined as

```
typedef struct _POINTFLOAT { // ptf
    FLOAT    x;         // The horizontal coordinate of a point
    FLOAT    y;         // The vertical coordinate of a point
} POINTFLOAT;
```

gmfCellIncX	The horizontal distance from the origin of the current character cell to the origin of the next character cell.
gmfCellIncY	The vertical distance from the origin of the current character cell to the origin of the next character cell.
Returns	True if the display lists could be created; False otherwise.

Example The following code can be found in glcode.c in either the MFCGL example program in Chapter 21, or glcode.c in the OWLGL example program in Chapter 22. These examples show how a font defined in a LOGFONT structure is created and selected into the device context, where it is then used to create a set of display lists that represent the entire ASCII character set for that font.

```
hDC = (HDC)pData;
hFont = CreateFontIndirect(&logfont);
SelectObject (hDC, hFont);
```

```
// create display lists for glyphs 0 through 255 with 0.1
// extrusion and default deviation. The display list numbering
// starts at 1000 (it could be any number).
wglUseFontOutlines(hDC, 0, 255, 1000, 0.0f, 0.3f, WGL_FONT_POLYGONS, agmf);

DeleteObject(hFont);
```

See Also   wglUseFontBitmaps, glIsList, glNewList, glCallList, glCallLists, glListBase, glDeleteLists, glEndList, glGenLists

5

ERRORS AND OTHER MESSAGES FROM OPENGL

5

ERRORS AND OTHER MESSAGES FROM OPENGL

What you'll learn in this chapter:

How To...	Functions You'll Use
Get the error code of the last OpenGL error	glGetError
Convert an error code into a textual description of the problem	gluErrorString
Get version and vendor information from OpenGL	glGetString, gluGetString
Make implementation-dependent performance hints	glHint

In any project, we want to write robust and well-behaved programs that respond politely to their users and have some amount of flexibility. Graphical programs that use OpenGL are no exception. Now we don't want to turn this chapter into a course on software engineering and quality assurance, but if you want your programs to run smoothly, you need to account for errors and unexpected circumstances. OpenGL provides you with two different methods of performing an occasional sanity check in your code.

The first of OpenGL's control mechanisms is *error detection*. If an error occurs, you need to be able to stop and say "Hey, an error occurred, and this is what it was." This is the only way in code that will let you know your rendering of the Space Station Freedom is now the Space Station Melted Crayola.

The second OpenGL sanity check is a simple solution to a common problem—something of which every programmer, good and bad, is sometimes guilty. Let's say you know that Microsoft's implementation of the Generic GDI version of OpenGL lets you get away with drawing in a double-buffered window using GDI, as long as you draw in the front buffer. Then you buy one of those fancy, warp drive accelerator cards, and the vendor throws in a new rendering engine. Worse, suppose your customer buys one of these cards. Will your code still work? Will it eat your image and spit out psychedelic rainbows? You may have a good reason for using such optimization tricks; it's certainly faster to use TextOut than to call wglUseFontBitmaps. (Of course, if you do have this fancy-dancy video card, TextOut may not be the fastest road to Rome anymore anyhow.) The simple way to guard against this type of catastrophe is to check the version and vendor of your OpenGL library. If your implementation is the generic Microsoft, cheat to your heart's content; otherwise, better stick to the documented way of doing things.

In summary, if you want to take advantage of vendor or version specific behavior, you should check in your code to make sure that the vendor and version are the same as that you designed for. Later, we'll discuss OpenGL Hints, which allow you to instruct the rendering engine to make tradeoffs for the sake of speed, or image quality. This would be the preferred means of using vendor specific optimizations.

When Bad Things Happen to Good Code

Internally, OpenGL maintains a set of six error status flags. Each flag represents a different type of error. Whenever one of these errors occurs, the corresponding flag is set. To see if any of these flags is set, call glGetError:

```
GLenum glGetError(void);
```

The glGetError function returns one of the values listed in Table 5-1, located in the Reference Section under glGetError. The GLU library defines three errors of its own, but these errors map exactly to two flags already present. If more than one of these flags is set, glGetError still returns only one distinct value. This value is then cleared when glGetError is called, and recalling glGetError will return either another error flag or GL_NO_ERROR. Usually, you will want to call glGetError in a loop that continues checking for error flags until the return value is GL_NO_ERROR.

Listing 5-1 is a section of code from the GLTELL example that loops, checking for error messages until there are none. Notice that the error string is placed in a control in a dialog box. You can see this in the output from the GLTELL program in Figure 5-1.

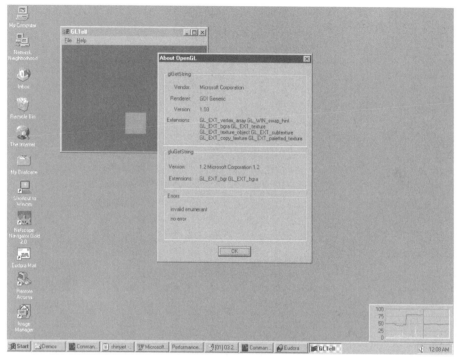

Figure 5-1 An About box describing the GL and GLU libraries, along with any recent errors

---

Listing 5-1 *Code sample that retrieves errors until there are no more errors*

```
// Display any recent error messages
      i = 0;
      do {
            glError = glGetError();

            SetDlgItemText(hDlg,IDC_ERROR1+i,gluErrorString(glError));
            i++;
            }
      while(i < 6 && glError != GL_NO_ERROR);
```

You can use another function in the GLU library, gluErrorString, to get a string describing the error flag:

```
const GLubyte* gluErrorString(GLenum errorCode);
```

This function takes as its only argument the error flag (returned from glGetError, or hand-coded), and returns a static string describing that error. For example, the error flag GL_INVALID_ENUM returns the string

```
invalid enumerant
```

You can take some peace of mind from the assurance that if an error is caused by an invalid call to an OpenGL function or command, that function or command is ignored. OpenGL may not behave as you intended, but it will continue to run. The only exception to this is GL_OUT_OF_MEMORY (or GLU_OUT_OF_MEMORY, which has the same value anyway). When this error occurs, the state of OpenGL is undefined—indeed, the state of your *program* may be undefined! With this error, it's best to clean up as gracefully as possible and terminate the program.

Who Am I and What Can I Do?

As mentioned in the introduction of this section, there are times when you want to take advantage of a known behavior in a particular implementation. If you know for a fact that you are using Microsoft's rendering engine, and the version number is the same as what you tested your program with, it's not unusual that you'll want to try some trick to enhance your program's performance. To be sure that the functionality you're exploiting exists on the machine running your program, you need a way to query OpenGL for the vendor and version number of the rendering engine. Both the GL library and GLU library can return version and vendor specific information about themselves.

For the GL library, you can call glGetString:

```
const GLubyte *glGetString(GLenum name);
```

This function returns a static string describing the requested aspect of the GL library. The valid parameter values are listed under glGetString in the Reference Section, along with the aspect of the GL library they represent.

The GLU library has a corresponding function, gluGetString:

```
const GLubyte *gluGetString(GLenum name);
```

It returns a string describing the requested aspect of the GLU library. The valid parameters are listed under gluGetString in the Reference Section, along with the aspect of the GLU library they represent.

Listing 5-2 is a section of code from the GLTELL sample program, a modified version of our faithful bouncing square. This time we've added a menu and an About box. The About box, shown earlier in Figure 5-1, displays information about the vendor and version of both the GL and GLU libraries. In addition, we've added an error to the code to produce a listing of error messages.

Listing 5-2 Example usage of glGetString and gluGetString

```
// glGetString demo
SetDlgItemText(hDlg,IDC_OPENGL_VENDOR,glGetString(GL_VENDOR));
SetDlgItemText(hDlg,IDC_OPENGL_RENDERER,glGetString(GL_RENDERER));
SetDlgItemText(hDlg,IDC_OPENGL_VERSION,glGetString(GL_VERSION));
SetDlgItemText(hDlg,IDC_OPENGL_EXTENSIONS,glGetString(GL_EXTENSIONS));

// gluGetString demo
SetDlgItemText(hDlg,IDC_GLU_VERSION,gluGetString(GLU_VERSION));
SetDlgItemText(hDlg,IDC_GLU_EXTENSIONS,gluGetString(GLU_EXTENSIONS));
```

Extensions to OpenGL

Take special note of the GL_EXTENSIONS and/or GLU_EXTENSIONS flags. Some vendors (including Microsoft, with the latest versions of OpenGL) may add extensions to OpenGL that offer vendor-specific optimizations, or popular OpenGL extensions that aren't yet part of the standard. These features can enhance your performance considerably. If you make use of these extension functions, however, you must test for the presence of the extensions (using GL_EXTENSIONS); and if they are not present, you must implement the feature by some other means.

The list of extensions returned will contain spaces between each entry. You will have to parse the string yourself to test for the presence of a particular extension library. For more information on OpenGL extensions, see the wglGetProcAddress function (Chapter 4), or your specific vendor's documentation. The Microsoft extensions are discussed and demonstrated in Appendix A.

Get a Clue with glHint

We have mentioned taking advantage of known anomalies in the OpenGL libraries. You can exploit other vendor-specific behaviors, as well. For one thing, you may want to perform renderings as quickly as possible on a generic implementation, but switch to a more accurate view for hardware-assisted implementations. Even without the vendor dependencies, you may simply want OpenGL to be a little less picky for the sake of speed—or to be *more* fastidious and produce a better image, no matter how long it takes.

The function glHint allows you to specify certain preferences of quality or speed for different types of operations. The function is defined as follows:

```
void glHint(GLenum target, GLenum mode );
```

The *target* parameter allows you to specify types of behavior you want to modify. These values, listed under glHint in the Reference Section, include hints for fog and anti-aliasing accuracy. The *mode* parameter tells OpenGL what you care most about—fastest render time and nicest output, for instance—or that you don't care. An example use might be rendering into a small preview window with lower accuracy to get a faster preview image, saving the higher accuracy and qualities for final output. Enumerated values for *mode* are also listed under glHint in the Reference Section.

For a demonstration of these settings on various images, see the supplementary sample program WINHINT in this chapter's subdirectory on the CD.

Bear in mind that not all implementations are required to support glHint, other than accepting input and not generating an error. This means your version of OpenGL may ignore any or all of these requests.

Summary

Even in an imperfect world, we can at least check for error conditions and possibly take action based on them. We can also determine vender and version information so that we can take advantage of known capabilities or watch out for known deficiencies. This chapter has shown you how to marshal your forces against these problems. You've also seen how you can ask OpenGL to prefer speed or quality in some types of operations. Again, this depends on the vendor and implementation details of your version of OpenGL.

Reference Section

GLGETERROR

Purpose	Returns information about the current error state.
Include File	<gl.h>
Syntax	GLenum glGetError(void);
Description	OpenGL maintains five error flags, listed in Table 5-1. When an error flag is set, it remains set until glGetError is called, at which time it will be set to GL_NO_ERROR. Multiple flags may be set simultaneously, in which case glGetError must be called again to clear any remaining errors. Generally, it is a good idea to call glGetError in a loop to ensure that all error flags have been cleared. If glGetError is called between glBegin and glEnd statements, the GL_INVALID_OPERATION flag is set.
Returns	One of the error flags in Table 5-1. In all cases except GL_OUT_OF_ MEMORY, the offending command is ignored and the condition of the OpenGL state variables, buffers, etc., is not affected. In the case of GL_OUT_OF_MEMORY, the state of OpenGL is undefined.
Example	See the GLTELL sample from Listing 5-1.
See Also	gluErrorString

Table 5-1 Valid error return codes from glGetError

Value	Meaning
GL_NO_ERROR	No errors have occurred.
GL_INVALID_ENUM	
GLU_INVALID_ENUM	An invalid value was specified for an enumerated argument.
GL_INVALID_VALUE	
GLU_INVALID_VALUE	A numeric argument was out of range.
GL_INVALID_OPERATION	An operation was attempted that is not allowed in the current state.
GL_STACK_OVERFLOW	A command was attempted that would have resulted in a stack overflow.
GL_STACK_UNDERFLOW	A command was attempted that would have resulted in a stack underflow.
GL_OUT_OF_MEMORY	
GLU_OUT_OF_MEMORY	There is insufficient memory to execute the requested command.

GLGETSTRING

Purpose	Returns a string describing some aspect of the OpenGL implementation.
Include File	<gl.h>
Syntax	const GLubyte *glGetString(GLenum name);
Description	This function returns a string describing some aspect of the current OpenGL implementation. This string is statically defined, and the return address cannot be modified.
Parameters	
name	GLenum: Identifies the aspect of the OpenGL implementation to describe. This may be one of the following values:

GL_VENDOR	Returns the name of the company responsible for this implementation.
GL_RENDERER	Returns the name of the renderer. This can vary with specific hardware configurations. GDI Generic specifies unassisted software emulation of OpenGL.
GL_VERSION	Returns the version number of this implementation.
GL_EXTENSIONS	Returns a list of supported extensions for this version and implementation. Each entry in the list is separated by a space.

Returns	A character string describing the requested aspect, or NULL if an invalid identifier is used.
Example	See the GLTELL sample from Listing 5-2.
See Also	gluGetString

glHint

Purpose	Allows the programmer to specify implementation-dependent performance hints.
Include File	<gl.h>
Syntax	void glHint(GLenum target, GLenum mode);
Description	Certain aspects of OpenGL behavior are open to interpretation on some implementations. This function allows some aspects to be controlled with performance hints that request optimization for speed or fidelity. There is no requirement that the glHint has any effect, and may be ignored for some implementations.
Parameters	
target	GLenum: Indicates the behavior to be controlled. This may be any of the following values:

GL_FOG_HINT	Influences accuracy of fog calculations
GL_LINE_SMOOTH_HINT	Influences quality of anti-aliased lines.
GL_PERSPECTIVE_CORRECTION_HINT	Influences quality of color and texture interpolation.
GL_POINT_SMOOTH_HINT	Influences quality of anti-aliased points.
GL_POLYGON_SMOOTH_HINT	Influences quality of anti-aliased polygons.

mode	GLenum: Indicates the desired optimized behavior. This may be any of the following values:

GL_FASTEST	The most efficient or quickest method should be used.
GL_NICEST	The most accurate or highest quality method should be used.
GL_DONT_CARE	No preference on the method used.

Returns	None.
Example	The following code is found in the WINHINT supplementary sample program. It tells OpenGL that it should render anti-aliased lines as quickly as possible, even if it has to sacrifice the image quality.

```
glHint(GL_LINE_SMOOTH_HINT, GL_FASTEST);
```

gluErrorString

Purpose	Retrieves a string that describes a particular error code.
Include File	<glu.h>
Syntax	const GLubyte* gluErrorString(GLenum errorCode);

Description	This function returns a string describing error code specified. This string is statically defined, and the return address cannot be modified. The returned string is ANSI. To return ANSI or UNICODE depending on the environment, call the macro glErrorStringWIN.
Parameters	
errorCode	GLenum: The error code to be described in the return string. Any of the codes in Table 5-1 may be used.
Returns	A string describing the error code specified.
Example	See the GLTELL sample from Listing 5-2.
See Also	glGetError

GLUGETSTRING

Purpose	Returns the version and extension information about the GLU library.
Include File	<glu.h>
Syntax	const GLubyte *gluGetString(GLenum name);
Description	This function returns a string describing either the version or extension information about the GLU library. This string is statically defined, and the return address cannot be modified.
Parameters	
name	GLenum: Identifies the aspect of the GLU library to describe. This may be one of the following values:

GLU_VERSION   Returns the version information for the GLU Library. The format of the return string is:

<version number><space><vendor information>

GLU_EXTENSIONS   Returns a list of supported extensions for this version of the GLU Library. Each entry in the list is separated by a space.

Returns	A character string describing the requested aspect, or NULL if an invalid identifier is used.
Example	See the GLTELL sample from Listing 5-2.
See Also	glGetString

PART II

USING OPENGL

USING OPENGL

It seems that every programming language class in college started with that same goofy *"How many miles per gallon did you get on the way to New York"* example program. First you needed to learn to use the terminal, then the editor, compiler, and linker, how the programs were structured, and finally some language syntax. Unfortunately, we must all learn to crawl before we can walk, and learning OpenGL is no exception.

Part I of this book introduced OpenGL, the hows and whys of 3D, and the format of OpenGL functions. Then we started gluing this to the Windows API, building Windows-based programs that used OpenGL to paint in the client area. We learned how to look for errors, how to interpret them, and how to make sure we don't take advantage of features that don't exist!

Now it's time to graduate from our baby walkers and start stumbling across the room. First, in Chapter 6, we'll cover all the OpenGL drawing primitives. You'll use these building blocks to make larger and more complex objects. Next you'll find out about all the things you can do in 3D space with your newfound object-building tools: translation, rotation, and other coordinate transformation goodies. Walking with more confidence, you'll be ready for Chapters 8 and 9, which give you color, shading, and lighting for photo-realistic effects. The remaining chapters offer advanced object-manipulation tools, techniques for juggling images and texture maps with ease, and some more specialized 3D object primitives.

When you're done with Part II, you'll be ready for your first 100-yard dash! By the end of the book, the Olympics!

Be sure and follow along with the tank/robot simulation development that starts in this section of the book. This special sample program won't be discussed in the chapters ahead, and can only be found on the CD, where the simulation will be enhanced with that chapter's techniques and functions. The readme.txt file for each step discusses the enhancements along the way.

Anybody else tired of bouncing squares? Read on! Now we're into the good stuff!

6

DRAWING IN 3D: LINES, POINTS, AND POLYGONS

6

DRAWING IN 3D: LINES, POINTS, AND POLYGONS

What you'll learn in this chapter:

How To...	Functions You'll Use
Draw points, lines, and shapes	glBegin/glEnd/glVertex
Set shape outlines to wireframe or solid objects	glPolygonMode
Set point sizes for drawing	glPointSize
Set line drawing width	glLineWidth
Perform hidden surface removal	glCullFace
Set patterns for broken lines	glLineStipple
Set polygon fill patterns	glPolygonStipple

If you've ever had a chemistry class (and probably even if you haven't), you know that all matter is made up of atoms, and that all atoms consist of only three things: protons, neutrons, and electrons. All the materials and substances you have ever come into contact with—from the petals of a rose to the sand on the beach—are just different arrangements of these three fundamental building blocks. Although this is a little over-simplified for most anyone beyond the third or fourth grade, it demonstrates a powerful principle: With just a few simple building blocks, you can create highly complex and beautiful structures.

The connection is fairly obvious. Objects and scenes that you create with OpenGL are also made up of smaller, simpler shapes, arranged and combined in various and unique ways. In this chapter we will explore these building blocks of 3D objects, called *primitives*. All primitives in OpenGL are one- or two-dimensional objects, ranging from single points to lines and complex polygons. In this chapter you will learn everything you need to know in order to draw objects in three dimensions from these simpler shapes.

Drawing Points in 3D

When you first learned to draw any kind of graphics on any computer system, you usually started with pixels. A pixel is the smallest element on your computer monitor, and on color systems that pixel can be any one of many available colors. This is computer graphics at its simplest: Draw a point somewhere on the screen, and make it a specific color. Then build on this simple concept, using your favorite computer language to produce lines, polygons, circles, and other shapes and graphics. Perhaps even a GUI…

With OpenGL, however, drawing on the computer screen is fundamentally different. You're not concerned with physical screen coordinates and pixels, but rather *positional coordinates* in your viewing volume. You let OpenGL worry about how to get your points, lines, and everything else translated from your established 3D space to the 2D image made by your computer screen.

This chapter and the next cover the most fundamental concepts of OpenGL or any 3D graphics toolkit. In the upcoming chapter, we'll go into substantial detail about how this transformation from 3D space to the 2D landscape of your computer monitor takes place, as well as how to manipulate (rotate, translate, and scale) your objects. For now, we shall take this ability for granted in order to focus on plotting and drawing in a 3D coordinate system. This may seem backwards, but if you first know how to draw something, and then worry about all the ways to manipulate your drawings, the material coming up in Chapter 7 will be more interesting and easier to learn. Once you have a solid understanding of graphics primitives and coordinate transformations, you will be able to quickly master any 3D graphics language or API.

Setting Up a 3D Canvas

Figure 6-1 shows a simple viewing volume that we will use for the examples in this chapter. The area enclosed by this volume is a Cartesian coordinate space that ranges from –100 to +100 on all three axes, x, y, and z. (For a review of Cartesian coordinates, see Chapter 2.) Think of this viewing volume as your three-dimensional canvas on which you will be drawing with OpenGL commands and functions.

We established this volume with a call to glOrtho(), much as we did for others in the previous chapters. Listing 6-1 shows the code for our ChangeSize() function that gets called when the window is sized (including when it is first created). This code looks a little different from that in previous chapters, and you'll notice some unfamiliar functions (glMatrixMode, glLoadIdentity). We'll spend more time on these in Chapter 7, exploring their operation in more detail.

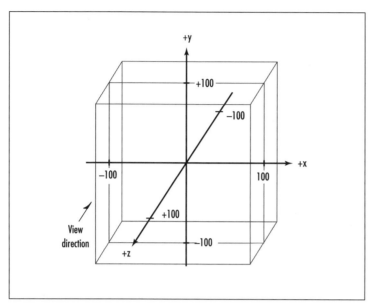

Figure 6-1 Cartesian viewing volume measuring 100 x 100 x 100

Listing 6-1 Code to establish the viewing volume in Figure 6-1

```
// Change viewing volume and viewport.  Called when window is resized
void ChangeSize(GLsizei w, GLsizei h)
        {
        GLfloat nRange = 100.0f;

        // Prevent a divide by zero
        if(h == 0)
                h = 1;

        // Set Viewport to window dimensions
        glViewport(0, 0, w, h);

        // Reset projection matrix stack
        glMatrixMode(GL_PROJECTION);
        glLoadIdentity();

        // Establish clipping volume (left, right, bottom, top, near, far)
        if (w <= h)
                glOrtho (-nRange, nRange, -nRange*h/w, nRange*h/w, -nRange, nRange);
        else
                glOrtho (-nRange*w/h, nRange*w/h, -nRange, nRange, -nRange, nRange);

        // Reset Model view matrix stack
        glMatrixMode(GL_MODELVIEW);
        glLoadIdentity();
        }
```

Why the Cart Before the Horse?

Look at any of the source code of this chapter, and you'll notice some new functions in the RenderScene() functions: glRotate(), glPushMatrix(), and glPopMatrix(). Though they're covered in more detail in Chapter 7, we're introducing them now. That's because they implement some important features that we wanted you to have as soon as possible. These functions let you plot and draw in 3D, and help you easily visualize your drawing from different angles. All of this chapter's sample programs employ the arrow keys for rotating the drawing around the x- and y-axes. Look at any 3D drawing dead-on (straight down the z-axis) and it may still look two-dimensional. But when you can spin the drawings around in space, it's much easier to see the effects of what you're drawing.

There is a lot to learn about drawing in 3D, and in this chapter we want you to focus on that. By changing only the drawing code for any of the examples that follow, you can start experimenting right away with 3D drawing and still get interesting results. Later, you'll learn how to manipulate drawings using the other functions.

A 3D Point: The Vertex

To specify a drawing point in this 3D "palette," we use the OpenGL function glVertex—without a doubt the most used function in all of the OpenGL API. This is the "lowest common denominator" of all the OpenGL primitives: a single point in space. The glVertex function can take from two to four parameters of any numerical type, from bytes to doubles, subject to the naming conventions discussed in Chapter 3.

The following single line of code specifies a point in our coordinate system located 50 units along the x-axis, 50 units along the y-axis, and 0 units out the z-axis:

```
glVertex3f(50.0f, 50.0f, 0.0f);
```

This point is illustrated in Figure 6-2. Here we chose to represent the coordinates as floating point values, as we shall do for the remainder of the book. Also, the form of glVertex() that we have used takes three arguments for the x, y, and z coordinate values, respectively.

Two other forms of glVertex take two and four arguments, respectively. We could represent the same point in Figure 6-2 with this code:

```
glVertex2f(50.0f, 50.0f);
```

This form of glVertex takes only two arguments that specify the x and y values, and assumes the z coordinate to be 0.0 always. The form of glVertex taking four arguments, glVertex4, uses a fourth coordinate value w, which is used for scaling purposes. You will learn more about this in Chapter 7 when we spend more time exploring coordinate transformations.

Draw Something!

Now we have a way of specifying a point in space to OpenGL. What can we make of it, and how do we tell OpenGL what to do with it? Is this vertex a point that should just be plotted? Is it the endpoint of a line, or the corner of a cube? The geometric

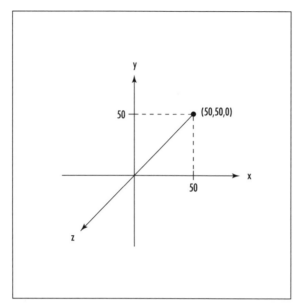

Figure 6-2 The point (50,50,0) as specified by
glVertex3f(50.0f, 50.0f, 0.0f)

definition of a vertex is not just a point in space, but rather *the point at which an inter-section of two lines or curves occurs*. This is the essence of primitives.

A primitive is simply the interpretation of a set or list of vertices into some shape drawn on the screen. There are ten primitives in OpenGL, from a simple point drawn in space to a closed polygon of any number of sides. You use the glBegin command to tell OpenGL to begin interpreting a list of vertices as a particular primitive. You then end the list of vertices for that primitive with the glEnd command. Kind of intuitive, don't you think?

Drawing Points

Let's begin with the first and simplest of primitives: points. Look at the following code:

```
glBegin(GL_POINTS);                            // Select points as the primitive
        glVertex3f(0.0f, 0.0f, 0.0f);          // Specify a point
        glVertex3f(50.0f, 50.0f, 50.0f);       // Specify another point
glEnd();                                       // Done drawing points
```

The argument to glBegin, GL_POINTS, tells OpenGL that the following vertices are to be interpreted and drawn as points. Two vertices are listed here, which translates to two specific points, both of which would be drawn.

This brings up an important point about glBegin and glEnd: You can list multiple primitives between calls as long as they are for the same primitive type. In this way, with a single glBegin/glEnd sequence you can include as many primitives as you like.

This next code segment is very wasteful and will execute more slowly than the preceding code:

```
glBegin(GL_POINTS);              // Specify point drawing
        glVertex3f(0.0f, 0.0f, 0.0f);
glEnd();

glBegin(GL_POINTS);              // Specify another point
        glVertex3f(50.0f, 50.0f, 50.0f);
glEnd();
```

Indenting Your Code

In the foregoing examples, did you notice the indenting style used for the calls to glVertex()? This convention is used by most OpenGL programmers to make the code easier to read. It is not required, but it does make it easier to find where primitives start and stop.

Our First Example

The code shown in Listing 6-2 draws some points in our 3D environment. It uses some simple trigonometry to draw a series of points that form a corkscrew path up the z-axis. This code is from the POINTS program, which is on the CD in the subdirectory for this chapter. All of the example programs use the framework we established in Chapters 4 and 5. Notice that in the SetupRC() function we are setting the current drawing color to green.

Listing 6-2 Rendering code to produce a spring-shaped path of points

```
// Define a constant for the value of PI
#define GL_PI 3.1415f

// This function does any needed initialization on the rendering
// context.
void SetupRC()
        {
        // Black background
        glClearColor(0.0f, 0.0f, 0.0f, 1.0f );

        // Set drawing color to green
        glColor3f(0.0f, 1.0f, 0.0f);
        }


// Called to draw scene
void RenderScene(void)
        {
        GLfloat x,y,z,angle; // Storage for coordinates and angles

        // Clear the window with current clearing color
```

```
glClear(GL_COLOR_BUFFER_BIT);

// Save matrix state and do the rotation
glPushMatrix();
glRotatef(xRot, 1.0f, 0.0f, 0.0f);
glRotatef(yRot, 0.0f, 1.0f, 0.0f);

// Call only once for all remaining points
glBegin(GL_POINTS);

z = -50.0f;
for(angle = 0.0f; angle <= (2.0f*GL_PI)*3.0f; angle += 0.1f)
        {
        x = 50.0f*sin(angle);
        y = 50.0f*cos(angle);

        // Specify the point and move the Z value up a little
        glVertex3f(x, y, z);
        z += 0.5f;
        }

// Done drawing points
glEnd();

// Restore transformations
glPopMatrix();

// Flush drawing commands
glFlush();
}
```

Only the code between calls to glBegin and glEnd is important for our purpose in this and the other examples for this chapter. This code calculates the x and y coordinates for an angle that spins between 0° and 360° three times. (We express this programmatically in radians rather than degrees; if you don't know trigonometry, you can take our word for it. If you're interested, see the box, "The Trigonometry of Radians/Degrees." Each time a point is drawn, the z value is increased slightly. When this program is run, all you will see is a circle of points, because you are initially looking directly down the z-axis. To better see the effect, use the arrow keys to spin the drawing around the x- and y-axes. This is illustrated in Figure 6-3.

One Thing at a Time
Again, don't get too distracted by the functions in this sample that we haven't covered yet (glPushMatrix, glPopMatrix, and glRotate). These functions are used to rotate the image around so you can better see the positioning of the points as they are drawn in 3D space. We will be covering these in some detail in Chapter 7. If we hadn't used these features now, you wouldn't be able to see the effects of your 3D drawings, and this and the following sample programs wouldn't be very interesting to look at. For the rest of the sample code in this chapter, we will only be showing the code that includes the glBegin and glEnd statements.

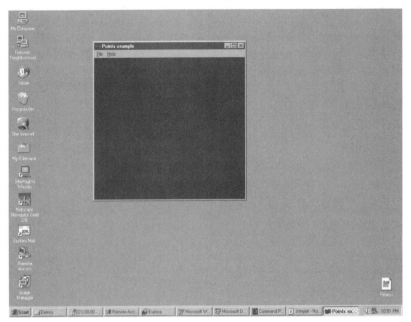

Figure 6-3 Output from the POINTS sample program

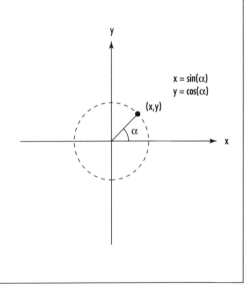

The Trigonometry of Radians/Degrees

The figure in this box shows a circle drawn in the xy plane. A line segment from the origin (0,0) to any point on the circle will make an angle (*a*) with the x-axis. For any given angle, the trigonometric functions Sine and Cosine will return the x and y values of the point on the circle. By stepping a variable that represents the angle all the way around the origin, we can calculate all the points on the circle. Note that the C runtime functions sin() and cos() accept angle values measured in radians instead of degrees. There are 2*PI radians in a circle, where PI is a nonrational number that is approximately 3.1415 (nonrational means there are an infinite number of values past the decimal point).

Setting the Point Size

When you draw a single point, the size of the point is one pixel by default. You can change this with the function glPointSize.

```
void glPointSize(GLfloat size);
```

The glPointSize function takes a single parameter that specifies the approximate diameter in pixels of the point drawn. Not all point sizes are supported, however, and you should check to make sure the point size you specify is available. Use the following code to get the range of point sizes, and the smallest interval between them:

```
GLfloat sizes[2];       // Store supported point size range
GLfloat step;           // Store supported point size increments

// Get supported point size range and step size
glGetFloatv(GL_POINT_SIZE_RANGE,sizes);
glGetFloatv(GL_POINT_SIZE_GRANULARITY,&step);
```

Here the *sizes* array will contain two elements that contain the smallest and the largest valid value for glPointsize. In addition, the variable *step* will hold the smallest step size allowable between the point sizes. The OpenGL specification only requires that one point size, 1.0, be supported. The Microsoft implementation of OpenGL allows for point sizes from 0.5 to 10.0, with 0.125 the smallest step size. Specifying a size out of range will not be interpreted as an error. Instead, the largest or smallest supported size will be used, whichever is closest to the value specified.

OpenGL State Variables

OpenGL maintains the state of many of its internal variables and settings. This collection of settings is called the OpenGL State Machine. The State Machine can be queried to determine the state of any of its variables and settings. Any feature or capability you enable or disable with glEnable/glDisable, as well as numeric settings set with glSet, can be queried with the many variations of glGet. Chapter 14 explores the OpenGL State Machine more completely.

Let's look at a sample that makes use of these new functions. The code shown in Listing 6-3 produces the same spiral shape as our first example, but this time the point sizes are gradually increased from the smallest valid size to the largest valid size. This example is from the program POINTSZ in the CD subdirectory for this chapter. The output from POINTSZ is shown in Figure 6-4.

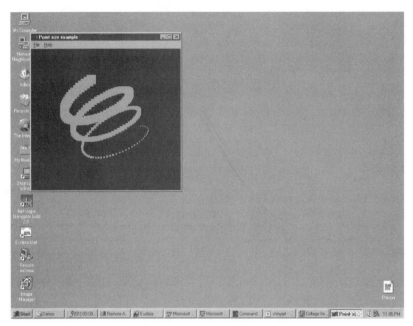

Figure 6-4 Output from POINTSZ program

Listing 6-3 Code from POINTSZ that produces a spiral with gradually increasing point sizes

```
// Define a constant for the value of PI
#define GL_PI 3.1415f

// Called to draw scene
void RenderScene(void)
        {
        GLfloat x,y,z,angle;    // Storage for coordinates and angles
        GLfloat sizes[2];       // Store supported point size range
        GLfloat step;           // Store supported point size increments
        GLfloat curSize;        // Store current point size
        ...
        ...

        // Get supported point size range and step size
        glGetFloatv(GL_POINT_SIZE_RANGE,sizes);
        glGetFloatv(GL_POINT_SIZE_GRANULARITY,&step);

        // Set the initial point size
        curSize = sizes[0];

        // Set beginning z coordinate
        z = -50.0f;

        // Loop around in a circle three times
        for(angle = 0.0f; angle <= (2.0f*GL_PI)*3.0f; angle += 0.1f)
```

```
      {
      // Calculate x and y values on the circle
      x = 50.0f*sin(angle);
      y = 50.0f*cos(angle);

      // Specify the point size before the primitive is specified
      glPointSize(curSize);

      // Draw the point
      glBegin(GL_POINTS);
              glVertex3f(x, y, z);
      glEnd();

      // Bump up the z value and the point size
      z += 0.5f;
      curSize += step;
      }
  ...
  ...
  }
```

This example demonstrates a couple of important things. For starters, notice that glPointSize must be called outside the glBegin/glEnd statements. Not all OpenGL functions are valid between these function calls. Though glPointSize affects all points drawn after it, you don't begin drawing points until you call glBegin(GL_POINTS). For a complete list of valid functions that you can call within a glBegin/glEnd sequence, see the Reference Section.

The most obvious thing you probably noticed about the POINTSZ excerpt is that the larger point sizes are represented simply by larger squares. This is the default behavior, but it typically is undesirable for many applications. Also, you may be wondering why you can increase the point size by a value less than one. If a value of 1.0 represents one pixel, how do you draw less than a pixel or, say, 2.5 pixels?

The answer is that the point size specified in glPointSize isn't the exact point size in pixels, but the approximate diameter of a circle containing all the pixels that will be used to draw the point. You can get OpenGL to draw the points as better points (that is, small filled circles) by enabling point smoothing, with a call to

```
glEnable(GL_POINT_SMOOTH);
```

Other functions affect how points and lines are smoothed, but this falls under the larger topic of anti-aliasing (Chapter 16). Anti-aliasing is a technique used to smooth out jagged edges and round out corners. We mention it now only in case you want to play with this on your own, and to whet your appetite for the rest of the book!

Drawing Lines in 3D

The GL_POINTS primitive we have been using thus far is pretty straightforward; for each vertex specified, it draws a point. The next logical step is to specify two vertices and draw a line between them. This is exactly what the next primitive, GL_LINES, does. The following short section of code draws a single line between two points (0,0,0) and (50, 50, 50):

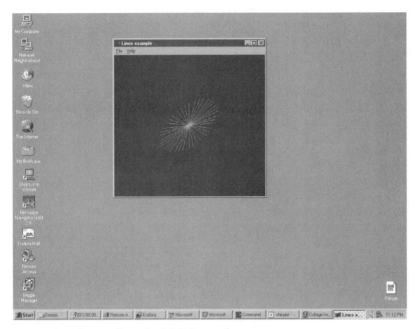

Figure 6-5 Output from the LINES sample program

```
glBegin(GL_LINES);
        glVertex3f(0.0f, 0.0f, 0.0f);
        glVertex3f(50.0f, 50.0f, 50.0f);
glEnd();
```

Note here that two vertices are used to specify a single primitive. For every two vertices specified, a single line is drawn. If you specify an odd number of vertices for GL_LINES, the last vertex is just ignored. Listing 6-4, from the LINES sample program on the CD, shows a more complex sample that draws a series of lines fanned around in a circle. The output from this program is shown in Figure 6-5.

Listing 6-4 Code from the sample program LINES that displays a series of lines fanned in a circle

```
// Call only once for all remaining points
glBegin(GL_LINES);

// All lines lie in the xy plane.
z = 0.0f;
for(angle = 0.0f; angle <= GL_PI*3.0f; angle += 0.5f)
        {
        // Top half of the circle
        x = 50.0f*sin(angle);
        y = 50.0f*cos(angle);
        glVertex3f(x, y, z);                  // First end point of line
```

```
                // Bottom half of the circle
                x = 50.0f*sin(angle+3.1415f);
                y = 50.0f*cos(angle+3.1415f);
                glVertex3f(x, y, z);                 // Second end point of line
                }

        // Done drawing points
        glEnd();
```

Line Strips and Loops

The next two OpenGL primitives build on GL_LINES by allowing you to specify a list of vertices through which a line is drawn. When you specify GL_LINE_STRIP, a line is drawn from one vertex to the next in a continuous segment. The following code draws two lines in the xy plane that are specified by three vertices. Figure 6-6 shows an example.

```
glBegin(GL_LINE_STRIP);
        glVertex3f(0.0f, 0.0f, 0.0f);   // V0
        glVertex3f(50.0f, 50.0f, 0.0f); // V1
        glVertex3f(50.0f, 100.0f, 0.0f);        // V2
glEnd();
```

The last line-based primitive is the GL_LINE_LOOP. This primitive behaves just like a GL_LINE_STRIP, but one final line is drawn between the last vertex specified and the first one specified. This is an easy way to draw a closed-line figure. Figure 6-7 shows a GL_LINE_LOOP drawn using the same vertices as for the GL_LINE_STRIP in Figure 6-6.

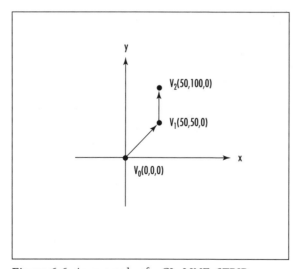

Figure 6-6 An example of a GL_LINE_STRIP specified by three vertices

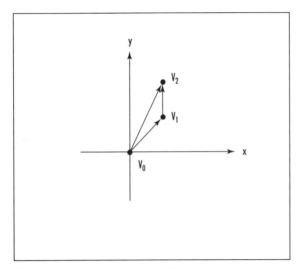

Figure 6-7 The same vertices from Figure 6-6, used by a GL_LINE_LOOP primitive

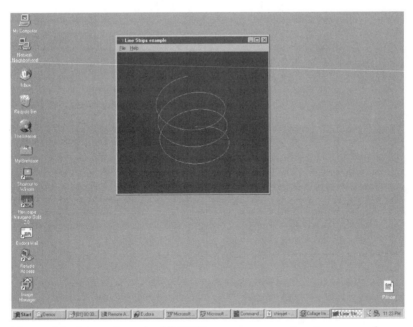

Figure 6-8 Output from the LSTRIPS program approximating a smooth curve

Approximating Curves with Straight Lines

The POINTS example program, shown earlier in Figure 6-3, showed you how to plot points along a spring-shaped path. You may have been tempted to push the points closer and closer together (by setting smaller values for the angle increment) to create a smooth spring-shaped curve instead of the broken points that only approximated the shape. This is a perfectly valid operation, but it can be quite slow for larger and more complex curves with thousands of points.

A better way of approximating a curve is to use a GL_LINE_STRIP to play connect-the-dots. As the dots move closer together, a smoother curve materializes, without your having to specify all those points. Listing 6-5 shows the code from Listing 6-2, with the GL_POINTS replaced by GL_LINE_STRIP. The output from this new program, LSTRIPS, is shown in Figure 6-8. As you can see, the approximation of the curve is quite good. You will find this handy technique almost ubiquitous among OpenGL programs.

Listing 6-5 Code from the sample program LSTRIPS, demonstrating Line Strips

```
// Call only once for all remaining points
glBegin(GL_LINE_STRIP);

z = -50.0f;
for(angle = 0.0f; angle <= (2.0f*GL_PI)*3.0f; angle += 0.1f)
        {
        x = 50.0f*sin(angle);
        y = 50.0f*cos(angle);

        // Specify the point and move the Z value up a little
        glVertex3f(x, y, z);
        z += 0.5f;
        }

// Done drawing points
glEnd();
```

Setting the Line Width

Just as you can set different point sizes, you can also specify various line widths when drawing lines. This is done with the glLineWidth function:

```
void glLineWidth(GLfloat width);
```

The glLineWidth function takes a single parameter that specifies the approximate width, in pixels, of the line drawn. Just like point sizes, not all line widths are supported, and you should check to make sure the line width you want to specify is available. Use the following code to get the range of line widths, and the smallest interval between them:

```
GLfloat sizes[2];       // Store supported line width range
GLfloat step;           // Store supported line width increments

// Get supported line width range and step size
glGetFloatv(GL_LINE_WIDTH_RANGE,sizes);
glGetFloatv(GL_LINE_WIDTH_GRANULARITY,&step);
```

Here the *sizes* array will contain two elements that contain the smallest and the largest valid value for glLineWidth. In addition, the variable *step* will hold the smallest step size allowable between the line widths. The OpenGL specification only requires that one line width, 1.0, be supported. The Microsoft implementation of OpenGL allows for line widths from 0.5 to 10.0, with 0.125 the smallest step size.

Listing 6-6 shows code for a more substantial example of glLineWidth. It's from the program LINESW and draws ten lines of varying widths. It starts at the bottom of the window at −90 on the y-axis and climbs the y-axis 20 units for each new line. Every time it draws a new line, it increases the line width by 1. Figure 6-9 shows the output for this program.

Listing 6-6 Drawing lines of various widths

```
// Called to draw scene
void RenderScene(void)
    {
    GLfloat y;                          // Storage for varying Y coordinate
    GLfloat fSizes[2];                  // Line width range metrics
    GLfloat fCurrSize;                  // Save current size

    ...
    ...
    ...

    // Get line size metrics and save the smallest value
    glGetFloatv(GL_LINE_WIDTH_RANGE,fSizes);
    fCurrSize = fSizes[0];

    // Step up Y axis 20 units at a time
    for(y = -90.0f; y < 90.0f; y += 20.0f)
        {
        // Set the line width
        glLineWidth(fCurrSize);

        // Draw the line
        glBegin(GL_LINES);
                glVertex2f(-80.0f, y);
                glVertex2f(80.0f, y);
        glEnd();

        // Increase the line width
        fCurrSize += 1.0f;
        }

    ...
    ...
    }
```

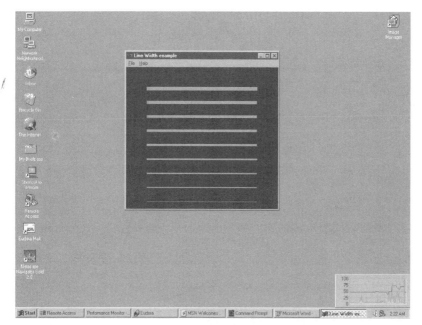

Figure 6-9 Demonstration of glLineWidth from LINESW program

Notice that we used glVertex2f() this time instead of glVertex3f() to specify the coordinates for our lines. As mentioned, this is only a convenience because we are drawing in the xy plane, with a z value of zero. To see that you are still drawing lines in three dimensions, simply use the arrow keys to spin your lines around. You will see easily that all the lines lie on a single plane.

Line Stippling

In addition to changing line widths, you can create lines with a dotted or dashed pattern, called *stippling*. To use line stippling, you must first enable stippling with a call to

```
glEnable(GL_LINE_STIPPLE);
```

Then the function glLineStipple establishes the pattern that the lines will use for drawing.

```
void glLineStipple(GLint factor, GLushort pattern);
```

Reminder
Any feature or ability that is enabled by a call to glEnable() can be disabled by a call to glDisable().

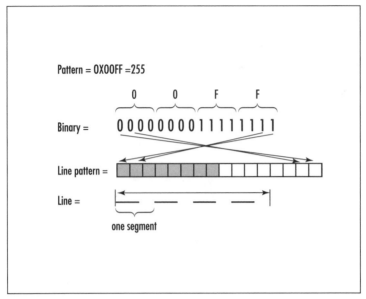

Figure 6-10 Stipple pattern is used to construct a line segment

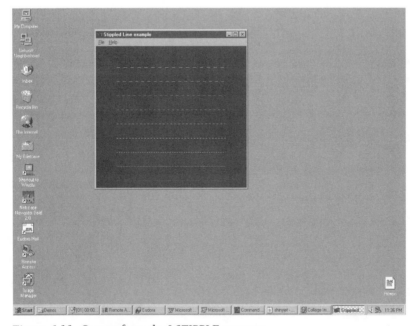

Figure 6-11 Output from the LSTIPPLE program

The *pattern* parameter is a 16-bit value that specifies a pattern to use when drawing the lines. Each bit represents a section of the line segment that is either on or off. By default, each bit corresponds to a single pixel, but the *factor* parameter serves as a multiplier to increase the width of the pattern. For example, setting *factor* to 5 would cause each bit in the pattern to represent five pixels in a row that would be either on or off. Furthermore, bit 0 (the least significant bit) of the pattern is used first to specify the line. Figure 6-10 illustrates a sample bit pattern applied to a line segment.

Why Are These Patterns Backward?
You might wonder why the bit pattern used for stippling is used in reverse when drawing the line. Internally, it's much faster for OpenGL to shift this pattern to the left one place, each time it needs to get the next mask value. For high-performance applications, reversing this pattern internally (to make it easier for humans to understand) can take up precious processor time.

Listing 6-7 shows a sample of using a stippling pattern that is just a series of alternating On and Off bits (0101010101010101). This program draws ten lines from the bottom of the window up the y-axis to the top. Each line is stippled with the pattern 0x5555, but for each new line the pattern multiplier is increased by 1. You can clearly see the effects of the widened stipple pattern in Figure 6-11.

Listing 6-7 Code from LSTIPPLE that demonstrates the effect of factor on the bit pattern

```
// Called to draw scene
void RenderScene(void)
        {
        GLfloat y;                      // Storage for varying Y coordinate
        GLint factor = 1;               // Stippling factor
        GLushort pattern = 0x5555;      // Stipple pattern

        ...
        ...

        // Enable Stippling
        glEnable(GL_LINE_STIPPLE);

        // Step up Y axis 20 units at a time
        for(y = -90.0f; y < 90.0f; y += 20.0f)
                {
                // Reset the repeat factor and pattern
                glLineStipple(factor,pattern);

                // Draw the line
                glBegin(GL_LINES);
                        glVertex2f(-80.0f, y);
                        glVertex2f(80.0f, y);
                glEnd();

                factor++;
                }
        ...
        ...
        }
```

Drawing Triangles in 3D

You've seen how to draw points and lines, and even how to draw some enclosed polygons with GL_LINE_LOOP. With just these primitives, you could easily draw any shape possible in three dimensions. You could, for example, draw six squares and arrange them so they form the sides of a cube.

You may have noticed, however, that any shapes you create with these primitives are not filled with any color—after all, you are only drawing lines. In fact, all the previous example draws is a wireframe cube, not a solid cube. To draw a solid surface, you need more than just points and lines; you need polygons. A polygon is a closed shape that may or may not be filled with the currently selected color, and it is the basis of all solid-object composition in OpenGL.

Triangles: Your First Polygon

The simplest polygon possible is the triangle, with only three sides. The GL_TRIANGLES primitive is used to draw triangles, and it does so by connecting three vertices together. The following code draws two triangles using three vertices each, as shown in Figure 6-12:

```
glBegin(GL_TRIANGLES);
        glVertex2f(0.0f, 0.0f);                 // V0
        glVertex2f(25.0f, 25.0f);               // V1
        glVertex2f(50.0f, 0.0f);                // V2

        glVertex2f(-50.0f, 0.0f);               // V3
        glVertex2f(-75.0f, 50.0f);              // V4
        glVertex2f(-25.0f, 0.0f);               // V5
glEnd();
```

Note that the triangles will be filled with the currently selected drawing color. If you don't specify a drawing color at some point, you can't be certain of the result (there is no *default* drawing color).

Choose the Fastest Primitives for Performance Tip
The triangle is the primitive of choice for the OpenGL programmer. You will find that, with a little work, any polygonal shape can be composed of one or more triangles placed carefully together. Most 3D accelerated hardware is highly optimized for the drawing of triangles. In fact, you will see many 3D benchmarks measured in triangles per second.

Winding

An important characteristic of any polygonal primitive is illustrated in Figure 6-12. Notice the arrows on the lines that connect the vertices. When the first triangle is drawn, the lines are drawn from V0 to V1, then to V2, and finally back to V0 to close the triangle. This path is in the order that the vertices are specified, and for this example, that order is clockwise from your point of view. The same directional characteristic is present for the second triangle, as well.

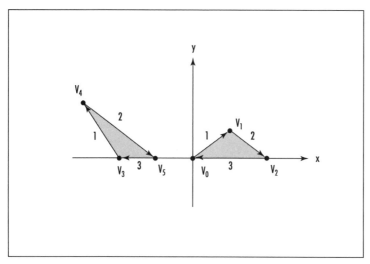

Figure 6-12 Two triangles drawn using GL_TRIANGLES

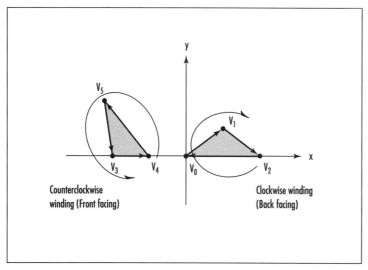

Figure 6-13 Two triangles with different windings

The combination of order and direction in which the vertices are specified is called *winding*. The triangles in Figure 6-12 are said to have clockwise winding because they are literally wound in the clockwise direction. If we reverse the positions of V4 and V5 on the triangle on the left, we get counterclockwise winding as shown in Figure 6-13.

OpenGL by default considers polygons that have counterclockwise winding to be *front facing.* This means that the triangle on the left in Figure 6-13 is showing us the front of the triangle, and the one on the right is showing the back side of the triangle.

Why is this important? As you will soon see, you will often want to give the front and back of a polygon different physical characteristics. You can hide the back of a polygon altogether, or give it a different color and reflective property as well (see Chapter 9). It's very important to keep the winding of all polygons in a scene consistent, using front-facing polygons to draw the outside surface of any solid objects. In the upcoming section on solid objects, we will demonstrate this principle using some models that are more complex.

If you need to reverse the default behavior of OpenGL, you can do so by calling the function

```
glFrontFace(GL_CW);
```

The GL_CW parameter tells OpenGL that clockwise-wound polygons are to be considered front facing. To change back to counterclockwise winding for the front face, use GL_CCW.

Triangle Strips

For many surfaces and shapes, you will need to draw several connected triangles. You can save a lot of time by drawing a strip of connected triangles with the GL_TRIAN-GLE_STRIP primitive. Figure 6-14 shows the progression of a strip of three triangles specified by a set of five vertices numbered V0 through V4. Here you see the vertices are not necessarily traversed in the same order they were specified. The reason for this is to preserve the winding (counterclockwise) of each triangle.

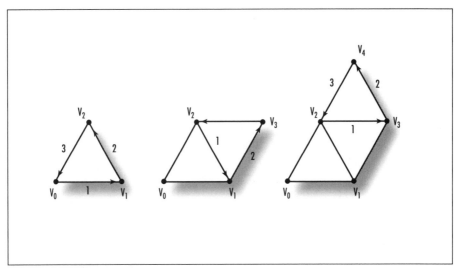

Figure 6-14 The progression of a GL_TRIANGLE_STRIP

(By the way, for the rest of our discussion of polygonal primitives, we won't be showing you any more code fragments to demonstrate the vertices and the glBegin statements. You should have the swing of things by now. Later, when we have a real sample program to work with, we'll resume the examples.)

There are two advantages to using a strip of triangles instead of just specifying each triangle separately. First, after specifying the first three vertices for the initial triangle, you only need to specify a single point for each additional triangle. This saves a lot of time (as well as data space) when you have many triangles to draw. The second advantage is that it's a good idea, as mentioned previously, to compose an object or surface out of triangles rather than some of the other primitives.

> Another advantage to composing large flat surfaces out of several smaller triangles is that when lighting effects are applied to the scene, the simulated effects can be better reproduced by OpenGL. You'll learn to apply this technique in Chapter 9.

Triangle Fans

In addition to triangle strips, you can use GL_TRIANGLE_FAN to produce a group of connected triangles that fan around a central point. Figure 6-15 shows a fan of three triangles produced by specifying four vertices. The first vertex, V0, forms the origin of the fan. After the first three vertices are used to draw the initial triangle, all subsequent vertices are used with the origin (V0) and the vertex immediately preceding it (Vn-1) to form the next triangle. Notice that the vertices are traversed in a clockwise direction, rather than counterclockwise.

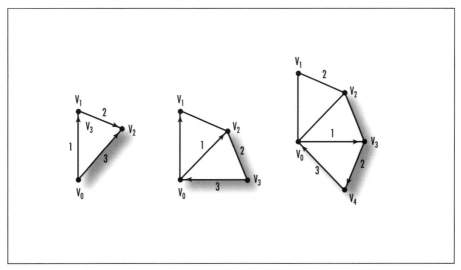

Figure 6-15 The progression of GL_TRIANGLE_FAN

Building Solid Objects

Composing a solid object out of triangles (or any other polygon) involves more than just assembling a series of vertices in a 3D coordinate space. Let's examine the example program TRIANGLE, which uses two triangle fans to create a cone in our viewing volume. The first fan produces the cone shape, using the first vertex as the point of the cone and the remaining vertices as points along a circle further down the z-axis. The second fan forms a circle and lies entirely in the xy plane, making up the bottom surface of the cone.

The output from TRIANGLE is shown in Figure 6-16. Here you are looking directly down the z-axis and can only see a circle composed of a fan of triangles. The individual triangles are emphasized by coloring them alternately green and red.

The code for the SetupRC and RenderScene functions is shown in Listing 6-8. (You will see some unfamiliar variables and specifiers that will be explained shortly.) This program demonstrates several aspects of composing 3D objects. Notice the Effects menu item; this will be used to enable and disable some 3D drawing features so we can explore some of the characteristics of 3D object creation.

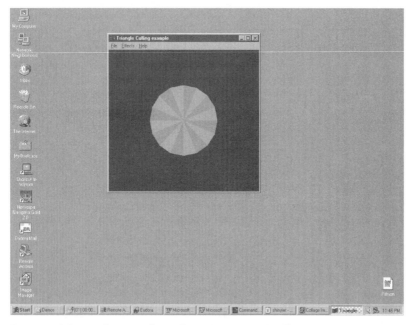

Figure 6-16 Initial output from the TRIANGLE sample program

Listing 6-8 Pertinent code for the TRIANGLE sample program

```
// This function does any needed initialization on the rendering
// context.
void SetupRC()
        {
        // Black background
        glClearColor(0.0f, 0.0f, 0.0f, 1.0f );

        // Set drawing color to green
        glColor3f(0.0f, 1.0f, 0.0f);

        // Set color shading model to flat
        glShadeModel(GL_FLAT);

        // Clockwise-wound polygons are front facing; this is reversed
        // because we are using triangle fans
        glFrontFace(GL_CW);
        }



// Called to draw scene
void RenderScene(void)
        {
        GLfloat x,y,angle;              // Storage for coordinates and angles
        int iPivot = 1;                 // Used to flag alternating colors

        // Clear the window and the depth buffer
        glClear(GL_COLOR_BUFFER_BIT | GL_DEPTH_BUFFER_BIT);

        // Turn culling on if flag is set
        if(bCull)
                glEnable(GL_CULL_FACE);
        else
                glDisable(GL_CULL_FACE);

        // Enable depth testing if flag is set
        if(bDepth)
                glEnable(GL_DEPTH_TEST);
        else
                glDisable(GL_DEPTH_TEST);

        // Draw the back side as a polygon only, if flag is set
        if(bOutline)
                glPolygonMode(GL_BACK,GL_LINE);
        else
                glPolygonMode(GL_BACK,GL_FILL);


        // Save matrix state and do the rotation
        glPushMatrix();
        glRotatef(xRot, 1.0f, 0.0f, 0.0f);
        glRotatef(yRot, 0.0f, 1.0f, 0.0f);
```

continued on next page

continued from previous page

```
// Begin a triangle fan
glBegin(GL_TRIANGLE_FAN);

// Pinnacle of cone is shared vertex for fan, moved up z-axis
// to produce a cone instead of a circle
glVertex3f(0.0f, 0.0f, 75.0f);

// Loop around in a circle and specify even points along the circle
// as the vertices of the triangle fan
for(angle = 0.0f; angle < (2.0f*GL_PI); angle += (GL_PI/8.0f))
        {
        // Calculate x and y position of the next vertex
        x = 50.0f*sin(angle);
        y = 50.0f*cos(angle);

        // Alternate color between red and green
        if((iPivot %2) == 0)
                glColor3f(0.0f, 1.0f, 0.0f);
        else
                glColor3f(1.0f, 0.0f, 0.0f);

        // Increment pivot to change color next time
        iPivot++;

        // Specify the next vertex for the triangle fan
        glVertex2f(x, y);
        }

// Done drawing fan for cone
glEnd();


// Begin a new triangle fan to cover the bottom
glBegin(GL_TRIANGLE_FAN);

// Center of fan is at the origin
glVertex2f(0.0f, 0.0f);
for(angle = 0.0f; angle < (2.0f*GL_PI); angle += (GL_PI/8.0f))
        {
        // Calculate x and y position of the next vertex
        x = 50.0f*sin(angle);
        y = 50.0f*cos(angle);

        // Alternate color between red and green
        if((iPivot %2) == 0)
                glColor3f(0.0f, 1.0f, 0.0f);
        else
                glColor3f(1.0f, 0.0f, 0.0f);

        // Increment pivot to change color next time
        iPivot++;

        // Specify the next vertex for the triangle fan
        glVertex2f(x, y);
        }

// Done drawing the fan that covers the bottom
glEnd();
```

```
// Restore transformations
glPopMatrix();

// Flush drawing commands
glFlush();
}
```

Setting Polygon Colors

Until now, we have set the current color only once and drawn only a single shape. Now, with multiple polygons, things get slightly more interesting. We want to use different colors so we can see our work more easily. Colors are actually specified per vertex, not per polygon. The shading model affects whether the polygon is then solidly colored (using the current color selected when the last vertex was specified), or smoothly shaded between the colors specified for each vertex.

The line *glShadeModel(GL_FLAT);* tells OpenGL to fill the polygons with the solid color that was current when the polygon's last vertex was specified. This is why we can simply change the current color to red or green before specifying the next vertex in our triangle fan. On the other hand, the line *glShadeModel(GL_SMOOTH);* would tell OpenGL to shade the triangles smoothly from each vertex, attempting to interpolate the colors between those specified for each vertex. You'll be learning much more about color and shading in Chapter 8.

Hidden Surface Removal

Hold down one of the arrow keys to spin the cone around, and don't select anything from the Effects menu yet. You'll notice something unsettling: The cone appears to be swinging back and forth plus and minus 180°, with the bottom of the cone always facing you, but not rotating a full 360°. Figure 6-17 shows this more clearly.

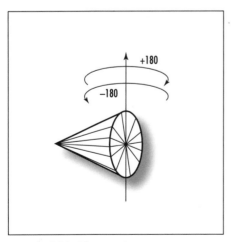

Figure 6-17 The rotating cone appears to be wobbling back and forth

This is occurring because the bottom of the cone is being drawn after the sides of the cone are drawn. This means, no matter how the cone is oriented, the bottom is then drawn on top of it, producing the "wobbling" illusion. This effect is not limited to just the various sides and parts of an object. If more than one object is drawn and one is in front of the other (from the viewer's perspective), the last object drawn will still appear over the previously drawn object.

You can correct this peculiarity with a simple technique called *hidden surface removal,* and OpenGL has functions that will do this for you behind the scenes. The concept is simple: When a pixel is drawn, it is assigned a value (called the z value) that denotes its distance from the viewer's perspective. Later, when another pixel needs to be drawn to that screen location, the new pixel's z value is compared to that of the pixel that is already stored there. If the new pixel's z value is higher, then it is closer to the viewer and thus in front of the previous pixel, so the previous pixel will be obscured by the new pixel. If the new pixel's z value is lower, then it must be behind the existing pixel and thus would not be obscured. This maneuver is accomplished internally by a depth buffer, which will be discussed in Chapter 15.

To enable depth testing, simply call

```
glEnable(GL_DEPTH_TEST);
```

This is done in Listing 6-8 when the bDepth variable is set to True, and depth testing is disabled if bDepth is False.

```
// Enable depth testing if flag is set
if(bDepth)
        glEnable(GL_DEPTH_TEST);
else
        glDisable(GL_DEPTH_TEST);
```

The bDepth variable is set when Depth Test is selected from the Effects menu. In addition, the depth buffer must be cleared each time the scene is rendered. The depth buffer is analogous to the color buffer in that it contains information about the distance of the pixels from the observer. This is used to determine if any pixels are hidden by pixels closer to the observer.

```
// Clear the window and the depth buffer
glClear(GL_COLOR_BUFFER_BIT | GL_DEPTH_BUFFER_BIT);
```

Figure 6-18 shows the Effects menu with depth testing enabled. It also shows the cone with the bottom correctly hidden behind the sides. You can see that depth testing is practically a prerequisite to creation of 3D objects out of solid polygons.

Culling: Hiding Surfaces for Performance

You can see that there are obvious visual advantages to not drawing a surface that is obstructed by another. Even so, you pay some performance overhead because every pixel drawn must be compared with the previous pixel's z value. Sometimes, however, you know that a surface will never be drawn anyway, so why specify it? The answer is that you may not wish to draw the back sides of the surface.

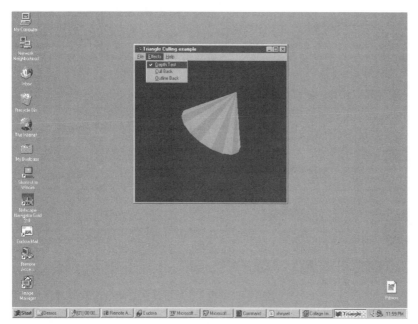

Figure 6-18 The bottom of the cone is now correctly placed behind the sides for this orientation

In our working example, the cone is a closed surface and we never see the inside. OpenGL is actually (internally) drawing the back sides of the far side of the cone, and then the front sides of the polygons facing us. Then, by a comparison of z buffer values, the far side of the cone is eliminated. Figures 6-19a and 6-19b show our cone at a particular orientation with depth testing turned on (a) and off (b). Notice that the green and red triangles that make up the cone sides change when depth testing is enabled. Without depth testing, the sides of the triangles at the far side of the cone show through.

Earlier in the chapter we explained how OpenGL uses winding to determine the front and back sides of polygons, and that it is important to keep the polygons that define the outside of your objects wound in a consistent direction. This consistency is what allows us to tell OpenGL to render only the front, only the back, or both sides of polygons. By eliminating the back sides of the polygons, we can drastically reduce the amount of necessary processing to render the image. Even though depth testing will eliminate the appearance of the inside of objects, internally OpenGL must take them into account unless we explicitly tell it not to.

The elimination of the front or back of polygons is called *culling*. Culling is enabled or disabled for our program by the following code fragment from Listing 6-8:

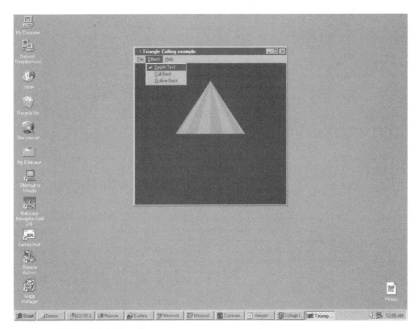

Figure 6-19a With depth testing

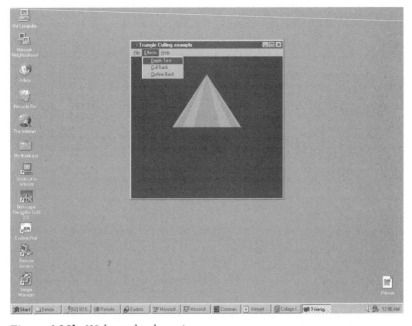

Figure 6-19b Without depth testing

```
// Clockwise-wound polygons are front facing; this is reversed
// because we are using triangle fans
glFrontFace(GL_CW);

...
...


// Turn culling on if flag is set
if(bCull)
        glEnable(GL_CULL_FACE);
else
        glDisable(GL_CULL_FACE);
```

Note that we first changed the definition of front-facing polygons to be those with clockwise winding (because our triangle fans are all wound clockwise).

Figure 6-20 demonstrates that the bottom of the cone is gone when culling is enabled. This is because we didn't follow our own rule about all the surface polygons having the same winding. The triangle fan that makes up the bottom of the cone is wound clockwise, like the fan that makes up the sides of the cone, but the front side of the cone's bottom section is facing the inside. See Figure 6-21.

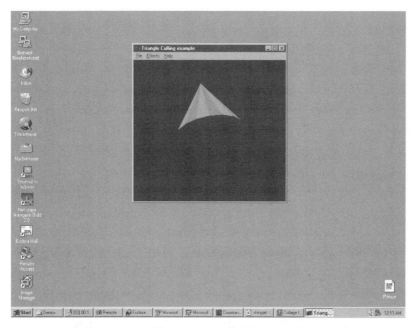

Figure 6-20 The bottom of the cone is culled because the front-facing triangles are inside

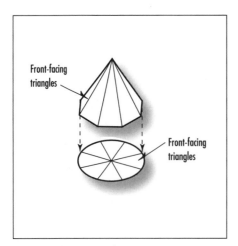

Figure 6-21 How the cone was
assembled from two triangle fans

We could have corrected this by changing the winding rule, by calling

```
glFrontFace(GL_CCW);
```

just before we drew the second triangle fan. But in this example we wanted to make it easy for you to see culling in action, as well as get set up for our next demonstration of polygon tweaking.

Polygon Modes

Polygons don't have to be filled with the current color. By default, polygons are drawn solid, but you can change this behavior by specifying that polygons are to be drawn as outlines or just points (only the vertices are plotted). The function glPolygonMode() allows polygons to be rendered filled, as outlines, or as points only. In addition, this rendering mode can be applied to both sides of the polygons or to just the front or back. The following code from Listing 6-8 shows the polygon mode being set to outlines or solid, depending on the state of the Boolean variable bOutline:

```
// Draw back side as a polygon only, if flag is set
if(bOutline)
        glPolygonMode(GL_BACK,GL_LINE);
else
        glPolygonMode(GL_BACK,GL_FILL);
```

Figure 6-22 shows the back sides of all polygons rendered as outlines. (We had to disable culling to produce this image; otherwise, the inside would be eliminated and you'd get no outlines.) Notice that the bottom of the cone is now wireframe instead of solid, and you can see up inside the cone where the inside walls are also drawn as wireframe triangles.

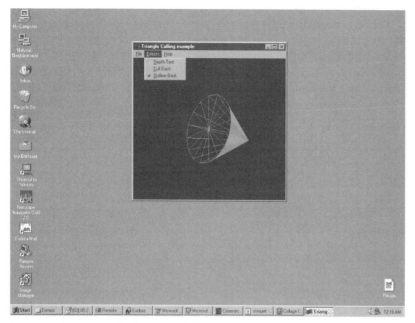

Figure 6-22 Using glPolygonMode() to render one side of the triangles as outlines

Other Primitives

Triangles are the preferred primitive for object composition since most OpenGL hardware specifically accelerates triangles, but they are not the only primitives available. Some hardware will provide for acceleration of other shapes as well, and programmatically it may be simpler to use a general-purpose graphics primitive. The remaining OpenGL primitives provide for rapid specification of a quadrilateral or quadrilateral strip, as well as a general-purpose polygon. If you know your code is going to be run in an environment that accelerates general-purpose polygons, these may be your best bet in terms of performance.

Four-Sided Polygons: Quads

The next most complex shape from a triangle is a *quadrilateral*, or a four-sided figure. OpenGL's GL_QUADS primitive draws a four-sided polygon. In Figure 6-23 a quad is drawn from four vertices. Note also that quads have clockwise winding.

Quad Strips

Just as you can for triangles, you can specify a strip of connected quadrilaterals with the GL_QUAD_STRIP primitive. Figure 6-24 shows the progression of a quad strip specified by six vertices. Quad strips, like single GL_QUADS, maintain a clockwise winding.

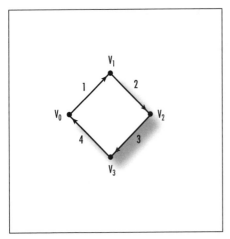

Figure 6-23 An example of GL_QUAD

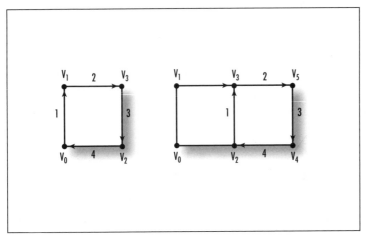

Figure 6-24 Progression of GL_QUAD_STRIP

General Polygons

The final OpenGL primitive is the GL_POLYGON, which can be used to draw a polygon having any number of sides. Figure 6-25 shows a polygon consisting of five vertices. Polygons created with GL_POLYGON have clockwise winding, as well.

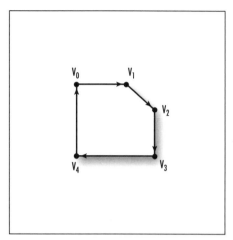

Figure 6-25 Progression of GL_POLYGON

What About Rectangles?
All ten of the OpenGL primitives are used with glBegin/glEnd to draw general-purpose polygonal shapes. One shape is so common, it has a special function instead of being a primitive; that shape is the rectangle. It was actually the first shape you learned to draw back in Chapter 3. The function glRect() provides an easy and convenient mechanism for specifying rectangles without having to resort to GL_QUAD.

Filling Polygons, or Stippling Revisited

There are two methods of applying a pattern to solid polygons. The customary method is texture mapping, where a bitmap is mapped to the surface of a polygon, and this is covered in Chapter 11. Another way is to specify a stippling pattern, as we did for lines. A polygon stipple pattern is nothing more than a 32 x 32 monochrome bitmap that is used for the fill pattern.

To enable polygon stippling, call

```
glEnable(GL_POLYGON_STIPPLE);
```

and then call

```
glPolygonStipple(pBitmap);
```

where pBitmap is a pointer to a data area containing the stipple pattern. Hereafter, all polygons will be filled using the pattern specified by pBitmap (GLubyte *). This pattern is similar to that used by line stippling, except the buffer is large enough to hold a 32 x 32-bit pattern. Also, the bits are read with the MSB (Most Significant Bit) first, which is just the opposite of line stipple patterns. Figure 6-26 shows a bit pattern for a campfire that we will use for a stipple pattern.

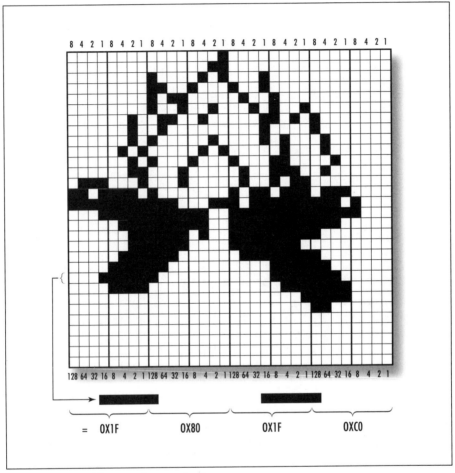

Figure 6-26 Building a polygon stipple pattern

Pixel Storage
As you will learn in Chapter 11, you can modify the way pixels for stipple patterns are interpreted, with the glPixelStore() function. For now, though, we will stick to simple polygon stippling.

To construct a mask to represent this pattern, we store one row at a time from the bottom up. Fortunately, unlike line-stipple patterns, the data is by default interpreted just as it is stored, with the most significant bit read first. Each byte can then be read from left to right and stored in an array of GLubyte large enough to hold 32 rows of 4 bytes apiece.

Listing 6-9 shows the code used to store this pattern. Each row of the array represents a row from Figure 6-26. The first row in the array is the last row of the figure, and so on, up to the last row of the array and the first row of the figure.

Suggestion: Come Back Later
If you are still uncertain about how this campfire bitmap is stored and interpreted, we suggest you come back and reread this material after you've finished Chapter 11, "Raster Graphics in OpenGL."

Listing 6-9 The mask definition for the campfire in Figure 6-26

```
// Bitmap of camp fire
GLubyte fire[] = { 0x00, 0x00, 0x00, 0x00,
                   0x00, 0x00, 0x00, 0x00,
                   0x00, 0x00, 0x00, 0x00,
                   0x00, 0x00, 0x00, 0x00,
                   0x00, 0x00, 0x00, 0x00,
                   0x00, 0x00, 0x00, 0x00,
                   0x00, 0x00, 0x00, 0xc0,
                   0x00, 0x00, 0x01, 0xf0,
                   0x00, 0x00, 0x07, 0xf0,
                   0x0f, 0x00, 0x1f, 0xe0,
                   0x1f, 0x80, 0x1f, 0xc0,
                   0x0f, 0xc0, 0x3f, 0x80,
                   0x07, 0xe0, 0x7e, 0x00,
                   0x03, 0xf0, 0xff, 0x80,
                   0x03, 0xf5, 0xff, 0xe0,
                   0x07, 0xfd, 0xff, 0xf8,
                   0x1f, 0xfc, 0xff, 0xe8,
                   0xff, 0xe3, 0xbf, 0x70,
                   0xde, 0x80, 0xb7, 0x00,
                   0x71, 0x10, 0x4a, 0x80,
                   0x03, 0x10, 0x4e, 0x40,
                   0x02, 0x88, 0x8c, 0x20,
                   0x05, 0x05, 0x04, 0x40,
                   0x02, 0x82, 0x14, 0x40,
                   0x02, 0x40, 0x10, 0x80,
                   0x02, 0x64, 0x1a, 0x80,
                   0x00, 0x92, 0x29, 0x00,
                   0x00, 0xb0, 0x48, 0x00,
                   0x00, 0xc8, 0x90, 0x00,
                   0x00, 0x85, 0x10, 0x00,
                   0x00, 0x03, 0x00, 0x00,
                   0x00, 0x00, 0x10, 0x00 };
```

To make use of this stipple pattern, we must first enable polygon stippling and then specify this pattern as the stipple pattern. The PSTIPPLE example program does this, and then draws a hexagon (stop sign) using the stipple pattern. Listing 6-10 is the pertinent code, and Figure 6-27 shows the output from PSTIPPLE.

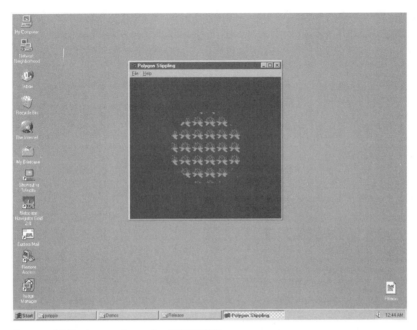

Figure 6-27 Output from the PSTIPPLE program

Listing 6-10 Code from PSTIPPLE that draws a stippled hexagon

```
// This function does any needed initialization on the rendering
// context.
void SetupRC()
        {
        // Black background
        glClearColor(0.0f, 0.0f, 0.0f, 1.0f );

        // Set drawing color to red
        glColor3f(1.0f, 0.0f, 0.0f);

        // Enable polygon stippling
        glEnable(GL_POLYGON_STIPPLE);

        // Specify a specific stipple pattern
        glPolygonStipple(fire);
        }


// Called to draw scene
void RenderScene(void)
        {
        // Clear the window
        glClear(GL_COLOR_BUFFER_BIT);

        ...
        ...
```

```
// Begin the stop sign shape,
// use a standard polygon for simplicity
glBegin(GL_POLYGON);
        glVertex2f(-20.0f, 50.0f);
        glVertex2f(20.0f, 50.0f);
        glVertex2f(50.0f, 20.0f);
        glVertex2f(50.0f, -20.0f);
        glVertex2f(20.0f, -50.0f);
        glVertex2f(-20.0f, -50.0f);
        glVertex2f(-50.0f, -20.0f);
        glVertex2f(-50.0f, 20.0f);
glEnd();

...
...

// Flush drawing commands
glFlush();
}
```

Figure 6-28 shows the hexagon rotated somewhat. You'll notice that the stipple pattern is still used, but the pattern is not rotated with the polygon. That's because the stipple pattern is only used for simple polygon filling on screen. If you need to map a bitmap to a polygon so that it mimics the polygon's surface, you will have to use texture mapping (Chapter 12).

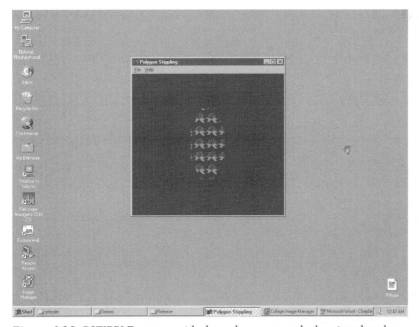

Figure 6-28 PSTIPPLE output with the polygon rotated, showing that the stipple pattern is not rotated

Polygon Construction Rules

When you are using many polygons to construct a complex surface, you'll need to remember two important rules.

The first rule is that all polygons must be planar. That is, all the vertices of the polygon must lie in a single plane, as illustrated in Figure 6-29. The polygon cannot twist or bend in space.

Here is yet another good reason to use triangles. No triangle can ever be twisted so that all three points do not line up in a plane, because mathematically it only takes three points to define a plane. (So if you can plot an invalid triangle, aside from winding it in the wrong direction, the Nobel Prize committee may just be looking for you!)

The second rule of polygon construction is that the polygon's edges must not intersect, and the polygon must be convex. A polygon intersects itself if any two of its lines cross. "Convex" means that the polygon cannot have any indentions. A more rigorous test of a convex polygon is to draw some lines through it. If any given line enters and leaves the polygon more than once, then the polygon is not convex. Figure 6-30 gives examples of good and bad polygons.

Why the Limitations on Polygons?
You may be wondering why OpenGL places the restrictions on polygon construction. Handling polygons can become quite complex, and OpenGL's restrictions allow it to use very fast algorithms for the rendering of these polygons. We predict that you'll not find these restrictions burdensome, and that you'll be able to build any shapes or objects you need using the existing primitives. (And you can use GL_LINES to draw an otherwise illegal shape, too.)

Subdivision and Edges

Even though OpenGL can only draw convex polygons, there's still a way to create a nonconvex polygon—by arranging two or more convex polygons together. For example, let's take a four-point star as shown in Figure 6-31. This shape is obviously not convex and thus violates OpenGL's rules for simple polygon construction. However, the star on the right is composed of six separate triangles, which are legal polygons.

When the polygons are filled, you won't be able to see any edges and the figure will seem to be a single shape on screen. However, if you use glPolygonMode to switch to an outline drawing, it would be distracting to see all those little triangles making up some larger surface area.

OpenGL provides a special flag called an *edge flag* for this purpose. By setting and clearing the edge flag as you specify a list of vertices, you inform OpenGL which line segments are considered border lines (lines that go around the border of your shape), and which ones are not (internal lines that shouldn't be visible). The glEdgeFlag()

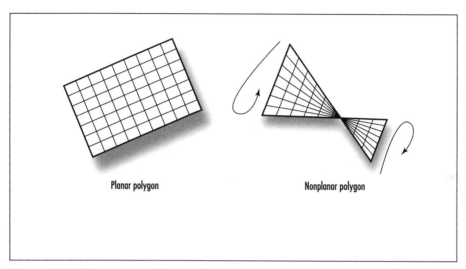

Figure 6-29 Planar vs. nonplanar polygons

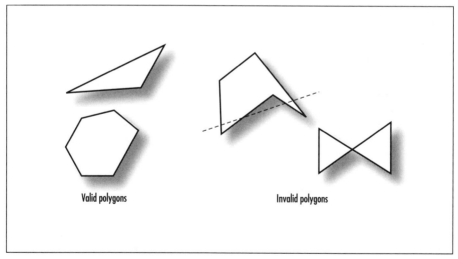

Figure 6-30 Some valid and invalid primitive polygons

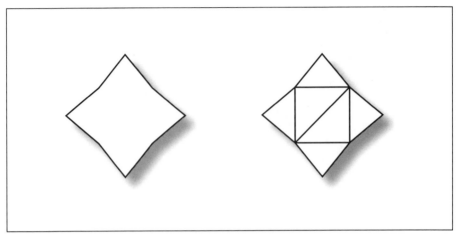

Figure 6-31 A nonconvex four-point star made up of six triangles

function takes a single parameter that sets the edge flag to True or False. When set to True, any vertices that follow mark the beginning of a boundary line segment. Listing 6-11 shows an example of this from the STAR example program on the CD.

Listing 6-11 Example usage of glEdgeFlag from the STAR program

```
// Begin the triangles
glBegin(GL_TRIANGLES);

        glEdgeFlag(bEdgeFlag);
        glVertex2f(-20.0f, 0.0f);
        glEdgeFlag(TRUE);
        glVertex2f(20.0f, 0.0f);
        glVertex2f(0.0f, 40.0f);

        glVertex2f(-20.0f,0.0f);
        glVertex2f(-60.0f,-20.0f);
        glEdgeFlag(bEdgeFlag);
        glVertex2f(-20.0f,-40.0f);
        glEdgeFlag(TRUE);

        glVertex2f(-20.0f,-40.0f);
        glVertex2f(0.0f, -80.0f);
        glEdgeFlag(bEdgeFlag);
        glVertex2f(20.0f, -40.0f);
        glEdgeFlag(TRUE);
```

```
        glVertex2f(20.0f, -40.0f);
        glVertex2f(60.0f, -20.0f);
        glEdgeFlag(bEdgeFlag);
        glVertex2f(20.0f, 0.0f);
        glEdgeFlag(TRUE);

        // Center square as two triangles
        glEdgeFlag(bEdgeFlag);
        glVertex2f(-20.0f, 0.0f);
        glVertex2f(-20.0f,-40.0f);
        glVertex2f(20.0f, 0.0f);

        glVertex2f(-20.0f,-40.0f);
        glVertex2f(20.0f, -40.0f);
        glVertex2f(20.0f, 0.0f);
        glEdgeFlag(TRUE);

// Done drawing Triangles
glEnd();
```

The Boolean variable bEdgeFlag is toggled on and off by a menu option to make the edges appear and disappear. If this flag is True, then all edges are considered boundary edges and will appear when the polygon mode is set to GL_LINES. In Figures 6-32a and 6-32b you can see the output from STAR, showing the wireframe star with and without edges.

Summary

We've covered a lot of ground in this chapter. At this point you can create your 3D space for rendering, and you know how to draw everything from points and lines to complex polygons. We've also shown you how to assemble these two dimensional primitives as the surface of three-dimensional objects.

We encourage you to experiment with what you have learned in this chapter. Use your imagination and create some of your own 3D objects before moving on to the rest of the book. You'll then have some personal samples to work with and enhance as you learn and explore new techniques throughout the book.

Here Comes the Tank/Robot Simulation!
Beginning with this chapter, we will begin constructing a tank and robot simulator as a supplementary example (found on the CD). The goal of this simulation is to have both the tank and robot roam around in a virtual landscape, allowing for viewpoints from the tank's or robot's perspective. The tank/robot simulator is not explained as part of the text, but the simulation will be gradually enhanced using the techniques presented in each chapter. You can start now and view some of the objects that will exist in the virtual world of our tank and robot. Observe and study how these objects are composed entirely of the primitives from this chapter.

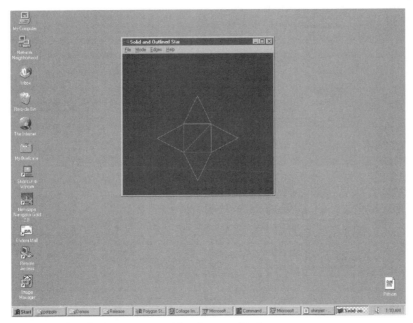

Figure 6-32a STAR program with edges enabled

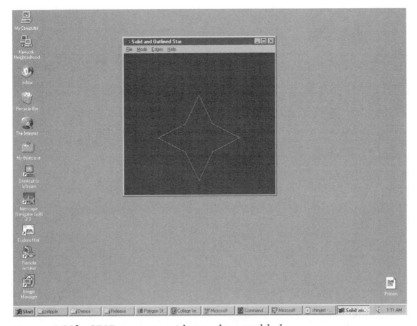

Figure 6-32b STAR program without edges enabled

Reference Section

GLBEGIN

Purpose	Used to denote the beginning of a group of vertices that define one or more primitives.
Include File	<gl.h>
Syntax	void glBegin(GLenum mode);
Description	This function is used in conjunction with glEnd to delimit the vertices of an OpenGL primitive. Multiple vertices sets may be included within a single glBegin/glEnd pair, as long as they are for the same primitive type. Other settings may also be made with additional OpenGL commands that affect the vertices following them. Only these OpenGL functions may be called within a glBegin/glEnd sequence: glVertex, glColor, glIndex, glNormal, glEvalCoord, glCallList, glCallLists, glTexCoord, glEdgeFlag, and glMaterial.
Parameters	
mode	GLenum: This value specifies the primitive to be constructed. It may be any of the values in Table 6-1.
Returns	None.
Example	You can find this ubiquitous function in literally every example and supplementary sample in this chapter. The following code shows a single point being drawn at the origin of the x,y,z coordinate system.

```
glBegin(GL_POINTS)
        glVertex3f(0.0f, 0.0f, 0.0f); //plots point at origin
glEnd();
```

See Also	glEnd, glVertex

Table 6-1 OpenGL Primitives Supported by glBegin()

Mode	Primitive Type
GL_POINTS	The specified vertices are used to create a single point each.
GL_LINES	The specified vertices are used to create line segments. Every two vertices specify a single and separate line segment. If the number of vertices is odd, the last one is ignored.
GL_LINE_STRIP	The specified vertices are used to create a line strip. After the first vertex, each subsequent vertex specifies the next point to which the line is extended.
GL_LINE_LOOP	Behaves as GL_LINE_STRIP, except a final line segment is drawn between the last and the first vertex specified. This is typically used to draw closed regions that may violate the rules regarding GL_POLYGON usage.
GL_TRIANGLES	The specified vertices are used to construct triangles. Every three vertices specify a new triangle. If the number of vertices is not evenly divisible by three, the extra vertices are ignored.

continued on next page

continued from previous page

Mode	Primitive Type
GL_TRIANGLE_STRIP	The specified vertices are used to create a strip of triangles. After the first three vertices are specified, each of any subsequent vertices is used with the two preceding ones to construct the next triangle. Each triplet of vertices (after the initial set) is automatically rearranged to ensure consistent winding of the triangles.
GL_TRIANGLE_FAN	The specified vertices are used to construct a triangle fan. The first vertex serves as an origin, and each vertex after the third is combined with the foregoing one and the origin. Any number of triangles may be fanned in this manner.
GL_QUADS	Each set of four vertices is used to construct a quadrilateral (a four-sided polygon). If the number of vertices is not evenly divisible by four, the remaining ones are ignored.
GL_QUAD_STRIP	The specified vertices are used to construct a strip of quadrilaterals. One quadrilateral is defined for each pair of vertices after the first pair. Unlike the vertex ordering for GL_QUADS, each pair of vertices is used in the reverse order specified, to ensure consistent winding.
GL_POLYGON	The specified vertices are used to construct a convex polygon. The polygon edges must not intersect. The last vertex is automatically connected to the first vertex to insure the polygon is closed.

GLCULLFACE

Purpose	Specifies whether the front or back of polygons should be eliminated from drawing.
Include File	<gl.h>
Syntax	void glCullFace(GLenum mode);
Description	This function disables lighting, shading, and color calculations and operations on either the front or back of a polygon. Eliminates unnecessary rendering computations because the back side of polygons will never be visible regardless of rotation or translation of the objects. Culling is enabled or disabled by calling glEnable and glDisable with the GL_CULL_FACE parameter. The front and back of the polygon are defined by use of glFrontFace() and by the order in which the vertices are specified (clockwise or counterclockwise winding).
Parameters	
mode	GLenum: Specifies which face of polygons should be culled. May be either GL_FRONT or GL_BACK.
Returns	None.
Example	The following code (from the TRIANGLE example in this chapter) shows how the color and drawing operations are disabled for the inside of the cone when the Boolean variable bCull is set to True.

```
// Clockwise-wound polygons are front facing; this is reversed
// because we are using triangle fans
glFrontFace(GL_CW);
```

```
...
...
...

// Turn culling on if flag is set
if(bCull)
        glEnable(GL_CULL_FACE);
else
        glDisable(GL_CULL_FACE);
```

See Also   glFrontFace, glLightModel

GLEDGEFLAG

Purpose   Flags polygon edges as either boundary or nonboundary edges. This can be used to determine whether interior surface lines are visible.

Include File   <gl.h>

Variations   void **glEdgeFlag**(GLboolean flag); void **glEdgeFlagv**(const GLboolean *flag);

Description   When two or more polygons are joined to form a larger region, the edges on the outside define the boundary of the newly formed region. This function flags inside edges as nonboundary. This is used only when the polygon mode is set to either GL_LINE or GL_POINT.

Parameters

flag   GLboolean: Sets the edge flag to this value, True or False.

*flag   const GLboolean *: A pointer to a value that is used for the edge flag.

Returns   None.

Example   The following code from the STAR program in this chapter sets the edge flag to False for triangle borders inside the region of the star. It draws the star either as a solid, an outline, or just the vertices.

```
// Draw back side as a polygon only, if flag is set
if(iMode == MODE_LINE)
        glPolygonMode(GL_FRONT_AND_BACK,GL_LINE);

if(iMode == MODE_POINT)
        glPolygonMode(GL_FRONT_AND_BACK,GL_POINT);

if(iMode == MODE_SOLID)
        glPolygonMode(GL_FRONT_AND_BACK,GL_FILL);


// Begin the triangles
glBegin(GL_TRIANGLES);

        glEdgeFlag(bEdgeFlag);
        glVertex2f(-20.0f, 0.0f);
        glEdgeFlag(TRUE);
        glVertex2f(20.0f, 0.0f);
        glVertex2f(0.0f, 40.0f);
```

continued on next page

continued from previous page

```
            glVertex2f(-20.0f,0.0f);
            glVertex2f(-60.0f,-20.0f);
            glEdgeFlag(bEdgeFlag);
            glVertex2f(-20.0f,-40.0f);
            glEdgeFlag(TRUE);

            glVertex2f(-20.0f,-40.0f);
            glVertex2f(0.0f, -80.0f);
            glEdgeFlag(bEdgeFlag);
            glVertex2f(20.0f, -40.0f);
            glEdgeFlag(TRUE);

            glVertex2f(20.0f, -40.0f);
            glVertex2f(60.0f, -20.0f);
            glEdgeFlag(bEdgeFlag);
            glVertex2f(20.0f, 0.0f);
            glEdgeFlag(TRUE);

            // Center square as two triangles
            glEdgeFlag(bEdgeFlag);
            glVertex2f(-20.0f, 0.0f);
            glVertex2f(-20.0f,-40.0f);
            glVertex2f(20.0f, 0.0f);

            glVertex2f(-20.0f,-40.0f);
            glVertex2f(20.0f, -40.0f);
            glVertex2f(20.0f, 0.0f);
            glEdgeFlag(TRUE);

    // Done drawing Triangles
    glEnd();
```

See Also   glBegin, glPolygonMode.

GLEND

Purpose	Terminates a list of vertices that specify a primitive initiated by glBegin.
Include File	<gl.h>
Syntax	void glEnd();
Description	This function is used in conjunction with glBegin to delimit the vertices of an OpenGL primitive. Multiple vertices sets may be included within a single glBegin/glEnd pair, as long as they are for the same primitive type. Other settings may also be made with additional OpenGL commands that affect the vertices following them. Only these OpenGL functions may be called within a glBegin/glEnd sequence: glVertex, glColor, glIndex, glNormal, glEvalCoord, glCallList, glCallLists, glTexCoord, glEdgeFlag, and glMaterial.
Returns	None.
Example	You can find this ubiquitous function in literally every example and supplementary sample in this chapter. The following code shows a single point being drawn at the origin of the x,y,z coordinate system.

```
glBegin(GL_POINTS)
        glVertex3f(0.0f, 0.0f, 0.0f);
glEnd();
```

See Also   glBegin, glVertex

GLFRONTFACE

Purpose   Defines which side of a polygon is the front or back.

Include File   <gl.h>

Syntax   void glFrontFace(GLenum mode);

Description   When a scene comprises objects that are closed (you cannot see the inside), color or lighting calculations on the inside of the object are unnecessary. The glCullFace function turns off such calculations for either the front or back of polygons. The glFrontFace function determines which side of the polygons is considered the front. If the vertices of a polygon as viewed from the front are specified so that they travel clockwise around the polygon, the polygon is said have clockwise winding. If the vertices travel counterclockwise, the polygon is said to have counterclockwise winding. This function allows you to specify either the clockwise or counterclockwise wound face to be the front of the polygon.

Parameters

mode   GLenum: Specifies the orientation of front-facing polygons: clockwise (GL_CW) or counterclockwise (GL_CCW).

Returns   None.

Example   The following code from the TRIANGLE example in this chapter shows how the color and drawing operations are disabled for the inside of the cone. It is also necessary to indicate which side of the triangles are the outside by specifying clockwise winding.

```
// Clockwise wound polygons are front facing, this is reversed
// because we are using triangle fans
glFrontFace(GL_CW);

...
...
...

// Turn culling on if flag is set
if(bCull)
        glEnable(GL_CULL_FACE);
else
        glDisable(GL_CULL_FACE);
```

See Also   glCullFace, glLightModel

GLGETPOLYGONSTIPPLE

Purpose	Returns the current polygon stipple pattern.
Include File	<gl.h>
Syntax	void glGetPolygonStipple(GLubyte *mask);
Description	This function returns a 32 x 32-bit pattern that represents the polygon stipple pattern. The pattern is copied to the memory location pointed to by mask. The packing of the pixels is affected by the last call to glPixelStore.
Parameters	
mask	GLubyte: A pointer to the polygon stipple pattern.
Returns	None.
Example	The following code segment retrieves the current stipple pattern:

```
GLubyte mask[32*4];    // 4 bytes = 32bits per row X 32 rows
...
...
glGetPolygonStipple(mask);
```

See Also	glPolygonStipple, glLineStipple, glPixelStore

GLLINESTIPPLE

Purpose	Specifies a line stipple pattern for line-based primitives GL_LINES, GL_LINE_STRIP, and GL_LINE_LOOP.
Include File	<gl.h>
Syntax	void glLineStipple(GLint factor, GLushort pattern);
Description	This function uses the bit pattern to draw stippled (dotted and dashed) lines. The bit pattern begins with bit 0 (the rightmost bit), so the actual drawing pattern is the reverse of what is actually specified. The factor parameter is used to widen the number of pixels drawn or not drawn along the line specified by each bit in pattern. By default, each bit in pattern specifies one pixel. To use line stippling, you must first enable stippling by calling

```
glEnable(GL_LINE_STIPPLE);
```

Line stippling is disabled by default. If you are drawing multiple line segments, the pattern is reset for each new segment. That is, if a line segment is drawn such that it is terminated halfway through pattern, the next line segment specified is unaffected.

Parameters	
factor	GLint: Specifies a multiplier that determines how many pixels will be affected by each bit in the pattern parameter. Thus the pattern width is

	multiplied by this value. The default value is 1 and the maximum value is clamped to 255.
pattern	GLushort: Sets the 16-bit stippling pattern. The least significant bit (bit 0) is used first for the stippling pattern. The default pattern is all 1's.
Returns	None.
Example	The following code from the LSTIPPLE example program show a series of lines drawn using a stipple pattern of 0x5555 (01010101), which draws a dotted line. The repeat factor is increased for each line drawn to demonstrate the widening of the dot pattern.

```
// Called to draw scene
void RenderScene(void)
        {
        GLfloat y;                      // Storage for varying Y coordinate
        GLint factor = 1;               // Stippling factor
        GLushort pattern = 0x5555;      // Stipple pattern

        ...
        ...

        // Enable Stippling
        glEnable(GL_LINE_STIPPLE);

        // Step up Y axis 20 units at a time
        for(y = -90.0f; y < 90.0f; y += 20.0f)
                {
                // Reset the repeat factor and pattern
                glLineStipple(factor,pattern);

                // Draw the line
                glBegin(GL_LINES);
                        glVertex2f(-80.0f, y);
                        glVertex2f(80.0f, y);
                glEnd();

                factor++;
                }
        ...
        ...
        }
```

See Also	glPolygonStipple

GLLINEWIDTH

Purpose	Sets the width of lines drawn with GL_LINES, GL_LINE_STRIP, or GL_LINE_LOOP.
Include File	<gl.h>
Syntax	void glLineWidth(GLfloat width);
Description	This function sets the width in pixels of lines drawn with any of the line-based primitives.

You can get the current line width setting by calling

```
GLfloat fSize;
...
glGetFloatv(GL_LINE_WIDTH, &fSize);
```

The current line-width setting will be returned in fSize. In addition, the minimum and maximum supported line widths can be found by calling

```
GLfloat fSizes[2];
...
glGetFloatv(GL_LINE_WIDTH_RANGE,fSizes);
```

In this instance, the minimum supported line width will be returned in fSizes[0], and the maximum supported width will be stored in fSizes[1]. Finally, the smallest supported increment between line widths can be found by calling

```
GLfloat fStepSize;
...
glGetFloatv(GL_LINE_WIDTH_GRANULARITY,&fStepSize);
```

For any implementation of OpenGL, the only line width guaranteed to be supported is 1.0. For the Microsoft Windows generic implementation, the supported line widths range from 0.5 to 10.0, with a granularity of 0.125.

Parameters

width   GLfloat: Sets the width of lines that are drawn with the line primitives. The default value is 1.0.

Returns   None.

Example   The following code from the LINESW example program demonstrates drawing lines of various widths.

```
void RenderScene(void)
        {
        GLfloat y;                  // Storage for varying Y coordinate
        GLfloat fSizes[2];          // Line width range metrics
        GLfloat fCurrSize;          // Save current size

        ...
        ...
        ...

        // Get line size metrics and save the smallest value
        glGetFloatv(GL_LINE_WIDTH_RANGE,fSizes);
        fCurrSize = fSizes[0];

        // Step up Y axis 20 units at a time
        for(y = -90.0f; y < 90.0f; y += 20.0f)
                {
                // Set the line width
                glLineWidth(fCurrSize);

                // Draw the line
                glBegin(GL_LINES);
```

```
            glVertex2f(-80.0f, y);
            glVertex2f(80.0f, y);
        glEnd();

        // Increase the line width
        fCurrSize += 1.0f;
        }


    ...
    ...
    }
```

See Also   glPointSize

GLPOINTSIZE

Purpose	Sets the point size of points drawn with GL_POINTS.
Include File	<gl.h>
Syntax	void glPointSize(GLfloat size);
Description	This function sets the diameter in pixels of points drawn with the GL_POINTS primitive. You can get the current pixel size setting by calling

```
GLfloat fSize;
...
glGetFloatv(GL_POINT_SIZE, &fSize);
```

The current pixel size setting will be returned in fSize. In addition, the minimum and maximum supported pixel sizes can be found by calling

```
GLfloat fSizes[2];
...
glGetFloatv(GL_POINT_SIZE_RANGE,fSizes);
```

In this instance, the minimum supported point size will be returned in fSizes[0], and the maximum supported size will be stored in fSizes[1]. Finally, the smallest supported increment between pixel sizes can be found by calling

```
GLfloat fStepSize;
...
glGetFloatv(GL_POINT_SIZE_GRANULARITY,&fStepSize);
```

For any implementation of OpenGL, the only point size guaranteed to be supported is 1.0. For the Microsoft Windows generic implementation, the point sizes range from 0.5 to 10.0, with a granularity of 0.125.

Parameters	
size	GLfloat: Sets the diameter of drawn points. The default value is 1.0.
Returns	None.
Example	The following code from the POINTSZ sample program from this chapter gets the point size range and granularity and uses them to gradually increase the size of points used to plot a spiral pattern.

```
GLfloat x,y,z,angle;    // Storage for coordinates and angles
GLfloat sizes[2];       // Store supported point size range
GLfloat step;           // Store supported point size increments
GLfloat curSize;        // Store current size

...
...

// Get supported point size range and step size
glGetFloatv(GL_POINT_SIZE_RANGE,sizes);
glGetFloatv(GL_POINT_SIZE_GRANULARITY,&step);

// Set the initial point size
curSize = sizes[0];

// Set beginning z coordinate
z = -50.0f;

// Loop around in a circle three times
for(angle = 0.0f; angle <= (2.0f*3.1415f)*3.0f; angle += 0.1f)
        {
        // Calculate x and y values on the circle
        x = 50.0f*sin(angle);
        y = 50.0f*cos(angle);

        // Specify the point size before the primitive
        glPointSize(curSize);

        // Draw the point
        glBegin(GL_POINTS);
                glVertex3f(x, y, z);
        glEnd();

        // Bump up the z value and the point size
        z += 0.5f;
        curSize += step;
        }
```

See Also   glLineWidth.

GLPOLYGONMODE

Purpose	Sets the rasterization mode used to draw polygons.
Include File	<gl.h>
Syntax	void glPolygonMode(GLenum face, GLenum mode);
Description	This function allows you to change how polygons are rendered. By default, polygons are filled or shaded with the current color or material properties. However, you may also specify that only the outlines or only the vertices are drawn. Furthermore, you may apply this specification to the front, back, or both sides of polygons.
Parameters	
face	GLenum: Specifies which face of polygons is affected by the mode change: GL_FRONT, GL_BACK, or GL_FRONT_AND_BACK.

mode	GLenum: Specifies the new drawing mode. GL_FILL is the default, producing filled polygons. GL_LINE produces polygon outlines, and GL_POINT only plots the points of the vertices. The lines and points drawn by GL_LINE and GL_POINT are affected by the edge flag set by glEdgeFlag.
Returns	None.
Example	The following code from the TRIANGLE example of this chapter sets the back side of polygons to be drawn as outlines or filled regions, depending on the value of the Boolean variable bOutline.

```
// Draw back side as a polygon only, if flag is set
if(bOutline)
        glPolygonMode(GL_BACK,GL_LINE);
else
        glPolygonMode(GL_BACK,GL_FILL);
```

See Also	glEdgeFlag, glLineStipple, glLineWidth, glPointSize, glPolygonStipple

GLPOLYGONSTIPPLE

Purpose	Sets the pattern used for polygon stippling.
Include File	<gl.h>
Syntax	void glPolygonStipple(const GLubyte *mask);
Description	A 32 x 32-bit stipple pattern may be used for filled polygons by using this function and enabling polygon stippling by calling glEnable(GL_POLYGON_STIPPLE). The 1's in the stipple pattern are filled with the current color, and 0's are not drawn.
Parameters	
*mask	const GLubyte: Points to a 32 x 32-bit storage area that contains the stipple pattern. The packing of bits within this storage area is affected by glPixelStore. By default, the MSB (Most Significant Bit) is read first when determining the pattern.
Returns	None.
Example	The following code from the PSTIPPLE program on the CD in this chapter's subdirectory enables polygon stippling, establishes a stipple pattern, and then draws a polygon in the shape of a hexagon (a stop sign).
See Also	glLineStipple, glGetPolygonStipple, glPixelStore

GLVERTEX

Purpose	Specifies the 3D coordinates of a vertex.
Include File	<gl.h>
Variations	void **glVertex2d**(GLdouble x, GLdouble y);
	void **glVertex2f**(GLfloat x, GLfloat y);

void **glVertex2i**(GLint x, GLint y);
void **glVertex2s**(GLshort x, GLshort y);
void **glVertex3d**(GLdouble x, GLdouble y, GLdouble z);
void **glVertex3f**(GLfloat x, GLfloat y, GLfloat z);
void **glVertex3i**(GLint x, GLint y, GLint z);
void **glVertex3s**(GLshort x, GLshort y, GLshort z);
void **glVertex4d**(GLdouble x, GLdouble y, GLdouble z, GLdouble w);
void **glVertex4f**(GLfloat x, GLfloat y, GLfloat z, GLfloat w);
void **glVertex4i**(GLint x, GLint y, GLint z, GLint w);
void **glVertex4s**(GLshort x, GLshort y, GLshort z, GLshort w);
void **glVertex2dv**(const GLdouble *v);
void **glVertex2fv**(const GLfloat *v);
void **glVertex2iv**(const GLint *v);
void **glVertex2sv**(const GLshort *v);
void **glVertex3dv**(const GLdouble *v);
void **glVertex3fv**(const GLfloat *v);
void **glVertex3iv**(const GLint *v);
void **glVertex3sv**(const GLshort *v);
void **glVertex4dv**(const GLdouble *v);
void **glVertex4fv**(const GLfloat *v);
void **glVertex4iv**(const GLint *v);
void **glVertex4sv**(const GLshort *v);

Description

This function is used to specify the vertex coordinates of the points, lines, and polygons specified by a previous call to glBegin. This function may not be called outside the scope of a glBegin/glEnd pair.

Parameters

x, y, z

The x, y, and z coordinates of the vertex. When z is not specified, the default value is 0.0.

w

The w coordinate of the vertex. This coordinate is used for scaling purposes and by default is set to 1.0. Scaling occurs by dividing the other three coordinates by this value.

*v

An array of values that contain the 2, 3, or 4 values needed to specify the vertex.

Returns

None.

Example

You can find this ubiquitous function in literally every example and supplementary sample in this chapter. The following code shows a single point being drawn at the origin of the x,y,z coordinate system.

```
glBegin(GL_POINTS)
        glVertex3f(0.0f, 0.0f, 0.0f);
glEnd();
```

See Also

glBegin, glEnd

7

MANIPULATING 3D SPACE: COORDINATE TRANSFORMATIONS

MANIPULATING 3D SPACE: COORDINATE TRANSFORMATIONS

What you'll learn in this chapter:

How to...	Functions You'll Use
Establish your position in the scene	gluLookAt/glTranslate/glRotate
Position objects within the scene	glTranslate/glRotate
Scale objects	glScale
Establish a perspective transformation	gluPerspective
Perform your own matrix transformations	glLoadMatrix/glMultMatrix

In Chapter 6, you learned how to draw points, lines, and various primitives in 3D. To turn a collection of shapes into a coherent scene, you must arrange them in relation to one another and to the viewer. In this chapter, you'll start moving shapes and objects around in your coordinate system. (Actually, you don't *move* the objects, but rather *shift the coordinate system* to create the view you want.) The ability to place and orient your objects in a scene is a crucial tool for any 3D graphics programmer. As you will see, it is actually very convenient to describe your objects' dimensions around the origin, and then translate and rotate the objects into the desired position.

Is This the Dreaded Math Chapter?

Yes, this is the dreaded math chapter. However, you can relax—we are going to take a more moderate approach to these principles than some texts.

The keys to object and coordinate transformations are two modeling matrices maintained by OpenGL. To familiarize you with these matrices, this chapter strikes a compromise between two extremes in computer graphics philosophy. On the one hand, we could warn you, "Please review a textbook on linear algebra before reading this chapter." On the other hand, we could perpetuate the deceptive reassurance that you can "learn to do 3D graphics without all those complex mathematical formulas." But we don't agree with either camp.

In reality, yes, you can get along just fine without understanding the finer mathematics of 3D graphics, just as you can drive your car every day without having to know anything at all about automotive mechanics and the internal combustion engine. But you'd better know enough about your car to realize that you need an oil change every so often, that you have to fill the tank with gas regularly and change the tires when they get bald. This makes you a responsible (and safe!) automobile owner. If you want to be a responsible and capable OpenGL programmer, the same standards apply. You want to understand at least the basics, so you know what can be done and what tools will best suit the job.

So, even if you don't have the ability to multiply two matrices in your head, you need to know what matrices are and that they are the means to OpenGL's 3D magic. But before you go dusting off that old linear algebra textbook (doesn't *everyone* have one?), have no fear—OpenGL will do all the math for you. Think of it as using a calculator to do long division when you don't know how to do it on paper. Though you don't have to do it yourself, you still know what it is and how to apply it. See—you *can* have your cake and eat it too!

Understanding Transformations

Transformations make possible the projection of 3D coordinates onto a 2D screen. Transformations also allow you to rotate objects around, move them about, and even stretch, shrink, and wrap them. Rather than modifying your object directly, a transformation modifies the coordinate system. Once a transformation rotates the coordinate system, then the object will appear rotated when it is drawn. There are three types of transformations that occur between the time you specify your vertices and the time they appear on the screen: viewing, modeling, and projection. In this section we will examine the principles of each type of transformation, which you will find summarized in Table 7-1.

Table 7-1 Summary of the OpenGL Transformations

Transformation	Use
Viewing	Specifies the location of the viewer or camera
Modeling	Moves objects around scene

Transformation	Use
Modelview	Describes the duality of viewing and modeling transformations
Projection	Clips and sizes the viewing volume
Viewport	Scales final output to the window

Eye Coordinates

An important concept throughout this chapter is that of *eye coordinates*. Eye coordinates are from the viewpoint of the observer, regardless of any transformations that may occur—think of them as "absolute" screen coordinates. Thus, eye coordinates are not real coordinates, but rather represent a virtual fixed coordinate system that is used as a common frame of reference. All of the transformations discussed in this chapter are described in terms of their effects relative to the eye coordinate system.

Figure 7-1 shows the eye coordinate system from two viewpoints. On the left (a), the eye coordinates are represented as seen by the observer of the scene (that is, perpendicular to the monitor). On the right (b), the eye coordinate system is rotated slightly so you can better see the relation of the z-axis. Positive x and y are pointed right and up, respectively, from the viewer's perspective. Positive z travels away from the origin toward the user, and negative z values travel farther away from the viewpoint into the screen.

When you draw in 3D with OpenGL, you use the Cartesian coordinate system. In the absence of any transformations, the system in use would be identical to the eye coordinate system. All of the various transformations change the current coordinate

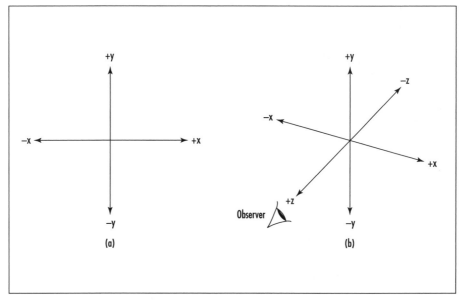

Figure 7-1 Two perspectives of eye coordinates

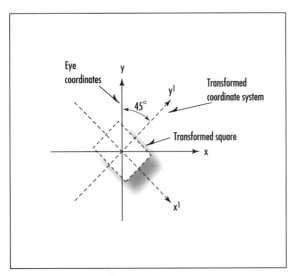

Figure 7-2 A coordinate system rotated with respect to eye coordinates

system with respect to the eye coordinates. This, in essence, is how you move and rotate objects in your scene—by moving and rotating the coordinate system with respect to eye coordinates. Figure 7-2 gives a two-dimensional example of the coordinate system rotated 45° clockwise by eye coordinates. A square plotted on this rotated coordinate system would also appear rotated.

In this chapter you'll study the methods by which you modify the current coordinate system before drawing your objects. You can even save the state of the current system, do some transformations and drawing, and then restore the state and start over again. By chaining these events, you will be able to place objects all about the scene and in various orientations.

Viewing Transformations

The *viewing transformation* is the first to be applied to your scene. It is used to determine the vantage point of the scene. By default, the point of observation is at the origin (0,0,0) looking down the negative z-axis ("into" the monitor screen). This point of observation is moved relative to the eye coordinate system to provide a specific vantage point. When the point of observation is located at the origin, then objects drawn with positive z values would be behind the observer.

The viewing transformation allows you to place the point of observation anywhere you want, and looking in any direction. Determining the viewing transformation is like placing and pointing a camera at the scene.

In the scheme of things, the viewing transformation must be specified before any other transformations. This is because it moves the currently working coordinate system in respect to the eye coordinate system. All subsequent transformations then occur based on the newly modified coordinate system. Later you'll see more easily how this works, when we actually start looking at how to make these transformations.

Modeling Transformations

Modeling transformations are used to manipulate your model and the particular objects within it. This transformation moves objects into place, rotates them, and scales them. Figure 7-3 illustrates three modeling transformations that you will apply to your objects. Figure 7-3a shows *translation,* where an object is moved along a given axis. Figure 7-3b shows a *rotation,* where an object is rotated about one of the axes. Finally, Figure 7-3c shows the effects of *scaling,* where the dimensions of the object are increased or decreased by a specified amount. Scaling can occur nonuniformly (the

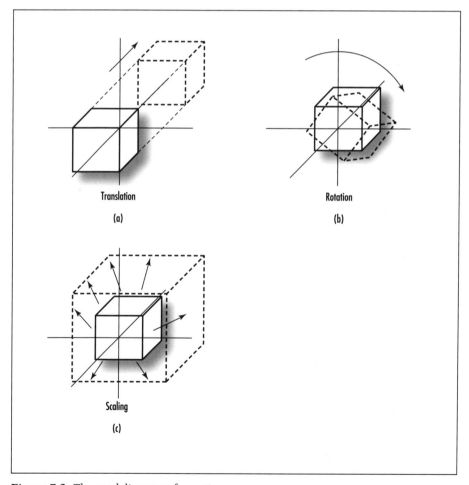

Translation

(a)

Rotation

(b)

Scaling

(c)

Figure 7-3 The modeling transformation

various dimensions can be scaled by different amounts), and this can be used to stretch and shrink objects.

The final appearance of your scene or object can depend greatly on the order in which the modeling transformations are applied. This is particularly true of translation and rotation. Figure 7-4a shows the progression of a square rotated first about the z-axis and then translated down the newly transformed x-axis. In Figure 7-4b, the same square is first translated down the x-axis and then rotated around the z-axis. The difference in the final dispositions of the square occurs because each transformation is performed with respect to the last transformation performed. In Figure 7-4a, the square is rotated with respect to the origin first. In 7-4b, after the square is translated, the rotation is then performed around the newly translated origin.

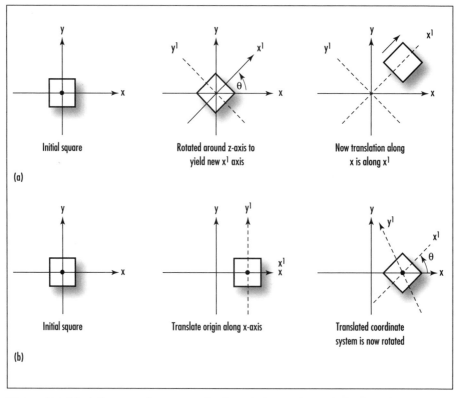

Figure 7-4 Modeling transforms: rotation/translation and translation/rotation

The Modelview Duality

The viewing and the modeling transformations are, in fact, the same in terms of their internal effects as well as the final appearance of the scene. The distinction between the two is made purely as a convenience for the programmer. There is no real difference between moving an object backward, and moving the reference system forward—as shown in Figure 7-5, the net effect is the same. (You experience this first-hand when you're sitting in your car at an intersection and you see the car next to you roll forward; it may seem to you that your own car is rolling backwards.). The term "modelview" is used here to indicate that you can think of this transformation either as the modeling transformation, or the viewing transformation, but in fact there is no distinction—thus, it is the modelview transformation.

The viewing transformation, therefore, is essentially nothing but a modeling transformation that you apply to a virtual object (the viewer) before drawing objects. As you will soon see, new transformations are repeatedly specified as you place more and more objects in the scene. The initial transformation provides a reference from which all other transformations are based.

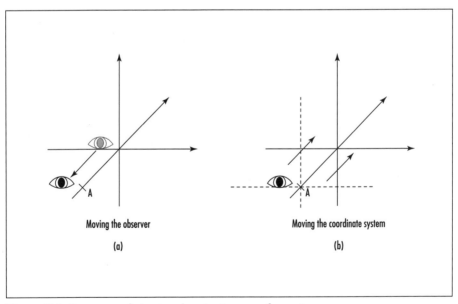

Figure 7-5 Two ways of viewing the viewing transformation

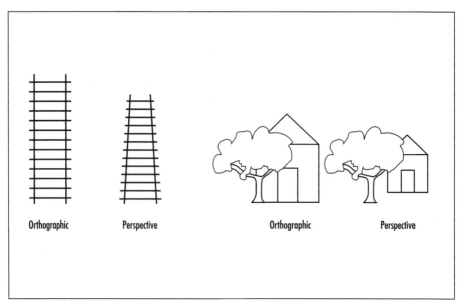

Orthographic Perspective Orthographic Perspective

Figure 7-6 Two examples of orthographic vs. perspective projections

Projection Transformations

The *projection transformation* is applied to your final Modelview orientation. This projection actually defines the viewing volume and establishes clipping planes. More specifically, the projection transformation specifies how a finished scene (after all the modeling is done) is translated to the final image on the screen. You will learn about two types of projections in this chapter: *orthographic* and *perspective*.

In an orthographic projection, all the polygons are drawn on screen with exactly the relative dimensions specified. This is typically used for CAD, or blueprint images where the precise dimensions are being rendered realistically.

A perspective projection shows objects and scenes more as they would appear in real life than in a blueprint. The trademark of perspective projections is *foreshortening,* which makes distant objects appear smaller than nearby objects of the same size. And parallel lines will not always be drawn parallel. In a railroad track, for instance, the rails are parallel, but with perspective projection they appear to converge at some distant point. We call this point the *vanishing point.*

The benefit of perspective projection is that you don't have to figure out where lines converge, or how much smaller distant objects are. All you need to do is specify the scene using the Modelview transformations, and then apply the perspective projection. It will work all the magic for you.

Figure 7-6 compares orthographic and perspective projections on two different scenes.

In general, you should use orthographic projections when you are modeling simple objects that are unaffected by the position and distance of the viewer. Orthographic views usually occur naturally when the ratio of the object's size to its distance from the viewer is quite small (say, a large object that's far away). Thus, an automobile viewed on a showroom floor can be modeled orthographically, but if you are standing directly in front of the car and looking down the length of it, perspective would come into play. Perspective projections are used for rendering scenes that contain many objects spaced apart, for walk-through or flying scenes, or for modeling any large objects that may appear distorted depending on the viewer's location. For the most part, perspective projections will be the most typical.

Viewport Transformations

When all is said and done, you end up with a two-dimensional projection of your scene that will be mapped to a window somewhere on your screen. This mapping to physical window coordinates is the last transformation that is done, and it is called the *viewport transformation*. The viewport was discussed briefly in Chapter 3, where you used it to stretch an image or keep a scene squarely placed in a rectangular window.

Matrix Munching

Now that you're armed with some basic vocabulary and definitions of transformations, you're ready for some simple matrix mathematics. Let's examine how OpenGL performs these transformations and get to know the functions you will call to achieve your desired effects.

The mathematics behind these transformations are greatly simplified by the mathematical notation of the matrix. Each of the transformations we have discussed can be achieved by multiplying a matrix that contains the vertices, by a matrix that describes the transformation. Thus all the transformations achievable with OpenGL can be described as a multiplication of two or more matrices.

What Is a Matrix?

A matrix is nothing more than a set of numbers arranged in uniform rows and columns—in programming terms, a two-dimensional array. A matrix doesn't have to be square, but each row or column must have the same number of elements as every other row or column in the matrix. Figure 7-7 presents some examples of matrices. (These don't represent anything in particular but only serve to demonstrate matrix structure.) Note that a matrix can have but a single column.

Our purpose here is not to go into the details of matrix mathematics and manipulation. If you want to know more about manipulating matrices and hand-coding some special transformations, see Appendix B for some good references.

The Transformation Pipeline

To effect the types of transformations described in this chapter, you will modify two matrices in particular: the Modelview matrix, and the Projection matrix. Don't worry, OpenGL gives you some high-level functions that you can call for these transformations. Only if you want to do something unusual do you need to call the lower-level functions that actually set the values contained in the matrices.

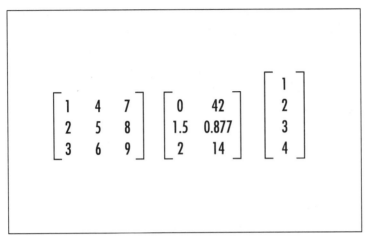

Figure 7-7 Examples of matrices

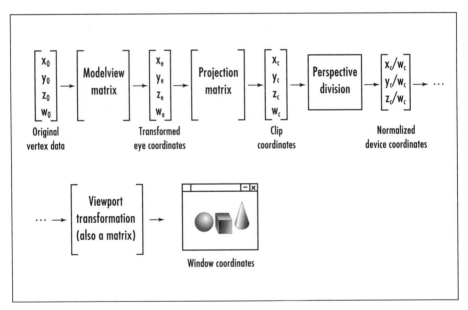

Figure 7-8 The vertex transformation pipeline

The road from raw vertex data to screen coordinates is a long one. Figure 7-8 is a flowchart of this process. First, your vertex is converted to a 1 x 4 matrix in which the first three values are the x, y, and z coordinates. The fourth number is a scaling factor that you can apply manually by using the vertex functions that take four values. This is the w coordinate, usually 1.0 by default. You will seldom modify this value directly but will apply one of the scaling functions to the Modelview matrix instead.

The vertex is then multiplied by the Modelview matrix, which yields the transformed eye coordinates. The eye coordinates are then multiplied by the Projection matrix to yield clip coordinates. This effectively eliminates all data outside the viewing volume. The clip coordinates are then divided by the w coordinate to yield normalized device coordinates. The w value may have been modified by the Projection matrix or the Modelview matrix, depending on the transformations that may have occurred. Again, OpenGL and the high-level matrix functions will hide all this from you.

Finally, your coordinate triplet is mapped to a 2D plane by the viewport transformation. This is also represented by a matrix, but not one that you will specify or modify directly. OpenGL will set it up internally depending on the values you specified to glViewport.

The Modelview Matrix

The Modelview matrix is a 4 x 4 matrix that represents the transformed coordinate system you are using to place and orient your objects. The vertices you provide for your primitives are used as a single-column matrix and multiplied by the Modelview matrix to yield new transformed coordinates in relation to the eye coordinate system.

In Figure 7-9, a matrix containing data for a single vertex is multiplied by the Modelview matrix to yield new eye coordinates. The vertex data is actually four elements, with an extra value w, that represents a scaling factor. This value is set by default to 1.0, and rarely will you change this yourself.

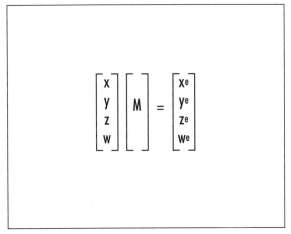

Figure 7-9 Matrix equation that applies the Modelview transformation to a single vertex

Translation

Let's take an example that modifies the Modelview matrix. Say you wanted to draw a cube using the AUX library's auxWireCube() function. You would simply call

```
auxWireCube(10.0f);
```

and you would have a cube centered at the origin that measures 10 units on a side. To move the cube up the y-axis by 10 units before drawing it, you would multiply the Modelview matrix by a matrix that describes a translation of 10 units up the y-axis, and then do your drawing. In skeleton form, the code looks like this:

```
// Construct a translation matrix for positive 10 Y
...

// Multiply it by the Modelview matrix
...

// Draw the cube
auxWireCube(10.0f);
```

Actually, such a matrix is fairly easy to construct, but it would require quite a few lines of code. Fortunately, a high-level function is provided that does this for you:

```
void glTranslatef(GLfloat x, GLfloat y, GLfloat z);
```

This function takes as parameters the amount to translate along the x, y, and z directions. It then constructs an appropriate matrix and does the multiplication. Now the pseudocode from above looks like the following, and the effect is illustrated in Figure 7-10.

```
// Translate up the y-axis 10 units
glTranslatef(0.0f, 10.0f, 0.0f);

// Draw the cube
auxWireCube(10.0f);
```

Rotation

To rotate an object about one of the three axes, you would have to devise a Rotation matrix to be multiplied by the Modelview matrix. Again, a high-level function comes to the rescue:

```
glRotatef((GLfloat angle, GLfloat x, GLfloat y, GLfloat z);
```

Here we are performing a rotation around the vector specified by the x, y, and z arguments. The angle of rotation is in the counterclockwise direction measured in degrees and specified by the argument angle. In the simplest of cases, the rotation is around one of the axes, so only that value needs to be specified.

You can also perform a rotation around an arbitrary axis by specifying x, y, and z values for that vector. To see the axis of rotation, you can just draw a line from the origin to the point represented by (x,y,z). The following code rotates the cube by 45° around an arbitrary axis specified by (1,1,1), as illustrated in Figure 7-11.

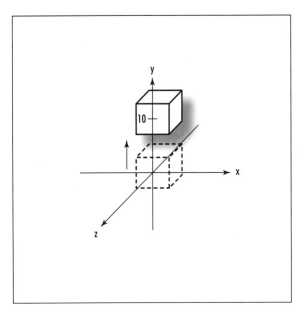

Figure 7-10 A cube translated 10 units in the positive y direction

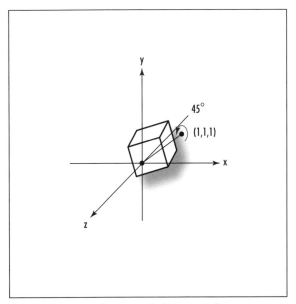

Figure 7-11 A cube rotated about an arbitrary axis

```
// Perform the transformation
glRotatef(90.0f, 1.0f, 1.0f, 1.0f);

// Draw the cube
auxWireCube(10.0f);
```

Scaling

A scaling transformation increases the size of your object by expanding all the vertices along the three axes by the factors specified. The function

```
glScalef(GLfloat x, GLfloat y, GLfloat z);
```

multiplies the x, y, and z values by the scaling factors specified.

Scaling does not have to be uniform. You can use it to stretch or squeeze objects, as well. For example, the following code will produce a cube that is twice as large along the x- and z-axis as the cubes discussed in the previous examples, but still the same along the y-axis. The result is shown in Figure 7-12.

```
// Perform the scaling transformation
glScalef(2.0f, 1.0f, 2.0f);

// Draw the cube
auxWireCube(10.0f);
```

The Identity Matrix

You may be wondering about now why we had to bother with all this matrix stuff in the first place. Can't we just call these transformation functions to move our objects

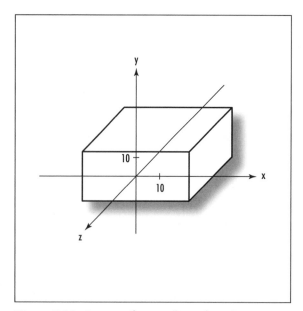

Figure 7-12 A nonuniform scaling of a cube

around and be done with it? Do we really need to know that it is the Modelview matrix that is being modified?

The answer is yes and no, but only if you are drawing a single object in your scene. This is because the effects of these functions are cumulative. Each time you call one, the appropriate matrix is constructed and multiplied by the current Modelview matrix. The new matrix then becomes the current Modelview matrix, which is then multiplied by the next transformation, and so on.

Suppose you want to draw two spheres—one 10 units up the positive y-axis, and one 10 units out the positive x-axis, as shown in Figure 7-13. You might be tempted to write code that looks something like this:

```
// Go 10 units up the y-axis
glTranslatef(0.0f, 10.0f, 0.0f);

// Draw the first sphere
auxSolidSphere(1.0f);

// Go 10 units out the x-axis
glTranslatef(10.0f, 0.0f, 0.0f);

// Draw the second sphere
auxSolidSphere(1.0f);
```

Consider, however, that each call to glTranslate is cumulative on the Modelview matrix, so the second call would translate 10 units in the positive x direction from the previous translation in the y direction. This would yield the results shown in Figure 7-14.

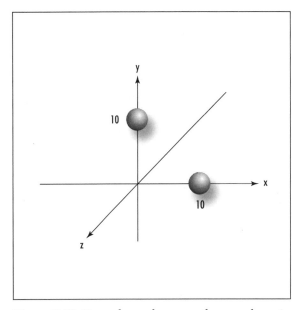

Figure 7-13 Two spheres drawn on the y- and x-axis

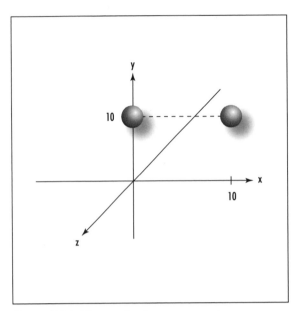

Figure 7-14 The result of two consecutive translations

You could make an extra call to glTranslate to back down the y-axis 10 units in the negative direction, but this would make some complex scenes very difficult to code and debug. A simpler method would be to reset the Modelview matrix to a known state—in this case, centered at the origin of our eye coordinate system.

This is done by loading the Modelview matrix with the Identity matrix. The Identity matrix specifies that no transformation is to occur, in effect saying that all the coordinates you specify when drawing are in eye coordinates. An Identity matrix contains all 0's with the exception of a diagonal row of ones. When this matrix is multiplied by any vertex matrix, the result is that the vertex matrix is unchanged. Figure 7-15 shows this equation.

As we've already stated, the details of performing matrix multiplication are outside the scope of this book. For now, just remember this: *Loading the Identity matrix means that no transformations are performed on the vertices.* In essence, you are resetting the Modelview matrix back to the origin.

The following two lines load the identity matrix into the Modelview matrix:

```
glMatrixMode(GL_MODELVIEW);
glLoadIdentity();
```

The first line specifies that the current operating matrix is the Modelview matrix. Once you set the current operating matrix (the matrix that your matrix functions are affecting), it remains the active matrix until you change it. The second line loads the current matrix (in this case, the Modelview matrix) with the identity matrix.

Now the following code will produce results as shown in Figure 7-13:

$$\begin{bmatrix} 8.0 \\ 4.5 \\ -2.0 \\ 1.0 \end{bmatrix} \begin{bmatrix} 1.0 & 0 & 0 & 0 \\ 0 & 1.0 & 0 & 0 \\ 0 & 0 & 1.0 & 0 \\ 0 & 0 & 0 & 1.0 \end{bmatrix} = \begin{bmatrix} 8.0 \\ 4.5 \\ -2.0 \\ 1.0 \end{bmatrix}$$

Figure 7-15 Multiplying a vertex matrix by the identity matrix yields the same vertex matrix

```
// Set current matrix to Modelview and reset
glMatrixMode(GL_MODELVIEW);
glLoadIdentity();

// Go 10 units up the y-axis
glTranslatef(0.0f, 10.0f, 0.0f);

// Draw the first sphere
auxSolidSphere(1.0f);

// Reset Modelview matrix again
glLoadIdentity();

// Go 10 units out the x-axis
glTranslatef(10.0f, 0.0f, 0.0f);

// Draw the second sphere
auxSolidSphere(1.0f);
```

The Matrix Stacks

It is not always desirable to reset the Modelview matrix to Identity before placing every object. Often you will want to save the current transformation state and then restore it after some objects have been placed. This is most convenient when you have initially transformed the Modelview matrix as your viewing transformation (and thus are no longer located at the origin).

To facilitate this, OpenGL maintains a matrix stack for both the Modelview and Projection matrices. A matrix stack works just like an ordinary program stack. You can push the current matrix onto the stack to save it, then make your changes to the current matrix. Popping the matrix off the stack then restores it. Figure 7-16 shows the stack principle in action.

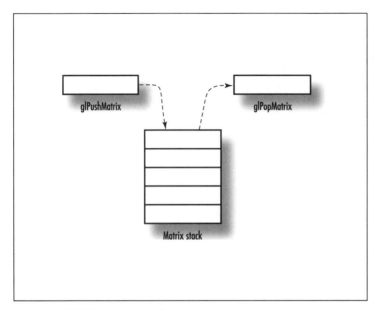

Figure 7-16 The matrix stack in action

Texture Matrix Stack

The texture stack is another matrix stack available to the programmer. This is used for the transformation of texture coordinates. Chapter 12 examines texture mapping and texture coordinates and contains a discussion of the texture matrix stack.

The stack depth can reach a maximum value that can be retrieved with a call to either

```
glGet(GL_MAX_MODELVIEW_STACK_DEPTH);
```

or

```
glGet(GL_MAX_PROJECTION_STACK_DEPTH);
```

If you exceed the stack depth, you'll get a GL_STACK_OVERFLOW; if you try to pop a matrix value off the stack when there is none, you will generate a GL_STACK_UNDERFLOW. The stack depth is implementation dependent. For the Microsoft software implementation these values are 32 for the Modelview and 2 for the Projection stack.

A Nuclear Example

Let's put to use what we have learned. In the next example, we will build a crude, animated model of an atom. This atom will have a single sphere at the center to represent

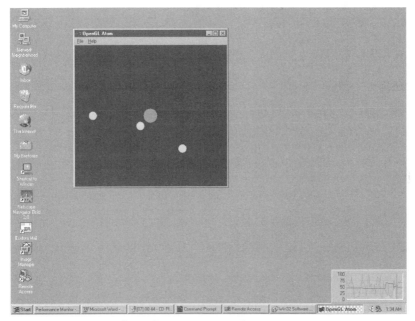

Figure 7-17 Output from the ATOM example program

the nucleus, and three electrons in orbit about the atom. Here we'll use an orthographic projection, as we have previously in this book. (Some other interesting projections are covered in the upcoming section, "Using Projections.")

Our ATOM program uses a timer to move the electrons four times a second (undoubtedly much slower than any real electrons!). Each time the Render function is called, the angle of revolution about the nucleus is incremented. Also, each electron lies in a different plane. Listing 7-1 shows the Render function for this example, and the output from the ATOM program is shown in Figure 7-17.

Listing 7-1 Render function from ATOM example program

```
// Called to draw scene
void RenderScene(void)
        {
        // Angle of revolution around the nucleus
        static float fElect1 = 0.0f;

        // Clear the window with current clearing color
        glClear(GL_COLOR_BUFFER_BIT | GL_DEPTH_BUFFER_BIT);

        // Reset the modelview matrix
        glMatrixMode(GL_MODELVIEW);
        glLoadIdentity();


        // Translate the whole scene out and into view
```

continued on next page

continued from previous page

```
// This is the initial viewing transformation
glTranslatef(0.0f, 0.0f, -100.0f);

// Red Nucleus
glRGB(255, 0, 0);
auxSolidSphere(10.0f);

// Yellow Electrons
glRGB(255,255,0);

// First Electron Orbit
// Save viewing transformation
glPushMatrix();

// Rotate by angle of revolution
glRotatef(fElect1, 0.0f, 1.0f, 0.0f);

// Translate out from origin to orbit distance
glTranslatef(90.0f, 0.0f, 0.0f);

// Draw the electron
auxSolidSphere(6.0f);

// Restore the viewing transformation
glPopMatrix();

// Second Electron Orbit
glPushMatrix();
glRotatef(45.0f, 0.0f, 0.0f, 1.0f);
glRotatef(fElect1, 0.0f, 1.0f, 0.0f);
glTranslatef(-70.0f, 0.0f, 0.0f);
auxSolidSphere(6.0f);
glPopMatrix();


// Third Electron Orbit
glPushMatrix();
glRotatef(360.0f, -45.0f, 0.0f, 0.0f, 1.0f);
glRotatef(fElect1, 0.0f, 1.0f, 0.0f);
glTranslatef(0.0f, 0.0f, 60.0f);
auxSolidSphere(6.0f);
glPopMatrix();


// Increment the angle of revolution
fElect1 += 10.0f;
if(fElect1 > 360.0f)
        fElect1 = 0.0f;

// Flush drawing commands
glFlush();
}
```

Let's examine the code for placing one of the electrons, a couple of lines at a time. The first line saves the current Modelview matrix by pushing the current transformation on the stack:

```
// First Electron Orbit
// Save viewing transformation
glPushMatrix();
```

Now the coordinate system is rotated around the y axis by an angle fElect1:

```
// Rotate by angle of revolution
glRotatef(fElect1, 0.0f, 1.0f, 0.0f);
```

Now the electron is drawn by translating down the newly rotated coordinate system:

```
// Translate out from origin to orbit distance
glTranslatef(90.0f, 0.0f, 0.0f);
```

Then the electron is drawn (as a solid sphere), and we restore the Modelview matrix by popping it off the matrix stack:

```
// Draw the electron
auxSolidSphere(6.0f);
```

```
// Restore the viewing transformation
glPopMatrix();
```

The other electrons are placed similarly.

Using Projections

In our examples so far we have used the Modelview matrix to position our vantage point of the viewing volume and to place our objects therein. The Projection matrix actually specifies the *size and shape* of our viewing volume.

Thus far in this book, we have created a simple parallel viewing volume using the function glOrtho, setting the near and far, left and right, and top and bottom clipping coordinates. When the Projection matrix is loaded with the Identity matrix, the diagonal line of 1's specifies that the clipping planes extend from the origin to positive 1 in all directions. The projection matrix does no scaling or perspective adjustments. As you will soon see, there are some alternatives to this approach.

Orthographic Projections

An orthographic projection, used for most of this book thus far, is square on all sides. The logical width is equal at the front, back, top, bottom, left, and right sides. This produces a parallel projection, which is useful for drawings of specific objects that do not have any foreshortening when viewed from a distance. This is good for CAD or architectural drawings, for which you want to represent the exact dimensions and measurements on screen.

Figure 7-18 shows the output from the example program ORTHO on the CD in this chapter's subdirectory. To produce this hollow, tube-like box, we used an orthographic projection just as we did for all our previous examples. Figure 7-19 shows the same box rotated more to the side so you can see how long it actually is.

In Figure 7-20, you're looking directly down the barrel of the tube. Because the tube does not converge in the distance, this is not an entirely accurate view of how such a tube would appear in real life. To add some perspective, we use a *perspective projection*.

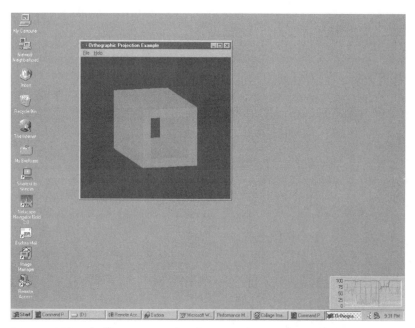

Figure 7-18 A hollow square tube shown with an orthographic projection

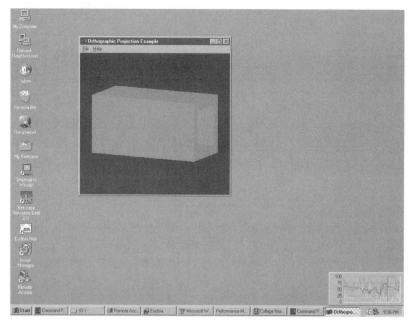

Figure 7-19 A side view showing the length of the square tube

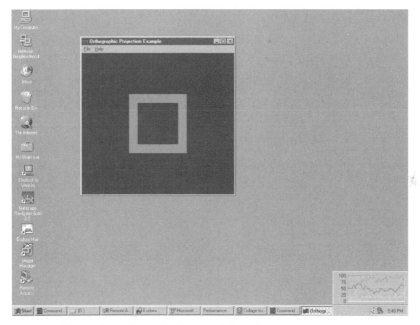

Figure 7-20 Looking down the barrel of the tube

Perspective Projections

A perspective projection performs perspective division to shorten and shrink objects that are farther away from the viewer. The width of the back of the viewing volume does not have the same measurements as the front of the viewing volume. Thus an object of the same logical dimensions will appear larger at the front of the viewing volume than if it were drawn at the back of the viewing volume.

The picture in our next example is of a geometric shape called a *frustum*. A frustum is a section of a pyramid viewed from the narrow end to the broad end. Figure 7-21 shows the frustum, with the observer in place.

You can define a frustum with the function glFrustum. Its parameters are the coordinates and distances between the front and back clipping planes. However, glFrustum is not very intuitive about setting up your projection to get the desired effects. The utility function gluPerspective is easier to use and somewhat more intuitive:

```
void gluPerspective(GLdouble fovy, GLdouble aspect, GLdouble zNear, GLdouble zFar);
```

Parameters for the gluPerspective function are a field-of-view angle in the vertical direction; the aspect ratio of the height to width; and the distances to the near and far clipping planes. See Figure 7-22. The aspect ratio is then found by dividing the width (w) by the height (h) of the front clipping plane.

Listing 7-2 shows how we change our orthographic projection from the previous examples to use a perspective projection. Foreshortening adds realism to our earlier

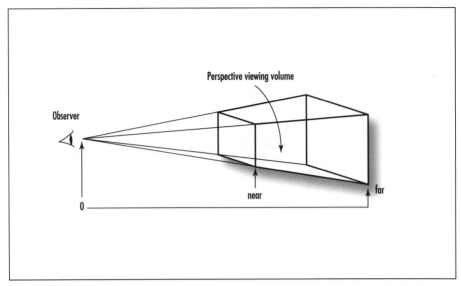

Figure 7-21 A perspective projection defined by a frustum

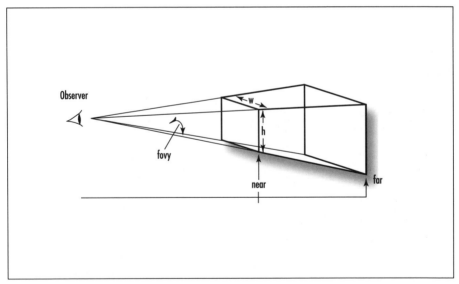

Figure 7-22 The frustum as defined by gluPerspective

orthographic projections of the square tube, as shown in Figures 7-23, 7-24, and 7-25. The only substantial change we made for our typical projection code in Listing 7-2 is the added call to gluPerspective.

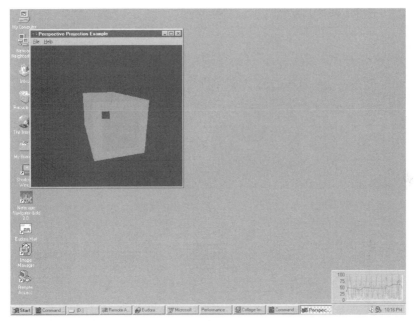

Figure 7-23 The square tube with a perspective projection

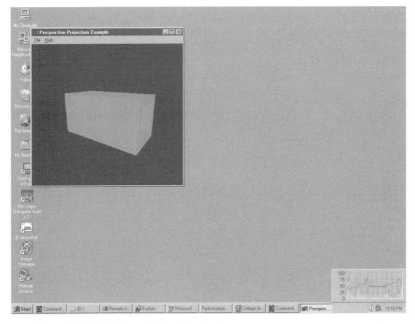

Figure 7-24 Side view with foreshortening

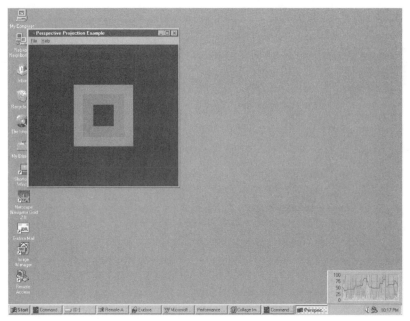

Figure 7-25 Looking down the barrel of the tube with perspective added

Listing 7-2 Setting up the perspective projection for the PERSPECT example program

```
// Change viewing volume and viewport.  Called when window is resized
void ChangeSize(GLsizei w, GLsizei h)
        {
        GLfloat fAspect;

        // Prevent a divide by zero
        if(h == 0)
                h = 1;

        // Set Viewport to window dimensions
        glViewport(0, 0, w, h);

        fAspect = (GLfloat)w/(GLfloat)h;

        // Reset coordinate system
        glMatrixMode(GL_PROJECTION);
        glLoadIdentity();

        // Produce the perspective projection
        gluPerspective(60.0f, fAspect, 1.0, 400.0);

        glMatrixMode(GL_MODELVIEW);
        glLoadIdentity();
        }
```

A Far-Out Example

For a complete example showing Modelview manipulation and perspective projections, we have modeled the Sun and the Earth/Moon system in revolution. We have enabled some lighting and shading for drama, so you can more easily see the effects of our operations. You'll be learning about shading and lighting in the next two chapters.

In our model, we have the Earth moving around the Sun, and the Moon revolving around the Earth. A light source is placed behind the observer to illuminate the Sun sphere. The light is then moved to the center of the Sun in order to light the Earth and Moon from the direction of the Sun, thus producing phases. This is a dramatic example of how easy it is to produce realistic effects with OpenGL.

Listing 7-3 shows the code that sets up our projection, and the rendering code that keeps the system in motion. A timer elsewhere in the program invalidates the window four times a second to keep the Render function in action. Notice in Figures 7-26 and 7-27 that when the Earth appears larger, it's on the near side of the Sun; on the far side, it appears smaller.

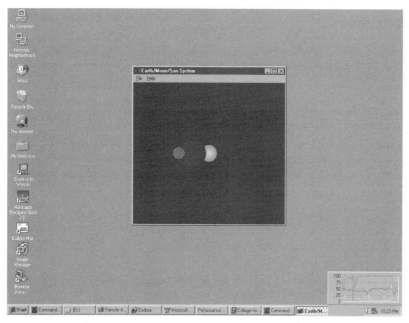

Figure 7-26 The Sun/Earth/Moon system with the Earth on the near side

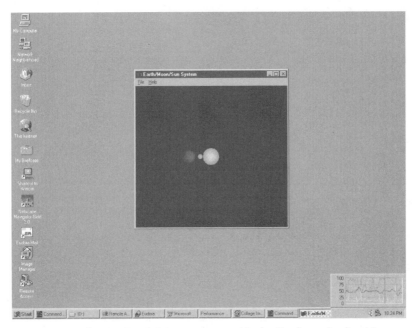

Figure 7-27 The Sun/Earth/Moon system with the Earth on the far side

Listing 7-3 Code that produces the Sun/Earth/Moon System

```
// Change viewing volume and viewport.  Called when window is resized
void ChangeSize(GLsizei w, GLsizei h)
        {
        GLfloat fAspect;

        // Prevent a divide by zero
        if(h == 0)
                h = 1;

        // Set Viewport to window dimensions
        glViewport(0, 0, w, h);

        // Calculate aspect ratio of the window
        fAspect = (GLfloat)w/(GLfloat)h;

        // Set the perspective coordinate system
        glMatrixMode(GL_PROJECTION);
        glLoadIdentity();

        // Field of view of 45 degrees, near and far planes 1.0 and 425
        gluPerspective(45.0f, fAspect, 1.0, 425.0);

        // Modelview matrix reset
        glMatrixMode(GL_MODELVIEW);
        glLoadIdentity();
        }
```

```
// Called to draw scene
void RenderScene(void)
        {
        // Earth and Moon angle of revolution
        static float fMoonRot = 0.0f;
        static float fEarthRot = 0.0f;

        // Clear the window with current clearing color
        glClear(GL_COLOR_BUFFER_BIT | GL_DEPTH_BUFFER_BIT);

        // Save the matrix state and do the rotations
        glMatrixMode(GL_MODELVIEW);
        glPushMatrix();

        // Set light position before viewing transformation
        glLightfv(GL_LIGHT0,GL_POSITION,lightPos);

        // Translate the whole scene out and into view
        glTranslatef(0.0f, 0.0f, -300.0f);

        // Set material color, Red
        // Sun
        glRGB(255, 255, 0);
        auxSolidSphere(15.0f);

        // Move the light after we draw the sun!
        glLightfv(GL_LIGHT0,GL_POSITION,lightPos);

        // Rotate coordinate system
        glRotatef(fEarthRot, 0.0f, 1.0f, 0.0f);

        // Draw the Earth
        glRGB(0,0,255);
        glTranslatef(105.0f,0.0f,0.0f);
        auxSolidSphere(15.0f);


        // Rotate from Earth-based coordinates and draw Moon
        glRGB(200,200,200);
        glRotatef(fMoonRot,0.0f, 1.0f, 0.0f);
        glTranslatef(30.0f, 0.0f, 0.0f);
        fMoonRot+= 15.0f;
        if(fMoonRot > 360.0f)
                fMoonRot = 0.0f;

        auxSolidSphere(6.0f);


        // Restore the matrix state
        glPopMatrix();  // Modelview matrix


        // Step earth orbit 5 degrees
        fEarthRot += 5.0f;
        if(fEarthRot > 360.0f)
                fEarthRot = 0.0f;

        // Flush drawing commands
        glFlush();
        }
```

Advanced Matrix Manipulation

You don't have to use the high-level functions to produce your transformations. We recommend that you do, however, because those functions often are highly optimized for their particular purpose, whereas the low-level functions are designed for general use. Two of these high-level functions make it possible for you to load your own matrix and multiply it into either the Modelview or Projection matrix stacks.

Loading a Matrix

You can load an arbitrary matrix into the Projection, Modelview, or Texture matrix stacks. First, declare an array to hold the 16 values of a 4 x 4 matrix. Make the desired matrix stack the current one, and call glLoadMatrix.

The matrix is stored in *column-major order,* which simply means that each column is traversed first from top to bottom. Figure 7-28 shows the matrix elements in numbered order. The following code shows an array being loaded with the Identity matrix, then being loaded into the Modelview matrix stack. This is equivalent to calling glLoadIdentity using the higher-level functions.

```
// Equivalent, but more flexible
glFloat m[] = { 1.0f, 0.0f, 0.0f, 0.0f,
                0.0f, 1.0f, 0.0f, 0.0f,
                0.0f, 0.0f, 1.0f, 0.0f,
                0.0f, 0.0f, 0.0f, 1.0f };

glMatrixMode(GL_MODELVIEW);
glLoadMatrixf(m);
```

$$\begin{bmatrix} a_0 & a_4 & a_8 & a_{12} \\ a_1 & a_5 & a_9 & a_{13} \\ a_2 & a_6 & a_{10} & a_{14} \\ a_3 & a_7 & a_{11} & a_{15} \end{bmatrix}$$

Figure 7-28 Column-major matrix ordering

Performing Your Own Transformations

You can load an array with an arbitrary matrix if you want, and multiply it, too, into one of the three matrix stacks. The following code shows a Transformation matrix that translates 10 units along the x-axis. This matrix is then multiplied into the Modelview matrix. You can also achieve this affect by calling glTranslatef.

```
// Define the Translation matrix
glFloat m[] = { 1.0f, 0.0f, 0.0f, 10.0f,
                0.0f, 1.0f, 0.0f, 0.0f,
                0.0f, 0.0f, 1.0f, 0.0f,
                0.0f, 0.0f, 0.0f, 1.0f };

// Multiply the translation matrix by the current modelview
// matrix. The new matrix becomes the modelview matrix
glMatrixMode(GL_MODELVIEW);
glMultMatrixf(m);
```

Other Transformations

There's no particular advantage in duplicating the functionality of gLoadIdentity or glTranslatef by specifying a matrix. The real reason for allowing manipulation of arbitrary matrices is to allow for complex matrix transformations. One such use is for drawing shadows, and you'll see that in action in Chapter 9. Some other uses are wrapping one object around another object, and certain lens effects. For information on these advanced uses, see Appendix B.

Summary

In this chapter, you've learned concepts crucial to using OpenGL for creation of 3D scenes. Even if you can't juggle matrices in your head, you now know what matrices are and how they are used to perform the various transformations. You've also learned how to manipulate the Modelview and Projection matrix stacks to place your objects in the scene and to determine how they are viewed on screen.

Finally, we also showed you the functions needed to perform your own matrix magic if you are so inclined. These functions allow you to create your own matrices and load them into the matrix stack, or multiply them by the current matrix first.

The tank/robot simulation at this point in the book will now allow you to move around in a three-dimensional world and explore objects placed all around. If you study the simulation code thus far, you will find excellent use of perspective projections, as well as the gluLookAt utility function that provides a simple way to specify your viewing transformation. Your 3D world is made of wire for now, but that will be changing very soon.

Reference Section

GLFRUSTUM

Purpose	Multiplies the current matrix by a Perspective matrix.
Include File	<gl.h>
Syntax	void glFrustum(GLdouble left, GLdouble right, GLdouble bottom, GLdouble top, GLdouble near, GLdouble far);
Description	This function creates a Perspective matrix that produces a perspective projection. The eye is assumed to be located at (0,0,0), with -far being the location of the far clipping plane, and -near specifying the location of the near clipping plane. This function can adversely affect the precision of the depth buffer if the ratio of far to near (far/near) is large.
Parameters	
left, right	GLdouble: Coordinates for the left and right clipping planes.
bottom, top	GLdouble: Coordinates for the bottom and top clipping planes.
near, far	GLdouble: Distance to the near and far clipping planes. Both of these values must be positive.
Returns	None.
Example	The code below sets up a Perspective matrix that defines a viewing volume from 0 to −100 on the z-axis. The x and y extents are 100 units in the positive and negative directions.

```
glLoadMatrix(GL_PROJECTION);
glLoadIdentify();
glFrustum(-100.0f, 100.0f, -100.0f, 100.0f, 0.0f, 100.0f);
```

See Also	glOrtho, glMatrixMode, glMultMatrix, glViewport

GLLOADIDENTITY

Purpose	Sets the current matrix to Identity.
Include File	<gl.h>
Syntax	void glLoadIdentity(void);
Description	This function replaces the current Transformation matrix with the Identity matrix. This essentially resets the coordinate system to eye coordinates.
Returns	None.
Example	The following code shows the Modelview matrix being set to identity:

```
glMatrixMode(GL_MODELVIEW);
glLoadIdentity();
```

See Also	glLoadMatrix, glMatrixMode, glMultMatrix, glPushMatrix

GLLOADMATRIX

Purpose	Sets the current matrix to the one specified.
Include File	<gl.h>
Variations	void **glLoadMatrixd**(const GLdouble *m); void **glLoadMatrixf**(const GLfloat *m);
Description	Replaces the current Transformation matrix with an arbitrary matrix supplied. It may be more efficient to use some of the other matrix manipulation functions such as glLoadIdentity, glRotate, glTranslate, and glScale.
Parameters	
*m	GLdouble or GLfloat: This array represents a 4 x 4 matrix that will be used for the current Transformation matrix. The array is stored in column-major order as 16 consecutive values.
Returns	None.
Example	The following two segments of code are equivalent. They both load the Modelview matrix with the Identity matrix.

```
// Efficient way
glMatrixMode(GL_MODELVIEW);
glLoadIdentity();

// Equivalent, but more flexible
glFloat m[] = { 1.0f, 0.0f, 0.0f, 0.0f,
                0.0f, 1.0f, 0.0f, 0.0f,
                0.0f, 0.0f, 1.0f, 0.0f,
                0.0f, 0.0f, 0.0f, 1.0f };

glMatrixMode(GL_MODELVIEW);
glLoadMatrixf(m);
```

See Also	glLoadIdentity, glMatrixMode, glMultMatrix, glPushMatrix

GLMATRIXMODE

Purpose	Specifies the current matrix (PROJECTION, MODELVIEW, TEXTURE).
Include File	<gl.h>
Syntax	void glMatrixMode(GLenum mode);
Description	This function is used to determine which matrix stack (GL_MODELVIEW, GL_PROJECTION, or GL_TEXTURE) will be used for matrix operations.
Parameters	
mode	GLenum: Identifies which matrix stack will be used for subsequent matrix operations. Any of the values in Table 7-2 are accepted.
Returns	None.
Example	The following common two lines of code select the Modelview matrix stack for matrix operations, then loads the Identity matrix.

```
glMatrixMode(GL_MODELVIEW);
glLoadMatrixf(m);
```

See Also   glLoadMatrix, glPushMatrix

Table 7-2 Valid Matrix Mode Identifiers for glMatrixMode()

Mode	Matrix Stack
GL_MODELVIEW	Matrix operations affect the Modelview matrix stack. (Used to move objects around scene.)
GL_PROJECTION	Matrix operations affect the Projection matrix stack. (Used to define clipping volume.)
GL_TEXTURE	Matrix operations affect the Texture matrix stack. (Manipulates texture coordinates.)

GLMULTMATRIX

Purpose   Multiplies the current matrix by the one specified.

Include File   <gl.h>

Variations   void **glMultMatrixd**(const GLdouble *m);
void **glMultMatrixf**(const GLfloat *m);

Description   This function multiplies the currently selected matrix stack with the one specified. The resulting matrix is then stored as the current matrix at the top of the matrix stack.

Parameters

m   GLdouble or GLfloat: This array represents a 4 x 4 matrix that will be multiplied by the current matrix. The array is stored in column-major order as 16 consecutive values.

Returns   None.

Example   The following code creates a Translation matrix and multiplies it by the current Modelview matrix. The newly created matrix replaces the values in the Modelview matrix. The multiplication shown here could also have been accomplished by calling glTranslate(10.0f, 0.0f, 0.0f);.

```
// Define the Translation matrix
glFloat m[] = { 1.0f, 0.0f, 0.0f, 10.0f,
                0.0f, 1.0f, 0.0f, 0.0f,
                0.0f, 0.0f, 1.0f, 0.0f,
                0.0f, 0.0f, 0.0f, 1.0f };

// Multiply the Translation matrix by the current Modelview
// matrix. The new matrix becomes the Modelview matrix
glMatrixMode(GL_MODELVIEW);
glMultMatrixf(m);
```

See Also   glMatrixMode, glLoadIdentity, glLoadMatrix, glPushMatrix

GLPOPMATRIX

Purpose	Pops the current matrix off the matrix stack.
Include File	<gl.h>
Syntax	void glPopMatrix(void);
Description	This function is used to pop the last (topmost) matrix off the current matrix stack. This is most often used to restore the previous condition of the current Transformation matrix if it was saved with a call to glPushMatrix.
Returns	None.
Example	The code below is from the ATOM example program for this chapter. This section saves the Modelview matrix state with a call to glPushMatrix (which is centered in the atom). Then the coordinate system is rotated and translated appropriately to place the electron, which is represented by a small sphere. The coordinate system is then restored by a call to glPopMatrix before the next electron is drawn.

```
// First Electron Orbit
glPushMatrix();
glRotatef(fElect1, 0.0f, 1.0f, 0.0f);
glTranslatef(90.0f, 0.0f, 0.0f);
auxSolidSphere(6.0f);
glPopMatrix();
```

See Also	glPushMatrix

GLPUSHMATRIX

Purpose	Pushes the current matrix onto the matrix stack.
Include File	<gl.h>
Syntax	void glPushMatrix(void);
Description	This function is used to push the current matrix onto the current matrix stack. This is most often used to save the current Transformation matrix so that it can be restored later with a call to glPopMatrix.
Returns	None.
Example	See glPopMatrix.
See Also	glPopMatrix

GLROTATE

Purpose	Rotates the current matrix by a Rotation matrix.
Include File	<gl.h>

Variations	void **glRotated**(GLdouble angle, GLdouble x, GLdouble y, GLdouble z); void **glRotatef**(GLfloat angle, GLfloat x, GLfloat y, GLfloat z);
Description	This function multiplies the current matrix by a Rotation matrix that performs a counterclockwise rotation around a directional vector that passes from the origin through the point (x,y,z). The newly rotated matrix becomes the current Transformation matrix.
Parameters	
angle	GLdouble or GLfloat: The angle of rotation in degrees. The angle produces a counterclockwise rotation.
x,y,z	GLdouble or GLfloat: A direction vector from the origin that is used as the axis of rotation.
Returns	None.
Example	The code below from the SOLAR example program places the Moon in orbit around the earth. The current Modelview matrix stack is centered at the Earth's position, when it is rotated by the current revolution of the Moon, then translated out to its position away from the Earth.

```
// Moon
glRGB(200,200,200);
glRotatef(fMoonRot,0.0f, 1.0f, 0.0f);
glTranslatef(30.0f, 0.0f, 0.0f);
fMoonRot+= 15.0f;
if(fMoonRot > 360.0)
        fMoonRot = 15.0f;

auxSolidSphere(6.0f);
```

See Also	glScale, glTranslate

GLSCALE

Purpose	Multiplies the current matrix by a Scaling matrix.
Include File	<gl.h>
Variations	void **glScaled**(GLdouble x, GLdouble y, GLdouble z); void **glScalef**(GLfloat x, GLfloat y, GLfloat z);
Description	This function multiplies the current matrix by a Scaling matrix. The newly scaled matrix becomes the current Transformation matrix.
Parameters	
x,y,z	GLdouble or GLfloat: Scale factors along the x, y, and z axes.
Returns	None.
Example	The following code modifies the Modelview matrix to produce flattened-out objects. The vertices of all subsequent primitives will be reduced by half in the y direction.

```
glMatrixMode(GL_MODELVIEW);
glLoadIdentity();

glScalef(1.0f, 0.5f, 1.0f);
```

See Also   glRotate, glTranslate

GLTRANSLATE

Purpose	Multiplies the current matrix by a Translation matrix.
Include File	<gl.h>
Variations	void **glTranslated**(GLdouble x, GLdouble y, GLdouble z); void **glTranslatef**(GLfloat x, GLfloat y, GLfloat z);
Description	This function multiplies the current matrix by a Translation matrix. The newly translated matrix becomes the current Transformation matrix.
Parameters	
x, y, z	GLdouble or GLfloat: The x, y, and z coordinates of a translation vector.
Returns	None.
Example	The following code is from the example program SOLAR. It places a blue sphere 105 units along the positive x-axis away from the origin.

```
// Earth
glColor3f(0.0f,0.0f,1.0f);
glTranslatef(105.0f,0.0f,0.0f);
auxSolidSphere(15.0f);
```

See Also   glRotate, glScale

GLULOOKAT

Purpose	Defines a viewing transformation.
Include File	<glu.h>
Syntax	void gluLookAt(GLdouble eyex, GLdouble eyey, GLdouble eyez, GLdouble centerx, GLdouble centery, GLdouble centerz, GLdouble upx, GLdouble upy, GLdouble upz);
Description	Defines a viewing transformation based on the position of the eye, the position of the center of the scene, and a vector pointing up from the viewer's perspective.
Parameters	
eyex, eyey, eyz	GLdouble: x, y, and z coordinates of the eye point.
centerx, centery, *centerz*	GLdouble: x, y, and z coordinates of the center of the scene being looked at.
upx, upy, upz	GLdouble: x, y, and z coordinates that specifies the up vector.

Returns	None.
Example	The following code is from the TANK example program. It shows how the viewing transformation is changed every time the tank or robot changes position.

```
// Reset the Modelview matrix
glMatrixMode(GL_MODELVIEW);
glLoadIdentity();

// Set viewing transformation based on position and direction.
gluLookAt(locX, locY, locZ, dirX, dirY, dirZ, 0.0f, 1.0f, 0.0f);
```

	Here locX through locY specify the location of the tank or robot (the observer's point of view), and dirX through dirZ represent the direction in which the tank is pointed. The last three values specify the direction pointed up, which for this simulation will always be in the positive y direction.
See Also	glFrustum, gluPerspective

GLUORTHO2D

Purpose	Defines a two-dimensional orthographic projection.
Include File	<glu.h>
Syntax	void gluOrtho2D(GLdouble left, GLdouble right, GLdouble bottom, GLdouble top);
Description	This function defines a 2D orthographic projection matrix. This projection matrix is equivalent to calling glOrtho with near and far set to 0 and 1, respectively.
Parameters	
left, right	GLdouble: Specifies the far-left and -right clipping planes.
bottom, top	GLdouble: Specifies the top and bottom clipping planes.
Returns	None.
Example	The following line of code sets up a 2D viewing volume that allows drawing in the xy plane from −100 to +100 along the x- and y-axis. Positive y will be up, and positive x will be to the right.

```
gluOrtho2D(-100.0, 100.0, -100.0, 100.0);
```

See Also	glOrtho, gluPerspective

GLUPERSPECTIVE

Purpose	Defines a viewing perspective Projection matrix.
Include File	<glu.h>

Syntax	void gluPerspective(GLdouble fovy, GLdouble aspect, GLdouble zNear, GLdouble zFar);
Description	This function creates a matrix that describes a viewing frustum in world coordinates. The aspect ratio should match the aspect ratio of the viewport (specified with glViewport). The perspective division is based on the field-of-view angle and the distance to the near and far clipping planes.
Parameters	
fovy	GLdouble: The field of view in degrees, in the y direction.
aspect	GLdouble: The aspect ratio. This is used to determine the field of view in the x direction. The aspect ratio is x/y.
zNear, zFar	GLdouble: The distance from the viewer to the near and far clipping plane. These values are always positive.
Returns	None.
Example	The following code is from the example program SOLAR. It creates a Perspective projection that makes planets on the far side of the Sun appear smaller than when on the near side.

```
// Change viewing volume and viewport.
// Called when window is resized
void ChangeSize(GLsizei w, GLsizei h)
        {
        GLfloat fAspect;

        // Prevent a divide by zero
        if(h == 0)
                h = 1;

        // Set Viewport to window dimensions
        glViewport(0, 0, w, h);

        // Calculate aspect ratio of the window
        fAspect = (GLfloat)w/(GLfloat)h;

        // Reset coordinate system
        glMatrixMode(GL_PROJECTION);
        glLoadIdentity();

        gluPerspective(45.0f, fAspect, 1.0, 425.0);

        // Modelview matrix reset
        glMatrixMode(GL_MODELVIEW);
        glLoadIdentity();
        }
```

See Also	glFrustum, gluOrtho2D

8

COLOR AND SHADING

8

COLOR AND SHADING

What you'll learn in this chapter:

How to...	Functions You'll Use
Specify a color in terms of RGB components	glColor
Set the shading model	glShadeModel
Create a 3-3-2 palette	CreatePalette
Make use of a palette	RealizePalette, SelectPalette, UpdateColors

At last we are going to talk about color! This is perhaps the single most important aspect of any graphics library—even above animation support. You must remember one thing as you develop graphics applications: In this case, the old adage isn't true; looks ARE everything! Don't let anyone tell you otherwise. Yes, it's true that features, performance, price, and reliability are important factors when you're selecting and working with a graphics application, but let's face it—on the scales of product evaluation, looks have the largest impact most of the time.

If you want to make a living in this field, you cannot develop just for the intellectual few who may think as you do. Go for the masses! Consider this: Black-and-white TVs were cheaper to make than color sets. Black-and-white video cameras, too, were cheaper and more efficient to make and use—and for a long time they were more reliable. But look around at our society today and draw your own conclusions. Of course, black-and-white has its place, but color is now paramount. (Then again, we wish they hadn't colorized all those Shirley Temple movies...)

What Is a Color?

First let's talk a little bit about color itself. How is a color made in nature, and how do we see colors? Understanding color theory and how the human eye sees a color scene will lend some insight into how you create a color programmatically. (If color theory is old hat to you, you can probably skip this section.)

Light as a Wave

Color is simply a wavelength of light that is visible to the human eye. If you had any physics classes in school, you may remember something about light being both a wave and a particle. It is modeled as a wave that travels through space much as a ripple through a pond; and it is modeled as a particle, such as a raindrop falling to the ground. If this seems confusing, you know why most people don't study quantum mechanics!

The light you see from nearly any given source is actually a mixture of many different *kinds* of light. These kinds of light are identified by their *wavelengths*. The wavelength of light is measured as the distance between the peaks of the light wave, as illustrated in Figure 8-1.

Wavelengths of visible light range from 390 nanometers (one billionth of a meter) for violet light, to 720 nanometers for red light; this range is commonly called the *spectrum*. You've undoubtedly heard the terms *ultraviolet* and *infrared*; these represent light not visible to the naked eye, lying beyond the ends of the spectrum You will recognize the spectrum as containing all the colors of the rainbow. See Figure 8-2.

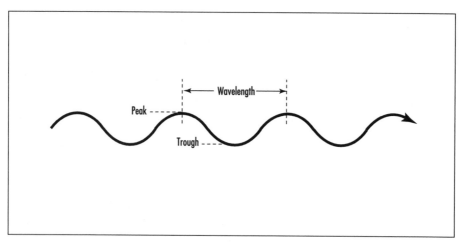

Figure 8-1 How a wavelength of light is measured

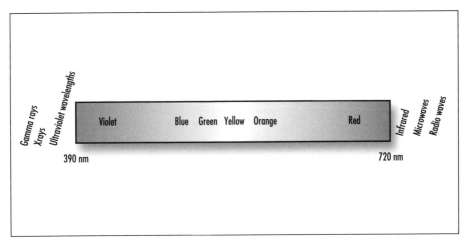

Figure 8-2 The spectrum of visible light

Light as a Particle

"OK, Mr. Smart Brain," you may ask, "If color is a wavelength of light and the only visible light is in this 'rainbow' thing, where is the brown for my Fig Newtons or the black for my coffee, or even the white of this page?" We'll begin answering that question by telling you that black is not a color; nor is white. Actually, black is the *absence* of color, and white is an *even combination* of all the colors at once. That is, a white object reflects all wavelengths of colors evenly, and a black object absorbs all wavelengths evenly.

As for the brown of those fig bars and the many other colors that you see, they are indeed colors. Actually, at the physical level they are *composite* colors. They are made of varying amounts of the "pure" colors found in the spectrum. To understand how this works, think of light as a particle. Any given object when illuminated by a light source is struck by "billions and billions" (my apologies to Carl Sagan) of photons, or tiny light particles. Remembering our physics mumbo jumbo, each of these photons is also a wave, which has a wavelength, and thus a specific color in the spectrum.

All physical objects are made up of atoms. The reflection of photons from an object depends on the kinds of atoms, the amount of each kind, and the arrangement of atoms in the object. Some photons will be reflected and some will be absorbed (the absorbed photons are usually converted to heat), and any given material or mixture of materials (such as your fig bar) will reflect more of some wavelengths than others. Figure 8-3 illustrates this principle.

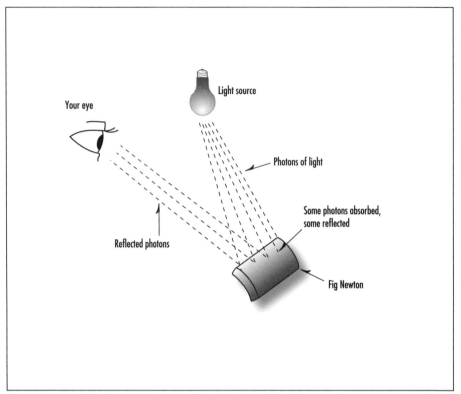

Figure 8-3 An object reflects some photons and absorbs others

Your Personal Photon Detector

The reflected light from your fig bar, when seen by your eye, is interpreted as color. The billions of photons enter your eye and are focused onto the back of your eye, where your retina acts as sort of a photographic plate. The retina's millions of *cone cells* are excited when struck by the photons, and this causes neural energy to travel to your brain, which interprets the information as light and color. The more photons that strike the cone cells, the more excited they get. This level of excitation is interpreted by your brain as the brightness of the light, which makes sense—the brighter the light, the more photons there are to strike the cone cells.

The eye has three kinds of cone cells. All of them respond to photons, but each kind responds most to a particular wavelength. One is more excited by photons that have reddish wavelengths, one by green wavelengths, and one by blue wavelengths. Thus light that is composed mostly of red wavelengths will excite red-sensitive cone cells more than the other cells, and your brain receives the signal that the light you are seeing is mostly reddish. You do the math—a combination of different wavelengths of various intensities will, of course, yield a mix of colors. All wavelengths equally repre-sented thus is perceived as white, and no light of any wavelength is black.

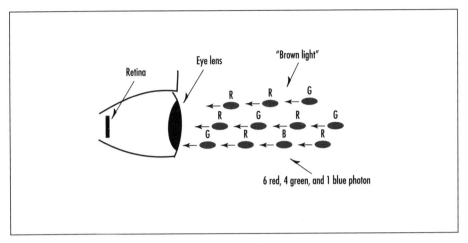

Figure 8-4 How the "color" brown is perceived by the eye

You can see that any "color" that your eye perceives is actually made up of light all over the visible spectrum. The "hardware" in your eye detects what it sees in terms of the relative concentrations and strengths of red, green, and blue light. Figure 8-4 shows how brown comprises a photon mix of 60% red photons, 40% green photons, and 10% blue photons.

The Computer as a Photon Generator

It makes sense that when we wish to generate a color with a computer, we do so by specifying separate intensities for red, green, and blue components of the light. It so happens that color computer monitors are designed to produce three kinds of light (can you guess which three?), each with varying degrees of intensity. In the back of your computer monitor is an electron gun that shoots electrons at the back of the screen you view. This screen contains phosphors that emit red, green, and blue light when struck by the electrons. The intensity of the light emitted varies with the intensity of the electron beam. These three color phosphors are then packed closely together to make up a single physical dot on the screen. See Figure 8-5.

You may recall that in Chapter 3 we explained how OpenGL defines a color exactly as intensities of red, green, and blue, with the glColor command. Here we will cover more thoroughly the two color modes supported by OpenGL.

- RGBA color mode is what we have been using all along for the examples in this book. When drawing in this mode, you set a color precisely by specifying it in terms of the three color components (Red, Green, and Blue).

- With *color index mode,* you choose a color while drawing by specifying an index into an array of available colors called a *palette.* Within this palette, you specify the exact color you want by setting the intensities of the red, green, and blue components.

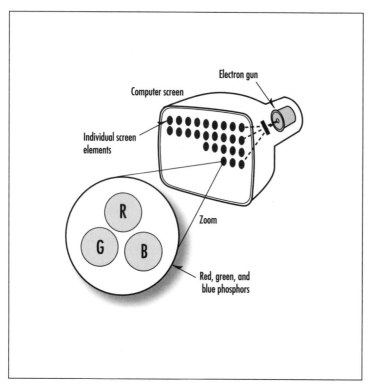

Figure 8-5 How a computer monitor generates colors

PC Color Hardware

There once was a time when state-of-the-art PC graphics hardware meant the Hercules graphics card. This card could produce bitmapped images with a resolution of 720 x 348. The drawback was that each pixel had only two states: on and off. At that time, bitmapped graphics of *any* kind on a PC was a big deal, and you could produce some great monochrome graphics. Your author even did some 3D graphics on a Hercules card back in college.

Actually predating the Hercules card was the CGA card, the Color Graphics Adapter. Introduced with the first IBM PC, this card could support resolutions of 320 x 200 pixels and could place any four of 16 colors on the screen at once. A higher resolution (640 x 200) with two colors was also possible, but wasn't as effective or cost conscious as the Hercules card (color monitors = $$$). CGA was puny by today's standards—it was even outmatched then by the graphics capabilities of a $200 Commodore 64 or Atari home computer. Lacking adequate resolution for business graphics or even modest modeling, CGA was used primarily for simple PC games or business applications that could benefit from colored text. Generally though, it was hard to make a good business justification for this more expensive hardware.

The next big breakthrough for PC graphics came when IBM introduced the Enhanced Graphics Adapter (EGA) card. This one could do more than 25 lines of colored text in new text modes, and for graphics could support 640 x 350-pixel bitmapped graphics in 16 colors! Other technical improvements eliminated some flickering problems of the CGA ancestor and provided for better and smoother animation. Now arcade-style games, real business graphics, and even 3D graphics became not only possible but even reasonable on the PC. This advance was a giant move beyond CGA, but still PC graphics were in their infancy.

The last mainstream PC graphics standard set by IBM was the VGA card (which stood for Vector Graphics Array rather than the commonly held Video Graphics Adapter). This card was significantly faster than the EGA, could support 16 colors at a higher resolution (640 x 480) and 256 colors at a lower resolution of 320 x 200. These 256 colors were selected from a palette of over 16 million possible colors. That's when the floodgates opened for PC graphics. Near photo-realistic graphics become possible on PCs. Ray tracers, 3D games, and photo-editing software began to pop up in the PC market.

IBM, as well, had a high-end graphics card—the 8514—for their "workstations." This card could do 1024 x 768 graphics at 256 colors. IBM thought this card would only be used by CAD and scientific applications! But one thing is certain about the consumer market: They always want more. It was this short-sightedness that cost IBM its role as standard-setter in the PC graphics market. Other vendors began to ship "Super-VGA" cards that could display higher and higher resolutions, with more and more colors. First 800 x 600, then 1024 x 768 and even higher, with first 256 colors, then 32,000, to 65,000. Today 24-bit color cards can display 16 million colors at resolutions up to 1024 x 768. Inexpensive PC hardware can support full color at VGA resolutions, or 800 x 600 Super-VGA resolutions. Most Windows PCs sold today can support at least 65,000 colors at resolutions of 1024 x 768.

All this power makes for some really cool possibilities—photo-realistic 3D graphics to name just one. When Microsoft ported OpenGL to the Windows platform, that enabled creation of high-end graphics applications for PCs. Today's Pentium and Pentium Pro PCs are still no match for modern SGI Workstations. But combine them with 3D-graphics accelerated graphics cards, and you can get the kind of performance possible only a few years ago on $100,000 graphics workstations—at a Wal-Mart Christmas special! In the very near future, typical home machines will be capable of very sophisticated simulations, games, and more. Our children will laugh at the term "virtual reality" in the same way we smile at those old *Buck Rogers* rocket ships.

PC Display Modes

Microsoft Windows revolutionized the world of PC graphics in two respects. First, it created a mainstream graphical operating environment that was adopted by the business world at large and, soon thereafter, the consumer market. Second, it made PC graphics significantly easier for programmers to do. With Windows, the hardware was "virtualized" by Windows display device drivers. Instead of having to write instructions directly to the video hardware, programmers today can write to a single API, and

Windows handles the specifics of talking to the hardware. Typically, Microsoft provides in the Windows base package (usually with vendor assistance) drivers for the more popular graphics cards. Hardware vendors with later hardware and software revisions ship their cards with Windows drivers and often provide updates to these drivers on BBSs or on the Internet.

There was a time when Windows shipped with drivers for the Hercules monochrome cards, and standard CGA, and EGA video adapters. Not anymore. Standard VGA is now considered the bottom of the barrel. New PCs sold today are capable of at least 640 x 480 resolution with 16 colors, and the choices of resolution and color depth go up from there.

Screen Resolution

Screen resolution for today's PCs can vary from 640 x 480 pixels up to 1280 x 1024 or more. Screen resolution, however, is not usually a prime limiting factor in writing graphics applications. The lower resolution of 640 x 480 is considered adequate for most graphics display tasks. More important is the size of the window, and this is taken into account easily with clipping volume and viewport settings (see Chapter 3). By scaling the size of the drawing to the size of the window, you can easily account for the various resolutions and window size combinations that can occur. Well-written graphics applications will display the same approximate image regardless of screen resolution. The user should automatically be able to see more and sharper details as the resolution increases.

Color Depth

If an increase in screen resolution or in the number of available drawing pixels in turn increases the detail and sharpness of the image, so too should an increase in available colors improve the clarity of the resulting image. An image displayed on a computer that can display millions of colors should look remarkably better than the same image displayed with only 16 colors. In programming, there are really only three color depths that you need to worry about: 4-bit, 8-bit, and 24-bit.

4-Bit Color

On the low end, your program may be run in a video mode that only supports 16 colors—called 4-bit mode because there are 4 bits devoted to color information for each pixel. These 4 bits represent a value from 0 to 15 that provides an index into a set of 16 predefined colors. With only 16 colors at your disposal, , there is little you can do to improve the clarity and sharpness of your image. It is generally accepted that most serious graphics applications can ignore the 16-color mode.

8-Bit Color

The 8-bit mode supports up to 256 colors on the screen. This is a substantial improvement, and when combined with *dithering* (explained later in this chapter) can produce satisfactory results for many applications. There are 8 bits devoted to each pixel, which are used to hold a value from 0 to 255 that references an index into a color table called the *palette*. The colors in this color table can be selected from over 16 million possible colors. If you need 256 shades of red, the hardware will support it.

Each color in the palette is selected by specifying 8 bits each for separate intensities of red, green, and blue, which means the intensity of each component can range from 0 to 255. This effectively yields a choice of over 16 million different colors for the palette. By selecting these colors carefully, near-photographic quality can be achieved on the PC screen.

24-Bit Color

The best quality image production available today on PCs is 24-bit color mode. In this mode, a full 24 bits are devoted to each pixel to hold eight bits of color data for each of the red, green, and blue color components (8 + 8 + 8 = 24). You have the capability to put any of over 16 million possible colors in every pixel on the screen. The most obvious drawback to this mode is the amount of memory required for high-resolution screens (over 2MB for a 1024 x 768 screen). Also indirectly, it is much slower to move larger chunks of memory around when doing animation, or just drawing on the screen. Fortunately, today's accelerated graphics adapters are optimized for these types of operations.

Other Color Depths

For saving memory or improving performance, many display cards also support various other color modes.

In the area of performance improvement, some cards support a 32-bit color mode sometimes called *true color* mode. Actually, the 32-bit color mode cannot display any more colors than the 24-bit mode, but it improves performance by aligning the data for each pixel on a 32-bit address boundary. Unfortunately, this results in a wasted 8-bits (1 byte) per pixel. On today's 32-bit Intel PCs, a memory address evenly divisible by 32 results in much faster memory access.

Two other popular display modes are sometimes supported to use memory more efficiently. The first is 15-bit color mode, which uses 5 bits each for storing red, green, and blue components. Each pixel can display any of 32,768 different colors. And in 16-bit mode, an additional bit is added for one of the color components (usually green), allowing one of 65,536 possible colors for each pixel. This last mode, especially, is practically as effective as 24-bit for photographic image reproduction. It is difficult to tell the difference between 16-bit and 24-bit color modes for most photographic images, although some banding may be observed on smoothly shaded surfaces with only 16 bits of color.

Programmatically, a color in the 15- or 16-bit color mode is set in the same way as for the 24-bit color modes—that is, as a set of three 8-bit intensities. The hardware or device driver takes this 24-bit color value and scales it to the nearest matching 15- or 16-bit color value before setting the pixel color.

Selecting a Color

You now know that OpenGL specifies an exact color as separate intensities of red, green, and blue components. You also know that Windows-supported PC hardware may be able to display nearly all of these combinations, or only a very few. How, then, do we specify a desired color in terms of these red, green, and blue components? And how will Windows fulfill this request using the colors it has available?

The Color Cube

Since a color is specified by three positive color values, we can model the available colors as a volume that we shall call the *RGB color space*. Figure 8-6 shows what this color space looks like at the origin with red, green, and blue as the axes. The red, green, and blue coordinates are specified just like x, y, and z coordinates. At the origin (0,0,0), the relative intensities of all the components is zero, and the resulting color is black. The maximum available on the PC for storage information is 24 bits, so with 8 bits for each component, let's say that a value of 255 along the axis would represent full saturation of that component. We would then end up with a cube measuring 255 on each side. The corner directly opposite black, where the concentrations are (0,0,0), is white with relative concentrations of (255,255,255). At full saturation (255) from the origin along each axis would lie the pure colors of red, green, and blue, respectively.

This "color cube" (Figure 8-7) then contains all the possible colors, either on the surface of the cube or within the interior of the cube. For example, all possible shades

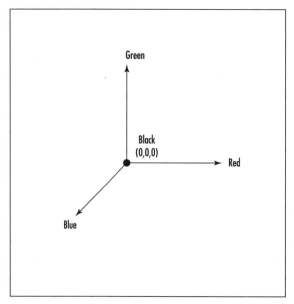

Figure 8-6 The origin of RGB color space

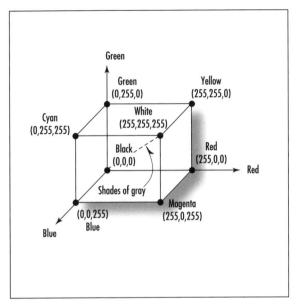

Figure 8-7 The RGB color space

of gray between black and white lie internally on the diagonal line between the corner (0,0,0) and (255,255,255).

Figure 8-8 is a screenshot of the smoothly shaded color cube produced by a sample program from this chapter, CCUBE. The surface of this cube shows the color variations from black on one corner to white on the opposite corner. Red, green, and blue are present on their corners 255 units from black. Additionally, the colors yellow, cyan, and magenta have corners showing the combination of the other three primary colors. This program will do an adequate job of rendering the color cube, even in a 16-color Windows display mode, and you'll learn how this is done later in this chapter. You can also spin the color cube around to examine all of its sides, by pressing the arrow keys.

Setting the Drawing Color

Let's briefly review the glColor() function. It is prototyped as follows:

```
void glColor<x><t>(red, green, blue, alpha);
```

In the function name, the <x> represents the number of arguments; it may be 3 for three arguments of red, green, and blue, or 4 for four arguments to include the alpha component. (The alpha component specifies the translucency of the color and will be covered in more detail in (Chapter 15.) For the time being, just use a three-argument version of the function.

The <t> in the function name specifies the argument's data type and can be b, d, f, i, s, ub, ui, us, for byte, double, float, integer, short, unsigned byte, unsigned integer,

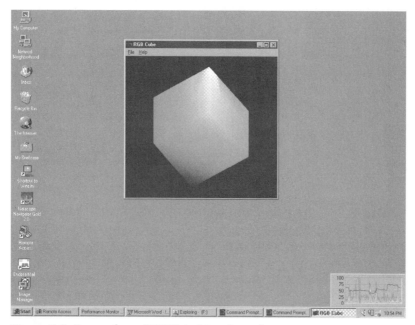

Figure 8-8 Output from CCUBE is this color cube

and unsigned short data types, respectively. Another version of the function has a v appended to the end; this version takes an array that contains the arguments (the v stands for vectored). In the Reference Section you will find an entry with more details on the glColor() function.

Most OpenGL programs that you'll see will use glColor3f and will specify the intensity of each component as 0.0 for none or 1.0 for full intensity. However, it may be easier, if you have Windows programming experience, to use the glColor3ub version of the function. This version takes three unsigned bytes, from 0 to 255, to specify the intensities of red, green, and blue. Using this version of the function is like using the Windows RGB macro to specify a color:

```
glColor3ub(0,255,128) = RGB(0,255,128)
```

In fact, this may make it easier for you to match your OpenGL colors to existing RGB colors used by your program for other non-OpenGL drawing tasks.

Remember that the RGB macro specifies a color to Windows but does not itself set the current drawing color, as glColor does. To do this, you'd use the RGB macro in conjunction with the creation of a GDI pen or brush.

Shading

Our previous working definition for glColor was that this function set the current drawing color, and all objects drawn after this command would have the last color specified. Now that we have discussed the OpenGL drawing primitives (Chapter 6), we can expand this definition to this: The glColor function sets the current color that is used for all vertices drawn after the command. So far, all of our examples have drawn wireframe objects, or solid objects with each face a different but solid color. If we specify a different color for each vertex of a primitive (either point, line, or polygon), what color is the interior?

Let's answer this question first regarding points. A point has only one vertex, and whatever color you specify for that vertex will be the resulting color for that point.

A line, however, has two vertices and each can be set to a different color. The color of the line depends on the *shading model*. Shading is simply defined as the smooth transition from one color to the next. Any two points in our RGB color space (Figure 8-7) can be connected by a straight line.

Smooth shading causes the colors along the line to vary as they do through the color cube from one color point to the other. In Figure 8-9, the color cube is shown with the black and white corners pointed out. Below it is a line with two vertices, one black and one white. The colors selected along the length of the line match the colors along the straight line in the color cube, from the black to the white corners. This results in a line that progresses from black through lighter and lighter shades of gray and eventually to white.

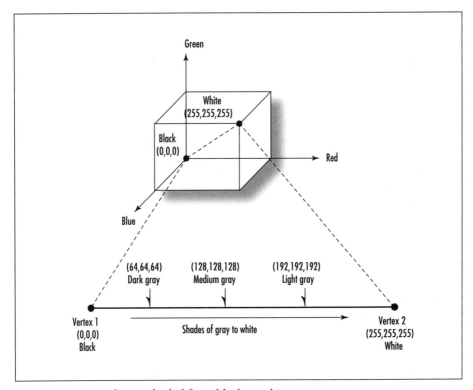

Figure 8-9 How a line is shaded from black to white

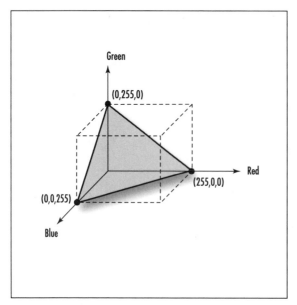

Figure 8-10 A triangle in RGB color space

You can do shading mathematically by finding the equation of the line connecting two points in the three-dimensional RGB color space. Then simply loop through from one end of the line to the other, retrieving coordinates along the way to provide the color of each pixel on the screen. Many good books on computer graphics will explain the algorithm to accomplish this and scale your color line to the physical line on the screen, etc. Fortunately, OpenGL will do all this for you!

The shading exercise becomes slightly more complex for polygons. A triangle, for instance, can also be represented as a plane within the color cube. Figure 8-10 shows a triangle with each vertex at full saturation for the red, green, and blue color components. The code to display this triangle is in Listing 8-1, and in the example program TRIANGLES on the CD.

Listing 8-1 Drawing a smooth-shaded triangle with red, green, and blue corners

```
// Enable smooth shading
    glShadeModel(GL_SMOOTH);
    // Draw the triangle
    glBegin(GL_TRIANGLES);
            // Red Apex
            glColor3ub((GLubyte)255,(GLubyte)0,(GLubyte)0);
            glVertex3f(0.0f,200.0f,0.0f);

            // Green on the right bottom corner
            glColor3ub((GLubyte)0,(GLubyte)255,(GLubyte)0);
            glVertex3f(200.0f,-70.0f,0.0f);
```

```
        // Blue on the left bottom corner
        glColor3ub((GLubyte)0,(GLubyte)0,(GLubyte)255);
        glVertex3f(-200.0f, -70.0f, 0.0f);
glEnd();
```

Setting the Shading Model

The first line of Listing 8-1 actually sets the shading model OpenGL uses to do smooth shading—the model we have been discussing. This is the default shading model, but it's a good idea to call this function anyway to ensure that your program is operating the way you intended.

(The other shading model that can be specified with glShadeModel is GL_FLAT for *flat shading.* Flat shading means that no shading calculations are performed on the interior of primitives. Generally, with flat shading the color of the primitive's interior is the color that was specified for the last vertex. The only exception is for a GL_POLY-GON primitive, in which case the color is that of the first vertex.)

Then the code in Listing 8-1 sets the top of the triangle to be pure red, the lower-right corner to be green, and the remaining bottom-left corner to be blue. Because smooth shading is specified, the interior of the triangle is shaded to provide a smooth transition between each corner.

The output from the TRIANGLE program is shown in Figure 8-11. This represents the plane shown graphically in Figure 8-10.

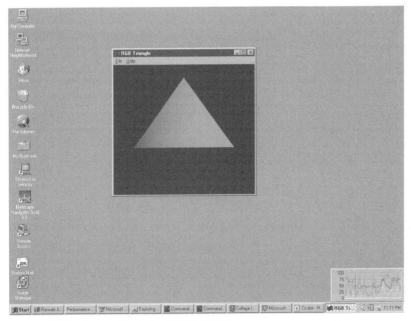

Figure 8-11 Output from the TRIANGLES program

Polygons, more complex than triangles, can also have different colors specified for each vertex. In these instances, the underlying logic for shading can become more intricate. Fortunately, you never have to worry about it with OpenGL. No matter how complex your polygon, OpenGL will successfully shade the interior points between each vertex.

Note that you will rarely wish to do this type of shading yourself, anyway. This is primarily used to produce lighting effects, and OpenGL once again comes to the rescue. We'll cover lighting in the Chapter 9.

Windows Palettes

The TRIANGLE and CCUBE example programs work reasonably well regardless of how many colors are available. If you can change the color depth of your system, try running these programs at the various color depths, starting at 16 colors and going up to 16 million if possible. You'll notice that the colors make a smooth transition regardless of color depth, but the higher color depths provide a smoother and more appealing image. Figures 8-12a and 8-12b show the output of the TRIANGLES sample with 16 colors and 16 million colors, respectively. Even though these pictures are not in color, you can see how much smoother the second triangle appears.

Color Matching

What happens when you try to draw a pixel of a particular color using the RGB values we have discussed? Internally, Windows defines a color using 8 bits each for the red, green, and blue components using the RGB macro, and you can use glColor3ub to duplicate this functionality within OpenGL.

If the PC graphics card is in 24-bit color mode, then each pixel is displayed precisely in the color specified by the 24-bit value (three 8-bit intensities). In the 15- and 16-bit color modes, Windows passes the 24-bit color value to the display driver, which converts the color to a 15- or 16-bit color value before displaying it. In 24-bit color mode, the RGB color cube measured 255 (or 8 bits) per side. In 15- or 16-bit

Figure 8-12a Output of the TRIANGLES sample with 16 colors

Figure 8-12b With 16 million colors the triangle is much smoother

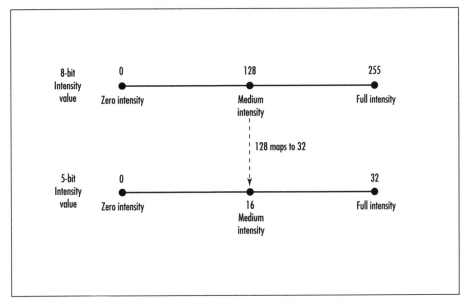

Figure 8-13 A medium-intensity red being mapped from an 8-bit value to a 5-bit value

color mode, the color cube measures 32 (5 bits) or 64 (6 bits) on a side. The device driver then matches the 24-bit color value to the nearest color match in the 15 or 16-bit color cube.

Figure 8-13 shows how an 8-bit red value might be mapped to a 5-bit red value.

At the low end of the scale, 4-bit color mode can only display 16 colors. These colors are fixed and cannot be modified. Internally, Windows still represents each color with a 24-bit RGB value. When you specify a color to use for drawing operations using the RGB macro or glColor3ub, Windows uses the nearest color of the 16 available to fulfill the request. If the color is being used for fill operations, the color is approximated by *dithering* the available colors.

Dithering

Having only 16 colors to work with makes the 4-bit color modes poorly suited for graphics. One thing the Windows GDI will do to help is to perform dithering on solid shapes and objects in this mode. Dithering is a means of placing different colors close together to produce the illusion of another composite color. For example, if you place yellow and blue squares together in a checkerboard pattern, the pattern will take on a greenish appearance. Without actually mixing the colors, the green would have a grainy appearance. By changing the proportion of yellow to green squares, you are effectively changing the intensities of yellow and green.

Windows uses dithering to produce colors not available in the current palette. In 16-color mode, image quality is typically very poor for more complex scenes. Figure

8-12 is a vivid demonstration of Windows dithering; we attempted to produce the RGB triangle on a system with only 16 colors. Generally, Windows does not perform dithering for OpenGL.

OpenGL can also do its own dithering, providing the command

```
glEnable(GL_DITHER);
```

This can sometimes improve image quality substantially in 8- and 15-bit color modes. You can see dithering in action in the example program DITHER from this chapter's subdirectory on the CD. This program draws a cube with sides of various colors and allows dithering to be enabled or disabled from the menu. When run in 8-bit color mode or better, dithering has little effect, but in the 4-bit, 16-color mode the dithered scene is remarkably different.

Advantages of a Palette in 8-Bit Mode

The 8-bit color modes can display 256 colors, and this results in a remarkable improvement for color graphics. When Windows is running in a color mode that supports 256 colors, it would make sense if those colors were evenly distributed across RGB color space. Then all applications would have a relatively wide choice of colors, and when a color was selected, the nearest available color would be used. Unfortunately, this is not very practical in the real world.

Since the 256 colors in the palette for the device can be selected from over 16 million different colors, an application can substantially improve the quality of its graphics by carefully selecting those colors—and many do. For example, to produce a seascape, additional shades of blue will be needed. CAD and modeling applications modify the palette to produce smooth shading of a surface of a particular single color. For example, the scene may require as many as 200 shades of gray to accurately render the image of a pipe's cross section. Thus, applications for the PC typically change this palette to meet their needs, resulting in near-photographic quality for many images and scenes. For 256 color bitmaps, the Windows .bmp format even has an array that's 256 entries long, containing 24-bit RGB values specifying the palette for the stored image.

An application can create a palette with the CreatePalette() function, identifying the palette by a handle of type HPALETTE. This function takes a logical palette structure (LOGPALETTE) that contains 256 entries, each specifying 8-bit values for red, green, and blue components. But before we examine palette creation, let's take a look at how multitasked applications can share the single system palette in 8-bit color mode.

Palette Arbitration

Windows multitasking allows many applications to be on screen at once. The hardware supports only 256 colors on screen at once, however, so all applications must share the same *system palette*. If one application changes the system palette, images in the other windows may have scrambled colors, producing some undesired psychedelic effects. To arbitrate palette usage among applications, Windows sends a set of messages. Applications are notified when another application has changed the system

palette, and they are notified when their window has received focus and palette modi-
fication is possible.

When an application receives keyboard or mouse input focus, Windows sends a
WM_QUERYNEWPALETTE message to the main window of the application. This
message asks the application if it wants to *realize* a new palette. Realizing a palette
means the application copies the palette entries from its private palette to the system
palette. To do this, the application must first select the palette into the device context
for the window being updated, and then call RealizePalette(). Listing 8-2 presents the
code for this message handler; it will be in all subsequent examples from this book.

Listing 8-2 Typical palette-arbitration code for Windows-based applications

```
static HPALETTE hPalette = NULL;         // Permenant palette handle


  ...
  ...
// Palette is created and referenced by hPalette
  ...
  ...
// Windows is telling the application that it may modify
// the system palette. This message in essance asks the
// application for a new palette.
case WM_QUERYNEWPALETTE:
        // If the palette was created.
        if(hPalette)
                {
                int nRet;

                // Selects the palette into the current device context
                SelectPalette(hDC, hPalette, FALSE);

                // Map entries from the currently selected palette to
                // the system palette. The return value is the number
                // of palette entries modified.
                nRet = RealizePalette(hDC);

                // Repaint, forces remap of palette in current window
                InvalidateRect(hWnd,NULL,FALSE);

                return nRet;
                }
        break;

// This window may set the palette, even though it is not the
// currently active window.
case WM_PALETTECHANGED:
        // Don't do anything if the palette does not exist, or if
        // this is the window that changed the palette.
        if((hPalette != NULL) && ((HWND)wParam != hWnd))
                {
                // Select the palette into the device context
                SelectPalette(hDC,hPalette,FALSE);

                // Map entries to system palette
                RealizePalette(hDC);
```

continued on next page

continued from previous page

```
                        // Remap the current colors to the newly realized palette
                        UpdateColors(hDC);
                        return 0;
                        }
            break;
```

Another message sent by Windows for palette realization is WM_PALET-TECHANGED. This message is sent to windows that can realize their palette but may not have the current focus. When this message is sent, you must also check the value of wParam. If wParam contains the handle to the current window receiving the message, then WM_QUERYNEWPALETTE has already been processed, and the palette does not need to be realized again.

Note also in Listing 8-2 that the value of hPalette is checked against NULL before either of these palette-realization messages is processed. If the application is not running in 8-bit color mode, then no palette needs to be created or realized by these functions. Structuring your code in this way makes it useful for displays that don't use palettes as well as those that do.

Creating a Palette

Unfortunately, palette considerations are a necessary evil if your application is to run on the 8-bit hardware that's still in use in some environments. So what do you do if your code is executing on a machine that only supports 256 colors?

For image reproduction, we recommend selecting a range of colors that closely match the original colors. For OpenGL rendering under most circumstances, however, you want the widest possible range of colors for general-purpose use. The trick is to select the palette colors so that they're evenly distributed throughout the color cube. Then, whenever a color is specified that is not already in the palette, Windows will select the nearest color in the color cube. As mentioned earlier, this is not ideal for some applications, but for OpenGL rendered scenes it is the best we can do. Unless there is substantial texture mapping in the scene with a wide variety of colors, results are usually acceptable.

Do You Need a Palette?

To determine if your application needs a palette, you can call DescribePixelFormat() after you have set the pixel format. Test the dwFlags member of the PIXELFORMAT-DECRIPTOR returned by DescribePixelFormat(), for the bit value PFD_NEED_PALETTE. If this bit is set, you will need to create a palette for use by your application. Listing 8-3 shows the necessary code for this test.

Listing 8-3 Testing to see if an application needs a palette

```
PIXELFORMATDESCRIPTOR pfd;      // Pixel Format Descriptor
int nPixelFormat;               // Pixel format index

// Get the pixel format index and retrieve the pixel format description
nPixelFormat = GetPixelFormat(hDC);
```

```
DescribePixelFormat(hDC, nPixelFormat, sizeof(PIXELFORMATDESCRIPTOR), &pfd);

// Does this pixel format require a palette?
if(!(pfd.dwFlags & PFD_NEED_PALETTE))
        return NULL;    // Does not need a palette

// Palette creation code
  ...
  ...
```

The Palette's Structure

To create a palette, you must first allocate memory for a LOGPALETTE structure. This structure is filled with the information that describes the palette, and then is passed to the Win32 function CreatePalette(). The LOGPALETTE structure is defined as follows:

```
typedef struct tagLOGPALETTE { // lgpl
    WORD           palVersion;
    WORD           palNumEntries;
    PALETTEENTRY palPalEntry[1];
} LOGPALETTE;
```

The first two members are the palette header and contain the palette version (always set to 0x300) and the number of color entries (256 for 8-bit modes). Each entry is then defined as a PALETTEENTRY structure that contains the RGB components of the color entry.

The following code allocates space for the logical palette:

```
LOGPALETTE *pPal;               // Pointer to memory for logical palette
  ...
  ...
// Allocate space for a logical palette structure plus all the palette
// entries
pPal = (LOGPALETTE*)malloc(sizeof(LOGPALETTE) + nColors*sizeof(PALETTEENTRY));
```

Here, nColors specifies the number of colors to place in the palette, which for our purposes is always 256.

Each entry in the palette then is a PALETTEENTRY structure, which is defined as follows:

```
typedef struct tagPALETTEENTRY { // pe
    BYTE peRed;
    BYTE peGreen;
    BYTE peBlue;
    BYTE peFlags;
} PALETTEENTRY;
```

The peRed, peGreen, and peBlue members specify an 8-bit value that represents the relative intensities of each color component. In this way, each of the 256 palette entries contains a 24-color definition. The peFlags member describes advanced usage of the palette entries. For OpenGL purposes you can just set this to NULL.

In addition to the 3-3-2 palette, Windows can support other 8-bit palettes for doing things such as specifying 200 shades of gray.

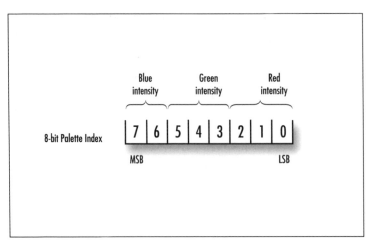

Figure 8-14 3-3-2 palette packing

The 3-3-2 Palette

Now comes the tricky part. Not only must our 256 palette entries be spread evenly throughout the RGB color cube, but they must be in a certain order. It is this order that enables OpenGL to find the color it needs, or the closest available color in the palette. Remember that in an 8-bit color mode you have 3 bits each for red and green, and 2 bits for blue. This is commonly referred to as a *3-3-2 palette*. So our RGB color cube measures 8 by 8 by 3 along the red, green, and blue axes, respectively.

To find the color needed in the palette, an 8-8-8 color reference (the 24-bit color mode setup) is scaled to a 3-3-2 reference. This 8-bit value is then the index into our palette array. The red intensities of 0–7 in the 3-3-2 palette must correspond to the intensities 0–255 in the 8-8-8 palette. Figure 8-14 illustrates how the red, green, and blue components are combined to make the palette index.

When we build the palette, we loop through all values from 0 to 255. We then decompose the index into the red, green, and blue intensities represented by these values (in terms of the 3-3-2 palette). Each component is multiplied by 255 and divided by the maximum value represented, which has the effect of smoothly stepping the intensities from 0 to 7 for red and green, and from 0 to 3 for the blue. Table 8-1 shows some sample palette entries, to demonstrate component calculation.

Table 8-1 A Few Sample Palette Entries for a 3-3-2 Palette

Palette Entry	Binary (B G R)	Blue Component	Green Component	Red Component
0	00 000 000	0	0	0
1	00 000 001	0	0	1*255/7
2	00 000 010	0	0	2*255/7

Palette Entry	Binary (B G R)	Blue Component	Green Component	Red Component
3	00 000 011	0	0	3*255/7
9	00 001 001	0	1*255/7	1*255/7
10	00 001 010	0	1*255/7	2*255/7
137	10 001 001	2*255/3	1*255/7	1*255/7
138	10 001 010	2*255/7	1*255/7	2*255/3
255	11 111 111	3*255/3	7*255/7	7*255/7

Building the Palette

Unfortunately, at this time OpenGL for Windows will only support 3-3-2 palettes in RGBA color mode. This is actually specified in the PIXELFORMATDESCRIPTOR returned by DescribePixelFormat(). The members cRedBits, cGreenBits, and cBluebits specify 3, 3, and 2, respectively, for the number of bits that can represent each component. Furthermore, the cRedShift, cGreenShift, and cBlueShift values specify how much to shift the respective component value to the left (in this case, 0, 3, and 6 for red, green, and blue shifts). These sets of values compose the palette index (Figure 8-14).

The code in Listing 8-4 creates a palette if needed and returns its handle. This function makes use of the component bit counts and shift information in the PIXELFORMATDESCRIPTOR to accommodate any subsequent palette requirements, such as a 2-2-2 palette.

Listing 8-4 Function to create a palette for OpenGL

```
// If necessary, creates a 3-3-2 palette for the device context listed.
HPALETTE GetOpenGLPalette(HDC hDC)
        {
        HPALETTE hRetPal = NULL;        // Handle to palette to be created
        PIXELFORMATDESCRIPTOR pfd;      // Pixel Format Descriptor
        LOGPALETTE *pPal;               // Pointer to memory for logical palette
        int nPixelFormat;               // Pixel format index
        int nColors;                    // Number of entries in palette
        int i;                          // Counting variable
        BYTE RedRange,GreenRange,BlueRange;
                                        // Range for each color entry (7,7,and 3)

        // Get the pixel format index and retrieve the pixel format description
        nPixelFormat = GetPixelFormat(hDC);
        DescribePixelFormat(hDC, nPixelFormat, sizeof(PIXELFORMATDESCRIPTOR), &pfd);

        // Does this pixel format require a palette?  If not, do not create a
        // palette and just return NULL
        if(!(pfd.dwFlags & PFD_NEED_PALETTE))
                return NULL;

        // Number of entries in palette. 8 bits yields 256 entries
        nColors = 1 << pfd.cColorBits;

        // Allocate space for a logical palette structure plus all the palette
```

continued on next page

continued from previous page

```
// entries
pPal = (LOGPALETTE*)malloc(sizeof(LOGPALETTE) + nColors*sizeof(PALETTEENTRY));

// Fill in palette header
pPal->palVersion = 0x300;               // Windows 3.0
pPal->palNumEntries = nColors;          // table size

// Build mask of all 1's. This creates a number represented by having
// the low order x bits set, where x = pfd.cRedBits, pfd.cGreenBits,and
// pfd.cBlueBits.
RedRange = (1 << pfd.cRedBits) -1;           // 7 for 3-3-2 palettes
GreenRange = (1 << pfd.cGreenBits) - 1;      // 7 for 3-3-2 palettes
BlueRange = (1 << pfd.cBlueBits) -1;         // 3 for 3-3-2 palettes

// Loop through all the palette entries
for(i = 0; i < nColors; i++)
        {
        // Fill in the 8-bit equivalents for each component
        pPal->palPalEntry[i].peRed = (i >> pfd.cRedShift) & RedRange;
        pPal->palPalEntry[i].peRed = (unsigned char)(
                (double) pPal->palPalEntry[i].peRed * 255.0 / RedRange);

        pPal->palPalEntry[i].peGreen = (i >> pfd.cGreenShift) & GreenRange;
        pPal->palPalEntry[i].peGreen = (unsigned char)(
                (double)pPal->palPalEntry[i].peGreen * 255.0 /GreenRange);

        pPal->palPalEntry[i].peBlue = (i >> pfd.cBlueShift) & BlueRange;
        pPal->palPalEntry[i].peBlue = (unsigned char)(
                (double)pPal->palPalEntry[i].peBlue * 255.0 / BlueRange);

        pPal->palPalEntry[i].peFlags = (unsigned char) NULL;
        }

// Create the palette
hRetPal = CreatePalette(pPal);

// Go ahead and select and realize the palette for this device context
SelectPalette(hDC,hRetPal,FALSE);
RealizePalette(hDC);

// Free the memory used for the logical palette structure
free(pPal);

// Return the handle to the new palette
return hRetPal;
}
```

Palette Creation and Disposal

The palette should be created and realized before the rendering context is created or made current. The function in Listing 8-4 requires only the device context, once the pixel format has been set. It will then return a handle to a palette if one is needed. Listing 8-5 shows the sequence of operations when the window is created and destroyed. This is similar to code presented previously for the creation and destruction of the rendering context, only now it also takes into account the possible existence of a palette.

Listing 8-5 A palette is created and destroyed

```
// Window creation, setup for OpenGL
case WM_CREATE:
        // Store the device context
        hDC = GetDC(hWnd);

        // Select the pixel format
        SetDCPixelFormat(hDC);

        // Create the palette if needed
        hPalette = GetOpenGLPalette(hDC);

        // Create the rendering context and make it current
        hRC = wglCreateContext(hDC);
        wglMakeCurrent(hDC, hRC);
        break;


// Window is being destroyed, cleanup
case WM_DESTROY:
        // Deselect the current rendering context and delete it
        wglMakeCurrent(hDC,NULL);
        wglDeleteContext(hRC);

        // If a palette was created, destroy it here
        if(hPalette != NULL)
                DeleteObject(hPalette);

        // Tell the application to terminate after the window
        // is gone.
        PostQuitMessage(0);
        break;
```

Some Restrictions Apply

Not all of your 256 palette entries will actually be mapped to the system palette. Windows reserves 20 entries for static system colors that include the standard 16 VGA/EGA colors. This protects the standard windows components (title bars, buttons, etc.) from alteration whenever an application changes the system palette. When your application realizes its palette, these 20 colors will not be overwritten. Fortunately, some of these colors already exist or are closely matched in the 3-3-2 palette. Those that don't are closely enough matched that you shouldn't be able to tell the difference.

Color Index Mode

OpenGL also supports the alternative *color index* mode. In this mode, you specify a color for drawing operations by specifying an index into an array of colors, rather than as an RGB triplet.

You cannot use color index mode and RGBA color mode together. This means if you use color index mode on a true-color device (or near true-color, such as a 16-bit color card), you won't have access to all the available colors. Under some implementations, the color index palette can be up to 4,096 entries long. The Microsoft implementation however, only supports 256 entries.

You can use color index mode to do contour mapping in which some function of the surface returns an index into the palette. It is somewhat faster than RGBA, and the limitations of the 3-3-2 palette do not exist. For example, if you need 200 shades of gray, you can have them. However, some of the lighting effects discussed in the next chapter are not available under color index mode either.

Why Use Color Index Mode?

There are really very few good reasons to use color index mode. Typically, this mode is used to get more control over the palette. You can also do *palette animation,* but only on devices that support palettes (8-bit display cards). This doesn't mean you can't use color index mode on these devices; it only means there is no corresponding hardware palette with which you can perform animation. Palette animation occurs when you change the entries in the palette, which causes a corresponding change in all screen pixels having that palette index. This can produce color cycling for some special effects.

Another reason to use color index mode is for applications that use color to indicate a third dimension—to indicate the pressure at certain spatialregions, for instance. You can also use this mode for false color images that do not require an organized palette. Finally, color index mode can be somewhat faster in 8-bit color modes because only one color channel (as opposed to three, one each for red, green, and blue) needs to be manipulated instead of three.

In addition to limiting the color selection, color index mode does not support some of OpenGL's other special effects—including many lighting effects and shading, fog, anti-aliasing, and alpha blending. Generally, it is better to use RGBA mode.

As mentioned, the most significant advantage of using color index mode is for more palette control on 8-bit display devices. The 3-3-2 palette limits your color choices, and if you want 200 shades of red to do really smooth shading on an 8-bit display, you are out of luck. In color index mode, however, the palette entries range from darkest to lightest colors. You can separate the palette into as many or as few bands as you like. The INDEX sample program displays a triangle shaded from black to bright red (see Figure 8-15). This shading is not possible in 8-bit color mode using at 3-3-2 palette.

Using Color Index Mode

To specify color index mode, all you need to do is set the iPixelType member of the PIXELFORMATDESCRIPTOR to PFD_TYPE_COLORINDEX. First, though, you need to create a palette. With color index mode, the palette is specific to the application. For our INDEX sample program, we want a palette consisting only of shades of red to do very smooth shading in an 8-bit color mode. Listing 8-6 is the code to create this palette.

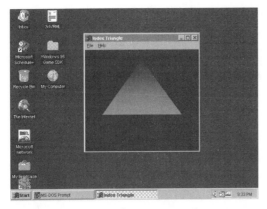

Figure 8-15 Output from INDEX showing over 200 shades of red for smooth shading

Listing 8-6 Code to create a palette consisting only of shades of red

```
// Creates a color ramp from black to bright red
HPALETTE GetRedPalette(HDC hDC)
        {
        HPALETTE hRetPal = NULL;         // Handle to palette to be created
        LOGPALETTE *pPal;                // Pointer to memory for logical palette
        int i;                                   // Counting variable


        // Allocate space for a logical palette structure plus all the palette
        // entries
        pPal =
                (LOGPALETTE*)malloc(sizeof(LOGPALETTE)+256*sizeof(PALETTEENTRY));

        // Fill in palette header
        pPal->palVersion = 0x300;        // Windows 3.0
        pPal->palNumEntries = 256;       // table size


        // Loop through all the palette entries, creating a graduated red
        // palette containing only shades of red
        for(i = 10; i < 246; i++)
                {
                pPal->palPalEntry[i].peRed = i; // Red intensity from 0 to 255
                pPal->palPalEntry[i].peGreen = 0;
                pPal->palPalEntry[i].peBlue = 0;
                pPal->palPalEntry[i].peFlags = (unsigned char) NULL;
                }

        // Create the palette
        hRetPal = CreatePalette(pPal);
```

continued on next page

continued from previous page

```
// Go ahead and select and realize the palette for this device context
SelectPalette(hDC,hRetPal,FALSE);
RealizePalette(hDC);

// Free the memory used for the logical palette structure
free(pPal);

// Return the handle to the new palette
return hRetPal;
}
```

Notice that this code always returns a palette. No check is made to see if the pixel format required a palette. This is because you can use color index mode even in the high-color modes. All of the other code concerning palette realization remains unaffected.

Show the Triangle

Now the code to render the triangle sets the color of the triangle's apex to color index 0, which is the darkest entry in the palette with 0 intensity (black). The color for the bottom two corners is set to palette index 255, the brightest shade of red. With smooth shading enabled, this code (Listing 8-7) produces the triangle seen in Figure 8-15.

Listing 8-7 Code to render the shaded triangle in the INDEX program

```
void RenderScene(void)
    {
    // Clear the window with current clearing color
    glClear(GL_COLOR_BUFFER_BIT);

    // Enable smooth shading
    glShadeModel(GL_SMOOTH);

    // Draw the triangle
    glBegin(GL_TRIANGLES);
            // Darkest Red Apex (black)
            glIndexi(0);
            glVertex3f(0.0f,200.0f,0.0f);

            // Brightest red bottom corners
            glIndexi(255);
            glVertex3f(200.0f,-70.0f,0.0f);
            glVertex3f(-200.0f, -70.0f, 0.0f);
    glEnd();

    // Flush drawing commands
    glFlush();
    }
```

Summary

This chapter covers one of the most important features supported by a graphics package: color. You have seen how to specify a color in terms of its RGB components, and how these components relate to one another in the RGB color cube. Your understanding of glColor has been expanded to include the coloring of vertices, and you have seen how this affects shading. We explained OpenGL's selection of colors in 4-, 8-, 16-, and 24-bit Windows color modes. We demonstrated the building of a 3-3-2 palette for use by OpenGL in 8-bit color modes. Finally, we took a brief look at color index mode and its utilization to gain better palette control in 8-bit color modes.

Good use of color and shading is a prerequisite for good 3D graphics. The upcoming chapter explains how OpenGL uses shading to produce lighting effects. You'll learn how to specify material colors and lighting conditions and allow OpenGL to select the drawing colors.

Reference Section

GLCLEARINDEX

Purpose	Sets the clear value for the color index buffers.
Include File	<gl.h>
Syntax	void glClearIndex(GLfloat color);
Description	This function specifies the color index to use in color index mode to clear the color buffers. This has the net effect of clearing the window and setting the background color to the color in the index specified by the *color* parameter.
Parameters	
color	GLfloat: The value to use when the color index buffers are cleared with glClear. The default is 0.
Returns	None.
Example	See the sample program INDEX in this chapter.
See Also	glClear, glGet

GLCOLOR

Purpose	Sets the current color when in RGBA color mode.
Include File	<gl.h>
Variations	void **glColor3b**(GLbyte red,GLbyte green, GLbyte blue);
	void **glColor3d**(GLdouble red, GLdouble green, GLdouble blue);
	void **glColor3f**(GLfloat red, GLfloat green, GLfloat blue);
	void **glColor3i**(GLint red, GLint green, GLint blue);
	void **glColor3s**(GLshort red, GLshort green, GLshort blue);
	void **glColor3ub**(GLubyte red, GLubyte green, GLubyte blue);
	void **glColor3ui**(GLuint red, GLuint green, GLuint blue);
	void **glColor3us**(GLushort red, GLushort green, GLushort blue);
	void **glColor4b**(GLbyte red, GLbyte green, GLbyte blue, GLbyte alpha);
	void **glColor4d**(GLdouble red, GLdouble green, GLdouble blue, GLdouble alpha);

void **glColor4f**(GLfloat red, GLfloat green, GLfloat blue, GLfloat alpha);
void **glColor4i**(GLint red, GLint green, GLint blue, GLint alpha);
void **glColor4s**(GLshort red, GLshort green, GLshort blue, GLshort alpha);
void **glColor4ub**(GLubyte red, GLubyte green, GLubyte blue, GLubyte alpha);
void **glColor4ui**(GLuint red, GLuint green, GLuint blue, GLuint alpha);
void **glColor4us**(GLushort red, GLushort green, GLushort blue, GLushort alpha);
void **glColor3bv**(const GLbyte *v);
void **glColor3dv**(const GLdouble *v);
void **glColor3fv**(const GLfloat *v);
void **glColor3iv**(const GLint *v);
void **glColor3sv**(const GLshort *v);
void **glColor3ubv**(const GLubyte *v);
void **glColor3uiv**(const GLuint *v);
void **glColor3usv**(const GLushort *v);
void **glColor4bv**(const GLbyte *v);
void **glColor4dv**(const GLdouble *v);
void **glColor4fv**(const GLfloat *v);
void **glColor4iv**(const GLint *v);
void **glColor4sv**(const GLshort *v);
void **glColor4ubv**(const GLubyte *v);
void **glColor4uiv**(const GLuint *v);
void **glColor4usv**(const GLushort *v);

Description   This function sets the current color by specifying separate red, green, and blue components of the color. Some functions also accept an alpha component. Each component represents the range of intensity from zero (0.0) to full intensity (1.0). Functions with the v suffix take a pointer to an array that specifies the components. Each element in the array must be of the same type. When the alpha component is not specified, it is implicitly set to 1.0. When non-floating point types are specified, the range from zero to the largest value represented by that type is mapped to the floating point range 0.0 to 1.0.

Parameters

red   Specifies the red component of the color.

green   Specifies the green component of the color.

blue   Specifies the blue component of the color.

alpha   Specifies the alpha component of the color. Used only in variations that take four arguments.

*v   A pointer to an array of red, green, blue, and possibly alpha values.

Returns   None.

Example   The following code from the CCUBE example in this chapter sets one of the corners of the color cube to white.

```
// Front face
glBegin(GL_POLYGON);

        // White
        glColor3ub((GLubyte) 255, (GLubyte)255, (GLubyte)255);
        glVertex3f(50.0f,50.0f,50.0f);
```

See Also   glIndex

GLCOLORMASK

Purpose	Enables or disables modification of color components in the color buffers.
Include File	<gl.h>
Syntax	void glColorMask(GLboolean bRed, GLboolean bGreen, GLboolean bBlue, GLboolean bAlpha);
Description	This function allows changes to individual color components in the color buffer to be disabled or enabled (all are enabled by default). For example, setting the bAlpha argument to GL_FALSE disallows changes to the alpha color component.
Parameters	
bRed	GLboolean: Specifies whether the red component may be modified.
bGreen	GLboolean: Specifies whether the green component may be modified.
bBlue	GLboolean: Specifies whether the blue component may be modified.
bAlpha	GLboolean: Specifies whether the alpha component may be modified.
Returns	None.
Example	See the sample program MASK on the CD for this chapter.
See Also	glColor, glIndex, glIndexMask, glDepthMask, glStencilMask

GLINDEX

Purpose	Sets the current color index to be used for color operations.
Include File	<gl.h>
Variations	void **glIndexd**(GLdouble c);
	void **glIndexf**(GLfloat c);
	void **glIndexi**(GLint c);
	void **glIndexs**(GLshort c);
	void **glIndexdv**(const GLdouble *c);
	void **glIndexfv**(const GLfloat *c);
	void **glIndexiv**(const GLint *c);
	void **glIndexsv**(const GLshort *c);

Description	This function changes the current color index to the one specified by *c*. This indexvalue is maintained internally as a floating point number.
Parameters	
c	The new color index to use for all subsequent operations.
*c	A pointer to the new color index to use for all subsequent operations.
Returns	None.
Example	The following code from the sample program INDEX draws a smoothly shaded triangle. The top of the triangle is set to color index 0 which has been set to zero, and the bottom corners to color index 255 which has been set to bright red.

```
// Draw the triangle
glBegin(GL_TRIANGLES);
        // Darkest Red Apex (black)
        glIndexi(0);
        glVertex3f(0.0f,200.0f,0.0f);

        // Brightest red bottom corners
        glIndexi(255);
        glVertex3f(200.0f,-70.0f,0.0f);
        glVertex3f(-200.0f, -70.0f, 0.0f);
glEnd();
```

See Also	glColor

GLINDEXMASK

Purpose	Protects individual bits in the color index buffer from being set.
Include File	<gl.h>
Syntax	void glIndexMask(GLuint mask);
Description	This function allows masking of individual bits in the color index buffer. Where the mask bit is set, the bits are writeable; where they are zero, they are write-protected from pixel operations. This function only applies to color index mode.
Parameters	
mask	GLuint: Specifies the binary bit mask to enable or disable writing to individual bits in the color index buffer.
Returns	None.
Example	See the sample program MASK on the CD for this chapter.
See Also	glIndex, glDepthMask, glStencilMask

GLLOGICOP

Purpose	Sets the logical pixel operation for color index mode.
Include File	<gl.h>

Syntax	void glLogicOp(GLenum opcode);
Description	The logical pixel operation defines the combination of pixel values. When a new color index value is specified for a pixel location, it is combined logically with the current color index value for that pixel. To enable logical pixel operations, call glEnable(GL_LOGIC_OP), to disable call glDisable(GL_LOGIC_OP). When logical pixel operations are enabled, incoming pixel values are combined with existing pixel values in the manner specified by *opcode*. When logical operations are not enabled, the net effect of pixel operations is as if GL_COPY were specified. Logical pixel operations are not supported in RGBA color mode.
Parameters	
opcode	GLEnum: Specifies the logical pixel mode to use. Any of the values listed in Table 8-2 are valid. This table lists the logical operation and the result of the operation, with s representing the source color index value, and d representing the destination color index value.
Returns	None.
Example	See the FLASHER example program from the CD. This example uses GL_XOR to produce smooth animation without double buffering.
See Also	glGet, glIsEnabled, glEnable, glDisable

Table 8-2 Valid Pixel Copy Operations

Opcode	Resulting Value
GL_CLEAR	0
GL_SET	1
GL_COPY	s
GL_COPY_INVERTED	!s
GL_NOOP	d
GL_INVERT	!d
GL_AND	s & d
GL_NAND	!(s & d)
GL_OR	s	d
GL_NOR	!(s | d)
GL_XOR	s ^ d
GL_EQUIV	!(s ^ d)
GL_AND_REVERSE	s & !d
GL_AND_INVERTED	!s & d
GL_OR_REVERSE	s	!d
GL_OR_INVERTED	!s	d

GLSHADEMODEL

Purpose	Sets default shading to flat or smooth.
Include File	<gl.h>
Syntax	void glShadeModel(GLenum mode);
Description	OpenGL primitives are always shaded, but the shading model may be flat (GL_FLAT) or smooth (GL_SMOOTH). In the simplest of scenarios, one color is set with glColor() before a primitive is drawn. This primitive is solid and flat (does not vary) throughout, regardless of the shading. If a different color is specified for each vertex, then the resulting image will vary with the shading model. With smooth shading, the color of the polygon's interior points are interpolated from the colors specified at the vertices. This means the color will vary from one color to the next between two vertices. The color variation follows a line through the color cube between the two colors. If lighting is enabled, OpenGL will do other calculations to determine the correct colors (see Chapter 9). In flat shading, the color specified for the last vertex is used throughout the region of the primitive. The only exception is for GL_POLYGON, in which case the color used throughout the region is the one specified for the first vertex.
Parameters	
mode	Specifies the shading model to use, either GL_FLAT or GL_SMOOTH. The default is GL_SMOOTH.
Returns	None.
Example	See the TRIANGLE and CCUBE examples from Chapter 8's subdirectory on the CD.
See Also	glColor, glLight, glLightModel

9

LIGHTING AND LAMPS

9

LIGHTING AND LAMPS

What you'll learn in this chapter:

How to...	Functions You'll Use
Set the lighting model	glLightModel
Set lighting parameters	glLight
Set material reflective properties	glColorMaterial, glMaterial
Use surface normals	glNormal

This chapter discusses lighting: in our opinion, the honey spot of OpenGL. You've been learning OpenGL from the ground up—how to put programs together, then how to assemble objects from primitives and manipulate them in 3D space. In Chapter 8 we showed you how to add color to your objects and do smooth shading. All well and good, but let's face it—any good summer co-op student with a good book on computer graphics could have put this much together themselves building only on the Windows GDI. To recoin a phrase, *"Where's the Beef?"*

To put it succinctly, the beef starts here. For most of the rest of this book, science takes a back seat and magic rules. According to Arthur C. Clarke, "Any sufficiently advanced technology is indistinguishable from magic." Of course there is no real magic involved in lighting, but it sure can seem that way at times. (If you *want* to dig into the mathematics, see Appendix B.)

Another name for this chapter might be "Adding Realism to Your Scenes." You see, there is more to an object's color in the real world than what we explained in Chapter

8. In addition to having a color, objects can appear shiny or dull or may even glow with their own light. An object's apparent color will vary with bright or dim lighting, and even the color of the light hitting an object will make a difference. An illuminated object can even be shaded across its surface when lit or viewed from an angle.

Most of the rest of Parts II and III are concerned with techniques that allow you to add more and more realism to your scenes. So put away your calculators (if you want), bring out your wizard's cap, and take a deep breath… The magic show starts here!

Light in the Real World

Real objects don't appear in a solid or shaded color based solely on their RGB value. Figure 9-1 shows the output from the program JET from the CD. It's a simple jet airplane, hand plotted with triangles using only the methods covered so far in this book. As usual, JET and the other programs in this chapter allow you to spin the object around by using the arrow keys to better see the effects.

The selection of colors is meant to highlight the three-dimensional structure of the jet. Aside from the crude assemblage of triangles, however, you can see that it looks hardly anything like a real object. Suppose you constructed a model of this airplane and painted each flat surface the colors represented. The model would still appear glossy or flat depending on the kind of paint used, and the color of each flat surface would vary with the angle of your view and any sources of light.

OpenGL does a very good job of approximating the real world in terms of lighting conditions. Unless an object emits its own light, it is illuminated by three different kinds of light: ambient, diffuse, and specular.

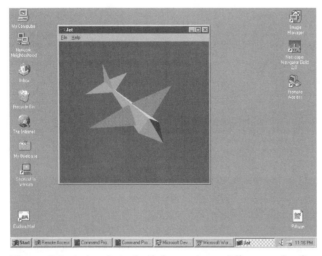

Figure 9-1 A simple jet built by setting a different color for each triangle

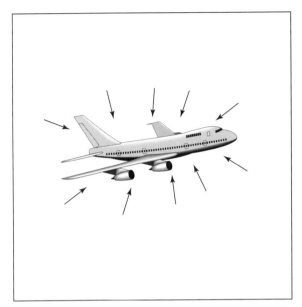

Figure 9-2 An object illuminated purely by ambient light

Ambient Light

Ambient light is light that doesn't come from any particular direction. It has a source, but the rays of light have bounced around the room or scene and become direction-less. Objects illuminated by ambient light are evenly lit on all surfaces in all directions. You can think of all previous examples in this book as being lit by a bright ambient light, because the objects were always visible and evenly colored (or shaded) regardless of their rotation or viewing angle. Figure 9-2 shows an object illuminated by ambient light.

Diffuse Light

Diffuse light comes from a particular direction but is reflected evenly off a surface. Even though the light is reflected evenly, the object surface is brighter if the light is pointed directly at the surface than if the light grazes the surface from an angle. A good example of a diffuse light source is fluorescent lighting, or sunlight streaming in a side window at noon. In Figure 9-3 the object is illuminated by a diffuse light source.

Specular Light

Like diffuse light, *specular light* is directional, but it is reflected sharply and in a particular direction. A highly specular light tends to cause a bright spot on the surface it

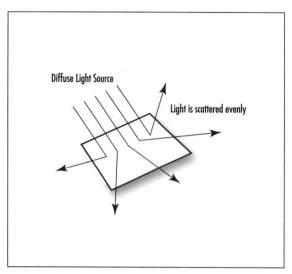

Figure 9-3 An object illuminated by a purely diffuse light source

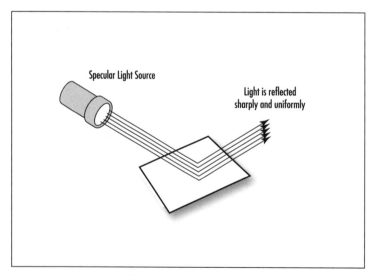

Figure 9-4 An object illuminated by a purely specular light source

shines upon, which is called the *specular highlight.* A spotlight and the Sun are examples of specular light. Figure 9-4 shows an object illuminated by a purely specular light source.

Put It All Together

No single light source is composed entirely of any of the three types of light just described. Rather, it is made up of varying intensities of each. For example, a red laser beam in a lab is composed of almost a pure-red specular component. However, smoke or dust particles scatter the beam, so it can be seen traveling across the room. This scattering represents the diffuse component of the light. If the beam is bright and no other light sources are present, you'd notice objects in the room taking on a red hue. This would be a very small ambient component of that light.

Thus a light source in a scene is said to be composed of three lighting components: ambient, diffuse, and specular. Just like the components of a color, each lighting component is defined with an RGBA value that describes the relative intensities of red, green, and blue light that make up that component. (We will ignore the alpha component until Chapter 15.) For example, our red laser light might be described by the component values in Table 9-1.

Table 9-1 Color and Light Distribution for a Red Laser Light Source

	Red	Green	Blue	Alpha
Specular	0.99	0.0	0.0	1.0
Diffuse	0.10	0.0	0.0	1.0
Ambient	0.05	0.0	0.0	1.0

Note that the red laser beam has no green or blue light. Also, note that specular, diffuse, and ambient light can each range in intensity from 0.0 to 1.0. You could interpret this table as saying that the red laser light in some scenes has a very high specular component, a small diffuse component, and a very small ambient component. Wherever it shines, you are probably going to see a reddish spot. Also, because of conditions (smoke, dust, etc.) in the room, the diffuse component will allow the beam to be seen traveling through the air. Finally, the ambient component—likely due to smoke or dust particles, as well—will scatter a tiny bit of light all about the room. Ambient and diffuse components of light are frequently combined because they are so similar in nature.

Materials in the Real World

Light is only part of the equation, though. In the real world, objects do have a color of their own. In Chapter 8, we described the color of an object as being defined by its reflected wavelengths of light. A blue ball reflects mostly blue photons and absorbs most others. This assumes that the light shining on the ball has blue photons in it to be reflected and detected by the observer. Generally, most scenes in the real world are illuminated by a white light containing an even mixture of all the colors. Under white light, therefore, most objects appear in their proper or "natural" colors. However, this is not always so; put the blue ball in a dark room with only a yellow light, and the ball would appear black to the viewer, because all the yellow light would be absorbed and there would be no blue to be reflected.

Material Properties

When we use lighting, we do not describe polygons as having a particular color, but rather as being made up of *materials* that have certain reflective properties. Instead of saying that a polygon is red, we say that the polygon is made of a material that reflects mostly red light. We are still saying that the surface is red, but now we must also specify the material's reflective properties for ambient, diffuse, and specular light sources. A material may be shiny and reflect specular light very well, while absorbing most of the ambient or diffuse light. Conversely, a flat colored object may absorb all specular light and won't be shiny under any circumstances. Another property to be specified is the emission property for objects that emit their own light, such as taillights or glow-in-the-dark watches.

Adding Light to Materials

Setting lighting and material properties to achieve the desired effect takes some practice. There are no color cubes or rules of thumb to give you quick and easy answers. This is where analysis gives way to art, and science yields to magic. The CD subdirectory for this chapter contains a supplementary sample program called MATLIGHT (for Materials and Lighting Studio). This program allows you to change material and lighting properties on the fly for a scene composed of some simple objects. You can use MATLIGHT to get a feel for the various lighting and material property settings. In addition, because the source is included, you can also substitute your own objects in MATLIGHT and work out the lighting and material details before committing your scene to code.

When drawing an object, OpenGL decides which color to use for each pixel in the object. That object has reflective "colors," and the light source has "colors" of its own. How does OpenGL determine which colors to use? Understanding this is not difficult, but it does take some simple grade-school multiplication. (See, that teacher *told* you you'd need it one day!)

Each vertex of your primitives is assigned an RGB color value based on the net effect of the ambient, diffuse, and specular illumination multiplied by the ambient, diffuse, and specular reflectance of the material properties. By making use of smooth shading between the vertices, the illusion of illumination is achieved!

Calculating Ambient Light Effects

First you need to put away the notion of color and instead think only in terms of red, green, and blue intensities. For an ambient light source of half-intensity red, green, and blue components, you'd have an RGB value for that source of (0.5, 0.5, 0.5). If this ambient light illuminates an object with ambient reflective properties specified in RGB terms of (.50, 1.0, .50), then the net "color" component from the ambient light would be

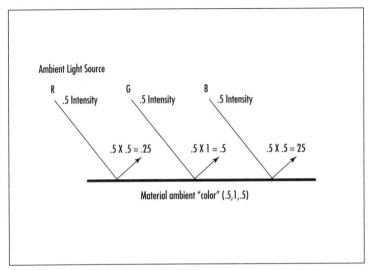

Figure 9-5 Calculating the ambient color component of an object

```
(0.50 * .50, 0.5 * 1.0, 0.50 * .50) = (0.25, 0.5, 0.25)
```

which would be the result of multiplying each of the ambient light source terms by each of the ambient material property terms. See Figure 9-5.

Thus, the material color components actually determine the percentage of incident light that is reflected. In our example, the ambient light had a red component that was at one-half intensity, and the material ambient property of .5 specified that one-half of that half-intensity light was reflected. Half of a half is a fourth, or 0.25.

Diffuse and Specular Effects

For ambient light, this is as simple as it gets. Diffuse light, too, has RGB intensities that interact in the same way with material properties. However, diffuse light is directional, and the intensity at the surface of the object will vary depending on the angle between the surface and the light source. The same goes for specular light sources and intensities. The net effect in terms of RGB values is figured the same way as for ambient light, with the intensity of the light source (adjusted for the angle of incidence) being multiplied by the material reflectance. Finally, all three RGB terms are added to yield a final color for the object. If any single color component is above 1.0, it is clamped to that value (you can't get more intense than full intensity!).

Generally, the ambient and diffuse components of light sources and materials are the same and have the greatest effect in determining the color of the object. Specular light and material properties tend to be light gray or white. The specular component depends significantly on the angle of incidence, and specular highlights on an object are usually white.

Adding Light to a Scene

This may seem like a lot of theory to digest all of a sudden. So let's slow down and start exploring some examples of the OpenGL code needed for lighting; this will also help reinforce what you've just learned. We will also be demonstrating some additional features and requirements of lighting in OpenGL. The next few examples build on our JET program. The initial version contains no lighting code and just draws triangles with hidden surface elimination enabled. But when we're done, the jet's metallic surface will glisten in the sunlight as you rotate it with the arrow keys.

Enable the Lighting

To tell OpenGL to use lighting calculations, call glEnable() with the GL_LIGHTING parameter, like this:

```
glEnable(GL_LIGHTING);
```

This alone tells OpenGL to use material properties and lighting parameters in determining the color for each vertex in your scene. However, without any specified material properties or lighting parameters, your object will remain dark and unlit as shown in Figure 9-6. Look at the code for any of the JET-based example programs, and you'll see that we have called a function SetupRC() right after creating the rendering context. This is where we will do any initialization of lighting parameters.

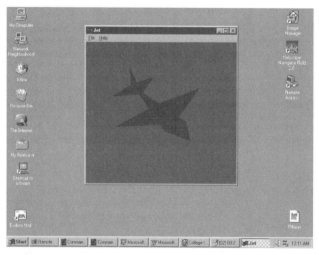

Figure 9-6 Jet with lighting enabled, but no light or material properties defined

Set Up the Lighting Model

After enabling lighting calculations, the first thing you need to do is set up the lighting model. The three parameters that affect the lighting model are set with the glLightModel() function.

The first lighting parameter used in our next example is GL_LIGHT_MODEL_AM-BIENT. This allows a global ambient light to be specified that illuminates all objects evenly from all sides. The following code specifies that a bright white light is to be used:

```
// Bright white light - full intensity RGB values
GLfloat ambientLight[] = { 1.0f, 1.0f, 1.0f, 1.0f };

// Enable lighting
glEnable(GL_LIGHTING);

// Set light model to use ambient light specified by ambientLight[]
glLightModelfv(GL_LIGHT_MODEL_AMBIENT,ambientLight);
```

The variation of glLightModel shown here, glLightModelfv, takes as its first parameter the lighting model parameter being modified or set, and then an array of the RGBA values that make up the light. The default RGBA values of this global ambient light are (0.2, 0.2, 0.2, 1.0), which is fairly dim. Other lighting model parameters allow you to determine if the front, back, or both sides of polygons are illuminated, and the calculation of specular lighting angles. See the Reference Section for more information on these parameters.

Set Material Properties

Now that we have an ambient light source, we need to set some material properties so that our polygons reflect light and we can see our jet. There are two ways to set material properties. The first is to use the function glMaterial before specifying each polygon or set of polygons. Examine the following code fragment:

```
Glfloat gray[] = { 0.75f, 0.75f, 0.75f, 1.0f };
...
...
glMaterialfv(GL_FRONT, GL_AMBIENT_AND_DIFFUSE, gray);

glBegin(GL_TRIANGLES);
        glVertex3f(-15.0f,0.0f,30.0f);
        glVertex3f(0.0f, 15.0f, 30.0f);
        glVertex3f(0.0f, 0.0f, -56.0f);
glEnd();
```

The first parameter to glMaterialfv specifies whether the front, back, or both (GL_FRONT, GL_BACK, or GL_FRONT_AND_BACK) take on the material properties specified. The second parameter tells which properties are being set; in this instance both the ambient and diffuse reflectances are being set to the same values. The final parameter is an array containing the RGBA values that make up these properties. All

...ified after the glMaterial call are affected by the last values set, until ....her ca ....glMaterial is made.

Under most circumstances, the ambient and diffuse components are the same, and unless you want specular highlights (sparkling, shiny spots), you don't need to define specular reflective properties. Even so, it would still be quite tedious if we had to define an array for every color in our object and call glMaterial() before each polygon or group of polygons.

This leads us to the second and preferred way of setting material properties, called *color tracking*. With color tracking you can tell OpenGL to set material properties by only calling glColor. To enable color tracking, call glEnable() with the GL_COLOR_MATERIAL parameter:

```
glEnable(GL_COLOR_MATERIAL);
```

Then the function glColorMaterial specifies the material parameters that will follow the values set by glColor.

For example, to set the ambient and diffuse properties of the fronts of polygons to track the colors set by glColor, call

```
glColorMaterial(GL_FRONT,GL_AMBIENT_AND_DIFFUSE);
```

The earlier code fragment setting material properties would then be as follows. This looks like more code, but it will actually save many lines of code and execute faster as the number of polygons grows.

```
// Enable color tracking
glEnable(GL_COLOR_MATERIAL);

// Front material ambient and diffuse colors track glColor
glColorMaterial(GL_FRONT,GL_AMBIENT_AND_DIFFUSE);

glMaterialfv(GL_FRONT, GL_AMBIENT_AND_DIFFUSE, gray);

...
...
glcolor3f(0.75f, 0.75f, 0.75f);
glBegin(GL_TRIANGLES);
        glVertex3f(-15.0f,0.0f,30.0f);
        glVertex3f(0.0f, 15.0f, 30.0f);
        glVertex3f(0.0f, 0.0f, -56.0f);
glEnd();
```

Listing 9-1 contains the code we add with the SetupRC function to our JET example, to set up a bright ambient light source, and to set the material properties that allow the object to reflect light and be seen. We have also changed the colors of the jet so that each section is a different color rather than each polygon. Notice in the final output (Figure 9-7) that it's not much different from the image before we had lighting. However, if we reduce the ambient light by half, we get the image shown in Figure 9-8. This is accomplished by setting the ambient light RGBA values to the following:

```
GLfloat ambientLight[] = { 0.5f, 0.5f, 0.5f, 1.0f };
```

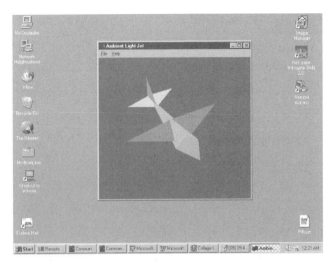

Figure 9-7 Output from completed AMBIENT example program

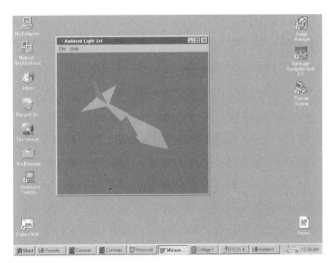

Figure 9-8 Output from AMBIENT when the light source is cut in half

You can see how we might reduce the ambient light in a scene to produce a dimmer image. This is useful for simulations in which dusk approaches gradually or when a more direct light source is blocked, as when an object is in the shadow of another, larger object.

Listing 9-1 Set up for ambient lighting conditions

```
// This function does any needed initialization on the rendering
// context.  Here it sets up and initializes the lighting for
// the scene.
void SetupRC()
        {
        // Light values
        // Bright white light
        GLfloat ambientLight[] = { 1.0f, 1.0f, 1.0f, 1.0f };

        glEnable(GL_DEPTH_TEST);        // Hidden surface removal
        glEnable(GL_CULL_FACE);         // Do not calculate inside of jet
        glFrontFace(GL_CCW);            // Counter clock-wise polygons face out

        // Lighting stuff
        glEnable(GL_LIGHTING); // Enable lighting

        // Set light model to use ambient light specified by ambientLight[]
        glLightModelfv(GL_LIGHT_MODEL_AMBIENT,ambientLight);

        glEnable(GL_COLOR_MATERIAL);    // Enable Material color tracking

        // Front material ambient and diffuse colors track glColor
        glColorMaterial(GL_FRONT,GL_AMBIENT_AND_DIFFUSE);

        // Nice light blue background
        glClearColor(0.0f, 0.0f, 05.f,1.0f);
        }
```

Using a Light Source

Manipulating the ambient light has its uses, but for most applications attempting to model the real world, one or more specific sources of light must be specified. In addition to their intensities and colors, these sources will have a location and a direction. The placement of these lights can dramatically affect the appearance of your scene.

OpenGL supports up to eight independent light sources located anywhere in your scene or out of the viewing volume. You can locate a light source an infinite distance away and make its light rays parallel, or make it a nearby light source radiating outward. You can also specify a spotlight with a specific cone of light radiating from it, as well as manipulate its characteristics.

Which Way Is Up?

When you specify a light source, you tell OpenGL where it is and in which direction it's shining. Often the light source will be shining in all directions, or it may be directional. Either way, for any object you draw, the rays of light from any source (other than a pure ambient source) will strike the surface of the polygons that make up the object at an angle. Of course, in the case of a directional light, the surface of all polygons may not necessarily be illuminated. To calculate the shading effects across the surface of the polygons, OpenGL must be able to calculate this angle.

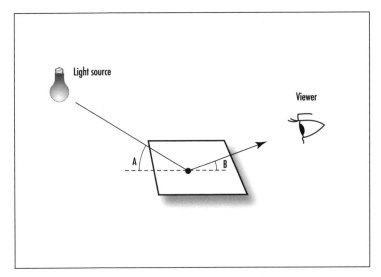

Figure 9-9 Light is reflected off objects at specific angles

In Figure 9-9, a polygon (a square) is being struck by a ray of light from some source. The ray makes an angle (A) with the plane as it strikes the surface. The light is then reflected at an angle (B) toward the viewer (or you wouldn't see it). These angles are used in conjunction with the lighting and material properties we have discussed thus far to calculate the apparent color of that location. It happens by design that the locations used by OpenGL are the vertices of the polygon. By calculating the apparent colors for each vertex and then doing smooth shading between them (explained in Chapter 8), the illusion of lighting is created. Magic!

From a programming standpoint, this presents a slight conceptual difficulty. Each polygon is created as a set of vertices, which are nothing more than points. Each vertex is then struck by a ray of light at some angle. How then do you (or OpenGL) calculate the angle between a point and a line (the ray of light)? Of course you can't geometrically find *the* angle between a single point and a line in 3D space, because there are an infinite number of possibilities. Therefore, you must associate with each vertex some piece of information that denotes a direction upward from the vertex and away from the surface of the primitive.

Surface Normals

A line from the vertex in this upward direction would then start in some imaginary plane (or your polygon) at a right angle. This line is called a *normal vector*. That word *vector* may sound like something the *Star Trek* crew members toss around, but it just means a line perpendicular to a real or imaginary surface. A vector is a line *pointed* in some direction, and the word *normal* is just another way for eggheads to say perpendicular (intersecting at a 90° angle). As if the word *perpendicular* weren't bad enough!

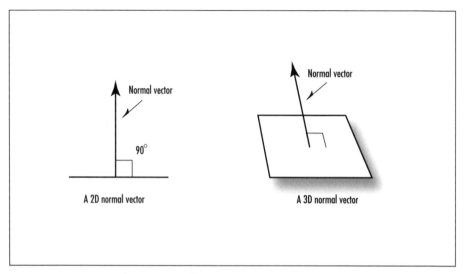

Figure 9-10 A 2D and a 3D normal vector

Therefore, a normal vector is a line pointed in a direction that is at a 90° angle to the surface of your polygon. Figure 9-10 presents examples of 2D and 3D normal vectors.

You may already be asking why we must specify a normal vector for each vertex. Why can't we just specify a single normal for a polygon and use it for each vertex? We can—and for our first few examples, we will. However, there are times when you don't want each normal to be exactly perpendicular to the surface of the polygon. You may have noticed that many surfaces are not flat! You can approximate these surfaces with flat, polygonal sections, but you will end up with a jagged or multifaceted surface. Later we'll discuss a technique to produce the illusion of smooth curves with straight lines by "tweaking" your surface normals (more magic!). But first things first.

Specifying a Normal

To see how we specify a normal for a vertex, let's take a look at Figure 9-11—a plane floating above the xz plane in 3D space. We've made this simple to demonstrate the concept. Notice the line through the vertex (1,1,0) that is perpendicular to the plane. If we select any point on this line, say (1,10,0), then the line from the first point (1,1,0) to the second point (1,10,0) is our normal vector. The second point specified actually indicates that the direction from the vertex is up in the y direction. This is also used to indicate the front and back sides of polygons, as the vector travels up and away from the front surface.

You can see that this second point is the number of units in the x, y, and z directions for some point on the normal vector away from the vertex. Rather than specifying two points for each normal vector, we can subtract the vertex from the second point on the normal, yielding a single coordinate triplet that indicates the x, y, and z steps away from the vertex. For our example this would be

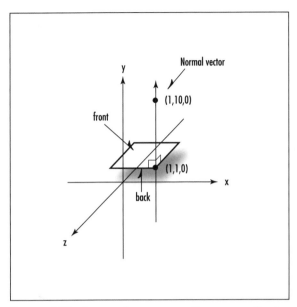

Figure 9-11 A normal vector traveling perpendicular
from the surface

$(1,10,0) - (1,1,0) = (1-1, 10-1, 0) = (0, 9, 0)$

Another way of looking at this is, if the vertex were translated to the origin, the point specified by subtracting the two original points would still specify the direction pointing away and at a 90° angle from the surface. Figure 9-12 shows the newly translated normal vector.

The vector is a directional quantity that tells OpenGL which direction the vertices (or polygon) face. This next code segment shows a normal vector being specified for one of the triangles in the JET example program:

```
glBegin(GL_TRIANGLES);
        glNormal3f(0.0f, -1.0f, 0.0f);
        glVertex3f(0.0f, 0.0f, 60.0f);
        glVertex3f(-15.0f, 0.0f, 30.0f);
        glVertex3f(15.0f,0.0f,30.0f);
glEnd();
```

The function glNormal3f takes the coordinate triplet that specifies a normal vector pointing in the direction perpendicular to the surface of this triangle. In this example, the normals for all three vertices have the same direction, which is down the negative y axis. This is a very simple example because the triangle is lying flat in the xz plane, and it actually represents a bottom section of the jet.

The prospect of specifying a normal for every vertex or polygon in your drawing may seem daunting, especially since very few surfaces will lie cleanly in one of the major planes. Never fear, we will shortly present a reusable function that you can call again and again to calculate your normals for you.

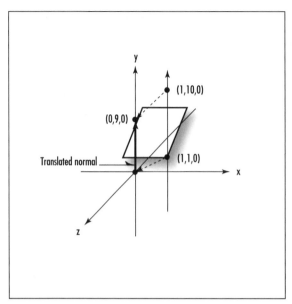

Figure 9-12 The newly translated normal vector

Polygon Winding
Take special note of the order of the vertices in the jet's triangle. If you viewed this triangle being drawn from the direction in which the normal vector points, the corners would appear counterclockwise around the triangle. This is called *polygon winding*. By default, the front of a polygon is defined as the side from which the vertices appear to be wound in a counterclockwise fashion.

Unit Normals

As OpenGL does its magic, all surface normals must eventually be converted to *unit normals*. A unit normal is just a normal vector that has a length of 1. The normal in Figure 9-12 has a length of 9. You can find the length of any normal by squaring each component, adding them together, and taking the square root. Divide each component of the normal by the length and you get a vector pointed in exactly the same direction, but only 1 unit long. In this case, our new normal vector would be specified as (0,1,0). This is called *normalization*. Thus, for lighting calculations, all normal vectors must be normalized. Talk about jargon!

You can tell OpenGL to convert your normals to unit normals automatically, by enabling normalization with glEnable and a parameter of GL_NORMALIZE:

```
glEnable(GL_NORMALIZE);
```

This does, however, have performance penalties. It's far better to calculate your normals ahead of time as unit normals instead of relying on OpenGL to do this for you.

Given any normal vector specified by a coordinate triplet that indicates the direction from the origin, you can easily find the equivalent unit normal vector with the function in Listing 9-2.

Listing 9-2 A function that reduces any normal vector to a unit normal vector

```
// Reduces a normal vector specified as a set of three coordinates,
// to a unit normal vector of length 1.
void ReduceToUnit(float vector[3])
        {
        float length;

        // Calculate the length of the vector
        length = (float)sqrt((vector[0]*vector[0]) +
                             (vector[1]*vector[1]) +
                             (vector[2]*vector[2]));

        // Keep the program from blowing up by providing an acceptable
        // value for vectors whose length may be calculated too close to zero.
        if(length == 0.0f)
                length = 1.0f;

        // Dividing each element by the length will result in a
        // unit normal vector.
        vector[0] /= length;
        vector[1] /= length;
        vector[2] /= length;
        }
```

Finding a Normal

Figure 9-13 presents another polygon that is not simply lying in one of the axis planes. The normal vector pointing away from this surface is more difficult to guess, so we need an easy way to calculate the normal for any arbitrary polygon in 3D coordinates.

You can easily calculate the normal vector for any polygon consisting of at least three points that lie in a single plane (a flat polygon). Figure 9-14 shows three points, P1, P2, and P3, that you can use to define two vectors: vector V1 from P1 to P2, and vector V2 from P1 to P2. Mathematically, two vectors in three-dimensional space define a plane (your original polygon lies in this plane). If you take the cross product of those two vectors (written mathematically as V1 X V2, the resulting vector is perpendicular to that plane (or normal). Figure 9-15 shows the vector V3 derived by taking the cross product of V1 and V2.

Don't worry if you don't know how to take the cross product of two vectors; all you need is the function in Listing 9-3. To use this function, pass it an array containing any three vertices from your polygon (specify in counterclockwise winding order), and an array that will contain the normal vector on return. The constant values x, y, and z are provided for your benefit if you want to see how the function works.

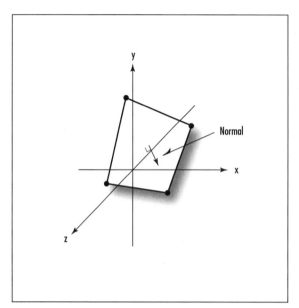

Figure 9-13 A nontrivial normal problem

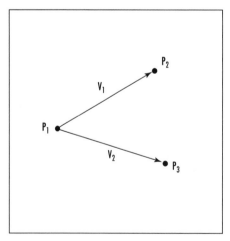

Figure 9-14 Two vectors defined by three points on a plane

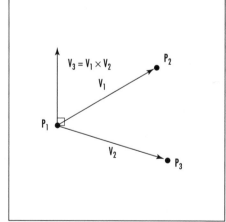

Figure 9-15 A normal vector as cross product of two vectors

Listing 9-3 Function to calculate a normal vector with any three vertices from a polygon

```
// Points p1, p2, & p3 specified in counterclockwise order
void calcNormal(float v[3][3], float out[3])
        {
        float v1[3],v2[3];
        static const int x = 0;
        static const int y = 1;
        static const int z = 2;

        // Calculate two vectors from the three points
        v1[x] = v[0][x] - v[1][x];
        v1[y] = v[0][y] - v[1][y];
        v1[z] = v[0][z] - v[1][z];

        v2[x] = v[1][x] - v[2][x];
        v2[y] = v[1][y] - v[2][y];
        v2[z] = v[1][z] - v[2][z];

        // Take the cross product of the two vectors to get
        // the normal vector which will be stored in out[]
        out[x] = v1[y]*v2[z] - v1[z]*v2[y];
        out[y] = v1[z]*v2[x] - v1[x]*v2[z];
        out[z] = v1[x]*v2[y] - v1[y]*v2[x];

        // Normalize the vector (shorten length to one)
        ReduceToUnit(out);
        }
```

Setting Up a Source

Now that you understand the requirements of setting up your polygons to receive and interact with a light source, it's time to turn on the lights! Listing 9-4 shows the SetupRC() function from the example program LITJET. Part of the setup process for this sample program creates a light source and places it to the upper-left, slightly behind the viewer. The light source GL_LIGHT0 has its ambient and diffuse components set to the intensities specified by the arrays ambientLight[], and diffuseLight[].This results in a moderate white light source.

```
GLfloat  ambientLight[] = { 0.3f, 0.3f, 0.3f, 1.0f };
GLfloat  diffuseLight[] = { 0.7f, 0.7f, 0.7f, 1.0f };
...
...
// Setup and enable light 0
glLightfv(GL_LIGHT0,GL_AMBIENT,ambientLight);
glLightfv(GL_LIGHT0,GL_DIFFUSE,diffuseLight);
```

The light is positioned by this code:

```
GLfloat lightPos[] = { -50.f, 50.0f, 100.0f, 1.0f };
...
...
glLightfv(GL_LIGHT0,GL_POSITION,lightPos);
```

Here lightPos[] contains the position of the light. The last value in this array is 1.0, which specifies that the designated coordinates are the position of the light source. If the last value in the array is 0.0, it indicates that the light is an infinite distance away along the vector specified by this array. We'll touch more on this later.

Finally, the light source GL_LIGHT0 is enabled:

```
glEnable(GL_LIGHT0);
```

Listing 9-4 Light and rendering context setup for LITJET

```
// This function does any needed initialization on the rendering
// context.  Here it sets up and initializes the lighting for
// the scene.
void SetupRC()
    {
    // Light values and coordinates
    GLfloat  ambientLight[] = { 0.3f, 0.3f, 0.3f, 1.0f };
    GLfloat  diffuseLight[] = { 0.7f, 0.7f, 0.7f, 1.0f };
    GLfloat  lightPos[] = { -50.f, 50.0f, 100.0f, 1.0f };

    glEnable(GL_DEPTH_TEST);        // Hidden surface removal
    glFrontFace(GL_CCW);            // Counter clock-wise polygons face out
    glEnable(GL_CULL_FACE);         // Do not calculate inside of jet

    // Enable lighting
    glEnable(GL_LIGHTING);

    // Setup and enable light 0
    glLightfv(GL_LIGHT0,GL_AMBIENT,ambientLight);
    glLightfv(GL_LIGHT0,GL_DIFFUSE,diffuseLight);
    glLightfv(GL_LIGHT0,GL_POSITION,lightPos);
    glEnable(GL_LIGHT0);

    // Enable color tracking
    glEnable(GL_COLOR_MATERIAL);

    // Set Material properties to follow glColor values
    glColorMaterial(GL_FRONT, GL_AMBIENT_AND_DIFFUSE);

    // Light blue background
    glClearColor(0.0f, 0.0f, 1.0f, 1.0f );
    }
```

Setting the Material Properties

Notice in Listing 9-4 that color tracking is enabled, and the properties to be tracked are the ambient and diffuse reflective properties for the front surface of the polygons. This is just as it was defined in the AMBIENT sample program:

```
// Enable color tracking
glEnable(GL_COLOR_MATERIAL);

// Set Material properties to follow glColor values
glColorMaterial(GL_FRONT, GL_AMBIENT_AND_DIFFUSE);
```

Specifying the Polygons

The rendering code from the first two JET samples changes considerably now, to support the new lighting model. Listing 9-5 is taken from the RenderScene() function from LITJET.

Listing 9-5 Code sample that sets color, calculates and specifies normals and polygons

```
float normal[3];        // Storage for calculated surface normal
...
...
// Set material color
glRGB(0, 255, 0);
glBegin(GL_TRIANGLES);
        glNormal3f(0.0f, -1.0f, 0.0f);
        glVertex3f(0.0f, 0.0f, 60.0f);
        glVertex3f(-15.0f, 0.0f, 30.0f);
        glVertex3f(15.0f,0.0f,30.0f);
//glEnd();


{
// Vertices for this triangle
float v[3][3] = {{ 15.0f, 0.0f, 30.0f},
                 { 0.0f, 15.0f, 30.0f},
                 { 0.0f, 0.0f, 60.0f}};

// Calculate the normal for the plane
calcNormal(v,normal);

// Draw the triangle using the plane normal
// for all the vertices
//glBegin(GL_TRIANGLES);
        glNormal3fv(normal);
        glVertex3fv(v[0]);
        glVertex3fv(v[1]);
        glVertex3fv(v[2]);
//glEnd();

}
```

You'll notice that we are calculating the normal vector using our code in Listing 9-3. Also, the material properties are now following the colors set by glColor (which is wrapped by our glRGB macro). One other thing you'll notice is that not every triangle is blocked by glBegin()/glEnd() functions. You can specify once that you are drawing triangles, and every three vertices will be used for a new triangle until you specify otherwise with glEnd(). For very large numbers of polygons, this can considerably boost performance by eliminating many unnecessary function calls.

Figure 9-16 shows the output from the completed LITJET example program. By rotating the jet around with the arrow keys, you can see the dramatic shading effects as the surface of the jet moves in the light.

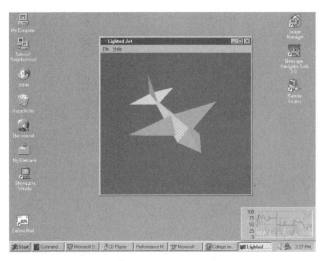

Figure 9-16 Output from LITJET sample

Performance Tip

The most obvious way to improve the performance of this code would be to calculate all the normal vectors ahead of time and store them for use in the Render function. Before you pursue this, read Chapter 10's material on display lists. Display lists provide a means of storing calculated values not only for the normal vectors, but for the polygon data as well. Remember, these examples are meant to demonstrate the concepts. They are not necessarily the most efficient code possible.

Lighting Effects

The ambient and diffuse light from the LITJET example are sufficient to provide the illusion of lighting. The surface of the jet appears shaded according to the angle of the incident light. As the jet rotates, these angles change and you can see the lighting effects changing in such a way that you can easily guess where the light is coming from.

We ignored the specular component of the light source, however, as well as the specular reflectivity of the material properties on the jet. Although the lighting effects are pronounced, the surface of the jet is rather flatly colored. Ambient and diffuse lighting and material properties are all you need if you are modeling clay, wood, cardboard, cloth, or some other flatly colored object. But for metallic surfaces like the skin of an airplane, some shine is often necessary.

Specular Highlights

Specular lighting and material properties add needed gloss to the surface of your objects. This shininess has a whitening effect on an object's color and can produce *specular highlights* when the angle of incident light is sharp in relation to the viewer. A specular highlight is what occurs when nearly all the light striking the surface of an object is reflected away. The white sparkle on a shiny red ball in the sunlight is good example of a specular highlight.

Specular Light

Adding a specular component to a light source is very easily done. The following code shows the light source setup for the LITJET program, modified to add a specular component to the light.

```
// Light values and coordinates
// Light values and coordinates
GLfloat   ambientLight[] = { 0.3f, 0.3f, 0.3f, 1.0f };
GLfloat   diffuseLight[] = { 0.7f, 0.7f, 0.7f, 1.0f };
GLfloat   specular[] = { 1.0f, 1.0f, 1.0f, 1.0f};
GLfloat   lightPos[] = { 0.0f, 150.0f, 150.0f, 1.0f };
...
...

// Enable lighting
glEnable(GL_LIGHTING);

// Setup and enable light 0
glLightfv(GL_LIGHT0,GL_AMBIENT,ambientLight);
glLightfv(GL_LIGHT0,GL_DIFFUSE,diffuseLight);
glLightfv(GL_LIGHT0,GL_SPECULAR,specular);
glLightfv(GL_LIGHT0,GL_POSITION,lightPos);
glEnable(GL_LIGHT0);
```

The specular[] array specifies a very bright white light source for the specular component of the light. Our purpose here is to model bright sunlight. The line

```
glLightfv(GL_LIGHT0,GL_SPECULAR,specular);
```

simply adds this specular component to the light source GL_LIGHT0.

If this were the only change you made to LITJET, you wouldn't see any difference in the jet's appearance. This is because we haven't yet defined any specular reflectance properties for the material properties.

Specular Reflectance

Adding specular reflectance to material properties is just as easy as adding the specular component to the light source. This next code segment shows the code from LITJET, again modified to add specular reflectance to the material properties.

```
// Light values and coordinates
GLfloat   specref[] = { 1.0f, 1.0f, 1.0f, 1.0f };

...
...


// Enable color tracking
glEnable(GL_COLOR_MATERIAL);

// Set Material properties to follow glColor values
```

continued on next page

continued from previous page

```
glColorMaterial(GL_FRONT, GL_AMBIENT_AND_DIFFUSE);

// All materials hereafter have full specular reflectivity
// with a high shine
glMaterialfv(GL_FRONT, GL_SPECULAR,specref);
glMateriali(GL_FRONT,GL_SHININESS,128);
```

As before, we enable color tracking so that the ambient and diffuse reflectance of the materials follow the current color set by the glColor() functions. (Of course, we don't want the specular reflectance to track glColor, because we are specifying it separately and it doesn't change.)

Now we've added an array specref[] that contains the RGBA values for our specular reflectance. This array of all 1's will produce a surface that reflects nearly all incident specular light. The line

```
glMaterialfv(GL_FRONT, GL_SPECULAR,specref);
```

sets the material properties for all subsequent polygons to have this reflectance. Since we do not call glMaterial again with the GL_SPECULAR property, all materials will have this property. We did this on purpose because we want the entire jet to appear made of metal or very shiny composites.

What we have done here in our setup routine is important: We have specified that the ambient and diffuse reflective material properties of all future polygons (until we say otherwise with another call to glMaterial or glColorMaterial) will change as the current color changes, but that the specular reflective properties will remain the same.

Specular Exponent

As stated earlier, high specular light and reflectivity brighten the colors of the object. For this example, the present extremely high specular light (full intensity) and specular reflectivity (full reflectivity) will result in a jet that appears almost totally white or gray except where the surface points away from the light source (in which case it would be black and unlit). To temper this effect, we use the next line of code after the specular component is specified, as follows:

```
glMateriali(GL_FRONT,GL_SHININESS,128);
```

The GL_SHININES property sets the specular exponent of the material, which specifies how small and focused the specular highlight is. A value of 0 specifies an unfocused specular highlight, which is actually what is producing the brightening of the colors evenly across the entire polygon. If you set this value, you reduce the size and increase the focus of the specular highlight, causing a shiny spot to appear. The larger the value, the more shiny and pronounced the surface. The range of this parameter is 1–128 for all implementations of OpenGL.

Listing 9-6 shows the new SetupRC code in the sample program SHINYJET. This is the only code that changed from LITJET (other than the title of the window) to produce a very shiny and glistening jet. Figure 9-17 shows the output from this program, but to fully appreciate the effect, you should run the program and hold down one of the arrow keys to spin the jet about in the sunlight.

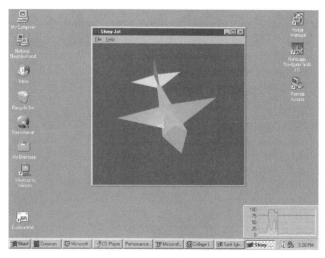

Figure 9-17 Output from the SHINYJET program

Listing 9-6 Setup from SHINYJET to produce specular highlights on the jet

```
// This function does any needed initialization on the rendering
// context.  Here it sets up and initializes the lighting for
// the scene.
void SetupRC()
        {
        // Light values and coordinates
        GLfloat    ambientLight[] = { 0.3f, 0.3f, 0.3f, 1.0f };
        GLfloat    diffuseLight[] = { 0.7f, 0.7f, 0.7f, 1.0f };
        GLfloat    specular[] = { 1.0f, 1.0f, 1.0f, 1.0f};
        Glfloat    lightPos[] = { 0.0f, 150.0f, 150.0f, 1.0f };
        GLfloat    specref[] =  { 1.0f, 1.0f, 1.0f, 1.0f };


        glEnable(GL_DEPTH_TEST);        // Hidden surface removal
        glFrontFace(GL_CCW);            // Counterclockwise polygons face out
        glEnable(GL_CULL_FACE);         // Do not calculate inside of jet

        // Enable lighting
        glEnable(GL_LIGHTING);

        // Set up and enable light 0
        glLightfv(GL_LIGHT0,GL_AMBIENT,ambientLight);
        glLightfv(GL_LIGHT0,GL_DIFFUSE,diffuseLight);
        glLightfv(GL_LIGHT0,GL_SPECULAR,specular);
        glLightfv(GL_LIGHT0,GL_POSITION,lightPos);
        glEnable(GL_LIGHT0);

        // Enable color tracking
        glEnable(GL_COLOR_MATERIAL);

        // Set Material properties to follow glColor values
```

continued on next page

continued from previous page

```
glColorMaterial(GL_FRONT, GL_AMBIENT_AND_DIFFUSE);

// All materials hereafter have full specular reflectivity
// with a high shine
glMaterialfv(GL_FRONT, GL_SPECULAR,specref);
glMateriali(GL_FRONT,GL_SHININESS,128);


// Light blue background
glClearColor(0.0f, 0.0f, 1.0f, 1.0f );
}
```

Normal Averaging

Earlier we mentioned that by "tweaking" your normals you can produce smooth surfaces with straight lines. This technique, known as *normal averaging,* produces some
interesting optical illusions. Say you have a surface like that shown in Figure 9-18,
with the usual surface normals.

Although the normals are shown in between the corners, they are actually specified
for each vertex. If you take into account that each vertex actually boarders another surface, you can specify the normal for that vertex as the average of the two normals at that
point for each surface. Figure 9-19 shows that for two adjoining surfaces, their common corner would have a different normal specified as each surface is drawn. If we take
the average of these two normals and use it when we specify each surface, the joining of
the two surfaces will *appear* less sharp after OpenGL does its surface shading.

Listing 9-7 shows the rendering function that creates the surface shown in Figure
9-18. (This code is from the example program WAVEY in the CD subdirectory for this
chapter.) The surface is created by stepping from left to right for the x coordinates, and
alternating up and down in the y coordinate direction. The z coordinates are constant,
with –50 being the front of the image and 50 being at the back.

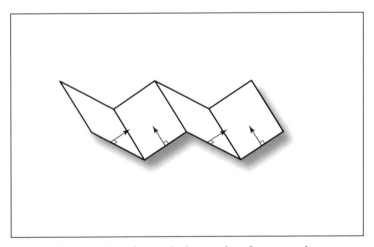

Figure 9-18 Jagged surface with the usual surface normals

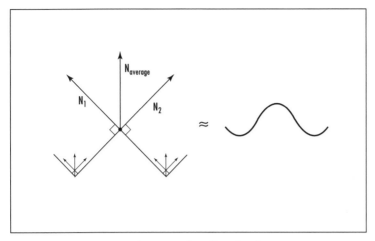

Figure 9-19 Averaging the normals will make sharp corners appear softer

Listing 9-7 The rendering function from the WAVEY example program

```
// Called to draw scene
void RenderScene(void)
        {
        float normal[3];      // Storage for calculate normal
        float v[4][3];        // Storage for rectangle coordinates
        float lastY;          // Left-hand side of rectangle
        float nextY;          // Right-hand side of rectangle
        float temp;           // Temporary storage for swapping
        float x;              // X coordinate storage


        // Menu state specifies if wireframe or not
        if(iState == WIRE)
                glPolygonMode(GL_FRONT_AND_BACK,GL_LINE);
        else
                glPolygonMode(GL_FRONT_AND_BACK,GL_FILL);


        // Menu state specifies if smooth or flat shading
        if(iState == SMOOTH || iState == AVERAGE)
                glShadeModel(GL_SMOOTH);
        else
                glShadeModel(GL_FLAT);


        // Clear the window with current clearing color
        glClear(GL_COLOR_BUFFER_BIT | GL_DEPTH_BUFFER_BIT);

        // Reset viewing volume and viewport
        ChangeSize(lastWidth,lastHeight);

        // Rotate the image according to accumulated angle set
```

continued on next page

continued from previous page

```
        // by the arrow key handlers
        glRotatef(xRot, 1.0f, 0.0f, 0.0f);
        glRotatef(yRot, 0.0f, 1.0f, 0.0f);

        // Set surface color to blue
        glRGB(0,0,255);

        // Initialize the y steppings
        lastY = 0.0f;
        nextY = 10.0f;

        // Loop through x coordinate from left to right, build
        // a rectangle with alternating slopes upward and downward
        for(x = -60.0f; x < 60.0f; x+= 20.0f)
                {
                // 1st Vertices
                v[0][0] = x;            // X coord for left
                v[0][1] = lastY;
                v[0][2] = 50.0f;        // Z coord for back

                // 2nd vertices
                v[1][0] = x;            // X coord for left
                v[1][1] = lastY;
                v[1][2] = -50.0f;       // Z coord for front

                // 3rd Vertices
                v[2][0] = x + 20.0f;    // X coord for right
                v[2][1] = nextY;
                v[2][2] = -50.0f;       // Z coord for front

                // 4th Vertices
                v[3][0] = x + 20.0f;    // X coord for right
                v[3][1] = nextY;
                v[3][2] = 50.0f;        // Z coord for back


                // Begin the polygon
                glBegin(GL_POLYGON);
                        if(iState != AVERAGE)
                                {
                                // Calculate and set the normal vector, unless
                                // averaging selected from the menu.
                                calcNormal(v,normal);
                                glNormal3fv(normal);
                                }
                        else    // Average normals. Here we cheat because we know
                                // the normal points either up or down
                                {
                                // Normal points straight up
                                if(nextY == 10)
                                        glNormal3f(0.0f,1.0f, 0.0f);
                                else
                                        // Normal points straight down
                                        glNormal3f(0.0f,-1.0f, 0.0f);
                                }

                // Specify the left two verticies
                glVertex3fv(v[0]);
```

```
                glVertex3fv(v[1]);

                // Do the same, but the normal on the other side points
                // the other direction
                if(iState == AVERAGE)
                        {
                        if(nextY == 10)
                                glNormal3f(0.0f,-1.0f, 0.0f); // points down
                        else
                                glNormal3f(0.0f,1.0f, 0.0f);  // points up
                        }

                // Specify the right two vertices
                glVertex3fv(v[2]);
                glVertex3fv(v[3]);
        glEnd();

        // Swap the y coordinate positions
        temp = lastY;
        lastY = nextY;
        nextY = temp;
        }

// Flush drawing commands
glFlush();
}
```

The WAVEY program has menu options to render just a wireframe image, do flat or smooth shading, and finally do the normal averaging. Figure 9-20 shows this folding image using flat shading, and Figure 9-21 is the same object with the normals averaged. You can see that the second image appears to have a smooth rippling effect across its surface.

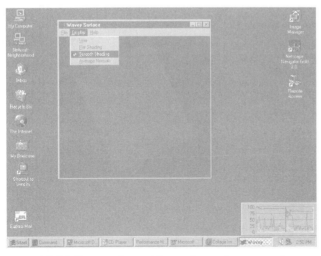

Figure 9-20 Bent surface with regular surface normals

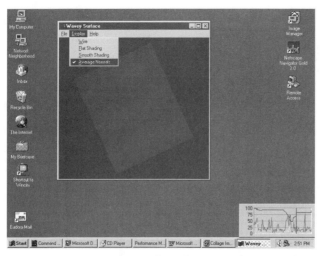

Figure 9-21 Bent surface with surface normals averaged together

Spotlights

So far, we have been specifying a light's position with glLight as follows:

```
// Array to specify position
GLfloat  lightPos[] = { 0.0f, 150.0f, 150.0f, 1.0f };

...
...

// Set the light position
glLightfv(GL_LIGHT0,GL_POSITION,lightPos);
```

The array lightPos[] contains the x, y, and z values that specify either the light's actual position in the scene, or the direction from which the light is coming. The last value, a 1.0 in this case, indicates that the light is actually present at this location. By default, the light will radiate equally in all directions from this location—but this can be changed to make a spotlight effect.

To make a light source an infinite distance away and coming from the direction specified by this vector, you would place a 0.0 in this last lightPos[] array element. A *directional light source,* as this is called, strikes the surface of your objects evenly. That is, all the light rays are parallel. In a *positional light source* on the other hand, the light rays diverge from the light source. The specular highlights achieved in the SHINYJET example would not be possible with a directional light source. Rather than the glistening spot, the entire face of the triangles that make up the jet would be white when they faced the light source dead on (the light rays strike the surface at a 90° angle).

Creating a Spotlight

Creating a spotlight is no different from creating any other directional light source. The code in Listing 9-8 shows the SetupRC() function from the SPOT example program. This program places a blue sphere in the center of the window. A spotlight is created that can be moved vertically with the up and down arrow keys, and horizontally with the left and right arrow keys. As the spotlight moves over the surface of the sphere, a specular highlight follows it on the surface.

Listing 9-8 Lighting setup for the SPOT sample program

```
// Light values and coordinates
GLfloat  lightPos[] = { 0.0f, 0.0f, 75.0f, 1.0f };
GLfloat  specular[] = { 1.0f, 1.0f, 1.0f, 1.0f};
GLfloat  specref[] =  { 1.0f, 1.0f, 1.0f, 1.0f };
GLfloat  ambientLight[] = { 0.5f, 0.5f, 0.5f, 1.0f};
GLfloat  spotDir[] = { 0.0f, 0.0f, -1.0f };


// This function does any needed initialization on the rendering
// context.  Here it sets up and initializes the lighting for
// the scene.
void SetupRC()
        {
        glEnable(GL_DEPTH_TEST);          // Hidden surface removal
        glFrontFace(GL_CCW);              // Counterclockwise polygons face out
        glEnable(GL_CULL_FACE);           // Do not try to display the back sides

        // Enable lighting
        glEnable(GL_LIGHTING);

        // Set up and enable light 0
        // Supply a slight ambient light so the objects can be seen
        glLightModelfv(GL_LIGHT_MODEL_AMBIENT, ambientLight);

        // The light is composed of just diffuse and specular components
        glLightfv(GL_LIGHT0,GL_DIFFUSE,ambientLight);
        glLightfv(GL_LIGHT0,GL_SPECULAR,specular);
        glLightfv(GL_LIGHT0,GL_POSITION,lightPos);

        // Specific spot effects
        // Cut off angle is 60 degrees
        glLightf(GL_LIGHT0,GL_SPOT_CUTOFF,60.0f);

        // Fairly shiny spot
        glLightf(GL_LIGHT0,GL_SPOT_EXPONENT,100.0f);

        // Enable this light in particular
        glEnable(GL_LIGHT0);

        // Enable color tracking
        glEnable(GL_COLOR_MATERIAL);

        // Set Material properties to follow glColor values
        glColorMaterial(GL_FRONT, GL_AMBIENT_AND_DIFFUSE);
```

continued on next page

continued from previous page

```
// All materials hereafter have full specular reflectivity
// with a high shine
glMaterialfv(GL_FRONT, GL_SPECULAR,specref);
glMateriali(GL_FRONT, GL_SHININESS,128);


// Black background
glClearColor(0.0f, 0.0f, 0.0f, 1.0f );
}
```

The following lines are actually what make a positional light source into a spotlight:

```
// Specific spot effects
// Cut off angle is 60 degrees
glLightf(GL_LIGHT0,GL_SPOT_CUTOFF,60.0f);

// Fairly shiny spot
glLightf(GL_LIGHT0,GL_SPOT_EXPONENT,100.0f);
```

The GL_SPOT_CUTOFF value specifies the radial angle of the cone of light emanating from the spotlight. For a normal positional light, this is 180° so that the light is not confined to a cone. Spotlights emit a cone of light, and objects outside this cone are not illuminated. Figure 9-22 shows how this angle translates to the cone width.

Drawing a Spotlight

When you place a spotlight in a scene, the light must come from somewhere. Just because you have a source of light at some location doesn't mean that you will see a bright spot there. For our SPOT example program, we placed a red cone at the spot-

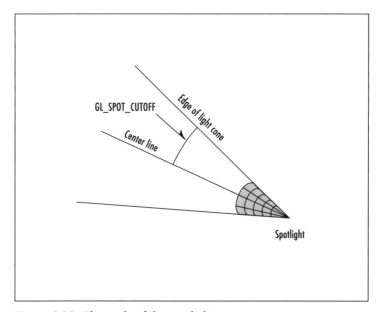

Figure 9-22 The angle of the spotlight's cone

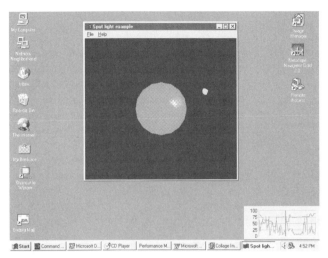

Figure 9-23 Output of the SPOT program demonstrating spotlights

light source to show where the light was coming from. Inside the end of this cone, we placed a bright yellow sphere to simulate a light bulb. Listing 9-9 shows the complete code to render the scene.

Make special note of the statement

```
glPushAttrib(GL_LIGHTING_BIT);
```

Just following this statement, we disable lighting and render a bright yellow sphere. Then we make a call to

```
glPopAttrib();
```

The first statement saves the state of all the lighting state variables. Then we can just disable lighting long enough to draw a yellow light bulb and put the lighting system back the way it was. See the Chapter 14 Reference Section entries for glPushAttrib and glPopAttrib for more information on saving and restoring state variables. A sample screen from our SPOT example program is shown in Figure 9-23.

Listing 9-9 The rendering function for SPOT, showing how the spotlight is moved

```
// Called to draw scene
void RenderScene(void)
    {
    // Clear the window with current clearing color
    glClear(GL_COLOR_BUFFER_BIT | GL_DEPTH_BUFFER_BIT);

    // Set material color and draw a sphere in the middle
    glRGB(0, 0, 255);
    auxSolidSphere(30.0f);
```

continued on next page

continued from previous page

```
        // Now place the light
        // Save the coordinate transformation
        glPushMatrix();
                // Rotate coordinate system
                glRotatef(yRot, 0.0f, 1.0f, 0.0f);
                glRotatef(xRot, 1.0f, 0.0f, 0.0f);

                // Specify new position and direction in rotated coords.
                glLightfv(GL_LIGHT0,GL_POSITION,lightPos);
                glLightfv(GL_LIGHT0,GL_SPOT_DIRECTION,spotDir);

                // Draw a red cone to enclose the light source
                glRGB(255,0,0);

                // Translate origin to move the cone out to where the light
                // is positioned.
                glTranslatef(lightPos[0],lightPos[1],lightPos[2]);
                auxSolidCone(4.0f,6.0f);

                // Draw a smaller displaced sphere to denote the light bulb
                // Save the lighting state variables
                glPushAttrib(GL_LIGHTING_BIT);

                        // Turn off lighting and specify a bright yellow sphere
                        glDisable(GL_LIGHTING);
                        glRGB(255,255,0);
                        auxSolidSphere(3.0f);

                // Restore lighting state variables
                glPopAttrib();

        // Restore coordinate transformations
        glPopMatrix();

        // Flush drawing commands
        glFlush();
        }
```

Shadows

A chapter on lighting naturally begs the topic of shadows. Adding shadows to your scenes can greatly improve their realism and visual effectiveness. In Figures 9-24a and 9-24b you see two views of a lighted cube, one without and one with a shadow (this is the example program from Chapter 2). The cube in Figure 9-24b with a shadow looks much more believable.

What Is a Shadow?

Conceptually, drawing a shadow is quite simple. A shadow is produced when an object keeps light from a light source from striking some object or surface behind the object casting the shadow. The area on the shadowed object's surface, outlined by the object casting the shadow, appears dark. We can produce a shadow programmatically by flattening the original object into the plane of the surface in which the object lies. The object is then drawn in black or some dark color, perhaps with some translucence (see the shadow sample in Chapter 16). Figure 9-25 illustrates this flattening.

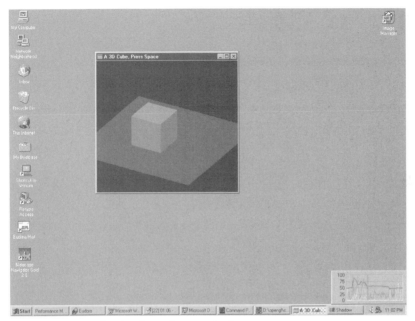

Figure 9-24a Lighted cube without a shadow

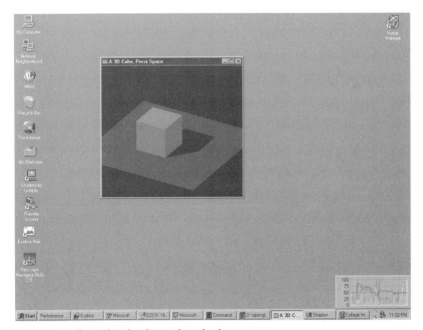

Figure 9-24b Lighted cube with a shadow

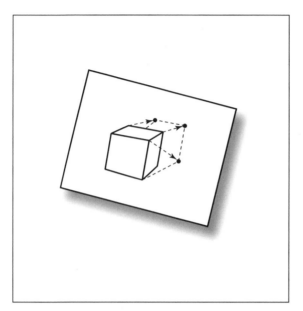

Figure 9-25 Flattening an object to create a shadow

The process of squishing an object against another surface is accomplished using some of those advanced matrix manipulations we explored in Chapter 7. Here we will boil it down to make it as simple as possible.

Squish Code

We need to flatten the Modelview projection matrix so that any and all objects drawn into it are now in this flattened two-dimensional world. No matter how the object is oriented, it will be squished into the plane in which the shadow lies. The second consideration is the distance and direction of the light source. The direction of the light source determines the shape of the shadow, and influences the size. If you've ever seen your shadow in the late or early morning hours, you know how long and warped your shadow can appear depending on the position of the Sun.

The function in Listing 9-10 takes three points that lie in the plane in which you want the shadow to appear, the position of the light source, and finally a pointer to a transformation matrix that this function will construct. Without delving too much into linear algebra, what this function does is deduce the coefficients of the equation of the plane in which the shadow will appear, and use it along with the lighting position to build a Transformation matrix. If you multiply this matrix by the current Modelview matrix, all further drawing will be flattened into this plane.

Listing 9-10 Function to make a shadow transformation matrix

```
// Creates a shadow projection matrix out of the plane equation
// coefficients and the position of the light. The return value is stored
// in destMat[][]
void MakeShadowMatrix(GLfloat points[3][3], GLfloat lightPos[4], GLfloat destMat[4][4])
        {
        GLfloat planeCoeff[4];
        GLfloat dot;

        // Find the plane equation coefficients
        // Find the first three coefficients the same way we
        // find a normal.
        calcNormal(points,planeCoeff);

        // Find the last coefficient by back substitutions
        planeCoeff[3] = - (
                (planeCoeff[0]*points[2][0]) + (planeCoeff[1]*points[2][1]) +
                (planeCoeff[2]*points[2][2]));


        // Dot product of plane and light position
        dot = planeCoeff[0] * lightPos[0] +
                        planeCoeff[1] * lightPos[1] +
                        planeCoeff[2] * lightPos[2] +
                        planeCoeff[3] * lightPos[3];

        // Now do the projection
        // First column
        destMat[0][0] = dot - lightPos[0] * planeCoeff[0];
        destMat[1][0] = 0.0f - lightPos[0] * planeCoeff[1];
        destMat[2][0] = 0.0f - lightPos[0] * planeCoeff[2];
        destMat[3][0] = 0.0f - lightPos[0] * planeCoeff[3];

        // Second column
        destMat[0][1] = 0.0f - lightPos[1] * planeCoeff[0];
        destMat[1][1] = dot - lightPos[1] * planeCoeff[1];
        destMat[2][1] = 0.0f - lightPos[1] * planeCoeff[2];
        destMat[3][1] = 0.0f - lightPos[1] * planeCoeff[3];

        // Third Column
        destMat[0][2] = 0.0f - lightPos[2] * planeCoeff[0];
        destMat[1][2] = 0.0f - lightPos[2] * planeCoeff[1];
        destMat[2][2] = dot - lightPos[2] * planeCoeff[2];
        destMat[3][2] = 0.0f - lightPos[2] * planeCoeff[3];

        // Fourth Column
        destMat[0][3] = 0.0f - lightPos[3] * planeCoeff[0];
        destMat[1][3] = 0.0f - lightPos[3] * planeCoeff[1];
        destMat[2][3] = 0.0f - lightPos[3] * planeCoeff[2];
        destMat[3][3] = dot - lightPos[3] * planeCoeff[3];
        }
```

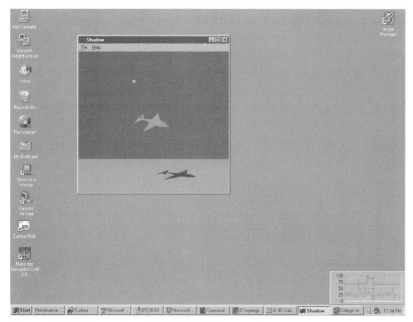

Figure 9-26 Output from the SHADOW example program

A Shadow Example

To demonstrate the use of the function in Listing 9-10, we will suspend our jet in air high above the ground. We'll place the light source directly above and a bit to the left of the jet. As you use the arrow keys to spin the jet around, the shadow cast by the jet will appear flattened on the ground below. The output from this SHADOW example program is shown in Figure 9-26.

The code in Listing 9-11 shows how the shadow projection matrix was created for this example. Note that we create the matrix once in SetupRC() and save it in a global variable.

Listing 9-11 Setting up the shadow projection matrix

```
GLfloat lightPos[] = { -75.0f, 150.0f, -50.0f, 0.0f };
...
...

// Transformation matrix to project shadow
GLfloat shadowMat[4][4];
...
...

// This function does any needed initialization on the rendering
// context.  Here it sets up and initializes the lighting for
// the scene.
void SetupRC()
```

```
{
// Any three points on the ground (counterclockwise order)
GLfloat points[3][3] = {{ -30.0f, -149.0f, -20.0f }, { -30.0f, -149.0f, 20.0f },
                        { 40.0f, -149.0f, 20.0f }};

glEnable(GL_DEPTH_TEST);          // Hidden surface removal
glFrontFace(GL_CCW);              // Counterclockwise polygons face out
glEnable(GL_CULL_FACE);           // Do not calculate inside of jet

// Enable lighting
glEnable(GL_LIGHTING);

...
// Code to setup lighting, etc.
...


// Light blue background
glClearColor(0.0f, 0.0f, 1.0f, 1.0f );

// Calculate projection matrix to draw shadow on the ground
MakeShadowMatrix(points, lightPos, shadowMat);
}
```

Listing 9-12 shows the rendering code for the SHADOW example. We first draw the jet as we normally would; then we restore the Modelview matrix and multiply it by the shadow matrix. This creates our squish Projection matrix. Then we draw the jet again (we've modified our code to accept a flag telling the DrawJet function to render in color or black). After restoring the Modelview matrix once again, we draw a small yellow sphere to approximate the position of the light, and then draw a plane below the jet to indicate the ground. This rectangle lies in the same plane in which our shadow will be drawn.

Listing 9-12 Render the jet and its shadow

```
// Called to draw scene
void RenderScene(void)
        {
        // Clear the window with current clearing color
        glClear(GL_COLOR_BUFFER_BIT | GL_DEPTH_BUFFER_BIT);

        // Save the matrix state and do the rotations
        glPushMatrix();

        // Draw jet at new orientation, put light in correct position
        // before rotating the jet
        glLightfv(GL_LIGHT0,GL_POSITION,lightPos);
        glRotatef(xRot, 1.0f, 0.0f, 0.0f);
        glRotatef(yRot, 0.0f, 1.0f, 0.0f);

        DrawJet(FALSE);

        // Restore original matrix state
        glPopMatrix();

        // Get ready to draw the shadow and the ground
```

continued on next page

continued from previous page

```
// First disable lighting and save the projection state
glPushAttrib(GL_LIGHTING_BIT);
glDisable(GL_LIGHTING);
glPushMatrix();

// Multiply by shadow projection matrix
glMultMatrixf((GLfloat *)shadowMat);

// Now rotate the jet around in the new flattened space
glRotatef(xRot, 1.0f, 0.0f, 0.0f);
glRotatef(yRot, 0.0f, 1.0f, 0.0f);

// Pass true to indicate drawing shadow
DrawJet(TRUE);

// Restore the projection to normal
glPopMatrix();

// Draw the light source
glPushMatrix();
glTranslatef(lightPos[0],lightPos[1], lightPos[2]);
glRGB(255,255,0);
auxSolidSphere(5.0f);
glPopMatrix();


// Draw the ground; we do manual shading to a darker green
// in the background to give the illusion of depth
glBegin(GL_QUADS);
        glRGB(0,128,0);
        glVertex3f(400.0f, -150.0f, -200.0f);
        glVertex3f(-400.0f, -150.0f, -200.0f);
        glRGB(0,255,0);
        glVertex3f(-400.0f, -150.0f, 200.0f);
        glVertex3f(400.0f, -150.0f, 200.0f);
glEnd();


// Restore lighting state variables
glPopAttrib();

// Flush drawing commands
glFlush();
}
```

Lighting and Color Index Mode

In Chapter 8, you learned that in color index mode, color is specified as an index into a palette rather than as components of red, green, and blue light. This has some obvious implications for lighting effects. Most of the lighting functions expect light and material properties to be specified in terms of these RGBA components.

Some consideration is made for color index mode by OpenGL, but in color index mode your lights may only contain diffuse and specular components. Material properties can include shininess, ambient, diffuse, and specular light, and although this may be enough to do some lighting, it is questionable whether it's actually worth the effort.

In order to do lighting, your palette must contain three color ramps for ambient, diffuse, and specular colorings. To achieve satisfactory results, your ramps will usually progress from black to shades of a single color and finally to white. It's possible to define these such that you produce a smoothly shaded object in a single color, but this has few if any practical applications.

Generally, most recognized OpenGL texts recommend that you avoid color index mode for lighting effects. Still, if you must use it, the CD contains a supplementary example called ILIGHT that shows how to use color index mode to illuminate a scene with some objects. However, all these objects are the same color!

Summary

In this chapter you have been introduced to some of the more magical and powerful capabilities of OpenGL. You've seen how to specify one or more light sources and define their lighting characteristics in terms of ambient, diffuse, and specular components. We explained how the corresponding material properties interact with these light sources, and demonstrated some special effects such as adding specular highlights and softening sharp edges.

Also covered were lighting positions, and creation and manipulation of spotlights. The high-level matrix munching function presented here will make shadow generation as easy as it gets. Finally, we explained why you should avoid color index mode for lighting effects. The demonstration programs in this chapter are fairly simple, but you'll find more samples on the CD in the subdirectory for this chapter. The programs on the CD further demonstrate all of these effects, including scenes with more than one light source.

Reference Section

GLCOLORMATERIAL

Purpose	Allows material colors to track the current color as set by glColor.
Include File	<gl.h>
Syntax	void glColorMaterial(GLenum face, GLenum mode);
Description	This function allows material properties to be set without having to call glMaterial directly. By using this function, certain material properties can be set to follow the current color as specified by glColor. By default, color tracking is disabled; to enable it, you must also call glEnable(GL_COLOR_MATERIAL). To disable color tracking again, call glDisable(GL_COLOR_MATERIAL).
Parameters	
face	GLenum: Specifies if the front (GL_FRONT), back (GL_BACK), or both (GL_FRONT_AND_BACK) should follow the current color.

mode	GLenum: Specifies which material property should be following the current color. This can be GL_EMISSION, GL_AMBIENT, GL_DIFFUSE, GL_SPECULAR, or GL_AMBIENT_AND_DIFFUSE.
Returns	None.
Example	The following code from the AMBIENT example program enables color tracking, then sets the front material parameters for ambient and diffuse reflectivity to follow the colors specified by glColor.

```
glEnable(GL_COLOR_MATERIAL);  // Enable Material color tracking

// Front material ambient and diffuse colors track glColor
glColorMaterial(GL_FRONT,GL_AMBIENT_AND_DIFFUSE);
```

See Also	glColor, glMaterial, glLight, glLightModel

GLCULLFACE

Purpose	Specifies whether the front or back of polygons should be eliminated from drawing.
Include File	<gl.h>
Syntax	void glCullFace(GLenum mode);
Description	This function disables lighting, shading, and color calculations and operations on either the front or back of a polygon. If, for instance, an object is closed in so that the back side of the polygons will never be visible regardless of rotation or translation, this will eliminate unnecessary computations in the display of the scene. Culling is enabled or disabled by calling glEnable and glDisable with the GL_CULL_FACE parameter. The front and back of the polygon are defined by use of the glFrontFace function and the order in which the vertices are specified (clockwise or counterclockwise winding).
Parameters	
mode	GLenum: Specifies which face of polygons should be culled. May be either GL_FRONT, or GL_BACK.
Returns	None.
Example	The following code from the AMBIENT example from this chapter shows how the color and drawing operations are disabled for the inside of the jet. It is also necessary to indicate which side of the polygon is the outside by specifying clockwise or counterclockwise winding.

```
glEnable(GL_CULL_FACE); // Do not calculate inside of jet
glFrontFace(GL_CCW);    // Counterclockwise polygons face out
```

See Also	glFrontFace, glLightModel

glFrontFace

Purpose	Defines which side of a polygon is the front or back.
Include File	<gl.h>
Syntax	void glFrontFace(GLenum mode);
Description	When a scene is made up of objects that are closed (you cannot see the inside), there is no need to do color or lighting calculations on the inside of the object. The glCullFace function will turn off such calculations for either the front or back of polygons. The glFrontFace function determines which side of the polygons is considered the front. If the vertices of a polygon are specified such that they travel around the polygon in a clockwise fashion, the polygon is said to have clockwise winding. If the vertices travel counterclockwise, the polygon is said to have counterclockwise winding. This function allows either the clockwise or counterclockwise wound face to be considered the front of the polygon.
Parameters	
mode	GLenum: Specifies the orientation of front facing polygons, clockwise (GL_CW) or counterclockwise (GL_CCW).
Returns	None.
Example	The following code from the AMBEINT example from this chapter shows how the color and drawing operations are disabled for the inside of the jet. It is also necessary to indicate which side of the polygon is the outside by specifying clockwise or counterclockwise winding.

```
glEnable(GL_CULL_FACE); // Do not calculate inside of jet
glFrontFace(GL_CCW);    // Counterclockwise polygons face out
```

See Also	glCullFace, glLightModel

glGetMaterial

Purpose	Returns the current material property settings.
Include File	<gl.h>
Variations	void **glGetMaterialfv**(GLenum face, GLenum pname, GLfloat *params);
	void **glGetMaterialiv**(GLenum face, GLenum pname, GLint *params);
Description	Use this function to query the current front or back material properties. The return values are stored at the address pointed to by *params*. For most properties this is an array of four values containing the RGBA components of the property specified.
Parameters	
face	GLenum: Specifies whether the front (GL_FRONT), or back (GL_BACK) material properties are being sought.

pname	GLenum: Specifies which material property is being queried. Valid values are: GL_AMBIENT, GL_DIFFUSE, GL_SPECULAR, GL_EMISSION, GL_SHININESS, and GL_COLOR_INDEXES.
params	GLint* or GLfloat*: An array of integer or floating point values representing the return values. For GL_AMBIENT, GL_DIFFUSE, GL_SPECULAR, and GL_EMISSION this is a four-element array containing the RGBA values of the property specified. For GL_SHININESS a single value representing the specular exponent of the material is returned. GL_COLOR_INDEXES returns an array of three elements containing the ambient, diffuse, and specular components in the form of color indexes. GL_COLOR_INDEXES is only used for color index lighting.
Returns	None.
Example	The following code shows how all the current material properties are read and stored.

```
// Storage for all the material properties
GLfloat mbientMat[4],diffuseMat[4],specularMat[4],emissionMat[4];
GLfloat shine;
...
...
// Read all the material properties
glGetMaterialfv(GL_FRONT,GL_AMBIENT,ambientMat);
glGetMaterialfv(GL_FRONT,GL_DIFFUSE,diffuseMat);
glGetMaterialfv(GL_FRONT,GL_SPECULAR,specularMat);
glGetMaterialfv(GL_FRONT,GL_EMISSION,emissionMat);
glGetMaterialfv(GL_FRONT,GL_SHININESS,&shine);
```

See Also	glMaterial

GLGETLIGHT

Purpose	Returns information about the current light source settings.
Include File	<gl.h>
Variations	void **glGetLightfv**(GLenum light, GLenum pname, GLfloat *params);
	void **glGetLightiv**(GLenum light, GLenum pname, GLint *params);
Description	Use this function to query the current settings for one of the eight supported light sources. The return values are stored at the address pointed to by *params*. For most properties this is an array of four values containing the RGBA components of the properties specified.
Parameters	
light	GLenum: The light source for which information is being requested. This will range from 0 to GL_MAX_LIGHTS (8 for Windows NT and Windows 95). Constant light values are enumerated from GL_LIGHT0 to GL_LIGHT7.
pname	GLenum: Specifies which property of the light source is being queried. Any of the following values are valid: GL_AMBIENT, GL_DIFFUSE,

GL_SPECULAR, GL_POSITION, GL_SPOT_DIRECTION, GL_SPOT_EXPONENT, GL_SPOT_CUTOFF, GL_CONSTANT_ATTENUATION, GL_LINEAR_ATTENUATION , and GL_QUADRATIC_ATTENUATION.

params   GLfloat* or GLint*: An array of integer or floating point values representing the return values. These return values will be in the form of an array of four, three, or a single value. Table 9-2 shows the return value meanings for each property.

Returns   None.

Example   The following code shows how all the lighting properties for the light source GL_LIGHT0 are retrieved and stored.

```
// Storage for the light properties
GLfloat ambientComp[4],diffuseComp[4],specularComp[4]
...
...
// Read the light components
glGetLightfv(GL_LIGHT0,GL_AMBIENT,ambientComp);
glGetLightfv(GL_FRONT,GL_DIFFUSE,diffuseComp);
glGetLightfv(GL_FRONT,GL_SPECULAR,specularComp);
```

See Also   glLight

Table 9-2 Valid Lighting Parameters for glGetLight

Property	Meaning of Return Values
GL_AMBIENT	Four RGBA components.
GL_DIFFUSE	Four RGBA components.
GL_SPECULAR	Four RGBA components.
GL_POSITION	Four elements that specify the position of the light source. The first three elements specify the position of the light. The fourth, if 1.0, specifies that the light is at this position. Otherwise, the light source is directional and all rays are parallel.
GL_SPOT_DIRECTION	Three elements specifying the direction of the spotlight. This vector will not be normalized, and will be in eye coordinates.
GL_SPOT_EXPONENT	A single value representing the spot exponent.
GL_SPOT_CUTOFF	A single value representing the cutoff angle of the spot source.
GL_CONSTANT_ATTENUATION	A single value representing the constant attenuation of the light.
GL_LINEAR_ATTENUATION	A single value representing the linear attenuation of the light.
GL_QUADRATIC_ATTENUATION	A single value representing the quadratic attenuation of the light.

GLLIGHT

Purpose   Sets light source parameters for one of the eight available light sources.

Include File   <gl.h>

Variations	void **glLightf**(GLenum light, GLenum pname, GLfloat param);
	void **glLighti**(GLenum light, GLenum pname, GLint param);
	void **glLightfv**(GLenum light, GLenum pname, const GLfloat *params);
	void **glLightiv**(GLenum light, GLenum pname, const GLint *params);

Description   Use this function to set the lighting parameters for one of the eight supported light sources. The first two variations of this function require only a single parameter value to set one of the following properties: GL_SPOT_EXPONENT, GL_SPOT_CUTOFF, GL_CONSTANT_ATTENUATION, GL_LINEAR_ATTENUATION, and GL_QUADRATIC_ATTENUATION. The second two variations are used for lighting parameters that require an array of multiple values. These include: GL_AMBIENT, GL_DIFFUSE, GL_SPECULAR, GL_POSITION, and GL_SPOT_DIRECTION. These variations may also be used with single valued parameters by specifying a single element array for *params.

Parameters

light   GLenum: Specifies which light source is being modified. This will range from 0 to GL_MAX_LIGHTS (8 for Windows NT and Windows 95). Constant light values are enumerated from GL_LIGHT0 to GL_LIGHT7.

pname   GLenum: Specifies which lighting parameter is being set by this function call. See Table 9-2 for a complete listing and the meaning of these parameters.

param   GLfloat, or GLint: For parameters that are specified by a single value, this specifies that value. These parameters are: GL_SPOT_EXPONENT, GL_SPOT_CUTOFF, GL_CONSTANT_ATTENUATION, GL_LINEAR_ATTENUATION, and GL_QUADRATIC_ATTENUATION. These parameters only have meaning for spot lights.

params   GLfloat*, or GLint*: An array of values that fully describe the parameters being set. See Table 9-2 for a listing and the meaning of these parameters.

Returns   None.

Example   The following code from the LITJET example program sets up a single light source to the upper-left behind the viewer. The light source is composed only of moderate ambient and diffuse components.

```
// Light values and coordinates
GLfloat  whiteLight[] = { 0.5f, 0.5f, 0.5f, 1.0f };
GLfloat lightPos[] = { -50.f, 50.0f, -100.0f, 0.0f };
...
...

// Enable lighting
glEnable(GL_LIGHTING);

// Set up and enable light 0
glLightfv(GL_LIGHT0,GL_AMBIENT_AND_DIFFUSE,whiteLight);
glLightfv(GL_LIGHT0,GL_POSITION,lightPos);
glEnable(GL_LIGHT0);
```

See Also   glGetLight

GLLIGHTMODEL

Purpose	Sets the lighting model parameters used by OpenGL.
Include File	<gl.h>
Variations	void **glLightModelf**(GLenum pname, GLfloat param)
	void **glLightModeli**(GLenum pname, GLint param);
	void **glLightModelfv**(GLenum pname, const GLfloat *params);
	void **glLightModeliv**(GLenum pname, const GLint *params);
Description	This function is used to set the lighting model parameters used by OpenGL. Any or all of three lighting model parameters may be set. GL_LIGHT_MODEL_AMBIENT is used to set a default ambient illumination for a scene. By default, this light has an RGBA value of (0.2, 0.2, 0.2, 1.0). Only the last two variations may be used to set this lighting model because they take pointers to an array that can contain the RGBA values. The GL_LIGHT_MODEL_TWO_SIDE parameter is specified to indicate whether both sides of polygons are illuminated. By default, only the front (defined by winding) of polygons is illuminated, using the front material properties as specified by glMaterial(). Finally, specifying a lighting model parameter of GL_LIGHT_MODEL_LOCAL_VIEWER modifies calculation of specular reflection angles, whether the view is down along the –z axis or from the origin of the eye coordinate system (see Chapter 6).
Parameters	
pname	GLenum: Specifies a lighting model parameter. GL_LIGHT_MODEL_AMBIENT, GL_LIGHT_MODEL_LOCAL_VIEWER, and GL_LIGHT_MODEL_TWO_SIDE are accepted.
param	GLfloat or GLint: For GL_LIGHT_MODEL_LOCAL_VIEWER, a value of 0.0 indicates that specular lighting angles take the view direction to be parallel to and in the direction of the –z axis. Any other value indicates that the view is from the origin of eye coordinate system. For GL_LIGHT_MODEL_TWO_SIDE, a value of 0.0 indicates that only the fronts of polygons are to be included in illumination calculations. Any other value indicates that both the front and back are included. This parameter has no effect on points, lines, or bitmaps.
params	GLfloat* or GLint*: For GL_LIGHT_MODEL_AMBIENT or GL_LIGHT_MODEL_LOCAL_VIEWER this points to an array of integers or floating point values, only the first element of which is used to set the parameter value. For GL_LIGHT_MODEL_AMBIENT this array points to four values that indicate the RGBA components of the ambient light.
Returns	None.
Example	The following code from this chapter's AMBIENT example sets up a global ambient light source consisting of a full-intensity white light.

```
// Bright white light
GLfloat ambientLight[] = { 1.0f, 1.0f, 1.0f, 1.0f };

glEnable(GL_DEPTH_TEST);        // Hidden surface removal
glEnable(GL_CULL_FACE);         // Do not calculate inside of jet
glFrontFace(GL_CCW);            // Counterclockwise polygons face out

// Enable lighting
glEnable(GL_LIGHTING);

// Set light model to use ambient light specified by ambientLight
glLightModelfv(GL_LIGHT_MODEL_AMBIENT,ambientLight);
```

See Also   glLight, glMaterial

GLMATERIAL

Purpose	Sets material parameters for use by the lighting model.
Include File	<gl.h>
Variations	void **glMaterialf**(GLenum face, GLenum pname, GLfloat param); void **glMateriali**(GLenum face,GLenum pname,GLint param); void **glMaterialfv**(GLenum face, GLenum pname, const GLfloat *params) void **glMaterialiv**(GLenum face, GLenum pname, const GLint *params);
Description	This function is used to set the material reflectance properties of polygons. The GL_AMBIENT, GL_DIFFUSE, and GL_SPECULAR properties affect how these components of incident light are reflected. GL_EMISSION is used for materials that appear to give off their own light. GL_SHININESS can vary from 0 to 128, with the higher values producing a larger specular highlight on the material surface. Finally, GL_COLOR_INDEXES is used for material reflectance properties in color Index mode.

Parameters

face	GLenum: Specifies whether the front, back, or both material properties of the polygons are being set by this function. May be either GL_FRONT, GL_BACK, or GL_FRONT_AND_BACK.
pname	GLenum: For the first two variations, this specifies the single-valued material parameter being set. Currently, the only single-valued material parameter is GL_SHININESS. The second two variations, which take arrays for their parameters, may set the following material properties: GL_AMBIENT, GL_DIFFUSE, GL_SPECULAR, GL_EMISSION, GL_SHININESS, GL_AMBIENT_AND_DIFFUSE, or GL_COLOR_INDEXES.
param	GLfloat or GLint: Specifies the value to which the parameter specified by *pname* (GL_SHININESS) will be set.
params	GLfloat* or GLint*: An array of floats or integers that contain the components of the property being set.

Returns	None.
Example	See the LITJET sample program from this chapter.
See Also	glGetMaterial, glColorMaterial, glLight, glLightModel

GLNORMAL

Purpose	Defines a surface normal for the next vertex or set of vertices specified.
Include File	<gl.h>
Variations	void **glNormal3b**(GLbyte nx, GLbyte ny, GLbyte nz);
	void **glNormal3d**(GLdouble nx, GLdouble ny, GLdouble nz);
	void **glNormal3f**(GLfloat nx, GLfloat ny, GLfloat nz);
	void **glNormal3i**(GLint nx, GLint ny, GLint nz);
	void **glNormal3s**(GLshort nx, GLshort ny, GLshort nz);
	void **glNormal3bv**(const GLbyte *v);
	void **glNormal3dv**(const GLdouble *v);
	void **glNormal3fv**(const GLfloat *v);
	void **glNormal3iv**(const GLint *v);
	void **glNormal3sv**(const GLshort *v);
Description	The normal vector specifies which direction is up and perpendicular to the surface of the polygon. This is used for lighting and shading calculations. Specifying a unit vector of length 1 will improve rendering speed. OpenGL will automatically convert your normals to unit normals if you enable this with glEnable(GL_NORMALIZE);
Parameters	
nx	Specifies the x magnitude of the normal vector.
ny	Specifies the y magnitude of the normal vector.
nz	Specifies the z magnitude of the normal vector.
v	Specifies an array of three elements containing the x, y, and z magnitudes of the normal vector.
Returns	None.
Example	The following code from the LITJET sample program from this chapter demonstrates setting a normal vector for each polygon before it is rendered.

```
// Vertices for this panel
float normal[3];
float v[3][3] = {{ 15.0f, 0.0f, 30.0f},
                 { 0.0f, 15.0f, 30.0f},
                 { 0.0f, 0.0f,  60.0f}};

// Calculate the normal for the plane
calcNormal(v,normal);
```

continued on next page

continued from previous page

```
            // Draw the triangle using the plane normal
            // for all the vertices
            glBegin(GL_TRIANGLES);
                    glNormal3fv(normal);
                    glVertex3fv(v[0]);
                    glVertex3fv(v[1]);
                    glVertex3fv(v[2]);
            glEnd();
```

See Also   glTexCoord, glVertex

10

3D MODELING AND OBJECT COMPOSITION

10

3D MODELING AND OBJECT COMPOSITION

What you'll learn in this chapter:

How to...	Functions You'll Use
Assemble polygons to create 3D objects	glBegin/glEnd/glVertex
Optimize object display with display lists	glNewList/glEndList/glCallList

Your quiver is quite full of OpenGL arrows by now and it's time to go hunting. Unlike previous chapters, this is going to be a project chapter, where you can put some of this stuff to practical use. We are going to define a problem or goal and pursue it to its logical end: a finished program. Along the way, you'll gain some insight in how to break your objects and scenes into smaller, more manageable pieces. We'll compose a complex object out of smaller, simpler objects, which in turn are composed of just the OpenGL primitives.

As a finishing touch we'll show you why and how to apply *display lists*. One of the biggest reasons for using display lists is speed, so for the icing on the cake, we'll even give you a crude but effective means of benchmarking your code.

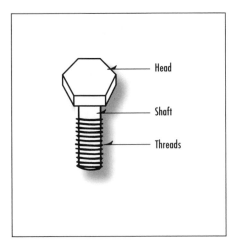

Figure 10-1 The hex bolt to be modeled in this chapter

Defining the Task

To demonstrate building a figure out of smaller simpler figures, we will use an interesting, yet simple example that creates a model of a metallic bolt (like those holding your disk drive together). Although this particular bolt may not exist in any hardware store, it will have the essential features. We shall make the bolt as simple as possible while still retaining the flavor of our task.

The bolt will have a six-sided head and a threaded shaft, like many typical steel bolts. Since this is a learning exercise, we'll simplify the threads by making them raised on the surface of the bolt shaft rather than carved out of the shaft.

Figure 10-1 is a rough sketch of what we're aiming for. We will build the three major components of this bolt—the head, the shaft, and the threads—individually and then put them together to form the final object.

Choosing a Projection

Before we start constructing, we need a projection, a frame of reference for placing the objects. For an example like this, an orthogonal projection is the best choice. This is a typical choice for applications such as CAD, in which an object is being modeled and measured exactly. This bolt has a specific width, height, and number of threads and is comparatively small. Using a perspective projection would make sense if we were modeling something larger such as a landscape, where the effect would be more apparent.

Listing 10-1 is the code that creates the viewing volume. It creates an orthogonal projection and represents a coordinate system that reaches 100 units along the x- and y-axis. An extra 100 units is supplied along the z-axis where the viewer will be located.

Listing 10-1 Setting up the orthogonal projection for this chapter's examples

```
// Change viewing volume and viewport.  Called when window is resized
void ChangeSize(GLsizei w, GLsizei h)
        {
        GLfloat nRange = 100.0f;

        // Prevent a divide by zero
        if(h == 0)
                h = 1;

        // Set Viewport to window dimensions
        glViewport(0, 0, w, h);

        // Reset coordinate system
        glMatrixMode(GL_PROJECTION);
        glLoadIdentity();

        // Establish clipping volume (left, right, bottom, top, near, far)
        if (w <= h)
                glOrtho (-nRange, nRange, -nRange*h/w, nRange*h/w, -nRange*2.0f, nRange*2.0f);
            else
                glOrtho (-nRange*w/h, nRange*w/h, -nRange, nRange, -nRange*2.0f, nRange*2.0f);

        glMatrixMode(GL_MODELVIEW);
        glLoadIdentity();
        }
```

Choosing the Lighting and Material Properties

With the projection chosen, the next step is to select a lighting model for our view of the bolt. Listing 10-2 is the code to set up the rendering context including the lighting and material properties. We make sure the ambient light is bright enough to see all the features, and include a specular component to make it glisten just as a real metal bolt would. The single light source is positioned to the upper-left of the viewer.

Listing 10-2 Setting up the rendering context and lighting conditions

```
// This function does any needed initialization on the rendering
// context.  Here it sets up and initializes the lighting for
// the scene.
void SetupRC()
        {
        // Light values and coordinates
        GLfloat   ambientLight[] = {0.4f, 0.4f, 0.4f, 1.0f };
        GLfloat   diffuseLight[] = {0.7f, 0.7f, 0.7f, 1.0f };
        GLfloat   specular[] = { 0.9f, 0.9f, 0.9f, 1.0f};
        GLfloat   lightPos[] = { -50.0f, 200.0f, 200.0f, 1.0f };
        GLfloat   specref[] =  { 0.6f, 0.6f, 0.6f, 1.0f };

        glEnable(GL_DEPTH_TEST);         // Hidden surface removal
        glEnable(GL_CULL_FACE); // Do not calculate inside of solid object
```

continued on next page

continued from previous page

```
// Enable lighting
glEnable(GL_LIGHTING);

// Set up light 0
glLightModelfv(GL_LIGHT_MODEL_AMBIENT,ambientLight);
glLightfv(GL_LIGHT0,GL_AMBIENT,ambientLight);
glLightfv(GL_LIGHT0,GL_DIFFUSE,diffuseLight);
glLightfv(GL_LIGHT0,GL_SPECULAR,specular);

// Position and turn on the light
glLightfv(GL_LIGHT0,GL_POSITION,lightPos);
glEnable(GL_LIGHT0);

// Enable color tracking
glEnable(GL_COLOR_MATERIAL);

// Set material properties to follow glColor values
glColorMaterial(GL_FRONT, GL_AMBIENT_AND_DIFFUSE);

// All materials hereafter have full specular reflectivity
// with a moderate shine
glMaterialfv(GL_FRONT, GL_SPECULAR,specref);
glMateriali(GL_FRONT,GL_SHININESS,64);

// Black background
glClearColor(0.0f, 0.0f, 0.0f, 1.0f );
}
```

Displaying the Results

Once we have determined the viewing, lighting, and material parameters, all that remains is to render the scene. Listing 10-3 shows the code outline used to display our bolt and bolt pieces. The SomeFunc() line is just a placeholder for function calls to render the head, shaft, and threads individually. We save the matrix state, perform any rotations (defined by the keyboard activity, as in all this book's previous examples), and call a function that renders some specific object or part of an object.

Listing 10-3 Rendering the object, allowing for rotated views

```
// Called to draw scene
void RenderScene(void)
    {
    // Clear the window with current clearing color
    glClear(GL_COLOR_BUFFER_BIT | GL_DEPTH_BUFFER_BIT);

    // Save the matrix state
    glMatrixMode(GL_MODELVIEW);
    glPushMatrix();

    // Rotate about x and y axes
    glRotatef(xRot, 1.0f, 0.0f, 0.0f);
    glRotatef(yRot, 0.0f, 1.0f, 0.0f);

    // Specific code to draw the object  ...
    ...
    ... SomeFunc();          // Place Holder
```

```
glPopMatrix();

// Flush drawing commands
glFlush();
}
```

Constructing a Model, One Piece at a Time

Any given programming task can be separated into smaller, more manageable tasks. This makes the smaller pieces easier to handle and code, and introduces some reusability into our code base, as well. Three-dimensional modeling is no exception, you will create large complex systems out of many smaller and more manageable pieces.

We have decided to break the bolt down into three pieces: head, shaft, and thread. Certainly this makes it much simpler for us to consider each section graphically, but it also give us three objects that we can reuse. In more complex modeling applications, this reusability is of crucial importance. In a CAD-type application, for example, you would probably have many different bolts to model—with various lengths, thickness, and thread density. Instead of the RenderHead() function that draws the head of the bolt in this example, you might want to write a function that takes parameters specifying the number of sides, thickness, and diameter of the bolt head.

Another thing we will do is model each piece of our bolt in coordinates that are most convenient for describing the object. Most often, objects are modeled around the origin and then translated and rotated into place. Later, when composing the final object, we can translate the components, rotate them, and even scale them if necessary to assemble our composite object.

The Head

The head of our bolt has six smooth sides and is smooth on top and bottom, as well. We can construct this solid object with two hexagons that represent the top and bottom of the head, and a series of quadrilaterals around the edges to represent the sides. We could use GL_QUAD and GL_POLYGON to draw this with a minimum number of vertices; however, as we've mentioned previously, you should always use triangles whenever possible. For any accelerated OpenGL hardware (and even some software routines), it may actually be faster to draw two triangles arranged together rather than a single quadrilateral.

Figure 10-2 illustrates how the bolt head will be constructed with triangles. We use a triangle fan with six triangles for the top and bottom sections of the head. Then each face of the side of the bolt is composed of two triangles.

A total of 24 triangles are used to draw the head of the bolt: 6 each on the top and bottom, and 12 more to compose the sides of the bolt head. Listing 10-4 is the function that renders the head of the bolt. Figure 10-3 shows the output of this program, HEAD, in this chapter's subdirectory on the CD. Notice that this code contains no functions that we haven't yet covered, but it's more substantial than any of the simpler chapter examples.

Figure 10-2 Triangle outline of bolt head

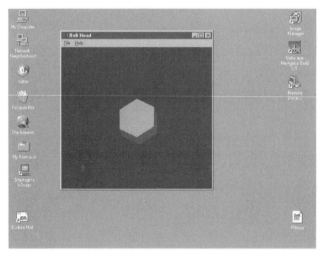

Figure 10-3 Output from the HEAD program

Listing 10-4 Rendering the head of the bolt

```
// Creates the head of the bolt
void RenderHead(void)
        {
        float x,y,angle;                        // Calculated positions
        float height = 25.0f;                   // Thickness of the head
        float diameter = 30.0f;                 // Diameter of the head
        float normal[3],corners[4][3];          // Storage of vertices and normals
        float step = (3.1415f/3.0f);            // step = 1/6th of a circle = hexagon
```

```
// Set material color for head of bolt
glColor3f(0.0f, 0.0f, 0.7f);

// Clockwise polygons face out, set for fans
glFrontFace(GL_CW);

// Begin a new triangle fan to cover the top
glBegin(GL_TRIANGLE_FAN);

        // All the normals for the top of the bolt point straight up
        // the z axis.
        glNormal3f(0.0f, 0.0f, 1.0f);

        // Center of fan is at the origin
        glVertex3f(0.0f, 0.0f, 0.0f);

        // Divide the circle up into 6 sections and start dropping
        // points to specify the fan
        for(angle = 0.0f; angle < (2.0f*3.1415f); angle += step)
                {
                // Calculate x and y position of the next vertex
                x = diameter*(float)sin(angle);
                y = diameter*(float)cos(angle);

                // Specify the next vertex for the triangle fan
                glVertex3f(x, y, 0.0f);
                }

        // Last vertex closes the fan
        glVertex3f(0.0f, diameter, 0.0f);

// Done drawing the fan that covers the bottom
glEnd();

// Now draw the bottom of the bolt head. Switch to
// clockwise polygons facing out.
glFrontFace(GL_CCW);

// Begin a new triangle fan to cover the bottom
glBegin(GL_TRIANGLE_FAN);

        // Normal for bottom points straight down the negative z axis
        glNormal3f(0.0f, 0.0f, -1.0f);

        // Center of fan is at the origin
        glVertex3f(0.0f, 0.0f, -height);

        // Divide the circle up into 6 sections and start dropping
        // points to specify the fan
        for(angle = 0.0f; angle < (2.0f*3.1415f); angle += step)
                {
                // Calculate x and y position of the next vertex
                x = diameter*(float)sin(angle);
                y = diameter*(float)cos(angle);

                // Specify the next vertex for the triangle fan
                glVertex3f(x, y, -height);
                }
```

continued on next page

continued from previous page

```
            // Last vertex, used to close the fan
            glVertex3f(0.0f, diameter, -height);

    // Done drawing the fan that covers the bottom
    glEnd();


    // Build the sides out of triangles (two each). Each face
    // will consist of two triangles arranged to form a
    // quadrilateral
    glBegin(GL_TRIANGLES);

        // Go around and draw the sides
        for(angle = 0.0f; angle < (2.0f*3.1415f); angle += step)
            {
            // Calculate x and y position of the next hex point
            x = diameter*(float)sin(angle);
            y = diameter*(float)cos(angle);

            // start at bottom of head
            corners[0][0] = x;
            corners[0][1] = y;
            corners[0][2] = -height;

            // extrude to top of head
            corners[1][0] = x;
            corners[1][1] = y;
            corners[1][2] = 0.0f;

            // Calculate the next hex point
            x = diameter*(float)sin(angle+step);
            y = diameter*(float)cos(angle+step);

            // Make sure we aren't done before proceeding
            if(angle+step < 3.1415*2.0)
                    {
                    // If we are done, just close the fan at a
                    // known coordinate.
                    corners[2][0] = x;
                    corners[2][1] = y;
                    corners[2][2] = 0.0f;

                    corners[3][0] = x;
                    corners[3][1] = y;
                    corners[3][2] = -height;
                    }
            else
                    {
                    // We aren't done, the points at the top and bottom
                    // of the head.
                    corners[2][0] = 0.0f;
                    corners[2][1] = diameter;
                    corners[2][2] = 0.0f;

                    corners[3][0] = 0.0f;
                    corners[3][1] = diameter;
                    corners[3][2] = -height;
                    }
```

```
                      // The normal vectors for the entire face will
                      // all point the same direction
                      calcNormal(corners, normal);
                      glNormal3fv(normal);

                      // Specify each triangle separately to lie next
                      // to each other.
                      glVertex3fv(corners[0]);
                      glVertex3fv(corners[1]);
                      glVertex3fv(corners[2]);

                      glVertex3fv(corners[0]);
                      glVertex3fv(corners[2]);
                      glVertex3fv(corners[3]);
                      }

     glEnd();
     }
```

The Shaft

The shaft of the bolt is nothing more than a cylinder with a bottom on it. We compose a cylinder by plotting xy values around in a circle, and then take two z values at these points and get polygons that approximate the wall of a cylinder. Once again, however, we will compose this wall entirely out of triangles. Figure 10-4 shows the outline of the cylinder.

We also create the bottom of the shaft with a triangle fan. Notice that the smaller the step size is around the circle, the smaller the flat facets that make up the cylinder wall and the more closely the wall will approximate a smooth curve.

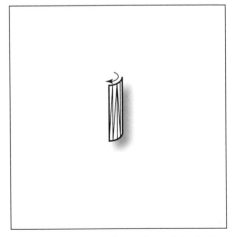

Figure 10-4 Triangle outline of the bolt shaft

Listing 10-5 is the code to produce this cylinder. Notice that the normals are not calculated for the triangles using the vertices of the triangles. We usually set the normal to be the same for all vertices, but here we'll break with this tradition to specify a new normal for each vertex. Since we are simulating a curved surface, the normal specified for each vertex would be normal to the actual curve.

Listing 10-5 Rendering the shaft of the bolt

```
// Creates the shaft of the bolt as a cylinder with one end
// closed.
void RenderShaft(void)
        {
        float x,y,angle;              // Used to calculate cylinder wall
        float height = 75.0f;         // Height of the cylinder
        float diameter = 20.0f;       // Diameter of the cylinder
        float normal[3],corners[4][3]; // Storage for vertices calculations
        float step = (3.1415f/50.0f);  // Approximate the cylinder wall with
                                       // 100 flat segments.


        // Set material color for head of screw
        glColor3f(0.0f, 0.0f, 0.7f);

        // counterclockwise polygons face out (the default for triangles)
        glFrontFace(GL_CCW);


        // First assemble the wall as 100 quadrilaterals formed by
        // placing adjoining triangles together
        glBegin(GL_TRIANGLES);

        // Go around and draw the sides
        for(angle = 0.0f; angle < (2.0f*3.1415f); angle += step)
                {
                // Calculate x and y position of the next vertex
                x = diameter*(float)sin(angle);
                y = diameter*(float)cos(angle);

                // Get the coordinate for this point and extrude the
                // length of the cylinder.
                corners[0][0] = x;
                corners[0][1] = y;
                corners[0][2] = -height;

                corners[1][0] = x;
                corners[1][1] = y;
                corners[1][2] = 0.0f;

                // Get the next point and do the same
                x = diameter*(float)sin(angle+step);
                y = diameter*(float)cos(angle+step);

                // If finished, use known starting point to close the surface
                if(angle+step < 3.1415*2.0) // Not Finished
                        {
                        corners[2][0] = x;
                        corners[2][1] = y;
```

```
               corners[2][2] = 0.0f;

               corners[3][0] = x;
               corners[3][1] = y;
               corners[3][2] = -height;
               }
    else
               {
               // Finished, use the starting point
               corners[2][0] = 0.0f;
               corners[2][1] = diameter;
               corners[2][2] = 0.0f;

               corners[3][0] = 0.0f;
               corners[3][1] = diameter;
               corners[3][2] = -height;
               }

    // Instead of using real normal to actual flat section,
    // use what the normal would be if the surface were really
    // curved. Since the cylinder goes up the z axis, the normal
    // points from the z axis out directly through each vertex.
    // Therefore we can use the vertex as the normal, as long as
    // we reduce it to unit length first.

    // First Triangle //////////////////////////////////////////
    // Fill the normal vector with the coordinate points
    normal[0] = corners[0][0];
    normal[1] = corners[0][1];
    normal[2] = corners[0][2];

    // Reduce to length of one and specify for this point
    ReduceToUnit(normal);
    glNormal3fv(normal);
    glVertex3fv(corners[0]);

    // Get vertex, calculate unit normal and go
    normal[0] = corners[1][0];
    normal[1] = corners[1][1];
    normal[2] = corners[1][2];
    ReduceToUnit(normal);
    glNormal3fv(normal);
    glVertex3fv(corners[1]);

    // Get vertex, calculate unit normal and go
    normal[0] = corners[2][0];
    normal[1] = corners[2][1];
    normal[2] = corners[2][2];
    ReduceToUnit(normal);
    glNormal3fv(normal);
    glVertex3fv(corners[2]);


    // Second Triangle /////////////////////////////////////////

    // Get vertex, calculate unit normal and go
    normal[0] = corners[2][0];
    normal[1] = corners[2][1];
    normal[2] = corners[2][2];
```

continued on next page

continued from previous page

```
                    ReduceToUnit(normal);
                    glNormal3fv(normal);
                    glVertex3fv(corners[2]);

                    // Get vertex, calculate unit normal and go
                    normal[0] = corners[3][0];
                    normal[1] = corners[3][1];
                    normal[2] = corners[3][2];
                    ReduceToUnit(normal);
                    glNormal3fv(normal);
                    glVertex3fv(corners[3]);

                    // Get vertex, calculate unit normal and go
                    normal[0] = corners[0][0];
                    normal[1] = corners[0][1];
                    normal[2] = corners[0][2];
                    ReduceToUnit(normal);
                    glNormal3fv(normal);
                    glVertex3fv(corners[0]);
                    }

    glEnd();            // Done with cylinder sides

    // Begin a new triangle fan to cover the bottom
    glBegin(GL_TRIANGLE_FAN);

    // Normal points down the z axis
    glNormal3f(0.0f, 0.0f, -1.0f);

    // Center of fan is at the origin
    glVertex3f(0.0f, 0.0f, -height);

    // Spin around, matching step size of cylinder wall
    for(angle = 0.0f; angle < (2.0f*3.1415f); angle += step)
            {
            // Calculate x and y position of the next vertex
            x = diameter*(float)sin(angle);
            y = diameter*(float)cos(angle);

            // Specify the next vertex for the triangle fan
            glVertex3f(x, y, -height);
            }

    // Close the fan
    glVertex3f(0.0f, diameter, -height);
    glEnd();
    }
```

Fortunately, the cylinder is wrapped symmetrically around the z-axis. Thus, the normal for each vertex can be found by normalizing (reducing to length 1) the vertex itself. Figure 10-5 shows the output from the SHAFT program.

The Thread

The thread is the most complex part of the bolt. It's composed of two planes arranged in a V shape that follows a corkscrew pattern up the length of the shaft. It is created as two flat segments arranged in a V pattern. Figure 10-6 illustrates the triangle outline of this shape and Listing 10-6 is the OpenGL code used to produce this shape.

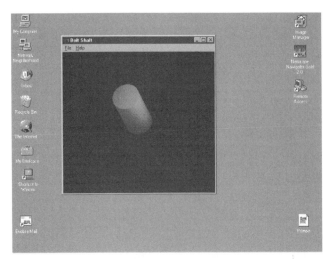

Figure 10-5 Output from the SHAFT program

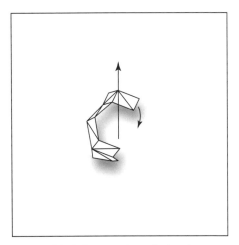

Figure 10-6 Progression of triangle
outline of thread

Listing 10-6 Rendering the thread of the bolt

```
// Creates the thread of the bolt
void RenderThread(void)
        {
        float x,y,z,angle;              // Calculate coordinates and step angle
        float height = 75.0f;           // Height of the threading
```

continued on next page

continued from previous page

```
float diameter = 20.0f;              // Diameter of the threading
float normal[3],corners[4][3];       // Storage for normal and corners
float step = (3.1415f/32.0f);        // One revolution
float revolutions = 7.0f;            // How many times around the shaft
float threadWidth = 2.0f;            // How wide is the thread
float threadThick = 3.0f;            // How thick is the thread
float zstep = .125f;                 // How much does the thread move up
                                     // the z axis each time a new segment
                                     // is drawn.


// 360 degrees in radians
#define PI2 (2.0f*3.1415f)

// Set material color for thread
glColor3f(0.0f, 0.0f, 0.4f);


z = -height+2;  // Starting spot almost to the end

// Go around and draw the sides until finished spinning up
for(angle = 0.0f; angle < PI2*revolutions; angle += step)
    {
    // Calculate x and y position of the next vertex
    x = diameter*(float)sin(angle);
    y = diameter*(float)cos(angle);

    // Store the next vertex next to the shaft
    corners[0][0] = x;
    corners[0][1] = y;
    corners[0][2] = z;

    // Calculate the position away from the shaft
    x = (diameter+threadWidth)*(float)sin(angle);
    y = (diameter+threadWidth)*(float)cos(angle);

    corners[1][0] = x;
    corners[1][1] = y;
    corners[1][2] = z;

    // Calculate the next position away from the shaft
    x = (diameter+threadWidth)*(float)sin(angle+step);
    y = (diameter+threadWidth)*(float)cos(angle+step);

    corners[2][0] = x;
    corners[2][1] = y;
    corners[2][2] = z + zstep;

    // Calculate the next position along the shaft
    x = (diameter)*(float)sin(angle+step);
    y = (diameter)*(float)cos(angle+step);

    corners[3][0] = x;
    corners[3][1] = y;
    corners[3][2] = z+ zstep;
```

```
        // We'll be using triangles, so make
        // counterclockwise polygons face out
        glFrontFace(GL_CCW);
        glBegin(GL_TRIANGLES);  // Start the top section of thread

                // Calculate the normal for this segment
                calcNormal(corners, normal);
                glNormal3fv(normal);

                // Draw two triangles to cover area
                glVertex3fv(corners[0]);
                glVertex3fv(corners[1]);
                glVertex3fv(corners[2]);

                glVertex3fv(corners[2]);
                glVertex3fv(corners[3]);
                glVertex3fv(corners[0]);

        glEnd();


        // Move the edge along the shaft slightly up the z axis
        // to represent the bottom of the thread
        corners[0][2] += threadThick;
        corners[3][2] += threadThick;

        // Recalculate the normal since points have changed. This
        // time it points in the opposite direction, so reverse it
        calcNormal(corners, normal);
        normal[0] = -normal[0];
        normal[1] = -normal[1];
        normal[2] = -normal[2];

        // Switch to clockwise facing out for underside of the
        // thread.
        glFrontFace(GL_CW);

        // Draw the two triangles
        glBegin(GL_TRIANGLES);
                glNormal3fv(normal);

                glVertex3fv(corners[0]);
                glVertex3fv(corners[1]);
                glVertex3fv(corners[2]);

                glVertex3fv(corners[2]);
                glVertex3fv(corners[3]);
                glVertex3fv(corners[0]);

        glEnd();

        // Creep up the z axis
        z += zstep;
        }
}
```

Figure 10-7 shows the output of the THREAD program.

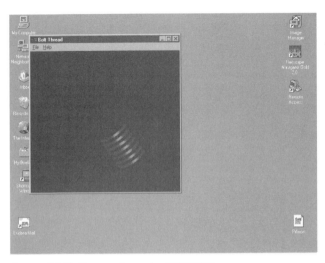

Figure 10-7 Output from the THREAD program

Putting the Model Together

The bolt is assembled by drawing all three sections in their appropriate location. All sections are translated appropriately up the z-axis. The shaft and threads are translated the same amount because essentially they occupy the same location. All that needs to be done is to put the pieces in the appropriate locations, and hidden surface removal will automatically eliminate hidden surfaces for us.

Listing 10-7 is the rendering code that manipulates and renders the three bolt components. Figure 10-8 shows the final output of the BOLT program.

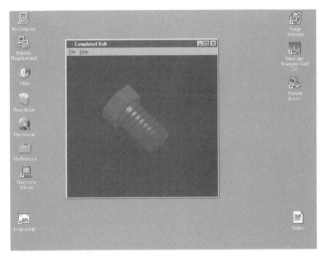

Figure 10-8 Output from the BOLT program

Listing 10-7 Rendering code to draw the completed bolt

```
// Called to draw the entire bolt
void RenderScene(void)
        {
        // Clear the window with current clearing color
        glClear(GL_COLOR_BUFFER_BIT | GL_DEPTH_BUFFER_BIT);

        // Save the matrix state and do the rotations
        glMatrixMode(GL_MODELVIEW);

        // Rotate and translate, then render the bolt head
        glPushMatrix();
                glRotatef(xRot, 1.0f, 0.0f, 0.0f);
                glRotatef(yRot, 0.0f, 1.0f, 0.0f);
                glTranslatef(0.0f, 0.0f, 55.0f);
                RenderHead();
        glPopMatrix();


        // Save matrix state, rotate, translate and draw the
        // shaft and thread together
        glPushMatrix();
        glRotatef(xRot, 1.0f, 0.0f, 0.0f);
        glRotatef(yRot, 0.0f, 1.0f, 0.0f);
        glTranslatef(0.0f, 0.0f, 40.0f);

        // Render just the hexagonal head of the nut
        RenderShaft();
        RenderThread();

        glPopMatrix();

        // Flush drawing commands
        glFlush();
```

A Makeshift Benchmark

Our final program produces a fairly good representation of the metal bolt we set out to model. Consisting of over 1,700 triangles, this is the most complex example in this book so far. Comparatively speaking, however, this number of triangles isn't anywhere close to the largest number of polygons you'll encounter when composing larger scenes and more complex objects. In fact, the latest 3D accelerated graphics cards are rated at hundreds of thousands of triangles per second, and that's for the cheap ones! One of the goals of this chapter is to introduce you to using display lists to optimize rendering speed. Before we can get into a comparison of rendering speeds, however, we will need a way to measure this—a benchmark.

When we get into the subject of display lists, we want you to be able to see that there is a performance difference rather than just take our word for it. So let's modify our BOLT program slightly. Rather than spinning the object about its axes when arrow keys are pressed, we'll have it spin repeatedly around just the y-axis in particular. As you might imagine, this turns the program into a continual triangle-generator that we can use to more easily see differences in performance. Listing 10-8 is the changed RenderScene() function used for SPINBOLT.

Listing 10-8 New RenderScene() function to spin bolt around the y-axis

```
// Called to draw the entire bolt
void RenderScene(void)
    {
    // Clear the window with current clearing color
    glClear(GL_COLOR_BUFFER_BIT | GL_DEPTH_BUFFER_BIT);

    // Make sure we have the correct matrix mode
    glMatrixMode(GL_MODELVIEW);

    // Rotate and translate the coordinate system
    glRotatef(5.0f, 0.0f, 1.0f, 0.0f);

    // Translate and render the head
    glTranslatef(0.0f, 0.0f, 55.0f);
    RenderHead();

    // Translate back some and render the shaft and thread
    glTranslatef(0.0f, 0.0f, -15.0f);
    RenderShaft();
    RenderThread();

    // Translate back some again for next pass
    glTranslatef(0.0f, 0.0f, -40.0f);

    // Flush drawing commands
    glFlush();
    }
```

This new rendering function does not save or restore the matrix state. We use glTranslate to manually restore the translation state of the matrix before leaving the function, but the effects of glRotate are cumulative. This causes the bolt to be rotated around its y-axis by 5° every time the bolt is rendered.

One simple animation technique would be to create a timer, and when the WM_TIMER message is received, invalidate the window causing a redraw. In this manner we can speed up and slow down the animation as desired. Our goal is not simple animation, however, but to get a feel for the rate of the rotations. A reasonable criterion is the amount of time required to spin the bolt completely around the y-axis (360°).

Using WM_TIMER messages would be a poor choice for benchmarking for two reasons. First, your window is not guaranteed to receive all the WM_TIMER messages (the OS could be too busy). And second, if you specify the time intervals, what good does it do to then measure those intervals with any confidence that they truly indicate performance?

What we really want to do is time the interval between the starting and stopping of rendering. This could provide a value that is too small for practical use, so we can just time the interval between a given number of renderings. By repeatedly rendering the scene a number of times and measuring the time it takes to perform these renderings, we have a fairly good benchmark.

Caution: This Is Only an Approximation!

This benchmark is very informal and uses a method of timing computer programs that's not accurate enough for publishing important results. We only use it here to demonstrate an easily detectable performance gain when using display lists. To compare your real programs (as well as the two presented here), you should at least have the rest of your system idle when running the test. Many factors can increase or decrease the values you get, but as long as conditions are more or less equal, you will see a time difference between the two bolt-spinning programs.

You might be tempted to just stack together a bunch of calls to RenderScene and obtain the time before and after to calculate the elapsed time. This would work, but closing the application would be very difficult because it would not have the chance to service any other messages (such as WM_CLOSE). The best way to get a Windows program to repeatedly paint its client area is to omit validation of the client area when the WM_PAINT handler is finished. If the client area is still invalid, Windows will just keep posting WM_PAINT messages to your application forever. In the midst of these WM_PAINT messages, other messages such as WM_CLOSE will still appear and be processed.

Listing 10-9 is the WM_PAINT handler for our new program, SPINBOLT.

Listing 10-9 WM_PAINT message handler for SPINBOLT

```
// Storage for timing values
static unsigned long ulStart = 0L;
static unsigned long ulFinish = 0L;
static double dTime = 0.0;

// Storage for performance statistics
char cBuffer[80];
RECT cRect;

   ...
   ...
   ...

      // The painting function.  This message sent by Windows
      // whenever the screen needs updating.
      case WM_PAINT:
            {
            // Count how many times rendered
            static iRenderCount = 0;

            // Get time at beginning of spin
            if(iRenderCount == 0)
                    ulStart = ulGetProfileTime();

            // Call OpenGL drawing code
```

continued on next page

continued from previous page

```
RenderScene();

// Bring image to front
SwapBuffers(hDC);

// Increment count. If 71 or over get the finish time
iRenderCount++;

if(iRenderCount > 71)
        {
        iRenderCount = 0;

        ulFinish = ulGetProfileTime();

        // Calculate the time in seconds
        dTime = ulFinish - ulStart;
        dTime /= 1000.0;
        }

// Display time (be sure and set background colors)
sprintf(cBuffer,"%3.1f Seconds for 360 degrees.",dTime);
GetClientRect(hWnd,&cRect);
SetBkColor(hDC,RGB(0,0,255));
SetTextColor(hDC,RGB(255,255,0));
TextOut(hDC,0,cRect.bottom-20,cBuffer,strlen(cBuffer));

// Do not validate, forcing a continuous repaint
}
break;
```

This message handler gets the current system time and counts the number of times it is called. After 71 times, it gets the new time, subtracts the difference, and displays the lapsed time. Remember that our bolt is rotating 5° each time it is rendered, so this technique effectively measures the amount of time it takes to spin the bolt 360°.

The function ulGetProfileTime simply gets the system time in clock ticks and converts it to thousandths of a second. (You can examine this yourself in the source listing if you want, but its operation is not germane to our discussion here.) SPINBOLT's output is shown in Figure 10-9. The time to spin the bolt around in this example was just under 15 seconds (on a 90MHz Pentium with no hardware 3D acceleration).

Improving Performance

You may have spotted a glaring performance problem with the WM_PAINT technique, however. Each time the bolt is drawn, a large number of calculations must be performed to redraw the thread, the shaft, and the bolt head. Among these calculations are some pretty expensive calls to sin() and cos().

What we need is a way of storing all these vertices and normals as they are calculated, so we can reuse them rather than go back through all that trigonometry to calculate spiral paths and such. OpenGL has just what we need: display lists. With a display list, you can record OpenGL function calls (and their results) and play them back at a later time. Display lists are faster than just reexecuting the same OpenGL functions singly. Further, non-OpenGL calls such as our trigonometry and normal cal-

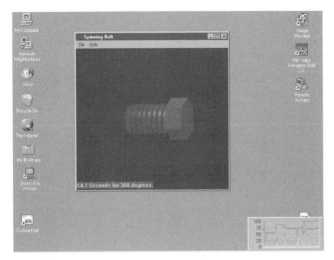

Figure 10-9 Output from the SPINBOLT program

culations are not stored, but their results, which are passed to the OpenGL functions, are. You should be getting an inkling of why display lists are such a good idea.

Human Beings and Computer Performance
A good rule of thumb in any type of software engineering is to work first on improvements that yield at least a 20% increase in performance. It is universally accepted that human beings, for the most part, have difficulty "detecting" an increase in software performance that is less than 20%. For OpenGL, this 20% value can often be attained quickly by using display lists when the number of polygons is high. It's a good idea to get in the habit of using them.

Creating a Display List

Creating a display list is a very straightforward process. Just as you delimit an OpenGL primitive with glBegin/glEnd, you delimit a display list with glNewList/glEndList. A display list, however, is named with an integer value that you supply. The following code represents a typical example of display list creation:

```
glNewList(1,GL_COMPILE);
     ...
     ...
// Some OpenGL Code
     ...
     ...
glEndList();
```

As the second parameter to glNewList, you can specify GL_COMPILE or GL_COM-PILE_AND_EXECUTE. This tells OpenGL whether to compile and store the OpenGL commands, or to compile, store, and execute the commands as they occur. Later, when you need to execute the display list, simply call

```
glCallList(1);
```

The identifier you supply is the same as that supplied in the corresponding call to glNewList.

Listing 10-10 is the code for our new example, SLSTBOLT, which makes use of display lists to produce the spinning bolt. Notice that you can nest calls to display lists. The maximum number of nested calls is 64 to prevent infinite recursion. In this code, we create a display list for each part of the bolt, and then one display list that does all the coordinate transformations and calls the lists to create the completed bolt.

Listing 10-10 New spinning bolt code using display lists

```
#define HEAD_LIST      1
#define SHAFT_LIST     2
#define THREAD_LIST    3
#define BOLT_LIST      4
  ...
  ...

// This function does any needed initialization on the rendering
// context.  Here it sets up and initializes the lighting for
// the scene, and creates display lists used later
void SetupRC()
        {
          ...
          ...
          ...

        // Create display list for Bolt head
        glNewList(HEAD_LIST,GL_COMPILE);
                RenderHead();
        glEndList();


        // Create display list for shaft
        glNewList(SHAFT_LIST,GL_COMPILE);
                RenderShaft();
        glEndList();


        // Create display list for thread
        glNewList(THREAD_LIST,GL_COMPILE);
                RenderThread();
        glEndList();


        // Create nested display list for entire bolt
        glNewList(BOLT_LIST,GL_COMPILE);

                // Clear the window with current clearing color
                glClear(GL_COLOR_BUFFER_BIT | GL_DEPTH_BUFFER_BIT);

                // Make sure we have the correct matrix mode
```

```
        glMatrixMode(GL_MODELVIEW);

        // Rotate and translate the coordinate system
        // Note this will be cumulative
        glRotatef(5.0f, 0.0f, 1.0f, 0.0f);

        // Translate and render the head
        glTranslatef(0.0f, 0.0f, 55.0f);
        glCallList(HEAD_LIST);

        // Translate back some and render the shaft and thread together
        glTranslatef(0.0f, 0.0f, -15.0f);
        glCallList(SHAFT_LIST);
        glCallList(THREAD_LIST);

        // Translate back again for next pass
        glTranslatef(0.0f, 0.0f, -40.0f);

// End Bolt list
glEndList();
}
// Called to draw the entire bolt
void RenderScene(void)
{
glCallList(BOLT_LIST);

// Flush drawing commands
glFlush();
}
```

You'll see that we defined some macros to identify the display lists more easily. These macros simply map to the numeric value that identifies the display list. Figure 10-10 shows the output from this new and improved spinning bolt program. The elapsed time for the example using display lists was just over 13 seconds, about a

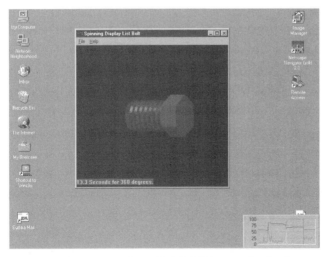

Figure 10-10 Output from SLSTBOLT using display lists

2-second improvement. This may not seem like much, but wait a few chapters and come back and try it again with special effects such as texture mapping or NURBS surfaces. As mentioned earlier, 1,700 triangles is really a very small portion of what some larger and more complex scenes will consist of.

The Tank Simulator

Try the tank simulator as it stood after the last chapter, and compare it to the one for this chapter. This version, which makes heavy use of display lists, consists of many thousands of triangles, and you won't need any benchmarking program or stopwatch to know that the performance has been enhanced!

Summary

We used this chapter to slow down somewhat and just talk about how to build a three-dimensional object, starting with using the OpenGL primitives to create simple 3D pieces, and then assembling them into a larger and more complex object. Learning the API is the easy part, but your level of experience in assembling 3D objects and scenes will be what differentiates you from your peers. Once an object or scene is broken down into small and potentially reusable components, you can save building time by using display lists. You'll find many more functions for utilizing and managing display lists in the Reference Section. You also learned a simple way to benchmark your OpenGL programs so you can get firsthand experience of the effects of optimizing your code.

Reference Section

GLCALLLIST

Purpose	Executes a display list.
Include File	<gl.h>
Syntax	void glCallList(GLuint list);
Description	Executes the display list identified by *list*. The OpenGL State Machine is not restored after this function is called, so it is a good idea to call glPushMatrix beforehand and glPopMatrix afterwards. Calls to glCallList may be nested. The function glGet with the argument GL_MAX_LIST_NESTING returns the maximum number of allowable nests. For Microsoft Windows, this value is 64.
Parameters	
list	GLuint: Identifies the display list to be executed.
Returns	None.

Example   The following code saves the matrix state before calling a display list. It then restores the state afterwards. This code is from the BOLTL example program from this chapter's subdirectory on the CD.

```
// Save the current transform state
glPushMatrix();

// Draw the bolt including nested display lists
glCallList(BOLT_HEAD);

// Restore state
glPopMatrix();
```

See Also   glCallLists, glDeleteLists, glGenLists, glNewList

GLCALLLISTS

Purpose   Executes a list of display lists.

Include File   <gl.h>

Syntax   void glCallLists(GLsizei n, GLenum type, const GLvoid *lists);

Description   This function calls the display lists listed in the *lists* array sequentially. This array can be of nearly any data type. The result is converted or clamped to the nearest integer value to determine the actual index of the display list. Optionally, the list values can be offset by a value specified by the function glListBase.

Parameters

n   GLsizei: Number of elements in the array of display lists.

type   GLenum: Specifies the datatype of the array stored at *lists*. This can be any one of the following values: GL_BYTE, GL_UNSIGNED_BYTE, GL_SHORT, GL_UNSIGNED_SHORT, GL_INT, GL_UNSIGNED_INT, GL_FLOAT, GL_2_BYTES, GL_3_BYTES, and GL_4_BYTES.

*lists   GLvoid: An array of elements of the type specified in *type*. The data type is *void* to allow any of the above data types to be used.

Returns   None.

Example   The following code shows how to call a list of display lists with a single call:

```
// Storage for the display list identifiers
int lists[50];
int i;
 ...
 ...
// Create list names
for(i = 0; i < 50; i++)
        lists[i] = i+1;

// Build some fifty display lists //////////
```

continued on next page

continued from previous page

```
// First list
glNewList(lists[0],GL_COMPILE);
            ...
            ...
glEndList();

// Second list
glNewList(lists[1],GL_COMPILE);
            ...
            ...
glEndList();

// And so on ...
  ...
  ...

// Call all fifty lists with a single call
glCallLists(50, GL_INT, lists);
```

See Also   glCallList, glDeleteLists, glGenLists, glListBase, glNewList

GLDELETELISTS

Purpose	Deletes a continuous range of display lists.
Include File	<gl.h>
Syntax	void glDeleteLists(GLuint list, GLsizei range);
Description	This function deletes a range of display lists. The range goes from an initial value and proceeds until the number of lists deleted as specified by *range* is completed. Deleting unused display lists can save considerable memory. Unused display lists in the range of those specified are ignored and do not cause an error.
Parameters	
list	GLuint: The integer name of the first display list to delete.
range	GLsizei: The number of display lists to be deleted following the initially specified list.
Returns	None.
Example	The following single line of code shows any and all display lists with identifiers between 1 and 50 being deleted:

```
glDeleteLists(1, 50);
```

See Also   glCallList, glCallLists, glGenLists, glIsList, glNewList

GLENDLIST

Purpose	Delimits the end of a display list.
Include File	<gl.h>

Syntax	void glEndList(void);
Description	Display lists are created by first calling glNewList. Thereafter, all OpenGL commands are compiled and placed in the display list. The glEndList function terminates the creation of this display list.
Returns	None.
Example	The following example code shows an example of a display list being delimited by glNewList and glEndList. This particular display list is composed by nesting two other display lists within it.

```
// Begin delimit of list
glNewList(BOLT_LIST,GL_COMPILE);

        // Display list calls two previously defined display lists
        glCallList(SHAFT_LIST);
        glCallList(THREAD_LIST);

// End this display list
glEndList();
```

See Also	glCallList, glCallLists, glDeleteLists, glGenLists, glIsList

GLGENLISTS

Purpose	Generates a continuous range of empty display lists.
Include File	<gl.h>
Syntax	GLuint glGenLists(GLsizei range);
Description	This function creates a range of empty display lists. The number of lists generated depends on the value specified in *range*. The return value is then the first display list in this range of empty display lists. The purpose of this function is to reserve a range of display list values for future use.
Parameters	
range	GLsizei: The number of empty display lists requested.
Returns	The first display list of the range requested. The display list values following the return value up to range -1 are created empty.
Example	The following code allocates an array of 25 integers that will be used to store 25 display lists. Each element in the array must be assigned a valid display list name that can be used later.

```
int lists[25];          // Space for 25 display lists
int first;              // Index of the first display list name available
int x;                  // Looping variable
  ...
  ...

// Get the first display list identifier
first = glGenLists(25);
```

continued on next page

continued from previous page

```
// Loop and assign each element in the array with a valid display list
for(x = 0; x < 25; x++)
lists[25] = first + x + 1;
```

See Also   glCallList, glCallLists, glDeleteLists, glNewList

GLISLIST

Purpose   Tests for the existence of a display list.

Include File   <gl.h>

Syntax   GLboolean glIsList(GLuint list);

Description   This function is used to find out if a display list exists for a given identifier.
                You can use this function to test display list values before using them.

Parameters

list   GLuint: The value of a potential display list. This function tests this value
                to see if a display list is defined for it.

Returns   GL_TRUE if the display list exists, otherwise GL_FALSE.

Example   The following code loops through an array that should contain valid dis-
                play lists. The display list identifier is tested for validity, and if valid it is
                called

```
                        int lists[25]; // Array of display lists
int x;                          // Looping variable
    ...
    ...

for(x = 0; x < 25; x++)
        if(glIsList(lists[x])
                glCallList();
```

See Also   glCallList, glCallLists, glDeleteLists, glGenLists, glNewList

GLLISTBASE

Purpose   Specifies an offset to be added to the list values specified in a call to
                glCallLists.

Include File   <gl.h>

Syntax   void glListBase(GLuint base);

Description   The function glCallLists calls a series of display lists listed in an array. This
                function sets an offset value that can be added to each display list name for
                this function. By default this is zero. You can retrieve the current value by
                calling glGet(GL_LIST_BASE).

Parameters

base   GLuint: Sets an integer offset value that will be added to display list names
                specified in calls to glCallLists. This value is zero by default.

Returns   None.

Example

The following code fragment creates 20 display lists numbered 0 through 19. An array of display list names (listA) is created that contains the numbers 0 through 9. Then glCallLists is used to execute all the display lists named in the listA array. Then, rather than reload the array with the next 10 display lists names, an offset value is specified with a call to glListBase. When glCallLists is called using the listA array, each element in listA will be offset by the value specified (10).

```
int listA[10];
int i;

for(i  = 0; i < 10;  i++)
        listA[i] = i;

// Build display Lists 1 - 20
glNewList(1,GL_COMPILE);
        ...
        ...
glEndList();

// Second list
glNewList(2,GL_COMPILE);
        ...
        ...
glEndList();

// And so on ...

// Call first ten lists
glCallLists(10,GL_INT,listA);

// Call next ten lists, using the same array
glListBase(10);
glCallIsts(10,GL_INT,listA);
```

See Also
glCallLists

GLNEWLIST

Purpose	Begins the creation or replacement of a display list.
Include File	<gl.h>
Syntax	void glNewList(GLuint list, GLenum mode);
Description	A display list is a group of OpenGL commands that are stored for execution on command. You can use display lists to speed up drawings that are computationally intensive or that require data to be read from a disk. The glNewList function begins a display list with an identifier specified by the integer list parameter. The display list identifier is used by glCallList and glCallLists to refer to the display list. If it's not unique, a previous display list may be overwritten. You can use glGenLists to reserve a range of display list names, and glIsList to test a display list identifier before using it. Display lists can be compiled only, or compiled and executed. After

glNewList is called, all OpenGL commands are stored in the display list in the order they were issued until glEndList is called. The following commands are executed when called and are never stored in the display list itself: glIsList, glGenLists, glDeleteLists, glFeedbackBuffer, glSelectBuffer, glRenderMode, glReadPixels, glPixelStore, glFlush, glFinish, glIsEnabled, and glGet.

Parameters

list   GLuint: The numerical name of the display list. If the display list already exists, it is replaced by the new display list.

mode   GLenum: Display lists may be compiled and executed later, or compiled and executed simultaneously. Specify GL_COMPILE to only compile the display list, or GL_COMPILE_AND_EXECUTE to execute the display list as it is being compiled.

Returns   None.

Example   The following is an example of a display list being delimited by glNewList and glEndList. This particular display list is composed by nesting two other display lists within it.

```
// Begin delimit of list
glNewList(BOLT_LIST,GL_COMPILE);

        // Display list calls two previously defined display lists
        glCallList(SHAFT_LIST);
        glCallList(THREAD_LIST);

// End this display list
glEndList();
```

See Also   glCallList, glCallLists, glDeleteLists, glGenLists, glIsList

11

RASTER GRAPHICS IN OPENGL

11

RASTER GRAPHICS IN OPENGL

What you'll learn in this chapter:

How to...	Functions You'll Use
Draw bitmap images	glBitmap/glRasterPos
Use bitmap fonts	wglUseFontBitmaps/glGenLists/glCallLists
Draw color images	glDrawPixels
Read and copy color images on the screen	glCopyPixels/glReadPixels
Read and write Windows bitmap files	LoadDIBitmap/SaveDIBitmap

You've probably heard a lot of sales hype lately about how much better it is to work with 3D graphics than with those old 2D graphics from years ago. While this is true for the most part, ultimately those 3D graphics are drawn in two dimensions on your screen. *Raster graphics* are two-dimensional arrays of colors and are used not only for displaying 3D graphics on the screen but also for printing images on raster printers or motion-picture film!

In addition to the vector and polygon functions we've examined so far, OpenGL provides several functions that directly manage 2D bitmaps and images. Those functions are the subject of this chapter.

Drawing Bitmaps

Bitmaps in OpenGL are two-color images that are used to quickly draw characters or symbols (such as icons) on the screen. This diverges from the (incorrect) Microsoft

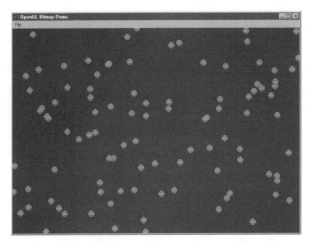

Figure 11-1 Output from glBitmap example

Windows definition that includes multicolored images, as well. OpenGL provides a single function to draw bitmaps: glBitmap. When you draw a bitmap with glBitmap, the first color (0) is transparent. The second color (1) is drawn using the current color and lighting material attributes.

Figure 11-1 shows an OpenGL bitmap image of smiley faces. The code (Listing 11-1) to draw this window consists of the bitmap data followed by a call to glBitmap.

Listing 11-1 Drawing the window of smiley faces

```
void
RepaintWindow(RECT *rect)    /* I - Client area rectangle */
{
  int             i;          /* Looping var */
  static GLubyte smiley[] = /* 16x16 smiley face */
  {
    0x03, 0xc0, 0, 0, /*       ****         */
    0x0f, 0xf0, 0, 0, /*      ********       */
    0x1e, 0x78, 0, 0, /*     ****  ****      */
    0x39, 0x9c, 0, 0, /*    ***  **  ***     */
    0x77, 0xee, 0, 0, /*   *** ****** ***    */
    0x6f, 0xf6, 0, 0, /*   ** ******** **    */
    0xff, 0xff, 0, 0, /* **************** */
    0xff, 0xff, 0, 0, /* **************** */
    0xff, 0xff, 0, 0, /* **************** */
    0xff, 0xff, 0, 0, /* **************** */
    0x73, 0xce, 0, 0, /*   ***  ****  ***    */
    0x73, 0xce, 0, 0, /*   ***  ****  ***    */
    0x3f, 0xfc, 0, 0, /*    ************     */
    0x1f, 0xf8, 0, 0, /*     **********      */
    0x0f, 0xf0, 0, 0, /*      ********       */
    0x03, 0xc0, 0, 0  /*       ****         */
  };
```

```
glViewport(0, 0, rect->right, rect->bottom);

glClearColor(0.0, 0.0, 0.0, 1.0);
glClear(GL_COLOR_BUFFER_BIT);

glMatrixMode(GL_PROJECTION);
glLoadIdentity();
glOrtho(0.0, rect->right - 1.0, 0.0, rect->bottom - 1.0, -1.0, 1.0);

/*
 * This bitmap is aligned to 4-byte boundaries...
 */

glPixelTransferi(GL_UNPACK_ALIGNMENT, 4);

glColor3f(1.0, 0.0, 0.0);
for (i = 0; i < 100; i ++)
{
   glRasterPos2i(rand() % rect->right, rand() % rect->bottom);
   glBitmap(16, 16, 8.0, 8.0, 0.0, 0.0, smiley);
};

glFinish();
}
```

In this example, we have defined a 16 x 16-pixel bitmap image of a smiley face. The bitmap is an array of 32 unsigned bytes (GLubyte), with bit 7 of the first byte corresponding to the *bottom-left* corner.

Some Things to Note About Bitmaps

OpenGL bitmaps are usually defined "upside down." That is, they are stored from bottom to top. (In fact, you can see that the happy face defined as "smiley" is upside down.) To define them from top to bottom, you must specify a negative height. Also, because of bugs in the Microsoft OpenGL libraries, you *must* align each scanline (row) of bitmap data to a 4-byte boundary. With a properly functioning OpenGL library, you could use the glPixelStore function described later in this chapter to change the bitmap alignment.

After defining a bitmap image to draw, we must specify the current *raster position* by calling the glRasterPos function:

```
glRasterPos2i(rand() % rect->right, rand() % rect->bottom);
```

In this example, we are positioning our smiley face randomly within the client area of our window with the bitmap offset by 8 pixels from the left and bottom. The raster position is specified in world/model coordinates, just like a glVertex position. In addition to setting the current raster position, glRasterPos also sets a *raster position valid* flag. This Boolean flag is True if the raster position lies inside the current viewport, and False otherwise.

A Note About Clipping

Polygons and other vector-drawing primitives will still be drawn if they lie partially out of the current viewport, and clipped to the edges of the viewport. Clipping for bitmaps works a little differently. If the raster position you specify lies outside of the current viewport, the bitmap will *not* be drawn.

To draw the bitmap, call the glBitmap function:

```
glBitmap(16, 16, 8.0, 8.0, 0.0, 0.0, smiley);
```

In this case we are drawing a 16 x 16 bitmap whose center lies at (8.0, 8.0) in the bitmap. After the bitmap is drawn, the raster position is moved (0.0, 0.0) pixels.

The prototype for this function is as follows:

```
glBitmap(GLsizei width, GLsizei height,
         GLfloat xorig, GLfloat yorig,
         GLfloat xmove, GLfloat ymove,
         const GLubyte *bits)
```

The width and height parameters specify the width and height of the bitmap. The bits parameter contains the bitmap you want to draw and is 32-bit aligned. The xorig and yorig parameters contain the center location of the bitmap. After the bitmap is drawn, the current raster position is moved by (xmove,ymove) pixels, and the raster position valid flag is left unchanged. The xmove and ymove parameters are normally used for bitmap fonts (described in the upcoming section) to advance to the next character "cell."

A Note About the Current Raster Position

As stated earlier, bitmaps will not be drawn if the raster position is outside the bitmap. However, since the raster position valid flag is left unchanged after a call to glBitmap, you can use glBitmap to position and draw bitmaps that are partially clipped on the edge of the current viewport. For example, here's how to draw the smiley bitmap just to the left of the current viewport:

```
glRasterPos2i(0, 0);
glBitmap(0, 0, 0.0, 0.0, -4.0, 0.0, NULL);
glBitmap(16, 16, 8.0, 8.0, 0.0, 0.0, smiley);
```

The NULL parameter in the first call to glBitmap simply specifies that there is no bitmap to draw. After the first call to glBitmap, the current raster position will be moved 4 pixels to the left (–4.0) before the real bitmap is drawn in the second call. This solution also applies to drawing pixmaps, explained later in this chapter.

Bitmap Fonts

One very important application of bitmaps is displaying character strings. Under ordinary circumstances, you would have to define a bitmap array for each character and then draw the bitmaps as necessary to display the string. Fortunately, the Microsoft

Windows Win32 libraries provide a function called wglUseFontBitmaps to generate these bitmaps from font files loaded on your system.

To use the font bitmaps, OpenGL provides three functions: glGenLists, glListBase and glCallLists (described in Chapter 10). The glGenLists function generates a contiguous series of OpenGL display list IDs that will hold the character bitmaps created by wglUseFontBitmaps.

```
GLuint  base;
HDC     hdc;

base = glGenLists(96);
wglUseFontBitmaps(hdc, 32, 96, base);
```

This creates 96 character bitmaps from the current font starting at character 32, the ASCII code for the space character. The base variable contains the first display list bitmap in the font—in this case, character 32 (ASCII space). To display a string of characters using these bitmaps, you use a combination of glListBase and glCallLists:

```
char *s;

glListBase(base - 32);
glCallLists(strlen(s), GL_UNSIGNED_BYTE, s);
```

The glListBase function sets the base display list ID. The glCallList and glCallLists functions will add this number to the display list ID(s) passed to them, effectively selecting the font you just defined. The glCallLists function calls a series of display lists based upon the array of characters (unsigned bytes) you pass in, which draws the character string.

Building a Simple Font Library

Certainly the wglCreateFontBitmaps function simplifies font creation, but you still have to do a lot just to output a character string. You can build a usable font library fairly easily, however. To start, you'll need a font creation function (Listing 11-2).

Listing 11-2 The beginning of the FontCreateBitmaps function

```
GLuint
FontCreateBitmaps(HDC    hdc,      /* I - Device Context */
                  char   *typeface, /* I - Font specification */
                  int    height,   /* I - Font height/size in pixels */
                  int    weight,   /* I - Weight of font (bold, etc) */
                  DWORD  italic)   /* I - Text is italic */
{
  Gluint base;                     /* Base display list for font */
  HFONT  font;                     /* Windows font ID */

  if ((base = glGenLists(96)) == 0)
    return (0);
```

The typeface argument is simply the name of the font, such as Courier or Helvetica, and specifies the style of character that you want. The height, weight, and italic arguments are passed directly to wglUseFontBitmaps and set the size and appearance of the characters.

Before you create the font bitmaps, you need to decide on a character set. Normally you'll use the ANSI or UNICODE character sets. The ANSI character set (ANSI_CHARSET) provides the standard 7-bit ASCII character set. To support international characters and diacritical marks, use the UNICODE character set instead (UNICODE_CHARSET). Some fonts use special character sets. The Symbol font, for example, provides Greek letters and many scientific symbols.

For this simple implementation, we will set the character set to ANSI_CHARSET for normal fonts, and SYMBOL_FONTSET for the Symbol font. See Listing 11-3.

Listing 11-3 Continuation of the FontCreateBitmaps function

```
if (stricmp(typeface, "symbol") == 0)
    font = CreateFont(height, 0, 0, 0, weight, italic, FALSE, FALSE,
                      SYMBOL_CHARSET, OUT_TT_PRECIS,
                      CLIP_DEFAULT_PRECIS, DRAFT_QUALITY,
                      DEFAULT_PITCH, typeface);
else
    font = CreateFont(height, 0, 0, 0, weight, italic, FALSE, FALSE,
                      ANSI_CHARSET, OUT_TT_PRECIS,
                      CLIP_DEFAULT_PRECIS, DRAFT_QUALITY,
                      DEFAULT_PITCH, typeface);

SelectObject(hdc, font);

wglUseFontBitmaps(hdc, 32, 96, base);

return (base);
}
```

If you need to use international characters, change the "normal" character set to UNICODE_CHARSET, and define 224 characters (256 minus 32), as shown here:

```
else
    font = CreateFont(height, 0, 0, 0, weight, italic, FALSE, FALSE,
                      UNICODE_CHARSET, OUT_TT_PRECIS,
                      CLIP_DEFAULT_PRECIS, DRAFT_QUALITY,
                      DEFAULT_PITCH, typeface);

SelectObject(hdc, font);

wglUseFontBitmaps(hdc, 32, 224, base);
```

To complement FontCreateBitmaps you'll need a font deletion function (Listing 11-4). Here the glDeleteLists function simply deletes the specified display lists, in this case our font bitmaps. As with the FontCreateBitmaps function, to make this function work with international character sets you need to change the number of display lists from 96 to 224.

Listing 11-4 FontDelete function

```
void
FontDelete(GLuint font) /* I - Font to delete */
{
  if (font == 0)
    return;

  glDeleteLists(font, 96);
}
```

Finally, to make drawing character strings easier, you can make put-string and printf-string functions. FontPuts (Listing 11-5) uses the glPushAttrib and glPopAttrib functions to save and restore the current display list base ID. If you forget to do this, you might inadvertently affect your other drawing code that uses display lists!

Listing 11-5 FontPuts function

```
void
FontPuts(GLuint font, /* I - Font to use */
         char   *s)   /* I - String to display */
{
  if (font == 0)
    return;

  if (s == NULL)
    return;

  glPushAttrib(GL_LIST_BIT);
    glListBase(font - 32);
    glCallLists(strlen(s), GL_UNSIGNED_BYTE, s);
  glPopAttrib();
}
```

> **A Note About glCallLists and Strings**
> It is important to remember that glCallLists and the font functions presented here do not handle control characters such as tab and newline. If you include control characters in the string you display, other display lists may be called that affect your final output. This behavior can be controlled by parsing the incoming string prior to using glCallLists. Newline and tab functionality can be simulated using the glBitmap technique outlined in the previous note, "A Note About the Current Raster Position," along with a call to glGetIntegerv (described in Chapter 14).

The FontPrintf function (Listing 11-6) uses the <stdarg.h> header file to manage the variable number of arguments needed for vsprintf, which formats the string to be drawn.

Listing 11-6 FontPrintf function

```
#define MAX_STRING 1024

void
FontPrintf(GLuint font,       /* I <?> - Font to use */
           char   *format,    /* I - printf() style format string */
           ...)               /* I - Other arguments as necessary */
{
  va_list    ap;                    /* Argument pointer */
  char       s[MAX_STRING + 1]; /* Output string */

  if (format == NULL)
    return;

  va_start(ap, format);       /* Start variable argument processing */
  vsprintf(s, format, ap);    /* Format the text into our output string */
  va_end(ap);                 /* End variable argument processing */

  FontPuts(font, s);
}
```

The complete code for FontCreate, FontDelete, FontPuts, and FontPrintf can be found in the CH11\FONT.C file. Prototypes are in the CH11\FONT.H file on the source code CD-ROM.

Pixmaps: Bitmaps with Color

Images with more than two colors are usually called *pixmaps* (short for pixel maps) and are used as background images or textures (covered in Chapter 12). In OpenGL, pixmaps are generally either 8-bit color index images or 24-bit RGB images.

Drawing Pixmaps

OpenGL provides a single function for drawing pixmaps called glDrawPixels. Like glBitmap, glDrawPixels uses the current raster position to define the lower-left corner of the image. You cannot specify a raster origin or movement as you can for glBitmap.

```
BITMAPINFO *BitmapInfo;
GLubyte    *BitmapBits;

glRasterPos2i(xoffset, yoffset);
glDrawPixels(BitmapInfo->bmiHeader.biWidth,
             BitmapInfo->bmiHeader.biHeight,
             GL_RGB, GL_UNSIGNED_BYTE, BitmapBits);
```

The glDrawPixels function accepts five arguments:

```
glDrawPixels(GLsizei width, GLsizei height,
             GLenum format, GLenum type,
             Glvoid *pixels)
```

The format parameter specifies the colorspace of the pixmap; valid formats are in Table 11-1. The GL_COLOR_INDEX format specifies that each color value in the pixmap is an index into the current Windows logical color palette. Color index images are often used for icons. The GL_LUMINANCE format maps each color value to a grayscale value on the screen, with the minimum value being completely black and the maximum value being completely white. The GL_RGB format specifies the exact red, green, and blue values for each pixel in the image.

Table 11-1 OpenGL Pixel Formats

Format	Description
GL_COLOR_INDEX	Color index pixels
GL_LUMINANCE	Grayscale pixels
GL_RGB	RGB pixels

The type parameter of glDrawPixels specifies the type and range of each color value or component, as listed in Table 11-2.

Table 11-2 OpenGL Pixel Types

Type	Description
GL_BYTE	Signed 8-bit values (from −128 to 127)
GL_UNSIGNED_BYTE	Unsigned 8-bit values (from 0 to 255)
GL_BITMAP	Bitmap image (from 0 to 1)

Remapping Colors

When using GL_COLOR_INDEX colors, you can remap the colors in your pixmap or bitmap using the glPixelMap or glPixelTransfer functions. The glPixelTransfer function lets you specify scaling and offsets for color index and RGB values. For example, here is the code to brighten an RGB image by 10%:

```
glPixelTransferf(GL_RED_SCALE, 1.1);
glPixelTransferf(GL_GREEN_SCALE, 1.1);
glPixelTransferf(GL_BLUE_SCALE, 1.1);
```

Similarly, to offset the color indices of a bitmap to the palette entries you have defined for it, use

```
glPixelTransferi(GL_INDEX_OFFSET, bitmap_entry);
```

In the "smiley" bitmap example (Listing 11-7), we might use this to remap the two colors in the bitmap to difference indices:

Listing 11-7 Repaint Window function to draw smiley faces

```
void
RepaintWindow(RECT *rect)    /* I - Client area rectangle */
{
  int            i;          /* Looping var */
  static GLubyte smiley[] = /* 16x16 smiley face */
  {
    0x03, 0xc0, 0, 0, /*       ****        */
    0x0f, 0xf0, 0, 0, /*     ********       */
    0x1e, 0x78, 0, 0, /*    ****  ****      */
    0x39, 0x9c, 0, 0, /*   ***  **  ***     */
    0x77, 0xee, 0, 0, /*  *** ****** ***    */
    0x6f, 0xf6, 0, 0, /*  ** ******** **    */
    0xff, 0xff, 0, 0, /* ****************   */
    0xff, 0xff, 0, 0, /* ****************   */
    0xff, 0xff, 0, 0, /* ****************   */
    0xff, 0xff, 0, 0, /* ****************   */
    0x73, 0xce, 0, 0, /*  ***  ****  ***    */
    0x73, 0xce, 0, 0, /*  ***  ****  ***    */
    0x3f, 0xfc, 0, 0, /*   ************     */
    0x1f, 0xf8, 0, 0, /*    **********      */
    0x0f, 0xf0, 0, 0, /*     ********       */
    0x03, 0xc0, 0, 0  /*       ****        */
  };


  glViewport(0, 0, rect->right, rect->bottom);

  glClearIndex(0.0);
  glClear(GL_COLOR_BUFFER_BIT);

  glMatrixMode(GL_PROJECTION);
  glLoadIdentity();
  glOrtho(0.0, rect->right - 1.0, 0.0, rect->bottom - 1.0, -1.0, 1.0);

 /*
  * This bitmap is aligned to 4-byte boundaries...
  */

  glPixelTransferi(GL_UNPACK_ALIGNMENT, 4);
  glPixelTransferi(GL_INDEX_OFFSET, 1);

  for (i = 0; i < 100; i ++)
  {
    glRasterPos2i(rand() % rect->right, rand() % rect->bottom);
    glDrawPixels(16, 16, GL_COLOR_INDEX, GL_BITMAP, smiley);
  };

  glFinish();
}
```

Color Mapping Tables

Sometimes it is necessary to apply color corrections that are more complicated than simple linear scale and offset. One application is gamma correction, in which the

Figure 11-2 Image without gamma correction (left) and with a gamma correction of 1.7 (right)

intensity of each color value is adjusted to a power curve that compensates for irregularities on your monitor or printer (see Figure 11-2). The glPixelMap function allows you to do this by specifying a lookup table, as follows:

```
GLfloat lut[256];
GLfloat gamma_value;
int            i;

gamma_value = 1.7; /* For NTSC video monitors */
for (i = 0; i < 256; i ++)
  lut[i] = pow(i / 255.0, 1.0 / gamma_value);

glPixelTransferi(GL_MAP_COLOR, GL_TRUE);
glPixelMap(GL_PIXEL_MAP_R_TO_R, 256, lut);
glPixelMap(GL_PIXEL_MAP_G_TO_G, 256, lut);
glPixelMap(GL_PIXEL_MAP_B_TO_B, 256, lut);
```

Scaling a Pixmap

Besides adjusting the colors of a pixmap, you can adjust the size of the pixmap using the glPixelZoom function. This function accepts two floating point parameters specifying the X and Y scaling factors for the image:

```
glPixelZoom(1.0, 1.0);   /* Don't scale the image */
glPixelZoom(-1.0, 1.0);  /* Flip the image horizontally */
glPixelZoom(1.0, -2.0);  /* Flip the image and double the height */
glPixelZoom(0.33, 0.33); /* Draw the image 1/3 size */
```

As you can see, glPixelZoom allows you to scale and flip an image just about any way you like. For other nonlinear effects, such as rippling water or perspective correction, you'll need to use texture mapping (Chapter 12).

Panning a Pixmap

The glPixelStore function can be used to pan inside an image. For example, to display the center 300 x 300 pixel area of a 640 x 480 pixel image, you would use

```
glPixelStorei(GL_UNPACK_ROW_LENGTH, 640);
glPixelStorei(GL_UNPACK_SKIP_PIXELS, (640 - 300) / 2);
glPixelStorei(GL_UNPACK_SKIP_ROWS, (480 - 300) / 2);
glDrawPixels(300, 300, GL_RGB, GL_UNSIGNED_BYTE, BitmapBits);
```

In this example, the GL_UNPACK_ROW_LENGTH value specifies the width of the original image in pixels. Set this when the width specified with glDrawPixels is different from the width of the image.

GL_UNPACK_SKIP_PIXELS specifies the number of pixels to skip on the left side of the image. Here we skip the first (640 – 300) / 2, or 170 pixels on the left side of the image to show the middle.

GL_UNPACK_SKIP_ROWS is similar but specifies the number of rows or scanlines in the image to skip. Normally, this value represents the number of rows from the bottom, but you can change this by specifying a negative Y scaling with glPixelZoom.

NOTE: The GL_UNPACK_ROW_LENGTH, GL_UNPACK_SKIP_PIXELS, and GL_UNPACK_SKIP_ROWS attributes refer to the original pixmap size in pixels, not the size after zooming!

Reading Pixmaps

OpenGL provides a function called glReadPixels that can read an image from the screen. Beyond the obvious application of saving your created image to disk, it can also be used for cool effects with texture mapping.

Unlike glDrawPixels, glReadPixels ignores the current raster position and requires you to specify an (x,y) viewport coordinate for the lower-left corner of the image to read. Listing 11-8 demonstrates how to read the current viewport into a Windows bitmap structure suitable for saving to a file or using as a texture.

Listing 11-8 ReadDIBitmap function

```
/*
 * 'ReadDIBitmap()' - Read the current OpenGL viewport into a
 *                    24-bit RGB bitmap.
 *
 * Returns the bitmap pixels if successful and NULL otherwise.
 */

void *
ReadDIBitmap(BITMAPINFO **info) /* 0 - Bitmap information */
{
  long    i, j,          /* Looping var */
          bitsize,       /* Total size of bitmap */
          width;         /* Aligned width of a scanline */
  GLint   viewport[4];   /* Current viewport */
  void    *bits;         /* RGB bits */
  GLubyte *rgb,          /* RGB looping var */
          temp;          /* Temporary var for swapping */
```

```
/*
 * Grab the current viewport...
 */

  glGetIntegerv(GL_VIEWPORT, viewport);

/*
 * Allocate memory for the header and bitmap...
 */

  if ((*info = (BITMAPINFO *)malloc(sizeof(BITMAPINFOHEADER))) == NULL)
  {
   /*
    * Couldn't allocate memory for bitmap info - return NULL...
    */

    return (NULL);
  };

  width   = viewport[2] * 3;      /* Real width of scanline */
  width   = (width + 3) & ~3;     /* Aligned to 4 bytes */
  bitsize = width * viewport[3]; /* Size of bitmap, aligned */

  if ((bits = calloc(bitsize, 1)) == NULL)
  {
   /*
    * Couldn't allocate memory for bitmap pixels - return NULL...
    */

    free(*info);
    return (NULL);
  };

/*
 * Read pixels from the framebuffer...
 */

  glFinish();                             /* Finish all OpenGL commands */
  glPixelStorei(GL_PACK_ALIGNMENT, 4); /* Force 4-byte alignment */
  glPixelStorei(GL_PACK_ROW_LENGTH, 0);
  glPixelStorei(GL_PACK_SKIP_ROWS, 0);
  glPixelStorei(GL_PACK_SKIP_PIXELS, 0);

  glReadPixels(0, 0, viewport[2], viewport[3], GL_RGB, GL_UNSIGNED_BYTE,
               bits);

/*
 * Swap red and blue for the bitmap...
 */

  for (i = 0; i < viewport[3]; i ++)
    for (j = 0, rgb = ((GLubyte *)bits) + i * width;
         j < viewport[2];
         j ++, rgb += 3)
    {
      temp   = rgb[0];
      rgb[0] = rgb[2];
      rgb[2] = temp;
    };
```

continued on next page

continued from previous page

```
/*
 * Finally, initialize the bitmap header information...
 */

(*info)->bmiHeader.biSize          = sizeof(BITMAPINFOHEADER);
(*info)->bmiHeader.biWidth         = viewport[2];
(*info)->bmiHeader.biHeight        = viewport[3];
(*info)->bmiHeader.biPlanes        = 1;
(*info)->bmiHeader.biBitCount      = 24;
(*info)->bmiHeader.biCompression   = BI_RGB;
(*info)->bmiHeader.biSizeImage     = bitsize;
(*info)->bmiHeader.biXPelsPerMeter = 2952; /* 75 DPI */
(*info)->bmiHeader.biYPelsPerMeter = 2952; /* 75 DPI */
(*info)->bmiHeader.biClrUsed       = 0;
(*info)->bmiHeader.biClrImportant  = 0;

return (bits);
}
```

The first thing you need to do is find out the size of the current viewport, using glGetIntegerv as shown just below. (This function is described in Chapter 14). This places the current X origin, Y origin, X size, and Y size into the viewport array, as shown in Table 11-3.

```
/*
 * Grab the current viewport...
 */

glGetIntegerv(GL_VIEWPORT, viewport);
```

Table 11-3 Viewport Array Definitions

Index	Description
0	X origin of viewport (pixels)
1	Y origin of viewport (pixels)
2	X size of viewport (pixels)
3	Y size of viewport (pixels)

Once you have the size of the viewport, you then allocate memory for the pixmap. It's important to note that Windows bitmaps (and OpenGL pixmaps by default) must have the beginning of each line at a 32-bit boundary. To accomplish this, we do the following:

```
width   = viewport[2] * 3;    /* Real width of scanline */
width   = (width + 3) & ~3;   /* Aligned to 4 bytes */
```

You must round the computed actual byte width of the viewport (in this case, 3 bytes for every pixel wide) up to the nearest 32-bit (or 4-byte) boundary. The total size of the pixmap then becomes

```
bitsize = width * viewport[3]; /* Size of bitmap, aligned */
```

After allocating memory for the pixmap, we call glReadPixels to get the contents of the current viewport and fill in the Windows BITMAPHEADER structure with all the necessary information.

Copying Pixmaps

OpenGL also provides a function to copy an area on the screen to another location— as needed, for instance, in scrolling or "magnifying glass" views:

```
int mousex, mousey;

glReadBuffer(GL_FRONT);
glDrawBuffer(GL_FRONT);
glPixelZoom(2.0, 2.0);
glRasterPos2i(0, 0);
glCopyPixels(mousex - 8, mousey - 8, 16, 16, GL_COLOR);
```

Here the glCopyPixels function copies pixels from the given location to the current raster position:

```
void glCopyPixels(GLint x, GLint y, GLsizei width, GLsizei height, GLenum type)
```

The x and y parameters specify the lower-left corner of the area to be copied. Width and height specify the size of the image to be copied. Pixels are copied from the specified (x,y) location to the current raster position. The type argument specifies which values are to be copied. For most applications, the pixel type is GL_COLOR to copy color indices or RGB values.

Pixel zoom is applied to the output pixels but not to the input pixels. In the example just above, a 16 x 16-pixel image will be copied to the lower-left corner of the window and scaled to 32 x 32 pixels. Offsets and sizes specified with calls to glPixelStore do not affect glCopyPixels. Changes made with glPixelTransfer and glPixelMap do, however.

A Bitmap File Viewer

Now that we've covered all the bitmap-related functions that are available, let's write a Windows .BMP file-viewing program using OpenGL. Our goals for this program are fairly straightforward:

- Load any Windows .BMP file
- Scale the image to the current window size
- Provide simple controls to change the image brightness and gamma correction
- Show a magnified view of the image underneath the mouse pointer
- Save the displayed image to disk
- Print the displayed image

The final code for this program can be found in CH11\OGLVIEW.C.

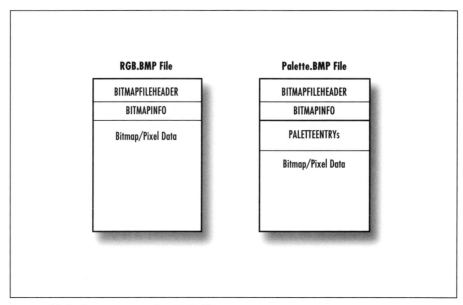

Figure 11-3 Organization of a .BMP file

About Windows Bitmap Files

Before we write the code, let's review the ubiquitous Windows bitmap format. Despite their limitations, Windows .BMP files are probably the most common and widely supported files used by PCs capable of from 2 to 16.7 million colors. With only a few exceptions, .BMP files do not utilize data compression schemes, so it's easy to read and use these files in your OpenGL programs.

A .BMP file is organized into three or four sections, depending on the type of colors used (see Figure 11-3). All .BMP files start with a BITMAPFILEHEADER structure containing an identification string ("BM") the total size of the file, and an offset to the actual image data. Here is that structure:

```
typedef struct
{
  WORD    bfType;            /* "BM" */
  DWORD   bfSize;            /* Size of file in bytes */
  WORD    bfReserved1;       /* Reserved, always 0 */
  WORD    bfReserved2;       /* Reserved, always 0 */
  DWORD   bfOffBits;         /* Offset to image in bytes */
} BITMAPFILEHEADER;
```

Following the file header is a BITMAPINFOHEADER structure that describes the contents of the image, as follows:

```
typedef struct
{
  DWORD     biSize;          /* Size of BITMAPINFOHEADER in bytes */
  LONG      biWidth;         /* Width of image in pixels */
  LONG      biHeight;        /* Height of image in pixels */
  WORD      biPlanes;        /* # of color planes (always 1) */
  WORD      biBitCount;      /* # of color bits */
  DWORD     biCompression;   /* Type of compression used */
  DWORD     biSizeImage;     /* Size of the image in bytes */
  LONG      biXPelsPerMeter; /* Horizontal pixels per meter */
  LONG      biYPelsPerMeter; /* Vertical pixels per meter */
  DWORD     biClrUsed;       /* Number of color used */
  DWORD     biClrImportant;  /* Number of 'important' colors */
} BITMAPINFOHEADER;
```

For color index (palette) images, a color palette follows the BITMAPINFOHEADER structure for every color in the image. Image data follows immediately after.

Reading the .BMP File

Because the .BMP file format is so simple, reading a .BMP file is almost trivial. You start by opening the file and reading a BITMAPFILEHEADER structure.

```
if ((fp = fopen(filename, "rb")) == NULL)
  return (NULL);

fread(&header, sizeof(BITMAPFILEHEADER), 1, fp);

if (header.bfType != 'MB') /* Check for BM reversed... */
{
 /*
  * Not a bitmap file - return NULL...
  */

  fclose(fp);
  return (NULL);
};
```

If the header looks good, you then read the BITMAPINFO structure along with any color palette definitions.

```
infosize = header.bfOffBits - sizeof(BITMAPFILEHEADER);
fread(*info, 1, infosize, fp);
```

And finally, you read the bitmap data and close the file.

```
if ((bitsize = (*info)->bmiHeader.biSizeImage) == 0)
  bitsize = ((*info)->bmiHeader.biWidth *
             (*info)->bmiHeader.biBitCount + 7) / 8 *
            abs((*info)->bmiHeader.biHeight);

fread(bits, 1, bitsize, fp);
fclose(fp);
```

Listing 11-9 contains the final code for LoadDIBitmap, with error checking.

Listing 11-9 LoadDIBitmap function

```c
void *
LoadDIBitmap(char          *filename, /* I - File to load */
             BITMAPINFO **info)     /* O - Bitmap information */
{
  FILE               *fp;         /* Open file pointer */
  void               *bits;       /* Bitmap pixel bits */
  long               bitsize,     /* Size of bitmap */
                     infosize;    /* Size of header information */
  BITMAPFILEHEADER header;         /* File header */


 /*
  * Try opening the file; use "rb" mode to read this *binary* file.
  */

  if ((fp = fopen(filename, "rb")) == NULL)
    return (NULL);

 /*
  * Read the file header and any following bitmap information...
  */

  if (fread(&header, sizeof(BITMAPFILEHEADER), 1, fp) < 1)
  {
   /*
    * Couldn't read the file header - return NULL...
    */

    fclose(fp);
    return (NULL);
  };

  if (header.bfType != 'MB') /* Check for BM reversed... */
  {
   /*
    * Not a bitmap file - return NULL...
    */

    fclose(fp);
    return (NULL);
  };

  infosize = header.bfOffBits - sizeof(BITMAPFILEHEADER);
  if ((*info = (BITMAPINFO *)malloc(infosize)) == NULL)
  {
   /*
    * Couldn't allocate memory for bitmap info - return NULL...
    */

    fclose(fp);
    return (NULL);
  };

  if (fread(*info, 1, infosize, fp) < infosize)
  {
```

```
  /*
   * Couldn't read the bitmap header - return NULL...
   */

  free(*info);
  fclose(fp);
  return (NULL);
};

/*
 * Now that we have all the header info read in, allocate memory for the
 * bitmap and read *it* in...
 */

if ((bitsize = (*info)->bmiHeader.biSizeImage) == 0)
  bitsize = ((*info)->bmiHeader.biWidth *
            (*info)->bmiHeader.biBitCount + 7) / 8 *
            abs((*info)->bmiHeader.biHeight);

if ((bits = malloc(bitsize)) == NULL)
{
  /*
   * Couldn't allocate memory - return NULL!
   */

  free(*info);
  fclose(fp);
  return (NULL);
};

if (fread(bits, 1, bitsize, fp) < bitsize)
{
  /*
   * Couldn't read bitmap - free memory and return NULL!
   */

  free(*info);
  free(bits);
  fclose(fp);
  return (NULL);
};

/*
 * OK, everything went fine - return the allocated bitmap...
 */

fclose(fp);
return (bits);
}
```

Writing the .BMP File

As they say in the car repair manuals, "Installation is the reverse of removal." To write a .BMP file, you simply add a BITMAPFILEHEADER structure to the bitmap in memory and write it to disk. Listing 11-10 is the SaveDIBitmap function.

Listing 11-10 SaveDIBitmap function

```
int
SaveDIBitmap(char        *filename, /* I - File to save to */
            BITMAPINFO *info,       /* I - Bitmap information */
            void        *bits)      /* I - Bitmap pixel bits */
{
  FILE              *fp;            /* Open file pointer */
  long              size,          /* Size of file */
                    infosize,      /* Size of bitmap info */
                    bitsize;       /* Size of bitmap pixels */
  BITMAPFILEHEADER header;         /* File header */


 /*
  * Try opening the file; use "wb" mode to write this *binary* file.
  */

  if ((fp = fopen(filename, "wb")) == NULL)
    return (-1);

  if (info->bmiHeader.biSizeImage == 0)/* Figure out the bitmap size */
    bitsize = (info->bmiHeader.biWidth *
               info->bmiHeader.biBitCount + 7) / 8 *
              abs(info->bmiHeader.biHeight);
  else
    bitsize = info->bmiHeader.biSizeImage;

  infosize = sizeof(BITMAPINFOHEADER);
  switch (info->bmiHeader.biCompression)
  {
    case BI_BITFIELDS :
        infosize += 12; /* Add 3 RGB doubleword masks */
        if (info->bmiHeader.biClrUsed == 0)
          break;
    case BI_RGB :
        if (info->bmiHeader.biBitCount > 8 &&
            info->bmiHeader.biClrUsed == 0)
          break;
    case BI_RLE8 :
    case BI_RLE4 :
        if (info->bmiHeader.biClrUsed == 0)
          infosize += (1 << info->bmiHeader.biBitCount) * 4;
        else
          infosize += info->bmiHeader.biClrUsed * 4;
        break;
  };

  size = sizeof(BITMAPFILEHEADER) + infosize + bitsize;

 /*
  * Write the file header, bitmap information, and bitmap pixel data...
  */

  header.bfType      = 'MB'; /* Non-portable... sigh */
  header.bfSize      = size;
  header.bfReserved1 = 0;
  header.bfReserved2 = 0;
  header.bfOffBits   = sizeof(BITMAPFILEHEADER) + infosize;
```

```
  if (fwrite(&header, 1, sizeof(BITMAPFILEHEADER), fp) <
          sizeof(BITMAPFILEHEADER))
  {
   /*
    * Couldn't write the file header - return...
    */

    fclose(fp);
    return (-1);
  };

  if (fwrite(info, 1, infosize, fp) < infosize)
  {
   /*
    * Couldn't write the bitmap header - return...
    */

    fclose(fp);
    return (-1);
  };

  if (fwrite(bits, 1, bitsize, fp) < bitsize)
  {
   /*
    * Couldn't write the bitmap - return...
    */

    fclose(fp);
    return (-1);
  };

 /*
  * OK, everything went fine - return...
  */

  fclose(fp);
  return (0);
}
```

Printing the Bitmap

Because Windows provides several convenient functions for printing within an application, it only makes sense to be able to print from our bitmap viewing program. For this example program, you will be using the standard GDI printing services.

The first thing you do is display a standard Windows print dialog using PrintDlg, as shown here:

```
memset(&pd, 0, sizeof(pd));
pd.lStructSize = sizeof(pd);
pd.hwndOwner   = owner;
pd.Flags       = PD_RETURNDC;
pd.hInstance   = NULL;
if (!PrintDlg(&pd))
  return (0);
```

If the PrintDlg function returns 0, the user has clicked the Cancel button. Otherwise, the PRINTDLG structure will contain a device context (HDC) handle that we can use for printing.

Next, you need to start the print job.

```
di.cbSize       = sizeof(DOCINFO);
di.lpszDocName  = "OpenGL Image";
di.lpszOutput   = NULL;
StartDoc(pd.hDC, &di);
```

After this, you draw the bitmap using the StretchBlt function and end the print job.

```
StretchBlt(pd.hDC, xoffset, yoffset, xsize, ysize,
           hdc, 0, 0, info->bmiHeader.biWidth,
           info->bmiHeader.biHeight, SRCCOPY);

EndPage(pd.hDC);
EndDoc(pd.hDC);
```

We compute the first 4 parameters to StretchBlt based on the size of the output page. Basically, we want to scale the image to the page yet keep the aspect ratio (width/height) the same.

```
xsize = rect.right;
ysize = xsize * info->bmiHeader.biHeight / info->bmiHeader.biWidth;
if (ysize > rect.bottom)
{
  ysize = rect.bottom;
  xsize = ysize * info->bmiHeader.biWidth / info->bmiHeader.biHeight;
};
```

The offsets are computed by taking half of the difference of widths and heights:

```
xoffset = (rect.right - xsize) / 2;
yoffset = (rect.bottom - ysize) / 2;
```

Normally you might pop up a "busy printing" dialog for the user, but in this case printing happens so fast it wouldn't be useful.

The final code for the PrintDIBitmap function is in Listing 11-11.

Listing 11-11 PrintDIBitmap function

```
int
PrintDIBitmap(HWND       owner, /* I - Owner/parent window */
              BITMAPINFO *info, /* I - Bitmap information */
              void       *bits) /* I - Bitmap pixel bits */
{
  PRINTDLG pd;                  /* Print dialog information */
  long     xsize,               /* Size of printed image */
           ysize,
           xoffset,             /* Offset from edges for image */
           yoffset;
  RECT     rect;                /* Page rectangle */
  DOCINFO  di;                  /* Document info */
  HDC      hdc;                 /* Device context for bitmap */
  HBITMAP  bitmap;              /* Bitmap image */
  HBRUSH   brush;               /* Background brush for page */
  HCURSOR  busy,                /* Busy cursor */
           oldcursor;           /* Old cursor */
```

```
/*
 * Range check...
 */

if (info == NULL || bits == NULL)
  return (0);

/*
 * Initialize a PRINTDLG structure before displaying a standard Windows
 * print dialog...
 */

memset(&pd, 0, sizeof(pd));
pd.lStructSize = sizeof(pd);
pd.hwndOwner   = owner;
pd.Flags       = PD_RETURNDC;
pd.hInstance   = NULL;
if (!PrintDlg(&pd))
  return (0);                       /* User chose 'cancel'... */

/*
 * OK, user wants to print, so set the cursor to 'busy' and start the
 * print job...
 */

busy      = LoadCursor(NULL, IDC_WAIT);
oldcursor = SetCursor(busy);

SetMapMode(pd.hDC, MM_TEXT);
di.cbSize      = sizeof(DOCINFO);
di.lpszDocName = "OpenGL Image";
di.lpszOutput  = NULL;

StartDoc(pd.hDC, &di);
StartPage(pd.hDC);

/*
 * Clear the background to white...
 */

rect.top    = 0;
rect.left   = 0;
rect.right  = GetDeviceCaps(pd.hDC, HORZRES);
rect.bottom = GetDeviceCaps(pd.hDC, VERTRES);
brush       = CreateSolidBrush(0x00ffffff);
FillRect(pd.hDC, &rect, brush);

/*
 * Stretch the bitmap to fit the page...
 */

hdc    = CreateCompatibleDC(pd.hDC);
bitmap = CreateDIBitmap(hdc, &(info->bmiHeader), CBM_INIT, bits, info,
                        DIB_RGB_COLORS);
SelectObject(hdc, bitmap);

xsize = rect.right;
ysize = xsize * info->bmiHeader.biHeight / info->bmiHeader.biWidth;
```

continued on next page

continued from previous page

```
if (ysize > rect.bottom)
{
  ysize = rect.bottom;
  xsize = ysize * info->bmiHeader.biWidth / info->bmiHeader.biHeight;
};

xoffset = (rect.right - xsize) / 2;
yoffset = (rect.bottom - ysize) / 2;

StretchBlt(pd.hDC, xoffset, yoffset, xsize, ysize,
           hdc, 0, 0, info->bmiHeader.biWidth, info->bmiHeader.biHeight,
           SRCCOPY);

/*
 * That's it.  End the print job and free anything we allocated...
 */

EndPage(pd.hDC);
EndDoc(pd.hDC);
DeleteDC(pd.hDC);

DeleteObject(bitmap);
DeleteObject(brush);
DeleteObject(busy);
DeleteDC(hdc);

/*
 * Restore the cursor and return...
 */

SetCursor(oldcursor);

return (1);
}
```

Displaying the Bitmap

The OpenGL part of our example program begins with displaying the .BMP file. Like most OpenGL programs, this one starts out by setting the current viewport and viewing transformations.

```
glViewport(0, 0, rect->right, rect->bottom);

glMatrixMode(GL_PROJECTION);
glLoadIdentity();
glOrtho(0.0, rect->right - 1.0, 0.0, rect->bottom - 1.0, -1.0, 1.0);
glMatrixMode(GL_MODELVIEW);
```

After this, you draw the bitmap. Here we are scaling the image to fit the current window while maintaining a 1:1 aspect ratio. The following code should look very familiar—you used it in the PrintDIBitmap function above:

```
xsize = rect->right;
ysize = BitmapInfo->bmiHeader.biHeight * xsize /
        BitmapInfo->bmiHeader.biWidth;
if (ysize > rect->bottom)
{
  ysize = rect->bottom;
```

```
    xsize = BitmapInfo->bmiHeader.biWidth * ysize /
            BitmapInfo->bmiHeader.biHeight;
};

xscale  = (float)xsize / (float)BitmapInfo->bmiHeader.biWidth;
yscale  = (float)ysize / (float)BitmapInfo->bmiHeader.biHeight;

xoffset = (rect->right - xsize) * 0.5;
yoffset = (rect->bottom - ysize) * 0.5;

glPixelStorei(GL_UNPACK_ALIGNMENT, 4);
glPixelZoom(xscale, yscale);
glRasterPos2i(xoffset, yoffset);
glDrawPixels(BitmapInfo->bmiHeader.biWidth,
            BitmapInfo->bmiHeader.biHeight,
            GL_RGB, GL_UNSIGNED_BYTE, BitmapBits);
```

Interestingly enough, the Windows StretchBlt function can display bitmap images faster than glDrawPixels. Of course, StretchBlt cannot perform the glPixelMap and glPixelTransfer functions, though.

The final code for the RepaintWindow function is in Listing 11-12.

Listing 11-12 RepaintWindow function

```
void
RepaintWindow(RECT *rect) /* I - Client area rectangle */
{
  GLint   xoffset,        /* X offset of image */
          yoffset;        /* Y offset of image */
  GLint   xsize,          /* X size of scaled image */
          ysize;          /* Y size of scaled image */
  GLfloat xscale,         /* Scaling in X direction */
          yscale;         /* Scaling in Y direction */

 /*
  * Reset the viewport and clear the window to white...
  */

  glViewport(0, 0, rect->right, rect->bottom);

  glMatrixMode(GL_PROJECTION);
  glLoadIdentity();
  glOrtho(0.0, rect->right - 1.0, 0.0, rect->bottom - 1.0, -1.0, 1.0);
  glMatrixMode(GL_MODELVIEW);

  glClearColor(1.0, 1.0, 1.0, 1.0);
  glClear(GL_COLOR_BUFFER_BIT);

 /*
  * If we have loaded a bitmap image, scale it to fit the window...
  */

  if (BitmapBits != NULL)
  {
    xsize = rect->right;
    ysize = BitmapInfo->bmiHeader.biHeight * xsize /
```

continued on next page

continued from previous page

```
              BitmapInfo->bmiHeader.biWidth;
  if (ysize > rect->bottom)
  {
    ysize = rect->bottom;
    xsize = BitmapInfo->bmiHeader.biWidth * ysize /
            BitmapInfo->bmiHeader.biHeight;
  };

  xscale  = (float)xsize / (float)BitmapInfo->bmiHeader.biWidth;
  yscale  = (float)ysize / (float)BitmapInfo->bmiHeader.biHeight;

  xoffset = (rect->right - xsize) * 0.5;
  yoffset = (rect->bottom - ysize) * 0.5;

  glPixelStorei(GL_UNPACK_ALIGNMENT, 4);
  glPixelZoom(xscale, yscale);
  glRasterPos2i(xoffset, yoffset);
  glDrawPixels(BitmapInfo->bmiHeader.biWidth,
               BitmapInfo->bmiHeader.biHeight,
               GL_RGB, GL_UNSIGNED_BYTE, BitmapBits);
  };

  glFinish();
}
```

Summary

In this chapter you have learned about most of the OpenGL bitmap functions. Beyond the simple application of character fonts, bitmaps can be full-color images for window backgrounds or texture images (explored in the chapter coming up). OpenGL functions such as glPixelMap, glPixelTransfer, and glPixelZoom can be used for special effects, as well.

Reference Section

GLCOPYPIXELS

Purpose	Copies a rectangular block of pixels in the frame buffer.
Include File	<GL/gl.h>
Syntax	void glCopyPixels(GLint x, GLint y, GLsizei width, GLsizei height, GLenum type);
Description	This function copies pixel data from the indicated area in the framebuffer to the current raster position. Use glRasterPos to set the current raster position. If the current raster position is not valid, then no pixel data is copied.
	Calls to glPixelMap, glPixelTransfer, and glPixelZoom affect the operation of glCopyPixels, as indicated in their pages in this Reference Section.

Parameters

x	GLint: The lower-left corner window horizontal coordinate.
y	GLint: The lower-left corner window vertical coordinate.
width	GLsizei: The width of the image in pixels.
height	GLsizei: The height of the image in pixels. If negative, the image is drawn from top to bottom. By default, images are drawn bottom to top.
type	GLenum: The type of pixel values to be copied. Valid types are as follows:

GL_COLOR	Color buffer values
GL_STENCIL	Stencil buffer values
GL_DEPTH	Depth buffer values

Returns	None.
Example	See the example in CH11\OGLVIEW.C.
See Also	glPixelMap, glPixelStore, glPixelTransfer, glPixelZoom

GLDRAWPIXELS

Purpose	Draws a block of pixels into the frame buffer.
Include File	<GL/gl.h>
Syntax	void glDrawPixels(GLsizei width, GLsizei height, GLenum format, GLenum type, const Glvoid *pixels);
Description	This function copies pixel data from memory to the current raster position. Use glRasterPos to set the current raster position. If the current raster position is not valid, then no pixel data is copied.
	Besides the format and type arguments, several other parameters define the encoding of pixel data in memory and control the processing of the pixel data before it is placed in the frame buffer. See the Reference Section pages for glPixelMap, glPixelStore, glPixelTransfer, and glPixelZoom.

Parameters

width	GLsizei: The width of the image in pixels.
height	GLsizei: The height of the image in pixels. If negative, the image is drawn from top to bottom. By default, images are drawn bottom to top.
format	GLenum: The colorspace of the pixels to be drawn. Valid formats are as follows:

GL_COLOR_INDEX	Color index pixels
GL_LUMINANCE	Grayscale pixels
GL_LUMINANCE_ALPHA	Grayscale + alpha pixels (2 components)
GL_RGB	RGB pixels (3 components)

GL_RGBA	RGBA pixels (4 components)
GL_RED	Red pixels
GL_GREEN	Green pixels
GL_BLUE	Blue pixels
GL_ALPHA	Alpha pixels
GL_STENCIL_INDEX	Stencil buffer values
GL_DEPTH_COMPONENT	Depth buffer values

type	GLenum: The data type of the pixels to be drawn. Valid types are as follows:
	GL_BYTE Signed 8-bit values (−128 to 127)
	GL_UNSIGNED_BYTE Unsigned 8-bit values (0 to 255)
	GL_BITMAP Bitmap image (0 to 1)
	GL_SHORT Signed 16-bit values (−32,768 to 32,767)
	GL_UNSIGNED_SHORT Unsigned 16-bit values (0 to 65,535)
	GL_INT Signed 32-bit values (−2,147,483,648 to 2,147,483,647)
	GL_UNSIGNED_INT Unsigned 32-bit values (0 to 4,294,967,295)
	GL_FLOAT 32-bit floating point values (GLfloat)

pixels	Glvoid *: A pointer to the pixel data for the image.
Returns	None.
Known Bugs	The GL_UNPACK_ALIGNMENT parameter for glPixelStore is presently ignored by glDrawPixels.
Example	See the example in CH11\OGLVIEW.C.
See Also	glPixelMap, glPixelStore, glPixelTransfer, glPixelZoom

GLPIXELMAP

Purpose	Defines a lookup table for pixel transfers.
Include File	<GL/gl.h>
Syntax	void glPixelMapfv(GLenum map, GLint mapsize, const GLfloat *values);
	void glPixelMapuiv(GLenum map, GLint mapsize, const GLuint *values);
	void glPixelMapusv(GLenum map, GLint mapsize, const GLushort *values);
Description	This function sets lookup tables for glCopyPixels, glDrawPixel, glReadPixels, glTexImage1D, and glTexImage2D. Lookup tables, or *maps*, are only used if the corresponding GL_MAP_COLOR or GL_MAP_STENCIL option is enabled with glPixelTransfer. Maps

are applied prior to drawing and after reading values from the framebuffer.

Parameters

map   GLenum: The type of map being defined. Valid maps are as follows:

GL_PIXEL_MAP_I_TO_I	Define a map for color indices.
GL_PIXEL_MAP_S_TO_S	Define a map for stencil values.
GL_PIXEL_MAP_I_TO_R	Define a map from color indices to red values.
GL_PIXEL_MAP_I_TO_G	Define a map from color indices to green values.
GL_PIXEL_MAP_I_TO_B	Define a map from color indices to blue values.
GL_PIXEL_MAP_I_TO_A	Define a map from color indices to alpha values.
GL_PIXEL_MAP_R_TO_R	Define a map for red values.
GL_PIXEL_MAP_G_TO_G	Define a map for green values.
GL_PIXEL_MAP_B_TO_B	Define a map for blue values.
GL_PIXEL_MAP_A_TO_A	Define a map for alpha values.

mapsize   GLint: The size of the lookup table.

values   GLfloat *, GLuint *, GLushort *: The lookup table.

Returns   None.

Example   See the example in CH11\OGLVIEW.C.

See Also   glCopyPixels, glDrawPixels, glPixelStore, glPixelTransfer, glReadPixels, glTexImage1D, glTexImage2D

GLPIXELSTORE

Purpose   Controls how pixels are stored or read from memory.

Include File   <GL/gl.h>

Syntax   void glPixelStorei(GLenum pname, GLint param);
void glPixelStoref(GLenum pname, GLfloat param);

Description   This function controls how pixels are stored with glReadPixels and read for glDrawPixels, glTexImage1D, and glTexImage2D. It does not affect the operation of glCopyPixels.

Parameters

pname   GLenum: The parameter to set. Valid names are as follows:

GL_PACK_SWAP_BYTES*	GL_TRUE	If True, all multibyte values have their bytes swapped when stored in memory.

GL_PACK_LSB_FIRST	GL_FALSE	If True, bitmaps have their leftmost pixel stored in bit 0 instead of bit 7.
GL_PACK_ROW_LENGTH	0	Set the pixel width of the image. If 0, the *width* argument is used instead.
GL_PACK_SKIP_PIXELS	0	Set the number of pixels to skip horizontally in the image.
GL_PACK_SKIP_ROWS	0	Set the number of pixels to skip vertically in the image.
GL_PACK_ALIGNMENT	4	Set the alignment of each scanline in the image. See Known Bugs section below.
GL_UNPACK_SWAP_BYTES (GL_TRUE for little-endian, GL_FALSE for big-endian)	GL_TRUE	If True, all multibyte values have their bytes swapped when read from memory.
GL_UNPACK_LSB_FIRST	GL_FALSE	If True, bitmaps have their leftmost pixel read from bit 0 instead of bit 7.
GL_UNPACK_ROW_LENGTH	0	Set the pixel width of the image. If 0, the *width* argument is used instead.
GL_UNPACK_SKIP_PIXELS	0	Set the number of pixels to skip horizontally in the image.
GL_UNPACK_SKIP_ROWS	0	Set the number of pixels to skip vertically in the image.
GL_UNPACK_ALIGNMENT	4	Set the alignment of each scanline in the image. See Known Bugs section below.

param   GLint, GLflet: The parameter value.

Returns   None.

Known Bugs   The GL_PACK_ALIGNMENT and GL_UNPACK_ALIGNMENT parameters for glPixelStore are presently ignored.

Example   See the example in CH11\BITMAP.C.

See Also   glDrawPixels, glReadPixels, glTexImage1D, glTexImage2D

GLPIXELTRANSFER

Purpose	Sets pixel transfer modes and options for glCopyPixels, glDrawPixels, glReadPixels, glTexImage1D, and glTexImage2D
Include File	<GL/gl.h>
Syntax	void glPixelTransferi(GLenum pname, GLint param); void glPixelTransferf(GLenum pname, GLfloat param);
Description	This function sets pixel transfer modes and options for glCopyPixels, glDrawPixels, glReadPixels, glTexImage1D, and glTexImage2D.
Parameters	
pname	GLenum: The transfer parameter to set. Valid names are as follows:

GL_MAP_COLOR	When set to GL_TRUE, enables pixel maps defined with glPixelMap for color indices and RGBA values.
GL_MAP_STENCIL	When set to GL_TRUE, enables pixel maps defined with glPixelMap for stencil values.
GL_INDEX_SHIFT	Specifies the amount to bitshift color indices. Positive values shift indices to the left. Negative values shift indices to the right.
GL_INDEX_OFFSET	Specifies an offset to be added to every color index.
GL_RED_SCALE	Specifies a floating point scaling factor for red color values.
GL_RED_BIAS	Specifies a bias that is added to every red color value.
GL_GREEN_SCALE	Specifies a floating point scaling factor for green color values.
GL_GREEN_BIAS	Specifies a bias that is added to every green color value.
GL_BLUE_SCALE	Specifies a floating point scaling factor for blue color values.
GL_BLUE_BIAS	Specifies a bias that is added to every blue color value.
GL_ALPHA_SCALE	Specifies a floating point scaling factor for alpha color values.
GL_ALPHA_BIAS	Specifies a bias that is added to every alpha color value.
GL_DEPTH_SCALE	Specifies a floating point scaling factor for depth values.
GL_DEPTH_BIAS	Specifies a bias that is added to every depth value.

param	GLint, GLfloat: The parameter value.

Returns	None.
Example	See the example in CH11\OGLVIEW.C.
See Also	glCopyPixels, glDrawPixels, glPixelMap, glReadPixels, glTexImage1D, glTexImage2D

GLPIXELZOOM

Purpose	Sets the scaling for pixel transfers.
Include File	<GL/gl.h>
Syntax	void glPixelZoom(GLfloat xfactor, GLfloat yfactor);
Description	This function sets pixel scaling for glCopyPixels, glDrawPixels, glReadPixels, glTexImage1D, and glTexImage2D.

Pixels are scaled using the "nearest neighbor" algorithm when they are read from memory or the framebuffer. In the case of glCopyPixels and glDrawPixels, the scaled pixels are drawn in the framebuffer at the current raster position.

For glReadPixels, pixels are written to the supplied memory buffer. When reading a zoomed image, you should compute the image size as follows:

```
int new_width, new_height;
int width, height;

new_width = xfactor * width + 0.5;
new_height = yfactor * height + 0.5;
```

Parameters	
xfactor	GLfloat: The horizontal scaling factor (1.0 is no scaling).
yfactor	GLfloat: The vertical scaling factor (1.0 is no scaling).
Returns	None.
Example	See the example in CH11\OGLVIEW.C.
See Also	glCopyPixels, glDrawPixels, glReadPixels, glTexImage1D, glTexImage2D

GLREADPIXELS

Purpose	Reads a block of pixels from the framebuffer.
Include File	<GL/gl.h>
Syntax	void glReadPixels(GLint x, GLint y, GLsizei width, GLsizei height, GLenum format, GLenum type, const Glvoid *pixels);
Description	This function copies pixel data from the framebuffer to memory. Besides the format and type arguments, several other parameters define the encoding of pixel data in memory and control the processing of the pixel data

before it is placed in the memory buffer. See the references for glPixelMap, glPixelStore, glPixelTransfer.

Parameters

x   GLint: The lower-left corner window horizontal coordinate.

y   GLint: The lower-left corner window vertical coordinate.

width   GLsizei: The width of the image in pixels.

height   GLsizei: The height of the image in pixels.

format   GLenum: The colorspace of the pixels to be read. Valid formats are as follows:

GL_COLOR_INDEX	Color index pixels
GL_LUMINANCE	Grayscale pixels
GL_LUMINANCE_ALPHA	Grayscale + alpha pixels (2 components)
GL_RGB	RGB pixels (3 components)
GL_RGBA	RGBA pixels (4 components)
GL_RED	Red pixels
GL_GREEN	Green pixels
GL_BLUE	Blue pixels
GL_ALPHA	Alpha pixels
GL_STENCIL_INDEX	Stencil buffer values
GL_DEPTH_COMPONENT	Depth buffer values

type   Glenum: The data type of the pixels to be drawn. Valid types are as follows:

GL_BYTE	Signed 8-bit values (−128 to 127)
GL_UNSIGNED_BYTE	Unsigned 8-bit values (0 to 255)
GL_BITMAP	Bitmap image (0 to 1)
GL_SHORT	Signed 16-bit values (−32768 to 32767)
GL_UNSIGNED_SHORT	Unsigned 16-bit values (0 to 65535)
GL_INT	Signed 32-bit values (−2147483648 to 2147483647)
GL_UNSIGNED_INT	Unsigned 32-bit values (0 to 4294967295)
GL_FLOAT	32-bit floating point values (GLfloat)

pixels   Glvoid *: A pointer to the pixel data for the image.

Returns   None.

Known Bugs   The GL_PACK_ALIGNMENT parameter for glPixelStore is presently ignored by glReadPixels.

Example   See the example in CH11\BITMAP.C.

See Also   glPixelMap, glPixelStore, glPixelTransfer

12

TEXTURE MAPPING

12

TEXTURE MAPPING

What you'll learn in this chapter:

How to...	Functions You'll Use
Drape images onto polygons (texture mapping)	glTexImage1D/glTexImage2D
Use .BMP files as textures	TextureLoadBitmap/TextureLoadMipmap
Use automatic texture coordinate generation	glTexGen

Texture mapping is probably the most significant advance in computer graphics in the last ten years. OpenGL provides texture image mapping functions that fit images onto polygons in your scene. How those images are put onto the polygons is up to you.

Texture mapping is used in games, including DOOM, for realistic images of rooms and monsters. Unlike OpenGL, these games use a texturing method called *raycasting* to map texture images onto polygons. Though raycasting is much faster on standard graphics cards than the texture mapping provided by OpenGL, it is also limited to flat surfaces in a 2D plane. That is, you can't look up or down. Texture mapping in OpenGL doesn't have this limitation, but you can expect it to work more slowly on standard graphics cards.

The good news is that some newer, affordable 3D graphics cards support OpenGL and hardware texturing. When a board supports hardware texture mapping, your CPU doesn't have to do all the texture mapping calculations and preparation—the graphics card does it for you.

The examples in this chapter will run on any Windows-compatible graphics card. If your graphics card supports 16- or 24-bit "true color" displays, you'll want to use them. Besides better-looking scenes, you'll find that the 16- and 24-bit modes are actually faster.

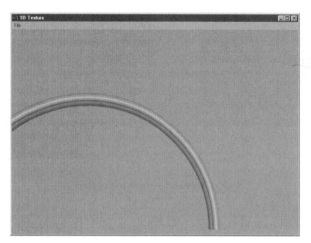

Figure 12-1 A 1D textured rainbow

The Basics of Texture Mapping

Texture mapping in OpenGL is fairly straightforward. To begin with, every texture is an image of some sort.

A 1D texture is an image with width but no height, or vise versa; 1D textures are a single pixel wide or high. You might think that 1D textures aren't very useful, but in fact they can take the place of more conventional color-shading techniques and accelerate rendering in the process! Figure 12-1 shows a 1D "ROY-G-BIV" (Red, Orange, Yellow - Green - Blue, Indigo, Violet) texture to display a rainbow. The texture image is a line of pixels (color values) covering the color spectrum seen in a rainbow. The equivalent nontextured scene would contain seven times the polygons of the textured one and require much more rendering time.

A 2D texture is an image that is more than 1 pixel wide and high and is generally loaded from a Windows .BMP file. Two-dimensional textures are commonly used to replace complex surface geometry (lots of polygons) on buildings, trees, and so forth. These 2D textures can also be used to add realistic background details, like the clouds in the sky in Figure 12-2.

The 1D and 2D textures you've seen so far are composed of RGB color values. Textures can also be composed of color indices or luminance (gray) levels, and can include alpha (transparency) values. The latter is useful for defining natural objects such as trees, because the alpha value can be used to make the tree visible but let the background show through. You'll learn more about this in Chapter 16.

Some hardware also supports 3D (volume) textures with OpenGL. Volume textures are used for viewing CAT, MRI, and other 3D "scans." Unfortunately, even a small 256 x 256 x 256 grayscale texture image will need a whopping 16 MB of memory. Currently an extension to OpenGL, 3D texturing may be included as a required feature in the OpenGL 1.1 specification.

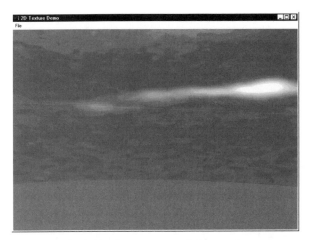

Figure 12-2 A 2D sky texture and the resulting scene

Defining Texture Images

Naturally, you must define a texture image before you can draw textured polygons in OpenGL. Texture images follow the same storage rules as bitmaps (discussed in Chapter 11).

A Note About Texture Images
The OpenGL standard requires that texture images' dimensions must be a power of 2. Texture images can also have 1 or 2 *border pixels* around their edges to define the color of polygons that fall outside the texture image.

Defining 1D Textures

OpenGL provides a single function for defining 1D textures: glTexImage1D. The glTexImage1D function accepts eight arguments:

```
void glTexImage1D(GLenum target, GLint level, GLint components,
                  GLsizei width, GLint border, GLenum format,
                  GLenum type, const GLvoid *pixels)
```

The target argument specifies which texture should be defined; this argument must be GL_TEXTURE_1D. The level argument indicates the texture image's level of detail and is usually 0. Other values are used for mipmapped textures (described later in this chapter). The components argument specifies the number of color values used for each pixel. For color index textures, components must be 1. Values of 3 and 4 are used for RGB and RGBA texture images, respectively.

Width and border specify the size of the texture image. The border value controls the number of border pixels OpenGL should expect (and use) and may have a value of 0, 1, or 2. The width parameter specifies the width of the main texture image (without the border pixels) and must be a power of 2.

The format argument indicates the type of color values to expect— GL_COLOR_INDEX, GL_LUMINANCE, GL_RGB, or GL_RGBA.

You'll find an example of defining a 1D texture in Listing 12-1 and in the example code CH12\TEX1D.C on the source code CD-ROM.

Listing 12-1 Defining a 1D texture image

```
void
LoadAllTextures(void)
{
  static unsigned char roygbiv_image[8][3] =
  {
    { 0x3f, 0x00, 0x3f }, /* Dark Violet (for 8 colors...) */
    { 0x7f, 0x00, 0x7f }, /* Violet */
    { 0xbf, 0x00, 0xbf }, /* Indigo */
    { 0x00, 0x00, 0xff }, /* Blue */
    { 0x00, 0xff, 0x00 }, /* Green */
    { 0xff, 0xff, 0x00 }, /* Yellow */
    { 0xff, 0x7f, 0x00 }, /* Orange */
    { 0xff, 0x00, 0x00 }  /* Red */
  };

  glNewList(RainbowTexture = glGenLists(1), GL_COMPILE);
    glTexParameteri(GL_TEXTURE_1D, GL_TEXTURE_MAG_FILTER, GL_LINEAR);
    glTexParameteri(GL_TEXTURE_1D, GL_TEXTURE_MIN_FILTER, GL_LINEAR);
    glTexImage1D(GL_TEXTURE_1D, 0, 3, 8, 0, GL_RGB, GL_UNSIGNED_BYTE,
                 roygbiv_image);
  glEndList();
}
```

The example code creates a display list containing the texture image and the desired magnification and minification filter, GL_LINEAR. The minification filter is used when the polygon to be drawn is smaller than the texture image, in this case 8 pixels. The magnification filter is used when the polygon is larger than the texture image. By designating the GL_LINEAR filter, you tell OpenGL to linearly interpolate color values in the texture image before drawing anything on the screen. The other filters you can use for GL_TEXTURE_MIN_FILTER are listed in Table 12-1.

Table 12-1 Texture Image Filters

Filter	Description
GL_NEAREST	Nearest-neighbor filtering.
GL_LINEAR	Linear interpolation.
GL_NEAREST_MIPMAP_NEAREST	Nearest-neighbor mipmapped filtering.
GL_NEAREST_MIPMAP_LINEAR	Linear interpolated mipmaps.

Filter	Description
GL_LINEAR_MIPMAP_NEAREST	Linear interpolation of mipmaps.
GL_LINEAR_MIPMAP_LINEAR	Linear interpolation of interpolated mipmaps.

GL_NEAREST filtering takes the closest pixel in the texture image rather than interpolating between pixels. You'll learn more about mipmap filtering later in the chapter.

Defining 2D Textures

To define a 2D texture image in OpenGL, you call glTexImage2D. The glTexImage2D function takes a height argument in addition to the ones that glTexImage1D uses, as follows:

```
void glTexImage2D(GLenum target, GLint level, GLint components,
                  GLsizei width, GLsizei height, GLint border,
                  GLenum format, GLenum type, const GLvoid *pixels)
```

Like glTexImage1D, the width and height arguments must be a power of 2.

Listing 12-2 shows how to load a sky texture image complete with clouds.

Listing 12-2 Defining a 2D texure image

```
void
LoadAllTextures(void)
{
  BITMAPINFO    *info;                      /* Bitmap information */
  void          *bits;                      /* Bitmap pixel bits */
  GLubyte       *rgb;                       /* Bitmap RGB pixels */


  /*
   * Try loading the bitmap and converting it to RGB...
   */

  bits = LoadDIBitmap('textures/sky.bmp', &info);
  if (bits == NULL)
    return;

  rgb = ConvertRGB(info, bits);
  if (rgb == NULL)
  {
    free(info);
    free(bits);

    return;
  };

  glNewList(SkyTexture = glGenLists(1), GL_COMPILE);
    glTexParameteri(GL_TEXTURE_2D, GL_TEXTURE_WRAP_S, GL_REPEAT);
    glTexParameteri(GL_TEXTURE_2D, GL_TEXTURE_WRAP_T, GL_REPEAT);
    glTexParameteri(GL_TEXTURE_2D, GL_TEXTURE_MAG_FILTER, GL_LINEAR);
    glTexParameteri(GL_TEXTURE_2D, GL_TEXTURE_MIN_FILTER, GL_NEAREST);

  /*
```

continued on next page

continued from previous page

```
 * Define the 2D texture image.
 */

    glPixelStorei(GL_UNPACK_ALIGNMENT, 4);        /* Force 4-byte alignment */
    glPixelStorei(GL_UNPACK_ROW_LENGTH, 0);
    glPixelStorei(GL_UNPACK_SKIP_ROWS, 0);
    glPixelStorei(GL_UNPACK_SKIP_PIXELS, 0);

    glTexImage2D(GL_TEXTURE_2D, 0, 3, info->bmiHeader.biWidth,
                 info->bmiHeader.biHeight, 0, GL_RGB, GL_UNSIGNED_BYTE, rgb);
  glEndList();

 /*
  * Free the bitmap and RGB images, then return 0 (no errors).
  */

    free(rgb);
    free(info);
    free(bits);
}
```

> **A Note About Textures**
>
> You'll notice that all the examples presented in this chapter use display lists to store texture images. Display lists generally speed up the drawing of static graphics commands, and texture images are no exception. In addition, the forthcoming OpenGL 1.1 API includes texture object support that optimizes texture images stored in display lists by keeping them loaded in the graphics hardware texture memory if available.

Drawing Textured Polygons

Once you have defined a texture, you still have to enable texturing. To enable 1D texturing, you'd use the following:

```
glDisable(GL_TEXTURE_2D);
glEnable(GL_TEXTURE_1D);
glTexEnvi(GL_TEXTURE_ENV, GL_TEXTURE_ENV_MODE, GL_DECAL);
```

The glEnable call enables 1D texturing. If you forget to enable texturing, none of your polygons will be textured! The glTexEnvi function sets texturing to "decal" mode, meaning that images are overlaid directly upon the polygons.

Other texturing modes are listed in Table 12-2.

Table 12-2 Texture Modes for GL_TEXTURE_ENV_MODE

Mode	Description
GL_MODULATE	Texture pixels "filter" existing pixel colors on the screen.
GL_DECAL	Texture pixels replace existing pixels on the screen.
GL_BLEND	Texture pixels "filter" existing pixels colors and are combined with a constant color.

The GL_MODULATE texture mode multiplies the current texture color (or luminance) by the color on the screen. For one-component (luminance) textures, this translates into a brightness filter that will vary the brightness of the screen image based upon the texture image. For three-component (RGB) textures, you can generate "colored lens filter" effects.

Unlike GL_MODULATE texturing, GL_BLEND texturing allows you to blend a constant color into the scene based upon the texture image. You'd use GL_BLEND texturing for things like clouds; the constant color would be off-white, and the texture image would be of a cloud.

Once you have defined the texturing mode to use, you can then proceed with the drawing of your polygons. Listing 12-3 shows how to draw the rainbow in Figure 12-1.

Listing 12-3 Drawing a 1D textured rainbow

```
glEnable(GL_TEXTURE_1D);
glCallList(RainbowTexture);
glBegin(GL_QUAD_STRIP);
  for (th = 0.0; th <= M_PI; th += (0.03125 * M_PI))
  {
  /*
   * Bottom edge of rainbow...
   */

    x = cos(th) * 50.0;
    y= sin(th) * 50.0;
    z = -50.0;
    glTexCoord1f(0.0);
    glVertex3f(x, y, z);

  /*
   * Top edge of rainbow...
   */

    x = cos(th) * 55.0;
    y = sin(th) * 55.0;
    z = -50.0;
    glTexCoord1f(1.0);
    glVertex3f(x, y, z);
  };
glEnd();
```

To position the ROY-G-BIV texture on the rainbow, you call glTexCoord. For 1D textures, you call one of the glTexCoord1f, glTexCoord1d, glTexCoord1s, or glTexCoord1i functions. A value of 0.0 represents the leftmost pixel in the image, and 1.0 represents the rightmost pixel. Values outside this range are handled differently depending on the value of the GL_TEXTURE_WRAP_S parameter. If GL_TEXTURE_WRAP_S is set to GL_CLAMP (the default), then texture coordinates are restricted to a range of 0.0 to 1.0, inclusive. When a polygon strays from the texture image, it is drawn using the color(s) along the texture image's edges (see Figure 12-3) or the texture image border colors, if defined. Texture coordinates are traditionally referred to as S and T, or (s,t) instead of X and Y.

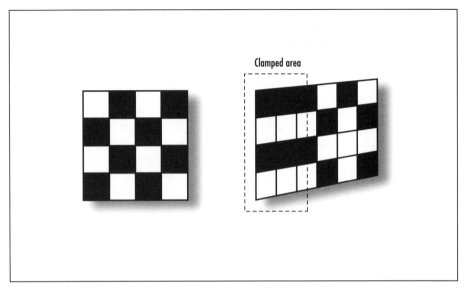

Figure 12-3 GL_CLAMP textures

If you use GL_REPEAT instead, the texture image is tiled over the polygon. Texture coordinates are used modulo 1.0—that is, the texture image repeats at regular intervals. GL_REPEAT texturing can be used to reduce the size of texture images on repetitive surfaces. The challenge with these kinds of textures is to make the edges of each tile blend into the next.

Automatically Generating Texture Coordinates
Generating texture coordinates can be a tedious task. Later in this chapter you'll learn about the glTexGen functions that can generate these coordinates automatically for you.

Mipmapped Textures

So far, we've dealt exclusively with single-texture images. That is, whenever we draw a textured polygon, the polygon is painted with a single 1D or 2D image. This is fine for some scenes, but animated displays often need various levels of detail depending on the distance from the viewer. For example, when walking through a virtual room, you might want a high-resolution image of a picture close up, but only the outline at a distance.

OpenGL supports textures with multiple images, called *mipmapped* textures. Mipmapping selects the texture image closest to the screen resolution for a polygon. Loading mipmapped textures takes slightly longer than standard textures, but the visual results are impressive. In addition, mipmapped textures can improve display performance by reducing the need for GL_LINEAR image filters.

What Does the 'Mip' in 'Mipmapped' Mean?
'mip' is latin for 'many'. 'Mipmapping' means 'many images'.

Mipmapped textures are defined by providing a specific level parameter for each image. For the ROY-G-BIV texture in the previous example, you would use the following:

```
static unsigned char roygbiv_image0[16][3];
static unsigned char roygbiv_image1[8][3];
static unsigned char roygbiv_image2[4][3];
static unsigned char roygbiv_image3[2][3];
static unsigned char roygbiv_image4[1][3];
glNewList(RainbowTexture = glGenLists(1), GL_COMPILE);
  glTexParameteri(GL_TEXTURE_1D, GL_TEXTURE_MAG_FILTER, GL_LINEAR);
  glTexParameteri(GL_TEXTURE_1D, GL_TEXTURE_MIN_FILTER,
               GL_NEAREST_MIPMAP_LINEAR);

  glTexImage1D(GL_TEXTURE_1D, 0, 3, 16, 0, GL_RGB, GL_UNSIGNED_BYTE,
               roygbiv_image0);
  glTexImage1D(GL_TEXTURE_1D, 1, 3, 8, 0, GL_RGB, GL_UNSIGNED_BYTE,
               roygbiv_image1);
  glTexImage1D(GL_TEXTURE_1D, 2, 3, 4, 0, GL_RGB, GL_UNSIGNED_BYTE,
               roygbiv_image2);
  glTexImage1D(GL_TEXTURE_1D, 3, 3, 2, 0, GL_RGB, GL_UNSIGNED_BYTE,
               roygbiv_image3);
  glTexImage1D(GL_TEXTURE_1D, 4, 3, 1, 0, GL_RGB, GL_UNSIGNED_BYTE,
               roygbiv_image4);
glEndList();
```

The image levels are specified in the first parameter to glTexImage1D(). The level 0 image is your *primary*, highest-resolution image for the texture. The level 1 image is half the size of the primary image, and so forth. When drawing polygons with a mipmapped texture, you need to use one of the minification filters (GL_TEXTURE_MIN_FILTER) in Table 12-3.

Table 12-3 Minification Filters

Filter	Description
GL_NEAREST_MIPMAP_NEAREST	Use the image nearest to the screen (polygon) resolution. Use the GL_NEAREST filter when texturing with this image.
GL_NEAREST_MIPMAP_LINEAR	Use the image nearest to the screen (polygon) resolution. Use the GL_LINEAR filter when texturing with this image.
GL_LINEAR_MIPMAP_NEAREST	Linearly interpolate between the two images nearest to the screen (polygon) resolution. Use the GL_NEAREST filter when texturing with this image.
GL_LINEAR_MIPMAP_LINEAR	Linearly interpolate between the two images nearest to the screen (polygon) resolution. Use the GL_LINEAR filter when texturing with this image.

The GL_LINEAR_MIPMAP_NEAREST and GL_LINEAR_MIPMAP_LINEAR filters can be very expensive in terms of display performance. GL_NEAREST_MIPMAP_ NEAREST is roughly equivalent to GL_NEAREST in performance, but generally produces much better results. Mipmap images are chosen by comparing the size of the polygon as it will be drawn on the screen, to the sizes of the mipmap images.

To make your life a bit easier, the OpenGL utility library (GLU32.LIB) provides two functions that automatically generate mipmapped images based on a single, high-resolution texture. In the following code, the gluBuild1DMipmaps and gluBuild2DMipmaps functions take the place of glTexImage1D and glTexImage2D:

```
/* 1D texture */
glTexParameteri(GL_TEXTURE_1D, GL_TEXTURE_MAG_FILTER, GL_LINEAR);
glTexParameteri(GL_TEXTURE_1D, GL_TEXTURE_MIN_FILTER,
                GL_NEAREST_MIPMAP_LINEAR);
gluBuild1DMipmaps(GL_TEXTURE_1D, 3, 8, 0, GL_RGB, GL_UNSIGNED_BYTE,
                roygbiv_image);

/* 2D texture */
glTexParameteri(GL_TEXTURE_2D, GL_TEXTURE_MAG_FILTER, GL_LINEAR);
glTexParameteri(GL_TEXTURE_2D, GL_TEXTURE_MIN_FILTER,
                GL_NEAREST_MIPMAP_NEAREST);
gluBuild2DMipmaps(GL_TEXTURE_2D, 3, info->bmiHeader.biWidth,
                info->bmiHeader.biHeight, 0, GL_RGB,
                GL_UNSIGNED_BYTE, rgb);
```

Because the gluBuild1DMipmaps and gluBuild2DMipmaps functions create images from one image, the appearance of some textured images may not be accurate. It's like drawing text characters at different sizes—scaling the bitmaps doesn't always generate good-looking results! When you run into this sort of problem, generate your mipmap images manually.

A Terrain Viewing Program

Our project for this chapter is a terrain viewing program that takes advantage of some of the texture-mapping features we have discussed. With this program, we'll want to accomplish the following:

- View textured terrain scenes

- Edit the terrain interactively in 3D

- Fly through the terrain

- Print the current scene

- Save the current scene to a .BMP file

The entire terrain program is listed at the end of this chapter, just before the Reference Section. A copy of the program is in the CH12 source directory on your CD-ROM. Double-click on the TEXSCENE.EXE program icon to try it out!

Defining the Terrain

To keep things simple, we'll define our terrain as a grid of elevation points with a texture attribute such as "this is water" or "this is a mountain." Each point in the grid will also have an associated lighting normal to add realism.

```
#define TERRAIN_SIZE 21

int     TerrainType[TERRAIN_SIZE][TERRAIN_SIZE];
GLfloat TerrainHeight[TERRAIN_SIZE][TERRAIN_SIZE];
GLfloat TerrainNormal[TERRAIN_SIZE][TERRAIN_SIZE][3];
```

Here the TerrainType array contains the type of terrain at each point and is assigned one of the following control IDs from our user-interface resource file:

IDC_GRASS	Grasslands
IDC_WATER	Water
IDC_TREES	Trees/woodland
IDC_ROCKS	Rocks/cliffs
IDC_MOUNTAINS	Mountains

Drawing Terrain

Our terrain drawing controls consist of a toolbar dialog window with five buttons that select the current type of terrain. To draw the terrain, you just click and drag in the main window (see Figure 12-4).

The heart of the drawing interface is in the DrawTerrain function. It uses the OpenGL *selection* mechanism to determine which terrain points are under the mouse pointer. Instead of drawing the terrain to the screen, selection rendering records "hits" inside the selection area (in this case, the mouse pointer) to a buffer you provide. In

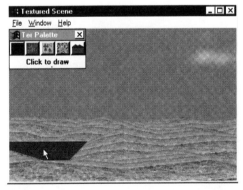

Figure 12-4 Textured terrain editing window

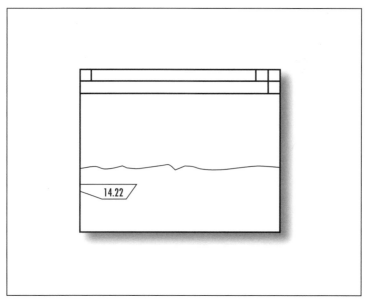

Figure 12-5 Picking a terrain cell

DrawTerrain, we record the (x,y) location of the terrain in the selection buffer, as in a "paint-by-numbers" book (see Figure 12-5). OpenGL selection is covered in more detail in Chapter 19.

Once we have the (x,y) terrain locations, we then reset the height and type of these points in the draw_cell function (Listing 12-4).

Listing 12-4 The draw_cell function

```
void
draw_cell(int x, /* I - Terrain X location */
          int y) /* I - Terrain Y location */
{
 /*
  * Range check the terrain location...
  */

  if (x < 0 || x >= TERRAIN_SIZE ||
      y < 0 || y >= TERRAIN_SIZE)
    return;

  if (TerrainType[y][x] == TerrainCurrent)
    return;       /* Already the right type */

  TerrainType[y][x] = TerrainCurrent;

 /*
  * Force a redraw...
  */
```

```
InvalidateRect(SceneWindow, NULL, TRUE);

/*
 * Set the height of the terrain 'cell'.  For water, the
 * height is constant at WATER_HEIGHT.  Other other types,
 * we add a random pertubation to make the terrain more
 * interesting/realistic.
 */

switch (TerrainCurrent)
{
    case IDC_WATER :
        TerrainHeight[y][x] = WATER_HEIGHT;
        break;
    case IDC_GRASS :
        TerrainHeight[y][x] = GRASS_HEIGHT + 0.1 * (rand() % 5);
        break;
    case IDC_TREES :
        TerrainHeight[y][x] = TREES_HEIGHT + 0.1 * (rand() % 5);
        break;
    case IDC_ROCKS :
        TerrainHeight[y][x] = ROCKS_HEIGHT + 0.1 * (rand() % 5);
        break;
    case IDC_MOUNTAINS :
        TerrainHeight[y][x] = MOUNTAINS_HEIGHT + 0.15 * (rand() % 5);
        break;
};
}
```

For the IDC_WATER terrain type, the point height is just set to WATER_HEIGHT (0.0). For other types, we add a small amount of random "jitter" to make the terrain look more realistic. Once the selected cell is drawn, we recompute the lighting normals using the new height values in UpdateNormals. Each lighting normal is calculated using the points above and to the right of the current point with the following formula:

```
N = lighting normal
H = height of current point
Hu = height of point above
Hr = height of point to the right

Nx = (Hr - H) / |N|
Ny = 1 / |N|
Nz = (Hu - H) / |N|
```

This is just a simplification of the cross product of adjacent terrain grid-cells. Once all the normals are recalculated, the scene is redrawn.

Drawing the Scene

Now that we've taken care of the drudge work, we can concentrate on displaying the terrain. You'll remember that besides displaying a pretty textured image, we also want to fly through this terrain. To accomplish this, we need to draw the terrain without textures—basically because texture mapping on a standard PC is too slow for animation. When the user isn't flying around (or drawing, for that matter), we want to draw with the textures. We will take care of this with a little conditional code and a few lighting parameters.

Also, because drawing the textured scene will be slower than the fly-through scene, we need to provide some feedback to the user that our program is doing something. For simplicity, we'll just draw to the front buffer (the visible one) when texturing, and to the back buffer (the invisible one for animation) when flying or drawing. This way, when the program updates the textured scene, the user will see the image being drawn. You'll learn more about buffers in Chapter 15.

The RepaintWindow function handles redrawing the terrain for the user. It starts off by selecting the front or back buffer (as described just above). Then it clears the color and depth bits, as follows:

```
glViewport(0, 0, rect->right, rect->bottom);

glClearColor(0.5, 0.5, 1.0, 1.0);

glEnable(GL_DEPTH_TEST);

if (Moving || Drawing)
{
  glDisable(GL_TEXTURE_2D);
  glDrawBuffer(GL_BACK);
}
else
{
  glEnable(GL_TEXTURE_2D);
  glTexEnvi(GL_TEXTURE_ENV, GL_TEXTURE_ENV_MODE, GL_DECAL);
  glDrawBuffer(GL_FRONT);
};

glClear(GL_COLOR_BUFFER_BIT | GL_DEPTH_BUFFER_BIT);
```

After this, RepaintWindow draws in the sky. For performance reasons, the sky is only drawn when the user is not flying over or drawing the terrain. Since the background is cleared to a light blue, this isn't really a problem. The sky is shaped like a pyramid and has the SKY.BMP texture image mapped to it for a nice, cloudy blue sky.

Once the sky is drawn, RepaintWindow starts drawing the terrain. The algorithm used is quite simple and basically generates strips of quadrilaterals (squares) along the terrain points. Each strip uses a different texture or lighting material color, so we have to issue glBegin/glEnd calls for each one. See Figure 12-6 for a graphical depiction of the algorithm.

As you can see, this algorithm won't track the terrain exactly, but it is fast and simple to implement. It scans the terrain from left to right and from bottom to top, and starts a new GL_QUAD_STRIP primitive whenever the terrain type changes. Along the way it assigns lighting normals and texture coordinates for each point on the terrain.

Automatically Generating Texture Coordinates

Generating all those texture coordinates can be tedious. Fortunately, OpenGL has an answer that we can use! In the current drawing code, we issue glTexCoord2i calls

```
glTexCoord2i(x * 2, y * 2);
```

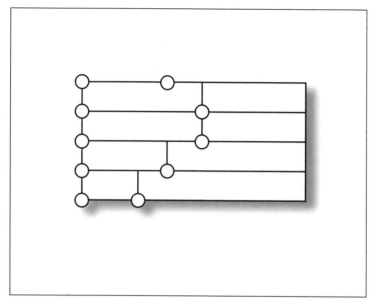

Figure 12-6 The terrain-drawing algorithm

for each and every point in the terrain. But instead of doing this for each point, we can use the glTexGen functions to define the S and T coordinates in terms of the X and Z position in the scene (Y is used for the height). To generate coordinates for our terrain, then, we can use the following:

```
static GLint s_vector[4] = { 2, 0, 0, 0 };
static GLint t_vector[4] = { 0, 0, 2, 0 };

glTexGeni(GL_S, GL_TEXTURE_GEN_MODE, GL_OBJECT_LINEAR);
glTexGeniv(GL_S, GL_OBJECT_PLANE, s_vector);

glTexGeni(GL_T, GL_TEXTURE_GEN_MODE, GL_OBJECT_LINEAR);
glTexGeniv(GL_T, GL_OBJECT_PLANE, t_vector);
```

Here the GL_OBJECT_LINEAR mapping mode maps the texture coordinates from object coordinates:

```
coordinate = X * vector[0] + Y * vector[1] +
             Z * vector[2] + W * vector[3]
```

The vector array is specified with glTexGen function:

```
void glTexGeniv(GLenum coord, GLenum pname, GLint *params)
```

where the coord parameter specifies which texture image coordinate to generate, GL_S or GL_T, and the pname parameter specifies the vector to define; in this case GL_OBJECT_PLANE. Finally, the params array specifies the object plane vector that is used to compute the texture coordinate.

The previous code for our terrain would generate these coordinates:

```
S = 2 * X
T = 2 * Z
```

To make OpenGL use these generated coordinates, you must enable texture coordinate generation, as follows:

```
glEnable(GL_TEXTURE_GEN_S);
glEnable(GL_TEXTURE_GEN_T);
```

The file TEXSCENE.C contains a version of our terrain viewing program that uses generated texture coordinates. The same techniques can be used with a 1D texture image. For the 1D image, you'd probably generate the S coordinate from the height (Y) to color the terrain based upon the height of the terrain. Generating texture coordinates is usually faster than specifying them manually in immediate mode, but is slower when using display lists.

Flying Through the Terrain

When the user is flying through the terrain, we need to regulate the flying speed based on the update rate of our scene. Rather than trying to maintain a fixed update rate—which can vary depending on the graphics card and CPU being used—we will measure the elapsed time from the last update to the current time. The FlyTerrain function manages this by measuring the time in milliseconds between each call, and moving the viewer forward at a fixed speed relative to the elapsed time.

Summary

In this chapter you've learned how to texture-map images onto polygons and other primitives using OpenGL. Texturing can provide that extra measure of realism that makes computer graphics so exciting to work with.

The OpenGL glTexParameter functions provide many ways to improve the quality of texture images when they are drawn. Mipmapped texture images provide multiple levels of detail that improve rendering quality and speed. Linear interpolation of texture images can improve certain types of textures, such as the sky texture used in the example project.

The glTexGen functions can simplify generation of texture coordinates by removing unnecessary or tedious calculations. By removing large amounts of conditional glTexCoord calls, automatic coordinate generation also simplifies programs that must display both textured and nontextured scenes

For games and other interactive, animated displays, you may want to support both textured and nontextured displays until accelerated OpenGL graphics boards become more widely available.

Now here is Listing 12-5, the complete terrain viewing program, TEXSCENE.C.

Listing 12-5 TEXSCENE.C: The terrain viewing program

```
#include 'texture.h'
#include 'texscene.h'
#include <stdarg.h>
#include <math.h>
#ifndef M_PI
#  define M_PI  (double)3.14159265358979323846
#endif /* !M_PI */


/*
 * Constants...
 */

#define TERRAIN_SIZE          21
#define TERRAIN_EDGE          ((TERRAIN_SIZE - 1) / 2)
#define TERRAIN_SCALE         (500.0 / TERRAIN_EDGE)

#define GRASS_HEIGHT          0.0
#define WATER_HEIGHT          0.0
#define TREES_HEIGHT          0.0
#define ROCKS_HEIGHT          0.5
#define MOUNTAINS_HEIGHT      1.0


/*
 * Globals...
 */

HWND          SceneWindow;          /* Scene window */
HPALETTE      ScenePalette;         /* Color palette (if necessary) */
HDC           SceneDC;              /* Drawing context */
HGLRC         SceneRC;              /* OpenGL rendering context */

GLuint        SkyTexture,           /* Sky texture image */
              GrassTexture,         /* Grass... */
              RocksTexture,         /* Rock... */
              WaterTexture,         /* Water... */
              TreesTexture,         /* Trees... */
              MountainsTexture;     /* Mountains... */

  HBITMAP     GrassDownBitmap,      /* Grass button down image */
              GrassUpBitmap,        /* Grass button up image */
              GrassSelectBitmap,    /* Grass button selected image */
              RocksDownBitmap,      /* ... */
              RocksUpBitmap,
              RocksSelectBitmap,
              WaterDownBitmap,
              WaterUpBitmap,
              WaterSelectBitmap,
              TreesDownBitmap,
              TreesUpBitmap,
              TreesSelectBitmap,
```

continued on next page

continued from previous page

```
                MountainsDownBitmap,
                MountainsUpBitmap,
                MountainsSelectBitmap;

HWND            TerrainWindow;          /* Terrain dialog */
int             TerrainCurrent = IDC_WATER;
int             TerrainType[TERRAIN_SIZE][TERRAIN_SIZE];
GLfloat         TerrainHeight[TERRAIN_SIZE][TERRAIN_SIZE];
GLfloat         TerrainNormal[TERRAIN_SIZE][TERRAIN_SIZE][3];

double          MoveTime;               /* Last update time */
GLboolean       Moving = GL_FALSE,      /* GL_TRUE if flying */
                Drawing = GL_FALSE;     /* GL_TRUE if drawing */
POINT           CenterMouseXY;          /* Initial mouse pos */
GLfloat         Position[3] = { 0.0, TERRAIN_SCALE, 0.0 };
                                        /* Viewer position */
GLfloat         Heading = 0.0,          /* Viewer heading */
                Pitch = 0.0,            /* Viewer pitch */
                Roll = 0.0;             /* Viewer roll */


/*
 * Local functions...
 */

void                    DisplayErrorMessage(char *, ...);
void                    MakePalette(int);
LRESULT CALLBACK        SceneProc(HWND, UINT, WPARAM, LPARAM);
UINT CALLBACK           TerrainDlgProc(HWND, UINT, WPARAM, LPARAM);
void                    InitializeTerrain(void);
void                    LoadAllTextures(void);
void                    LoadAllBitmaps(HINSTANCE);
void                    DrawTerrain(int, int);
void                    FlyTerrain(int, int);
void                    RepaintWindow(RECT *);
void                    SaveBitmapFile(void);
void                    PrintBitmap(void);
double                  GetClock(void);


/*
 * 'WinMain()' - Main entry...
 */

int APIENTRY
WinMain(HINSTANCE hInst,                /* I - Current process instance */
        HINSTANCE hPrevInstance,        /* I - Parent process instance */
        LPSTR     lpCmdLine,            /* I - Command-line arguments */
        int       nCmdShow)             /* I - Show window at startup? */
{
  MSG           msg;                    /* Window UI event */
  WNDCLASS      wc;                     /* Window class */
  POINT         pos;                    /* Current mouse pos */


  /*
   * Initialize the terrain to all grasslands...
   */
```

```
  InitializeTerrain();

/*
 * Register main window...
 */

  wc.style          = 0;
  wc.lpfnWndProc    = (WNDPROC)SceneProc;
  wc.cbClsExtra     = 0;
  wc.cbWndExtra     = 0;
  wc.hInstance      = hInst;
  wc.hIcon          = NULL;
  wc.hCursor        = LoadCursor(NULL, IDC_ARROW);
  wc.hbrBackground  = 0;
  wc.lpszMenuName   = MAKEINTRESOURCE(IDR_MENU1);
  wc.lpszClassName  = 'Textured Scene';

  if (RegisterClass(&wc) == 0)
  {
    DisplayErrorMessage('Unable to register window class!');
    return (FALSE);
  };

/*
 * Then create it...
 */

  SceneWindow = CreateWindow('Textured Scene', 'Textured Scene',
                             WS_OVERLAPPEDWINDOW | WS_CLIPCHILDREN | WS_CLIPSIBLINGS,
                             32, 32, 400, 300,
                             NULL, NULL, hInst, NULL);

  if (SceneWindow == NULL)
  {
    DisplayErrorMessage('Unable to create window!');
    return (FALSE);
  };

  ShowWindow(SceneWindow, nCmdShow);
  UpdateWindow(SceneWindow);

/*
 * Load the bitmaps for the buttons, and then create the terrain
 * editing dialog.
 */

  LoadAllBitmaps(hInst);

  TerrainWindow = CreateDialog(hInst, MAKEINTRESOURCE(IDD_TERRAIN_DIALOG),
                               SceneWindow, (DLGPROC)TerrainDlgProc);

/*
 * Loop on events until the user quits this application...
 */

  while (TRUE)
  {
    /*
```

continued on next page

continued from previous page

```
  * Process all messages in the queue...
  */

  while (!Moving ||
         PeekMessage(&msg, NULL, 0, 0, PM_NOREMOVE) == TRUE)
    if (GetMessage(&msg, NULL, 0, 0))
    {
      TranslateMessage(&msg);
      DispatchMessage(&msg);
    }
    else
      return (1);

  /*
   * Handle flying as necessary...
   */

  GetCursorPos(&pos);
  FlyTerrain(pos.x, pos.y);
  };

  return (msg.wParam);
}


/*
 * 'DisplayErrorMessage()' - Display an error message dialog.
 */

void
DisplayErrorMessage(char *format,       /* I - printf() style format string */
                    ...)                /* I - Other arguments as necessary */
{
  va_list     ap;                       /* Argument pointer */
  char        s[1024];                  /* Output string */


  if (format == NULL)
    return;

  va_start(ap, format);
  vsprintf(s, format, ap);
  va_end(ap);

  MessageBeep(MB_ICONEXCLAMATION);
  MessageBox(NULL, s, 'Error', MB_OK | MB_ICONEXCLAMATION);
}


/*
 * 'MakePalette()' - Make a color palette for RGB colors if necessary.
 */

void
MakePalette(int pf)                      /* I - Pixel format ID */
{
  PIXELFORMATDESCRIPTOR pfd;             /* Pixel format information */
  LOGPALETTE            *pPal;           /* Pointer to logical palette */
  int                   nColors;         /* Number of entries in palette */
```

```
    int                 i,              /* Color index */
                        rmax,           /* Maximum red value */
                        gmax,           /* Maximum green value */
                        bmax;           /* Maximum blue value */


   /*
    * Find out if we need to define a color palette...
    */

   DescribePixelFormat(SceneDC, pf, sizeof(PIXELFORMATDESCRIPTOR), &pfd);

   if (!(pfd.dwFlags & PFD_NEED_PALETTE))
   {
     ScenePalette = NULL;
     return;
   };

   /*
    * Allocate memory for a color palette...
    */

   nColors = 1 << pfd.cColorBits;

   pPal = (LOGPALETTE *)malloc(sizeof(LOGPALETTE) +
                              nColors * sizeof(PALETTEENTRY));

   pPal->palVersion    = 0x300;
   pPal->palNumEntries = nColors;

   /*
    * Get the maximum values for red, green, and blue.  Then build 'nColors'
    * colors...
    */

   rmax = (1 << pfd.cRedBits) - 1;
   gmax = (1 << pfd.cGreenBits) - 1;
   bmax = (1 << pfd.cBlueBits) - 1;

   for (i = 0; i < nColors; i ++)
   {
     pPal->palPalEntry[i].peRed   = 255 * ((i >> pfd.cRedShift) & rmax) / rmax;
     pPal->palPalEntry[i].peGreen = 255 * ((i >> pfd.cGreenShift) & gmax) / gmax;
     pPal->palPalEntry[i].peBlue  = 255 * ((i >> pfd.cBlueShift) & bmax) / bmax;

     pPal->palPalEntry[i].peFlags = 0;
   };

   /*
    * Create, select, and realize the palette...
    */

   ScenePalette = CreatePalette(pPal);
   SelectPalette(SceneDC, ScenePalette, FALSE);
   RealizePalette(SceneDC);

   free(pPal);
}
```

continued on next page

continued from previous page

```
/*
 * 'SceneProc()' - Handle window events in the viewing window.
 */

LRESULT CALLBACK
SceneProc(HWND    hWnd,          /* I - Window triggering this event */
          UINT    uMsg,          /* I - Message type */
          WPARAM  wParam,        /* I - 'word' parameter value */
          LPARAM  lParam)        /* I - 'long' parameter value */
{
  int                     pf;    /* Pixel format ID */
  PIXELFORMATDESCRIPTOR   pfd;   /* Pixel format information */
  PAINTSTRUCT             ps;    /* WM_PAINT message info */
  RECT                    rect;  /* Current client area rectangle */


  switch (uMsg)
  {
    case WM_CREATE :
      /*
       * 'Create' message.  Get device and rendering contexts, and
       * setup the client area for OpenGL drawing...
       */

      SceneDC = GetDC(hWnd);

      pfd.nSize        = sizeof(pfd);
      pfd.nVersion     = 1;
      pfd.dwFlags      = PFD_DRAW_TO_WINDOW | PFD_SUPPORT_OPENGL | PFD_DOUBLEBUFFER;
                                             /* Do OpenGL drawing */
      pfd.dwLayerMask  = PFD_MAIN_PLANE;     /* Main drawing plane */
      pfd.iPixelType   = PFD_TYPE_RGBA;      /* RGB color buffer */
      pfd.cColorBits   = 0;                  /* Best color buffer please */
      pfd.cDepthBits   = 32;                 /* Need a depth buffer */
      pfd.cStencilBits = 0;                  /* No stencil buffer */
      pfd.cAccumBits   = 0;                  /* No accumulation buffer */

      pf = ChoosePixelFormat(SceneDC, &pfd);
      if (pf == 0)
        DisplayErrorMessage('texscene was unable to choose a suitable pixel format!');
      else if (!SetPixelFormat(SceneDC, pf, &pfd))
        DisplayErrorMessage('texscene was unable to set the pixel format!');

      MakePalette(pf);

      SceneRC = wglCreateContext(SceneDC);
      wglMakeCurrent(SceneDC, SceneRC);

      /*
       * Load all the texture images into display lists...
       */

      LoadAllTextures();
      break;

    case WM_SIZE :
    case WM_PAINT :
      /*
       * Repaint the client area with our bitmap...
       */
```

```
        BeginPaint(hWnd, &ps);

        GetClientRect(hWnd, &rect);
        RepaintWindow(&rect);

        EndPaint(hWnd, &ps);
        break;

    case WM_COMMAND :
        /*
         * Handle menu selections...
         */

        switch (LOWORD(wParam))
        {
          case IDM_FILE_SAVEAS :
              SaveBitmapFile();
              break;
          case IDM_FILE_PRINT :
              PrintBitmap();
              break;
          case IDM_FILE_EXIT :
              DestroyWindow(SceneWindow);
              break;

          case IDM_WINDOW_TERRAIN :
              /*
               * Toggle the terrain dialog window on and off...
               */

              if (GetMenuState(GetMenu(SceneWindow), IDM_WINDOW_TERRAIN,
                               MF_BYCOMMAND) & MF_CHECKED)
              {
                CheckMenuItem(GetMenu(SceneWindow), IDM_WINDOW_TERRAIN,
                              MF_BYCOMMAND | MF_UNCHECKED);
                ShowWindow(TerrainWindow, SW_HIDE);
              }
              else
              {
                CheckMenuItem(GetMenu(SceneWindow), IDM_WINDOW_TERRAIN,
                              MF_BYCOMMAND | MF_CHECKED);
                ShowWindow(TerrainWindow, SW_SHOW);
              };
              break;
        };
        break;

    case WM_QUIT :
    case WM_CLOSE :
        /*
         * Destroy the windows and bitmaps and exit...
         */

        DestroyWindow(SceneWindow);
        DestroyWindow(TerrainWindow);

        DeleteObject(GrassDownBitmap);
        DeleteObject(GrassSelectBitmap);
        DeleteObject(GrassUpBitmap);
        DeleteObject(WaterDownBitmap);
```

continued on next page

continued from previous page

```
        DeleteObject(WaterSelectBitmap);
        DeleteObject(WaterUpBitmap);
        DeleteObject(RocksDownBitmap);
        DeleteObject(RocksSelectBitmap);
        DeleteObject(RocksUpBitmap);
        DeleteObject(TreesDownBitmap);
        DeleteObject(TreesSelectBitmap);
        DeleteObject(TreesUpBitmap);
        DeleteObject(MountainsDownBitmap);
        DeleteObject(MountainsSelectBitmap);
        DeleteObject(MountainsUpBitmap);

        exit(0);
        break;

    case WM_DESTROY :
      /*
       * Release and free the device context, rendering
       * context, and color palette...
       */

      if (SceneRC)
        wglDeleteContext(SceneRC);

      if (SceneDC)
        ReleaseDC(SceneWindow, SceneDC);

      if (ScenePalette)
        DeleteObject(ScenePalette);

      PostQuitMessage(0);
      break;

    case WM_QUERYNEWPALETTE :
      /*
       * Realize the color palette if necessary...
       */

      if (ScenePalette)
      {
        SelectPalette(SceneDC, ScenePalette, FALSE);
        RealizePalette(SceneDC);

        InvalidateRect(hWnd, NULL, FALSE);
        return (TRUE);
      };
      break;

    case WM_PALETTECHANGED:
      /*
       * Reselect our color palette if necessary...
       */

      if (ScenePalette && (HWND)wParam != hWnd)
      {
        SelectPalette(SceneDC, ScenePalette, FALSE);
        RealizePalette(SceneDC);

        UpdateColors(SceneDC);
```

```
    };
    break;

case WM_LBUTTONDOWN :
  /*
   * The left mouse button just was pressed.  If we have
   * the terrain dialog window open, then this signifies
   * the beginning of drawing.
   *
   * Otherwise, set the 'Moving' flag to true to indicate
   * flying.
   */

  SetCapture(SceneWindow);

  if (IsWindowVisible(TerrainWindow))
  {
    DrawTerrain(LOWORD(lParam), HIWORD(lParam));
    Drawing = GL_TRUE;
  }
  else
  {
    GetCursorPos(&CenterMouseXY);
    Moving    = GL_TRUE;
    MoveTime = GetClock();
  };
  break;

case WM_MOUSEMOVE :
  /*
   * The mouse pointer moved.  If we are in the process of
   * drawing some terrain, do it.
   *
   * Otherwise, ignore the message because we fly from the
   * main loop.
   */

  if (Drawing)
    DrawTerrain(LOWORD(lParam), HIWORD(lParam));
  break;

case WM_LBUTTONUP :
  /*
   * The user released the left mouse button.  Stop drawing
   * or flying...
   */

  Moving  = GL_FALSE;
  Drawing = GL_FALSE;
  ReleaseCapture();

  InvalidateRect(SceneWindow, NULL, TRUE);
  break;

default :
  /*
   * Pass all other messages through the default window
   * procedure...
   */
```

continued on next page

continued from previous page

```
          return (DefWindowProc(hWnd, uMsg, wParam, lParam));
    };

    return (FALSE);
}


/*
 * 'TerrainDlgProc()' - Process messages in the terrain dialog window.
 */

UINT CALLBACK
TerrainDlgProc(HWND    hWnd,      /* I - Source window */
               UINT    uMsg,      /* I - Message type */
               WPARAM  wParam,    /* I - 'word' parameter value */
               LPARAM  lParam)    /* I - 'long' parameter value */
{
  HDC                  hdc;    /* Drawing context for buttons */
  LPDRAWITEMSTRUCT     lpdis;  /* Button state info */
  UINT                 idCtl;  /* Button ID */


  switch (uMsg)
  {
    case WM_DRAWITEM :
        /*
         * Windows wants us to draw a button.  Figure out which
         * button it is, and display as necessary...
         */

        idCtl = (UINT)wParam;
        lpdis = (LPDRAWITEMSTRUCT)lParam;
        hdc   = CreateCompatibleDC(lpdis->hDC);

        switch (idCtl)
        {
          case IDC_WATER :
              if (lpdis->itemState & ODS_SELECTED)
                SelectObject(hdc, WaterDownBitmap);
              else if (TerrainCurrent == IDC_WATER)
                SelectObject(hdc, WaterSelectBitmap);
              else
                SelectObject(hdc, WaterUpBitmap);
              break;
          case IDC_GRASS :
              if (lpdis->itemState & ODS_SELECTED)
                SelectObject(hdc, GrassDownBitmap);
              else if (TerrainCurrent == IDC_GRASS)
                SelectObject(hdc, GrassSelectBitmap);
              else
                SelectObject(hdc, GrassUpBitmap);
              break;
          case IDC_TREES :
              if (lpdis->itemState & ODS_SELECTED)
                SelectObject(hdc, TreesDownBitmap);
              else if (TerrainCurrent == IDC_TREES)
                SelectObject(hdc, TreesSelectBitmap);
              else
```

```
                SelectObject(hdc, TreesUpBitmap);
            break;
        case IDC_ROCKS :
            if (lpdis->itemState & ODS_SELECTED)
              SelectObject(hdc, RocksDownBitmap);
            else if (TerrainCurrent == IDC_ROCKS)
              SelectObject(hdc, RocksSelectBitmap);
            else
              SelectObject(hdc, RocksUpBitmap);
            break;
        case IDC_MOUNTAINS :
            if (lpdis->itemState & ODS_SELECTED)
              SelectObject(hdc, MountainsDownBitmap);
            else if (TerrainCurrent == IDC_MOUNTAINS)
              SelectObject(hdc, MountainsSelectBitmap);
            else
              SelectObject(hdc, MountainsUpBitmap);
            break;
    };

    /*
     * Stretch the bitmap to fit the button area...
     */

    StretchBlt(lpdis->hDC, lpdis->rcItem.left,
               lpdis->rcItem.top, lpdis->rcItem.right,
               lpdis->rcItem.bottom,
               hdc, 0, 0, 24, 24, SRCCOPY);
    DeleteDC(hdc);
    break;

case WM_CLOSE :
    /*
     * Close the window (hide it) and turn the check mark off
     * in the main menu.
     */

    ShowWindow(TerrainWindow, SW_HIDE);
    CheckMenuItem(GetMenu(SceneWindow), IDM_WINDOW_TERRAIN,
                  MF_BYCOMMAND | MF_UNCHECKED);
    break;

case WM_COMMAND :
    /*
     * A button was selected - choose the new current terrain
     * type.
     */

    switch (LOWORD(wParam))
    {
      case IDC_GRASS :
      case IDC_TREES :
      case IDC_ROCKS :
      case IDC_WATER :
      case IDC_MOUNTAINS :
          TerrainCurrent = LOWORD(wParam);

          InvalidateRect(TerrainWindow, NULL, TRUE);
          UpdateWindow(TerrainWindow);
```

continued on next page

continued from previous page

```
                return (TRUE);
        };
        break;
  };

  return (FALSE);
}


/*
 * 'LoadAllBitmaps()' - Load bitmap images for the terrain control buttons.
 */

void
LoadAllBitmaps(HINSTANCE hInstance)    /* I - Process instance */
{
  GrassDownBitmap    = LoadBitmap((HANDLE)hInstance,
                                  MAKEINTRESOURCE(IDB_GRASS_DOWN));
  GrassSelectBitmap = LoadBitmap((HANDLE)hInstance,
                                  MAKEINTRESOURCE(IDB_GRASS_SELECT));
  GrassUpBitmap      = LoadBitmap((HANDLE)hInstance,
                                  MAKEINTRESOURCE(IDB_GRASS_UP));

  WaterDownBitmap    = LoadBitmap((HANDLE)hInstance,
                                  MAKEINTRESOURCE(IDB_WATER_DOWN));
  WaterSelectBitmap = LoadBitmap((HANDLE)hInstance,
                                  MAKEINTRESOURCE(IDB_WATER_SELECT));
  WaterUpBitmap      = LoadBitmap((HANDLE)hInstance,
                                  MAKEINTRESOURCE(IDB_WATER_UP));

  RocksDownBitmap    = LoadBitmap((HANDLE)hInstance,
                                  MAKEINTRESOURCE(IDB_ROCKS_DOWN));
  RocksSelectBitmap = LoadBitmap((HANDLE)hInstance,
                                  MAKEINTRESOURCE(IDB_ROCKS_SELECT));
  RocksUpBitmap      = LoadBitmap((HANDLE)hInstance,
                                  MAKEINTRESOURCE(IDB_ROCKS_UP));

  TreesDownBitmap    = LoadBitmap((HANDLE)hInstance,
                                  MAKEINTRESOURCE(IDB_TREES_DOWN));
  TreesSelectBitmap = LoadBitmap((HANDLE)hInstance,
                                  MAKEINTRESOURCE(IDB_TREES_SELECT));
  TreesUpBitmap      = LoadBitmap((HANDLE)hInstance,
                                  MAKEINTRESOURCE(IDB_TREES_UP));

  MountainsDownBitmap   = LoadBitmap((HANDLE)hInstance,
                                     MAKEINTRESOURCE(IDB_MOUNTAINS_DOWN));
  MountainsSelectBitmap = LoadBitmap((HANDLE)hInstance,
                                     MAKEINTRESOURCE(IDB_MOUNTAINS_SELECT));
  MountainsUpBitmap     = LoadBitmap((HANDLE)hInstance,
                                     MAKEINTRESOURCE(IDB_MOUNTAINS_UP));
}


/*
 * 'LoadAllTextures()' - Load texture images for the scene.
 */

void
LoadAllTextures(void)
```

```
{
  glNewList(SkyTexture = glGenLists(1), GL_COMPILE);
    glTexParameteri(GL_TEXTURE_2D, GL_TEXTURE_WRAP_S, GL_REPEAT);
    glTexParameteri(GL_TEXTURE_2D, GL_TEXTURE_WRAP_T, GL_REPEAT);
    TextureLoadBitmap('textures/sky.bmp');
    glTexParameteri(GL_TEXTURE_2D, GL_TEXTURE_MAG_FILTER, GL_LINEAR);
  glEndList();

  glNewList(RocksTexture = glGenLists(1), GL_COMPILE);
    glTexParameteri(GL_TEXTURE_2D, GL_TEXTURE_WRAP_S, GL_REPEAT);
    glTexParameteri(GL_TEXTURE_2D, GL_TEXTURE_WRAP_T, GL_REPEAT);
    TextureLoadMipmap('textures/rock.bmp');
    glTexParameteri(GL_TEXTURE_2D, GL_TEXTURE_MAG_FILTER, GL_NEAREST);
    glTexParameteri(GL_TEXTURE_2D, GL_TEXTURE_MIN_FILTER, GL_NEAREST_MIPMAP_LINEAR);
  glEndList();

  glNewList(GrassTexture = glGenLists(1), GL_COMPILE);
    glTexParameteri(GL_TEXTURE_2D, GL_TEXTURE_WRAP_S, GL_REPEAT);
    glTexParameteri(GL_TEXTURE_2D, GL_TEXTURE_WRAP_T, GL_REPEAT);
    TextureLoadMipmap('textures/grass.bmp');
    glTexParameteri(GL_TEXTURE_2D, GL_TEXTURE_MAG_FILTER, GL_NEAREST);
    glTexParameteri(GL_TEXTURE_2D, GL_TEXTURE_MIN_FILTER, GL_NEAREST_MIPMAP_LINEAR);
  glEndList();

  glNewList(WaterTexture = glGenLists(1), GL_COMPILE);
    glTexParameteri(GL_TEXTURE_2D, GL_TEXTURE_WRAP_S, GL_REPEAT);
    glTexParameteri(GL_TEXTURE_2D, GL_TEXTURE_WRAP_T, GL_REPEAT);
    TextureLoadMipmap('textures/water.bmp');
    glTexParameteri(GL_TEXTURE_2D, GL_TEXTURE_MAG_FILTER, GL_NEAREST);
    glTexParameteri(GL_TEXTURE_2D, GL_TEXTURE_MIN_FILTER, GL_NEAREST_MIPMAP_LINEAR);
  glEndList();

  glNewList(TreesTexture = glGenLists(1), GL_COMPILE);
    glTexParameteri(GL_TEXTURE_2D, GL_TEXTURE_WRAP_S, GL_REPEAT);
    glTexParameteri(GL_TEXTURE_2D, GL_TEXTURE_WRAP_T, GL_REPEAT);
    TextureLoadMipmap('textures/trees.bmp');
    glTexParameteri(GL_TEXTURE_2D, GL_TEXTURE_MAG_FILTER, GL_NEAREST);
    glTexParameteri(GL_TEXTURE_2D, GL_TEXTURE_MIN_FILTER, GL_NEAREST_MIPMAP_LINEAR);
  glEndList();

  glNewList(MountainsTexture = glGenLists(1), GL_COMPILE);
    glTexParameteri(GL_TEXTURE_2D, GL_TEXTURE_WRAP_S, GL_REPEAT);
    glTexParameteri(GL_TEXTURE_2D, GL_TEXTURE_WRAP_T, GL_REPEAT);
    TextureLoadMipmap('textures/mountain.bmp');
    glTexParameteri(GL_TEXTURE_2D, GL_TEXTURE_MAG_FILTER, GL_NEAREST);
    glTexParameteri(GL_TEXTURE_2D, GL_TEXTURE_MIN_FILTER, GL_NEAREST_MIPMAP_LINEAR);
  glEndList();
}


/*
 * 'UpdateNormals()' - Update the lighting normals for the
 *                     terrain...
 */

void
UpdateNormals(void)
{
  int        x, y;          /* Terrain (x,y) location */
```

continued on next page

continued from previous page

```
GLfloat         (*n)[3],      /* Current terrain normal */
                nx, ny, nz,   /* Normal components */
                d,            /* Normal magnitude */
                *height;      /* Current terrain height */


/*
 * Loop through the terrain arrays and regenerate the
 * lighting normals based on the terrain height.
 */

n      = TerrainNormal[0];
height = TerrainHeight[0];
for (y = 0; y < (TERRAIN_SIZE - 1); y ++, n ++, height ++)
{
  for (x = 0; x < (TERRAIN_SIZE - 1); x ++, n ++, height ++)
  {
    /*
     * Compute the cross product of the vectors above and to
     * the right (simplified for this special case).
     */

    nx = height[0] - height[1];
    ny = -1.0;
    nz = height[0] - height[TERRAIN_SIZE];

    d = -sqrt(nx * nx + ny * ny + nz * nz);

    n[0][0] = nx / d; /* Normalize the normal vector */
    n[0][1] = ny / d;
    n[0][2] = nz / d;
  };

  /*
   * Compute the cross product of the vectors above and to
   * the left (simplified for this special case) for the last
   * column in the grid.
   */

  nx = height[0] - height[-1];
  ny = -1.0;
  nz = height[0] - height[TERRAIN_SIZE];

  d = -sqrt(nx * nx + ny * ny + nz * nz);

  n[0][0] = nx / d;    /* Normalize the normal vector */
  n[0][1] = ny / d;
  n[0][2] = nz / d;
};

/*
 * Set the top row of normals to be the same as the second-to-
 * last row of normals.
 */

for (x = 0; x < TERRAIN_SIZE; x ++, n ++)
{
  n[0][0] = n[-TERRAIN_SIZE][0];
  n[0][1] = n[-TERRAIN_SIZE][1];
```

```
    n[0][2] = n[-TERRAIN_SIZE][2];
  };
}


/*
 * 'InitializeTerrain()' - Initialize the terrain arrays...
 */

void
InitializeTerrain(void)
{
  int   x, y;              /* Terrain (x,y) location */

 /*
  * Fill the terrain array with grass...
  */

  TerrainCurrent = IDC_WATER;

  for (y = 0; y < TERRAIN_SIZE; y ++)
    for (x = 0; x < TERRAIN_SIZE; x ++)
    {
      TerrainType[y][x]   = IDC_GRASS;
      TerrainHeight[y][x] = GRASS_HEIGHT + 0.1 * (rand() % 5);
    };

 /*
  * Update the lighting normals...
  */

  UpdateNormals();
}


/*
 * 'draw_cell()' - Draw (fill-in) a single terrain cell...
 */

void
draw_cell(int x,          /* I - Terrain X location */
          int y)          /* I - Terrain Y location */
{
 /*
  * Range check the terrain location...
  */

  if (x < 0 || x >= TERRAIN_SIZE ||
      y < 0 || y >= TERRAIN_SIZE)
    return;

  if (TerrainType[y][x] == TerrainCurrent)
    return;                /* Already the right type */

  TerrainType[y][x] = TerrainCurrent;

 /*
  * Force a redraw...
```

continued on next page

continued from previous page

```
    */

    InvalidateRect(SceneWindow, NULL, TRUE);

   /*
    * Set the height of the terrain 'cell'.  For water, the
    * height is constant at WATER_HEIGHT.  For other types,
    * we add a random pertubation to make the terrain more
    * interesting/realistic.
    */

    switch (TerrainCurrent)
    {
      case IDC_WATER :
          TerrainHeight[y][x] = WATER_HEIGHT;
          break;
      case IDC_GRASS :
          TerrainHeight[y][x] = GRASS_HEIGHT + 0.1 * (rand() % 5);
          break;
      case IDC_TREES :
          TerrainHeight[y][x] = TREES_HEIGHT + 0.1 * (rand() % 5);
          break;
      case IDC_ROCKS :
          TerrainHeight[y][x] = ROCKS_HEIGHT + 0.1 * (rand() % 5);
          break;
      case IDC_MOUNTAINS :
          TerrainHeight[y][x] = MOUNTAINS_HEIGHT + 0.15 * (rand() % 5);
          break;
    };
}


/*
 * 'DrawTerrain()' - Draw a terrain cell at the given mouse
 *                   position.
 */

void
DrawTerrain(int mousex,         /* I - Horizontal mouse position */
            int mousey)         /* I - Vertical mouse position */
{
  int           i,              /* Looping var */
                count,          /* Selection count */
                x, y;           /* Terrain (x,y) location */
  GLfloat       *height;        /* Current height */
  GLuint        buffer[100];    /* Selection buffer */
  GLint         viewport[4];    /* OpenGL viewport */


  /*
   * Get the current OpenGL viewport and make the vertical
   * mouse position start from the bottom of the viewport.
   */

  glGetIntegerv(GL_VIEWPORT, viewport);
  mousey = viewport[3] - 1 - mousey;

  /*
   * Begin selection into a 100 'hit' buffer...
```

```
*
* Allow picks within 4 pixels of the current mouse position.
*/

glSelectBuffer(100, buffer);
glRenderMode(GL_SELECT);

glInitNames();
glMatrixMode(GL_PROJECTION);
glLoadIdentity();
gluPickMatrix((GLdouble)mousex, (GLdouble)mousey, 4.0, 4.0,
             viewport);
gluPerspective(45.0, (float)viewport[2] / (float)viewport[3],
             0.1, 1000.0);

glMatrixMode(GL_MODELVIEW);
glPushMatrix();
 /*
  * Rotate/translate for the current viewing position and
  * orientation.
  */

  glRotatef(Roll, 0.0, 0.0, 1.0);
  glRotatef(Pitch, -1.0, 0.0, 0.0);
  glRotatef(Heading, 0.0, 1.0, 0.0);
  glTranslatef(-Position[0],
               -Position[1],
               -Position[2]);
  glScalef(TERRAIN_SCALE, TERRAIN_SCALE, TERRAIN_SCALE);

 /*
  * Draw the terrain into the selection buffer.  This is
  * done differently than the RepaintWindow() function does
  * so that we can select individual cells rather than whole
  * strips of one type.
  *
  * The select buffer has names pushed on the stack for both
  * the X and Y locations in the terrain...
  */

  height = TerrainHeight[0];
  glPushName(0);
  for (y = 0; y < (TERRAIN_SIZE - 1); y ++, height ++)
  {
    glLoadName(y);
    glPushName(0);

    for (x = 0; x < (TERRAIN_SIZE - 1); x ++, height ++)
    {
      glLoadName(x);
      glBegin(GL_POLYGON);
        glVertex3f((GLfloat)(x - TERRAIN_EDGE),
                   height[0],
                   (GLfloat)(y - TERRAIN_EDGE));
        glVertex3f((GLfloat)(x - TERRAIN_EDGE),
                   height[TERRAIN_SIZE],
                   (GLfloat)(y - TERRAIN_EDGE + 1));

        glVertex3f((GLfloat)(x - TERRAIN_EDGE + 1),
```

continued on next page

415

continued from previous page

```
                      height[1],
                      (GLfloat)(y - TERRAIN_EDGE));
          glVertex3f((GLfloat)(x - TERRAIN_EDGE + 1),
                      height[TERRAIN_SIZE + 1],
                      (GLfloat)(y - TERRAIN_EDGE + 1));
        glEnd();
      };

      glPopName();
    };
    glPopName();
  glPopMatrix();
  glFinish();

 /*
  * Get the 'hits' in the selection buffer...
  */

  count = glRenderMode(GL_RENDER);
  for (i = 0; i < count; i += 3)
  {
    if (buffer[i] == 0)
      continue;

   /*
    * Each 'hit' will contain the following parameters:
    *
    * 0 - count (2)
    * 1 - Z minimum value
    * 2 - Z maximum value
    * 3 - Y location in terrain
    * 4 - X location in terrain
    */

    x = buffer[i + 4];
    y = buffer[i + 3];
    i += buffer[i];

   /*
    * Fill-in the 4 corners of the selected cell...
    */

    draw_cell(x, y);
    draw_cell(x + 1, y);
    draw_cell(x, y + 1);
    draw_cell(x + 1, y + 1);

   /*
    * Update lighting normals for the terrain.
    */

    UpdateNormals();
  };
}


 /*
  * 'FlyTerrain()' - Fly using the given mouse position.
  */
```

```
void
FlyTerrain(int mousex,          /* I - Horizontal mouse position */
           int mousey)          /* I - Vertical mouse position */
{
  RECT          rect;           /* Current client rectangle */
  GLfloat       movex, movey;   /* Scale mouse movement */
  double        curtime,        /* Current time in seconds */
                distance;       /* Distance to move */
  GLfloat       cheading,       /* Cosine of heading */
                sheading,       /* Sine of heading */
                cpitch,         /* Cosine of pitch */
                spitch;         /* Sine of pitch */


 /*
  * Get the current system time to figure out how far to move.
  */

  curtime  = GetClock();
  distance = 10.0 * (curtime - MoveTime);
  MoveTime = curtime;

 /*
  * See how far the mouse pointer is from the 'center' (click)
  * position.
  */

  movex = 0.05 * (mousex - CenterMouseXY.x);
  movey = 0.05 * (mousey - CenterMouseXY.y);

 /*
  * Adjust roll, pitch, and heading according to the current
  * mouse inputs and orientation.
  */

  Roll    += movex;
  Pitch   += movey * cos(Roll * M_PI / 180.0);
  Heading += movey * sin(Roll * M_PI / 180.0);

  if (Heading < 0.0)
    Heading += 360.0;
  else if (Heading >= 360.0)
    Heading -= 360.0;

  if (Pitch < -180.0)
    Pitch += 360.0;
  else if (Pitch >= 180.0)
    Pitch -= 360.0;

  if (Roll < -180.0)
    Roll += 360.0;
  else if (Roll >= 180.0)
    Roll -= 360.0;

 /*
  * Move based upon the current orientation...
  */

  cheading = cos(Heading * M_PI / 180.0);
```

continued on next page

continued from previous page

```
  sheading = sin(Heading * M_PI / 180.0);
  cpitch   = cos(Pitch * M_PI / 180.0);
  spitch   = sin(Pitch * M_PI / 180.0);

  Position[0] += distance * sheading * cpitch;
  Position[2] -= distance * cheading * cpitch;
  Position[1] += distance * spitch;

 /*
  * Redraw the window using the new position and orientation...
  */

  GetClientRect(SceneWindow, &rect);
  RepaintWindow(&rect);
}


/*
 * 'RepaintWindow()' - Redraw the client area with our scene.
 */

void
RepaintWindow(RECT *rect)        /* I - Client area rectangle */
{
  int            i;              /* Looping var */
  int            x, y;           /* Terrain (x,y) location */
  int            last_type;      /* Previous terrain type */
  int            *type;          /* Current terrain type */
  GLfloat        *height,        /* Current terrain height */
                 (*n)[3];        /* Current terrain normal */
  static GLfloat        sky_top[4][3] =
  {                             /* Sky coordinates */
    { -TERRAIN_EDGE, TERRAIN_SIZE * 0.8, -TERRAIN_EDGE },
    {  TERRAIN_EDGE, TERRAIN_SIZE * 0.8, -TERRAIN_EDGE },
    {  TERRAIN_EDGE, TERRAIN_SIZE * 0.8,  TERRAIN_EDGE },
    { -TERRAIN_EDGE, TERRAIN_SIZE * 0.8,  TERRAIN_EDGE }
  };
  static GLfloat        sky_bottom[4][3] =
  {
    { -TERRAIN_EDGE, 0.0, -TERRAIN_EDGE },
    {  TERRAIN_EDGE, 0.0, -TERRAIN_EDGE },
    {  TERRAIN_EDGE, 0.0,  TERRAIN_EDGE },
    { -TERRAIN_EDGE, 0.0,  TERRAIN_EDGE }
  };
  static GLfloat        sunpos[4] = { 0.0, 1.0, 0.0, 0.0 };
  static GLfloat        suncolor[4] = { 64.0, 64.0, 64.0, 1.0 };
  static GLfloat        sunambient[4] = { 0.001, 0.001, 0.001, 1.0 };


 /*
  * Reset the viewport and clear the window to light blue...
  */

  glViewport(0, 0, rect->right, rect->bottom);

  glClearColor(0.5, 0.5, 1.0, 1.0);

  glEnable(GL_DEPTH_TEST);

  if (Moving || Drawing)
```

```
{
 /*
  * Don't texture while flying or drawing; it's too slow...
  * Also, draw to the back buffer for smooth animation.
  */

  glDisable(GL_TEXTURE_2D);
  glDrawBuffer(GL_BACK);
}
else
{
 /*
  * Enable textures when we've stopped moving or drawing.
  * This generates a nice scene that we can printout or
  * save to a bitmap file...
  *
  * Because it takes longer, we draw to the front buffer
  * so the user can see some progress...
  */

  glEnable(GL_TEXTURE_2D);
  glTexEnvi(GL_TEXTURE_ENV, GL_TEXTURE_ENV_MODE, GL_DECAL);
  glDrawBuffer(GL_FRONT);
};

glClear(GL_COLOR_BUFFER_BIT | GL_DEPTH_BUFFER_BIT);

/*
 * Setup viewing transformations for the current position and
 * orientation...
 */

glMatrixMode(GL_PROJECTION);
glLoadIdentity();
gluPerspective(45.0, (float)rect->right / (float)rect->bottom,
               0.1, 1000.0);

glMatrixMode(GL_MODELVIEW);
glPushMatrix();
  glRotatef(Roll, 0.0, 0.0, 1.0);
  glRotatef(Pitch, -1.0, 0.0, 0.0);
  glRotatef(Heading, 0.0, 1.0, 0.0);
  glTranslatef(-Position[0],
               -Position[1],
               -Position[2]);
  glScalef(TERRAIN_SCALE, TERRAIN_SCALE, TERRAIN_SCALE);

  if (!(Moving || Drawing))
  {
    /*
     * Draw the sky...
     */

    glDisable(GL_LIGHTING);
    glCallList(SkyTexture);
    glBegin(GL_QUAD_STRIP);
      for (i = 0; i < 4; i ++)
      {
        glTexCoord2f((float)i, 0.0);
        glVertex3fv(sky_bottom[i]);
```

continued on next page

continued from previous page

```
        glTexCoord2f((float)i, 0.8);
        glVertex3fv(sky_top[i]);
      };

      glTexCoord2f(4.0, 0.0);
      glVertex3fv(sky_bottom[0]);

      glTexCoord2f(4.0, 0.8);
      glVertex3fv(sky_top[0]);
    glEnd();

    glBegin(GL_TRIANGLE_FAN);
      glTexCoord2f(0.5, 1.0);
      glVertex3f(0.0, TERRAIN_SIZE, 0.0);

      for (i = 0; i < 4; i ++)
      {
        glTexCoord2f((float)i, 0.8);
        glVertex3fv(sky_top[i]);
      };

      glTexCoord2f(4.0, 0.8);
      glVertex3fv(sky_top[0]);
    glEnd();
  };

/*
 * Setup lighting...
 */

  glEnable(GL_LIGHTING);
  glLightModeli(GL_LIGHT_MODEL_TWO_SIDE, GL_TRUE);

  glEnable(GL_LIGHT0);
  glLightfv(GL_LIGHT0, GL_POSITION, sunpos);
  glLightfv(GL_LIGHT0, GL_DIFFUSE, suncolor);
  glLightfv(GL_LIGHT0, GL_AMBIENT, sunambient);

  if (Moving || Drawing)
    glEnable(GL_COLOR_MATERIAL);
  else
    glDisable(GL_COLOR_MATERIAL);

/*
 * Then the terrain...
 */

  type   = TerrainType[0];
  height = TerrainHeight[0];
  n      = TerrainNormal[0];
  for (y = 0; y < (TERRAIN_SIZE - 1); y ++)
  {
    last_type = -1;

    for (x = 0; x < TERRAIN_SIZE; x ++, type ++, height ++, n ++)
    {
      if (last_type != *type)
      {
```

```
/*
 * If the type of terrain changes, end any existing
 * strip of quads and reset color/texture parameters...
 */

if (last_type != -1)
  glEnd();

switch (*type)
{
  case IDC_WATER :
      if (Moving || Drawing)
        glColor3f(0.0, 0.0, 0.5);
      else
        glCallList(WaterTexture);
      break;
  case IDC_GRASS :
      if (Moving || Drawing)
        glColor3f(0.0, 0.5, 0.0);
      else
        glCallList(GrassTexture);
      break;
  case IDC_ROCKS :
      if (Moving || Drawing)
        glColor3f(0.25, 0.25, 0.25);
      else
        glCallList(RocksTexture);
      break;
  case IDC_TREES :
      if (Moving || Drawing)
        glColor3f(0.0, 0.25, 0.0);
      else
        glCallList(TreesTexture);
      break;
  case IDC_MOUNTAINS :
      if (Moving || Drawing)
        glColor3f(0.2, 0.1, 0.05);
      else
        glCallList(MountainsTexture);
      break;
};

glBegin(GL_QUAD_STRIP);
if (last_type != -1)
{
 /*
  * Start from the previous location to prevent
  * holes...
  */

  glTexCoord2i(x * 2 - 2, y * 2);
  glNormal3fv(n[-1]);
  glVertex3f((GLfloat)(x - TERRAIN_EDGE - 1),
             height[-1],
             (GLfloat)(y - TERRAIN_EDGE));
  glTexCoord2i(x * 2 - 2, y * 2 + 2);
  glNormal3fv(n[TERRAIN_SIZE - 1]);
  glVertex3f((GLfloat)(x - TERRAIN_EDGE - 1),
             height[TERRAIN_SIZE - 1],
```

continued on next page

continued from previous page

```
                            (GLfloat)(y - TERRAIN_EDGE + 1));
        };

        last_type = *type;
      };

      glTexCoord2i(x * 2, y * 2);
      glNormal3fv(n[0]);
      glVertex3f((GLfloat)(x - TERRAIN_EDGE),
                 height[0],
                 (GLfloat)(y - TERRAIN_EDGE));
      glTexCoord2i(x * 2, y * 2 + 2);
      glNormal3fv(n[TERRAIN_SIZE]);
      glVertex3f((GLfloat)(x - TERRAIN_EDGE),
                 height[TERRAIN_SIZE],
                 (GLfloat)(y - TERRAIN_EDGE + 1));
    };

    glEnd();
  };
  glPopMatrix();

 /*
  * While we fly or draw we're double-buffering.  Swap buffers
  * as necessary...
  */

  glFinish();
  if (Moving || Drawing)
    SwapBuffers(SceneDC);
}


/*
 * 'SaveBitmapFile()' - Save the currently displayed scene to disk.
 */

void
SaveBitmapFile(void)
{
  char          title[256],    /* Title of file */
                filename[256], /* Name of file */
                directory[256]; /* Current directory */
  OPENFILENAME  ofn;           /* Filename dialog structure */
  void          *bits;         /* Screen bitmap bits */
  BITMAPINFO    *info;         /* Screen bitmap info */


 /*
  * Grab the screen bitmap...
  */

  bits = ReadDIBitmap(&info);
  if (bits == NULL)
  {
    DisplayErrorMessage('Unable to get OpenGL bitmap from screen!');
    return;
  };
```

```
/*
 * Pop up a filename dialog...
 */

strcpy(directory, '.');
strcpy(filename, 'untitled.bmp');
strcpy(title, '');

memset(&ofn, 0, sizeof(ofn));

ofn.lStructSize      = sizeof(ofn);
ofn.hwndOwner        = SceneWindow;
ofn.lpstrFilter      = 'Bitmaps\0*.BMP\0\0';
ofn.nFilterIndex     = 1;
ofn.lpstrFile        = filename;
ofn.nMaxFile         = sizeof(filename) - 1;
ofn.lpstrFileTitle   = title;
ofn.nMaxFileTitle    = sizeof(title) - 1;
ofn.lpstrInitialDir  = directory;
ofn.lpstrTitle       = 'Save Bitmap File';
ofn.Flags            = OFN_HIDEREADONLY | OFN_PATHMUSTEXIST |
                       OFN_NONETWORKBUTTON;

if (GetSaveFileName(&ofn))
{
  /*
   * Save the named bitmap to disk...
   */

  if (SaveDIBitmap(filename, info, bits))
    DisplayErrorMessage('Could not save to file \'%s\' -\n%s',
                        filename, strerror(errno));
};

/*
 * Free memory and return...
 */

free(info);
free(bits);
}


/*
 * 'PrintBitmap()' - Print the currently displayed scene.
 */

void
PrintBitmap(void)
{
  void        *bits;          /* Screen bitmap bits */
  BITMAPINFO  *info;          /* Screen bitmap info */

  /*
   * Grab the screen bitmap...
   */
```

continued on next page

continued from previous page

```
  bits = ReadDIBitmap(&info);
  if (bits == NULL)
  {
    DisplayErrorMessage('Unable to get OpenGL bitmap from screen!');
    return;
  };

 /*
  * Print the bitmap...
  */

  PrintDIBitmap(SceneWindow, info, bits);

 /*
  * Free memory and return...
  */

  free(info);
  free(bits);
}


/*
 * 'GetClock()' - Return an increasing clock time in milliseconds...
 */

double
GetClock(void)
{
  SYSTEMTIME    curtime;         /* Current system time */

  GetSystemTime(&curtime);
  return (curtime.wHour * 3600.0 +
          curtime.wMinute * 60.0 +
          curtime.wSecond +
          curtime.wMilliseconds * 0.001);
}
```

Reference Section

GLTEXCOORD

Purpose	Specifies the current texture image coordinate for textured polygon rendering.
Include File	<GL/gl.h>
Syntax	void glTexCoord1{dfis}(TYPE s);
	void glTexCoord1{dfis}v(TYPE *s);
	void glTexCoord2{dfis}(TYPE s, TYPE t);
	void glTexCoord2{dfis}v(TYPE *st);
	void glTexCoord3{dfis}(TYPE s, TYPE t, TYPE r);
	void glTexCoord3{dfis}v(TYPE *stq);

void glTexCoord4{dfis}(TYPE s, TYPE t, TYPE r, TYPE q);
void glTexCoord4{dfis}v(TYPE *strq);

Description	These functions set the current texture image coordinate in 1–4 dimensions. For example, the s and t parameters correspond to the horizontal and vertical image coordinates of a 2D texture image.
Parameters	
s	The horizontal texture image coordinate.
t	The vertical texture image coordinate.
r	The texture image depth coordinate.
q	The texture image "time" coordinate.
Returns	None.
Example	See the example in CH12\TEXSCENE.C on the source code CD-ROM.
See Also	glTexEnv, glTexGen, glTexImage1D, glTexImage2D, glTexParameter

GLTEXENV

Purpose	Sets texturing parameters.
Include File	<GL/gl.h>
Syntax	void glTexEnvf(GLenum target, GLenum pname, GLfloat param);
	void glTexEnvfv(GLenum target, GLenum pname, GLfloat *param);
	void glTexEnvi(GLenum target, GLenum pname, GLint param);
	void glTexEnviv(GLenum target, GLenum pname, GLint *param);
Description	The glTexEnv functions set texture-mapping parameters that control how texture images are mapped to polygons. The GL_DECAL texturing mode uses a texture image directly to draw polygon. GL_BLEND and GL_MODULATE texture modes use the GL_TEXTURE_ENV_COLOR color and the current framebuffer to determine what pixels are textured.
Parameters	
target	GLenum: The texture environment to define; must be GL_TEXTURE_ENV.
pname	GLenum: The parameter name to define. Valid names are as follows:

GL_TEXTURE_ENV_MODE   Specifies the type of texturing to do.

GL_TEXTURE_ENV_COLOR   Specifies the color to use for blending.

param	The parameter value. For GL_TEXTURE_ENV_COLOR, param is a pointer to an RGBA color value. For GL_TEXTURE_ENV_MODE, it can be one of the following constants:

GL_DECAL   Texture images are directly mapped to the framebuffer.

GL_BLEND   Texture images are blended with a constant color (GL_TEXTURE_ENV_ COLOR) before being mapped to the framebuffer.

	GL_MODULATE	Texture images are multiplied with the framebuffer before being mapped to it.
Returns	None.	
Example	See the example in CH12\TEXSCENE.C on the source code CD-ROM.	
See Also	glTexCoord, glTexGen, glTexImage1D, glTexImage2D, glTexParameter	

GLTEXGEN

Purpose	Defines parameters for texture coordinate generation.
Include File	<GL/gl.h>
Syntax	void glTexGend(GLenum coord, GLenum pname, GLdouble param);
	void glTexGenf(GLenum coord, GLenum pname, GLfloat param);
	void glTexGeni(GLenum coord, GLenum pname, GLint param);
	void glTexGendv(GLenum coord, GLenum pname, GLdouble *param);
	void glTexGenfv(GLenum coord, GLenum pname, GLfloat *param);
	void glTexGeniv(GLenum coord, GLenum pname, GLint *param);
Description	This function sets parameters for texture coordinate generation when one or more of GL_TEXTURE_GEN_S, GL_TEXTURE_GEN_T, GL_TEXTURE_GEN_R, or GL_TEXTURE_GEN_Q is enabled with glEnable.

When GL_TEXTURE_GEN_MODE is set to GL_OBJECT_LINEAR, texture coordinates are generated by multiplying the current object (vertex) coordinates by the constant vector specified by GL_OBJECT_PLANE:

```
coordinate = v[0] * p[0] + v[1] * p[1] + v[2] * p[2] + v[3] * p[3]
```

For GL_EYE_LINEAR, the eye coordinates (object coordinate multiplied through the GL_MODELVIEWmatrix) are used.

When GL_TEXTURE_GEN_MODE is set to GL_SPHERE_MAP, coordinates are generated in a sphere about the current viewing position or origin.

Parameters	
coord	GLenum: The texture coordinate to map. Must be one of GL_S, GL_T, GL_R, or GL_Q.
pname	GLenum: The parameter to set. Must be one of GL_TEXTURE_GEN_MODE, GL_OBJECT_PLANE, or GL_EYE_PLANE.
param	The parameter value. For GL_TEXTURE_GEN_MODE, param is one of the following:
	GL_OBJECT_LINEAR Texture coordinates are calculated from object (vertex) coordinates.
	GL_EYE_LINEAR Texture coordinates are calculated by eye coordinates (object coordinates multiplied through the GL_MODELVIEW matrix).

GL_SPHERE_MAP	Texture coordinates are generated in a sphere around the viewing position.

For GL_OBJECT_PLANE and GL_EYE_PLANE, *param* is a 4-element array that is used as a multiplier for object or eye coordinates.

Returns	None.
Example	See the example in CH12\TEXSCEN2.C on the source code CD-ROM.
See Also	glTexCoord, glTexEnv, glTexImage1D, glTexImage2D, glTexParameter

GLTEXIMAGE1D

Purpose	Defines a one-dimensional texture image.
Include File	<GL/gl.h>
Syntax	void glTexImage1D(GLenum target, GLint level, Glint components, GLsizei width, GLint border GLenum format, GLenum type, const GLvoid *pixels);
Description	This function defines a one-dimensional texture image. The image data is subject to modes defined with glPixelMap, glPixelStore, and glPixelTransfer.
Parameters	
target	GLenum: Must be GL_TEXTURE_1D.
level	GLint: The level of detail. Usually 0 unless mipmapping is used.
components	GLint: The number of color components, from 1 to 4.
width	GLsizei: The width of the texture image. This must be a power of 2 or follow the formula $2^n + 2*border$.
border	GLint: The width of the border. Must be 0, 1, or 2.
format	GLenum: The format of the pixel data. Valid formats are as follows:

GL_COLOR_INDEX	Pixel values are color indices.
GL_RED	Pixel values are red intensities.
GL_GREEN	Pixel values are green intensities.
GL_BLUE	Pixel values are blue intensities.
GL_ALPHA	Pixel values are alpha intensities.
GL_RGB	Pixel values are RGB colors.
GL_RGBA	Pixel values are RGBA colors.
GL_LUMINANCE	Pixel values are grayscale colors.
GL_ALPHA_LUMINANCE	Pixel values are alpha and grayscale colors.

type	GLenum: The data type of each pixel value (see *glDrawPixels*).
pixels	GLvoid *: The pixel data.
Returns	None.

Known Bugs	The GL_PACK_ALIGNMENT and GL_UNPACK_ALIGNMENT parameters for glPixelStore are presently ignored.
Example	See the example in CH12\TEX1D.C on the source code CD-ROM.
See Also	glPixelMap, glPixelStore, glPixelTransfer, glTexImage2D

GLTEXIMAGE2D

Purpose	Defines a two-dimensional texture image.
Include File	<GL/gl.h>
Syntax	void glTexImage2D(GLenum target, GLint level, Glint components, GLsizei width, GLsizei height, GLint border GLenum format, GLenum type, const GLvoid *pixels);
Description	This function defines a two-dimensional texture image. The image data is subject to modes defined with glPixelMap, glPixelStore, and glPixelTransfer.

Parameters

target	GLenum: Must be GL_TEXTURE_2D.
level	GLint: The level of detail. Usually 0 unless mipmapping is used.
components	GLint: The number of color components, from 1 to 4.
width	GLsizei: The width of the texture image. This must be a power of 2 or follow the formula $2^n + 2*border$.
height	GLsizei: The height of the texture image. This must be a power of two or follow the formula $2^m + 2*border$.
border	GLint: The width of the border. Must be 0, 1, or 2.
format	GLenum: The format of the pixel data. Valid formats are as follows:

GL_COLOR_INDEX	Pixel values are color indices.
GL_RED	Pixel values are red intensities.
GL_GREEN	Pixel values are green intensities.
GL_BLUE	Pixel values are blue intensities.
GL_ALPHA	Pixel values are alpha intensities.
GL_RGB	Pixel values are RGB colors.
GL_RGBA	Pixel values are RGBA colors.
GL_LUMINANCE	Pixel values are grayscale colors.
GL_ALPHA_LUMINANCE	Pixel values are alpha and grayscale colors.

type	GLenum: The data type of each pixel value (see *glDrawPixels*).
pixels	GLvoid *: The pixel data.
Returns	None.
Known Bugs	The GL_PACK_ALIGNMENT and GL_UNPACK_ALIGNMENT parameters for glPixelStore are presently ignored.

Example	See the example in CH12\TEX2D.C on the source code CD-ROM.
See Also	glPixelMap, glPixelStore, glPixelTransfer, glTexImage1D

GLTEXPARAMETER

Purpose	Sets texture image parameters.
Include File	<GL/gl.h>
Syntax	void glTexParameterf(GLenum target, GLenum pname, GLfloat param);
	void glTexParameterfv(GLenum target, GLenum pname, GLfloat *param);
	void glTexParameteri(GLenum target, GLenum pname, GLint param);
	void glTexParameteriv(GLenum target, GLenum pname, GLint *param);
Description	This function sets filter and repetition parameters for texture images.
Parameters	
target	GLenum: Must be one of GL_TEXTURE_1D or GL_TEXTURE_2D.
pname	GLenum: The texturing parameter to set. Valid names are:

Parameter	Description
GL_TEXTURE_MIN_FILTER	Specifies the texture image minification (reduction) method or filter.
GL_TEXTURE_MAX_FILTER	Specifies the texture image magnification (enlargement) method or filter.
GL_TEXTURE_WRAP_S	Specifies handling of texture S coordinates outside the range of 0.0 to 1.0.
GL_TEXTURE_WRAP_T	Specifies handling of texture T coordinates outside the range of 0.0 to 1.0.
GL_BORDER_COLOR	Specifies a border color for textures without borders.

param	For GL_TEXTURE_MIN_FILTER, *param* is one of the following:
	For GL_TEXTURE_MAX_FILTER, *param* is either GL_NEAREST or GL_LINEAR.GL_TEXTURE_WRAP_S and GL_TEXTURE_WRAP_T can be set to GL_REPEAT or GL_CLAMP. GL_REPEAT causes the texture image to be repeated over the polygon. GL_CLAMP uses the specified border pixels or a constant border color (see below) on areas that fall outside of the 0.0–1.0 texture coordinate range.
	For GL_BORDER_COLOR, *param* is an RGBA color array that is used as a constant border color when a texture image has no border pixels defined.
Returns	None.
Example	See the example in CH12\TEXSCENE.C on the source code CD-ROM.
See Also	glTexCoord, glTexEnv, glTexGen, glTexImage1D, glTexImage2D

13

QUADRICS: SPHERES, CYLINDERS, AND DISKS

13

QUADRICS: SPHERES, CYLINDERS, AND DISKS

What you'll learn in this chapter:

How to...	Functions You'll Use
Create quadrics to draw simple geometric shapes	gluNewQuadric
Control the quality of drawn shapes	
Draw the shapes using different OpenGL primitives	gluQuadricDrawStyle
Use lighting and texturing with quadrics	gluQuadricNormals/gluQuadricTexture

We can hear you asking: "What the heck are quadrics?" Well, quadrics are a part of the OpenGL Utility Library (GLU32.LIB) that supports the drawing of simple three-dimensional geometric shapes. In particular, functions are provided to draw cones, cylinders, disks, and spheres. In this chapter we'll explore the practical uses of these quadric functions in your programs.

Creating a Quadric

Every quadric you draw on the screen has a *state* (or collection of settings) associated with it. The gluNewQuadric function creates an opaque state variable that describes the current drawing style, orientation, lighting mode, texturing mode, and callback functions, as follows:

```
GLUquadricObj *obj;

obj = gluNewQuadric();
```

Note that a quadric state does not include the geometric shape to be drawn. Instead, it describes *how* to draw geometric shapes. This allows you to reuse quadrics for many different kinds of shapes.

Changing the Way Quadrics Are Drawn

Once you have created a quadric, you can customize the drawing of shapes by changing the quadric state. The GLU functions for this are gluQuadricDrawStyle, gluQuadricNormals, gluQuadricOrientation, and gluQuadricTexture.

```
void gluQuadricDrawStyle(GLUquadricObj *obj, GLenum drawStyle)
void gluQuadricNormals(GLUquadricObj *obj, GLenum normals)
void gluQuadricOrientation(GLUquadricObj *obj, GLenum orientation)
void gluQuadricTexture(GLUquadricObj *obj, GLboolean textureCoords)
```

The gluQuadricDrawStyle function selects the type of OpenGL drawing primitives that are used to draw the shape. The default style is to fill shapes using polygon and strip primitives (GLU_FILL). Table 13-1 shows the possible styles.

Table 13-1 Quadric Drawing Styles

Style	Description
GLU_FILL	Quadrics are drawn filled in, using polygon and strip primitives.
GLU_LINE	Quadrics are drawn "wireframe," using line primitives.
GLU_SILHOUETTE	Quadrics are drawn using line primitives; only the outside edges are drawn.
GLU_POINT	Quadrics are drawn using point primitives.

Lighting normals are usually generated automatically for quadrics. The gluQuadricNormals function controls calculation of normals. Table 13-2 lists the possible lighting calculations.

Table 13-2 Quadric Lighting Normal Modes

Normal Mode	Description
GLU_NONE	No lighting normals are generated.
GLU_FLAT	Lighting normals are generated for each polygon to create a faceted appearance.
GLU_SMOOTH	Lighting normals are generated for each vertex to create a smooth appearance.

To control the direction of lighting normals, the gluQuadricOrientation function is provided to make normals point outwards (GLU_OUTSIDE) or inwards (GLU_INSIDE). This has particular application with spheres (if you are inside or outside the sphere).

Finally, texture coordinates can be generated automatically for your quadrics. The gluQuadricTexture function enables (GL_TRUE) or disables (GL_FALSE) texture coordinate generation. We'll cover exactly how texture coordinates are chosen as we start drawing quadrics on the screen.

As you may remember, texture coordinates are used for texture mapping images onto polygons (see Chapter 12).

Drawing Cylinders

Cylinders are drawn using gluCylinder. A cylinder drawn with this function is essentially a tube that runs along the z-axis (see Figure 13-1). The ends of the cylinder are *never* filled in!

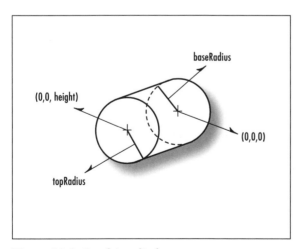

Figure 13-1 Quadric cylinders

```
void gluCylinder(GLUquadricObj *obj,
                 GLdouble baseRadius,
                 GLdouble topRadius,
                 GLdouble height,
                 GLint slices,
                 GLint stacks)
```

The baseRadius and topRadius arguments specifiy the radius of the cylinder at the bottom and top of the cylinder. The height argument specifies the actual height (or length) of the tube.

The slices and stacks arguments control how many subdivisions (sides) are generated around and along the cylinder. Generally, you will make slices a number around 20 to give the cylinder a smooth appearance. Values below this will yield a faceted appearance; values greater than 20 may cause display jitter. When you utilize spotlighting or a lot of specular highlights, you will also want the stacks argument set high, usually the same as the height argument. Otherwise, set stacks to 2 to cover the top and bottom of the cylinder.

Cylinders can also be employed for the generation of faceted surfaces, such as a pencil or a tool socket.

Drawing Cones

While the OpenGL Utility Library does not include a special cone-drawing function, the gluCylinder function can be used to make cones simply by specifying a topRadius or bottomRadius of 0.0.

Texturing and Cylinders

When texturing a gluCylinder shape, textures are wrapped from the forward edge (0,radius,0) of the cylinder. This means your texture images should be *upside-down* to display properly on the cylinder. We'll use textures with cylinders in the pencil project in this chapter.

Drawing Disks

Disks are round, flat shapes that may contain holes. Examples of disks include coins and washers.

```
void gluDisk(GLUquadricObj *obj,
             GLdouble innerRadius,
             GLdouble outerRadius,
             GLint slices,
             GLint loops)
```

The innerRadius and outerRadius arguments control the size of the hole and disk, respectively. If the innerRadius argument is 0.0, the disk is drawn as a solid circle (see Figure 13-2).

The slices argument sets the number of sides the disk has and generally should be a number around 20 to make the disk look round. The loops argument controls the number of concentric rings that are drawn for the disk (between the inner and outer

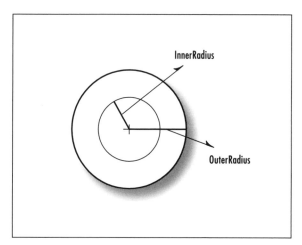

Figure 13-2 Quadric disks

radii); this usually should be set to 1 for circles and 2 for washers. As is true for cylinders, using larger values for loops will improve specular lighting and spotlight effects.

Disks and Textures

Texture images for disks are mapped so that the texture image just touches the cylinder at the edges. The top of the texture image is mapped to the top of the disk, the left side to the left side of the disk, and so forth.

Drawing Partial Disks

The OpenGL Utility Library also provides a function to display partial disks. When drawing a partial disk, you specify a start angle and sweep angle for the disk. The startAngle argument specifies a clockwise angle in degrees from the top of the disk. The sweepAngle argument specifies the number of degrees of arc to draw. For instance, 90° would be a quarter disk, and so forth.

```
void gluPartialDisk(GLUquadricObj *obj,
            GLdouble innerRadius,
            GLdouble outerRadius,
            GLint slices,
            GLint loops,
            GLdouble startAngle,
            GLdouble sweepAngle)
```

Drawing Spheres

Spheres are hollow balls or globes. When you draw a sphere, you specify the radius of the sphere.

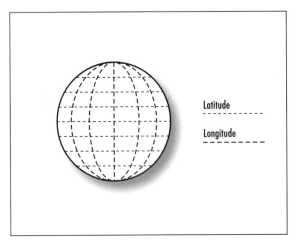

Figure 13-3 A quadric sphere

```
void gluSphere(GLUquadricObj *obj,
               GLdouble radius,
               GLint slices,
               GLint stacks)
```

If you think of the sphere as a globe, the slices argument represents the number of lines of longitude, and the stacks argument represents the number of lines of latitude (see Figure 13-3).

Spheres and Textures

Texture images are mapped to spheres using longitude and latitude coordinates. A world map image would wrap perfectly around the sphere.

Drawing a Pencil

To close this chapter, we'll write a little program that rotates an image of a pencil (see Figure 13-4). The pencil consists of three cylinders and two texture images. The first texture image has the typical symbol for a #2 pencil, and the words "OpenGL Country Club" wrapped around the pencil. For the end and the sharpened point of the pencil, we'll use a second image of wood with exposed lead (well, carbon).

The point of the pencil, obviously, is a cone. The end of the pencil isn't quite as obvious. Since it's flat, you might expect to use a disk for the end. Unfortunately, the result of the way texture images are applied to disks doesn't look right with our texture image (see Figure 13-5). So instead, the end is made using a cylinder with a height and topRadius of 0.0.

Since quadrics are drawn from (0, 0, 0), you have to translate the coordinates of the pieces prior to drawing them. For example, to draw the body of the pencil you would do this:

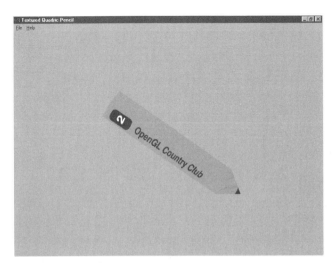

Figure 13-4 Quadric pencil window

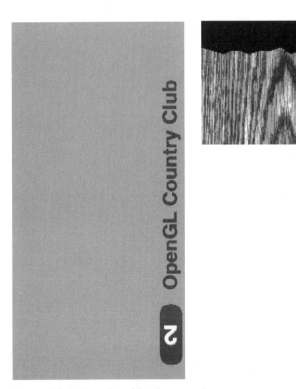

Figure 13-5 Pencil and lead texture images

```
glPushMatrix();
  glTranslatef(0.0, 0.0, -20.0);
  gluCylinder(PencilObj, 5.0, 5.0, 40.0, 6, 2);
glPopMatrix();
```

In the pencil drawing program, Listing 13-1, the RepaintWindow function handles drawing everything. The first thing we display is the body of the pencil, which is a six-sided cylinder.

```
gluQuadricNormals(PencilObj, GLU_FLAT);
glCallList(PencilTexture);

glPushMatrix();
  glTranslatef(0.0, 0.0, -20.0);

  gluCylinder(PencilObj, 5.0, 5.0, 40.0, 6, 2);
glPopMatrix();
```

Next, we display the point and end of the pencil using the "lead" texture image. Again, we'll use six-sided cylinders to do the work we need.

```
gluQuadricNormals(PencilObj, GLU_SMOOTH);
glCallList(LeadTexture);

glPushMatrix();
  glTranslatef(0.0, 0.0, 20.0);

  gluCylinder(PencilObj, 5.0, 0.0, 7.5, 6, 2);
glPopMatrix();

glPushMatrix();
  glTranslatef(0.0, 0.0, -20.0);

  gluCylinder(PencilObj, 5.0, 0.0, 0.0, 6, 2);
glPopMatrix();
```

Summary

In this chapter we've covered the quadric drawing functions. OpenGL quadrics are geometric shapes that form the basic "building blocks" of many objects, both manufactured and natural. Using the quadric drawing functions is a convenient and fast way to avoid writing a lot of extra code for drawing these shapes.

Now here's Listing 13-1, the pencil program.

Listing 13-1 The pencil drawing program

```
/*
 * Include necessary headers.
 */

#include "texture.h"
#include "pencil.h"
#include <stdarg.h>
```

```
/*
 * Globals...
 */

HWND            PencilWindow;           /* Scene window */
HPALETTE        PencilPalette;          /* Color palette (if necessary) */
HDC             PencilDC;               /* Drawing context */
HGLRC           PencilRC;               /* OpenGL rendering context */

GLuint          PencilTexture,          /* Pencil texture image */
                LeadTexture;            /* Lead... */

GLfloat         PencilRoll = 0.0,       /* Pencil orientation */
                PencilPitch = 90.0,
                PencilHeading = 0.0;
GLUquadricObj   *PencilObj;


/*
 * Local functions...
 */

void                    DisplayErrorMessage(char *, ...);
void                    MakePalette(int);
LRESULT CALLBACK        PencilProc(HWND, UINT, WPARAM, LPARAM);
void                    LoadAllTextures(void);
void                    RepaintWindow(RECT *);
void                    PrintBitmap(void);


/*
 * 'WinMain()' - Main entry...
 */

int APIENTRY
WinMain(HINSTANCE hInst,                 /* I - Current process instance */
        HINSTANCE hPrevInstance,         /* I - Parent process instance */
        LPSTR     lpCmdLine,             /* I - Command-line arguments */
        int       nCmdShow)              /* I - Show window at startup? */
{
  MSG           msg;                     /* Window UI event */
  WNDCLASS      wc;                      /* Window class */
  RECT          rect;                    /* Current client area rectangle */

  /*
   * Register main window...
   */

  wc.style          = 0;
  wc.lpfnWndProc    = (WNDPROC)PencilProc;
  wc.cbClsExtra     = 0;
  wc.cbWndExtra     = 0;
  wc.hInstance      = hInst;
  wc.hIcon          = NULL;
  wc.hCursor        = LoadCursor(NULL, IDC_ARROW);
  wc.hbrBackground  = 0;
```

continued on next page

continued from previous page

```
  wc.lpszMenuName  = MAKEINTRESOURCE(IDR_MENU1);
  wc.lpszClassName = "Textured Quadric Pencil";

  if (RegisterClass(&wc) == 0)
  {
    DisplayErrorMessage("Unable to register window class!");
    return (FALSE);
  };

/*
 * Then create it...
 */

  PencilWindow = CreateWindow("Textured Quadric Pencil", "Textured Quadric Pencil",
                             WS_OVERLAPPEDWINDOW | WS_CLIPCHILDREN | WS_CLIPSIBLINGS,
                             32, 32, 400, 300,
                             NULL, NULL, hInst, NULL);

  if (PencilWindow == NULL)
  {
    DisplayErrorMessage("Unable to create window!");
    return (FALSE);
  };

  ShowWindow(PencilWindow, nCmdShow);
  UpdateWindow(PencilWindow);

/*
 * Loop on events until the user quits this application...
 */

  while (TRUE)
  {
   /*
    * Process all messages in the queue...
    */

    while (PeekMessage(&msg, NULL, 0, 0, PM_NOREMOVE) == TRUE)
      if (GetMessage(&msg, NULL, 0, 0))
      {
        TranslateMessage(&msg);
        DispatchMessage(&msg);
      }
      else
        return (1);

   /*
    * Spin the pencil...
    */

    PencilRoll    += 1.0;
    PencilPitch   += 2.0;
    PencilHeading += 3.0;

    GetClientRect(PencilWindow, &rect);
    RepaintWindow(&rect);
  };

  return (msg.wParam);
}
```

```
/*
 * 'DisplayErrorMessage()' - Display an error message dialog.
 */

void
DisplayErrorMessage(char *format,        /* I - printf() style format string */
                    ...)                 /* I - Other arguments as necessary */
{
  va_list       ap;                      /* Argument pointer */
  char          s[1024];                 /* Output string */


  if (format == NULL)
    return;

  va_start(ap, format);
  vsprintf(s, format, ap);
  va_end(ap);

  MessageBeep(MB_ICONEXCLAMATION);
  MessageBox(NULL, s, "Error", MB_OK | MB_ICONEXCLAMATION);
}


/*
 * 'MakePalette()' - Make a color palette for RGB colors if necessary.
 */

void
MakePalette(int pf)                       /* I - Pixel format ID */
{
  PIXELFORMATDESCRIPTOR pfd;              /* Pixel format information */
  LOGPALETTE            *pPal;            /* Pointer to logical palette */
  int                   nColors;         /* Number of entries in palette */
  int                   i,               /* Color index */
                        rmax,            /* Maximum red value */
                        gmax,            /* Maximum green value */
                        bmax;            /* Maximum blue value */

 /*
  * Find out if we need to define a color palette...
  */

  DescribePixelFormat(PencilDC, pf, sizeof(PIXELFORMATDESCRIPTOR), &pfd);

  if (!(pfd.dwFlags & PFD_NEED_PALETTE))
  {
    PencilPalette = NULL;
    return;
  };

 /*
  * Allocate memory for a color palette...
  */

  nColors = 1 << pfd.cColorBits;

  pPal = (LOGPALETTE *)malloc(sizeof(LOGPALETTE) +
                              nColors * sizeof(PALETTEENTRY));
```

continued on next page

continued from previous page

```
  pPal->palVersion    = 0x300;
  pPal->palNumEntries = nColors;

 /*
  * Get the maximum values for red, green, and blue.  Then build 'nColors'
  * colors...
  */

  rmax = (1 << pfd.cRedBits) - 1;
  gmax = (1 << pfd.cGreenBits) - 1;
  bmax = (1 << pfd.cBlueBits) - 1;

  for (i = 0; i < nColors; i ++)
  {
    pPal->palPalEntry[i].peRed   = 255 * ((i >> pfd.cRedShift) & rmax) / rmax;
    pPal->palPalEntry[i].peGreen = 255 * ((i >> pfd.cGreenShift) & gmax) / gmax;
    pPal->palPalEntry[i].peBlue  = 255 * ((i >> pfd.cBlueShift) & bmax) / bmax;

    pPal->palPalEntry[i].peFlags = 0;
  };

 /*
  * Create, select, and realize the palette...
  */

  PencilPalette = CreatePalette(pPal);
  SelectPalette(PencilDC, PencilPalette, FALSE);
  RealizePalette(PencilDC);

  free(pPal);
}


/*
 * 'PencilProc()' - Handle window events in the viewing window.
 */

LRESULT CALLBACK
PencilProc(HWND    hWnd,        /* I - Window triggering this event */
           UINT    uMsg,        /* I - Message type */
           WPARAM  wParam,      /* I - 'word' parameter value */
           LPARAM  lParam)      /* I - 'long' parameter value */
{
  int                 pf;       /* Pixel format ID */
  PIXELFORMATDESCRIPTOR pfd;     /* Pixel format information */
  PAINTSTRUCT         ps;       /* WM_PAINT message info */
  RECT                rect;     /* Current client area rectangle */


  switch (uMsg)
  {
    case WM_CREATE :
       /*
        * 'Create' message.  Get device and rendering contexts, and
        * setup the client area for OpenGL drawing...
        */

        PencilDC = GetDC(hWnd);
```

```
      pfd.nSize        = sizeof(pfd);
      pfd.nVersion     = 1;
      pfd.dwFlags      = PFD_DRAW_TO_WINDOW | PFD_SUPPORT_OPENGL | PFD_DOUBLEBUFFER;
                                               /* Do OpenGL drawing */
      pfd.dwLayerMask  = PFD_MAIN_PLANE;       /* Main drawing plane */
      pfd.iPixelType   = PFD_TYPE_RGBA;        /* RGB color buffer */
      pfd.cColorBits   = 0;                    /* Best color buffer please */
      pfd.cDepthBits   = 32;                   /* Need a depth buffer */
      pfd.cStencilBits = 0;                    /* No stencil buffer */
      pfd.cAccumBits   = 0;                    /* No accumulation buffer */

      pf = ChoosePixelFormat(PencilDC, &pfd);
      if (pf == 0)
        DisplayErrorMessage("texscene was unable to choose a suitable pixel format!");
      else if (!SetPixelFormat(PencilDC, pf, &pfd))
        DisplayErrorMessage("texscene was unable to set the pixel format!");

      MakePalette(pf);

      PencilRC = wglCreateContext(PencilDC);
      wglMakeCurrent(PencilDC, PencilRC);

      /*
       * Load all the texture images into display lists...
       */

      LoadAllTextures();
      PencilObj = gluNewQuadric();
      gluQuadricTexture(PencilObj, GL_TRUE);
      break;

case WM_SIZE :
case WM_PAINT :
   /*
    * Repaint the client area with our bitmap...
    */

   BeginPaint(hWnd, &ps);

   GetClientRect(hWnd, &rect);
   RepaintWindow(&rect);

   EndPaint(hWnd, &ps);
   break;

case WM_COMMAND :
   /*
    * Handle menu selections...
    */

   switch (LOWORD(wParam))
   {
     case IDM_FILE_PRINT :
         PrintBitmap();
         break;
     case IDM_FILE_EXIT :
         DestroyWindow(PencilWindow);
         break;
   };
   break;
```

continued on next page

continued from previous page

```
    case WM_QUIT :
    case WM_CLOSE :
        /*
         * Destroy the windows and bitmaps and exit...
         */

        DestroyWindow(PencilWindow);

        exit(0);
        break;

    case WM_DESTROY :
        /*
         * Release and free the device context, rendering
         * context, and color palette...
         */

        if (PencilRC)
          wglDeleteContext(PencilRC);

        if (PencilDC)
          ReleaseDC(PencilWindow, PencilDC);

        if (PencilPalette)
          DeleteObject(PencilPalette);

        PostQuitMessage(0);
        break;

    case WM_QUERYNEWPALETTE :
        /*
         * Realize the color palette if necessary...
         */

        if (PencilPalette)
        {
          SelectPalette(PencilDC, PencilPalette, FALSE);
          RealizePalette(PencilDC);

          InvalidateRect(hWnd, NULL, FALSE);
          return (TRUE);
        };
        break;

    case WM_PALETTECHANGED:
        /*
         * Reselect our color palette if necessary...
         */

        if (PencilPalette && (HWND)wParam != hWnd)
        {
          SelectPalette(PencilDC, PencilPalette, FALSE);
          RealizePalette(PencilDC);

          UpdateColors(PencilDC);
        };
        break;

    default :
```

```
        /*
         * Pass all other messages through the default window
         * procedure...
         */

        return (DefWindowProc(hWnd, uMsg, wParam, lParam));
  };

  return (FALSE);
}


/*
 * 'LoadAllTextures()' - Load texture images for the scene.
 */

void
LoadAllTextures(void)
{
  glNewList(PencilTexture = glGenLists(1), GL_COMPILE);
    glTexParameteri(GL_TEXTURE_2D, GL_TEXTURE_WRAP_S, GL_REPEAT);
    glTexParameteri(GL_TEXTURE_2D, GL_TEXTURE_WRAP_T, GL_REPEAT);
    TextureLoadBitmap("textures/pencil.bmp");
  glEndList();

  glNewList(LeadTexture = glGenLists(1), GL_COMPILE);
    glTexParameteri(GL_TEXTURE_2D, GL_TEXTURE_WRAP_S, GL_REPEAT);
    glTexParameteri(GL_TEXTURE_2D, GL_TEXTURE_WRAP_T, GL_REPEAT);
    TextureLoadBitmap("textures/lead.bmp");
  glEndList();
}


/*
 * 'RepaintWindow()' - Redraw the client area with our pencil.
 */

void
RepaintWindow(RECT *rect)          /* I - Client area rectangle */
{
 /*
  * Reset the viewport and clear the window to light blue...
  */

  glViewport(0, 0, rect->right, rect->bottom);

  glClearColor(0.7, 0.7, 1.0, 1.0);
  glClear(GL_COLOR_BUFFER_BIT | GL_DEPTH_BUFFER_BIT);

 /*
  * Setup viewing transformations for the current position and
  * orientation...
  */

  glMatrixMode(GL_PROJECTION);
  glLoadIdentity();
  gluPerspective(45.0, (float)rect->right / (float)rect->bottom,
                 0.1, 1000.0);
```

continued on next page

continued from previous page

```
  glEnable(GL_LIGHTING);
  glEnable(GL_LIGHT0);
  glEnable(GL_DEPTH_TEST);
  glEnable(GL_TEXTURE_2D);
  glTexEnvi(GL_TEXTURE_ENV, GL_TEXTURE_ENV_MODE, GL_DECAL);

  glMatrixMode(GL_MODELVIEW);
  glPushMatrix();
    glTranslatef(0.0, 0.0, -80.0);
    glRotatef(PencilHeading, 0.0, -1.0, 0.0);
    glRotatef(PencilPitch, 1.0, 0.0, 0.0);
    glRotatef(PencilRoll, 0.0, 0.0, -1.0);

  /*
   * First the pencil body - this uses a 6-sided cylinder...
   */

    gluQuadricNormals(PencilObj, GLU_FLAT);
    glCallList(PencilTexture);

    glPushMatrix();
      glTranslatef(0.0, 0.0, -20.0);

      gluCylinder(PencilObj, 5.0, 5.0, 40.0, 6, 2);
    glPopMatrix();

  /*
   * Then the ends - a cone at the tip and a flat cone at the base...
   */

    gluQuadricNormals(PencilObj, GLU_SMOOTH);
    glCallList(LeadTexture);

    glPushMatrix();
      glTranslatef(0.0, 0.0, 20.0);

      gluCylinder(PencilObj, 5.0, 0.0, 7.5, 6, 2);
    glPopMatrix();

    glPushMatrix();
      glTranslatef(0.0, 0.0, -20.0);

    /*
     * Normally we might use a disk shape for this, but unfortunately the texture
     * coordinates don't match up...
     */
      gluCylinder(PencilObj, 5.0, 0.0, 0.0, 6, 2);
    glPopMatrix();
  glPopMatrix();
  /*
   * Swap buffers and return...
   */

  glFinish();
  SwapBuffers(PencilDC);
}
```

```
/*
 * 'PrintBitmap()' - Print the currently displayed scene.
 */

void
PrintBitmap(void)
{
  void        *bits;        /* Screen bitmap bits */
  BITMAPINFO  *info;        /* Screen bitmap info */

 /*
  * Grab the screen bitmap...
  */

  bits = ReadDIBitmap(&info);
  if (bits == NULL)
  {
    DisplayErrorMessage("Unable to get OpenGL bitmap from screen!");
    return;
  };

 /*
  * Print the bitmap...
  */

  PrintDIBitmap(PencilWindow, info, bits);

 /*
  * Free memory and return...
  */

  free(info);
  free(bits);
}
```

Reference Section

GLUCYLINDER

Purpose	Draws a quadric cylinder.
Include File	<GL/glu.h>
Syntax	void gluCylinder(GLUquadricObj *obj, GLdouble baseRadius, GLdouble topRadius, GLdouble height, GLint slices, GLint stacks);
Description	This function draws a hollow cylinder with no ends along the z-axis. If topRadius or bottomRadius is 0, a cone is drawn instead. The cylinder is projected height units along the positive z-axis. The slices argument controls the number of sides along the cylinder. The stacks argument controls the number of segments along the z-axis (across the cylinder) that are generated.

Parameters

obj	GLUquadricObj *: The quadric state information to use for rendering.
baseRadius	GLdouble: The radius of the base (Z=0) of the cylinder.
topRadius	GLdouble: The radius of the top (Z=height) of the cylinder.
height	GLdouble: The height or length of the cylinder along the z-axis.
slices	GLint: The number of sides on the cylinder.
stacks	GLint: The number of segments in the cylinder along the z-axis.
Returns	None.
Example	See the example in CH13\PENCIL.C.
See Also	gluDeleteQuadric, gluNewQuadric, gluQuadricCallback, gluQuadricDrawStyle, gluQuadricNormals, gluQuadricOrientation, gluQuadricTexture

GLUDELETEQUADRIC

Purpose	Deletes a quadric state object.
Include File	<GL/glu.h>
Syntax	void gluDeleteQuadric(GLUquadricObj *obj);
Description	This function deletes a quadric state object. Once an object has been deleted it cannot be used for drawing again.
Parameters	
obj	GLUquadricObj *: The quadric state object to delete.
Returns	None.
See Also	gluNewQuadric, gluQuadricCallback, gluQuadricDrawStyle, gluQuadricNormals, gluQuadricOrientation, gluQuadricTexture

GLUDISK

Purpose	Draws a quadric disk.
Include File	<GL/glu.h>
Syntax	void gluDisk(GLUquadricObj *obj, GLdouble innerRadius, GLdouble outerRadius, GLint slices, GLint loops);
Description	This function draws a disk perpendicular to the z-axis. If innerRadius is 0, a solid (filled) circle is drawn instead of a washer. The slices argument controls the number of sides on the disk. The loops argument controls the number of rings generated out from the z-axis.
Parameters	
obj	GLUquadricObj *: The quadric state information to use for rendering.
innerRadius	GLdouble: The inside radius of the disk.
outerRadius	GLdouble: The outside radius of the disk.

slices	GLint: The number of sides on the cylinder.
loops	GLint: The number of rings out from the z-axis.
Returns	None.
See Also	gluDeleteQuadric, gluNewQuadric, gluQuadricCallback, gluQuadricDrawStyle, gluQuadricNormals, gluQuadricOrientation, gluQuadricTexture

gluNewQuadric

Purpose	Creates a new quadric state object.
Include File	<GL/glu.h>
Syntax	GLUquadricObj *gluNewQuadric(void);
Description	This function creates a new opaque quadric state object to be used for drawing. The quadric state object contains specifications that determine how subsequent images will be drawn.
Parameters	None.
Returns	GLUquadricObj *: NULL if no memory is available; otherwise, a valid quadric state object pointer.
Example	See the example in CH13\PENCIL.C.
See Also	gluDeleteQuadric, gluQuadricCallback, gluQuadricDrawStyle, gluQuadricNormals, gluQuadricOrientation, gluQuadricTexture

gluPartialDisk

Purpose	Draws a partial quadric disk.
Include File	<GL/glu.h>
Syntax	void gluPartialDisk(GLUquadricObj *obj, GLdouble innerRadius, GLdouble outerRadius, GLint slices, GLint loops, GLdouble startAngle, GLdouble sweepAngle);
Description	This function draws a partial disk perpendicular to the z-axis. If innerRadius is 0, a solid (filled) circle is drawn instead of a washer. The slices argument controls the number of sides on the disk. The loops argument controls the number of rings out from the z-axis that are generated. The startAngle argument specifies the starting angle of the disk with 0° at the top of the disk and 90° at the right of the disk. The sweepAngle argument specifies the portion of the disk in degrees.
Parameters	
obj	GLUquadricObj *: The quadric state information to use for rendering.
innerRadius	GLdouble: The inside radius of the disk.
outerRadius	GLdouble: The outside radius of the disk.
slices	GLint: The number of sides on the cylinder.

loops	GLint: The number of rings out from the z-axis.
startAngle	GLdouble: The start angle of the partial disk.
sweepAngle	GLdouble: The angular size of the partial disk.
Returns	None.
See Also	gluDeleteQuadric, gluNewQuadric, gluQuadricCallback, gluQuadricDrawStyle, gluQuadricNormals, gluQuadricOrientation, gluQuadricTexture

GLUQUADRICCALLBACK

Purpose	Defines a quadric callback function.
Include File	<GL/glu.h>
Syntax	void gluQuadricCallback(GLUquadricObj *obj, GLenum which, void (*fn)());
Description	This function defines callback functions to be used when drawing quadric shapes. At present, the only defined callback function is GLU_ERROR, which is called whenever an OpenGL or GLU error occurs.
Parameters	
obj	GLUquadricObj *: The quadric state information to use for rendering.
which	GLenum: The callback function to define. Must be GLU_ERROR.
fn	void (*)(): The callback function (receives one GLenum containing the error).
Returns	None.
See Also	gluDeleteQuadric, gluNewQuadric, gluQuadricDrawStyle, gluQuadricNormals, gluQuadricOrientation, gluQuadricTexture

GLUQUADRICDRAWSTYLE

Purpose	Sets the drawing style of a quadric state object.	
Include File	<GL/glu.h>	
Syntax	void gluQuadricDrawStyle(GLUquadricObj *obj, GLenum drawStyle);	
Description	This function selects a drawing style for all quadric shapes.	
Parameters		
obj	GLUquadricObj *: The quadric state information to use for rendering.	
drawStyle	GLenum: The drawing style. Valid styles are as follows:	
	GLU_FILL	Quadrics are drawn filled, using polygon and strip primitives.
	GLU_LINE	Quadrics are drawn "wireframe," using line primitives.
	GLU_SILHOUETTE	Quadrics are drawn using line primitives; only the outside edges are drawn.
	GLU_POINT	Quadrics are drawn using point primitives.

Returns	None.
See Also	gluDeleteQuadric, gluNewQuadric, gluQuadricCallback, gluQuadricNormals, gluQuadricOrientation, gluQuadricTexture

GLUQUADRICNORMALS

Purpose	Sets the type of lighting normals used for quadric objects.
Include File	<GL/glu.h>
Syntax	void gluQuadricNormals(GLUquadricObj *obj, GLenum normals);
Description	This function sets the type of lighting normals that are generated when drawing shapes using the specified quadric state object.
Parameters	
obj	GLUquadricObj *: The quadric state information to use for rendering.
normals	GLenum: The type of normals to generate. Valid types are as follows:

GLU_NONE	No lighting normals are generated.
GLU_FLAT	Lighting normals are generated for each polygon to generate a faceted appearance.
GLU_SMOOTH	Lighting normals are generated for each vertex to generate a smooth appearance.

Returns	None.
Example	See the example in CH13\PENCIL.C.
See Also	gluDeleteQuadric, gluNewQuadric, gluQuadricCallback, gluQuadricDrawStyle, gluQuadricOrientation, gluQuadricTexture

GLUQUADRICORIENTATION

Purpose	Sets the orientation of lighting normals for quadric objects.
Include File	<GL/glu.h>
Syntax	void gluQuadricOrientation(GLUquadricObj *obj, GLenum orientation);
Description	This function sets the direction of lighting normals for hollow objects. The orientation parameter may be GLU_OUTSIDE to point lighting normals outward, or GLU_INSIDE to point them inward.
Parameters	
obj	GLUquadricObj *: The quadric state information to use for rendering.
orientation	GLenum: The orientation of lighting normals, GLU_OUTSIDE or GLU_INSIDE. The default is GLU_OUTSIDE.
Returns	None.
See Also	gluDeleteQuadric, gluNewQuadric, gluQuadricCallback, gluQuadricDrawStyle, gluQuadricNormals, gluQuadricTexture

GLUQUADRICTEXTURE

Purpose	Enables or disables texture coordinate generation for texture-mapping images onto quadrics.
Include File	<GL/glu.h>
Syntax	void gluQuadricTexture(GLUquadricObj *obj, GLboolean textureCoords);
Description	This function controls whether or not texture coordinates are generated for quadric shapes.
Parameters	
obj	GLUquadricObj *: The quadric state information to use for rendering.
textureCoords	GLboolean: GL_TRUE if texture coordinates should be generated; GL_FALSE otherwise.
Returns	None.
See Also	gluDeleteQuadric, gluNewQuadric, gluQuadricCallback, gluQuadricDrawStyle, gluQuadricNormals, gluQuadricOrientation

GLUSPHERE

Purpose	Draws a quadric sphere.
Include File	<GL/glu.h>
Syntax	void gluSphere(GLUquadricObj *obj, GLdouble radius, GLint slices, GLint stacks);
Description	This function draws a hollow sphere centered at the origin. The slices argument controls the number of lines of longitude on the sphere. The stacks argument controls the number of lines of latitude on the sphere.
Parameters	
obj	GLUquadricObj *: The quadric state information to use for rendering.
radius	GLdouble: The radius of the sphere.
slices	GLint: The number of lines of longitude on the sphere.
stacks	GLint: The number of lines of latitude on the sphere.
Returns	None.
See Also	gluDeleteQuadric, gluNewQuadric, gluQuadricCallback, gluQuadricDrawStyle, gluQuadricNormals, gluQuadricOrientation, gluQuadricTexture

PART III

ADVANCED TOPICS AND SPECIAL EFFECTS

III

ADVANCED TOPICS AND SPECIAL EFFECTS

If you've been reading this book from front to back as a tutorial, you are now quite well grounded in the use of OpenGL for a variety of purposes. In the third part of this book, we are going to cover a few remaining topics that will enhance your knowledge and understanding of OpenGL. We will also be covering some special effects and capabilities of the API that may take a little more time to digest than the previous material.

First, we visit the OpenGL State Machine in Chapter 14. Until now we have taken this for granted and covered some of the variables only when they have been relevant to our discussion. Now a look at the entire concept and how to take advantage of it is in order. Then a more complete discussion of the OpenGL buffers (Chapter 15) will be in order.

Many scenes and objects can benefit by some of the visual fine-tuning that is afforded by the techniques presented in Chapter 16. Here you will see how to soften or sharpen images, and how to create some spectacular effects made possible with translucence.

Complex surface generation can be a real headache. Chapter 17 will give you some high-level tools that can make these surfaces easier to create. Useful techniques for breaking down your polygons into smaller ones are shown in Chapter 18, and in Chapter 19 you'll learn how to interact with your scenes and objects using the OpenGL features of selection and feedback.

Finally, we will end our coverage of the API with a closer look at just one use for OpenGL. You'll see how Virtual Reality over the Internet has its roots in an OpenGL C++ class library called Open Inventor.

14

THE OPENGL STATE MACHINE

14

THE OPENGL STATE MACHINE

What you'll learn in this chapter:

How to...	Functions You'll Use
Enable and disable rendering options	glEnable/glDisable
Query the state of rendering options	glIsEnabled/glGetInteger/glGetFloat/glGetDouble
Save and restore some or all of the current state	glPushAttrib/glPopAttrib

The *rendering state* is one of the things that make OpenGL so fast and efficient at drawing 3D graphics. This state is grouped logically into different categories such as color, lighting, texturing, and so forth. Each rendering context (HRC) that you create has its own rendering state specific to a window or off-screen bitmap.

Unlike most of the other chapters, this chapter does not contain any complete example programs. Rather, you will find these state functions used in examples for every other chapter in the book.

Basic OpenGL State Functions

OpenGL's two functions that enable and disable rendering features are called, appropriately enough, glEnable and glDisable. You pass these functions a single enumerated constant, such as GL_DEPTH_TEST, as follows:

```
glEnable(GL_DEPTH_TEST);    /* Enable depth buffer testing */
glDisable(GL_DEPTH_TEST);   /* Disable depth buffer testing */
```

You can retrieve the current state using glIsEnabled, glIsDisabled, and glGetBooleanv, as in the following:

```
GLboolean state;

/*
 * GL_TRUE if depth testing is enabled...
 */
state = glIsEnabled(GL_DEPTH_TEST);

/*
 * GL_TRUE if depth testing is disabled...
 */
state = glIsDisabled(GL_DEPTH_TEST);

/*
 * Returns Boolean state value; GL_TRUE if depth testing is enabled...
 */
glGetBooleanv(GL_DEPTH_TEST, &state);
```

Most OpenGL state variables are Boolean values, on or off. Some, like the current viewport, are an array of integers, or an array of floating point numbers for the current RGBA color. To address these types of state values, OpenGL adds glGetDoublev, glGetFloatv, and glGetInteger:

```
GLint    istate[4];
GLfloat  fstate[4];
GLdouble dstate[3];

glGetIntegerv(GL_VIEWPORT, istate);
glGetFloatv(GL_CURRENT_COLOR, fstate);
glGetDoublev(GL_CURRENT_NORMAL, dstate);
```

You'll learn more about the various state variables further into the chapter.

Saving and Restoring States

Just as OpenGL maintains a stack of Projection, Modelview, and Texture matrices, it has a stack for the current rendering state. Unlike the matrix stack, the state stack gives you much more control over exactly what you save (push) or restore (pop) from the stack; see Figure 14-1.

The OpenGL functions to save and restore rendering state attributes are glPushAttrib and glPopAttrib. The glPushAttrib function works a lot like glPushMatrix, except that you can select the state values to put on the stack! To save all of the current rendering state, you would call

```
glPushAttrib(GL_ALL_ATTRIB_BITS);
```

Usually, however, you're only interested in saving a specific set of information, such as the current color, line width, and so forth. OpenGL defines many constants for specific types of information (see Table 14-1). For example:

```
glPushAttrib(GL_CURRENT_BIT);   /* Save current drawing color, etc */
glPushAttrib(GL_LIGHTING_BIT); /* Save current lighting settings */
glPushAttrib(GL_TEXTURING_BIT);/* Save current texturing settings */
```

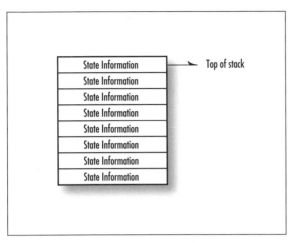

Figure 14-1 OpenGL attribute stack

Once you have done your rendering, you restore those state bits with glPopAttrib. This function accepts no arguments and restores only what was saved with the last glPushAttrib.

Table 14-1 glPushAttrib attribute bits

Attribute Bit	Description
GL_ACCUM_BUFFER_BIT	Accumulation buffer clear value.
GL_COLOR_BUFFER_BIT	Alpha test state, function, and values. Blending state, function, and values. GL_DITHER state. Current drawing buffer(s). Current logical operation state and function. Current RGBA/index clear color and write masks.
GL_CURRENT_BIT	Current RGBA color or color index. Current lighting normal and texture coordinate. Current raster position, GL_CURRENT_RASTER_POSITION_VALID, and GL_EDGE_FLAG. GL_DEPTH_BUFFERBITGL_DEPTH_TEST state, depth buffer function, depth buffer clear value, and GL_DEPTH_WRITEMASK state.
GL_ENABLE_BIT	GL_ALPHA_TEST, GL_AUTO_NORMAL, and GL_BLEND state. User-defined clipping plane state. GL_COLOR_MATERIAL, GL_CULL_FACE, GL_DEPTH_TEST, GL_DITHER, GL_FOG, GL_LIGHTi, GL_LIGHTING, GL_LINE_SMOOTH, GL_LINE_STIPPLE, GL_LOGIC_OP, GL_MAP1_x, GL_MAP2_x, GL_NORMALIZE, GL_POINT_SMOOTH, GL_POLYGON_SMOOTH, GL_POLYGON_STIPPLE, GL_SCISSOR_TEST, GL_STENCIL_TEST, GL_TEXTURE_1D, GL_TEXTURE_2D, and GL_TEXTURE_GEN_x states.
GL_EVAL_BIT	GL_MAP1_x and GL_MAP2_x state, 1D and 2D grid endpoints and divisions, GL_AUTO_NORMAL state.
GL_FOG_BIT	GL_FOG state, fog color, fog density, linear fog start, linear fog end, fog index, GL_FOG_MODE value.

continued on next page

continued from previous page

Attribute Bit	Description
GL_HINT_BIT	GL_PERSPECTIVE_CORRECTION_HINT, GL_POINT_SMOOTH_HINT, GL_LINE_SMOOTH_HINT, GL_POLYGON_SMOOTH_HINT, and GL_FG_HINT state.
GL_LIGHTING_BIT	GL_COLOR_MATERIAL state. GL_COLOR_MATERIAL_FACE value. Color material parameters that are tracking the ambient scene color. GL_LIGHT_MODEL_LOCAL_VIEWER and GL_LIGHT_MODEL_TWO_SIDE values. GL_LIGHTING and GL_LIGHTx states. All light parameters. GL_SHADE_MODEL value.
GL_LINE_BIT	GL_LINE_SMOOTH and GL_LINE_STIPPLE states. Line stipple pattern and repeat counter. Line width.
GL_LIST_BIT	GL_LIST_BASE value.
GL_PIXEL_MODE_BIT	GL_RED_BIAS, GL_RED_SCALE, GL_GREEN_BIAS, GL_GREEN_SCALE, GL_BLUE_BIAS, GL_BLUE_SCALE, GL_ALPHA_BIAS, GL_ALPHA_SCALE, GL_DEPTH_BIAS, GL_DEPTH_SCALE, GL_INDEX_OFFSET, GL_INDEX_SHIFT, GL_MAP_COLOR, GL_MAP_DEPTH, GL_ZOOM_X, GL_ZOOM_Y, and GL_READ_BUFFER settings.
GL_POINT_BIT	GL_POINT_SMOOTH state, point size.
GL_POLYGON_BIT	GL_CULL_FACE, GL_CULL_FACE_MODE, GL_FRONT_FACE, GL_POLYGON_MODE, GL_POLYGON_SMOOTH, GL_POLYGON_STIPPLE.
GL_POLYGON_STIPPLE_BIT	Polygon stipple image.
GL_SCISSOR_BIT	GL_SCISSOR_TEST state, scissor box.
GL_STENCIL_BUFFER_BIT	GL_STENCIL_TEST state. Stencil function and reference value. Stencil value mask. Stencil fail, pass, and depth buffer pass action. Stencil buffer clear value and writemask.
GL_TEXTURE_BIT	Enable bits for all texture coordinates. Border color for each texture image. Minification filter and magnification filter. Texture coordinates and wrap modes. Color and mode for each texture environment. GL_TEXTURE_GEN_x, GL_TEXTURE_GEN_MODE settings. glTexGen plane equations.
GL_TRANSFORM_BIT	Coefficients of the six clipping planes, enable bits for the clipping planes, GL_MATRIX_MODE setting, GL_NORMALIZE state.
GL_VIEWPORT_BIT	Depth range, viewport origin, and extent.

Drawing States

OpenGL has a large number of states associated with drawing actions for the basic glBegin/glEnd primitives. Most are saved with a call to glPushAttrib(GL_CURRENT_BIT | GL_LINE_BIT). See Table 14-2.

Table 14-2 Drawing state variables

State Variable	Description
GL_ALPHA_TEST	Do alpha value testing.
GL_BLEND	Perform pixel blending operations.
GL_CLIP_PLANEx	Clip drawing operations outside the specified clipping plane.

State Variable	Description
GL_CULL_FACE	Cull back- or front-facing polygons.
GL_DITHER	Dither color values.
GL_LINE_SMOOTH	Anti-alias lines.
GL_LINE_STIPPLE	Apply a bit pattern to lines.
GL_LOGIC_OP	Do logical operations on pixels when drawing.
GL_POINT_SMOOTH	Anti-alias points.
GL_POLYGON_SMOOTH	Anti-alias polygons.
GL_POLYGON_STIPPLE	Apply a bit pattern to polygons.
GL_SCISSOR_TEST	Clip drawing outside the glScissor region.

Depth Buffer States

The most common mistake made by beginning OpenGL programmers is to forget to enable depth testing with glEnable(GL_DEPTH_TEST). Without depth testing, hidden surface removal is not performed using the depth buffer (see Chapter 15). Calling glPushAttrib with GL_DEPTH_BUFFER_BIT takes care of saving the GL_DEPTH_TEST state.

Stencil Buffer States

The stencil buffer supports many special effects, including shadows. Like the depth buffer, however, the stencil buffer is very easy to control. Save stencil buffer state information with glPushAttrib(GL_STENCIL_BUFFER_BIT). which saves the current GL_STENCIL_TEST value.

Lighting States

Of all the OpenGL features, lighting has the most OpenGL state information. The state information for lighting includes the current lighting environment (model) settings for color and lighting mode; material definitions; the color, position, and direction of light; and other parameters. Moreover, OpenGL adds even *more* state information with automatic lighting normal generation.

Table 14-3 lists all the available variables. At the very minimum, you'll need to call glEnable(GL_LIGHTING) and glEnable(GL_LIGHT0). To save the current lighting state, call glPushAttrib(GL_LIGHTING_BIT | GL_EVAL_BIT).

Table 14-3 Lighting State Variables

State Variable	Description
GL_AUTO_NORMAL	Automatically generate lighting normals from glMap parameters.
GL_COLOR_MATERIAL	Assign material colors from the current drawing color.
GL_LIGHTING	Enable lighting calculations.
GL_LIGHTx	Enable light x.

continued on next page

continued from previous page

State Variable	Description
GL_MAP1_NORMAL	Enable mapping of lighting normals from 1D coordinates.
GL_MAP2_NORMAL	Enable mapping of lighting normals from 2D coordinates.
GL_NORMALIZE	Normalize all lighting normals prior to doing calculations.

Texturing States

In terms of complexity, texturing in OpenGL is second only to lighting. Table 14-4 lists the available variables.

To save the current texturing parameters, call glEnable with GL_TEXTURE_BIT and GL_EVAL_BIT. When you're enabling texturing, make sure to enable only one of the texturing modes—*either* GL_TEXTURE_1D *or* GL_TEXTURE_2D. The OpenGL spec states that 2D texturing overrides 1D texturing, but some implementations do not comply with this.

Table 14-4 Texturing State Variables

State Variable	Description
GL_MAP1_TEXTURE_COORD_1	The s texture coordinate will be generated by calls to glEvalPoint1, glEvalMesh1, and glEvalCoord1.
GL_MAP1_TEXTURE_COORD_2	The s and t texture coordinates will be generated by calls to glEvalPoint1, glEvalMesh1, and glEvalCoord1.
GL_MAP1_TEXTURE_COORD_3	The s, t, and r texture coordinates will be generated by calls to glEvalPoint1, glEvalMesh1, and glEvalCoord1.
GL_MAP1_TEXTURE_COORD_4	The s, t, r, and q texture coordinates will be generated by calls to glEvalPoint1, glEvalMesh1, and glEvalCoord1.
GL_MAP2_TEXTURE_COORD_1	The s texture coordinate will be generated by calls to glEvalPoint2, glEvalMesh2, and glEvalCoord2.
GL_MAP2_TEXTURE_COORD_2	The s and t texture coordinates will be generated by calls to glEvalPoint2, glEvalMesh2, and glEvalCoord2.
GL_MAP2_TEXTURE_COORD_3	The s, t, and r texture coordinates will be generated by calls to glEvalPoint2, glEvalMesh2, and glEvalCoord2.
GL_MAP2_TEXTURE_COORD_4	The s, t, r, and q texture coordinates will be generated by calls to glEvalPoint2, glEvalMesh2, and glEvalCoord2.
GL_TEXTURE_1D	Enable 1D texturing unless 2D texturing is enabled.
GL_TEXTURE_2D	Enable 2D texturing.
GL_TEXTURE_GEN_Q	Automatically generate the q texture coordinate from calls to glVertex.
GL_TEXTURE_GEN_R	Automatically generate the r texture coordinate from calls to glVertex.
GL_TEXTURE_GEN_S	Automatically generate the s texture coordinate from calls to glVertex.
GL_TEXTURE_GEN_T	Automatically generate the t texture coordinate from calls to glVertex.

Pixel States

Pixel transfer, storage, and mapping modes are probably the least understood and least optimized OpenGL features. Save them with a call to glPushAttrib(GL_PIXEL_BIT). There are no glEnable states for these modes.

Reference Section

GLDISABLE, GLENABLE

Purpose	Disables or enables an OpenGL feature.
Include File	<GL/gl.h>
Syntax	void glDisable(GLenum feature);
	glEnable
Description	glDisable disables an OpenGL drawing feature, and glEnable enables an OpenGL drawing feature.
Parameters	
feature	GLenum: The feature to disable or enable, from Table 14-5.
Returns	None.
See Also	glIsEnabled, glPopAttrib, glPushAttrib

Table 14-5 Features Enabled/Disabled by glEnable/glDisable

Feature	Description
GL_AUTO_NORMAL	Automatically generate lighting normals from *glMap* parameters.
GL_COLOR_MATERIAL	Assign material colors from the current drawing color.
GL_LIGHTING	Enable lighting calculations.
GL_LIGHTx	Enable light *x*.
GL_MAP1_NORMAL	Enable mapping of lighting normals from 1D coordinates.
GL_MAP2_NORMAL	Enable mapping of lighting normals from 2D coordinates.
GL_NORMALIZE	Normalize all lighting normals prior to doing calculations.
GL_MAP1_TEXTURE_COORD_1	The s texture coordinate will be generated by calls to glEvalPoint1, glEvalMesh1, and glEvalCoord1.
GL_MAP1_TEXTURE_COORD_2	The s and t texture coordinates will be generated by calls to glEvalPoint1, glEvalMesh1, and glEvalCoord1.
GL_MAP1_TEXTURE_COORD_3	The s, t, and r texture coordinates will be generated by calls to glEvalPoint1, glEvalMesh1, and glEvalCoord1.
GL_MAP1_TEXTURE_COORD_4	The s, t, r, and q texture coordinates will be generated by calls to glEvalPoint1, glEvalMesh1, and glEvalCoord1.
GL_MAP2_TEXTURE_COORD_1	The s texture coordinate will be generated by calls to glEvalPoint2, glEvalMesh2, and glEvalCoord2.

continued on next page

continued from previous page

Feature	Description
GL_MAP2_TEXTURE_COORD_2	The s and t texture coordinates will be generated by calls to glEvalPoint2, glEvalMesh2, and glEvalCoord2.
GL_MAP2_TEXTURE_COORD_3	The s, t, and r texture coordinates will be generated by calls to glEvalPoint2, glEvalMesh2, and glEvalCoord2.
GL_MAP2_TEXTURE_COORD_4	The s, t, r, and q texture coordinates will be generated by calls to glEvalPoint2, glEvalMesh2, and glEvalCoord2.
GL_TEXTURE_1D	Enable 1D texturing unless 2D texturing is enabled.
GL_TEXTURE_2D	Enable 2D texturing.
GL_TEXTURE_GEN_Q	Automatically generate the q texture coordinate from calls to glVertex.
GL_TEXTURE_GEN_R	Automatically generate the r texture coordinate from calls to glVertex.
GL_TEXTURE_GEN_S	Automatically generate the s texture coordinate from calls to glVertex.
GL_TEXTURE_GEN_T	Automatically generate the t texture coordinate from calls to glVertex.
GL_STENCIL_TEST	Enable stencil buffer comparisons.
GL_DEPTH_TEST	Enable depth buffer comparisons.
GL_ALPHA_TEST	Do alpha value testing.
GL_BLEND	Perform pixel blending operations.
GL_CLIP_PLANEx	Clip drawing operations outside the specified clipping plane.
GL_CULL_FACE	Cull back- or front-facing polygons.
GL_DITHER	Dither color values.
GL_LINE_SMOOTH	Anti-alias lines.
GL_LINE_STIPPLE	Apply a bit pattern to lines.
GL_LOGIC_OP	Do logical operations on pixels when drawing.
GL_POINT_SMOOTH	Anti-alias points.
GL_POLYGON_SMOOTH	Anti-alias polygons.
GL_POLYGON_STIPPLE	Apply a bit pattern to polygons.
GL_SCISSOR_TEST	Clip drawing outside the glScissor region.

GLISENABLED

Purpose	Tests if an OpenGL feature is enabled.
Include File	<GL/gl.h>
Syntax	GLboolean glIsEnabled(GLenum feature);
Description	This function returns GL_TRUE if the specified feature has been enabled and GL_FALSE otherwise.
Parameters	
feature	GLenum: The feature to test (see glEnable).
Returns	GLboolean: GL_TRUE if the feature is enabled, GL_FALSE otherwise.
See Also	glDisable, glEnable, glPopAttrib, glPushAttrib

glPopAttrib

Purpose	Restores state information saved with glPushAttib.
Include File	<GL/gl.h>
Syntax	void glPopAttrib(void);
Description	glPopAttrib restores previously saved state information from a call to glPushAttrib. If the attribute stack is empty, the current OpenGL error state is set and the call is ignored.
Parameters	None.
Returns	None.
See Also	glDisable, glEnable, glIsEnabled, glPushAttrib

glPushAttrib

Purpose	Saves OpenGL state information.
Include File	<GL/gl.h>
Syntax	void glPushAttrib(GLuint bits);
Description	This function saves OpenGL state information specified by *bits*. If the attribute stack is full, the current OpenGL error state is set and the top of the stack is overwritten.
Parameters	
bits	GLuint: The state information to save (see Table 14-1).
Returns	None.
See Also	glDisable, glEnable, glIsEnabled, glPopAttrib

15

BUFFERS: NOT JUST FOR ANIMATION

15

BUFFERS: NOT JUST FOR ANIMATION

What you'll learn in this chapter:

How to...	Functions You'll Use
Set up buffers	ChoosePixelFormat/SetPixelFormat
Use the depth buffer	glEnable/glDepthFunc/glDepthRange
Use the stencil buffer	glEnable/glStencilFunc
Use the accumulation buffer	glEnable/glAccum

In the previous chapters, we've used buffers for color and depth information. OpenGL provides several kinds of buffers that are linked by the OpenGL graphics context:

- Color buffer
- Depth buffer
- Stencil buffer
- Accumulation buffer

Each buffer has specific capabilities beyond simple double-buffering for animation and depth-buffering for hidden surface removal as described in this chapter.

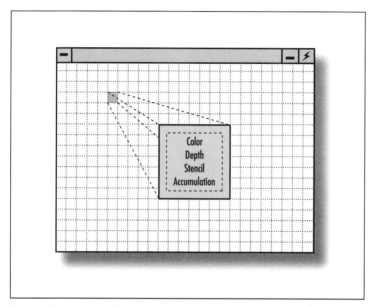

Figure 15-1 OpenGL buffer organization

What Are Buffers?

A buffer in OpenGL is essentially a two-dimensional array of values that correspond to a pixel in a window or off-screen image. Each buffer has the same number of columns and rows (width and height) as the current client area of a window but holds a different range and type of values. See Figure 15-1.

Configuring Buffers

Before using OpenGL, you must configure the window's hardware device context (HDC) for the buffers and color mode you require. The PIXELFORMATDESCRIPTOR structure contains this information. Here's the typical way this buffer is set up:

```
// This structure holds buffer, layer, and color mode information.
PIXELFORMATDESCRIPTOR pfd;


// First initialize the pfd size and version...
pfd.nSize       = sizeof(pfd);
pfd.nVersion    = 1;

// Next, layer and buffering information...
pfd.dwFlags     = PFD_DRAW_TO_WINDOW | PFD_SUPPORT_OPENGL;
pfd.dwLayerMask = PFD_MAIN_PLANE;
pfd.iLayerType  = PFD_MAIN_PLANE;

// The pixel type indicates whether we use color indices or RGBA
pfd.iPixelType  = PFD_TYPE_RGBA;
```

```
// Now we specify the *minimum* number of bitplanes we need for
// each buffer.  Windows will choose the closest pixel format
// satisfying our minimum requirements.
pfd.cColorBits   = 8;
pfd.cDepthBits   = 16;
pfd.cAccumBits   = 0;
pfd.cStencilBits = 0;
```

The dwFlags bitfield specifies that we want to draw into the window using OpenGL. It also tells Windows the number of color buffers we require. See Table 15-1.

Table 15-1 PIXELFORMATDESCRIPTOR Option Flags

Flag	Description
PFD_DRAW_TO_WINDOW	Draw into a window.
PFD_DRAW_TO_BITMAP	Draw into an off-screen bitmap.
PFD_SUPPORT_GDI	The color buffer supports GDI drawing commands.
PFD_SUPPORT_OPENGL	The buffers support OpenGL drawing commands.
PFD_DOUBLEBUFFER	The color values are double buffered.
PFD_STEREO	Two sets of buffers are available (left and right).
PFD_DOUBLE_BUFFER_DONTCARE	It doesn't matter if the color values are double buffered.
PFD_STEREO_DONTCARE	It doesn't matter if the buffers are in stereo.

The dwLayerMask and iLayerType fields specify the drawing planes that are to be used and are usually set to PFD_MAIN_PLANE. Some OpenGL graphics cards provide auxiliary buffers above and below the normal Windows color plane allowing you to draw menus or other graphical constructs without overwriting the main image. The generic implementation provided by Microsoft does not support auxiliary drawing planes.

The iPixelType field specifies how color values are represented and can be one of the two values in Table 15-2.

Table 15-2 PIXELFORMATDESCRIPTOR Pixel Types

Pixel Type	Description
PFD_TYPE_RGBA	Colors are composed of red, green, blue, and alpha values.
PFD_TYPE_COLORINDEX	Colors are composed of an index value in the current logical palette.

The cColorBits, cDepthBits, cAccumBits, and cStencilBits fields specify the size of each buffer for the window. Specifying 0 for a field disables that buffer, except for cColorBits. If you specify 0 for cColorBits, Windows will provide the minimum number of bits available—usually 4 or 8 bits (16 or 256 colors). When iPixelType is set to PFD_TYPE_RGBA, the cColorBits field specifies the total number of red, green, and blue color bits. The current generic implementation of OpenGL provided by Microsoft does not support alpha color bits.

Once you have filled in all the necessary PIXELFORMATDESCRIPTOR information, you can set the pixel format for the window with a few simple calls, as shown here:

```
// The device context refers to the graphics driver for this window.
HDC                     hdc;

// This integer holds the Windows pixel format code
int                     pf;


// Choose and select the pixel format...
pf = ChoosePixelFormat(hdc, &pfd);
if (pf == 0)
{
  // Could not find the pixel format...
  MessageBox(NULL, "ChoosePixelFormat failed!", "Error", MB_OK);
}
else if (!SetPixelFormat(hdc, pf, &pfd))
{
  // Could not set the pixel format...
  MessageBox(NULL, "SetPixelFormat failed!", "Error", MB_OK);
}
```

After calling ChoosePixelFormat, the PIXELFORMATDESCRIPTOR information is filled with the actual hardware values that were chosen. On return, the dwFlags field can contain three additional flags that require your attention; they are listed in Table 15-3.

Table 15-3 PIXELFORMATDESCRIPTOR Return Values

Return Value	Description
PFD_GENERIC_FORMAT	The requested format is supported by the generic implementation.
PFD_NEED_PALETTE	The RGBA color buffer will be drawn on a palette-managed device and requires a logical palette.
PFD_NEED_SYSTEM_PALETTE	The color values require a fixed system palette to display correctly. Call SetSystemPaletteUse() to force a one-to-one mapping of the logical palette and the system palette.

If PFD_NEED_PALETTE is set, you should define a logical palette as specified by the cRedBits, cRedShift, cGreenBits, cGreenShift, cBlueBits, and cBlueShift fields. Following is an example of a defined palette.

```
HDC                     hdc;
PIXELFORMATDESCRIPTOR   pfd;
HPALETTE                palette;
LOGPALETTE              *pal;
int                     i,
                        pf,
                        num_colors,
                        red, num_reds,
                        blue, num_blues,
                        green, num_greens;
```

```
// Get the current pixel format information
pf = GetPixelFormat(hdc);
DescribePixelFormat(hdc, pf, sizeof(PIXELFORMATDESCRIPTOR), &pfd);

// Check to see if we need to make a palette
if (pfd.dwFlags & PFD_NEED_PALETTE)
{
  // Yes, we do.  First, allocate logical color palette entries...
  num_colors = 1 << pfd.cColorBits;
  pal        = (PLOGPALETTE)LocalAlloc(LMEM_FIXED, sizeof(LOGPALETTE) +
                                    num_colors * sizeof(PALETTEENTRY));

  pal->palVersion    = 0x300;
  pal->palNumEntries = num_colors;

  num_reds   = (1 << pfd.cRedBits) - 1;
  num_greens = (1 << pfd.cGreenBits) - 1;
  num_blues  = (1 << pfd.cBlueBits) - 1;

  for (blue = 0, i = 0; blue <= num_blues; blue ++)
    for (green = 0; green <= num_greens; green ++)
      for (red = 0; red <= num_reds; red ++, i ++)
      {
        pal->palPalEntry[i].peRed   = 255 * red / num_reds;
        pal->palPalEntry[i].peGreen = 255 * green / num_greens;
        pal->palPalEntry[i].peBlue  = 255 * blue / num_blues;
        pal->palPalEntry[i].peFlags = 0;
      }

  palette = CreatePalette(pal);
  SelectPalette(hdc, palette, FALSE);
  RealizePalette(hdc);

  LocalFree(pal);
}
```

The Color Buffer

The color buffer holds pixel color information. Each pixel can contain a color index or red/green/blue/alpha (RGBA) values that describes the appearance of that pixel. RGBA pixels are displayed directly using the closest available color(s) on the screen. The generic OpenGL implementation from Microsoft does not support alpha color values at this time.

The appearance of color index pixels is determined by looking up the index in an RGB color table. Under Windows these color tables are implemented using a logical color palette. Color index mode is very useful for displaying tabular data graphically (for example, stress or force meters), as shown in the second depth buffer example in "Another Application of the Depth Buffer."

Double Buffering

Double buffering provides an additional off-screen color buffer that is often used for animation. With double buffering you can draw a scene off screen and quickly "swap" it onto the screen, eliminating the annoying flicker that would otherwise be present.

Double buffering only affects the color buffer and does not provide a second depth, accumulation, or stencil buffer. If you choose a pixel format with double buffering, OpenGL selects the "back" buffer for drawing. You can change this using the glDrawBuffer function to specify one of the values in Table 15-4.

Table 15-4 glDrawBuffer Values

Buffer	Description
GL_FRONT	Draw only to the front (visible) color buffer.
GL_BACK	Draw only to the back (hidden) color buffer.
GL_FRONT_AND_BACK	Draw to both the front and back color buffers.

Stereo Buffering

Stereo buffering provides an additional color buffer in single-buffered mode and two additional color buffers in double-buffered mode, to generate a left- and right-eye screen image. (See Table 15-5.) True three-dimensional images can be generated by choosing the correct viewing positions for each eye, usually offset by a few "inches" to simulate the distance between our eyes. Stereo buffering is not available on most PC graphics cards.

In addition to specifying the front or back buffer for drawing, the glDrawBuffer function can select the left- or right-eye buffers.

Table 15-5 Stereo Buffer Values

Buffer	Description
GL_LEFT_FRONT	Draw only to the left-front buffer.
GL_LEFT_BACK	Draw only to the left-back buffer.
GL_RIGHT_FRONT	Draw only to the right-front buffer.
GL_RIGHT_BACK	Draw only to the right-back buffer.
GL_FRONT	Draw to both the left- and right-front buffers.
GL_BACK	Draw to both the left- and right-back buffers.

Swapping Buffers

Open GL does support double buffering, but there is no OpenGL function to actually swap the front and back buffers! Fortunately, every windowing system with OpenGL support has a function call to accomplish this. Under Windows, this call is

```
SwapBuffers(hdc);
```

where hdc is the device context for the window in which you are drawing. If you have chosen a stereo-buffered pixel format, both the left and right eyes are swapped by the one call.

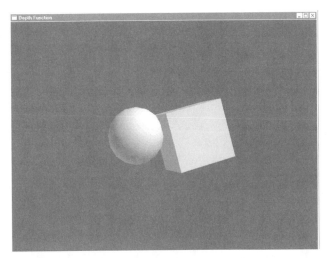

Figure 15-2a Typical depth buffering with GL_LESS

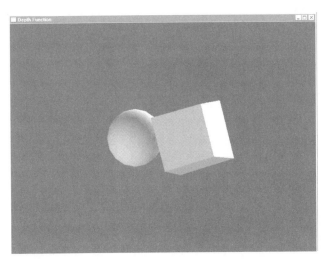

Figure 15-2b Typical depth buffering with GL_GREATER

The Depth Buffer

The depth buffer holds distance values for each pixel. Each value represents the pixel's distance from the viewer and is scaled to fill the current near/far clipping volume. The software implementation of OpenGL under Windows supports both 16- and 32-bit depth values.

The depth buffer is normally used to perform hidden surface removal. Hidden surface removal is a process that occurs naturally in the real world; when one solid (opaque) object is placed in front of another, the nearer object will hide some or all of the one behind it.

In OpenGL, the depth buffer can also be used for some interesting effects, such as cutting away the front of objects to show the inner surfaces (see Figures 15-2a and 15-2b).

Depth Comparisons

When you draw in a window using OpenGL, the Z position of each pixel is compared with the value in the depth buffer. If the result of the comparison is True, the pixel is stored in the color buffer along with its depth. OpenGL defines eight depth-comparison functions that can be used for depth buffering (Table 15-6).

The default comparison function is GL_LESS. To change it, call glDepthFunc:

```
glDepthFunc(function);
```

Using the GL_LESS function, pixels in a polygon are drawn if the depth value of the pixel is less than the depth value in the depth buffer.

Table 15-6 Depth Comparison Functions

Name	Function
GL_NEVER	Always False.
GL_LESS	True if source Z < depth Z.
GL_EQUAL	True if source Z = depth Z.
GL_LEQUAL	True if source Z <= depth Z.
GL_GREATER	True if source Z > depth Z.
GL_NOTEQUAL	True if source Z != depth Z.
GL_GEQUAL	True if source Z >= depth Z.
GL_ALWAYS	Always True.

Depth Values

When using the GL_EQUAL and GL_NOTEQUAL depth comparisons, it is sometimes necessary to alter the range of depth values used, in order to reduce the number of available values (keeping the number of values to a minimum). Use glDepth Range, as follows:

```
glDepthRange(near, far);
```

The near and far parameters are floating point numbers between 0.0 and 1.0, inclusive. The defaults are 0.0 for near and 1.0 for far. Normally, near is less than far, but you may also reverse the order to achieve special effects (or use the GL_GREATER and GL_GEQUAL functions). Reducing the range of values stored in the depth buffer does not affect clipping, but it will make the depth buffer less accurate and can lead to errors in hidden surface removal in the display.

Some depth comparisons need a different initial depth value. By default, the depth buffer is cleared to 1.0 with the glClear function. To specify a different value, use the glClearDepth function:

```
glClearDepth(depth);
```

The depth parameter is a floating point number between 0.0 and 1.0, inclusive, unless you have defined a smaller range with glDepthRange. In general, use a value of 0.0 for GL_GREATER and GL_GEQUAL comparisons, and 1.0 for GL_LESS and GL_LEQUAL comparisons.

Applications of the Depth Buffer

The usual application of the depth buffer is to remove hidden surfaces. As noted earlier, the depth buffer can also be used to cut away the front parts of a scene. Listing 15-1 demonstrates this type of application. The key to this program is the use of glDepthFunc and glClearDepth:

```
glDepthFunc(depth_function);
```

Here we use a global variable to hold the current depth function. The depth_function variable is initialized to GL_LESS when the program starts. When the user presses the D key, the toggle_depth callback function switches this between GL_GREATER and GL_LESS.

```
if (depth_function == GL_LESS)
  glClearDepth(1.0);
else
  glClearDepth(0.0);
```

The glClearDepth call is needed to provide the correct initial depth value for the window, since the depth value is 1.0 by default. Nothing would be drawn when the depth function is set to GL_GREATER, because no pixel could possibly have a depth value greater than 1.0.

Listing 15-1 Depth buffer example using glDepthFunc

```
/*
 * "depth.c" - A test program demonstrating the use of glDepthFunc().
 *
 * Press the 'd' key to toggle between GL_LESS and GL_GREATER depth
 * tests.  Press the 'ESC' key to quit.
 */

#include <GL/glaux.h>

/*
 * These #define constants are provided for compatibility between MS Windows
 * and the rest of the world.
 *
 * CALLBACK and APIENTRY are function modifiers under MS Windows.
 */

#ifndef WIN32
```

continued on next page

continued from previous page

```
#   define CALLBACK
#   define APIENTRY
#endif /* !WIN32 */


GLenum depth_function = GL_LESS;         /* Current depth function */


/*
 * 'reshape_scene()' - Change the size of the scene...
 */

void CALLBACK
reshape_scene(GLsizei width,     /* I - Width of the window in pixels */
              GLsizei height)  /* I - Height of the window in pixels */
{
 /*
  * Reset the current viewport and perspective transformation...
  */

  glViewport(0, 0, width, height);

  glMatrixMode(GL_PROJECTION);
  glLoadIdentity();
  gluPerspective(22.5, (float)width / (float)height, 0.1, 1000.0);

  glMatrixMode(GL_MODELVIEW);
}


/*
 * 'draw_scene()' - Draw a scene containing a cube with a sphere in front of
 *                  it.
 */

void CALLBACK
draw_scene(void)
{
  static float red_light[4] = { 1.0, 0.0, 0.0, 1.0 };
  static float red_pos[4] = { 1.0, 1.0, 1.0, 0.0 };
  static float blue_light[4] = { 0.0, 0.0, 1.0, 1.0 };
  static float blue_pos[4] = { -1.0, -1.0, -1.0, 0.0 };


 /*
  * Enable drawing features that we need...
  */

  glEnable(GL_DEPTH_TEST);
  glEnable(GL_LIGHTING);
  glEnable(GL_LIGHT0);
  glEnable(GL_LIGHT1);

  glShadeModel(GL_SMOOTH);
  glDepthFunc(depth_function);

 /*
  * Clear the color and depth buffers...
  */
```

```
      if (depth_function == GL_LESS)
        glClearDepth(1.0);
      else
        glClearDepth(0.0);

      glClearColor(0.0, 0.0, 0.0, 0.0);
      glClear(GL_COLOR_BUFFER_BIT | GL_DEPTH_BUFFER_BIT);

     /*
      * Draw the cube and sphere in different colors...
      *
      * We have positioned two lights in this scene.  The first is red and
      * located above, to the right, and behind the viewer.  The second is blue
      * and located below, to the left, and in front of the viewer.
      */

      glLightfv(GL_LIGHT0, GL_DIFFUSE, red_light);
      glLightfv(GL_LIGHT0, GL_POSITION, red_pos);

      glLightfv(GL_LIGHT1, GL_DIFFUSE, blue_light);
      glLightfv(GL_LIGHT1, GL_POSITION, blue_pos);

      glPushMatrix();
        glTranslatef(-1.0, 0.0, -20.0);
        auxSolidSphere(1.0);
      glPopMatrix();

      glPushMatrix();
        glTranslatef(1.0, 0.0, -20.0);
        glRotatef(15.0, 0.0, 1.0, 0.0);
        glRotatef(15.0, 0.0, 0.0, 1.0);
        auxSolidCube(2.0);
      glPopMatrix();

      glFlush();
    }


    /*
     * 'toggle_depth()' - Toggle the depth function between GL_LESS and GL_GREATER.
     */

    void CALLBACK
    toggle_depth(void)
    {
      if (depth_function == GL_LESS)
        depth_function = GL_GREATER;
      else
        depth_function = GL_LESS;
    }


    /*
     * 'main()' - Initialize the window and display the scene until the user presses
     *            the ESCape key.
     */

    void
    main(void)
```

continued on next page

continued from previous page

```
{
  auxInitDisplayMode(AUX_RGB | AUX_SINGLE | AUX_DEPTH);
  auxInitWindow(?Depth Function?);

  auxKeyFunc(AUX_d, toggle_depth);
  auxReshapeFunc(reshape_scene);

  auxMainLoop(draw_scene);
}


/*
 * End of "depth.c".
 */
```

Another Application of the Depth Buffer

The depth buffer can also be used to generate a contour mapping of a scene, which shows different colors for each depth. Contour maps can be generated using the glReadPixels function and by specifying the depth component as the value of interest, as follows:

```
glReadPixels(x, y, width, height, GL_DEPTH_COMPONENT, type, pixels);
```

The returned depth values can then be scaled and assigned to color values that can be displayed as a contour image, especially in color index mode, like this:

```
#define WIDTH 320
#define HEIGHT 200
GLfloat pixels[WIDTH * HEIGHT];
int i;

// draw the scene...
glEnable(GL_DEPTH_TEST);
...
// Grab the depth buffer
glReadPixels(0, 0, WIDTH, HEIGHT, GL_DEPTH_COMPONENT, GL_FLOAT,
             pixels);
// Convert depth values to color indices
for (i = 0; i < (WIDTH * HEIGHT); i ++)
  pixels[i] = pixels[i] * 255.0; // Assume 256 color palette
// Display the new pixels on the screen
glDisable(GL_DEPTH_TEST);
glDrawPixels(0, 0, WIDTH, HEIGHT, GL_COLOR_INDEX, GL_FLOAT, pixels);
```

In a real application, you'd probably want to provide some user control over the color palette and range of values. You can also use RGBA color values to enhance a scene, using glBlendFunc to mix the "normal" image with the "depth" image.

Cutting Away Parts of a Scene

Let's see how to cut away parts of a scene—an engine block, for instance—to show some internal operation that would not normally be visible. Listing 15-2 is an example of using the depth buffer for this purpose.

The heart of this program is the draw_scene function, which draws a picture of a cube and sphere being cut by a moving plane. To cut away parts of the scene, we first draw the cutting plane. Instead of drawing to the color buffer, we begin by disabling drawing to the color buffer with glDrawBuffer.

```
glDrawBuffer(GL_NONE);

glBegin(GL_POLYGON);
   glVertex3f(-100.0, 100.0, cutting_plane);
   glVertex3f(100.0, 100.0, cutting_plane);
   glVertex3f(100.0, -100.0, cutting_plane);
   glVertex3f(-100.0, -100.0, cutting_plane);
glEnd();

glDrawBuffer(GL_BACK);
```

Once the cutting plane is drawn, we reenable color buffer drawing and proceed with drawing the cube and sphere. The invisible plane we drew will restrict what is drawn on the screen to polygons that lie behind it, effectively cutting away parts of the scene.

Listing 15-2 Using glDrawBuffer to cut away selected pieces of an object

```
/*
 * "depthcut.c" - A test program demonstrating the use of glDepthFunc() and
 *                glDrawBuffer() to cut away parts of a scene.
 *
 * Press the 'd' key to toggle between GL_LESS and GL_GREATER depth
 * tests.  Press the 'ESC' key to quit.
 */

#include <GL/glaux.h>

/*
 * These #define constants are provided for compatibility between MS Windows
 * and the rest of the world.
 *
 * CALLBACK and APIENTRY are function modifiers under MS Windows.
 */

#ifndef WIN32
#  define CALLBACK
#  define APIENTRY
#endif /* !WIN32 */


GLenum          depth_function = GL_LESS;      /* Current depth function */
GLfloat         cutting_plane = -15.0,         /* Cutting plane distance */
                cutting_dir   = -1.0;          /* Cutting plane direction */


/*
 * 'reshape_scene()' - Change the size of the scene...
 */

void CALLBACK
reshape_scene(GLsizei width,     /* I - Width of the window in pixels */
              GLsizei height)    /* I - Height of the window in pixels */
{
```

continued on next page

continued from previous page

```
  /*
   * Reset the current viewport and perspective transformation...
   */

  glViewport(0, 0, width, height);

  glMatrixMode(GL_PROJECTION);
  glLoadIdentity();
  gluPerspective(22.5, (float)width / (float)height, 0.1, 1000.0);

  glMatrixMode(GL_MODELVIEW);
}


/*
 * 'draw_scene()' - Draw a scene containing a cube with a sphere in front of
 *                  it.
 */

void CALLBACK
draw_scene(void)
{
  static float  red_light[4] = { 1.0, 0.0, 0.0, 1.0 };
  static float  red_pos[4]   = { 1.0, 1.0, 1.0, 0.0 };
  static float  blue_light[4] = { 0.0, 0.0, 1.0, 1.0 };
  static float  blue_pos[4]   = { -1.0, -1.0, -1.0, 0.0 };


  /*
   * Enable drawing features that we need...
   */

  glEnable(GL_DEPTH_TEST);
  glEnable(GL_LIGHTING);
  glEnable(GL_LIGHT0);
  glEnable(GL_LIGHT1);

  glShadeModel(GL_SMOOTH);
  glDepthFunc(depth_function);

  /*
   * Clear the color and depth buffers...
   */

  if (depth_function == GL_LESS)
    glClearDepth(1.0);
  else
    glClearDepth(0.0);

  glClearColor(0.0, 0.0, 0.0, 0.0);
  glClear(GL_COLOR_BUFFER_BIT | GL_DEPTH_BUFFER_BIT);

  /*
   * Draw the cutting plane.  Note that we disable drawing into the normal color buffer
   * while we do this...
   */

  glDrawBuffer(GL_NONE);
```

```
  glBegin(GL_POLYGON);
    glVertex3f(-100.0, 100.0, cutting_plane);
    glVertex3f(100.0, 100.0, cutting_plane);
    glVertex3f(100.0, -100.0, cutting_plane);
    glVertex3f(-100.0, -100.0, cutting_plane);
  glEnd();

  glDrawBuffer(GL_BACK);

 /*
  * Draw the cube and sphere in different colors...
  *
  * We have positioned two lights in this scene.  The first is red and
  * located above, to the right, and behind the viewer.  The second is blue
  * and located below, to the left, and in front of the viewer.
  */

  glLightfv(GL_LIGHT0, GL_DIFFUSE, red_light);
  glLightfv(GL_LIGHT0, GL_POSITION, red_pos);

  glLightfv(GL_LIGHT1, GL_DIFFUSE, blue_light);
  glLightfv(GL_LIGHT1, GL_POSITION, blue_pos);

  glPushMatrix();
    glTranslatef(-1.0, 0.0, -20.0);
    auxSolidSphere(1.0);
  glPopMatrix();

  glPushMatrix();
    glTranslatef(1.0, 0.0, -20.0);
    glRotatef(15.0, 0.0, 1.0, 0.0);
    glRotatef(15.0, 0.0, 0.0, 1.0);
    auxSolidCube(2.0);
  glPopMatrix();

  auxSwapBuffers();
}


/*
 * 'toggle_depth()' - Toggle the depth function between GL_LESS and GL_GREATER.
 */

void CALLBACK
toggle_depth(void)
{
  if (depth_function == GL_LESS)
    depth_function = GL_GREATER;
  else
    depth_function = GL_LESS;
}


/*
 * 'move_plane()' - Move the cutting plane while we are idle...
 */

void CALLBACK
```

continued on next page

continued from previous page

```
move_plane(void)
{
  cutting_plane += cutting_dir;

 /*
  * Reverse directions as needed...
  */

  if (cutting_plane <= -30.0 ||
      cutting_plane >= -15.0)
    cutting_dir = -cutting_dir;

  draw_scene();
}


/*
 * 'main()' - Initialize the window and display the scene until the user presses
 *            the ESCape key.
 */

void
main(void)
{
  auxInitDisplayMode(AUX_RGB | AUX_DOUBLE | AUX_DEPTH);
  auxInitWindow("Depth Function");

  auxKeyFunc(AUX_d, toggle_depth);
  auxReshapeFunc(reshape_scene);
  auxIdleFunc(move_plane);

  auxMainLoop(draw_scene);
}


/*
 * End of "depthcut.c".
 */
```

The Stencil Buffer

The stencil buffer provides many options to restrict drawing on the screen and has many applications that the depth buffer just can't do. At its simplest level, the stencil buffer can be used to block out certain areas on the screen. For example, a flight simulation program might use the stencil buffer to restrict drawing operations to the inside of the aircraft's round controls such as the artificial horizon and airspeed indicators.

Perhaps the most exciting application of the stencil buffer is for shadows. Depending on your graphics hardware, you can generate *hard and soft shadows* from multiple light sources, making your scenes much more realistic and exciting.

Using the Stencil Buffer

To use the stencil buffer, you have to first request one. For Windows, this means setting the cStencilBits field in the Pixel Format Descriptor (PFD) for your window, as in

```
pfd.cStencilBits = 1;
```

Once you have requested a stencil buffer, you must enable stenciling by calling glEnable(GL_STENCIL_TEST). Without this call, *all* stencil buffer operations are disabled.

Stencil Buffer Functions

There are four stenciling functions in OpenGL:

```
void glClearStencil(GLint s)
void glStencilFunc(GLenum func, GLint ref, GLuint mask)
void glStencilMask(GLuint mask)
void glStencilOp(GLenum fail, GLenum zfail, GLzpass)
```

The glClearStencil function is similar to glClearColor, glClearDepth, and glClearIndex; it provides the initial value that is stored in the stencil buffer when glClear(GL_STENCIL_BIT) is called. By default, a 0 stencil value is stored in the stencil buffer. Unlike the depth and color buffers, you don't always clear the stencil buffer every time you redisplay your scene. In the flight simulator example mentioned earlier, the aircraft control area might never change position or size, so redrawing into the stencil buffer would be unnecessary.

Drawing into the Stencil Buffer

Once you have enabled the GL_STENCIL_TEST attribute with glEnable, you'll still need to set up *how* the stencil buffer operates. By default, it does nothing, allowing drawing to occur anywhere on the screen without updating the stencil buffer. To make stenciling work effectively, however, we need to put values into the stencil buffer. The glStencilFunc and glStencilOp functions handle this interaction.

The glStencilFunc *function* defines a comparison function, reference value, and mask for all stencil buffer operations. The valid functions are in Table 15-7.

Table 15-7 Stenciling Functions

Function	Description
GL_NEVER	The stencil test always fails (no drawing occurs).
GL_LESS	Passes if the reference value is less than the stencil value.
GL_LEQUAL	Passes if the reference value is less than or equal to the stencil value.
GL_GREATER	Passes if the reference value is greater than the stencil value.
GL_GEQUAL	Passes if the reference value is greater than or equal to the stencil value.
GL_EQUAL	Passes if the reference value is equal to the stencil value.
GL_NOTEQUAL	Passes if the reference value is not equal to the stencil value.
GL_ALWAYS	The default; stencil test always passes (drawing always occurs).

Coupled with the stencil function is the stencil *operation*, defined with glStencilOp. Valid operations are in Table 15-8.

Table 15-8 Stenciling Operations

Operation	Description
GL_KEEP	Keep the current stencil buffer contents.
GL_ZERO	Set the stencil buffer value to 0.
GL_REPLACE	Set the stencil buffer value to the function reference value.
GL_INCR	Increment the current stencil buffer value.
GL_DECR	Decrement the current stencil buffer value.
GL_INVERT	Bitwise invert the current stencil buffer value.

Normally a mask image is used to outline the area in which drawing is to take place. Here is an example of drawing a mask image into the stencil buffer:

```
glStencilFunc(GL_ALWAYS, 1, 1);
glStencilOp(GL_REPLACE, GL_REPLACE, GL_REPLACE);
```

Then you would issue drawing commands that store a value of 1 in the stencil buffer. To draw using the stencil buffer mask, do the following prior to drawing the scene:

```
glStencilFunc(GL_EQUAL, 1, 1);
glStencilOp(GL_KEEP, GL_KEEP, GL_KEEP);
```

Because this operates with all OpenGL drawing functions including glBitmap, you can use the stencil buffer to create many special "hole" effects for animations! Listing 15-3 contains a version of DEPTHCUT.C called STENCILCT.C that uses the stencil buffer instead of the depth buffer to cut away the middle of the cube.

Following is the heart of this program, which uses the functions described above:

```
glStencilFunc(GL_ALWAYS, 1, 1);
glStencilOp(GL_REPLACE, GL_REPLACE, GL_REPLACE);

glPushMatrix();
  glTranslatef(-1.0, 0.0, -20.0);
  auxSolidSphere(1.0);
glPopMatrix();
```

Once the stencil image is drawn, we draw the cube wherever the sphere was *not* drawn:

```
glStencilFunc(GL_NOTEQUAL, 1, 1);        /* Draw where sphere isn't */
glStencilOp(GL_KEEP, GL_KEEP, GL_KEEP);

...

glPushMatrix();
  glTranslatef(1.0, 0.0, -20.0);
  glRotatef(15.0, 0.0, 1.0, 0.0);
  glRotatef(15.0, 0.0, 0.0, 1.0);
  auxSolidCube(2.0);
glPopMatrix();
```

Listing 15-3 STENCILCT.C, a stencil buffer example

```
/*
 * "stencilct.c" - A test program demonstrating the use of glStencilFunc()
 *                 and glStencilOp() to cut away the middle of a cube.
 */

#include <GL/glaux.h>

/*
 * These #define constants are provided for compatibility between MS Windows
 * and the rest of the world.
 *
 * CALLBACK and APIENTRY are function modifiers under MS Windows.
 */

#ifndef WIN32
#   define CALLBACK
#   define APIENTRY
#endif /* !WIN32 */


/*
 * 'reshape_scene()' - Change the size of the scene...
 */

void CALLBACK
reshape_scene(GLsizei width,     /* I - Width of the window in pixels */
              GLsizei height)    /* I - Height of the window in pixels */
{
  /*
   * Reset the current viewport and perspective transformation...
   */

  glViewport(0, 0, width, height);

  glMatrixMode(GL_PROJECTION);
  glLoadIdentity();
  gluPerspective(22.5, (float)width / (float)height, 0.1, 1000.0);

  glMatrixMode(GL_MODELVIEW);
}


/*
 * 'draw_scene()' - Draw a scene containing a cube with a sphere in front of
 *                  it.
 */

void CALLBACK
draw_scene(void)
{
  static float  red_light[4] = { 1.0, 0.0, 0.0, 1.0 };
  static float  red_pos[4] = { 1.0, 1.0, 1.0, 0.0 };
  static float  blue_light[4] = { 0.0, 0.0, 1.0, 1.0 };
  static float  blue_pos[4] = { -1.0, -1.0, -1.0, 0.0 };
```

continued on next page

continued from previous page

```
/*
 * Enable drawing features that we need...
 */

glEnable(GL_DEPTH_TEST);
glEnable(GL_STENCIL_TEST);
glEnable(GL_LIGHTING);
glEnable(GL_LIGHT0);
glEnable(GL_LIGHT1);

glShadeModel(GL_SMOOTH);

/*
 * Clear the color, depth, and stencil buffers...
 */

glClearColor(0.0, 0.0, 0.0, 0.0);
glClear(GL_COLOR_BUFFER_BIT | GL_DEPTH_BUFFER_BIT |
        GL_STENCIL_BUFFER_BIT);

/*
 * Draw the sphere that will be cutting away parts of the cube...
 */

glStencilFunc(GL_ALWAYS, 1, 1);
glStencilOp(GL_REPLACE, GL_REPLACE, GL_REPLACE);

glPushMatrix();
  glTranslatef(-1.0, 0.0, -20.0);
  auxSolidSphere(1.0);
glPopMatrix();

/*
 * Clear the color and depth buffers once again...
 */

glClearColor(0.0, 0.0, 0.0, 0.0);
glClear(GL_COLOR_BUFFER_BIT | GL_DEPTH_BUFFER_BIT);

/*
 * Draw the cube...
 *
 * We have positioned two lights in this scene.  The first is red and
 * located above, to the right, and behind the viewer.  The second is blue
 * and located below, to the left, and in front of the viewer.
 */

glStencilFunc(GL_NOTEQUAL, 1, 1);
glStencilOp(GL_KEEP, GL_KEEP, GL_KEEP);

glLightfv(GL_LIGHT0, GL_DIFFUSE, red_light);
glLightfv(GL_LIGHT0, GL_POSITION, red_pos);

glLightfv(GL_LIGHT1, GL_DIFFUSE, blue_light);
glLightfv(GL_LIGHT1, GL_POSITION, blue_pos);

glPushMatrix();
  glTranslatef(1.0, 0.0, -20.0);
  glRotatef(15.0, 0.0, 1.0, 0.0);
```

```
    glRotatef(15.0, 0.0, 0.0, 1.0);
    auxSolidCube(2.0);
  glPopMatrix();

  auxSwapBuffers();
}


/*
 * 'main()' - Initialize the window and display the scene until the user presses
 *            the ESCape key.
 */

int APIENTRY
WinMain(HINSTANCE hInstance,
        HINSTANCE hPrev,
        LPSTR     lpCmdLine,
        int       nCmdShow)
{
  auxInitDisplayMode(AUX_RGB | AUX_DOUBLE | AUX_DEPTH | AUX_STENCIL);
  auxInitWindow("Stenciling");

  auxReshapeFunc(reshape_scene);
  auxMainLoop(draw_scene);
}


/*
 * End of "stencilct.c".
 */
```

The Accumulation Buffer

The accumulation buffer provides support for many special effects such as motion blur and depth of field. It also supports full-screen anti-aliasing, although other methods (such as multisampling) are better suited to this task.

The accumulation buffer is considerably less complex than the other buffers discussed so far. It has a single function, *glAccum*, that manages all accumulation buffer actions. The actions that can be performed are in Table 15-9.

Table 15-9 Accumulation Operations

Operation	Description
GL_ACCUM	Add scaled color-buffer values to the accumulation buffer.
GL_LOAD	Load scaled color-buffer values into the accumulation buffer, replacing whatever had been there before.
GL_ADD	Add a constant color to the accumulation buffer's values.
GL_MULT	Multiply color values in the accumulation buffer by a constant color (filtering effects).
GL_RETURN	Copy the accumulation buffer into the main color buffer.

The normal way you use the accumulation buffer is to render multiple views into it and display the final composite scene with glAccum(GL_RETURN, 1.0).

Using the Accumulation Buffer for Motion Blur

As a coworker of ours once said, "It's *easy* to make any application of the accumulation buffer *look* like motion blur!" The problem is akin to what happens when your hands shake as you take a picture with a camera—too much jitter will blur the image.

You'll find that rendering motion blur is a little more complicated than just drawing a sequence of frames with the camera moving between each frame. We perceive motion blur when an object moves faster than our eyes can track it. In essence, the picture changes as the brain is "processing" the image, but the focus on the moving target is never lost. In a camera, light entering the lens exposes the film for a finite amount of time. Depending on the camera and photographer, the amount of blur seen may be small around the edges, or it could streak across the image.

When you simulate motion blur with computer graphics, it is important to remember that the current (or final) position of the object you are blurring *must* look more solid (or focused) than the rest of the frames. The easiest way to accomplish this is to use a larger color scaling factor when accumulating the current frame so that more of the color values from the final frame used will stand out from the rest. A typical implementation looks something like this:

```
/* Draw the current frame */
draw_frame(0);
/* Load the accumulation buffer with 50% of the current frame */
glAccum(GL_LOAD, 0.5);

/* Draw the last 10 frames and accumulate 5% for each */
for (i = 1; i <= 10; i ++)
{
  draw_frame(-i);
  glAccum(GL_ACCUM, 0.05);
};

/* Display the final scene */
glAccum(GL_RETURN, 1.0);
```

Notice that you don't have to use glClear to initialize the accumulation buffer contents, as you do with the color, depth, and stencil buffers. Instead, most often you'll use glAccum(GL_LOAD, s) on the first frame of the scene. The program in Listing 15-4 demonstrates motion blur on the cube and sphere.

Listing 15-4 MOTION.C: Motion blur using the accumulation buffer

```
/*
 * "motion.c" - A test program demonstrating the use of glAccum() for
 *              motion blur.
 */

#include <GL/glaux.h>
```

```
/*
 * These #define constants are provided for compatibility between MS Windows
 * and the rest of the world.
 *
 * CALLBACK and APIENTRY are function modifiers under MS Windows.
 */

#ifndef WIN32
#  define CALLBACK
#  define APIENTRY
#endif /* !WIN32 */

GLfloat rotation = 0.0;


/*
 * 'reshape_scene()' - Change the size of the scene...
 */

void CALLBACK
reshape_scene(GLsizei width,     /* I - Width of the window in pixels */
              GLsizei height)    /* I - Height of the window in pixels */
{
  /*
   * Reset the current viewport and perspective transformation...
   */

  glViewport(0, 0, width, height);

  glMatrixMode(GL_PROJECTION);
  glLoadIdentity();
  gluPerspective(22.5, (float)width / (float)height, 0.1, 1000.0);

  glMatrixMode(GL_MODELVIEW);
}


/*
 * 'draw_scene()' - Draw a scene containing a cube with a sphere in front of
 *                  it.
 */

void CALLBACK
draw_scene(void)
{
  GLfloat       frame;
  static float  red_light[4] = { 1.0, 0.0, 0.0, 1.0 };
  static float  red_pos[4]   = { 1.0, 1.0, 1.0, 0.0 };
  static float  blue_light[4] = { 0.0, 0.0, 1.0, 1.0 };
  static float  blue_pos[4]   = { -1.0, -1.0, -1.0, 0.0 };


  /*
   * Enable drawing features that we need...
   */

  glEnable(GL_DEPTH_TEST);
  glEnable(GL_LIGHTING);
```

continued on next page

continued from previous page

```
  glEnable(GL_LIGHT0);
  glEnable(GL_LIGHT1);

  glShadeModel(GL_SMOOTH);

 /*
  * Clear the color and depth buffers...
  */

  glClearColor(0.0, 0.0, 0.0, 0.0);
  glClear(GL_COLOR_BUFFER_BIT | GL_DEPTH_BUFFER_BIT);

 /*
  * Draw the cube and sphere in different colors...
  *
  * We have positioned two lights in this scene.  The first is red and
  * located above, to the right, and behind the viewer.  The second is blue
  * and located below, to the left, and in front of the viewer.
  */

  glLightfv(GL_LIGHT0, GL_DIFFUSE, red_light);
  glLightfv(GL_LIGHT0, GL_POSITION, red_pos);

  glLightfv(GL_LIGHT1, GL_DIFFUSE, blue_light);
  glLightfv(GL_LIGHT1, GL_POSITION, blue_pos);

 /*
  * Draw the objects 11 times starting at the current rotation...
  */

  for (frame = 0.0; frame <= 11.0; frame ++)
  {
    glPushMatrix();
      glTranslatef(0.0, 0.0, -20.0);
      glRotatef(rotation - frame, 0.0, 1.0, 0.0);

      glPushMatrix();
        glTranslatef(-1.0, 0.0, 0.0);
        auxSolidSphere(1.0);
      glPopMatrix();

      glPushMatrix();
        glTranslatef(1.0, 0.0, 0.0);
        glRotatef(15.0, 0.0, 1.0, 0.0);
        glRotatef(15.0, 0.0, 0.0, 1.0);
        auxSolidCube(2.0);
      glPopMatrix();
    glPopMatrix();

   /*
    * Accumulate 50% the first time, 5% every other time...
    */

    if (frame == 0.0)
      glAccum(GL_LOAD, 0.5);
    else
      glAccum(GL_ACCUM, 0.05);
  };
```

```
/*
 * Copy the accumulated results back to the color buffer...
 */

  glAccum(GL_RETURN, 1.0);

  auxSwapBuffers();
}


/*
 * 'rotate_objects()' - Rotate while we are idle...
 */

void CALLBACK
rotate_objects(void)
{
  rotation += 2.0;
  if (rotation >= 360.0)
    rotation -= 360.0;

  draw_scene();
}


/*
 * 'main()' - Initialize the window and display the scene until the user presses
 *            the ESCape key.
 */

int APIENTRY
WinMain(HINSTANCE hInstance,
        HINSTANCE hPrev,
        LPSTR     lpCmdLine,
        int       nCmdShow)
{
  auxInitDisplayMode(AUX_RGB | AUX_DOUBLE | AUX_DEPTH | AUX_ACCUM);
  auxInitWindow("Motion Blur");

  auxReshapeFunc(reshape_scene);
  auxIdleFunc(rotate_objects);

  auxMainLoop(draw_scene);
}


/*
 * End of "motion.c".
 */
```

Using the Accumulation Buffer for Anti-Aliasing

Another application of the accumulation buffer is full-scene anti-aliasing. The basic strategy is to jitter the image one-half a pixel in several directions, to blur the *edges* of an image but not the solid areas. Accumulating as little as four of these "jittered" scenes will produce remarkably smoother images. The Microsoft Visual C++ compiler includes many OpenGL examples that use jitter for anti-aliasing. See the file

OPENGL\BOOK\JITTER.H from the Visual C++ CD-ROM for many different sets of jitter values.

Anti-aliasing with the accumulation buffer does carry a price in speed, however. If you want to do any real-time anti-aliased animation, you'll have to look at graphics hardware that supports *multisampling* to do your anti-aliasing for you. The accumulation buffer is just too slow for interactive work.

If you are generating stills or stop-motion animations, the accumulation buffer will give you anti-aliasing and simulated depth-of-field that simply are not possible with multisampling.

Reference Section

GLAccum

Purpose	Operates on the accumulation buffer to establish pixel values.
Include File	<GL/gl.h>
Syntax	void glAccum(GLenum func, GLfloat value);
Description	This function operates on the accumulation buffer. Except for GL_RETURN, color values are scaled by the *value* parameter and added or stored into the accumulation buffer. For GL_RETURN, the accumulation buffer's color values are scaled by the *value* parameter and stored in the current color buffer.
Parameters	
func	GLenum: The accumulation function to apply. Valid functions are as follows:

GL_ACCUM	Add scaled color-buffer values to the accumulation buffer.
GL_LOAD	Load scaled color-buffer values into the accumulation buffer, replacing whatever was there before.
GL_ADD	Add a constant color to the accumulation buffer values.
GL_MULT	Multiply color values in the accumulation buffer by a constant color (filtering effects).
GL_RETURN	Copy the accumulation buffer into the main color buffer.

Returns	None.
Example	See the CH15\MOTION.C example on the source code CD-ROM.
See Also	ChoosePixelFormat, SetPixelFormat

GLClearColor

Purpose	Specifies a color value for the color buffer.
Include File	<GL/gl.h>

Syntax	void glClearColor(GLfloat red, GLfloat green, GLfloat blue, GLfloat alpha);
Description	This function sets the color value that will be used when clearing the color buffer with glClear(GL_COLOR_BUFFER_BIT).
Parameters	
red	GLfloat: The red color value for the color buffer.
green	GLfloat: The green color value for the color buffer.
blue	GLfloat: The blue color value for the color buffer.
alpha	GLfloat: The alpha color value for the color buffer.
Returns	None.
See Also	ChoosePixelFormat, SetPixelFormat

glClearDepth

Purpose	Specifies a depth value for the depth buffer.
Include File	<GL/gl.h>
Syntax	void glClearDepth(GLclampd depth);
Description	This function sets the depth value that will be used when clearing the depth buffer with glClear(GL_DEPTH_BUFFER_BIT).
Parameters	
depth	GLclampd: The clear value for the depth buffer.
Returns	None.
See Also	ChoosePixelFormat, SetPixelFormat

glClearIndex

Purpose	Specifies a color index value for the color buffer.
Include File	<GL/gl.h>
Syntax	void glClearIndex(GLfloat index);
Description	This function sets the color index value that will be used when clearing the color buffer with glClear(GL_COLOR_BUFFER_BIT).
Parameters	
index	GLfloat: The color index value for the color buffer.
Returns	None.
See Also	ChoosePixelFormat, SetPixelFormat

GLCLEARSTENCIL

Purpose	Specifies a stencil value for the stencil buffer.
Include File	<GL/gl.h>
Syntax	void glClearStencil(GLint value);
Description	This function sets the stencil value that will be used when clearing the stencil buffer with glClear(GL_STENCIL_BUFFER_BIT).
Parameters	
value	GLint: The clear value for the stencil buffer.
Returns	None.
See Also	ChoosePixelFormat, SetPixelFormat

GLDRAWBUFFER

Purpose	Selects a color buffer for drawing.
Include File	<GL/gl.h>
Syntax	void glDrawBuffer(GLenum mode);
Description	This function selects a color buffer for subsequent drawing operations. You will typically call it to select the front or back color-buffer in a double-buffered drawing context.
Parameters	
mode	GLenum: A constant (see Table 15-10) selecting the color buffer to draw into. For example, to select the back color-buffer for drawing, you would use:
	glDrawBuffer(GL_BACK)
Returns	None.
Known Bugs	The generic Microsoft implementation does not support stereo drawing buffers or *mode* value GL_NONE.
Example	See the CH15\DEPTHCUT.C example on the source code CD-ROM.
See Also	ChoosePixelFormat, SetPixelFormat

Table 15-10 Valid Modes for glDrawBuffer

Mode Value	Meaning
GL_NONE	Do not draw into any color buffer.
GL_FRONT	Draw into the front color buffer.
GL_BACK	Draw into the back color buffer (double-buffered contexts only).
GL_FRONT_AND_BACK	Draw into both the front and back color buffers (double-buffered contexts only).
GL_LEFT	Draw into the left-eye color buffer (stereo contexts only; selects front and back buffers when double-buffered).

Mode Value	Meaning
GL_RIGHT	Draw into the right-eye color buffer (stereo contexts only; selects front and back buffers when double-buffered).
GL_BACK_LEFT	Draw into the back color buffer for the left eye (stereo, double-buffered contexts only) .
GL_BACK_RIGHT	Draw into the back color buffer for the right eye (stereo, double-buffered contexts only).
GL_FRONT_LEFT	Draw into the front color buffer for the left eye (stereo, double-buffered contexts only).
GL_FRONT_RIGHT	Draw into the front color buffer for the right eye (stereo, double-buffered contexts only).

glDepthFunc

Purpose	Sets the depth test function.
Include File	<GL/gl.h>
Syntax	void glDepthFunc(GLenum func);
Description	This function sets the depth buffer test function for hidden surface removal.
Parameters	
func	GLenum: The depth buffer comparison function to use. Valid functions are as follows:

GL_NEVER	Always False
GL_LESS	True if source Z < depth Z
GL_EQUAL	True if source Z = depth Z
GL_LEQUAL	True if source Z <= depth Z
GL_GREATER	True if source Z > depth Z
GL_NOTEQUAL	True if source Z != depth Z
GL_GEQUAL	True if source Z >= depth Z
GL_ALWAYS	Always True

Returns	None.
Example	See the CH15\DEPTH.C example on the source code CD-ROM.
See Also	ChoosePixelFormat, SetPixelFormat

glDepthRange

Purpose	Sets the range of depth values in the depth buffer.
Include File	<GL/gl.h>
Syntax	void glDepthRange(GLclampd near, GLclampd far);
Description	This function sets the range of depth buffer values that will be used for depth comparisons for hidden surface removal. It is legal for *near* to be greater than *far*.

## CHAPTER 15

Parameters

near	GLclampd: the near depth value.
far	GLclampd: the far depth value.
Returns	None.
Example	See the CH15\DEPTH.C example on the source code CD-ROM.
See Also	ChoosePixelFormat, SetPixelFormat

16

VISUAL EFFECTS: BLENDING AND FOG

16

VISUAL EFFECTS: BLENDING AND FOG

What you'll learn in this chapter:

How to...	Functions You'll Use
Display transparent or translucent lines and polygons	glBlendFunc
Add weather haze and fog effects	glFog

This chapter introduces the color blending and fog functions provided by OpenGL, both of which can be used to add that last bit of realism you need.

The color blending functions support effects such as transparency that can be used to simulate windows, drink glasses, and other transparent objects. The fog functions add a variable amount of color to the polygons you draw, producing a scene that looks "hazy" or just downright dreary!

Something to remember when using these special effects is that they don't look good on an 8-bit display. Make sure your programs contain the option of disabling these effects when running on 8-bit displays.

Blending

Blending in OpenGL provides pixel-level control of RGBA color storage in the color buffer. Blending operations cannot be used in color index mode and are disabled in color index windows.

To enable blending in RGBA windows, you must first call glEnable(GL_BLEND). After this, you call glBlendFunc with two arguments: the source and the destination colors' blending functions (see Tables 16-1 and 16-2). By default, these arguments are GL_ONE and GL_ZERO, respectively, which is equivalent to glDisable(GL_BLEND).

Table 16-1 Blending Functions for Source Color

Function	Blend Factor
GL_ZERO	Source color = 0,0,0,0.
GL_ONE	Uses <?> Source color.
GL_DST_COLOR	Source color is multiplied by the destination pixel color.
GL_ONE_MINUS_DST_COLOR	Source color is multiplied by (1,1,1,1 − destination color).
GL_SRC_ALPHA	Source color multiplied by source alpha.
GL_ONE_MINUS_SRC_ALPHA	Source color multiplied by (1 − source alpha).
GL_DST_ALPHA	Source color multiplied by destination alpha; not supported by Microsoft OpenGL.
GL_ONE_MINUS_DST_ALPHA	Source color multiplied by (1 − destination alpha); not supported by Microsoft OpenGL.
GL_SRC_ALPHA_SATURATE	Source color multiplied by the minimum of the source and (1 − destination) alphas; not supported by Microsoft OpenGL.

Table 16-2 Blending Functions for Destination Color

Function	Blend Factor
GL_ZERO	Destination color = 0,0,0,0.
GL_ONE	Use <?> Destination color.
GL_SRC_COLOR	Destination color is multiplied by the source pixel color.
GL_ONE_MINUS_SRC_COLOR	Destination color is multiplied by (1,1,1,1 − source color).
GL_SRC_ALPHA	Destination color multiplied by source alpha.
GL_ONE_MINUS_SRC_ALPHA	Destination color multiplied by (1 − source alpha).
GL_DST_ALPHA	Destination color multiplied by destination alpha; not supported by Microsoft OpenGL.
GL_ONE_MINUS_DST_ALPHA	Destination color multiplied by (1 − destination alpha); not supported by Microsoft OpenGL.
GL_SRC_ALPHA_SATURATE	Destination color multiplied by the minimum of the source and (1 − destination) alphas; not supported by Microsoft OpenGL.

Using Blending for Transparency

Transparency is perhaps the most typical use of blending, often used for windows, bottles, and other 3D objects that you can see through. Transparency can also be used to combine multiple images, or for "soft" brushes in a paint program.

Following are the blending functions for all of these applications:

```
glEnable(GL_BLEND);
glBlendFunc(GL_SRC_ALPHA, GL_ONE_MINUS_SRC_ALPHA);
```

This combination takes the source color and scales it based on the alpha component, and then adds the destination pixel color scaled by 1 minus the alpha value. Stated more simply, this blending function takes a fraction of the current drawing color and overlays it on the pixel on the screen. The alpha component of the color can be from 0 (completely transparent) to 1 (completely opaque), as follows:

```
Rd = Rs * As + Rd * (1 - As)
Gd = Gs * As + Gd * (1 - As)
Bd = Bs * As + Bd * (1 - As)
```

Because only the *source* alpha component is used, you do not need a graphics board that supports alpha color planes in the color buffer. This is important because the standard Microsoft OpenGL implementation does not support alpha color planes.

Something to remember with alpha-blended transparency is that the normal depth-buffer test can interfere with the effect you're trying to achieve. To make sure that your transparent polygons and lines are drawn properly, always draw them from back to front.

Listing 16-1 shows the code that was used to draw the transparent teapot in Figure 16-1. In the draw_scene function, we draw the two teapots from back to front to ensure that the rear teapot can be seen through the front one. You'll notice some artifacts remain visible in the front teapot where the surface polygons intersect. You can't eliminate these completely, but you can reduce them by sorting the polygons by depth first and enabling back-face culling with glEnable(GL_CULL_FACE).

The first thing draw_scene does is set the blending function to do transparency based on the drawing (source) color's alpha component:

```
glBlendFunc(GL_SRC_ALPHA, GL_ONE_MINUS_SRC_ALPHA);
```

Figure 16-1 Transparent teapot using blending

Next, the opaque teapot is drawn with blending disabled so that we can always see the teapot through the transparent one:

```
glDisable(GL_BLEND);
glColor3f(1.0, 1.0, 0.0);
auxSolidTeapot(1.0);
```

Finally, blending is enabled and the transparent teapot is drawn with an alpha (transparency) value of 0.25:

```
glEnable(GL_BLEND);
glColor4f(1.0, 1.0, 1.0, 0.25);
auxSolidTeapot(1.0);
```

Listing 16-1 BLENDPOT.C: Using glBlendFunc for transparency

```
/*
 * "blendpot.c" - A test program demonstrating the use of glBlendFunc() for
 *                transparency.
 */

#include <GL/glaux.h>

/*
 * These #define constants are provided for compatibility between MS Windows
 * and the rest of the world.
 *
 * CALLBACK and APIENTRY are function modifiers under MS Windows.
 */

#ifndef WIN32
#   define CALLBACK
#   define APIENTRY
#endif /* !WIN32 */

GLfloat rotation = 0.0;


/*
 * 'reshape_scene()' - Change the size of the scene...
 */

void CALLBACK
reshape_scene(GLsizei width,    /* I - Width of the window in pixels */
              GLsizei height)   /* I - Height of the window in pixels */
{
  /*
   * Reset the current viewport and perspective transformation...
   */

  glViewport(0, 0, width, height);

  glMatrixMode(GL_PROJECTION);
  glLoadIdentity();
  gluPerspective(22.5, (float)width / (float)height, 0.1, 1000.0);

  glMatrixMode(GL_MODELVIEW);
}
```

```
/*
 * 'draw_scene()' - Draw a scene containing a cube with a sphere in front of
 *                  it.
 */

void CALLBACK
draw_scene(void)
{
  GLfloat      frame;
  static float red_light[4] = { 1.0, 0.0, 0.0, 1.0 };
  static float red_pos[4] = { 1.0, 1.0, 1.0, 0.0 };
  static float blue_light[4] = { 0.0, 0.0, 1.0, 1.0 };
  static float blue_pos[4] = { -1.0, -1.0, -1.0, 0.0 };


 /*
  * Enable drawing features that we need...
  */

  glEnable(GL_DEPTH_TEST);
  glEnable(GL_LIGHTING);
  glEnable(GL_LIGHT0);
  glEnable(GL_LIGHT1);

  glShadeModel(GL_SMOOTH);

 /*
  * Clear the color and depth buffers...
  */

  glClearColor(0.0, 0.0, 0.0, 0.0);
  glClear(GL_COLOR_BUFFER_BIT | GL_DEPTH_BUFFER_BIT);

 /*
  * Draw the cube and sphere in different colors...
  *
  * We have positioned two lights in this scene.  The first is red and
  * located above, to the right, and behind the viewer.  The second is blue
  * and located below, to the left, and in front of the viewer.
  */

  glLightfv(GL_LIGHT0, GL_DIFFUSE, red_light);
  glLightfv(GL_LIGHT0, GL_POSITION, red_pos);

  glLightfv(GL_LIGHT1, GL_DIFFUSE, blue_light);
  glLightfv(GL_LIGHT1, GL_POSITION, blue_pos);

  glEnable(GL_COLOR_MATERIAL);
  glBlendFunc(GL_SRC_ALPHA, GL_ONE_MINUS_SRC_ALPHA);

  glPushMatrix();
    glTranslatef(0.0, 0.0, -15.0);
    glRotatef(-rotation, 0.0, 1.0, 0.0);

    glDisable(GL_BLEND);
    glColor3f(1.0, 1.0, 0.0);
    auxSolidTeapot(1.0);
  glPopMatrix();
```

continued on next page

continued from previous page

```
  glPushMatrix();
    glTranslatef(0.0, 0.0, -10.0);
    glRotatef(rotation, 0.0, 1.0, 0.0);

    glEnable(GL_BLEND);
    glColor4f(1.0, 1.0, 1.0, 0.25);
    auxSolidTeapot(1.0);
  glPopMatrix();

  auxSwapBuffers();
}


/*
 * 'rotate_objects()' - Rotate while we are idle...
 */

void CALLBACK
rotate_objects(void)
{
  rotation += 2.0;
  if (rotation >= 360.0)
    rotation -= 360.0;

  draw_scene();
}


/*
 * 'main()' - Initialize the window and display the scene until the user presses
 *            the ESCape key.
 */

void
main(void)
{
  auxInitDisplayMode(AUX_RGB | AUX_DOUBLE | AUX_DEPTH);
  auxInitWindow("Blended Teapot");

  auxReshapeFunc(reshape_scene);
  auxIdleFunc(rotate_objects);

  auxMainLoop(draw_scene);
}


/*
 * End of "blendpot.c".
 */
```

Using Blending with Anti-Aliasing

The appearance of anti-aliased points, lines, and polygons can be enhanced by using the same two blending functions as for transparency, GL_SRC_ALPHA and GL_ONE_MINUS_SRC_ALPHA. On systems with hardware-assisted anti-aliasing and blending, blending will produce results similar to full-screen anti-aliased scenes made using the accumulation buffer. At the same time, blending is several times faster than accumulation because the scene needs to be drawn only once.

To draw a scene using blending and anti-aliased primitives, call the following functions:

```
glEnable(GL_BLEND);
glBlendFunc(GL_SRC_ALPHA, GL_ONE_MINUS_SRC_ALPHA);
glEnable(GL_LINE_SMOOTH);
glEnable(GL_POINT_SMOOTH);
glEnable(GL_POLYGON_SMOOTH);
```

Using Blending for a Paint Program

The same techniques used for 3D graphics can be applied to 2D graphics. In the case of paint programs, we can use blending to create soft-edged "brushes." To start, we will define *alpha images* of each brush. An alpha image contains alpha values but no RGB (color) values and will define how much color actually is drawn on the page (see Figure 16-2).

To "paint" using this brush image, we're going to use a different set of blending functions:

```
glBlendFunc(GL_SRC_COLOR, GL_ONE_MINUS_SRC_ALPHA);
```

Instead of the GL_SRC_ALPHA function for the source color, we use the GL_SRC_COLOR function, which uses the current color instead of the alpha component. Thus, the color that will be applied is as follows:

```
R = Rs * Ab + Rd * (1.0 - Ab)
G = Gs * Ab + Gd * (1.0 - Ab)
B = Bs * Ab + Bd * (1.0 - Ab)
```

That is, the alpha values from the brush image will be used instead of the current alpha color value!

Listing 16-2 is a simple "paint" program that uses a 7 x 7 pixel brush image for painting. The main event loop handles drawing in the window. When you hold the left

Figure 16-2 Alpha "brush" image

mouse button down, the event loop will call the DrawXY function to paint at the current mouse position:

```
glRasterPos2i(mousex, mousey);
glDrawPixels(7, 7, GL_LUMINANCE_ALPHA, GL_UNSIGNED_BYTE, BlendBrush[0]);
```

The RepaintWindow function clears the client area whenever the window is resized or needs to be redrawn:

```
glViewport(0, 0, rect->right, rect->bottom);
glOrtho(0.0, (float)rect->right, (float)rect->bottom, 0.0, -1.0, 1.0);

glClearColor(0.0, 0.0, 0.0, 1.0);
glClear(GL_COLOR_BUFFER_BIT);

glEnable(GL_BLEND);
glBlendFunc(GL_SRC_ALPHA, GL_ONE_MINUS_SRC_ALPHA);
```

Unfortunately, this means you'll lose your painting. A real paint application could use glReadPixels to copy the drawn pixels to an off-screen buffer, which could be used to redraw the screen later using glDrawPixels.

Listing 16-2 BLENDRAW.C: Paint program using glBlendFunc

```
/*
 * Include necessary headers.
 */

#include <windows.h>
#include <GL/gl.h>
#include "blendraw.h"
#include <stdarg.h>
#include <math.h>
#ifndef M_PI
#  define M_PI  (double)3.14159265358979323846
#endif /* !M_PI */


/*
 * Globals...
 */

HWND            BlendWindow;       /* Blend window */
HPALETTE        BlendPalette;      /* Color palette (if necessary) */
HDC             BlendDC;           /* Drawing context */
HGLRC           BlendRC;           /* OpenGL rendering context */

unsigned char   BlendBrush[7][16] =
{
  { 0xff, 0x00, 0xff, 0x00, 0xff, 0x08, 0xff, 0x10, 0xff, 0x08, 0xff, 0x00, 0xff, 0x00 },
  { 0xff, 0x00, 0xff, 0x08, 0xff, 0x10, 0xff, 0x20, 0xff, 0x10, 0xff, 0x08, 0xff, 0x00 },
  { 0xff, 0x08, 0xff, 0x10, 0xff, 0x20, 0xff, 0x40, 0xff, 0x20, 0xff, 0x10, 0xff, 0x08 },
  { 0xff, 0x10, 0xff, 0x20, 0xff, 0x40, 0xff, 0x80, 0xff, 0x40, 0xff, 0x20, 0xff, 0x10 },
  { 0xff, 0x08, 0xff, 0x10, 0xff, 0x20, 0xff, 0x40, 0xff, 0x20, 0xff, 0x10, 0xff, 0x08 },
  { 0xff, 0x00, 0xff, 0x08, 0xff, 0x10, 0xff, 0x20, 0xff, 0x10, 0xff, 0x08, 0xff, 0x00 },
  { 0xff, 0x00, 0xff, 0x00, 0xff, 0x08, 0xff, 0x10, 0xff, 0x08, 0xff, 0x00, 0xff, 0x00 },
};
```

```
GLboolean        Drawing = GL_FALSE;      /* GL_TRUE if drawing */


/*
 * Local functions...
 */

void                  DisplayErrorMessage(char *, ...);
void                  MakePalette(int);
LRESULT CALLBACK      BlendProc(HWND, UINT, WPARAM, LPARAM);
void                  DrawXY(int, int);
void                  RepaintWindow(RECT *);


/*
 * 'WinMain()' - Main entry...
 */

int APIENTRY
WinMain(HINSTANCE hInst,                /* I - Current process instance */
        HINSTANCE hPrevInstance,        /* I - Parent process instance */
        LPSTR     lpCmdLine,            /* I - Command-line arguments */
        int       nCmdShow)             /* I - Show window at startup? */
{
  MSG        msg;                       /* Window UI event */
  WNDCLASS   wc;                        /* Window class */
  POINT      pos;                       /* Current mouse pos */


 /*
  * Register main window...
  */

  wc.style         = 0;
  wc.lpfnWndProc   = (WNDPROC)BlendProc;
  wc.cbClsExtra    = 0;
  wc.cbWndExtra    = 0;
  wc.hInstance     = hInst;
  wc.hIcon         = NULL;
  wc.hCursor       = LoadCursor(NULL, IDC_ARROW);
  wc.hbrBackground = 0;
  wc.lpszMenuName  = MAKEINTRESOURCE(IDR_MENU1);
  wc.lpszClassName = "Blend Paint";

  if (RegisterClass(&wc) == 0)
  {
    DisplayErrorMessage("Unable to register window class!");
    return (FALSE);
  };

 /*
  * Then create it...
  */

  BlendWindow = CreateWindow("Blend Paint", "Blend Paint",
                             WS_OVERLAPPEDWINDOW | WS_CLIPCHILDREN | WS_CLIPSIBLINGS,
                             32, 32, 400, 300,
                             NULL, NULL, hInst, NULL);
```

continued on next page

continued from previous page

```
  if (BlendWindow == NULL)
  {
    DisplayErrorMessage("Unable to create window!");
    return (FALSE);
  };

  ShowWindow(BlendWindow, nCmdShow);
  UpdateWindow(BlendWindow);

 /*
  * Loop on events until the user quits this application...
  */

  while (GetMessage(&msg, NULL, 0, 0))
  {
    TranslateMessage(&msg);
    DispatchMessage(&msg);
  };

  return (msg.wParam);
}


/*
 * 'DisplayErrorMessage()' - Display an error message dialog.
 */

void
DisplayErrorMessage(char *format,        /* I - printf() style format string */
                    ...)                 /* I - Other arguments as necessary */
{
  va_list       ap;                      /* Argument pointer */
  char          s[1024];                 /* Output string */


  if (format == NULL)
    return;

  va_start(ap, format);
  vsprintf(s, format, ap);
  va_end(ap);

  MessageBeep(MB_ICONEXCLAMATION);
  MessageBox(NULL, s, "Error", MB_OK | MB_ICONEXCLAMATION);
}


/*
 * 'MakePalette()' - Make a color palette for RGB colors if necessary.
 */

void
MakePalette(int pf)                      /* I - Pixel format ID */
{
  PIXELFORMATDESCRIPTOR pfd;             /* Pixel format information */
  LOGPALETTE            *pPal;           /* Pointer to logical palette */
  int                   nColors;         /* Number of entries in palette */
  int                   i,               /* Color index */
                        rmax,            /* Maximum red value */
```

```
                     gmax,            /* Maximum green value */
                     bmax;            /* Maximum blue value */


/*
 * Find out if we need to define a color palette...
 */

DescribePixelFormat(BlendDC, pf, sizeof(PIXELFORMATDESCRIPTOR), &pfd);

if (!(pfd.dwFlags & PFD_NEED_PALETTE))
{
  BlendPalette = NULL;
  return;
};

/*
 * Allocate memory for a color palette...
 */

nColors = 1 << pfd.cColorBits;

pPal = (LOGPALETTE *)malloc(sizeof(LOGPALETTE) + nColors * sizeof(PALETTEENTRY));

pPal->palVersion    = 0x300;
pPal->palNumEntries = nColors;

/*
 * Get the maximum values for red, green, and blue.  Then build 'nColors'
 * colors...
 */

rmax = (1 << pfd.cRedBits) - 1;
gmax = (1 << pfd.cGreenBits) - 1;
bmax = (1 << pfd.cBlueBits) - 1;

for (i = 0; i < nColors; i ++)
{
  pPal->palPalEntry[i].peRed   = 255 * ((i >> pfd.cRedShift) & rmax) / rmax;
  pPal->palPalEntry[i].peGreen = 255 * ((i >> pfd.cGreenShift) & gmax) / gmax;
  pPal->palPalEntry[i].peBlue  = 255 * ((i >> pfd.cBlueShift) & bmax) / bmax;

  pPal->palPalEntry[i].peFlags = 0;
};

/*
 * Create, select, and realize the palette...
 */

BlendPalette = CreatePalette(pPal);
SelectPalette(BlendDC, BlendPalette, FALSE);
RealizePalette(BlendDC);

free(pPal);
}


/*
 * 'BlendProc()' - Handle window events in the viewing window.
 */
```

continued on next page

continued from previous page

```
LRESULT CALLBACK
BlendProc(HWND   hWnd,          /* I - Window triggering this event */
          UINT   uMsg,          /* I - Message type */
          WPARAM wParam,        /* I - 'word' parameter value */
          LPARAM lParam)        /* I - 'long' parameter value */
{
  int                    pf;    /* Pixel format ID */
  PIXELFORMATDESCRIPTOR  pfd;   /* Pixel format information */
  PAINTSTRUCT            ps;    /* WM_PAINT message info */
  RECT                   rect;  /* Current client area rectangle */


  switch (uMsg)
  {
    case WM_CREATE :
      /*
       * 'Create' message.  Get device and rendering contexts, and
       * setup the client area for OpenGL drawing...
       */

        BlendDC = GetDC(hWnd);

        pfd.nSize        = sizeof(pfd);
        pfd.nVersion     = 1;
        pfd.dwFlags      = PFD_DRAW_TO_WINDOW | PFD_SUPPORT_OPENGL;
                                         /* Do OpenGL drawing */
        pfd.dwLayerMask  = PFD_MAIN_PLANE;    /* Main drawing plane */
        pfd.iPixelType   = PFD_TYPE_RGBA;     /* RGB color buffer */
        pfd.cColorBits   = 0;                 /* Best color buffer please */
        pfd.cDepthBits   = 0;                 /* Don't need a depth buffer */
        pfd.cStencilBits = 0;                 /* No stencil buffer */
        pfd.cAccumBits   = 0;                 /* No accumulation buffer */

        pf = ChoosePixelFormat(BlendDC, &pfd);
        if (pf == 0)
          DisplayErrorMessage("texscene was unable to choose a suitable pixel format!");
        else if (!SetPixelFormat(BlendDC, pf, &pfd))
          DisplayErrorMessage("texscene was unable to set the pixel format!");

        MakePalette(pf);

        BlendRC = wglCreateContext(BlendDC);
        wglMakeCurrent(BlendDC, BlendRC);
        break;

    case WM_SIZE :
    case WM_PAINT :
      /*
       * Repaint the client area with our bitmap...
       */

        BeginPaint(hWnd, &ps);

        GetClientRect(hWnd, &rect);
        RepaintWindow(&rect);

        EndPaint(hWnd, &ps);
        break;
```

```
case WM_COMMAND :
    /*
     * Handle menu selections...
     */

    switch (LOWORD(wParam))
    {
      case IDM_FILE_EXIT :
          DestroyWindow(BlendWindow);
          break;
    };
    break;

case WM_QUIT :
case WM_CLOSE :
    /*
     * Destroy the windows and bitmaps and exit...
     */

    DestroyWindow(BlendWindow);

    exit(0);
    break;

case WM_DESTROY :
    /*
     * Release and free the device context, rendering
     * context, and color palette...
     */

    if (BlendRC)
      wglDeleteContext(BlendRC);

    if (BlendDC)
      ReleaseDC(BlendWindow, BlendDC);

    if (BlendPalette)
      DeleteObject(BlendPalette);

    PostQuitMessage(0);
    break;

case WM_QUERYNEWPALETTE :
    /*
     * Realize the color palette if necessary...
     */

    if (BlendPalette)
    {
      SelectPalette(BlendDC, BlendPalette, FALSE);
      RealizePalette(BlendDC);

      InvalidateRect(hWnd, NULL, FALSE);
      return (TRUE);
    };
    break;

case WM_PALETTECHANGED:
```

continued on next page

continued from previous page

```
      /*
       * Reselect our color palette if necessary...
       */

      if (BlendPalette && (HWND)wParam != hWnd)
      {
        SelectPalette(BlendDC, BlendPalette, FALSE);
        RealizePalette(BlendDC);

        UpdateColors(BlendDC);
      };
      break;

  case WM_LBUTTONDOWN :        /* Left button = red */
      Drawing = GL_TRUE;
      glColorMask(GL_TRUE, GL_FALSE, GL_FALSE, GL_TRUE);
      DrawXY(LOWORD(lParam), HIWORD(lParam));
      break;

  case WM_MBUTTONDOWN :        /* Middle button = green */
      Drawing = GL_TRUE;
      glColorMask(GL_FALSE, GL_TRUE, GL_FALSE, GL_TRUE);
      DrawXY(LOWORD(lParam), HIWORD(lParam));
      break;

  case WM_RBUTTONDOWN :        /* Right button = blue */
      Drawing = GL_TRUE;
      glColorMask(GL_FALSE, GL_FALSE, GL_TRUE, GL_TRUE);
      DrawXY(LOWORD(lParam), HIWORD(lParam));
      break;

  case WM_MOUSEMOVE :
      if (Drawing)
        DrawXY(LOWORD(lParam), HIWORD(lParam));
      break;

  case WM_LBUTTONUP :
  case WM_MBUTTONUP :
  case WM_RBUTTONUP :
      Drawing = GL_FALSE;
      break;

  default :
      /*
       * Pass all other messages through the default window
       * procedure...
       */

      return (DefWindowProc(hWnd, uMsg, wParam, lParam));
  };

  return (FALSE);
}


/*
 * 'DrawXY()' - Draw at the given mouse position.
 */
```

```
void
DrawXY(int mousex,              /* I - Horizontal mouse position */
       int mousey)             /* I - Vertical mouse position */
{
  glRasterPos2i(mousex, mousey);
  glDrawPixels(7, 7, GL_LUMINANCE_ALPHA, GL_UNSIGNED_BYTE, BlendBrush[0]);

  glFinish();
}


/*
 * 'RepaintWindow()' - Redraw the client area.
 */

void
RepaintWindow(RECT *rect)        /* I - Client area rectangle */
{
 /*
  * Reset the viewport and clear the window to white...
  */

  glViewport(0, 0, rect->right, rect->bottom);
  glOrtho(0.0, (float)rect->right, (float)rect->bottom, 0.0, -1.0, 1.0);

  glClearColor(0.0, 0.0, 0.0, 1.0);
  glColorMask(GL_TRUE, GL_TRUE, GL_TRUE, GL_TRUE);
  glClear(GL_COLOR_BUFFER_BIT);

  glEnable(GL_BLEND);
  glBlendFunc(GL_SRC_ALPHA, GL_ONE_MINUS_SRC_ALPHA);

  glFinish();
}
```

Fog

OpenGL provides depth-cueing (shading based upon distance) and atmospheric effects through the *glFog* function. Essentially, fog provides a way of adding (*mixing*) a predefined color with each vertex or texture image based upon the distance from the user. Fog is often used in flight simulators and animation packages to provide the final real-world look to computer graphics.

OpenGL supports three kinds of fog: GL_LINEAR for depth-cueing, GL_EXP for heavy fog or clouds, and GL_EXP2 for smoke and weather haze. Figure 16-3 shows GL_LINEAR fog; later, in Figure 16-5, you can see the effect of GL_EXP fog.

You choose the type of fog (or fog mode) using glFogi:

```
glFogi(GL_FOG_MODE, GL_LINEAR);
```

```
glFogi(GL_FOG_MODE, GL_EXP);
```

```
glFogi(GL_FOG_MODE, GL_EXP2);
```

Once you have chosen the fog type, you must choose a fog color that will be mixed with your scene using the glFogfv or glFogiv functions:

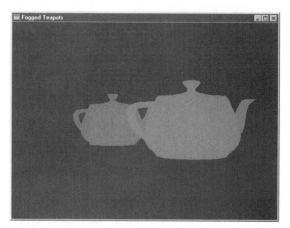

Figure 16-3 Depth-cued teapots using glFog

```
GLfloat fog_color[4] = { r, g, b, a };
glFogfv(GL_FOG_COLOR, fog_color);

GLint fog_color[4] = { r, g, b, a };
glFogiv(GL_FOG_COLOR, fog_color);
```

For depth-cueing, you'll generally want to make the fog color the same as the background (black, in Figure 16-3). This will make the depth-cueing look "correct" to the eye—that is, objects farther away will appear to fade into the background. For some applications, you might want to give the fog a bright color such as yellow, instead, so that things stand out more against the background.

Drawing Depth-Cued Teapots

Listing 16-3 draws two teapots using depth-cueing. The draw_scene function handles all graphics drawing and starts by setting the fog color to black and the fog mode to GL_LINEAR.

```
static float    fog_color[4] = { 0.0, 0.0, 0.0, 0.0 };

glEnable(GL_FOG);
glFogf(GL_FOG_MODE, GL_LINEAR);
glFogfv(GL_FOG_COLOR, fog_color);
```

Finally, it draws both teapots at different distances from the viewer. The results are visibly obvious.

Listing 16-3 FOGPOT.C: Depth-cued teapots using glFog

```
#include <GL/glaux.h>

/*
 * These #define constants are provided for compatibility between MS Windows
 * and the rest of the world.
```

```
 *
 * CALLBACK and APIENTRY are function modifiers under MS Windows.
 */

#ifndef WIN32
#   define CALLBACK
#   define APIENTRY
#endif /* !WIN32 */

GLfloat rotation = 0.0;


/*
 * 'reshape_scene()' - Change the size of the scene...
 */

void CALLBACK
reshape_scene(GLsizei width,     /* I - Width of the window in pixels */
              GLsizei height)    /* I - Height of the window in pixels */
{
 /*
  * Reset the current viewport and perspective transformation...
  */

  glViewport(0, 0, width, height);

  glMatrixMode(GL_PROJECTION);
  glLoadIdentity();
  gluPerspective(22.5, (float)width / (float)height, 0.1, 1000.0);

  glMatrixMode(GL_MODELVIEW);
}


/*
 * 'draw_scene()' - Draw a scene containing a cube with a sphere in front of
 *                  it.
 */

void CALLBACK
draw_scene(void)
{
  static float  red_light[4] = { 1.0, 0.0, 0.0, 1.0 };
  static float  red_pos[4] = { 1.0, 1.0, 1.0, 0.0 };
  static float  blue_light[4] = { 0.0, 0.0, 1.0, 1.0 };
  static float  blue_pos[4] = { -1.0, -1.0, -1.0, 0.0 };
  static float  fog_color[4] = { 0.0, 0.0, 0.0, 0.0 };


 /*
  * Enable drawing features that we need...
  */

  glEnable(GL_DEPTH_TEST);
  glEnable(GL_LIGHTING);
  glEnable(GL_LIGHT0);
  glEnable(GL_LIGHT1);

  glShadeModel(GL_SMOOTH);
```

continued on next page

continued from previous page

```
  /*
   * Clear the color and depth buffers...
   */

  glClearColor(0.0, 0.0, 0.0, 0.0);
  glClear(GL_COLOR_BUFFER_BIT | GL_DEPTH_BUFFER_BIT);

  /*
   * Draw the cube and sphere in different colors...
   *
   * We have positioned two lights in this scene.  The first is red and
   * located above, to the right, and behind the viewer.  The second is blue
   * and located below, to the left, and in front of the viewer.
   */

  glLightfv(GL_LIGHT0, GL_DIFFUSE, red_light);
  glLightfv(GL_LIGHT0, GL_POSITION, red_pos);

  glLightfv(GL_LIGHT1, GL_DIFFUSE, blue_light);
  glLightfv(GL_LIGHT1, GL_POSITION, blue_pos);

  glEnable(GL_COLOR_MATERIAL);

  glEnable(GL_FOG);
  glFogf(GL_FOG_MODE, GL_LINEAR);
  glFogfv(GL_FOG_COLOR, fog_color);

  glPushMatrix();
    glTranslatef(-1.0, 0.0, -15.0);
    glRotatef(-rotation, 0.0, 1.0, 0.0);

    glColor3f(1.0, 1.0, 0.0);
    auxSolidTeapot(1.0);
  glPopMatrix();

  glPushMatrix();
    glTranslatef(1.0, 0.0, -10.0);
    glRotatef(rotation, 0.0, 1.0, 0.0);

    glColor3f(0.0, 1.0, 1.0);
    auxSolidTeapot(1.0);
  glPopMatrix();

  auxSwapBuffers();
}


/*
 * 'rotate_objects()' - Rotate while we are idle...
 */

void CALLBACK
rotate_objects(void)
{
  rotation += 2.0;
  if (rotation >= 360.0)
    rotation -= 360.0;

  draw_scene();
}
```

```
/*
 * 'main()' - Initialize the window and display the scene until the user presses
 *            the ESCape key.
 */

void
main(void)
{
  auxInitDisplayMode(AUX_RGB | AUX_DOUBLE | AUX_DEPTH);
  auxInitWindow("Fogged Teapots");

  auxReshapeFunc(reshape_scene);
  auxIdleFunc(rotate_objects);

  auxMainLoop(draw_scene);
}
```

Other Types of Fog

For the other fog types, you'll probably make the fog color white or some other light color. In addition to the fog color, GL_EXP and GL_EXP2 fog types have an additional density parameter:

```
glFogf(GL_FOG_DENSITY, density);
```

The density parameter can be any number greater than 0.0, but typically you'll keep it less than 0.1. Figure 16-4 shows how the density of fog affects how much of the fog color is used.

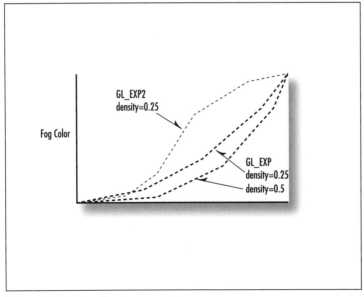

Figure 16-4 Fog density over distance

Fog Distance

The fog *distance* is the transformed Z component of all glVertex calls. This Z coordinate lies in the range 0.0 to 1.0 and is the same number that is stored in the depth buffer. The fog distance and density determine how much fog color is mixed in, as shown here:

$$f_{exp} = e^{-(densityz)}$$

$$f_{exp2} = e^{-(densityz)^2}$$

$$f_{linear} = \frac{end - z}{end - start}$$

By default, fog is applied at all depths from 0.0 to 1.0. The GL_FOG_START and GL_FOG_END parameters restrict the range of depth values used for fog calculations. This is typically used to more accurately model fog density when the immediate area in front of the viewer is not covered (for example, when flying through clouds, the breaks between clouds will not be as dense).

Revisiting the Terrain Viewing Program

Weather haze effects are the perfect addition to the terrain viewing program of Chapter 12. In Figure 16-5 you can see the fantastic improvement in image quality. This was achieved by adding the following three lines of code:

```
glFogf(GL_FOG_DENSITY, 0.0025);
glFogi(GL_FOG_MODE, GL_EXP);
glFogfv(GL_FOG_COLOR, fogcolor);
```

The fog color in this case was defined as a solid white RGBA color (1.0, 1.0, 1.0, 1.0). To improve the output even more at the expense of speed, we can also call

```
glHint(GL_FOG_HINT, GL_NICEST);
```

This forces fog to be evaluated at every *pixel* rather than every *vertex*. Unfortunately, for most scenes this means 100 times as many calculations must be performed! Now here is Listing 16-4, with the updated RepaintWindow function.

Figure 16-5 Weather haze using glFog

Listing 16-4 FOGSCENE.C: Updated RepaintWindow function using glFog for the terrain viewing program

```
/*
 * 'RepaintWindow()' - Redraw the client area with our scene.
 */

void
RepaintWindow(RECT *rect)        /* I - Client area rectangle */
{
  int           i;               /* Looping var */
  int           x, y;            /* Terrain (x,y) location */
  int           last_type;       /* Previous terrain type */
  int           *type;           /* Current terrain type */
  GLfloat       *height,         /* Current terrain height */
                (*n)[3];         /* Current terrain normal */
  static GLfloat        sky_top[4][3] =
  {                              /* Sky coordinates */
    { -TERRAIN_EDGE, TERRAIN_SIZE * 0.8, -TERRAIN_EDGE },
    {  TERRAIN_EDGE, TERRAIN_SIZE * 0.8, -TERRAIN_EDGE },
    {  TERRAIN_EDGE, TERRAIN_SIZE * 0.8,  TERRAIN_EDGE },
    { -TERRAIN_EDGE, TERRAIN_SIZE * 0.8,  TERRAIN_EDGE }
  };
  static GLfloat        sky_bottom[4][3] =
  {
```

continued on next page

continued from previous page

```
      { -TERRAIN_EDGE, 0.0, -TERRAIN_EDGE },
      {  TERRAIN_EDGE, 0.0, -TERRAIN_EDGE },
      {  TERRAIN_EDGE, 0.0,  TERRAIN_EDGE },
      { -TERRAIN_EDGE, 0.0,  TERRAIN_EDGE }
    };
    static GLfloat        sunpos[4] = { 0.0, 1.0, 0.0, 0.0 };
    static GLfloat        suncolor[4] = { 64.0, 64.0, 64.0, 1.0 };
    static GLfloat        sunambient[4] = { 0.001, 0.001, 0.001, 1.0 };
    static GLfloat        fogcolor[4] = { 1.0, 1.0, 1.0, 1.0 };


  /*
   * Reset the viewport and clear the window to light blue...
   */

  glViewport(0, 0, rect->right, rect->bottom);

  glClearColor(0.5, 0.5, 1.0, 1.0);

  glEnable(GL_DEPTH_TEST);
  glEnable(GL_FOG);
  glFogf(GL_FOG_DENSITY, 0.0025);
  glFogi(GL_FOG_MODE, GL_EXP);
  glFogfv(GL_FOG_COLOR, fogcolor);

  if (Moving || Drawing)
  {
   /*
    * Don't texture while flying or drawing; it's too slow...
    * Also, draw to the back buffer for smooth animation.
    */

    glDisable(GL_TEXTURE_2D);
    glDrawBuffer(GL_BACK);
  }
  else
  {
   /*
    * Enable textures when we've stopped moving or drawing.
    * This generates a nice scene that we can print out or
    * save to a bitmap file...
    *
    * Because it takes longer, we draw to the front buffer
    * so the user can see some progress...
    */

    glEnable(GL_TEXTURE_2D);
    glTexEnvi(GL_TEXTURE_ENV, GL_TEXTURE_ENV_MODE, GL_DECAL);
    glDrawBuffer(GL_FRONT);
  };

  glClear(GL_COLOR_BUFFER_BIT | GL_DEPTH_BUFFER_BIT);

  /*
   * Setup viewing transformations for the current position and
   * orientation...
   */

  glMatrixMode(GL_PROJECTION);
```

```
glLoadIdentity();
gluPerspective(45.0, (float)rect->right / (float)rect->bottom,
               0.1, 1000.0);

glMatrixMode(GL_MODELVIEW);
glPushMatrix();
  glRotatef(Roll, 0.0, 0.0, 1.0);
  glRotatef(Pitch, -1.0, 0.0, 0.0);
  glRotatef(Heading, 0.0, 1.0, 0.0);
  glTranslatef(-Position[0],
               -Position[1],
               -Position[2]);
  glScalef(TERRAIN_SCALE, TERRAIN_SCALE, TERRAIN_SCALE);

  if (!(Moving || Drawing))
  {
   /*
    * Draw the sky...
    */

    glDisable(GL_LIGHTING);
    glCallList(SkyTexture);
    glBegin(GL_QUAD_STRIP);
      for (i = 0; i < 4; i ++)
      {
        glTexCoord2f((float)i, 0.0);
        glVertex3fv(sky_bottom[i]);

        glTexCoord2f((float)i, 0.8);
        glVertex3fv(sky_top[i]);
      };

      glTexCoord2f(4.0, 0.0);
      glVertex3fv(sky_bottom[0]);

      glTexCoord2f(4.0, 0.8);
      glVertex3fv(sky_top[0]);
    glEnd();

    glBegin(GL_TRIANGLE_FAN);
      glTexCoord2f(0.5, 1.0);
      glVertex3f(0.0, TERRAIN_SIZE, 0.0);

      for (i = 0; i < 4; i ++)
      {
        glTexCoord2f((float)i, 0.8);
        glVertex3fv(sky_top[i]);
      };

      glTexCoord2f(4.0, 0.8);
      glVertex3fv(sky_top[0]);
    glEnd();
  };

 /*
  * Setup lighting...
  */

  glEnable(GL_LIGHTING);
```

continued on next page

continued from previous page

```
    glLightModeli(GL_LIGHT_MODEL_TWO_SIDE, GL_TRUE);

    glEnable(GL_LIGHT0);
    glLightfv(GL_LIGHT0, GL_POSITION, sunpos);
    glLightfv(GL_LIGHT0, GL_DIFFUSE, suncolor);
    glLightfv(GL_LIGHT0, GL_AMBIENT, sunambient);

    if (Moving || Drawing)
      glEnable(GL_COLOR_MATERIAL);
    else
      glDisable(GL_COLOR_MATERIAL);

   /*
    * Then the terrain...
    */

    type   = TerrainType[0];
    height = TerrainHeight[0];
    n      = TerrainNormal[0];
    for (y = 0; y < (TERRAIN_SIZE - 1); y ++)
    {
      last_type = -1;

      for (x = 0; x < TERRAIN_SIZE; x ++, type ++, height ++, n ++)
      {
        if (last_type != *type)
        {
         /*
          * If the type of terrain changes, end any existing
          * strip of quads and reset color/texture parameters...
          */

          if (last_type != -1)
            glEnd();

          switch (*type)
          {
            case IDC_WATER :
                if (Moving || Drawing)
                  glColor3f(0.0, 0.0, 0.5);
                else
                  glCallList(WaterTexture);
                break;
            case IDC_GRASS :
                if (Moving || Drawing)
                  glColor3f(0.0, 0.5, 0.0);
                else
                  glCallList(GrassTexture);
                break;
            case IDC_ROCKS :
                if (Moving || Drawing)
                  glColor3f(0.25, 0.25, 0.25);
                else
                  glCallList(RocksTexture);
                break;
            case IDC_TREES :
                if (Moving || Drawing)
                  glColor3f(0.0, 0.25, 0.0);
                else
```

```
                      glCallList(TreesTexture);
                  break;
              case IDC_MOUNTAINS :
                  if (Moving || Drawing)
                    glColor3f(0.2, 0.1, 0.05);
                  else
                    glCallList(MountainsTexture);
                  break;
            };

            glBegin(GL_QUAD_STRIP);
            if (last_type != -1)
            {
             /*
              * Start from the previous location to prevent
              * holes...
              */

             glTexCoord2i(x * 2 - 2, y * 2);
             glNormal3fv(n[-1]);
             glVertex3f((GLfloat)(x - TERRAIN_EDGE - 1),
                        height[-1],
                        (GLfloat)(y - TERRAIN_EDGE));
             glTexCoord2i(x * 2 - 2, y * 2 + 2);
             glNormal3fv(n[TERRAIN_SIZE - 1]);
             glVertex3f((GLfloat)(x - TERRAIN_EDGE - 1),
                        height[TERRAIN_SIZE - 1],
                        (GLfloat)(y - TERRAIN_EDGE + 1));
            };

            last_type = *type;
          };

          glTexCoord2i(x * 2, y * 2);
          glNormal3fv(n[0]);
          glVertex3f((GLfloat)(x - TERRAIN_EDGE),
                     height[0],
                     (GLfloat)(y - TERRAIN_EDGE));
          glTexCoord2i(x * 2, y * 2 + 2);
          glNormal3fv(n[TERRAIN_SIZE]);
          glVertex3f((GLfloat)(x - TERRAIN_EDGE),
                     height[TERRAIN_SIZE],
                     (GLfloat)(y - TERRAIN_EDGE + 1));
        };

        glEnd();
      };
  glPopMatrix();

 /*
  * While we fly or draw we're double-buffering.  Swap buffers
  * as necessary...
  */

  glFinish();
  if (Moving || Drawing)
    SwapBuffers(SceneDC);
}
```

Summary

Blending and fog complete the OpenGL library and are yet another source for making the images you generate more realistic. Blending provides transparency effects and improves anti-aliasing of points, lines, and polygons. Fog supports a variety of depth-cueing and weather effects that make images look *less* exact and, ironically, more like the real world.

Reference Section

GLBLENDFUNC

Purpose	Sets color blending functions.
Include File	<GL/gl.h>
Syntax	void glBlendFunc(GLenum sfactor, GLenum dfactor);
Description	This function sets the source and destination blending factors for color blending. You must call glEnable(GL_BLEND) to enable color blending. Blending is only available in RGBA drawing contexts. The default settings for blending are glBlendFunc(GL_ONE, GL_ZERO).
Parameters	
sfactor	GLenum: The source color's blending function.
dfactor	GLenum: The destination pixel color's blending function.
Returns	None.
Example	See the example in CH16\BLENDPOT.C on the CD.

GLFOG

Purpose	Specifies fog parameters.
Include File	<GL/gl.h>
Syntax	void glFogf(GLenum pname, GLfloat param);
	void glFogfv(GLenum pname, GLfloat *params);
	void glFogi(GLenum pname, GLint param);
	void glFogiv(GLenum pname, GLint *params);
Description	The *glFog* functions set fog parameters. To draw using fog you must call glEnable(GL_FOG).
Parameters	
pname	GLenum: The parameter to set. Valid names are as follows:
	GL_FOG_COLOR The color of the fog; must be an array of 4 numbers representing the RGBA color.

GL_FOG_DENSITY	The fog density; a number greater than 0.0. The density is only used for the GL_EXP and GL_EXP2 fog modes.
GL_FOG_END	The farthest distance to which the fog is applied. This is a transformed Z (depth) value from 0.0 to 1.0.
GL_FOG_INDEX	The color index to use for fog if the OpenGL drawing context is in color index mode.
GL_FOG_MODE	The fog type; specifies the formula used to render fog effects (GL_LINEAR, GL_EXP, or GL_EXP2).
GL_FOG_START	The closest distance to which fog is applied. This is a transformed Z (depth) value from 0.0 to 1.0.

param	GLfloat, GLint: The parameter value.
params	GLfloat *, GLint *: A pointer to the parameter array.
Returns	None.
Example	See the example in CH16\FOGSCENE.C on the CD.

17

CURVES AND SURFACES: WHAT THE #%@!&* ARE NURBS?

17

CURVES AND SURFACES: WHAT THE #%@!&* ARE NURBS?

What you'll learn in this chapter:

How to...	Functions You'll Use
Use maps to render Bézier curves and surfaces	glMap, glEvalCoord
Use evaluators to simplify surface mapping	glMapGrid, glEvalMesh
Create NURBS surfaces	gluNewNurbsRenderer, gluBeginSurface, gluNurbsSurface, gluEndSurface, gluDeleteNurbsRenderer
Create trimming curves	gluBeginTrim, gluPwlCurve, gluEndTrim

For most applications that make use of 3D graphics, you'll need smooth curves and surfaces. Making use of the techniques discussed elsewhere in this book, you could divide such a surface into many smaller quads or triangles, then calculate the normals at the various vertices, and apply lighting—producing what appears to be a very smooth and flowing surface. Or, with little more than basic algebra you could even write code that evaluates an equation for a surface and uses something like triangle strips or quads to generate a surface with either a fine or coarse visual resolution.

Suppose, however, you want to create a curve or surface and you don't have an algebraic equation to start with. It's far from a trivial task to figure it out in reverse, starting from what you visualize as the end result and working down to a second- or third-order polynomial. Taking a rigorous mathematical approach is time consuming and error prone, even with the aid of a computer. And forget about doing it in your head.

Recognizing this fundamental need in the art of computer-generated graphics, Pierre Bézier, an automobile designer for Renault in the 1970s, created a set of mathematical models that could represent curves and surfaces by specifying only a small set of control points. In addition to simplifying the representation of curved surfaces, the models facilitated interactive adjustments to the shape of the curve or surface..

Other types of curves and surfaces, and indeed a whole new vocabulary for computer-generated surfaces soon evolved. The mathematics behind this magic show are no more complex than the matrix manipulations in Chapter 7, and an intuitive understanding of these curves is easy to grasp. As we did in Chapter 7, we will take the approach that you can do a lot with these functions without a deep understanding of their mathematics.

Curves and Surfaces

A curve has a single starting point, a length, and an endpoint. It's really just a line that squiggles about in 3D space. A surface, on the other hand, has width and length and thus a surface area. We'll begin by showing you how to draw some smooth curves in 3D space, and then extend this to surfaces. But first let's establish some common vocabulary and math fundamentals.

Parametric Representation

When you think of straight lines, you may think of this famous equation:

$$Y = mX + b$$

Here m equals the slope of the line, and b is the Y intercept of the line (the place where the line crosses the y-axis). This may take you back to your eighth-grade algebra class, where you also learned about the equations for parabolas, hyperbolas, exponential curves, and so on. All of these equations expressed Y (or X) in terms of some function of X (or Y).

Another way of expressing the equation for a curve or line is as a *parametric equation*. A parametric equation expresses both X and Y in terms of another variable that varies across some predefined range of values, that is not explicitly a part of the geometry of the curve. Sometimes in physics, for example, the X, Y, and Z coordinates of a particle may be in terms of some functions of time, where time is expressed in seconds. In the following, f(), g(), and h() are unique functions that vary with time (t):

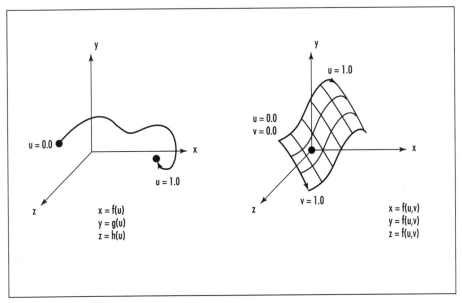

Figure 17-1 Parametric representations of curves and surfaces

$$X = f(t)$$
$$Y = g(t)$$
$$Z = h(t)$$

When we define a curve in OpenGL, we will also define it as a parametric equation. The parametric parameter of the curve, which we'll call u, and its range of values will be the domain of that curve. Surfaces will be described using two parametric parameters: u and v. Figure 17-1 shows both a curve and a surface defined in terms of u and v domains. The important thing to realize here is that the parametric parameters (u and v) represent the extents of the equations that describe the curve; they do not reflect actual coordinate values.

Control Points

Curves are represented by a number of control points that influence the shape of the curve. For the Bézier curves, the first and last control points are actually part of the curve. The other control points act as magnets, pulling the curve towards them. Figure 17-2 shows some examples of this concept, with varying numbers of control points.

The *order* of the curve is represented by the number of control points used to describe its shape. The *degree* is one less than the order of the curve. The mathematical meaning of these terms pertains to the parametric equations that exactly describe the curve, with the order being the number of coefficients, and the degree being the highest exponent of the parametric parameter. If you want to read more about the mathematical basis of Bézier curves, see Appendix B.

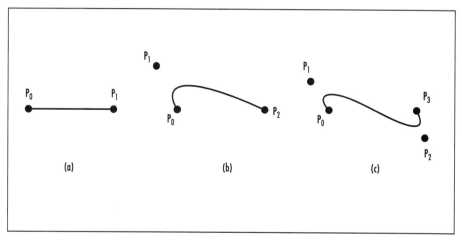

Figure 17-2 How control points affect curve shape

The curve in Figure 17-2(b) is called a quadratic curve (degree 2), and Figure 17-2(c) is called a cubic (degree 3). Cubic curves are the most typical. Theoretically, you could define a curve of any order, but higher-order curves start to oscillate uncontrollably and can vary wildly with the slightest change to the control points.

Continuity

If two curves placed side by side share an endpoint (called the *breakpoint*), they together form a piecewise curve. The *continuity* of these curves at this breakpoint describes how smooth the transition is between them. The four categories of continuity are none (C0), positional (C1), tangential (C2), and curvature (C3).

As you can see in Figure 17-3, no continuity is when the two curves don't meet at all. Positional continuity is achieved when the curves at least meet and share a common endpoint. Tangential continuity occurs when the two curves have the same tangent at the breakpoint. Finally, curvature continuity means the two curves' tangents also have the same rate of change at the breakpoint (thus an even smoother transition).

When assembling complex surfaces or curves from many pieces, you will usually strive for C2 or C3 continuity. You'll see later that some parameters for curve and surface generation can be chosen to produce the desired continuity.

Evaluators

OpenGL contains several functions that make it very easy to draw Bézier curves and surfaces by specifying the control points and the range for the parametric u and v parameters. Then, by calling the appropriate evaluation function (the evaluator), the points that make up the curve or surface are generated. We'll start with a 2D example of a Bézier curve and then extend this to three dimensions to create a Bézier surface.

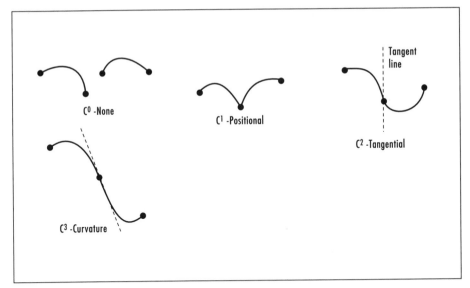

Figure 17-3 Continuity of piecewise curves

A 2D Curve

The best way to get started is with an example, explaining it line by line. Listing 17-1 shows some code from the example program BEZIER in this chapter's subdirectory on the CD. This program specifies four control points for a Bézier curve and then renders the curve using an evaluator. The output from Listing 17-1 is shown in Figure 17-4.

Listing 17-1 Code from BEZIER that draws a Bézier curve with four control points

```
// The number of control points for this curve
GLint nNumPoints = 4;

GLfloat ctrlPoints[4][3]= {{  -4.0f, 0.0f, 0.0f},      // Endpoint
                           { -6.0f, 4.0f, 0.0f},      // Control Point
                           {  6.0f, -4.0f, 0.0f},  // Control Point
                           {  4.0f, 0.0f, 0.0f }}; // Endpoint
...
...

// This function is used to superimpose the control points over the curve
void DrawPoints(void)
        {
        int i;  // Counting variable

        // Set point size larger to make more visible
        glPointSize(5.0f);

        // Loop through all control points for this example
        glBegin(GL_POINTS);
                for(i = 0; i < nNumPoints; i++)
```

continued on next page

continued from previous page

```
                                glVertex2fv(ctrlPoints[i]);
        glEnd();
        }


// Change viewing volume and viewport.  Called when window is resized
void ChangeSize(GLsizei w, GLsizei h)
        {
        // Prevent a divide by zero
        if(h == 0)
                h = 1;

        // Set Viewport to window dimensions
        glViewport(0, 0, w, h);
        glMatrixMode(GL_PROJECTION);
        glLoadIdentity();

        gluOrtho2D(-10.0f, 10.0f, -10.0f, 10.0f);

        // Modelview matrix reset
        glMatrixMode(GL_MODELVIEW);
        glLoadIdentity();
        }

// Called to draw scene
void RenderScene(void)
        {
        int i;

        // Clear the window with current clearing color
        glClear(GL_COLOR_BUFFER_BIT);

        // Sets up the Bézier
        // This actually only needs to be called once and could go in
        // the setup function
        glMap1f(GL_MAP1_VERTEX_3,       // Type of data generated
        0.0f,                           // Lower u range
        100.0f,                         // Upper u range
        3,                              // Distance between points in the data
        nNumPoints,                     // Number of control points
        &ctrlPoints[0][0]);             // Array of control points

        // Enable the evaluator
        glEnable(GL_MAP1_VERTEX_3);

        // Use a line strip to "connect the dots"
        glBegin(GL_LINE_STRIP);
                for(i = 0; i <= 100; i++)
                        {
                        // Evaluate the curve at this point
                        glEvalCoord1f((GLfloat) i);
                        }
        glEnd();

        // Draw the Control Points
        DrawPoints();

        // Flush drawing commands
        glFlush();
        }
```

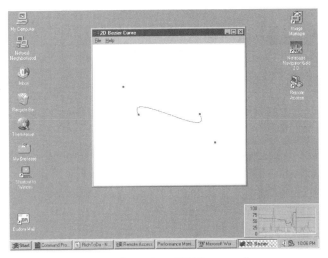

Figure 17-4 Output from the BEZIER example program

The first thing we do in Listing 17-1 is define the control points for our curve:

```
// The number of control points for this curve
GLint nNumPoints = 4;

GLfloat ctrlPoints[4][3]= {{  -4.0f, 0.0f, 0.0f},      // Endpoint
                           { -6.0f, 4.0f, 0.0f},      // Control Point
                           {  6.0f, -4.0f, 0.0f},     // Control Point
                           {  4.0f, 0.0f, 0.0f }};    // Endpoint
```

We defined global variables for the number of control points and the array of control points. To experiment, you can change these by adding more control points, or just modifying the position of these points.

The function DrawPoints() is pretty straightforward. We call this function from our rendering code to display the control points along with the curve. This also is very useful when you are experimenting with control-point placement. Our standard ChangeSize() function establishes a 2D orthographic projection that spans from –10 to +10 in the x and y directions.

Finally, we get to the rendering code. The function RenderScene() first calls glMap1f (after clearing the screen) to create a mapping for our curve:

```
// Called to draw scene
void RenderScene(void)
        {
        int i;

        // Clear the window with current clearing color
        glClear(GL_COLOR_BUFFER_BIT);

        // Sets up the Bézier
        // This actually only needs to be called once and could go in
        // the setup function
```

continued on next page

continued from previous page

```
glMap1f(GL_MAP1_VERTEX_3,    // Type of data generated
0.0f,                        // Lower u range
100.0f,                      // Upper u range
3,                           // Distance between points in the data
nNumPoints,                  // Number of control points
&ctrlPoints[0][0]);          // Array of control points
...
...
```

The first parameter to glMap1f, GL_MAP1_VERTEX_3, sets up the evaluator to generate vertex coordinate triplets (x, y, and z), as opposed to GL_MAP1_VERTEX_4 which would generate the coordinates and an alpha component. You can also have the evaluator generate other values, such as texture coordinates and color information. See the Reference Section for details.

The next two parameters specify the lower and upper bounds of the parametric u value for this curve. The lower value specifies the first point on the curve, and the upper value specifies the last point on the curve. All the values in between correspond to the other points along the curve. Here we set the range to 0–100.

The fourth parameter to glMap1f specifies the number of floating point values between the vertices in the array of control points. Each vertex consists of three floating point values (for x, y, and z), so we set this value to 3. This flexibility allows the control points to be placed in an arbitrary data structure, as long as they occur at regular intervals.

The last parameter is a pointer to a buffer containing the control points used to define the curve. Here, we pass a pointer to the first element of the array. Once the mapping for the curve is created, we enable the evaluator to make use of this mapping. This is maintained through a state variable, and the following function call is all that is needed to enable the evaluator to produce points along the curve:

```
// Enable the evaluator
glEnable(GL_MAP1_VERTEX_3);
```

The function glEvalCoord1f takes a single argument: a parametric value along the curve. This function then evaluates the curve at this value and calls glVertex internally for that point. By looping through the domain of the curve and calling glEvalCoord to produce vertices, we can draw the curve with a simple line strip:

```
// Use a line strip to "connect the dots"
glBegin(GL_LINE_STRIP);
        for(i = 0; i <= 100; i++)
            {
            // Evaluate the curve at this point
            glEvalCoord1f((GLfloat) i);
            }
glEnd();
```

Finally, we wish to display the control points themselves:

```
// Draw the Control Points
DrawPoints();

// Flush drawing commands
glFlush();
}
```

Evaluating a Curve

OpenGL can make things even easier than this. We set up a grid with the function glMapGrid, which tells OpenGL to create an evenly spaced grid of points over the u domain (the parametric argument of the curve). Then we call glEvalMesh to "connect the dots" using the primitive specified (GL_LINE or GL_POINTS). The following two function calls:

```
// Use higher level functions to map to a grid, then evaluate the
// entire thing.

// Map a grid of 100 points from 0 to 100
glMapGrid1d(100,0.0,100.0);

// Evaluate the grid, using lines
glEvalMesh1(GL_LINE,0,100);
```

completely replace this code:

```
// Use a line strip to "connect-the-dots"
glBegin(GL_LINE_STRIP);
        for(i = 0; i <= 100; i++)
                {
                // Evaluate the curve at this point
                glEvalCoord1f((GLfloat) i);
                }
glEnd();
```

As you can see, this is more compact and efficient, but its real benefit comes when evaluating surfaces rather than curves.

A 3D Surface

Creating a 3D Bézier surface is much like the 2D version. In addition to defining points along the u domain, we must define them along the v domain as well.

Listing 17-2 is from our next example program, BEZ3D, and displays a wire mesh of a 3D Bézier surface. The first change from the preceding example is that we have defined three more sets of control points for the surface along the v domain. To keep this surface simple, the control points are the same except for the Z value. This will create a uniform surface, as if we simply extruded a 2D Bézier along the Z axis.

Listing 17-2 BEZ3D code to create a Bézier surface

```
// The number of control points for this curve
GLint nNumPoints = 3;

GLfloat ctrlPoints[3][3][3]= {{{  -4.0f, 0.0f, 4.0f},          // V = 0
                    { -2.0f, 4.0f, 4.0f},
                    {  4.0f, 0.0f, 4.0f }},

                    {{  -4.0f, 0.0f, 0.0f},          // V = 1
                    { -2.0f, 4.0f, 0.0f},
                    {  4.0f, 0.0f, 0.0f }},
```

continued on next page

continued from previous page

```
                                    {{ -4.0f, 0.0f, -4.0f},      // V = 2
                                     { -2.0f, 4.0f, -4.0f},
                                     {  4.0f, 0.0f, -4.0f }}};
...
...

// Called to draw scene
void RenderScene(void)
        {
        //int i;

        // Clear the window with current clearing color
        glClear(GL_COLOR_BUFFER_BIT);

        // Save the modelview matrix stack
        glMatrixMode(GL_MODELVIEW);
        glPushMatrix();

        // Rotate the mesh around to make it easier to see
        glRotatef(45.0f, 0.0f, 1.0f, 0.0f);
        glRotatef(60.0f, 1.0f, 0.0f, 0.0f);

        // Sets up the Bézier
        // This actually only needs to be called once and could go in
        // the setup function
        glMap2f(GL_MAP2_VERTEX_3,     // Type of data generated
        0.0f,                         // Lower u range
        10.0f,                        // Upper u range
        3,                            // Distance between points in the data
        3,                            // Dimension in u direction (order)
        0.0f,                         // Lower v range
        10.0f,                        // Upper v range
        9,                            // Distance between points in the data
        3,                            // Dimension in v direction (order)
        &ctrlPoints[0][0][0]);        // array of control points

        // Enable the evaluator
        glEnable(GL_MAP2_VERTEX_3);

        // Use higher level functions to map to a grid, then evaluate the
        // entire thing.

        // Map a grid of 100 points from 0 to 100
        glMapGrid2f(10,0.0f,10.0f,10,0.0f,10.0f);

        // Evaluate the grid, using lines
        glEvalMesh2(GL_LINE,0,10,0,10);

        // Draw the Control Points
        DrawPoints();

        // Restore the modelview matrix
        glPopMatrix();

        // Flush drawing commands
        glFlush();
        }
```

Our rendering code is different now, too. In addition to rotating the figure for better effect, we call glMap2f instead of glMap1f. This specifies control points along two domains (u and v) instead of just one (u).

```
// Sets up the Bézier
// This actually only needs to be called once and could go in
// the setup function
glMap2f(GL_MAP2_VERTEX_3,        // Type of data generated
0.0f,                            // Lower u range
10.0f,                           // Upper u range
3,                               // Distance between points in the data
3,                               // Dimension in u direction (order)
0.0f,                            // Lower v range
10.0f,                           // Upper v range
9,                               // Distance between points in the data
3,                               // Dimension in v direction (order)
&ctrlPoints[0][0][0]);          // array of control points
```

We must still specify the lower and upper range for u; and the distance between points in the u domain is still 3. Now, however, we must also specify the lower and upper range in the v domain. The distance between points in the v domain is now 9 values, because we have a three-dimensional array of control points, with each span in the u domain being three points of three values each (3 x 3 = 9). Then we tell glMap2f how many points in the v direction are specified for each u division, followed by a pointer to the control points themselves.

The two-dimensional evaluator is enabled just like the one-dimensional one, and we call glMapGrid2f with the number of divisions in the u and v direction.

```
// Enable the evaluator
glEnable(GL_MAP2_VERTEX_3);

// Use higher level functions to map to a grid, then evaluate the
// entire thing.

// Map a grid of 10 points from 0 to 10
glMapGrid2f(10,0.0f,10.0f,10,0.0f,10.0f);
```

After the evaluator is set up, we can call the two-dimensional (meaning u and v) version of glEvalMesh to evaluate our surface grid. Here we evaluate using lines, and specify the u and v domains values to range from 0 to 10.

```
// Evaluate the grid, using lines
glEvalMesh2(GL_LINE,0,10,0,10);
```

The end result is shown in Figure 17-5.

Lighting and Normal Vectors

Another valuable features of evaluators is the automatic generation of surface normals. By simply changing this code:

```
// Evaluate the grid, using lines
glEvalMesh2(GL_LINE,0,10,0,10);
```

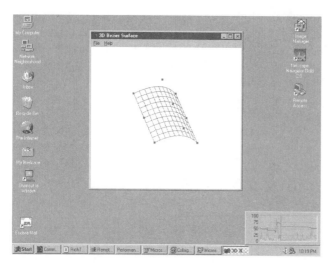

Figure 17-5 Output from the BEZ3D program

to this:

```
// Evaluate the grid, using lines
glEvalMesh2(GL_FILL,0,10,0,10);
```

and then calling

```
glEnable(GL_AUTO_NORMAL);
```

in our initialization code, we enable easy lighting of surfaces generated by evaluators. Figure 17-6 shows the same surface as Figure 17-5, but with lighting enabled and automatic normalization turned on. The code for this program is found in BEZLIT in the CD subdirectory for this chapter. The program is only slightly modified from BEZ3D.

NURBS

You can use evaluators to your heart's content to evaluate Bézier surfaces of any degree, but for more complex curves you will have to assemble your Bézier's piecewise. As you add more control points, it becomes difficult to create a curve that has good continuity. A higher level of control is available through the glu library's NURBS functions. NURBS stands for *non-uniform rational B-spline*. Mathematicians out there might know immediately that this is just a more generalized form of curves and surfaces that can produce Bézier curves and surfaces, as well as some other kinds (mathematically speaking). They allow you to tweak the influence of the control points you specified for the evaluators, to produce smoother curves and surfaces with larger numbers of control points.

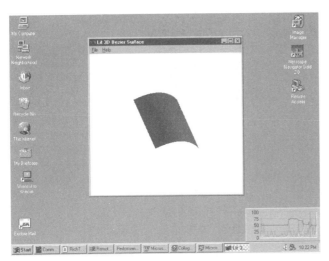

Figure 17-6 Output from BEZLIT program

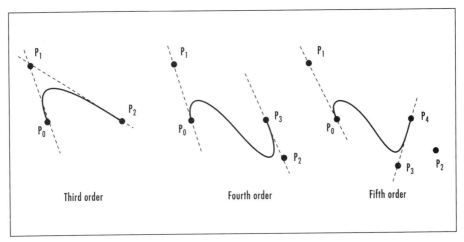

Figure 17-7 Bézier continuity as the order of the curve increases

From Bézier to B-Splines

A Bézier curve is defined by two points that act as endpoints, and any number of other control points that influence the shape of the curve. The three Bézier curves in Figure 17-7 have 3, 4, and 5 control points specified. The curve is tangent to a line that connects the endpoints with their adjacent control points. For quadratic (3 points) and cubic (4 points) curves, the resulting Béziers are quite smooth, usually with a continuity of C3 (curvature). For higher numbers of control points, however, the smoothness begins to break down as the additional control points pull and tug on the curve.

B-splines (bi-cubic splines), on the other hand, work much as the Bézier curves do, but the curve is broken down into segments. The shape of any given segment is influenced only by the nearest four control points, producing a piecewise assemblage of a curve with each segment exhibiting characteristics much like a fourth-order Bézier curve. This means a long curve with many control points is inherently smoother, with the junction between each segment exhibiting C3 continuity. It also means that the curve does not necessarily have to pass through any of the control points.

Knots

The real power of NURBS is that you can tweak the influence of the four control points for any given segment of a curve to produce the smoothness needed. This control is done via a sequence of values called *knots*.

Two knot values are defined for every control point. The range of values for the knots matches the u or v parametric domain, and must be nondescending. This is because the knot values determine the influence of the control points that fall within that range in u/v space. Figure 17-8 shows a curve demonstrating the influence of control points over a curve having four units in the u parametric domain. Points in the middle of the u domain have a greater pull on the curve, and only points between 0 and 3 have any effect on the shape of the curve.

The key here is that one of these influence curves exists at each control point along the u/v parametric domain. The knot sequence then defines the strength of the influ-

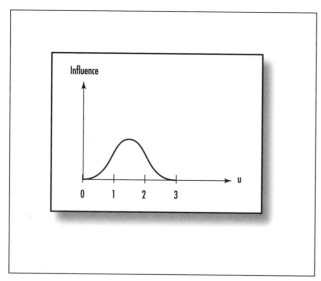

Figure 17-8 Control point influence along u parameter

ence of points within this domain. If a knot value is repeated, then points near this parametric value have even greater influence. The repeating of knot values is called *knot multiplicity*. Higher knot multiplicity decreases the curvature of the curve or surface within that region.

Creating a NURBS Surface

The glu NURBS functions provide a useful high-level facility for rendering surfaces. You don't have to explicitly call the evaluators or establish the mappings or grids. To render a NURBS, you first create a NURBS object that you will reference whenever you call the NURBS-related functions to modify the appearance of the surface or curve.

The function gluNewNurbsRenderer creates a renderer for the NURB, and gluDeleteNurbsRenderer destroys it. The following code fragments demonstrate these functions in use:

```
// NURBS object pointer
GLUnurbsObj *pNurb = NULL;
...
...

// Setup the NURBS object
    pNurb = gluNewNurbsRenderer();


...
// Do your NURBS things...
...
...

// Delete the NURBS object if it was created
if(pNurb)
        gluDeleteNurbsRenderer(pNurb);
```

NURBS Properties

Once you have created a NURBS renderer, you can set various high-level NURBS properties for the NURB, like this:

```
// Set sampling tolerance
gluNurbsProperty(pNurb, GLU_SAMPLING_TOLERANCE, 25.0f);

// Fill to make a solid surface (use GLU_OUTLINE_POLYGON to create a
// polygon mesh)
gluNurbsProperty(pNurb, GLU_DISPLAY_MODE, (GLfloat)GLU_FILL);
```

You will typically call these functions in your setup routine, rather than repeatedly in your rendering code. In this example, the GLU_SAMPLING_TOLERANCE defines how fine the mesh that defines the surface is, and GLU_FILL tells OpenGL to fill in the mesh instead of generating a wireframe.

Define the Surface

The surface definition is passed as arrays of control points and knot sequences to the gluNurbsSurface function. As shown here, this function is also bracketed by calls to gluBeginSurface and gluEndSurface:

```
// Render the NURB
// Begin the NURB definition
gluBeginSurface(pNurb);

// Evaluate the surface
gluNurbsSurface(pNurb,              // pointer to NURBS renderer
    8, Knots,                       // No. of knots and knot array u direction
    8, Knots,                       // No. of knots and knot array v direction
    4 * 3,                          // Distance between control points in u dir.
    3,                              // Distance between control points in v dir.
    &ctrlPoints[0][0][0],           // Control points
    4, 4,                           // u and v order of surface
    GL_MAP2_VERTEX_3);              // Type of surface

// Done with surface
gluEndSurface(pNurb);
```

You can make more calls to gluNurbsSurface to create any number of NURBS surfaces, but the properties you set for the NURBS renderer will still be in effect. Often this is desired, anyway—you rarely want two surfaces (perhaps joined) to have different fill styles (one filled, and one a wire mesh).

Using the control points and knot values shown in the next code segment, we produce the NURBS surface shown in Figure 17-9. This NURBS program is found in this chapter's subdirectory on the CD.

```
// Mesh extends four units -6 to +6 along x and y axis
// Lies in Z plane
//              u  v  (x,y,z)
GLfloat ctrlPoints[4][4][3]= {{{  -6.0f, -6.0f, 0.0f},          // u = 0,       v = 0
                              {   -6.0f, -2.0f, 0.0f}, //                       v = 1
                              {   -6.0f,  2.0f, 0.0f}, //                       v = 2
                              {   -6.0f,  6.0f, 0.0f}}, //                      v = 3

                             {{  -2.0f, -6.0f, 0.0f},          // u = 1         v = 0
                              {   -2.0f, -2.0f, 8.0f}, //                       v = 1
                              {   -2.0f,  2.0f, 8.0f}, //                       v = 2
                              {   -2.0f,  6.0f, 0.0f}}, //                      v = 3

                             {{   2.0f, -6.0f, 0.0f },          // u =2         v = 0
                              {    2.0f, -2.0f, 8.0f }, //                      v = 1
                              {    2.0f,  2.0f, 8.0f }, //                      v = 2
                              {    2.0f,  6.0f, 0.0f }}, //                     v = 3

                             {{   6.0f, -6.0f, 0.0f},          // u = 3         v = 0
                              {    6.0f, -2.0f, 0.0f}, //                       v = 1
                              {    6.0f,  2.0f, 0.0f}, //                       v = 2
                              {    6.0f,  6.0f, 0.0f}}}; //                     v = 3

// Knot sequence for the NURB
GLfloat Knots[8] = {0.0f, 0.0f, 0.0f, 0.0f, 1.0f, 1.0f, 1.0f, 1.0f};
```

Trimming

Trimming means creating cutout sections from NURBS surfaces. This is often used for literally trimming sharp edges of a NURBS surface. You can also create holes in your surface just as easily. The output from the NURBT program is shown in Figure 17-10.

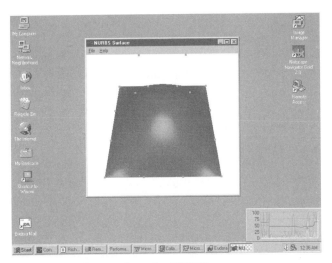

Figure 17-9 Output from the NURBS program

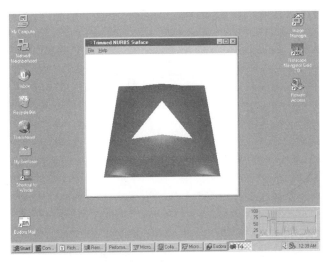

Figure 17-10 Output from the NURBT program

This is the same NURBS surface used in the preceding sample (without the control points shown), with a triangular region removed. This program, too, is on the CD.

Listing 17-3 is the code that was added to the NURBS example program to produce this trimming effect. Within the gluBeginSurface/gluEndSurface delimiters, we call gluBeginTrim and specify a trimming curve with gluPwlCurve, and finish the trimming curve with gluEndTrim.

Listing 17-3 Modifications to NURBS to produce trimming

```
// Outside trimming points to include entire surface
GLfloat outsidePts[5][2] = /* counter clockwise */
     {{0.0f, 0.0f}, {1.0f, 0.0f}, {1.0f, 1.0f}, {0.0f, 1.0f}, {0.0f, 0.0f}};

// Inside trimming points to create triangle shaped hole in surface
GLfloat insidePts[4][2] = /* clockwise */
    {{0.25f, 0.25f}, {0.5f, 0.5f}, {0.75f, 0.25f}, { 0.25f, 0.25f}};
...
...
...

// Render the NURB
// Begin the NURB definition
gluBeginSurface(pNurb);

// Evaluate the surface
gluNurbsSurface(pNurb,          // pointer to NURBS renderer
    8, Knots,                   // No. of knots and knot array u direction
    8, Knots,                   // No. of knots and knot array v direction
    4 * 3,                      // Distance between control points in u dir.
    3,                          // Distance between control points in v dir.
    &ctrlPoints[0][0][0],       // Control points
    4, 4,                       // u and v order of surface
    GL_MAP2_VERTEX_3);          // Type of surface

// Outer area, include entire curve
gluBeginTrim (pNurb);
gluPwlCurve (pNurb, 5, &outsidePts[0][0], 2, GLU_MAP1_TRIM_2);
gluEndTrim (pNurb);

// Inner triangluar area
gluBeginTrim (pNurb);
gluPwlCurve (pNurb, 4, &insidePts[0][0], 2, GLU_MAP1_TRIM_2);
gluEndTrim (pNurb);


// Done with surface
gluEndSurface(pNurb);
```

Within the gluBeginTrim/gluEndTrim delimiters, you can specify any number of curves as long as they form a closed loop in a piecewise fashion. You can also use gluNurbsCurve to define a trimming region or part of a trimming region. These trimming curves must, however, be in terms of the unit parametric u and v space. This means the entire u/v domain is scaled from 0.0 to 1.0.

The gluPwlCurve defines a piecewise linear curve—nothing more than a list of points connected end to end. In this scenario, the inner trimming curve forms a triangle, but with many points you could create an approximation of any curve needed.

Trimming a curve trims away surface area that is to the right of the curve's winding. Thus a clockwise-wound trimming curve will discard its interior. Typically an outer trimming curve is specified, which encloses the entire NURBS parameter space. Then smaller trimming regions are specified within this region with clockwise winding. Figure 17-11 illustrates this relationship.

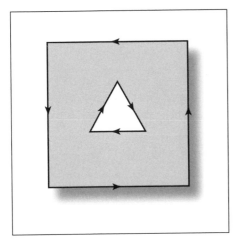

Figure 17-11 Area inside clockwise-wound curves is trimmed away

Summary

This chapter could easily have been the most intimidating in the entire book. As you have seen, however, the concepts that lie behind these curves and surfaces are not at all difficult to understand. Appendix B suggests further reading if you want in-depth mathematical information.

The examples from this chapter give you a good starting point for experimenting with NURBS. Try adjusting the control points and knot sequences to create warped or rumpled surfaces. Also try some quadratic surfaces and some with higher order than the cubic surfaces. Additional examples can also be found on the accompanying CD.

Watch out—one pitfall to avoid as you play with these curves is trying too hard to create one complex surface out of a single NURB. You'll find greater power and flexibility if you compose complex surfaces out of several smaller and easy-to-handle NURBS or Bézier surfaces.

Reference Section

GlEvalCoord

Purpose	Evaluates 1D and 2D maps that have been previously enabled.
Include File	<gl.h>
Variations	void **glEvalCoord1d**(GLdouble u);
	void **glEvalCoord1f**(GLfloat u);
	void **glEvalCoord2d**(GLdouble u, GLdouble v);
	void **glEvalCoord2f**(GLfloat u, GLfloat v);

void **glEvalCoord1dv**(const GLdouble *u);
void **glEvalCoord1fv**(const GLfloat *u);
void **glEvalCoord2dv**(const GLdouble *u);
void **glEvalCoord2fv**(const GLfloat *u);

Description   This function uses a previously enabled evaluator (set up with glMap) to produce vertex, color, normal, or texture values based on the parametric u/v values. The type of data and function calls simulated are specified by the glMap1 and glMap2 functions.

Parameters

u,v   These parameters specify the v and/or u parametric value that is to be evaluated along the curve or surface.

Returns   None.

Example   The following code from the BEZIER example program produces equivalent calls to glVertex3f each time glEvalCoord1f is called. The exact vertex produced is from the equation for the curve at the parametric value i.

```
// Use a line strip to "connect the dots"
glBegin(GL_LINE_STRIP);
        for(i = 0; i <= 100; i++)
                {
                // Evaluate the curve at this point
                glEvalCoord1f((GLfloat) i);
                }
glEnd();
```

See Also   glEvalMesh, glEvalPoint, glMap1, glMap2, glMapGrid

GLEVALMESH

Purpose   Computes a 1D or 2D grid of points or lines.
Include File   <gl.h>
Variations   void **glEvalMesh1**(GLenum mode, GLint i1, GLint i2);
                    void **glEvalMesh2**(GLenum mode, GLint i1, GLint i2, GLint j1, GLint j2);
Description   This function is used with glMapGrid to efficiently create a mesh of evenly spaced u and v domain values. glEvalMesh actually evaluates the mesh and produces the points, line segments, or filled polygons.

Parameters

mode   GLdouble: Specifies whether the mesh should be computed as points (GL_POINT), lines (GL_LINE), or filled meshes for surfaces (GL_FILL).

i1,i2   GLint: Specifies the first and last integer values for the u domain.

j1,j2   GLint: Specifies the first and last integer values for the v domain.

Returns   None.

Example   The following code from the BEZIER example program creates a grid map from 0 to 100 with 100 partitions. The call to glEvalMesh then evaluates the grid and draws line segments between each point on the curve.

```
// Use higher level functions to map to a grid, then evaluate the
// entire thing.

// Map a grid of 100 points from 0 to 100
glMapGrid1d(100,0.0,100.0);

// Evaluate the grid, using lines
glEvalMesh1(GL_LINE,0,100);
```

See Also   glBegin, glEvalCoord, glEvalPoint, glMap1, glMap2, glMapGrid

GLEVALPOINT

Purpose	Generates and evaluates a single point in a mesh.
Include File	<gl.h>
Variations	void **glEvalPoint1**(GLint i);
	void **glEvalPoint2**(GLint i, GLint j);
Description	This function can be used in place of glEvalMesh to evaluate a domain at a single point. The evaluation produces a single primitive, GL_POINTS. The first variation (glEvalPoint1) is used for curves, and the second (glEvalPoint2) is for surfaces.
Parameters	
i,j	GLint: Specifies the u and v domain parametric values.
Returns	None.
Example	The following code renders the Bézier curve in the example program BEZIER as a series of points rather than line segments. Here we have commented out the code that is no longer needed from the previous example for glEvalCoord.

```
// Use a line strip to "connect the dots"
// glBegin(GL_LINE_STRIP);
        for(i = 0; i <= 100; i++)
                {
                // Evaluate the curve at this point
                //glEvalCoord1f((GLfloat) i);
                glEvalPoint1(i);
                }
// glEnd();
```

See Also   glEvalCoord, glEvalMesh, glMap1, glMap2, glMapGrid

GLGETMAP

Purpose	Returns evaluator parameters.
Include File	<gl.h>
Variations	void **glGetMapdv**(GLenum target, GLenum query, GLdouble *v);
	void **glGetMapfv**(GLenum target, GLenum query, GLfloat *v);
	void **glGetMapiv**(GLenum target, GLenum query, GLint *v);

Description	This function retrieves map settings that were set by the glMap functions. See glMap1 and glMap2 in this section for explanations of the types of maps.
Parameters	
target	GLenum: The name of the map; the following maps are defined: GL_MAP1_COLOR_4, GL_MAP1_INDEX, GL_MAP1_NORMAL, GL_MAP1_TEXTURE_COORD_1, GL_MAP1_TEXTURE_COORD_2, GL_MAP1_TEXTURE_COORD_3, GL_MAP1_TEXTURE_COORD_4, GL_MAP1_VERTEX_3, GL_MAP1_VERTEX_4, GL_MAP2_COLOR_4 , GL_MAP2_INDEX, GL_MAP2_NORMAL, GL_MAP2_TEXTURE_COORD_1, GL_MAP2_TEXTURE_COORD_2, GL_MAP2_TEXTURE_COORD_3, GL_MAP2_TEXTURE_COORD_4, GL_MAP2_VERTEX_3, and GL_MAP2_VERTEX_4. See glMap in this section for an explanation of these map types.
query	GLenum: Specifies which map parameter to return in *v. May be one of the following values:
	GL_COEFF : Returns an array containing the control points for the map. Coordinates are returned in row-major order. 1D maps return order control points, and 2D maps return u-order times the v-order control points.
	GL_ORDER: Returns the order of the evaluator function. For 1D maps, this is a single value. For 2D maps, two values are returned (an array) that contain first the u-order, then the v-order.
	GL_DOMAIN: Returns the linear parametric mapping parameters. For 1D evaluators, this is the lower and upper u value. For 2D maps, it's lower and upper u followed by lower and upper v.
*v	Pointer to storage that will contain the requested parameter. The data type of this storage should match the function used (double, float, or integer).
Returns	None.
Example	The following code shows mapping parameters being designated and later retrieved (probably in another function). In comments we show the contents of the buffer.

```
glMap2f(GL_MAP2_VERTEX_3,      // Type of data generated
        0.0f,                  // Lower u range
        10.0f,                 // Upper u range
        3,                     // Distance between points in the data
        3,                     // Dimension in u direction (order)
        0.0f,                  // Lower v range
        10.0f,                 // Upper v range
        9,                     // Distance between points in the data
        3,                     // Dimension in v direction (order)
        &ctrlPoints[0][0][0]); // array of control points
```

```
   ...
   ...
   ...

float parametricRange[4];

glGetMapfv(GL_MAP2_VERTEX_3,GL_DOMAIN,parametricRange);

/* Now parametricRange[0] = 0.0                // Lower u
        parametricRange[1] = 10.0             // Upper u
        parametricRange[2] = 0.0              // Lower v
        parametricRange[3] = 10.0             // Upper v

*/
```

See Also   glEvalCoord, glMap1, glMap2

GLMAP

Purpose	Defines a 1D or 2D evaluator.
Include File	<gl.h>
Variations	void **glMap1d**(GLenum target, GLdouble u1, GLdouble u2, GLint ustride, GLint uorder, const GLdouble *points); void **glMap1f**(GLenum target, GLfloat u1, GLfloat u2, GLint ustride, GLint uorder, const GLfloat *points); void **glMap2d**(GLenum target, GLdouble u1, GLdouble u2, GLint ustride, GLint uorder, GLdouble v1, GLdouble v2, GLint vstride, GLint vorder, const GLdouble *points); void **glMap2f**(GLenum target, GLfloat u1, GLfloat u2, GLint ustride, GLint uorder, GLfloat v1, GLfloat v2, GLint vstride, GLint vorder, const GLfloat *points);
Description	These functions define 1D or 2D evaluators. The glMap1x functions are used for 1D evaluators (curves), and the glMap2x functions are used for 2D evaluators (surfaces). Evaluators produce vertex or other information (see the target parameter below) evaluated along one or two dimensions of a parametric range (u and v).
Parameters	
target	GLenum: Specifies what kind of values are produced by the evaluator. Valid values for 1D and 2D evaluators are as follows:

GL_MAP1_VERTEX_3 (or GL_MAP2_VERTEX_3): Control points are three floats that represent x, y, and z coordinate values. glVertex3 commands are generated internally when the map is evaluated.

GL_MAP1_VERTEX_4 (or GL_MAP2_VERTEX_4): Control points are four floats that represent x, y, z, and w coordinate values. glVertex4 commands are generated internally when the map is evaluated.

GL_MAP1_INDEX (or GL_MAP2_INDEX): The generated control points are single floats that represent a color index value. glIndex commands are generated internally when the map is evaluated. *Note:* The current color index is not changed as it would be if glIndex were called directly.

GL_MAP1_COLOR_4 (or GL_MAP2_COLOR_4): The generated control points are four floats that represent red, green, blue, and alpha components. glColor4 commands are generated internally when the map is evaluated. *Note:* The current color is not changed as it would be if glColor4f were called directly.

GL_MAP1_NORMAL (or GL_MAP2_NORMAL): The generated control points are three floats that represent the x, y, and z components of a normal vector. glNormal commands are generated internally when the map is evaluated. *Note:* The current normal is not changed as it would be if glNormal were called directly.

GL_MAP1_TEXTURE_COORD_1 (or GL_MAP2_TEXTURE_COORD_1): The generated control points are single floats that represent the s texture coordinate. glTexCoord1 commands are generated internally when the map is evaluated. *Note:* The current texture coordinates are not changed as they would be if glTexCoord were called directly.

GL_MAP1_TEXTURE_COORD_2 (or GL_MAP2_TEXTURE_COORD_2): The generated control points are two floats that represent the s and t texture coordinates. glTexCoord2 commands are generated internally when the map is evaluated. *Note:* The current texture coordinates are not changed as they would be if glTexCoord were called directly.

GL_MAP1_TEXTURE_COORD_3 (or GL_MAP2_TEXTURE_COORD_3): The generated control points are three floats that represent the s, t, and r texture coordinates. glTexCoord3 commands are generated internally when the map is evaluated. *Note:* The current texture coordinates are not changed as they would be if glTexCoord were called directly.

GL_MAP1_TEXTURE_COORD_4 (or GL_MAP2_TEXTURE_COORD_4): The generated control points are four floats that represent the s, t, r, and q texture coordinates. glTexCoord4 commands are generated internally when the map is evaluated. *Note:* The current texture coordinates are not changed as they would be if glTexCoord were called directly.

u1,u2	Specifies the linear mapping of the parametric u parameter.
v1,v2	Specifies the linear mapping of the parametric v parameter. This is only used for 2D maps.
ustride, vstride	Specifies the number of floats or doubles between control points in the *points* data structure. The coordinates for each point occupy consecutive memory locations, but this parameter allows the points to be spaced as needed to let the data come from an arbitrary data structure.
uorder, vorder	Specifies the number of control points in the u and v direction.

*points	A memory pointer that points to the control points. This may be a 2D or 3D array or any arbitrary data structure.
Returns	None.
Example	The following code is from the example program BEZ3D from this chapter. It establishes a quadratic Bézier spline mapping.

```
// The number of control points for this curve
GLint nNumPoints = 3;

GLfloat ctrlPoints[3][3][3]= {{{  -4.0f, 0.0f, 4.0f},
                               { -2.0f, 4.0f, 4.0f},
                               {  4.0f, 0.0f, 4.0f }},

                              {{  -4.0f, 0.0f, 0.0f},
                               { -2.0f, 4.0f, 0.0f},
                               {  4.0f, 0.0f, 0.0f }},

                              {{  -4.0f, 0.0f, -4.0f},
                               { -2.0f, 4.0f, -4.0f},
                               {  4.0f, 0.0f, -4.0f }}};

...
...


        // Sets up the Bézier
        // This actually only needs to be called once and could go in
        // the setup function
        glMap2f(GL_MAP2_VERTEX_3,     // Type of data generated
        0.0f,                         // Lower u range
        10.0f,                        // Upper u range
        3,                            // Distance between points in the data
        3,                            // Dimension in u direction (order)
        0.0f,                         // Lower v range
        10.0f,                        // Upper v range
        9,                            // Distance between points in the data
        3,                            // Dimension in v direction (order)
        &ctrlPoints[0][0][0]); // array of control points
```

See Also	glBegin, glColor, glEnable, glEvalCoord, glEvalMesh, glEvalPoint, glMapGrid, glNormal, glTexCoord, glVertex

GLMAPGRID

Purpose	Defines a 1D or 2D mapping grid.
Include File	<gl.h>
Variations	void **glMapGrid1d**(GLint un, GLdouble u1, GLdouble u2);
	void **glMapGrid1f**(GLint un, GLfloat u1, GLfloat u2);
	void **glMapGrid2d**(GLint un, GLdouble u1, GLdouble u2, GLint vn, GLdouble v1, GLdouble v2);

void **glMapGrid2f**(GLint un, GLfloat u1, GLfloat u2, GLint vn, GLfloat v1, GLfloat v2);

Description This function establishes a 1D or 2D mapping grid. This is used with glMap and glEvalMesh to efficiently evaluate a mapping and create a mesh of coordinates.

Parameters

un,vn GLint: Specifies the number of grid subdivisions in the u or v direction.

u1,u2 Specifies the lower and upper grid domain values in the u direction.

v1,v2 Specifies the lower and upper grid domain values in the v direction.

Returns None.

Example The following code from the BEZ3D example program shows a 3D Bézier mapping being established and a mesh being created and evaluated for it.

```
// Sets up the Bézier
// This actually only needs to be called once and could go in
// the setup function
glMap2f(GL_MAP2_VERTEX_3,      // Type of data generated
        0.0f,                  // Lower u range
        10.0f,                 // Upper u range
        3,                     // Distance between points in the data
        3,                     // Dimension in u direction (order)
        0.0f,                  // Lower v range
        10.0f,                 // Upper v range
        9,                     // Distance between points in the data
        3,                     // Dimension in v direction (order)
        &ctrlPoints[0][0][0]); // array of control points

// Enable the evaluator
glEnable(GL_MAP2_VERTEX_3);

// Use higher level functions to map to a grid, then evaluate the
// entire thing.

// Map a grid of 10 points from 0 to 10
glMapGrid2f(10,0.0f,10.0f,10,0.0f,10.0f);

// Evaluate the grid, using lines
glEvalMesh2(GL_LINE,0,10,0,10);
```

See Also glEvalCoord, glEvalMesh, glEvalPoint, glMap1, glMap2

GLU**B**EGIN**C**URVE

Purpose Begins a NURBS curve definition.

Include File <glu.h>

Syntax void gluBeginCurve(GLUnurbsObj *nObj);

Description This function is used with gluEndCurve to delimit a NURBS curve definition.

Parameters

nObj GLUnurbsObj: Specifies the NURBS object.

Returns	None.
Example	The following code from the example program NURBC from the CD demonstrates this function delimiting the NURBS curve definition.

```
// Render the NURB
// Begin the NURB definition
gluBeginCurve(pNurb);

// Evaluate the surface
gluNurbsCurve(pNurb,
8, Knots,
        3,
&ctrlPoints[0][0],
4,
GL_MAP1_VERTEX_3);

// Done with surface
gluEndCurve(pNurb);
```

See Also	gluEndCurve

GLUBEGINSURFACE

Purpose	Begins a NURBS surface definition.
Include File	<glu.h>
Syntax	void gluBeginSurface(GLUnurbsObj *nObj);
Description	This function is used with gluEndSurface to delimit a NURBS surface definition.
Parameters	
nObj	GLUnurbsObj: Specifies the NURBS object.
Returns	None.
Example	The following code from the example program NURBS from this chapter demonstrates this function delimiting the NURBS surface definition.

```
// Render the NURB
// Begin the NURB definition
gluBeginSurface(pNurb);

// Evaluate the surface
gluNurbsSurface(pNurb,
8, Knots,
8, Knots,
4 * 3,
3,
&ctrlPoints[0][0][0],
4, 4,
GL_MAP2_VERTEX_3);

// Done with surface
gluEndSurface(pNurb);
```

See Also	gluEndSurface

GLUBEGINTRIM

Purpose	Begins a NURBS trimming loop definition.
Include File	<glu.h>
Syntax	void gluBeginTrim(GLUnurbsObj *nObj);
Description	This function is used with gluEndTrim to delimit a trimming curve definition. A trimming curve is a curve or set of joined curves defined with gluNurbsCurve or gluPwlCurve. The gluBeginTrim and gluEndTrim functions must reside inside the gluBeginSurface/gluEndSurface delimiters. When you use trimming, the direction of the curve specifies which portions of the surface are trimmed. Surface area to the left of the traveling direction of the trimming curve is left untrimmed. Thus clockwise-wound trimming curves eliminate the area inside them, while counter clockwise-wound trimming curves eliminate the area outside them.
Parameters	
nObj	GLUnurbsObj: Specifies the NURBS object.
Returns	None.
Example	The following code from this chapter's NURBT example program shows two trimming curves being applied to a NURBS surface. The outer trimming curve includes the entire surface area. The inner curve is actually triangular in shape and creates a cut-away section in the surface.

```
// Render the NURB
// Begin the NURB definition
gluBeginSurface(pNurb);

// Evaluate the surface
gluNurbsSurface(pNurb,
        8, Knots,
        8, Knots,
        4 * 3,
        3,
        &ctrlPoints[0][0][0],
        4, 4,
        GL_MAP2_VERTEX_3);

// Outer area, include entire curve
gluBeginTrim (pNurb);
gluPwlCurve (pNurb, 5, &outsidePts[0][0], 2, GLU_MAP1_TRIM_2);
gluEndTrim (pNurb);

// Inner triangluar area
gluBeginTrim (pNurb);
gluPwlCurve (pNurb, 4, &insidePts[0][0], 2, GLU_MAP1_TRIM_2);
gluEndTrim (pNurb);
```

See Also	gluEndTrim

gluDeleteNurbsRenderer

Purpose	Destroys a NURBS object.
Include File	<glu.h>
Syntax	void gluDeleteNurbsRenderer(GLUnurbsObj *nobj);
Description	This function deletes the NURBS object specified and frees any memory associated with it.
Parameters	
nObj	GLUnurbsObj*: Specifies the NURBS object to delete.
Returns	None.
Example	Following is from the example program NURBS. It shows the NURBS object being deleted when the main window is destroyed. Note the pointer was initialized to NULL when the program begins, and thus is not deleted unless it was successfully created.

```
// Window is being destroyed, cleanup
case WM_DESTROY:
        // Deselect the current rendering context and delete it
        wglMakeCurrent(hDC,NULL);
        wglDeleteContext(hRC);

        // Delete the NURBS object if it was created
        if(pNurb)
                gluDeleteNurbsRenderer(pNurb);

        // Tell the application to terminate after the window
        // is gone.
        PostQuitMessage(0);
        break;
```

See Also	gluNewNurbsRenderer

gluEndCurve

Purpose	Ends a NURBS curve definition.
Include File	<glu.h>
Syntax	void gluEndCurve(GLUnurbsObj *nobj);
Description	This function is used with gluBeginCurve to delimit a NURBS curve definition.
Parameters	
nObj	GLUnurbsObj: Specifies the NURBS object.
Returns	None.
Example	See the example for gluBeginCurve.
See Also	gluBeginCurve

GLUENDSURFACE

Purpose	Ends a NURBS surface definition.
Include File	<glu.h>
Syntax	void gluEndSurface(GLUnurbsObj *nObj);
Description	This function is used with gluBeginSurface to delimit a NURBS surface definition.
Parameters	
nObj	GLUnurbsObj*: Specifies the NURBS object.
Returns	None.
Example	See the example for gluBeginSurface.
See Also	gluBeginSurface

GLUENDTRIM

Purpose	Ends a NURBS trimming loop definition.
Include File	<glu.h>
Syntax	void gluEndTrim(GLUnurbsObj *nobj);
Description	This function is used with gluBeginTrim to mark the end of a NURBS trimming loop. See gluBeginTrim for more information on trimming loops.
Parameters	
nObj	GLUnurbsObj*: Specifies the NURBS object.
Returns	None.
Example	See the example for gluBeginTrim.
See Also	gluBeginTrim

GLUGETNURBSPROPERTY

Purpose	Retrieves a NURBS property.
Include File	<gl.h>
Syntax	void gluGetNurbsProperty(GLUnurbsObj *nObj, GLenum property, GLfloat *value);
Description	This function retrieves the NURBS property specified for a particular NURBS object. See gluNurbsProperty for an explanation of the various properties.
Parameters	
nObj	GLUnurbsObj: Specifies the NURBS object.

property	GLenum: The NURBS property to be retrieved. Valid properties are GLU_SAMPLING_TOLERANCE, GLU_DISPLAY_MODE, GLU_CULLING, GLU_AUTO_LOAD_MATRIX, GLU_PARAMETRIC_TOLERANCE, GLU_SAMPLING_METHOD, GLU_U_STEP, and GLU_V_STEP. See the gluNurbsProperty function for details on these properties.
Returns	None.
Example	Following example shows how the NURBS property GLU_SAMPLING_TOLERANCE is set to 25. Later in the program (presumably in some other function), gluGetNurbsProperty is called to query the sampling tolerance.

```
gluNurbsProperty(pNurb, GLU_SAMPLING_TOLERANCE, 25.0f);

...
...
GLfloat fTolerance;
...

gluGetNurbsProperty(pNurb, GLU_SAMPLING_TOLERANCE, &fTolerance);
```

See Also	gluNewNurbsRenderer, gluNurbsProperty

GLULOADSAMPLINGMATRICES

Purpose	Loads NURBS sampling and culling matrices.
Include File	<gl.h>
Syntax	void gluLoadSamplingMatrices(GLUnurbsObj *nObj, const GLfloat modelMatrix[16], const GLfloat projMatrix[16], const GLint viewport[4]);
Description	This function is used to recompute the sampling and culling matrices for a NURBS surface. The sampling matrix is used to determine how finely the surface must be tessellated to satisfy the sampling tolerance. The culling matrix is used to determine if the surface should be culled before rendering. Usually this function does not need to be called, unless the GLU_AUTO_LOAD_MATRIX property is turned off. This might be the case when using selection and feedback modes.
Parameters	
nObj	GLUnurbsObj*: Specifies the NURBS object.
modelMatrix	GLfloat[16]: Specifies the Modelview matrix.
projMatrix	GLfloat[16]: Specifies the Projection matrix.
viewport	GLint[4]: Specifies a viewport.
Returns	None.

Example   The following code can be used to manually set up and use the sampling and culling matrices.

```
GLfloat fModelView[16],fProjection[16],fViewport[4];
...
...

pNurb = glNewNurbsRenderer(.....);
...
...

// Get the current matrix and viewport info
glGetFloatv(GL_MODELVIEW_MATRIX,fModelView);
glGetFloatv(GL_PROJECTION_MATRIX,fProjection);
glGetIntegerv(GL_VIEWPORT,fViewport);


...
...
// Load the matrices manually
gluLoadSamplingMatrices(pNurb,fModelView,fProjection,fViewport);
```

See Also   gluNewNurbsRenderer, gluNurbsProperty

GLUNEWNURBSRENDERER

Purpose   Creates a NURBS object.

Include File <glu.h>

Syntax   GLUnurbsObj* gluNewNurbsRenderer(void);

Description   This function creates a NURBS rendering object. This object is used to control the behavior and characteristics of NURBS curves and surfaces. The functions that allow the NURBS properties to be set all require this pointer. You must delete this object with gluDeleteNurbsRenderer when you are finished rendering your NURBS.

Returns   A pointer to a new NURBS object. This object will be used when you call the rendering and control functions.

Example   This code demonstrates the creation of a NURBS object:

```
// Setup the Nurbs object

// Start by creating it
pNurb = gluNewNurbsRenderer();

// Set NURBS properties
gluNurbsProperty(pNurb, GLU_SAMPLING_TOLERANCE, 25.0f);
gluNurbsProperty(pNurb, GLU_DISPLAY_MODE, (GLfloat)GLU_FILL);

.. other properties
...
...
```

See Also   gluDeleteNurbsRenderer

gluNurbsCallback

Purpose	Defines a callback for a NURBS function.
Include File	<glu.h>
Syntax	void gluNurbsCallback(GLUnurbsObj *nObj, GLenum which, void (*fn)( ));
Description	This function sets a NURBS callback function. The only supported callback is GL_ERROR. When an error occurs, this function is called with an argument of type GLenum. One of 37 NURBS errors can be specified by the defines GLU_NURBS_ERROR1 - GLU_NURBS_ERROR37. A character string definition of the error can be retrieved with the function gluErrorString(). These are listed in Table 17-1.
Parameters	
nObj	GLUnurbsObj*: Specifies the NURBS object.
which	GLEnum: Specifies the callback being defined. The only valid value is GLU_ERROR.
fn	void *(): Specifies the function that should be called for the callback.
Returns	None.
Example	The following is an example error handler for NURBS errors. Some code that installs the error handler is also shown. You can see this in the NURBS example program.

```
// NURBS callback error handler
void CALLBACK NurbsErrorHandler(GLenum nErrorCode)
        {
        char cMessage[64];

        // Extract a text message of the error
        strcpy(cMessage,"NURBS error occured: ");
        strcat(cMessage,gluErrorString(nErrorCode));

        // Display the message to the user
        MessageBox(NULL,cMessage,NULL,MB_OK | MB_ICONEXCLAMATION);
        }


    . . .
    . . .
    . . .

// Setup the Nurbs object
    pNurb = gluNewNurbsRenderer();

        // Install error handler to notify user of NURBS errors
        gluNurbsCallback(pNurb, GLU_ERROR, NurbsErrorHandler);

    gluNurbsProperty(pNurb, GLU_SAMPLING_TOLERANCE, 25.0f);
        ... Other properties
        ...
```

See Also	gluErrorString

Table 17-1 NURBS Error Codes

Error Code	Definition
GLU_NURBS_ERROR1	Spline order un-supported.
GLU_NURBS_ERROR2	Too few knots.
GLU_NURBS_ERROR3	Valid knot range is empty.
GLU_NURBS_ERROR4	Decreasing knot sequence knot.
GLU_NURBS_ERROR5	Knot multiplicity greater than order of spline.
GLU_NURBS_ERROR6	endcurve() must follow bgncurve().
GLU_NURBS_ERROR7	bgncurve() must precede endcurve().
GLU_NURBS_ERROR8	Missing or extra geometric data.
GLU_NURBS_ERROR9	Can't draw pwlcurves.
GLU_NURBS_ERROR10	Missing or extra domain data.
GLU_NURBS_ERROR11	Missing or extra domain data.
GLU_NURBS_ERROR12	endtrim() must precede endsurface().
GLU_NURBS_ERROR13	bgnsurface() must precede endsurface().
GLU_NURBS_ERROR14	Curve of improper type passed as trim curve.
GLU_NURBS_ERROR15	bgnsurface() must precede bgntrim().
GLU_NURBS_ERROR16	endtrim() must follow bgntrim().
GLU_NURBS_ERROR17	bgntrim() must precede endtrim().
GLU_NURBS_ERROR18	Invalid or missing trim curve.
GLU_NURBS_ERROR19	bgntrim() must precede pwlcurve().
GLU_NURBS_ERROR20	pwlcurve referenced twice.
GLU_NURBS_ERROR21	pwlcurve and nurbscurve mixed.
GLU_NURBS_ERROR22	Improper usage of trim data type.
GLU_NURBS_ERROR23	nurbscurve referenced twice.
GLU_NURBS_ERROR24	nurbscurve and pwlcurve mixed.
GLU_NURBS_ERROR25	nurbssurface referenced twice.
GLU_NURBS_ERROR26	Invalid property.
GLU_NURBS_ERROR27	endsurface() must follow bgnsurface().
GLU_NURBS_ERROR28	Intersecting or misoriented trim curves.
GLU_NURBS_ERROR29	Intersecting trim curves.
GLU_NURBS_ERROR30	UNUSED.
GLU_NURBS_ERROR31	Unconnected trim curves.
GLU_NURBS_ERROR32	Unknown knot error.
GLU_NURBS_ERROR33	Negative vertex count encountered.
GLU_NURBS_ERROR34	Negative byte-stride encountered.
GLU_NURBS_ERROR35	Unknown type descriptor.
GLU_NURBS_ERROR36	Null control point reference.
GLU_NURBS_ERROR 37	Duplicate point on pwlcurve.

GLUNURBSCURVE

Purpose	Defines the shape of a NURBS curve.
Include File	<glu.h>
Syntax	void gluNurbsCurve(GLUnurbsObj *nObj, GLint nknots, GLfloat *knot, GLint stride, GLfloat *ctlarray, GLint order, GLenum type);
Description	This function defines the shape of a NURBS curve. The definition of this curve must be delimited by gluBeginCurve and gluEndCurve.
Parameters	
nObj	GLUnurbsObj*: Pointer to the NURBS object (created with gluNewNurbsRenderer).
nkots	GLint: The number of knots in *knots*. This is the number of control points plus order.
knots	GLfloat*: An array of knot values in nondescending order.
stride	GLint: Specifies the offset, as a number of single-precision floating point values, between control points.
ctlArray	GLfloat*: Pointer to an array or data structure containing the control points for the NURBS surface.
order	GLint: The order of the NURBS surface. Order is 1 more than the degree.
type	GLenum: The type of surface. This can be any of the two-dimensional evaluator types: GL_MAP2_VERTEX_3, GL_MAP2_VERTEX_4, GL_MAP2_INDEX, GL_MAP2_COLOR_4, GL_MAP2_NORMAL, GL_MAP2_TEXTURE_COORD_1, GL_MAP2_TEXTURE_COORD_2, GL_MAP2_TEXTURE_COORD_3, and GL_MAP2_TEXTURE_COORD_4.
Returns	None.
Example	See the example for gluBeginCurve.
See Also	gluBeginCurve,gluEndCurve, gluNurbsSurface

GLUNURBSPROPERTY

Purpose	Sets a NURBS property.
Include File	<glu.h>
Syntax	void gluNurbsProperty(GLUnurbsObj *nObj, GLenum property, GLfloat value);
Description	This function sets the properties of the NURBS object. Valid properties are as follows: GLU_SAMPLING_TOLERANCE: Sets the maximum length in pixels to use when using the GLU_PATH_LENGTH sampling method. The default is 50.0.

GLU_DISPLAY_MODE: Defines how the NURBS surface is rendered. The value parameter may be GLU_FILL to use filled and shaded polygons, GLU_OUTLINE_POLYGON to draw just the outlines of the polygons (after tessellation), and finally GLU_OUTLINE_PATCH to draw just the outlines of user defined patches and trim curves. The default is GLU_FILL.

GLU_CULLING: The value parameter is interpreted as a Boolean value that indicates whether the NURBS curve should be discarded if its control points are outside the viewport.

GLU_PARAMETRIC_TOLERANCE: Sets the maximum pixel distance used when the sampling method is set to GLU_PARAMETRIC_ERROR. The default is 0.5. This property was introduced in GLU version 1.1.

GLU_SAMPLING_METHOD: Specifies how to tessellate the NURBS surface. This property was introduced in GLU version 1.1. The following values are valid:

GLU_PATH_LENGTH specifies that surfaces rendered with the maximum pixel length of the edges of the tessellation polygons are not greater than the value specified by GLU_SAMPLING_TOLERANCE.

GLU_PARAMETRIC_ERROR specifies that the surface is rendered with the value of GLU_PARAMETRIC_TOLERANCE designating the maximum distance, in pixels, between the tessellation polygons and the surfaces they approximate.

GLU_DOMAIN_DISTANCE specifies, in parametric coordinates, how many sample points per unit length to take in the u and v dimensions. The default is GLU_PATH_LENGTH.

GLU_U_STEP: Sets the number of sample points per unit length taken along the u dimension in parametric coordinates. This value is used when GLU_SAMPLING_METHOD is set to GLU_DOMAIN_DISTANCE. The default is 100. This property was introduced in GLU version 1.1.

GLU_V_STEP: Sets the number of sample points per unit length taken along the v dimension in parametric coordinates. This value is used when GLU_SAMPLING_METHOD is set to GLU_DOMAIN_DISTANCE. The default is 100. This property was introduced in GLU version 1.1.

GLU_AUTO_LOAD_MATRIX: The value parameter is interpreted as a Boolean value. When set to GL_TRUE, it causes the NURBS code to download the Projection matrix, the Modelview matrix, and the viewport from the OpenGL server to compute sampling and culling matrices for each NURBS curve. Sampling and culling matrices are required to determine the tessellation of a NURBS surface into line segments or polygons and to cull a NURBS surface if it lies outside of the viewport. If this mode is set to GL_FALSE, the user needs to provide these matrices and a viewport for the NURBS renderer to use in constructing sampling and culling matrices. This can be done with the gluLoadSamplingMatrices function. The default value for this mode GL_TRUE. Changing this mode does not affect the sampling and culling matrices until gluLoadSamplingMatrices is called.

Parameters	
nObj	GLUnurbsObj*: The NURB object that is having a property modified (this is created by calling glNewNurbsRenderer).
property	GLenum: The property to be set or modified. This may be any of the following values: GLU_SAMPLING_TOLERANCE, GLU_DISPLAY_MODE, GLU_CULLING, GLU_AUTO_LOAD_MATRIX, GLU_PARAMETRIC_TOLERANCE, GLU_SAMPLING_METHOD, GLU_U_STEP, and GLU_V_STEP.
value	GLfloat: The value to which the indicated property is being set.
Returns	None.
Example	The following code from this chapter's NURBS program sets the NURBS display property to render the surface as a wire mesh.

```
gluNurbsProperty(pNurb, GLU_DISPLAY_MODE, GLU_OUTLINE_POLYGON);
```

See Also	gluGetNurbsProperty, gluGetString, gluLoadSamplingMatrices, gluNewNurbsRenderer

GLUNURBSSURFACE

Purpose	Defines the shape of a NURBS surface.
Include File	<glu.h>
Syntax	void gluNurbsSurface(GLUnurbsObj *nObj, GLint uknotCount, GLfloat *uknot, GLint vknotCount, GLfloat *vknot, GLint uStride, GLint vStride, GLfloat *ctlArray, GLint uorder, GLint vorder, GLenum type);
Description	This function defines the shape of a NURBS surface. Must be delimited by gluBeginSurface and gluEndSurface. The shape of the surface is defined before any trimming takes place. A NURBS surface can be trimmed by using the gluBeginTrim/gluEndTrim and gluNurbsCurve and/or gluPwlCurve to do the trimming.
Parameters	
nObj	GLUnurbsObj*: Pointer to the NURBS object (created with gluNewNurbsRenderer).
uknotCount	GLint: The number of knots in the parametric u direction.
uknot	GLfloat*: An array of knot values that represent the knots in the u direction. These values must be nondescending. The length of the array is specified in uknotCount.
vknotCount	GLint: The number of knots in the parametric v direction.

vknot	GLfloat*: An array of knot values that represent the knots in the v direction. These values must be nondescending. The length of the array is specified in vknotCount.
uStride	GLint: Specifies the offset, as a number of single-precision, floating point values, between successive control points in the parametric u direction in ctlarray.
vStride	GLint: Specifies the offset, as a number of single-precision, floating point values, between successive control points in the parametric v direction in ctlarray.
ctlArray	GLfloat*: Pointer to an array containing the control points for the NURBS surface. The offsets between successive control points in the parametric u and v directions are given by uStride and vStride.
uorder	GLint: The order of the NURBS surface in the parametric u direction. The order is 1 more than the degree; hence a surface that is cubic in u has a u order of 4.
vorder	GLint: The order of the NURBS surface in the parametric v direction. The order is 1 more than the degree; hence a surface that is cubic in v has a v order of 4.
type	GLenum: The type of surface. This can be any of the 2D evaluator types: GL_MAP2_VERTEX_3, GL_MAP2_VERTEX_4, GL_MAP2_INDEX, GL_MAP2_COLOR_4, GL_MAP2_NORMAL, GL_MAP2_TEXTURE_COORD_1, GL_MAP2_TEXTURE_COORD_2, GL_MAP2_TEXTURE_COORD_3, and GL_MAP2_TEXTURE_COORD_4.
Returns	None.
Example	See the example for gluBeginSurface.
See Also	gluBeginSurface, gluBeginTrim, gluNewNurbsRenderer, gluNurbsCurve, gluPwlCurve

GLUPWLCURVE

Purpose	Specifies a piecewise NURBS trimming curve.
Include File	<glu.h>
Syntax	void gluPwlCurve(GLUnurbsObj *nObj, GLint count, GLfloat *array, GLint stride, GLenum type);
Description	This function defines a piecewise linear trimming curve for a NURBS surface. The array of points are in terms of the parametric u and v coordinate space. This space is a unit square exactly 1 unit in length along both axes. Clockwise-wound trimming curves eliminate the enclosed area; counterclockwise trimming curves discard the exterior area. Typically, a trimming region is first established around the entire surface area that trims away all

points not on the surface. Then smaller trimming areas wound clockwise are placed within it to cut away sections of the curve. Trimming curves can be piecewise. This means one or more calls to gluPwlCurve or gluNurbsCurve can be called to define a trimming region as long as they share endpoints and define a close region in u/v space.

Parameters

nObj	GLUnurbsObj*: Specifies the NURBS object being trimmed.
count	GLint: Specifies the number of points on the curve listed in *array*.
array	GLfloat*: Specifies the array of boundary points for this curve.
stride	GLint: Specifies the offset between points on the curve.
type	GLenum: Specifies the type of curve. May be GLU_MAP1_TRIM_2, used when the trimming curve is specified in terms of u and v coordinates; or GLU_MAP1_TRIM_3, used when a w (scaling) coordinate is also specified.

Returns   None.

Example   The following code from this chapter's program NURBT shows a NURBS curve being trimmed with a triangular shaped region. A large trimming area encloses the surface that includes all the area within it. A secondary trimming area defines a triangle and discards any surface area within it.

```
// Outside trimming points to include entire surface
GLfloat outsidePts[5][2] = /* counter clockwise */
      {{0.0f, 0.0f}, {1.0f, 0.0f}, {1.0f, 1.0f}, {0.0f, 1.0f}, {0.0f, 0.0f}};

// Inside trimming points to create triangle shaped hole in surface
GLfloat insidePts[4][2] = /* clockwise */
    {{0.25f, 0.25f}, {0.5f, 0.5f}, {0.75f, 0.25f}, { 0.25f, 0.25f}};

...
...

// Render the NURB
// Begin the NURB definition
gluBeginSurface(pNurb);

// Evaluate the surface
gluNurbsSurface(pNurb,
      8, Knots,
      8, Knots,
      4 * 3,
      3,
      &ctrlPoints[0][0][0],
      4, 4,
      GL_MAP2_VERTEX_3);

// Outer area, include entire curve
gluBeginTrim (pNurb);
gluPwlCurve (pNurb, 5, &outsidePts[0][0], 2, GLU_MAP1_TRIM_2);
gluEndTrim (pNurb);
```

continued on next page

continued from previous page

```
// Inner triangluar area
gluBeginTrim (pNurb);
gluPwlCurve (pNurb, 4, &insidePts[0][0], 2, GLU_MAP1_TRIM_2);
gluEndTrim (pNurb);


// Done with surface
gluEndSurface(pNurb);
```

See Also   gluBeginTrim, gluEndTrim, gluNurbsCurve

18

POLYGON TESSELLATION

18

POLYGON TESSELLATION

What you'll learn in this chapter:

How to...	Functions You'll Use
Use the OpenGL Utility library to draw complex polygons	gluBegin/gluEnd
Use the OpenGL Utility library to draw complex surfaces	gluNextContour

The OpenGL Utility library (glu32.lib) includes a robust polygon tessellation interface that can handle rendering of complex polygons and surfaces. What is tessellation, you ask? According to the *American Heritage Dictionary:*

> **tes·sel·late** *verb, transitive*
> **tes·sel·lat·ed, tes·sel·lat·ing, tes·sel·lates**
>
> To form into a mosaic pattern, as by using small squares of stone or glass.
>
> **teś sel·lá tion** *noun* [1]

A computer graphics tessellator takes one or more connected sets of points and forms a series of polygons that fill to form the described shape. In place of stone and glass, it uses triangles and pixels. A polygon tessellator is specially designed to manage the drawing of polygons that have unusual attributes such as holes.

Complex Polygons

What makes polygons complex? Well, in OpenGL a complex polygon is one that is either concave (the polygon contains a "dent") or has holes in it. Figure 18-1

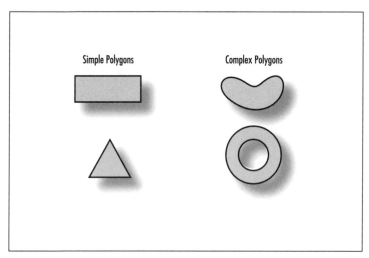

Figure 18-1 Simple and complex polygons

contains some simple and complex polygons that you may need to render at some time.

OpenGL's GL_POLYGON primitive can only render simple, *convex* polygons. A polygon is convex if no point lies inside a line between any two vertices. That is, if you can draw a line between two vertices of a polygon and the line goes into empty space outside the polygon edge, the polygon is *not* convex; it is concave or complex.

Concave polygons are nonconvex polygons that have no unfilled holes in their interiors. The top-right polygon in Figure 18-1 is concave, but the one below it is not because it contains a hole in the middle of the filled area.

Complex polygons have holes or twists in them. The lower-right polygon in Figure 18-1 is complex.

Drawing Concave Polygons

Drawing concave polygons with the glu is not difficult. The first thing you must do is create a tessellator object, as shown here:

```
GLUtriangulatorObj *tess;

tess = gluNewTess();
```

The GLUtriangulatorObj structure contains state information that is used by the tessellator to render the polygon.

Next, you call a sequence of gluBeginPolygon, gluTessVertex, and gluEndPolygon to render the polygon:

```
GLdouble vertices[100][3];

gluBeginPolygon(tess);
```

```
    gluTessVertex(tess, vertices[0], NULL);
    gluTessVertex(tess, vertices[1], NULL);
    ...
    gluTessVertex(tess, vertices[99], NULL);
gluEndPolygon(tess);
```

After the gluEndPolygon call, the tessellator does its work and generates a series of triangles, triangle strips, and triangle fans. Because this process can take a long time, it's a good idea to put tessellated polygons into display lists to improve display performance (see Chapter 10).

Drawing Complex Polygons

Drawing complex polygons is a little more involved than for concave polygons but is not as hard as it would seem. Complex polygons can have holes and twists in them, so the gluNextContour function is provided to identify the type of path you are defining. Table 18-1 lists the path types for glNextContour.

Table 18-1 gluNextContour path types

Path Type	Description
GLU_EXTERIOR	The path lies on the exterior of the polygon.
GLU_INTERIOR	The path lies on the interior of the polygon (hole).
GLU_UNKNOWN	You don't know what the path is; the library will attempt to figure it out.
GLU_CCW	This should only be used once and defines that counterclockwise paths are exterior paths and clockwise ones are interior.
GLU_CW	This should only be used once and defines that counterclockwise paths are exterior paths and clockwise ones are interior.

For the example shown in Figure 18-2, we will define an exterior path for the outline, and an interior path for the triangular hole in the middle (see Figure 18-3).

To draw the letter *A*, we call gluNextContour only once before providing the interior points. The example in Listing 18-1, LETTER.C, uses this code to display a rotating *A*.

```
tess = gluNewTess();
gluBeginPolygon(tess);
    gluTessVertex(tess, outside[0], outside[0]);
    gluTessVertex(tess, outside[1], outside[1]);
    gluTessVertex(tess, outside[2], outside[2]);
    gluTessVertex(tess, outside[3], outside[3]);
    gluTessVertex(tess, outside[4], outside[4]);
    gluTessVertex(tess, outside[5], outside[5]);
    gluTessVertex(tess, outside[6], outside[6]);
gluNextContour(tess, GLU_INTERIOR);
    gluTessVertex(tess, inside[0], inside[0]);
    gluTessVertex(tess, inside[1], inside[1]);
    gluTessVertex(tess, inside[2], inside[2]);
gluEndPolygon(tess);
gluDeleteTess(tess);
```

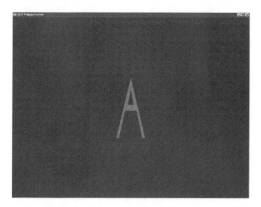

Figure 18-2 The letter *A* as a complex polygon

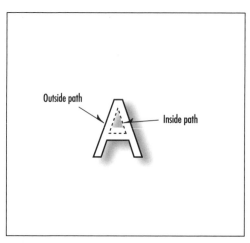

Figure 18-3 Polygon paths for the letter *A*

Listing 18-1 LETTER.C: Tessellating the polygon for the letter **A**

```
/*
 * "letter.c" - A test program demonstrating the use of the GLU polygon
 *              tessellator.
 */

#include <GL/glaux.h>

/*
 * These #define constants are provided for compatibility between MS Windows
 * and the rest of the world.
 *
```

```
 * CALLBACK and APIENTRY are function modifiers under MS Windows.
 */

#ifndef WIN32
#  define CALLBACK
#  define APIENTRY
#endif /* !WIN32 */

GLfloat rotation = 0.0;


/*
 * 'reshape_scene()' - Change the size of the scene...
 */

void CALLBACK
reshape_scene(GLsizei width,     /* I - Width of the window in pixels */
              GLsizei height)    /* I - Height of the window in pixels */
{
 /*
  * Reset the current viewport and perspective transformation...
  */

  glViewport(0, 0, width, height);

  glMatrixMode(GL_PROJECTION);
  glLoadIdentity();
  gluPerspective(22.5, (float)width / (float)height, 0.1, 1000.0);

  glMatrixMode(GL_MODELVIEW);
}


/*
 * 'draw_scene()' - Draw a scene containing the letter A.
 */

void CALLBACK
draw_scene(void)
{
  GLUtriangulatorObj   *tess;
  static GLdouble      outside[7][3] =
  {
    { 0.0, 1.0, 0.0 },
    { -0.5, -1.0, 0.0 },
    { -0.4, -1.0, 0.0 },
    { -0.2, -0.1, 0.0 },
    { 0.2, -0.1, 0.0 },
    { 0.4, -1.0, 0.0 },
    { 0.5, -1.0, 0.0 }
  };
  static GLdouble      inside[3][3] =
  {
    { 0.0, 0.6, 0.0 },
    { -0.1, 0.1, 0.0 },
    { 0.1, 0.1, 0.0 }
  };
  static float  red_light[4] = { 1.0, 0.0, 0.0, 1.0 };
  static float  red_pos[4] = { 1.0, 1.0, 1.0, 0.0 };
  static float  blue_light[4] = { 0.0, 0.0, 1.0, 1.0 };
```

continued on next page

CHAPTER 18

continued from previous page

```
  static float  blue_pos[4] = { -1.0, -1.0, -1.0, 0.0 };


/*
 * Enable drawing features that we need...
 */

  glEnable(GL_DEPTH_TEST);
  glEnable(GL_LIGHTING);
  glEnable(GL_LIGHT0);
  glEnable(GL_LIGHT1);

  glShadeModel(GL_SMOOTH);

/*
 * Clear the color and depth buffers...
 */

  glClearColor(0.0, 0.0, 0.0, 0.0);
  glClear(GL_COLOR_BUFFER_BIT | GL_DEPTH_BUFFER_BIT);

/*
 * Draw the cube and sphere in different colors...
 *
 * We have positioned two lights in this scene.  The first is red and
 * located above, to the right, and behind the viewer.  The second is blue
 * and located below, to the left, and in front of the viewer.
 */

  glLightfv(GL_LIGHT0, GL_DIFFUSE, red_light);
  glLightfv(GL_LIGHT0, GL_POSITION, red_pos);

  glLightfv(GL_LIGHT1, GL_DIFFUSE, blue_light);
  glLightfv(GL_LIGHT1, GL_POSITION, blue_pos);

  glEnable(GL_COLOR_MATERIAL);

  glPushMatrix();
    glTranslatef(0.0, 0.0, -15.0);
    glRotatef(-rotation, 0.0, 1.0, 0.0);

    glColor3f(0.0, 1.0, 0.0);

    tess = gluNewTess();
    gluTessCallback(tess, GLU_BEGIN, glBegin);
    gluTessCallback(tess, GLU_VERTEX, glVertex3dv);
    gluTessCallback(tess, GLU_END, glEnd);
    gluBeginPolygon(tess);
      gluTessVertex(tess, outside[0], outside[0]);
      gluTessVertex(tess, outside[1], outside[1]);
      gluTessVertex(tess, outside[2], outside[2]);
      gluTessVertex(tess, outside[3], outside[3]);
      gluTessVertex(tess, outside[4], outside[4]);
      gluTessVertex(tess, outside[5], outside[5]);
      gluTessVertex(tess, outside[6], outside[6]);
    gluNextContour(tess, GLU_INTERIOR);
```

```
      gluTessVertex(tess, inside[0], inside[0]);
      gluTessVertex(tess, inside[1], inside[1]);
      gluTessVertex(tess, inside[2], inside[2]);
    gluEndPolygon(tess);
    gluDeleteTess(tess);
  glPopMatrix();

  auxSwapBuffers();
}


/*
 * 'rotate_objects()' - Rotate while we are idle...
 */

void CALLBACK
rotate_objects(void)
{
  rotation += 2.0;
  if (rotation >= 360.0)
    rotation -= 360.0;

  draw_scene();
}


/*
 * 'main()' - Initialize the window and display the scene until the user presses
 *            the ESCape key.
 */

void
main(void)
{
  auxInitDisplayMode(AUX_RGB | AUX_DOUBLE | AUX_DEPTH);
  auxInitWindow("GLU Polygon Letter");

  auxReshapeFunc(reshape_scene);
  auxIdleFunc(rotate_objects);

  auxMainLoop(draw_scene);
}
```

Callback Functions

The glu defines several callback functions that can be used for special effects. The gluTessCallback function allows you to change these functions to do something of your own. It takes three arguments:

```
void gluTessCallback(GLUtriangulatorObj *tobj, GLenum which, void (*fn)());
```

The which argument specifies the callback function to define and must be one of the arguments in Table 18-2.

Table 18-2 Tessellator Callback Functions

which argument	Description
GLU_BEGIN	Specifies a function that is called to begin a GL_TRIANGLES, GL_TRIANGLE_STRIP, or GL_TRIANGLE_FAN primitive. The function must accept a single GLenum parameter that specifies the primitive to be rendered and is usually set to glBegin.
GLU_EDGE_FLAG	Specifies a function that marks whether succeeding GLU_VERTEX callbacks refer to original or generated vertices. The function must accept a single GLboolean argument that is GL_TRUE for original and GL_FALSE for generated vertices.
GLU_VERTEX	Specifies a function that is called before every vertex is sent, usually with glVertex3dv. The function receives a copy of the third argument to gluTessVertex.
GLU_END	Specifies a function that marks the end of a drawing primitive, usually glEnd. It takes no arguments.
GLU_ERROR	Specifies a function that is called when an error occurs. It must take a single argument of type GLenum.

Normally, you will use the GLU_BEGIN, GLU_END, GLU_VERTEX, and GLU_ERROR callback. GLU_BEGIN, GLU_END, and GLU_VERTEX correspond to glBegin, glEnd, and glVertex3dv, respectively. A simple function to display errors sent from the tessellator is in Listing 18-2.

Listing 18-2 A simple tessllator error-callback function

```
void
tess_error_callback(GLenum error)
{
  MessageBeep(MB_ICONEXCLAMATION);
  MessageBox(NULL, gluErrorString(error), "GLU Error", MB_OK |
          MB_ICONEXCLAMATION);
}
```

Summary

The OpenGL polygon tessellator can be used to render a variety of complex polygons that OpenGL's GL_POLYGON primitive just can't handle. Polygon tessellation does come at a price, and you will want to put these tessellated polygons into display lists to get good performance from them.

The callback mechanism allows for some control over the generated results but does not affect the tessellation algorithms used. Callback functions are rarely used because of this.

Reference Section

GLUBEGINPOLYGON

Purpose	Starts tessellation of a complex polygon.
Include File	<GL/glu.h>
Syntax	void gluBeginPolygon(GLUtriangulator *tobj);
Description	This function starts tessellation of a complex polygon.
Parameters	
tobj	GLUtriangulatorObj *: The tessellator object to use for the polygon.
Returns	None.
Example	See the example in CH18\LETTER.C on the CD.
See Also	gluEndPolygon, gluNextContour, gluTessVertex

GLUDELETETESS

Purpose	Deletes a tessellator object.
Include File	<GL/glu.h>
Syntax	void gluDeleteTess(GLUtriangulatorObj *tobj);
Description	The *gluDeleteTess* function frees all memory associated with a tessellator object.
Parameters	
tobj	GLUtriangulatorObj *: The tessellator object to delete.
Returns	None.
Example	See the example in CH18\LETTER.C on the CD.
See Also	gluNewTess

GLUENDPOLYGON

Purpose	Ends tessellation of a complex polygon and renders it.
Include File	<GL/glu.h>
Syntax	void gluEndPolygon(GLUtriangulator *tobj);
Description	This function ends tessellation of a complex polygon and renders the final result.
Parameters	
tobj	GLUtriangulatorObj *: The tessellator object to use for the polygon.

Returns	None.
Example	See the example in CH18\LETTER.C on the CD.
See Also	gluBeginPolygon, gluNextContour, gluTessVertex

GLUNEWTESS

Purpose	Creates a tessellator object.
Include File	<GL/glu.h>
Syntax	GLUtriangulatorObj *gluNewTess(void);
Description	The *gluNewTess* function creates a tessellator object.
Parameters	None.
Returns	GLUtriangulatorObj *: The new tessellator object.
Example	See the example in CH18\LETTER.C on the CD.
See Also	gluDeleteTess

GLUNEXTCONTOUR

Purpose	Specifies a new contour or hole in a complex polygon.
Include File	<GL/glu.h>
Syntax	void gluNextContour(GLUtriangulator *tobj, GLenum type);
Description	This function specifies a new contour or hole in a complex polygon.
Parameters	
tobj	GLUtriangulatorObj *: The tessellator object to use for the polygon.
type	GLenum: The type of contour. Valid types are in Table 18-1 earlier in chapter.
Returns	None.
Example	See the example in CH18\LETTER.C on the CD.
See Also	gluBeginPolygon, gluEndPolygon, gluTessVertex

GLUTESSCALLBACK

Purpose	To specify a callback function for tessellation.
Include File	<GL/glu.h>
Syntax	void gluTessCallback(GLUtriangulator *tobj, GLenum which, void (*fn)());
Description	This function specifies a callback function for various tesselation functions. Callback functions do not replace or change the tessellator performance. Rather, they provide the means to add information to the tessellated output (such as color or texture coordinates).

Parameters

tobj	GLUtriangulatorObj *: The tessellator object to use for the polygon.
which	GLenum: The callback function to define. Valid functions are in Table 18-2 earlier in chapter.
fn	void (*)(): The function to call.
Returns	None.

GLUTESSVERTEX

Purpose	Adds a vertex to the current polygon path.
Include File	<GL/glu.h>
Syntax	void gluTessVertex(GLUtriangulator *tobj, GLdouble v[3], void *data);
Description	This function adds a vertex to the current tessellator path. The *data* argument is passed through to the GL_VERTEX callback function..

Parameters

tobj	GLUtriangulatorObj *: The tessellator object to use for the polygon.
v	GLdouble[3]: The 3D vertex.
data	void *: A data pointer to be passed to the GL_VERTEX callback function.
Returns	None.
Example	See the example in CH18\LETTER.C on the CD.
See Also	gluBeginPolygon, gluEndPolygon, gluNextContour

19

INTERACTIVE GRAPHICS

19

INTERACTIVE GRAPHICS

What you'll learn in this chapter:

How to...	Functions You'll Use
Assign OpenGL selection names to primitives or groups of primitives	glInitNames/glPushName/glPopName
Use selection to determine which objects are under the mouse	glSelectBuffer/glRenderMode
Use feedback to get information about where objects are drawn	glFeedbackBuffer/gluPickMatrix

Thus far you have learned to create some sophisticated 3D graphics using OpenGL, and many applications do no more than generate these scenes. But many graphics applications (notably, games) will require more interaction with the scene itself. In addition to the menu and dialog boxes, you'll need to provide a way for the user to interact with a graphical scene. Under Windows, this is usually done with a mouse.

Selection, a very powerful feature of OpenGL, allows you to take a mouse click at some position over a window and determine which of your objects are beneath it. The act of selecting a specific object on the screen is called *picking.* With Open GL's selection feature, you can specify a viewing volume and determine which objects fall within that viewing volume. A powerful utility function produces a matrix for you, based purely on screen coordinates and the pixel dimensions you specify; you use this matrix to create a smaller viewing volume placed beneath the mouse cursor. Then you use selection to test this viewing volume to see which objects are contained by it.

Feedback allows you to get information from OpenGL about how your vertices are transformed and illuminated when they are drawn to the framebuffer. You can use this information to transmit rendering results over a network, send them to a plotter, or add GDI graphics to your OpenGL scene that appear to interact with the OpenGL objects. Feedback does not serve the same purpose as selection, but the mode of operation is very similar and they work productively together. You'll see this teamwork later in a specific example.

Selection

Selection is actually a rendering mode, but in selection mode no pixels are actually copied to the framebuffer. Instead, primitives that are drawn within the viewing volume (and thus would normally appear in the framebuffer) produce "hit" records in a selection buffer.

You must set up this selection buffer in advance, and name your primitives or groups of primitives (your objects) so they can be identified in the selection buffer. You then parse the selection buffer to determine which objects intersected the viewing volume. This has marginal value unless you modify the viewing volume before entering selection mode and calling your drawing code to determine which objects are in some restricted area of your scene. In one common scenario, you specify a viewing volume that corresponds to the mouse pointer, and then check to see which named objects the mouse is pointing to.

Naming Your Primitives

You can name every single primitive used to render your scene of objects, but this is rarely useful. More often you will name groups of primitives, thus creating names for the specific objects or pieces of objects in your scene. Object names, like display list names, are nothing more than unsigned integers.

The names list is maintained on the name stack. After you initialize the name stack, you can push names on the stack or simply replace the name currently on top of the stack. When a hit occurs during selection, all the names on the names stack are copied into the selection buffer. Thus, a single hit can return more than one name if needed.

For our first example, we'll keep things simple. We'll create a simplified (and not to scale) model of the inner planets of the solar system. When the left mouse button is down, we'll display a message box describing which planet was clicked on. Listing 19-1 shows some of the rendering code for our example program, PLANETS. We have created macro definitions for the Sun, Mercury, Venus, Earth, and Mars.

Listing 19-1 Naming the Sun and planets in the PLANETS program

```
#define SUN         1
#define MERCURY     2
#define VENUS       3
#define EARTH       4
#define MARS        5

. . .
. . .
```

```
// Called to draw scene
void RenderScene(void)
        {
        // Clear the window with current clearing color
        glClear(GL_COLOR_BUFFER_BIT | GL_DEPTH_BUFFER_BIT);

        // Save the matrix state and do the rotations
        glMatrixMode(GL_MODELVIEW);
        glPushMatrix();

        // Translate the whole scene out and into view
        glTranslatef(0.0f, 0.0f, -300.0f);

        // Initialize the names stack
        glInitNames();
        glPushName(0);


        // Set material color, Yellow
        // Sun
        glRGB(255, 255, 0);
        glLoadName(SUN);
        auxSolidSphere(15.0f);

        // Draw Mercury
        glRGB(128,0,0);
        glPushMatrix();
        glTranslatef(24.0f, 0.0f, 0.0f);
        glLoadName(MERCURY);
        auxSolidSphere(2.0f);
        glPopMatrix();

        // Draw Venus
        glPushMatrix();
        glRGB(128,128,255);
        glTranslatef(60.0f, 0.0f, 0.0f);
        glLoadName(VENUS);
        auxSolidSphere(4.0f);
        glPopMatrix();

        ...
        ...     Other planets
        ...

        // Restore the matrix state
        glPopMatrix();  // Modelview matrix

        // Flush drawing commands
        glFlush();
        }
```

In PLANETS, the glInitNames function initializes and clears the names stack, and glPushName pushes 0 on the stack to put at least one entry on the stack. For the Sun and each planet, we call glLoadName to name the object or objects about to be drawn. This name, in the form of an unsigned integer, is not pushed on the name stack but rather replaces the current name on top of the stack. Later we'll discuss keeping an actual stack of names. For now, we just replace the top name of the name stack each time we draw an object (the Sun or a particular planet).

Working with Selection Mode

As mentioned, OpenGL can operate in three different rendering modes. The default mode is GL_RENDER, in which all the drawing actually occurs on screen. To use selection, we must change the rendering mode to selection by calling the OpenGL function:

```
glRenderMode(GL_SELECTION);
```

When we actually want to draw again, we call

```
glRenderMode(GL_RENDER);
```

to place OpenGL back in rendering mode. The third rendering mode is GL_FEED-BACK, discussed later in this chapter.

The naming code in Listing 19-1 has no effect unless we first switch the rendering mode to selection mode. Most often, you will use the same function to render the scene in both GL_RENDER mode and GL_SELECTION modes, as we have done here.

Listing 19-2 is the code that is triggered by the clicking of the left mouse button. This code gets the mouse coordinates from lParam and passes them to ProcessSelection, which will process the mouse click for this example.

Listing 19-2 Code that responds to the left mouse button click

```
case WM_LBUTTONDOWN:
        {
        int xPos = LOWORD(lParam);   // horizontal position of cursor
        int yPos = HIWORD(lParam);   // vertical position of cursor

        // Render in selection mode and display results
        ProcessSelection(xPos, yPos);
        }
```

The Selection Buffer

The selection buffer is filled with hit records during the rendering process. A hit record is generated whenever a primitive or collection of primitives is rendered that would have been contained in the viewing volume. Under normal conditions, this is simply anything that would have appeared on screen.

The selection buffer is an array of unsigned integers, and each hit record occupies at least four elements of the array. The first array index contains the number of names that are on the names stack when the hit occurs. For the PLANETS example (Listing 19-1), this will always be 1. The next two entries contain the minimum and maximum window z coordinates of all the vertices contained by the viewing volume since the last hit record. This value, which ranges from [0,1], is scaled to the size of an unsigned integer ($2^{32}-1$) for storage in the selection buffer. This pattern, illustrated in Figure 19-1, is then repeated for all the hit records contained in the selection buffer.

The format of the selection buffer gives you no way of knowing how many hit records you will need to parse. This is because the selection buffer is not actually filled

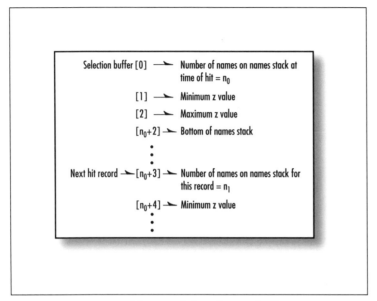

Figure 19-1 Hit record format of the selection buffer

until you switch the rendering mode back to GL_RENDER. When you do this with the glRenderMode function, the return value of glRenderMode returns the number of hit records copied.

Listing 19-3 shows the processing function called when a mouse click occurs for the PLANETS example program. It shows the selection buffer being allocated and specified with glSelectBuffer. This function takes two arguments: the length of the buffer and a pointer to the buffer itself.

Listing 19-3 Function to process the mouse click

```
// Process the selection, which is triggered by a right mouse
// click at (xPos, yPos).
#define BUFFER_LENGTH 64
void ProcessSelection(int xPos, int yPos)
        {
        // Space for selection buffer
        GLuint selectBuff[BUFFER_LENGTH];

        // Hit counter and viewport storage
        GLint hits, viewport[4];

        // Set up selection buffer
        glSelectBuffer(BUFFER_LENGTH, selectBuff);

        // Get the viewport
        glGetIntegerv(GL_VIEWPORT, viewport);
```

continued on next page

continued from previous page

```
// Switch to projection and save the matrix
glMatrixMode(GL_PROJECTION);
glPushMatrix();

// Change render mode
glRenderMode(GL_SELECT);

// Establish new clipping volume to be unit cube around
// mouse cursor point (xPos, yPos) and extending two pixels
// in the vertical and horizontal direction
glLoadIdentity();
gluPickMatrix(xPos, yPos, 2,2, viewport);

// Apply perspective matrix
gluPerspective(45.0f, fAspect, 1.0, 425.0);

// Draw the scene
RenderScene();

// Collect the hits
hits = glRenderMode(GL_RENDER);

// If a single hit occurred, display the info.
if(hits == 1)
        ProcessPlanet(selectBuff[3]);

// Restore the projection matrix
glMatrixMode(GL_PROJECTION);
glPopMatrix();

// Go back to modelview for normal rendering
glMatrixMode(GL_MODELVIEW);
}
```

Picking

Picking occurs when you use the mouse position to create and use a modified viewing volume during selection. By creating a smaller viewing volume positioned in your scene under the mouse position, only objects that would be drawn within that viewing volume will generate hit records. By examining the selection buffer, you can then see which objects, if any, were clicked on by the mouse.

The gluPickMatrix function is a handy utility that will create a matrix describing the new viewing volume:

```
void gluPickMatrix(GLdouble x, GLdouble y, GLdouble width, GLdouble height, GLint viewport[4]);
```

The x and y parameters are the center of the desired viewing volume in window coordinates. The mouse position can be plugged in here, and the viewing volume will be centered directly underneath the mouse. The width and height parameters then specify the dimensions of the viewing volume in window pixels. For clicks near an object, use a large value; for clicks right next to the object or directly on the object, use a smaller value. The viewport array contains the window coordinates of the currently defined viewport. This can easily be obtained by calling

```
glGetIntegerv(GL_VIEWPORT, viewport);
```

To use gluPickMatrix, you should first save the current Projection matrix state (thus saving the current viewing volume). Then call glLoadIdentity to create a unit-viewing volume. Calling gluPickMatrix then translates this viewing volume to the correct location. Finally, you must apply any further perspective projections you may have applied to your original scene; otherwise, you won't get a true mapping. Here's how it's done for the PLANETS example (from Listing 19-3):

```
// Switch to projection and save the matrix
glMatrixMode(GL_PROJECTION);
glPushMatrix();

// Change render mode
glRenderMode(GL_SELECT);

// Establish new clipping volume to be unit cube around
// mouse cursor point (xPos, yPos) and extending two pixels
// in the vertical and horizontal direction
glLoadIdentity();
gluPickMatrix(xPos, yPos, 2,2, viewport);

// Apply perspective matrix
gluPerspective(45.0f, fAspect, 1.0, 425.0);

// Draw the scene
RenderScene();

// Collect the hits
hits = glRenderMode(GL_RENDER);
```

In this segment, the viewing volume is saved first. Then selection mode is entered, the viewing volume is modified to include only the area beneath the mouse cursor, and the scene is redrawn by calling RenderScene. After the scene is rendered, we call glRenderMode again to place OpenGL back into normal rendering mode and get a count of generated hit records.

In the next segment, if a hit occurred (for this example, there is either one hit or none), we pass the entry in the selection buffer that contains the name of the object selected or our ProcessPlanet function. Finally, we restore the Projection matrix (thus the old viewing volume is restored) and switch the active matrix stack back to the Modelview matrix, which is usually the default.

```
// If a single hit occurred, display the info.
if(hits == 1)
        ProcessPlanet(selectBuff[3]);

// Restore the projection matrix
glMatrixMode(GL_PROJECTION);
glPopMatrix();

// Go back to modelview for normal rendering
glMatrixMode(GL_MODELVIEW);
```

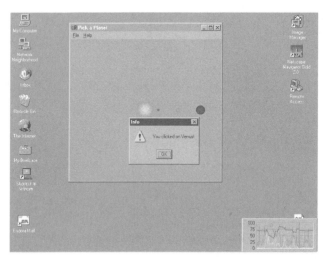

Figure 19-2 Output from PLANETS, after clicking on a planet

The ProcessPlanet function simply displays a message box telling which planet was clicked on. This code is not shown because it is fairly trivial, consisting of no more than a switch and some message-box function calls.

The output from PLANETS is shown in Figure 19-2, where you can see the result of clicking on the second planet from the Sun.

Hierarchical Picking

For the PLANETS example, we didn't push any names on the stack, but rather just replaced the existing one. This single name residing on the name stack was then the only name returned in the selection buffer. We can also get multiple names when a selection hit occurs, by placing more than one name on the name stack. This is useful, for instance, in drill-down situations when you need to know not only that a particular bolt was selected, but that it belonged to a particular wheel, on a particular car, and so forth.

To demonstrate multiple names being returned on the names stack, we will stick with the astronomy theme of our previous example. Figure 19-3 shows two planets (okay, so use a little imagination)—a large blue planet with a single moon, and a smaller red planet with two moons.

Rather than just identify the planet or moon that's clicked on, we want to also identify the planet that is associated with the particular moon. The code in Listing 19-4 shows our new rendering code for this scene. We push the names of the moons onto the names stack so that it will contain the name of the planet as well as the name of the moon when selected.

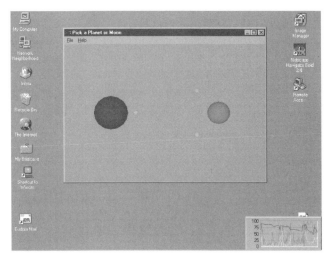

Figure 19-3 Two planets with their respective moons

Listing 19-4 Rendering code for the MOONS example program

```
#define EARTH    1
#define MARS        2
#define MOON1   3
#define MOON2   4


// Called to draw scene
void RenderScene(void)
        {
        // Clear the window with current clearing color
        glClear(GL_COLOR_BUFFER_BIT | GL_DEPTH_BUFFER_BIT);

        // Save the matrix state and do the rotations
        glMatrixMode(GL_MODELVIEW);
        glPushMatrix();

        // Translate the whole scene out and into view
        glTranslatef(0.0f, 0.0f, -300.0f);

        // Initialize the names stack
        glInitNames();
        glPushName(0);


        // Draw the Earth
        glPushMatrix();
        glRGB(0,0,255);
        glTranslatef(-100.0f,0.0f,0.0f);
        glLoadName(EARTH);
        auxSolidSphere(30.0f);
```

continued on next page

continued from previous page

```
// Draw the Moon
glTranslatef(45.0f, 0.0f, 0.0f);
glRGB(220,220,220);
glPushName(MOON1);
auxSolidSphere(5.0f);
glPopName();
glPopMatrix();

// Draw Mars
glRGB(255,0,0);
glPushMatrix();
glTranslatef(100.0f, 0.0f, 0.0f);
glLoadName(MARS);
auxSolidSphere(20.0f);

// Draw Moon1
glTranslatef(-40.0f, 40.0f, 0.0f);
glRGB(220,220,220);
glPushName(MOON1);
auxSolidSphere(5.0f);
glPopName();

// Draw Moon2
glTranslatef(0.0f, -80.0f, 0.0f);
glPushName(MOON2);
auxSolidSphere(5.0f);
glPopName();
glPopMatrix();


// Restore the matrix state
glPopMatrix();  // Modelview matrix

// Flush drawing commands
glFlush();
}
```

Now in our ProcessSelection function, we still call the ProcessPlanet function that we wrote, but this time we pass the entire selection buffer:

```
// If a single hit occurred, display the info.
if(hits == 1)
        ProcessPlanet(selectBuff);
```

Listing 19-5 shows the more substantial ProcessPlanet function for this example. In this instance, the bottom name on the names stack will always be the name of the planet because it was pushed on first. If a moon is clicked on, it will also be on the names stack. This function displays the name of the planet selected, and if it was a moon, that information is also displayed. A sample output is shown in Figure 19-4.

Listing 19-5 Code that parses the selection buffer for the MOONS sample program

```
// Parse the selection buffer to see which planet/moon was selected
void ProcessPlanet(GLuint *pSelectBuff)
        {
        int id,count;
        char cMessage[64];
```

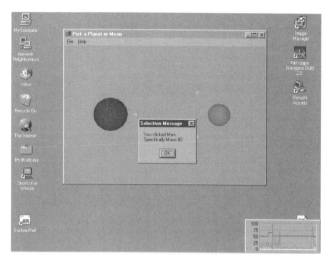

Figure 19-4 Sample output from the MOONS sample program

```
// How many names on the name stack
count = pSelectBuff[0];

// Bottom of the name stack
id = pSelectBuff[3];

// Select on earth or mars, whichever was picked
switch(id)
        {
        case EARTH:
                strcpy(cMessage,"You clicked Earth.");

                // If there is another name on the name stack,
                // then it must be the moon that was selected
                // This is what was actually clicked on
                if(count == 2)
                        strcat(cMessage,"\nSpecifically the moon.");

                break;

        case MARS:
                strcpy(cMessage,"You clicked Mars.");

                // We know the name stack is only two deep. The precise
                // moon that was selected will be here.
                if(count == 2)
                        {
                        if(pSelectBuff[4] == MOON1)
                                strcat(cMessage,"\nSpecifically Moon #1.");
                        else
                                strcat(cMessage,"\nSpecifically Moon #2.");
                        }
                break;
```

continued on next page

continued from previous page

```
                // If nothing was clicked we shouldn't be here!
                default:
                        strcpy(cMessage,"Error - Nothing was clicked on!");
                        break;
        }

        // Display the message about planet and moon selection
        MessageBox(NULL,cMessage,"Selection Message",MB_OK);
        }
```

Feedback

Feedback, like selection, is a rendering mode that does not produce output in the form of pixels on the screen. Instead, information is written to a feedback buffer about how the scene would have been rendered. This information includes transformed vertex data in window coordinates, color data resulting from lighting calculations, and texture data.

Feedback mode is entered just like selection mode, by calling glRenderMode with a GL_FEEDBACK argument. You must reset the rendering mode to GL_RENDER to fill the feedback buffer and return to normal rendering mode.

The Feedback Buffer

The feedback buffer is an array of floating point values specified with the glFeedback function:

```
void glFeedbackBuffer(GLsizei size, GLenum type, GLfloat *buffer);
```

This function takes the size of the feedback buffer, the type and amount of drawing information wanted, and finally a pointer to the buffer itself.

Valid values for type are shown in Table 19-1. The type of data specifies how much data is placed in the feedback buffer for each vertex. Color data (C) is represented by a single value in color index mode, or four values for RGBA color mode.

Table 19-1 Feedback Buffer Types

Type	Vertex Coordinates	Color Data	Texture Data	Total Values
GL_2D	x, y	N/A	N/A	2
GL_3D	x, y, z	N/A	N/A	3
GL_3D_COLOR	x, y, z	C	N/A	3 + C
GL_3D_COLOR_TEXTURE	x, y, z	C	4	7 + C
GL_4D_COLOR_TEXTURE	x, y, z, w	C	4	8 + C

Feedback Data

The feedback buffer contains a list of tokens followed by vertex data and possibly color and texture data. You can parse for these tokens (see Table 19-2) to determine the types of primitives that would have been rendered.

Table 19-2 Feedback Buffer Tokens

Token	Primitive
GL_POINT_TOKEN	Points
GL_LINE_TOKEN	Line
GL_LINE_RESET_TOKEN	Line segment when line stipple is reset
GL_POLYGON_TOKEN	Polygon
GL_BITMAP_TOKEN	Bitmap
GL_DRAW_PIXEL_TOKEN	Pixel rectangle drawn
GL_COPY_PIXEL_TOKEN	Pixel rectangle copied
GL_PASS_THROUGH_TOKEN	User-defined marker

The point, bitmap, and pixel tokens are followed by data for a single vertex, and possibly color and texture data. This depends on the data type from Table 19-1 specified in the call to glFeedbackBuffer. The line tokens return two sets of vertex data, and the polygon token is immediately followed by the number of vertices that follow. The user-defined marker (GL_PASS_THROUGH_TOKEN) is followed by a single floating point value that is user defined. Figure 19-5 shows an example of a feedback buffer's memory layout if a GL_3D type were specified.

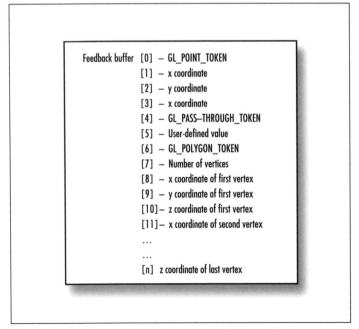

Figure 19-5 An example memory layout for a feedback buffer

PassThrough Markers

When your rendering code is executing, the feedback buffer is filled with tokens and vertex data as each primitive is specified. Just as you can in selection mode, you can flag certain primitives by naming them. In feedback mode you can set markers between your primitives, as well. This is done by calling glPassThrough:

```
void glPassThrough(GLfloat token );
```

This function places a GL_PASS_THROUGH_TOKEN in the feedback buffer, followed by the value you specify when calling the function. This is somewhat similar to naming primitives in selection mode. It's the only way of labeling objects in the feedback buffer.

An Example

An excellent use of feedback is to obtain window coordinate information regarding any objects that you render. You can then use this information to place controls near the objects in the window, or other windows around them.

To demonstrate feedback, we will use selection to determine which of two objects on the screen have been clicked on by the user. Then we will enter feedback mode and render the scene again to obtain the vertex information in window coordinates. Using this data, we will determine the minimum and maximum x and y values for the object, and use those values to draw a focus rectangle around the object. The end result is graphical selection and deselection of one or both objects.

Label the Objects for Feedback

Listing 19-6 shows the rendering code for our example program, SELECT. *Don't confuse this with a demonstration of selection mode!* Even though selection mode is employed in our example to select an object on the screen, we are demonstrating the process of getting enough information about that object—using feedback—to draw a rectangle around it using normal Windows GDI commands. Notice the use of glPassThrough to label the objects in the feedback buffer, right after the calls to glLoadName to label the objects in the selection buffer.

Listing 19-6 Rendering code for the SELECT example program

```
#define CUBE          1
#define SPHERE  2

// Called to draw scene
void RenderScene(void)
        {
        // Clear the window with current clearing color
        glClear(GL_COLOR_BUFFER_BIT | GL_DEPTH_BUFFER_BIT);

        // Save the matrix state and do the rotations
        glMatrixMode(GL_MODELVIEW);
        glPushMatrix();
```

```
// Translate the whole scene out and into view
glTranslatef(-80.0f, 0.0f, -300.0f);

// Initialize the names stack
glInitNames();
glPushName(0);


// Set material color, Yellow
// Cube
glRGB(255, 255, 0);
glLoadName(CUBE);
glPassThrough((GLfloat)CUBE);
auxSolidCube(75.0f);


// Draw Sphere
glRGB(128,0,0);
glTranslatef(130.0f, 0.0f, 0.0f);
glLoadName(SPHERE);
glPassThrough((GLfloat)SPHERE);
auxSolidSphere(50.0f);

// Restore the matrix state
glPopMatrix();  // Modelview matrix

// Flush drawing commands
glFlush();
}
```

Step 1: Select the Object

Figure 19-6 shows the output from this rendering code, displaying a cube and a sphere. When the user clicks on one of the objects, the function ProcessSelection is called (Listing 19-7). This is very similar to the selection code in the previous two examples.

Listing 19-7 Selection processing for the SELECT example program

```
// Process the selection, which is triggered by a right mouse
// click at (xPos, yPos).
#define BUFFER_LENGTH 64
void ProcessSelection(int xPos, int yPos)
    {
    // Space for selection buffer
    GLuint selectBuff[BUFFER_LENGTH];

    // Hit counter and viewport storage
    GLint hits, viewport[4];

    // Set up selection buffer
    glSelectBuffer(BUFFER_LENGTH, selectBuff);

    // Get the viewport
    glGetIntegerv(GL_VIEWPORT, viewport);

    // Switch to projection and save the matrix
```

continued on next page

continued from previous page

```
glMatrixMode(GL_PROJECTION);
glPushMatrix();

// Change render mode
glRenderMode(GL_SELECT);

// Establish new clipping volume to be unit cube around
// mouse cursor point (xPos, yPos) and extending two pixels
// in the vertical and horizontal direction
glLoadIdentity();
gluPickMatrix(xPos, yPos, 2,2, viewport);

// Apply perspective matrix
gluPerspective(60.0f, fAspect, 1.0, 425.0);

// Draw the scene
RenderScene();

// Collect the hits
hits = glRenderMode(GL_RENDER);

// Restore the projection matrix
glMatrixMode(GL_PROJECTION);
glPopMatrix();

// Go back to modelview for normal rendering
glMatrixMode(GL_MODELVIEW);

// If a single hit occurred, display the info.
if(hits == 1)
        MakeSelection(selectBuff[3]);
}
```

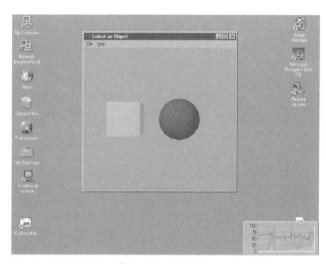

Figure 19-6 Output from the SELECT program after the
sphere has been clicked

Step 2: Get Feedback on the Object

Now that we have determined which object was clicked on, we set up the feedback buffer, and render again in feedback mode. Listing 19-8 is the code that sets up feedback mode for this example and calls RenderScene to redraw the scene. This time, however, the glPassThrough functions put markers for the objects in the feedback buffer.

Listing 19-8 Load and parse the feedback buffer

```
// Go into feedback mode and draw a rectangle around the object
#define FEED_BUFF_SIZE 4096
void MakeSelection(int nChoice)
        {
        // Space for the feedback buffer
        GLfloat feedBackBuff[FEED_BUFF_SIZE];

        // Storage for counters, etc.
        int size,i,j,count;

        // Min and max x and y values for 2D vertex positions
        float nMaxX,nMaxY,nMinX,nMinY;

        // Initial minimum and maximum values
        nMaxX = nMaxY = -999999.0f;
        nMinX = nMinY =  999999.0f;

        // Set the feedback buffer
        glFeedbackBuffer(FEED_BUFF_SIZE,GL_2D, feedBackBuff);

        // Enter feedback mode
        glRenderMode(GL_FEEDBACK);

        // Redraw the scene
        RenderScene();

        // Leave feedback mode
        size = glRenderMode(GL_RENDER);


        // Parse the feedback buffer and get the
        // min and max X and Y window coordinates
        i = 0;
        while(i < FEED_BUFF_SIZE)
                {
                // Search for appropriate token
                if(feedBackBuff[i] == GL_PASS_THROUGH_TOKEN)
                        if(feedBackBuff[i+1] == (GLfloat)nChoice)
                        {
                        i+= 2;
                        // Loop until next token is reached
                        while(feedBackBuff[i] != GL_PASS_THROUGH_TOKEN)
                                {
                                // Just get the polygons
                                if(feedBackBuff[i] == GL_POLYGON_TOKEN)
                                        {
```

continued on next page

continued from previous page

```
                                    // Get all the values for this polygon
                                    // How many vertices
                                    count = (int)feedBackBuff[++i];
                                    i++;

                                    // Loop for each vertex
                                    for(j = 0; j < count; j++)
                                        {
                                        // Min and Max X
                                        if(feedBackBuff[i] > nMaxX)
                                                nMaxX = feedBackBuff[i];

                                        if(feedBackBuff[i] < nMinX)
                                                nMinX = feedBackBuff[i];

                                        i++;

                                        // Min and Max Y
                                        if(feedBackBuff[i] > nMaxY)
                                                nMaxY = feedBackBuff[i];

                                        if(feedBackBuff[i] < nMinY)
                                                nMinY = feedBackBuff[i];

                                        i++;
                                        }
                            }
                    else
                            i++;    // Get next index and keep looking
                    }
            break;
            }
        i++;
        }

    // Draw focus rectangle
    HighLight((int)floor(nMinX+0.5), (int)floor(nMinY+0.5),
            (int)floor(nMaxX+0.5), (int)floor(nMaxY+0.5));
    }
```

Once the feedback buffer is filled, we search it for GL_PASS_THROUGH_TOKEN. When we find one, we get the next value and determine if it is the one we are looking for. If so, the only thing that remains is to loop through all the polygons for this object and get the minimum and maximum window x and y values. The HighLight function uses the Win32 function DrawFocusRect to draw a rectangle around the outside of the object that was clicked on. This function uses XOR drawing mode, so calling it twice causes the rectangle to disappear. This allows you to select by clicking on an object, and deselect by clicking again.

Summary

Selection and feedback are two very powerful features of OpenGL that give you the ability to facilitate the user's active interaction with the scene. Selection and picking are used to identify an object or region of a scene in OpenGL coordinates rather than just window coordinates. Feedback returns valuable information about how an object or primitive is actually drawn in the window. You can use this information to supplement OpenGL's graphics with Windows-specific graphics and operations that appear to interact with your OpenGL graphics.

Reference Section

GLFEEDBACKBUFFER

Purpose	Sets the feedback mode.
Include File	<gl.h>
Syntax	void glFeedbackBuffer(GLsizei size, GLenum type, GLfloat *buffer);
Description	This function establishes the feedback buffer and the type of vertex information desired. Feedback is a rendering mode; rather than rendering to the framebuffer, OpenGL sends vertex data to the buffer specified here. These blocks of data can include x, y, z, and w coordinate positions (in window coordinates); color data for color index mode or RGBA color mode; and finally texture coordinates. The amount and type of information desired is specified by the type argument.
Parameters	
size	GLsizei: The maximum number of entries allocated for *buffer*. If a block of data written to the feedback would overflow the amount of space allocated, only the part of the block that will fit in the buffer is written.
type	GLenum: Specifies the kind of vertex data to be returned in the feedback buffer. Each vertex generates a block of data in the feedback buffer. For each of the following types, the block of data contains a primitive token identifier followed by the vertex data. The vertex data specifically will include the following:

GL_2D: x and y coordinate pairs.

GL_3D: x, y, and z coordinate triplets.

GL_3D_COLOR: x, y, z coordinates, and color data (one value for Color Index, four for RGBA).

GL_3D_COLOR_TEXTURE: x, y, z coordinates, color data (one or four values), and four texture coordinates.

GL_4D_COLOR_TEXTURE: x, y, z, and w coordinates, color data (one or four values), and four texture coordinates.

buffer	GLfloat*: Buffer where feedback data will be stored.
Returns	None.

Example
The following code from the SELECT sample program initializes the feed-back buffer with glFeedbackBuffer, then switches to feedback mode, renders the scene, and fills the feedback buffer by switching back to rendering mode.

```
#define FEED_BUFF_SIZE  4096
...
...

// Space for the feedback buffer
GLfloat feedBackBuff[FEED_BUFF_SIZE];

...
...

// Set the feedback buffer
glFeedbackBuffer(FEED_BUFF_SIZE,GL_2D, feedBackBuff);

// Enter feedback mode
glRenderMode(GL_FEEDBACK);

// Redraw the scene
RenderScene();

// Leave feedback mode
size = glRenderMode(GL_RENDER);
```

See Also
glPassThrough, glRenderMode, glSelectBuffer

GLINITNAMES

Purpose	Initializes the name stack.
Include File	<gl.h>
Syntax	void glInitNames(void);
Description	The name stack is used to allow drawing primitives or groups of primitives, to be named with an unsigned integer when rendered in selection mode. Each time a primitive is named, its name is pushed on the names stack with glPushName, or the current name is replaced with glLoadName. This function sets the name stack to its initial condition with no names on the stack.
Returns	None.
Example	The following code is from the example program PLANETS. It initializes the names stack and places a single value on the stack.

```
// Initialize the names stack
glInitNames();
glPushName(0);
```

See Also
glInitNames, glPushName, glRenderMode, glSelectBuffer

GLLOADNAME

Purpose	Loads a name onto the name stack.
Include File	<gl.h>
Syntax	void glLoadName(GLuint name);
Description	This function places the name specified on the top of the names stack. The name stack is used to name primitives or groups of primitives when rendered in selection mode. The current name on the names stack is actually replaced by the name specified with this function.
Parameters	
name	GLuint: Specifies the name to be placed on the names stack. Selection names are unsigned integers.
Returns	None.
Example	The following code from the PLANETS example program shows a name being loaded on the name stack just before an object is rendered.

```
// Set material color, Yellow
// Sun
glRGB(255, 255, 0);
glLoadName(SUN);
auxSolidSphere(15.0f);
```

See Also	glInitNames, glPushName, glRenderMode, glSelectBuffer

GLPASSTHROUGH

Purpose	Places a marker in the feedback buffer.
Include File	<gl.h>
Syntax	void glPassThrough(GLfloat token);
Description	When OpenGL is placed in feedback mode, no pixels are drawn to the framebuffer.Instead, information about the drawing primitives is placed in a feedback buffer. This function allows you to place the token GL_PASS_THROUGH_TOKEN in the midst of the feedback buffer, which will be followed by the floating point value specified by this function. This function is called in your rendering code and has no effect unless in feedback mode.
Parameters	
token	GLfloat: A value to be placed in the feedback buffer following the GL_PASS_THROUGH_TOKEN.
Returns	None.

Example   The following code from the SELECT example program demonstrates
                    glPassThrough and glLoadName being used together to identify an object.
                    This marks the object in both the selection and feedback buffers.

```
// Set material color, Yellow
// Cube
glRGB(255, 255, 0);
glLoadName(CUBE);
glPassThrough((GLfloat)CUBE);
auxSolidCube(75.0f);
```

See Also   glFeedbackBuffer, glRenderMode

GLPOPNAME

Purpose   Pops (removes) the top entry from the name stack.

Include File   <gl.h>

Syntax   void glPopName(void);

Description   The names stack is used during selection to identify drawing commands.
                    This function removes a name from the top of the names stack. The cur-
                    rent depth of the name stack can be retrieved by calling glGet with
                    GL_NAME_STACK_DEPTH.

Returns   None.

Example   The following code from the MOONS example program uses the name
                    stack to place the name of a planet and its moon on the name stack for
                    selection. This code in particular shows one moon's name being popped
                    off the name stack before the name of the next moon is pushed on.

```
// Draw Mars
glRGB(255,0,0);
glPushMatrix();
glTranslatef(100.0f, 0.0f, 0.0f);
glLoadName(MARS);
auxSolidSphere(20.0f);

// Draw Moon1
glTranslatef(-40.0f, 40.0f, 0.0f);
glRGB(220,220,220);
glPushName(MOON1);
auxSolidSphere(5.0f);
glPopName();

// Draw Moon2
glTranslatef(0.0f, -80.0f, 0.0f);
glPushName(MOON2);
auxSolidSphere(5.0f);
glPopName();
glPopMatrix();
```

See Also   glInitNames, glLoadName, glRenderMode, glSelectBuffer, glPushName

GLPUSHNAME

Purpose	Specifies a name that will be pushed on the name stack.
Include File	<gl.h>
Syntax	void glPushName(GLuint name);
Description	The names stack is used during selection to identify drawing commands. This function pushes a name on the names stack to identify any subsequent drawing commands. The names stack maximum depth can be retrieved by calling glGet with GL_MAX_NAME_STACK_DEPTH, and the current depth by calling glGet with GL_NAME_STACK_DEPTH. The maximum depth of the names stack can vary with implementation, but all implementations must support at least 64 entries.
Parameters	
name	GLuint: The name to be pushed onto the names stack.
Returns	None.
Example	The following code from the MOONS example program uses the name stack to place the name of a planet and its moon on the name stack for selection. This code in particular shows the names of the moons being pushed on the names stack after the name of the planet. This moon's name is then popped off before the next moon's name is pushed on.

```
// Draw Mars
glRGB(255,0,0);
glPushMatrix();
glTranslatef(100.0f, 0.0f, 0.0f);
glLoadName(MARS);
auxSolidSphere(20.0f);

// Draw Moon1
glTranslatef(-40.0f, 40.0f, 0.0f);
glRGB(220,220,220);
glPushName(MOON1);
auxSolidSphere(5.0f);
glPopName();

// Draw Moon2
glTranslatef(0.0f, -80.0f, 0.0f);
glPushName(MOON2);
auxSolidSphere(5.0f);
glPopName();
glPopMatrix();
```

See Also	glInitNames, glLoadName, glRenderMode, glSelectBuffer, glPopName

GLRENDERMODE

Purpose	Sets one of three rasterization modes.
Include File	<gl.h>

Syntax	GLint glRenderMode(GLenum mode);
Description	OpenGL operates in three modes when you call your drawing functions:

GL_RENDER: Render mode (the default). Drawing functions result in pixels in the framebuffer.

GL_SELECT: Selection mode. No changes to the framebuffer are made. Rather, hit records are written to the selection buffer that record primitives that would have been drawn within the viewing volume. The selection buffer must be allocated and specified first with a call to glSelectBuffer. GL_FEEDBACK: Feedback mode. No changes to the framebuffer are made. Instead coordinates and attributes of vertices that would have been rendered in render mode are written to a feedback buffer. The feedback buffer must be allocated and specified first with a call to glFeedbackBuffer.

Parameters

mode   GLenum: Specifies the rasterization mode. May be any one of GL_RENDER, GL_SELECT, and GL_FEEDBACK. The default value is GL_RENDER.

Returns   The return value depends on the rasterization mode that was set the last time this function was called:

GL_RENDER: Zero.

GL_SELECT: The number of hit records written to the selection buffer.

GL_FEEDBACK: The number of values written to the feedback buffer. Note, this is not the same as the number of vertices written.

Example   The following code shows glRenderMode being called to enter selection mode for the PLANETS example program. The function is called again with an argument of GL_RENDER to enter rendering mode and to write the hit records into the selection buffer.

```
// Process the selection, which is triggered by a right mouse
// click at (xPos, yPos).
#define BUFFER_LENGTH 64
void ProcessSelection(int xPos, int yPos)
    {
    // Space for selection buffer
    GLuint selectBuff[BUFFER_LENGTH];

    // Hit counter and viewport storage
    GLint hits, viewport[4];

    // Set up selection buffer
    glSelectBuffer(BUFFER_LENGTH, selectBuff);

    // Get the viewport
    glGetIntegerv(GL_VIEWPORT, viewport);

    // Switch to projection and save the matrix
    glMatrixMode(GL_PROJECTION);
    glPushMatrix();
```

```
// Change render mode
glRenderMode(GL_SELECT);

// Establish new clipping volume to be unit cube around
// mouse cursor point (xPos, yPos) and extending two pixels
// in the vertical and horizontal direction
glLoadIdentity();
gluPickMatrix(xPos, yPos, 2,2, viewport);

// Apply perspective matrix
gluPerspective(45.0f, fAspect, 1.0, 425.0);

// Draw the scene
RenderScene();

// Collect the hits
hits = glRenderMode(GL_RENDER);

// If a single hit occurred, display the info.
if(hits == 1)
        ProcessPlanet(selectBuff[3]);

// Restore the projection matrix
glMatrixMode(GL_PROJECTION);
glPopMatrix();

// Go back to modelview for normal rendering
glMatrixMode(GL_MODELVIEW);
}
```

See Also   glFeedbackBuffer, glInitNames, glLoadName, glPassThrough, glPushName, glSelectBuffer

GLSELECTBUFFER

Purpose   Sets the buffer to be used for selection values.

Include File   <gl.h>

Syntax   void glSelectBuffer(GLsizei size, GLuint *buffer);

Description   When OpenGL is in selection mode (GL_SELECT), drawing commands do not produce pixels in the framebuffer. Instead they produce hit records that are written to the selection buffer that is established by this function. Each hit record consists of the following data:

1. The number of names on the names stack when the hit occurred.

2. The minimum and maximum z values of all the vertices of the primitives that intersected the viewing volume. This value is scaled to range from 0.0 to 1.0.

3. The contents of the name stack at the time of the hit, starting with the bottommost element.

Parameters

size   GLsize: The number of values that can be written into the buffer established by *buffer.*

buffer   GLuint*: A pointer to memory that will contain the selection hit records.

Returns   None.

Example   The following code shows the selection buffer being created for the PLANETS example program.

```
// Process the selection, which is triggered by a right mouse
// click at (xPos, yPos).
#define BUFFER_LENGTH 64
void ProcessSelection(int xPos, int yPos)
    {
    // Space for selection buffer
    GLuint selectBuff[BUFFER_LENGTH];

    ...
    ...

    // Set up selection buffer
    glSelectBuffer(BUFFER_LENGTH, selectBuff);
```

See Also   glFeedbackBuffer, glInitNames, glLoadName, glPushName, glRenderMode

GLUPICKMATRIX

Purpose   Defines a picking region that can be used to identify user selections.

Include File   <glu.h>

Syntax   void **gluPickMatrix**(GLdouble x, GLdouble y, GLdouble width, GLdouble height, GLint viewport[4]);

Description   This function creates a matrix that will define a smaller viewing volume based on screen coordinates for the purpose of selection. By using the mouse coordinates with this function in selection mode, you can determine which of your objects are under or near the mouse cursor. The matrix created is multiplied by the current projection matrix. Typically you should call glLoadIdentity before calling this function, then multiply the perspective matrix that you used to create the viewing volume in the first place. If you are using gluPickMatrix to pick NURBS surfaces, you must turn off the NURBS property GLU_AUTO_LOAD_MATRIX before using this function.

Parameters

x,y   GLdouble: The center of the picking region in window coordinates.

width,height   GLdouble: The width and height of the desired picking region in window coordinates.

viewport   GLint[4]: The current viewport. You can get the current viewport by calling glGetIntegerv with GL_VIEWPORT.

Returns   None.

Example   The following code is from the PLANETS example program. It uses this
                  function to create a new clipping volume that will cover an area of the
                  window only 2 pixels by 2 pixels, centered on the mouse cursor. This is
                  used to select the object that is directly underneath the mouse cursor.

```
// Hit counter and viewport storage
GLint hits, viewport[4];

// Set up selection buffer
glSelectBuffer(BUFFER_LENGTH, selectBuff);

// Get the viewport
glGetIntegerv(GL_VIEWPORT, viewport);

// Switch to projection and save the matrix
glMatrixMode(GL_PROJECTION);
glPushMatrix();

// Change render mode
glRenderMode(GL_SELECT);

// Establish new clipping volume to be unit cube around
// mouse cursor point (xPos, yPos) and extending two pixels
// in the vertical and horizontal direction
glLoadIdentity();
gluPickMatrix(xPos, yPos, 2,2, viewport);

// Apply perspective matrix
gluPerspective(45.0f, fAspect, 1.0, 425.0);

// Draw the scene
RenderScene();

// Collect the hits
hits = glRenderMode(GL_RENDER);

// If a single hit occurred, display the info.
if(hits == 1)
        ProcessPlanet(selectBuff[3]);

// Restore the projection matrix
glMatrixMode(GL_PROJECTION);
glPopMatrix();

// Go back to modelview for normal rendering
glMatrixMode(GL_MODELVIEW);
```

See Also   glGet, glLoadIdentity, glMultMatrix, glRenderMode, gluPerspective

20

OPENGL ON THE 'NET: VRML

20

OPENGL ON THE 'NET: VRML

OpenGL has been put to many uses. This chapter is about one use in particular that has recently become widely popular: *virtual reality*.

OpenGL is ideally suited for a variety of graphical and modeling purposes, and it is the enabling technology behind the pseudorealism of virtual reality. These computer-generated "worlds," in which many of the user's senses can be immersed, contain three-dimensional scenes that include sound and sometimes feeling and resistance via tactile feedback mechanisms. Some products offer technology as diverse as tactile feedback gloves, three-dimensional goggles, and arcade-style computer games that allow realistic movement in all directions.

The Internet, which is far more mature technologically than is virtual reality, has recently become the popular playground of the modern computer enthusiast—not to mention a necessity for the professional, academic, and military users for which it was originally intended. Few of us today are unfamiliar with the term *cyberspace*—a virtual world of its own with many places to visit and people to meet—and most of us have spent at least some time *surfing* this network of computers and information resources.

In this chapter we will briefly discuss an implementation of virtual reality over the Internet that has its origins in OpenGL. For the sake of brevity, we will assume you have some familiarity with the Internet, the World-Wide Web (the Web or WWW), and the Web browsers that facilitate navigation across the World-Wide Web.

When Worlds Collide

It didn't take long for someone to make the connection between cyberspace and virtual reality. If in cyberspace you are traveling around the world, visiting different places and accessing various types of information, it makes sense to be able to do this in a visual environment rather than with textual displays that are so hard to muddle through.

Graphical navigation of the Internet first began when Tim Berners-Lee at the European Center for Nuclear Physics (CERN) in Geneva devised a set of protocols that made it possible to easily encode the connection between various files contained in FTP archives. These connections link documents to other documents of interest, allowing navigation from one document to another, even across directories, computers, and continents. These protocols use Universal Resource Locators (URLs) to identify document locations and were the genesis of the World-Wide Web.

Soon thereafter, Marc Anderson (who later founded Netscape Communications Corporation) created a Web browser that could mix various kinds of files, including text and graphics, into a single presentation. This browser was NCSA Mosaic, and it could represent the relationships within a document to other documents, as well as provide a protocol for formatting the documents with embedded images and different types of text. The Internet hasn't been the same since. In less than a year, the Internet went from being a technical thing-a-ma-bob to something anyone can use with point-and-click ease.

Two-Dimensional Navigation

Web pages comprise mostly text documents in a special format called HTML (HyperText Markup Language). HTML documents can embed other documents, graphics, even video and sound, as well as hypertext links to other documents and Web sites. Figure 20-1 shows a typical Web home page; this one belongs to Silicon Graphics and is fairly graphics heavy. By clicking on a button for a subject of interest to you, or on a "hot spot" on the larger image, you are transported to another page containing the linked information of interest and/or a whole new set of categories and links to other pages.

Enter VRML

The graphical yet two-dimensional method of Web navigation became immensely popular in just a couple of years. "Navigating" through cyberspace in this manner was very efficient as long as the information you were seeking could be represented as a document. However, the world is not a library, and Internet entrepreneurs were pushing the limits of what could be accomplished effectively with two-dimensional document-centric navigation.

Then in 1994 (not that long ago!), Mark Pesce and Tony Parisi created a new type of Web document and browser that could navigate in three dimensions. On Valentine's Day 1994, the first virtual reality Web site was up and running. It was three-dimensional, and it allowed you to navigate a 3D scene and click on objects of interest that were linked to other 3D scenes or HTML Web pages.

These 3D files were modeled with a new scripting language, VRML (originally meaning Virtual Reality Markup Language and eventually Virtual Reality Modeling Language). Silicon Graphics (SGI), a world leader in computer graphics technology,

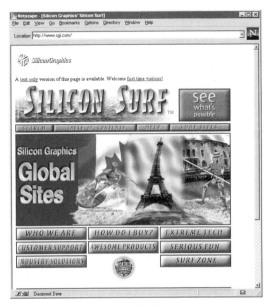

Figure 20-1 A typical Web home page
with hypertext links

graciously placed their Open Inventor scene-description language file format in the
public domain, and it became the basis for VRML version 1.0.

About Open Inventor

Open Inventor is a much higher-level interface for 3D modeling than is provided by the OpenGL API
alone. Open Inventor is actually a C++ class library built on top of OpenGL. Programmers use this library,
or tools that use the library, to create complex 3D scenes and objects that often aren't practical by hand,
using OpenGL alone. Open Inventor objects (in the C++ sense) have a feature called *persistence* that
allows them to be saved to disk and reloaded later. SGI provided the VRML developer community with
free source code. This was used to parse the native scene-description script used by Open Inventor for per-
sistent storage of 3D scenes and objects (in binary), into more meaningful information about the location
and characteristics of the objects that make up the scene. Open Inventor is discussed in more detail later
in this chapter.

Fueled by free source code from SGI, by April of 1995 VRML became the darling of
the popular Internet press. VRML browsers from multiple vendors appeared on the
market, for all of the popular platforms including PCs. Now the technology existed for
users to do more than just select items from a menu. Now they could actually walk
through a library or museum or even a shopping mall, and pick up and examine items
of interest.

WebSpace

Silicon Graphics was naturally the first to have a fully compliant, commercially available VRML Web browser. WebSpace was its name, and it set the standard by which all other VRML browsers were to be compared. WebSpace was developed to run on SGI's own workstations, but a third party, Template Graphics Software, has been allowed to develop a version for Microsoft Windows and other platforms. All versions of this browser now fully support the VRML 1.0 standard and make use of OpenGL to render the scenes.

Installation

WebSpace can be installed as a helper application in most WWW browsers. For installation instructions, see the README file for your browser. WebSpace loads VRML files with a .wrl extension as well as Open Inventor scene files with an .iv extension. In addition, the latest version of WebSpace from Template Graphics will automatically load .wrl files that have been compressed with gzip, a popular Internet file-compression format. This makes for substantially smaller files and thus faster loading.

WebSpace on CD

A copy of Template Graphics's Windows version of WebSpace is available on this book's CD in the Chapter 20 subdirectory. The software and sample VRML scenes are courtesy of Silicon Graphics Inc. and Template Graphics Software. These files are provided as shareware. *If you use this software for more than evaluation purposes, you should register your copy. See the README file for licensing information.*

The Walk Viewer

There are two modes of operation for navigation in WebSpace. The first is the Walk Viewer, which lets you actually navigate through the model presented, such as a museum or architectural model. The second is the Examiner Viewer, which is used to examine objects in WebSpace, such as an airplane, tool, or piece of furniture. You'll see both of these modes in action shortly.

Figure 20-2 shows WebSpace viewing a sample VRML scene in the Walk Viewer mode. This mode is used when the browser is being used to travel through a 3D scene. It could be a simple 3D terrain, an architectural view of a building, a shopping mall, or even a small city area (as shown).

Detailed Use Instructions

This chapter is an introduction to VRML and Virtual Reality on the Internet. We used WebSpace as our baseline to demonstrate the concepts of 3D Web navigation. For more detailed information on use and features of the WebSpace browser, see the README and help files that accompany the program.

Figure 20-2 WebSpace in the Walk
Viewer mode

Some objects in the scene may be hot-linked to other sites or to HTML documents, just like a 2D Web page. The controls at the bottom of the window are collectively called the Dashboard; they are used to navigate throughout the scene. The diamond on the far left is the Seek tool; it helps you rapidly navigate to a point of interest in the scene. To use the Seek Tool, simply click on it to activate the Seek mode and then click anywhere else in the scene. The navigator smoothly proceeds to that place without your having to use any of the other navigation tools.

The tool on the far right is an Arrow Pad that is used to slide the view of the scene vertically or horizontally. This view is only a translation along the x- or y-axis (side-to-side or up-and-down). The camera point of view is not tilted or rotated in any way.

Finally, in the center of the dashboard is the Joystick—used to move forward and backward through the scene, turn left and right, and tilt the view up and down. Simply click on the joystick and drag it up or down to move forward or backwards, and left or right to twist the view to the left or right.

3D Navigation
The 3D interface of WebSpace may seem somewhat primitive to up-to-the-minute Internet users. It's reminiscent of a flight simulator or arcade game, and could use some improvement in its ease of use. You can expect dramatic improvements in the coming years as more browsers are introduced.

There is a red knob on the right side of the joystick, called the Tilt Knob, that is used to tilt the view up or down. Click on the Tilt Knob and drag it up or down to view the ceiling or floor, respectively. In Figure 20-3, the Tilt Knob is being used to look up at the top of some buildings.

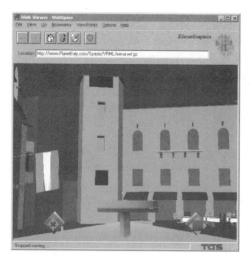

Figure 20-3 Using the Tilt Knob to look "up" at the rooftops

The Examiner Viewer

The Examiner Viewer mode is for exploring an object, rather than traveling through a virtual scene. Figure 20-4 shows WebSpace examining a model of the first Kitty Hawk airplane. Imagine walking through a virtual museum in the Walk Viewer, then clicking on a small picture of the plane. When the browser switches to the Examiner mode, you get a closer look at the plane. In addition, there may be other hypertext links to a report about flight, or the Wright brothers.

You'll notice the Dashboard in Figure 20-4 looks similar to that of the Walk Viewer, but the joystick is now replaced by a Trackball and Thumbwheel. The Thumbwheel lets you move the object closer or farther away from the point of view. Click on the Thumbwheel and drag up to move the object farther away, or down to move the object closer. Figure 20-5 shows the Kitty Hawk airplane at a greater distance.

With the Trackball you rotate the viewed object in any direction. Click anywhere on the Trackball, and drag it to spin the object being viewed. If you release the left mouse button while moving the mouse, the Trackball will continue to spin the principle object.

Open Inventor and VRML

To understand the relationship between Open Inventor and VRML, you may want a little more background on Open Inventor. This object-oriented library and tool set is implemented using OpenGL. The programming library is almost always used from C++, but C bindings exist, as well. This object-oriented approach provides a much higher level of control over the objects and scenes being composed.

Figure 20-4 Examiner Viewer

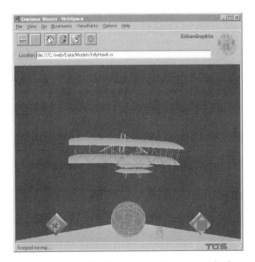

Figure 20-5 The Examiner Viewer with the object at a greater distance away from the viewer

When OpenGL is used to create a scene or object, each function and command has an immediate effect on the frame buffer. Unless you are using double buffering, the results of each action are immediately visible on screen. This is known as *immediate mode rendering*.

Open Inventor, on the other hand, operates in what is sometimes called a *retained* mode. In this mode you use various commands and functions to compose a scene database. This database of objects and materials is then rendered all at once to create the scene. The real power of retained mode is that individual objects in the scene can be manipulated very easily programmatically. Furthermore, relationships between objects can be established that allow the manipulation of one object to affect other objects (such as linked assemblages or mechanical models). Object engines can also be used within the database to perform rotations, animations, and other actions. This information is then embedded within the scene description, and no further programming is necessary on the part of the developer.

The VRML 1.0 specification is based entirely on the Open Inventor 3D file interchange format. This file format, which is nothing more than the scene database in a standardized layout, allows 3D graphics designers to easily exchange objects and scenes when using Open Inventor-based tools. It's easy to store a single object or an entire scene filled with objects, in a single file.

Summary

WebSpace is not the only way to visit cyberspace in 3D. Many other vendors (including Microsoft) have hopped on the bandwagon and developed their own VRML viewers.. WebSpace does offer the unique advantage of compatibility with nearly any Web browser and will load and view both VRML and Open Inventor files, either uncompressed or compressed.

Even as this chapter went to production, the battle was raging over who will set the standards for VRML version 2.0. These newer versions will add new features for animation and multimedia enhancements to 3D scenes viewed over the Internet.

Is virtual reality over the Internet just a passing fad or the beginning of a revolution? Only time will tell, but there is a universal law at play here: "Demand will always consume available bandwidth," whether it's processing power, communication speed, or graphics capabilities. As computer networks manage more speed and work with better graphics hardware, you can be reasonably certain that virtual reality is here to stay. It is only going to get faster, more realistic, and more capable of simulating the world in which we live.

PART IV

OPENGL WITH. . .

IV

OPENGL
WITH. . .

In the fourth and last part of this book, we are going to take a look at some general programming issues that arise when using OpenGL. Two chapters will help C++ programmers who are using the most popular C++ frameworks in use for Windows programmers, MFC and OWL. We won't be leaving out the 4GL and other visual programmers, either. In Chapter 23 we introduce you to an OpenGL OCX that will facilitate the use of OpenGL from almost any 32-bit Windows programming environment.

Finally, no book on Windows and OpenGL would be complete without addressing the interaction of OpenGL with the other graphics APIs. In addition to GDI, this group includes the DirectX architecture and 3DDDI.

21

MFC-BASED OPENGL PROGRAMMING

21

MFC-BASED OPENGL PROGRAMMING

What you'll learn in this chapter:

How to...	Functions You'll Use
Set MFC window styles to support OpenGL	PreCreateWindow
Create and set up the rendering context	OnCreate
Clean up the rendering context when the program terminates	OnDestroy
Place your projection and viewport code	OnSize
Place your rendering code	OnDraw
Prevent screen flicker between renderings	OnEraseBkgnd
Place your palette management code	OnQueryNewPalette, OnPaletteChanged

It is an undeniable fact that a large and growing number of developers are using C++ for Windows development. Throughout this book, however, we have presented all our source code in C. Fortunately, most C++ programmers can easily follow C source code. On the other hand, unfortunately, the converse is not necessarily true (many C programmers cannot follow C++ as easily). This is not to say that C++ is especially harder to grasp and use, but if you picked up this book on graphics programming, you want to learn graphics programming, you probably don't want to have to learn some new syntax along the way as well.

Although any of the samples in this book can be compiled with a C++ compiler as well as a C compiler, most C++ programmers developing for Windows are not writing

C code. Most are using a commercial C++ application framework package, or their own C++ class hierarchy. The point is, most C++ applications don't have windows procedures like the ones in this book, nor do they have those "case statements from hell" that handle every conceivable message that may be posted to a window.

The purpose of this short chapter is to give C++ programmers using a popular application framework a starting place for their OpenGL programs. The application framework for this chapter is the Microsoft Foundation Classes (MFC). The samples and screenshots for this chapter were prepared using Microsoft's Visual C++ 4.0. Other compilers and environments that support MFC should work similarly.

Note: If you are using OWL (Borland's Object Windows Library), coverage of it is included in Chapter 22.

For the purposes of this chapter, we will assume that you are already familiar with the following:

■ Visual C++ and MFC for building Windows NT and Windows 95 applications

■ Chapter 4 of this book, covering OpenGL for Windows and the creation and use of rendering contexts

■ The palette handling material in Chapter 8

Isolate Your OpenGL Code

For any application, it is good design practice to keep your source code as modular as possible. By isolating functional pieces, it becomes much easier to reuse and maintain the code. By isolating your "pure" OpenGL code into a separate module, you can efficiently replace this module with specific code, while retaining the functionality of the rest of the application. Our sample here makes it relatively simple to take any C program in this book and convert it to C++, using MFC and our test application shell.

We start by declaring three functions in a C source file called glcode.c. The file glcode.h contains the declarations for these functions and is included for access in our CView-derived class file.

```
// glcode.h
// Declarations for external OpenGL module.  These functions are
// defined in glcode.c and are called appropriately by the CView
// derived classes.

extern "C" {
        void GLSetupRC(void *pData);
        void GLRenderScene(void *pData);
        void GLResize(GLsizei h, GLsizei w);
        }
```

The GLSetupRC function is where we will place any code that does initialization for our rendering context. This may be as simple as setting the clear color, or as complex as establishing our lighting conditions. The GLRenderScene function will be called by the OnDraw member function of our CView derived class to do the actual rendering. Finally, GLResize will be called by the WM_SIZE handler, passing the new width and height of the window client area. Here you can do any necessary recalculations to establish the viewing volume and viewport.

Notice that the GLSetupRC and GLRenderScene functions take void pointers. This allows you to pass data of any type to your rendering code without changing the interface. Although we could have made the glcode file a C++ file instead of a C file, it's easier to move existing C code from any source and include it in the MFC program. Visual C++ will just compile this module as a C file and link it into the rest of the application.

We don't present the glcode.c file here because the code for our sample is quite lengthy, but you can browse it from the CD to gain general familiarity. Also, we'll reuse the same file for our OWL sample in the next chapter.

Starting with AppWizard

Many an application written with Visual C++ started life with the AppWizard. The document-view architecture can be compared favorably to the model-view architecture of other object-oriented programming environments. Even for quick-and-dirty applications or experimental projects, the AppWizard can provide a fully functional SDI (Single Document Interface), MDI (Multiple Document Interface), or dialog-based application shell in less than a minute. It makes sense to start here, building a sample SDI MFC application that uses OpenGL. To create a sample OpenGL scene, we'll add features and functionality to the CView class. You can use the same methods to add OpenGL functionality to any CWnd-derived class.

Build the Shell

We start by building an SDI shell application with AppWizard, skipping all the options for database access and OLE functionality. Figure 21-1 shows the initial shell SDI application created by AppWizard.

You might also want to turn off the option to add Print and Print Preview. OpenGL scenes can only be rendered to a printer device context if the printer is a color printer supporting four or more bitplanes of color depth (16 or more colors). Printing to a monochrome laser or dot-matrix printer is possible but cumbersome. See the supplementary program GLPRINT in the \OpenGL11 subdirectory for an example of printing OpenGL scenes using the new features in OpenGL version 1.1.

Add the Libraries

Before we start adding any OpenGL code to this shell, we have to add the OpenGL libraries to the project. You do this by selecting Build/Settings from your main menu. The dialog in Figure 21-2 illustrates where to put the OpenGL library names. You may have other libraries you will want to include, depending on your application. These are only the libraries you'll need for OpenGL.

You'll also need to add the OpenGL header files to the project. The easiest place to put these (so you can then just forget about them) is in stdafx.h. Just add the following two headers, and they will be included in the precompiled header file as well:

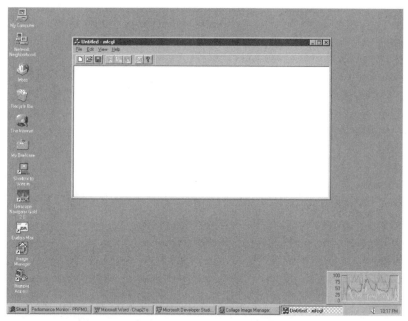

Figure 21-1 Initial AppWizard SDI shell application

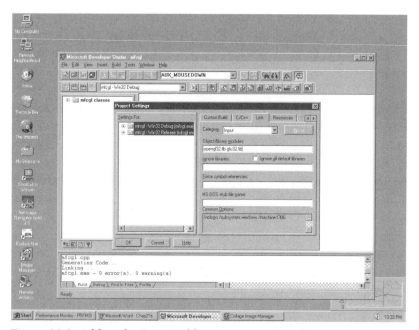

Figure 21-2 Adding the OpenGL libraries to your Visual C++ project.

```
#include <gl\gl.h>              // OpenGL Libraries
#include <gl\glu.h>             // GLU OpenGL Libraries
```

Get CView Ready for OpenGL

When you use the document-view architecture encouraged by AppWizard's SDI application generation, you end up with a class derived from CView that is responsible for the presentation layer of your application. In our example, that class is named CMfcglView. It's declared in the file mfcglView.h and implemented in the file mfcglView.cpp.

The earliest requirement of any window that will be used for OpenGL is that the window styles WS_CLIPCHILDREN and WS_CLIPSIBLINGS be set. We can do this easily in the virtual member function PreCreateWindow of our derived CView class, which is already provided in the file mfcglView.cpp. This function lets us modify the CREATESTRUCT information before the window is created. One of the members of this structure contains the windows styles used on creation. We can simply add these style bits by performing a logical OR, like this:

```
BOOL CMfcglView::PreCreateWindow(CREATESTRUCT& cs)
        {
        // Add Window styles required for OpenGL before window is created
        cs.style |= (WS_CLIPCHILDREN | WS_CLIPSIBLINGS | CS_OWNDC);

        return CView::PreCreateWindow(cs);
        }
```

Notice that we also set the style for CS_OWNDC, so the window can have its own private device context. Although this is not strictly necessary, it saves time and works better with MFC. Some device context pointers returned by MFC functions are temporary and cannot be stored for later use. It's better to get it once and keep it.

Space in the CMfcglView class is allocated to store the device context and the rendering context, with the following code from MfcglView.h:

```
public:
        HGLRC m_hRC;            // Rendering Context
        HDC m_hDC;              // Device Context
```

Pixel Format and Rendering Context

Now that we have a window with the correct styles necessary for OpenGL, we need to set the OpenGL pixel format. Since the device context is required to create a pixel format, we'll wait to do this until after the window is created. We can use the Class Wizard to add a message map entry that will be called when the window receives the WM_CREATE message. Figure 21-3 shows the relevant Class Wizard dialog, containing an entry for WM_DESTROY, as well.

Setting the pixel format within the WM_CREATE handler is relatively straightforward. Listing 21-1 shows our message handler with the code that selects the pixel format for the device context.

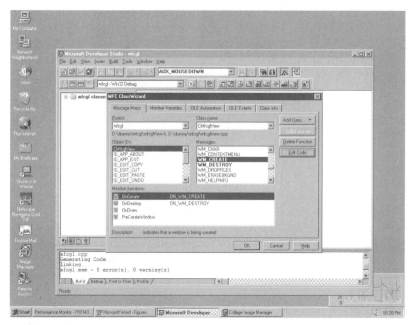

Figure 21-3 Adding the message maps for WM_CREATE and WM_DESTROY

Listing 21-1 WM_CREATE message handler that sets the Pixel Format

```
int CMfcglView::OnCreate(LPCREATESTRUCT lpCreateStruct)
      {
      if (CView::OnCreate(lpCreateStruct) == -1)
            return -1;

      int nPixelFormat;                         // Pixel format index
      m_hDC = ::GetDC(m_hWnd);                   // Get the device context

      static PIXELFORMATDESCRIPTOR pfd = {
            sizeof(PIXELFORMATDESCRIPTOR),       // Size of this structure
            1,                                   // Version of this structure
      PFD_DRAW_TO_WINDOW |                       // Draw to Window (not bitmap)
            PFD_SUPPORT_OPENGL |                 // Support OpenGL in window
            PFD_DOUBLEBUFFER,                    // Double-buffered mode
            PFD_TYPE_RGBA,                       // RGBA color mode
            24,                                  // Want 24bit color
            0,0,0,0,0,0,                         // Not used to select mode
            0,0,                                 // Not used to select mode
            0,0,0,0,0,                           // Not used to select mode
            32,                                  // Size of depth buffer
            0,                                   // Not used to select mode
            0,                                   // Not used to select mode
            PFD_MAIN_PLANE,                      // Draw in main plane
            0,                                   // Not used to select mode
            0,0,0 };                             // Not used to select mode
```

```
// Choose a pixel format that best matches that described in pfd
nPixelFormat = ChoosePixelFormat(m_hDC, &pfd);

// Set the pixel format for the device context
VERIFY(SetPixelFormat(m_hDC, nPixelFormat, &pfd));

// Create the rendering context
m_hRC = wglCreateContext(m_hDC);

// Make the rendering context current, perform initialization, then
// deselect it
VERIFY(wglMakeCurrent(m_hDC,m_hRC));
GLSetupRC();
wglMakeCurrent(NULL,NULL);

return 0;
}
```

Notice that we store the device context and rendering contexts in the class variables m_hDC and m_hRC. Immediately after creating the rendering context, we make it current and call the external function GLSetupRC. This function will do any initialization we need for the rendering context, after which we make it not current. This allows us to use more than one rendering context in case we need multiple windows that use OpenGL. (We won't for our sample, but if you build on this, it's wise to have the option for more than one OpenGL window without the need to recode what you already have.)

Clean Up the Rendering Context

We should go ahead and add the code to clean up and delete the rendering context before we forget. We do this in the WM_DESTROY handler, added in Figure 21-3. We also release the device context obtained for the window.

```
// The window is being destroyed, delete the rendering context,
// and release the device context
void CMfcglView::OnDestroy()
        {
        wglDeleteContext(m_hRC);
        ReleaseDC(m_hWnd,m_hDC);

        CView::OnDestroy();
        }
```

Handling Window Resizing

When the window size changes, the WM_SIZE message is posted to the window. We add a handler for this message with Class Wizard, and call the external function GLResize, passing the new width and height of the window. The rendering context must be made current before calling this function, or the OpenGL function calls in GLResize will have no effect on the rendering context. Here's the code:

```
void CMfcglView::OnSize(UINT nType, int cx, int cy)
        {
        CView::OnSize(nType, cx, cy);
```

continued on next page

continued from previous page

```
        VERIFY(wglMakeCurrent(m_hDC,m_hRC));
        GLResize(cx, cy);
        VERIFY(wglMakeCurrent(NULL,NULL));
        }
```

Rendering the Scene

Now we are ready to add the code that actually draws the OpenGL scene. The member function OnDraw is called whenever the window receives a WM_PAINT message. Here we make the rendering context current and call the GLRenderScene function, which contains only OpenGL function calls. Since we earlier requested a double-buffered window, we call SwapBuffers afterward and then again make the rendering context not current.

```
// Called when window receives WM_PAINT, render our scene
void CMfcglView::OnDraw(CDC* pDC)
        {
        // Make the rendering context current
        wglMakeCurrent(m_hDC,m_hRC);

        // Call our external OpenGL code
        GLRenderScene(NULL);

        // Swap our scene to the front
        SwapBuffers(m_hDC);

        // Allow other rendering contexts to coexist
        wglMakeCurrent(m_hDC,NULL);
        }
```

Don't Erase First

Whenever the window is resized or invalidated, MFC will erase the window background before repainting. Since our OpenGL background is black, this erasing (which sets the window to white) will cause a flicker every time OnDraw is called.

To keep the window from flickering, we override the default handling of WM_ERASEBACKGROUND. Usually, the window is erased before being repainted after a resize. If we return FALSE from this function, however, the window will never be erased before a repaint and there won't be any flicker. Usually this function returns CView::OnEraseBkgnd(pDC), which implements the default behavior of erasing the background, but you can just return FALSE to prevent this behavior.

```
// Override to keep the background from being erased every time
// the window is repainted
BOOL CMfcglView::OnEraseBkgnd(CDC* pDC)
        {
        return FALSE;
        }
```

CPalette Handling

Our finishing touch in the MFC sample is creating and realizing the RGB palette on devices that use palettes (256 color cards). Instead of maintaining a handle to the palette as in Chapter 8, here we'll create an MFC object of type CPalette.

For our function in Listing 21-2 we declare an instance of CPalette in mfcglView.h:

```
CPalette m_GLPalette;   // Logical Palette
```

and then manually add a member function to CMfcGlView that initializes the palette. This code is nearly identical to the function GetOpenGLPalette presented in Chapter 8, except that a CPalette object is constructed instead of a handle to a palette returned.

Listing 21-2 CPalette creation and initialization code

```
// Initializes the CPalette object
void CMfcglView::InitializePalette(void)
        {
        PIXELFORMATDESCRIPTOR pfd;      // Pixel format descriptor
        LOGPALETTE *pPal;               // Pointer to memory for logical palette
        int nPixelFormat;               // Pixel format index
        int nColors;                    // Number of entries in palette
        int i;                          // Counting variable

        BYTE RedRange,GreenRange,BlueRange;
                                // Range for each color entry (7,7,and 3)

        // Get the pixel format index and retrieve the pixel format description
        nPixelFormat = GetPixelFormat(m_hDC);
        DescribePixelFormat(m_hDC, nPixelFormat, sizeof(PIXELFORMATDESCRIPTOR), &pfd);

        // Does this pixel format require a palette?  If not, do not create a
        // palette and just return NULL
        if(!(pfd.dwFlags & PFD_NEED_PALETTE))
                return;

        // Number of entries in palette.  8-bit yields 256 entries
        nColors = 1 << pfd.cColorBits;

        // Allocate space for a logical palette structure plus all the
        // palette entries
        pPal = (LOGPALETTE*)malloc(sizeof(LOGPALETTE) +nColors*sizeof(PALETTEENTRY));

        // Fill in palette header
        pPal->palVersion = 0x300;       // Windows 3.0
        pPal->palNumEntries = nColors;  // table size

        // Build mask of all 1's.  This creates a number represented by having
        // the low-order x bits set, where x = pfd.cRedBits, pfd.cGreenBits,
        // and pfd.cBlueBits.
        RedRange = (1 << pfd.cRedBits) - 1;
        GreenRange = (1 << pfd.cGreenBits) - 1;
        BlueRange = (1 << pfd.cBlueBits) - 1;

        // Loop through all the palette entries
        for(i = 0; i < nColors; i++)
                {
                // Fill in the 8-bit equivalents for each component
                pPal->palPalEntry[i].peRed = (i >> pfd.cRedShift) & RedRange;
                pPal->palPalEntry[i].peRed = (unsigned char)(
                        (double) pPal->palPalEntry[i].peRed * 255.0 / RedRange);

                pPal->palPalEntry[i].peGreen = (i >> pfd.cGreenShift) & GreenRange;
```

continued on next page

continued from previous page

```
            pPal->palPalEntry[i].peGreen = (unsigned char)(
                    (double)pPal->palPalEntry[i].peGreen * 255.0/ GreenRange);

            pPal->palPalEntry[i].peBlue = (i >> pfd.cBlueShift) & BlueRange;
            pPal->palPalEntry[i].peBlue = (unsigned char)(
                    (double)pPal->palPalEntry[i].peBlue * 255.0 / BlueRange);

            pPal->palPalEntry[i].peFlags = (unsigned char) NULL;
            }

    // Create the palette
    m_GLPalette.CreatePalette(pPal);

    // Go ahead and select and realize the palette for this device context
    SelectPalette(m_hDC,(HPALETTE)m_GLPalette,FALSE);
    RealizePalette(m_hDC);

    // Free the memory used for the logical palette structure
    free(pPal);
    }
```

Using the Class Wizard again to add message response functions for WM_QUERYNEWPALETTE and WM_PALETTECHANGED, our code to realize the palette is shown in Listing 21-3.

Listing 21-3 Code to realize CPalette for the view class

```
BOOL CMfcglView::OnQueryNewPalette()
        {
        // If the palette was created.
        if((HPALETTE)m_GLPalette)
                {
                int nRet;

                // Selects the palette into the current device context
                SelectPalette(m_hDC, (HPALETTE)m_GLPalette, FALSE);

                // Map entries from the currently selected palette to
                // the system palette.  The return value is the number
                // of palette entries modified.
                nRet = RealizePalette(m_hDC);

                // Repaint, forces remap of palette in current window
                InvalidateRect(NULL,FALSE);

                return nRet;
                }

        return CView::OnQueryNewPalette();
        }


void CMfcglView::OnPaletteChanged(CWnd* pFocusWnd)
        {
        if(((HPALETTE)m_GLPalette != NULL) && (pFocusWnd != this))
                {
                // Select the palette into the device context
```

```
SelectPalette(m_hDC,(HPALETTE)m_GLPalette,FALSE);

// Map entries to system palette
RealizePalette(m_hDC);

// Remap the current colors to the newly realized palette
UpdateColors(m_hDC);
return;
}

CView::OnPaletteChanged(pFocusWnd);
}
```

This code to realize the palette is very much like that in Chapter 8. Here, though, Windows does not send these messages to the CView-derived class directly, but rather to the application's CMainFrame class. This is because Windows only sends palette messages to the application's main window; it is this window's responsibility to route the messages to any child windows that need to be notified.

So use the Class Wizard once again to add the two palette message handlers to the CMainFrame class. These handlers simply find the active view and post the palette messages to it unchanged, allowing the view to respond as needed. These message handlers are listed in Listing 21-4.

Listing 21-4 CMainFrame code to route palette-handling messages to the view

```
// Route message to CView-derived class
void CMainFrame::OnPaletteChanged(CWnd* pFocusWnd)
    {
    CView* pView = GetActiveView();
    if (pView)
            {
            // OnPaletteChanged is not public, so send a message.
            pView->SendMessage(WM_PALETTECHANGED,
                    (WPARAM)(pFocusWnd->GetSafeHwnd()),
                    (LPARAM)0);
            }
    }

// Route message to CView-derived class.
BOOL CMainFrame::OnQueryNewPalette()
    {
    CView* pView = GetActiveView();
    if (pView)
            {
            // OnQueryNewPalette is not public, so send a message.
            return pView->SendMessage(WM_QUERYNEWPALETTE,
                    (WPARAM)0,
                    (LPARAM)0);
            }

    return FALSE;
    }
```

We also added a WM_TIMER handler and created a timer in our view class to create an animated OpenGL scene (Figure 21-4). The timer function simply invalidates

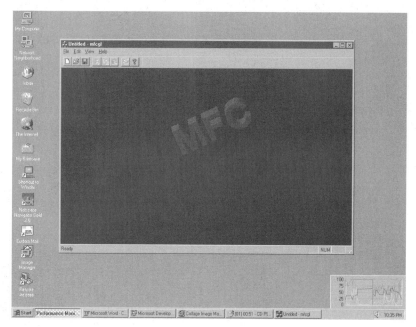

Figure 21-4 Final animated output of our MFC sample

the window, forcing a repaint. In our glcode.c module the rendering function increments a rotation angle each time the screen is redrawn, thus creating the animation effect. All of this code is in the \MFCGL directory on the CD.

Summary

This chapter covered the specific mechanics of using OpenGL from an MFC-based program, demonstrating where to set the Windows styles required for OpenGL, where and when to set the pixel format, and creation of the rendering context. The example program also illustrates when and where to make the rendering context current, and how to realize an MFC CPalette when needed.

You should be able to take the sample application from this chapter and easily add your own custom OpenGL code. In addition, the framework—with all the OpenGL code in the glcode.c module—makes it easy to port existing C/OpenGL samples to our MFC shell program. You can study additional examples in many of the sample programs in this book, which are implemented in C, and in C++ using MFC and OWL (see Chapter 22).

22

OWL-BASED OPENGL PROGRAMMING

22

OWL-BASED OPENGL PROGRAMMING

What you'll learn in this chapter:

How to...	Functions You'll Use
Set OWL window styles to support OpenGL	EvCreate
Create and set up the rendering context	EvCreate
Clean up the rendering context when the program terminates	EvDestroy
Place your projection and viewport code	EvSize
Place your rendering code	EvPaint
Prevent screen flicker between renderings	EvEraseBkgnd
Place your palette-management code	EvQueryNewPalette, EvPaletteChanged

It is an undeniable fact that a large and growing number of developers are using C++ for Windows development. Throughout this book, however, we have presented all our source code in C. Fortunately, most C++ programmers can easily follow C source code. On the other hand, if you picked up this book to learn graphics programming, you probably don't want to have to learn some new syntax along the way.

Although any of the samples in this book can be compiled with a C++ compiler as well as a C compiler, most C++ programmers developing for Windows are not writing C code. Most are using a commercial C++ application framework package, or their own C++ class hierarchy. The point is, most C++ applications don't have windows procedures like the ones in this book, nor do they have those "case statements from hell" that handle every conceivable message that may be posted to a window. Instead, there is a framework of classes that embody the Windows screen objects, with member functions handling the processing of messages.

The purpose of this short chapter is to give C++ programmers using a popular application framework a starting place for their OpenGL programs. The application framework for this chapter is Borland's Object Windows Library (OWL). The samples and screenshots for this chapter were prepared using Borland C++ 5.0. If you are using MFC (Microsoft Foundation Classes), see Chapter 21.

For the purposes of this chapter, we will assume that you are already familiar with the following:

- Borland C++ and OWL for building Windows NT and Windows 95 applications

- Chapter 4 of this book, covering OpenGL for Windows and the creation and use of rendering contexts

- The palette handling material in Chapter 8

Isolate Your OpenGL Code

For any application, it is good design practice to keep your source code as modular as possible. By isolating functional pieces, it becomes much easier to reuse and maintain the code. By isolating your "pure" OpenGL code into a separate module, you can efficiently replace this module with specific code, while retaining the functionality of the rest of the application. Our sample here makes it relatively simple to take any C program in this book and convert it to C++, using OWL and our test application shell.

We start by declaring three functions in a C source file called glcode.c. The file glcode.h contains the declarations for these functions and is included for access in our TWindowView-derived class file.

```
// glcode.h
// Declarations for external OpenGL module.  These functions are
// defined in glcode.c and are called appropriately by the TWindowView
// derived classes.

extern "C" {
        void GLSetupRC(void *pData);
        void GLRenderScene(void *pData);
        void GLResize(GLsizei h, GLsizei w);
        }
```

The GLSetupRC function is where we will place any code that does initialization for our rendering context. This may be as simple as setting the clear color, or as complex as establishing our lighting conditions. The GLRenderScene function will be called by the WM_PAINT handler of our TWindowView-derived class to do the actual rendering. Finally, GLResize will be called by the WM_SIZE handler, passing the new width and height of the window client area. Here you can do any necessary recalculations to establish the viewing volume and viewport.

Notice that the GLSetupRC and GLRenderScene functions take void pointers. This allows you to pass data of any type to your rendering code without changing the interface. Although we could have made the glcode file a C++ file instead of a C file, it's easier to move existing C code from any source and include it in the OWL program. Borland C++ will just compile this module as a C file and link it into the rest of the application.

We don't present the glcode.c file here because the code for our sample is quite lengthy, but we'll use basically the same file for both the OWL and MFC sample programs.

Starting with AppExpert

Many an application written with Visual C++ started life with the AppExpert. The document-view architecture endorsed by AppExpert can be compared favorably to the model-view architecture of other object-oriented programming environments. Even for quick-and-dirty applications or experimental projects, the AppExpert can provide a fully functional SDI (Single Document Interface), MDI (Multiple Document Interface), or dialog-based application shell in less than a minute. It makes sense to start here, building a sample SDI OWL application that uses OpenGL. To create a sample OpenGL scene, we'll add features and functionality to the TWindowView class. You can use the same methods to add OpenGL functionality to any TWindow-derived class.

Build the Shell

We'll start by building an SDI shell application with AppExpert, skipping most of the options for OLE functionality, drag and drop, and so forth. Figure 22-1 shows the first AppExpert dialog to create our shell OWL application.

You might also want to turn off the option to add Print and Print Preview. OpenGL scenes can only be rendered to a printer device context if the printer is a color printer supporting four or more bitplanes of color depth (16 or more colors). Printing to a monochrome laser or dot-matrix printer is possible but cumbersome. See the supplementary program GLPRINT in the \OpenGL11 subdirectory for an example of printing OpenGL scenes using the new features in OpenGL version 1.1.

You can leave the Application options at their default values, or go in and unselect the tool bars, status bars, and so forth. In addition, it's important to select the window styles for Clip Children and Clip Siblings (which are required for OpenGL programs) in the MainWindow Basic Options page. Finally, select the SDI Client page and specify that the main window be derived from TWindowView, as shown in Figure 22-2.

Figure 22-3 shows the shell application after it has been built.

Add the Headers

Before we start adding any OpenGL code to this shell, we have to add the OpenGL headers to the project. Add these two headers to the top of the owlglapp.h header file:

```
#include <gl\gl.h>        // OpenGL Libraries
#include <gl\glu.h>       // GLU OpenGL Libraries
```

This will define the OpenGL functions and commands for all our OWL-based files for this project.

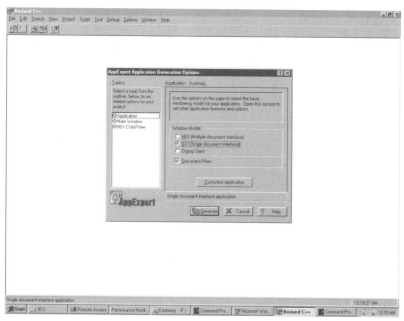

Figure 22-1 Starting a new SDI application with AppExpert

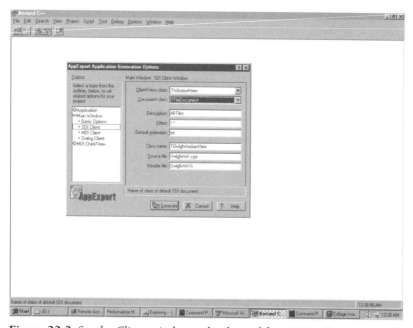

Figure 22-2 Set the Client window to be derived from TWindowView

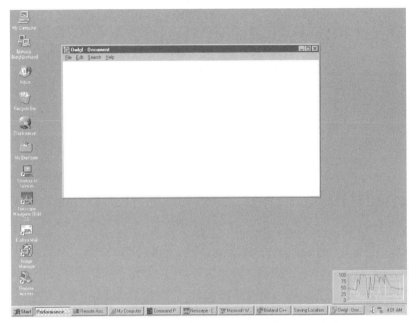

Figure 22-3 AppExpert-generated vanilla SDI application shell

As a general rule, Borland automatically links to an import library that contains all the Win32 API functions. Sometimes these libraries will be out of sync with later releases of the operating system, and you will need to create your own import libraries and link to them. (See the discussion of Borland C++ in the Introduction to the book.)

Add the Message Handlers

We finish fleshing out our OpenGL-capable shell with OWL by adding message handlers for at least the first five of the messages listed in Table 22-1. These first five are required for a well-behaved OpenGL Windows application. The palette messages are only necessary if you are including palette-handling code so your application can run on 8-bit color systems. The WM_TIMER message is optional, as well, but is useful when you need to do timed events or animations. Our example later in this chapter makes use of WM_TIMER to produce an animated effect.

Table 22-1 Typical Messages Handled by an OpenGL Application

Message	Purpose
WM_CREATE	Window creation. Sets required window styles and creates the rendering context.
WM_DESTROY	Cleans up by deleting the rendering context.
WM_ERASEBKGND	Tells Windows GDI not to erase the background when the window needs to be redrawn.
WM_PAINT	Handles any required painting or repainting of window. Call the OpenGL rendering code here.

continued on next page

continued from previous page

Message	Purpose
WM_SIZE	Calls code to modify OpenGL viewport information.
WM_QUERYNEWPALETTE	Application gets the chance to realize its palette.
WM_PALETTECHANGED	Application gets the chance to respond to palette changes.
WM_TIMER	For timed events such as animation.

Figure 22-4 shows the ClassExpert window being used to add these messages.

Fleshing Out the Shell

At this point we have a complete skeleton application, with message handlers defined for window initialization and cleanup, painting, resizing, and palette handling. To this shell we will add the code that enables OpenGL to render in the window. This is accomplished by calling the Win32 functions specific for OpenGL, and then calling our OpenGL-specific code in the glcode.c module at the appropriate places.

Get TWindowView Ready for OpenGL

AppExpert generates a class, TOwlglWindowView, derived directly from TWindowView. This class is responsible for the client window area of the application. In our example, that class is declared in the file owlglwnv.h and implemented in the file owlglwnv.cpp.

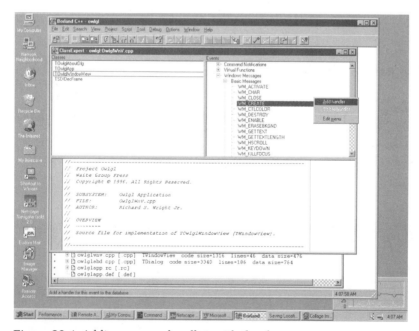

Figure 22-4 Adding message handlers with the class expert

Now we fill in the code for the WM_CREATE handler. As noted earlier in this Chapter, the first requirement of any window that will be used for OpenGL is that the window styles WS_CLIPCHILDREN and WS_CLIPSIBLINGS are set when the window is created. Since we have already set these styles in the AppExpert before generating this program, we don't need to do anything further for this requirement. However, should you need to set this programatically, you can do it easily in the WM_CREATE handler, as follows:

```
int TOwlglWindowView::EvCreate(CREATESTRUCT& cs)
        {
        int result;

        // Add Styles for OpenGL windows
        cs.style |= (WS_CLIPCHILDREN | WS_CLIPSIBLINGS | CS_OWNDC);
        result = TWindowView::EvCreate(cs);
         ...
         ...
```

Notice that we also set the style for CS_OWNDC, so the window can have its own private device context. Although this is not strictly necessary, it saves time and works better with OWL. Some device context pointers returned by OWL functions are temporary and cannot be stored for later use (this is also true for MFC, by the way). So it's better to get it once and keep it.

Space in the TOwlglWindowView class is allocated to store the device context, the rendering context, and the palette, with the following code from owlglwnv.h:

```
public:
        HGLRC m_hRC;                    // Rendering context
        HDC m_hDC = NULL;               // Device context
        TPalette *m_pPalette;           // 3-3-2 Palette
```

Pixel Format and Rendering Context

In the remainder of our WM_CREATE handler, we will set the pixel format and create a rendering context for the window. Since the device context is required to create a pixel format, we'll wait to do this until after the window is created. Setting the Pixel Format within the WM_CREATE handler is done the same way as for any of the C program examples presented in this book after Chapter 3 (remember we ditched the AUX library after this). Listing 22-1 shows our finished message handler, with the code that selects the pixel format for the device context.

Listing 22-1 WM_CREATE message handler that sets the pixel format

```
// Handles WM_CREATE message
int TOwlglWindowView::EvCreate(CREATESTRUCT far& createStruct)
{
  int result;

  createStruct.style |= (WS_CLIPCHILDREN | WS_CLIPSIBLINGS | CS_OWNDC);

  result = TWindowView::EvCreate(createStruct);
```

continued on next page

continued from previous page

```
// Select pixel format/rendering context
static PIXELFORMATDESCRIPTOR pfd = {
    sizeof(PIXELFORMATDESCRIPTOR),  // Size of this structure
    1,                              // Version of this structure
    PFD_DRAW_TO_WINDOW |            // Draw to window (not to bitmap)
    PFD_SUPPORT_OPENGL |            // Support OpenGL calls in window
    PFD_DOUBLEBUFFER,               // Double-buffered mode
    PFD_TYPE_RGBA,                  // RGBA color mode
    24,                             // Want 24-bit color
    0,0,0,0,0,0,                    // Not used to select mode
    0,0,                            // Not used to select mode
    0,0,0,0,0,                      // Not used to select mode
    32,                             // Size of depth buffer
    0,                              // Not used to select mode
    0,                              // Not used to select mode
    PFD_MAIN_PLANE,                 // Draw in main plane
    0,                              // Not used to select mode
    0,0,0 };                        // Not used to select mode

// Get the device context
m_hDC = ::GetDC(this->GetHandle());

// Choose a pixel format that best matches that described in pfd
int nPixelFormat = ChoosePixelFormat(m_hDC, &pfd);

// Set the pixel format for the device context
SetPixelFormat(m_hDC, nPixelFormat, &pfd);

// Create a 3-3-2 palette
SetupPalette(m_hDC);

// Create the rendering context
m_hRC = wglCreateContext(m_hDC);

// Make the rendering context current and perform initializion.
wglMakeCurrent(m_hDC,m_hRC);
GLSetupRC(m_hDC);

// Set a timer for 200 milliseconds
SetTimer(200,101,NULL);

return result;
}
```

Immediately after creating the rendering context, we make it current and call the external function GLSetupRC(). This function will do any initialization we need for the rendering context, after which we make it not current. This allows us to use more than one rendering context in case we need multiple windows that use OpenGL. (We won't for our sample, but if you build on this, it's wise to have the option for more than one OpenGL window without the need to recode what you already have.)

Clean Up the Rendering Context

We should go ahead and add the code to clean up and delete the rendering context before we forget. We do this in the WM_DESTROY handler, as shown in Listing 22-2.

Listing 22-2 WM_DESTROY handler cleans up rendering context

```
// Handles WM_DESTROY message
void TOwlglWindowView::EvDestroy()
{
// Kill the timer
KillTimer(101);

        // Free the rendering context
        wglMakeCurrent(NULL,NULL);
        wglDeleteContext(m_hRC);

        // Release the device context
        ::ReleaseDC(this->GetHandle(),m_hDC);

        TWindowView::EvDestroy();
}
```

Handling Window Resizing

When the window size changes, the WM_SIZE message is posted to the window. We added a handler for this message with ClassExpert, and call the external function GLResize(), passing the new width and height of the window. The rendering context must be made current before calling this function, or the OpenGL function calls in GLResize will have no effect on the rendering context for this window. This code is in Listing 22-3.

Listing 22-3 WM_SIZE handler that adjusts the OpenGL viewport

```
// Handles WM_SIZE message
void TOwlglWindowView::EvSize(uint sizeType, TSize& size)
{
        TWindowView::EvSize(sizeType, size);

        // Make the rendering context current, and call function
        // to make adjustments to OpenGL viewport
        wglMakeCurrent(m_hDC,m_hRC);
        GLResize(size.cx, size.cy);
        wglMakeCurrent(m_hDC,NULL);
}
```

Rendering the Scene

Now we are ready to add the code that actually draws the OpenGL scene. The member function EvPaint was added by ClassExpert and is called whenever the window receives a WM_PAINT message. Here we make the rendering context current and call the GLRenderScene function, which contains only OpenGL function calls. The code for our EvPaint() function is in Listing 22-4.

Note that since we earlier requested a double-buffered window, we have to call SwapBuffers() afterward. Also, any WM_PAINT handler needs to validate the window so that Windows knows you are finished drawing in it. If you don't do this, Windows will continually post WM_PAINT messages to your window.

Listing 22-4 Code for handling WM_PAINT for our OWL-based OpenGL sample

```
// Handles WM_PAINT message
void TOwlglWindowView::EvPaint()
{
        // Make the rendering context current, and call OpenGL Rendering code
        wglMakeCurrent(m_hDC,m_hRC);
        GLRenderScene(NULL);
        wglMakeCurrent(NULL,m_hRC);

        // Finally swap buffers since this rendering context is double buffered
        SwapBuffers(m_hDC);

        // Validate the window
        Validate();
}
```

No Flickering Allowed

Whenever the window is resized or invalidated, Windows will erase the window background before repainting. Since our OpenGL background is black, this erasing (which sets the window to white) will cause a flicker every time EvPaint is called. Even if that weren't so, we are using SwapBuffer() to get our image in the window, which updates the entire client region anyway.

To keep the window from flickering, we override the default handling of WM_ERASEBACKGROUND. Usually, the window is erased before being repainted after a resize. If we return FALSE from this function, however, the window will never be erased before a repaint, and there won't be any flicker. Usually this function returns TWindowView::EvEraseBkgnd(dc), but you can just return FALSE to get this behavior. See Listing 22-5.

Listing 22-5 Preventing the window from being erased everytime it is redrawn

```
// Handles WM_ERASEBACKGROUND message
bool TOwlglWindowView::EvEraseBkgnd(HDC dc)
        {
        return FALSE;   // Do not erase background
        }
```

Keep It Moving

Though certainly not a requirement, the example for this chapter uses a timer to invalidate the window every 200 milliseconds (thus forcing a repaint from our OpenGL code). The code in glcode.c rotates a figure every time it is called. This has the effect of displaying a smoothly rotating set of objects—in this case, three particular 3D letters. Implementing a timer is simple: You set a timer in the EvCreate() function, add a handler for WM_TIMER, and then kill the timer in the EvDestroy handler. This is standard Windows programming, and the pertinent code is shown in Listing 22-6.

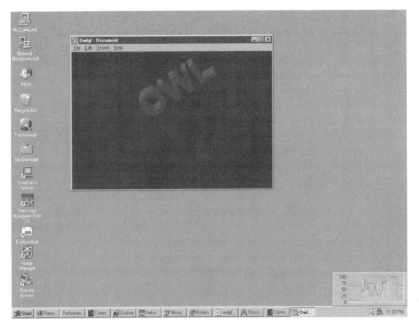

Figure 22-5 Animated output from the OWL-based OpenGL program

The output from our program thus far is shown in Figure 22-5.

Listing 22-6 Code that creates/destroys a timer to do some animation

```
// Handles WM_CREATE message
int TOwlglWindowView::EvCreate(CREATESTRUCT far& createStruct)
        {
        ...
        ...

        // Set a timer for 200 milliseconds
        SetTimer(200,101,NULL);
        ...
        ...


// Handles WM_TIMER message
void TOwlglWindowView::EvTimer(uint timerId)
        {
        TWindowView::EvTimer(timerId);

        // Force a repaint
        Invalidate();
        }


// Handles WM_DESTROY message
```

continued on next page

continued from previous page

```
void TOwlglWindowView::EvDestroy()
        {
        // Kill the timer
        KillTimer(101);
          ...
          ...
```

TPalette Handling

Our finishing touch for the OWL sample is creating and realizing the RGB palette on devices that use palettes (256-color cards). Instead of maintaining a handle to the palette as in Chapter 8, here we'll create an OWL object of type TPalette.

We declare a pointer to a TPalette in owlglwnv.h:

```
TPalette *m_pPalette;   // Logical Palette
```

and then manually add a member function to TOwlglWindowView that initializes the palette. This code, shown in Listing 22-7, is nearly identical to the function GetOpenGLPalette presented in Chapter 8, except that a TPalette object is constructed instead of a handle to a palette returned.

Listing 22-7 TPalette creation and initialization code

```
// Create the palette if necessary
void TOwlglWindowView::SetupPalette(HDC hDC)
        {
        PIXELFORMATDESCRIPTOR pfd;      // Pixel format descriptor
        LOGPALETTE *pPal;               // Pointer to memory for logical palette
        int nPixelFormat;               // Pixel format index
        int nColors;                    // Number of entries in palette
        int i;                          // Counting variable

        BYTE RedRange,GreenRange,BlueRange;       // Range for each color entry
                                                  //              (7,7,and 3)

        // Get the pixel format index and retrieve the pixel format description
        nPixelFormat = GetPixelFormat(hDC);
        DescribePixelFormat(hDC, nPixelFormat,
                sizeof(PIXELFORMATDESCRIPTOR), &pfd);

        // Does this pixel format require a palette?  If not, do not create a
        // palette and just return
        if(!(pfd.dwFlags & PFD_NEED_PALETTE))
                return;

        // Number of entries in palette.  8-bit yields 256 entries
        nColors = 1 << pfd.cColorBits;

        // Allocate space for a logical palette structure plus all the
        // palette entries
        pPal = (LOGPALETTE*)malloc(sizeof(LOGPALETTE)
        +nColors*sizeof(PALETTEENTRY));

        // Fill in palette header
```

```
pPal->palVersion = 0x300;        // Windows 3.0
pPal->palNumEntries = nColors;   // table size

// Build mask of all 1's.  This creates a number represented by having
// the low-order x bits set, where x = pfd.cRedBits, pfd.cGreenBits,
// and pfd.cBlueBits.
RedRange = (1 << pfd.cRedBits) - 1;
GreenRange = (1 << pfd.cGreenBits) - 1;
BlueRange = (1 << pfd.cBlueBits) - 1;

// Loop through all the palette entries
for(i = 0; i < nColors; i++)
        {
        // Fill in the 8-bit equivalents for each component
        pPal->palPalEntry[i].peRed = (i >> pfd.cRedShift) & RedRange;
        pPal->palPalEntry[i].peRed = (unsigned char)(
                (double) pPal->palPalEntry[i].peRed * 255.0 / RedRange);

        pPal->palPalEntry[i].peGreen = (i >> pfd.cGreenShift) & GreenRange;
        pPal->palPalEntry[i].peGreen = (unsigned char)(
                (double)pPal->palPalEntry[i].peGreen * 255.0/ GreenRange);

        pPal->palPalEntry[i].peBlue = (i >> pfd.cBlueShift) & BlueRange;
        pPal->palPalEntry[i].peBlue = (unsigned char)(
                (double)pPal->palPalEntry[i].peBlue * 255.0 / BlueRange);

        pPal->palPalEntry[i].peFlags = (unsigned char) NULL;
        }

// Create the palette
m_pPalette = new TPalette(pPal);

// Go ahead and select and realize the palette for this device context
if(SelectPalette(hDC,m_pPalette->GetHandle(),FALSE) == NULL)
        ::MessageBox(NULL,"Cannot select Palette in Palette Creation", "Error",MB_OK);

if(RealizePalette(hDC) == NULL)
        ::MessageBox(NULL,"Cannot realize Palette in Palette Creation", "Error",MB_OK);

// Free the memory used for the logical palette structure
free(pPal);
}
```

Don't forget to call this function in the WM_CREATE handler. This should be done before the rendering context is created:

```
// Set the pixel format for the device context
SetPixelFormat(m_hDC, nPixelFormat, &pfd);

// Create a 3-3-2 palette
SetupPalette(m_hDC);

// Create the rendering context
m_hRC = wglCreateContext(m_hDC);
```

Having used the ClassExpert to add message-response functions for WM_QUERYNEWPALETTE and WM_PALETTECHANGED, our code to realize the palette is shown in Listing 22-8.

Listing 22-8 Code to realize TPalette for the TWindowView class

```
// Handles WM_QUERYNEWPALETTE message
bool TOwlglWindowView::EvQueryNewPalette()
        {
        bool result;

        // Only if palette was created
        if(m_pPalette != NULL)
                {
                int nRet;

                // Select the palette into the current device context
                if(SelectPalette(m_hDC, m_pPalette->GetHandle(),FALSE) == NULL)
                        ::MessageBox(NULL,"Cannot select Palette","Error",MB_OK);

                // Map entries from the currently selected palette to
                // the system palette.  The return value is the number
                // of palette entries modified.
                nRet = RealizePalette(m_hDC);

                if(nRet == 0)
                        ::MessageBox(NULL,"Cannot realize Palette","Error",MB_OK);

                // Repaint, forces remap of palette in current window
                Invalidate();

                return nRet;
                }

        // Call default function
        result = TWindowView::EvQueryNewPalette();
        return result;
        }



// Handles WM_PALETTECHANGED message
void TOwlglWindowView::EvPaletteChanged(THandle hWndPalChg)
        {
        // Only if palette created, or not this window
        if((m_pPalette != NULL) && (hWndPalChg != this->HWindow))
                {
                // Select the palette into the device context
                ::SelectPalette(m_hDC,m_pPalette->GetHandle(),FALSE);

                // Map entries to system palette
                ::RealizePalette(m_hDC);

                // Remap the current colors to the newly realized palette
                ::UpdateColors(m_hDC);
                return;
                }

        // Call default handler
        TWindowView::EvPaletteChanged(hWndPalChg);
        }
```

The code to realize the palette is very much like that in Chapter 8. Here, though, Windows does not send these messages to the TWindowView-derived class directly, but rather to the application's class TDecoratedFrame (SDIDecFrame, for our example). This is because Windows only sends palette messages to the application's main window. It is this window's responsibility to route the messages to any child windows that need to be notified.

So use the Class Expert once again to add the two palette messages to the SDIDecFrame class. These message handlers, shown in Listing 22-9, simply find the child TWindowView and post the palette messages to it unchanged, allowing the window to respond as needed.

Listing 22-9 CMainFrame code to route palette-handling messages to the view

```
// Route WM_QUERYNEWPALETTE to child
bool SDIDecFrame::EvQueryNewPalette()
    {
    bool result;
    TWindow *pGLWindow;

    // Get the child SDI window
    pGLWindow = GetClientWindow();

    // Send the message
    if(pGLWindow)
            pGLWindow->SendMessage(WM_QUERYNEWPALETTE,0,0);

    return TRUE;
    }

// Route the WM_PALETTECHANGES to child
void SDIDecFrame::EvPaletteChanged(THandle hWndPalChg)
    {
    TWindow *pGLWindow;

    // Get the child SDI window
    pGLWindow = GetClientWindow();

    // Send the message
    if(pGLWindow)
            pGLWindow->SendMessage(WM_PALETTECHANGED, (UINT)hWndPalChg, (UINT)0);
    }
```

Summary

This chapter covered the specific mechanics of using OpenGL from an OWL-based program, demonstrating where to set the Windows styles required for OpenGL, where and when to set the pixel format, and creation of the rendering context. The example program also illustrates when and where to make the rendering context current, and how to realize an OWL TPalette when needed.

You should be able to take the sample application from this chapter and easily add your own custom OpenGL code. In addition, the framework—with all the OpenGL code in the glcode.c module—makes it easy to port existing C/OpenGL samples to our OWL shell program. You can study additional examples in many of the sample programs in this book, which are implemented in C, and in C++ using OWL and MFC (see Chapter 21).

23

VISUAL BASIC AND 4GL-BASED OPENGL PROGRAMMING

23

VISUAL BASIC AND 4GL-BASED OPENGL PROGRAMMING

Other than Chapters 21 and 22, this book has focused on the OpenGL API from the standpoint of a C program. No consideration of Windows programming is complete, however, without a discussion of the many 4GLs and other visual environments popular today. In this chapter we will briefly discuss the requirements of using the OpenGL API from some of these environments. In addition, we will demonstrate an OpenGL OCX (OLE custom control) that is included with this book for two widely used Win32 development environments: Microsoft's Visual Basic 4.0 and Borland's Delphi 2.0.

For the purposes of this chapter we will assume you have a working knowledge of your particular environment (Visual Basic or Delphi), and how to use and call OCX methods. Even if you have no experience with OCX controls, you may be surprised by how easy they are to use.

Low-Level Access Required

Any Windows development language or environment can make use of OpenGL, provided it supports low-level access to the Win32 API and other libraries contained in DLLs. Most environments and tools allow this in order that applications can be integrated with other libraries, or simply so that the developer can take advantage of new operating systems features introduced after the tool is released.

The entire OpenGL API is contained in two DLLs: opengl32.dll and glu32.dll. Just as most Win32 APIs are accessed directly from DLLs, such as user32.dll, gdi32.dll, and others, you can also get to OpenGL functions and commands from a high-level language environment. Each tool and environment takes a different approach to accessing functions in external DLLs. Usually, you need to specify the function name, its arguments, return type, and in which DLL file the function is contained.

There are two disadvantages to using these methods for using OpenGL from one of the aforementioned environments. First, it is extremely tedious! Every OpenGL function needs to be defined and exported for a given environment. In addition, the argument and return types must be mapped to the native data types of the particular environment. Not only the functions must be defined, but so must all those state variables and flags (GL_ACCUM, GL_LOAD, and on and on) from the header files. This is further compounded by the fact that you must do it for each and every environment that would make use of OpenGL!

The second disadvantage is the requirement of Win32 that OpenGL-enabled windows have the Windows styles WS_CLIPCHILDREN and WS_CLIPSIBLINGS set. Some of these environments make it very difficult to get to any low-level window styles unless they're on a proprietary check box somewhere. The worst case is that you may even have to export CreateWindow from Windows itself and call it from within your program.

If you're going through all this trouble to use OpenGL from say, Visual Basic, you might just as well write a DLL in C that does all your OpenGL rendering, and then call into it from your high-level environment. This answer, though it's probably the most optimal in terms of performance, is something of a cop-out that leaves non-C/C++ programmers out of the picture.

But if you bought this book to learn about OpenGL, and you have been able to follow the samples and function definitions, there is still hope!

The Magic of Objects

The term *object oriented* is perhaps, along with *client/server*, one of the most abused and misused buzzwords of the 1990s. We want to avoid a serious debate on this issue, but we think one important new technology holds significant promise for code reuse.

That technology is OLE (Object Linking and Embedding)—or, more importantly for this chapter, the OCX (OLE Custom Control). When Microsoft introduced Visual Basic and made development of custom controls possible through VBXs, a new industry was born almost overnight. New companies and fortunes were made supplying Visual Basic developers with new and interesting widgets. Soon competing environments (PowerBuilder, Delphi, and others) allowed VBXs to be used for their applications. This further fueled the fire of component reuse.

Plug and Play

These so-called plug-and-play software components revolutionized application development for 16-bit Windows. The successor to VBXs was the OCX, which makes use of OLE automation to create a framework for highly portable and reusable software modules. Microsoft has of late made OCX development possible for 16-bit Windows, but the original target was the new generation of 32-bit Windows operating systems.

By packaging your code into an OCX, it can be used by any environment that supports OCXs. This includes MFC-based C++ applications, as well as Visual Basic 4.0, Borland's Delphi 2.0, PowerBuilder, and others. Furthermore, no special consideration is necessary for the host environment. You just register the OCX with the operating system, and all its methods are available. Code that interfaces with the OCX will, naturally, be dependent on the syntax of the environment, but the control itself is merely "installed" into your environment and is ready for use.

Wrap It Up

By wrapping the OpenGL API with an OCX control, we have effectively solved both disadvantages of using OpenGL from a high-level visual language. Now all the functions are defined for us, and we even have a window readily available to do our drawing! Moreover, now we can use OpenGL from any environment that supports OCX controls!

There is one caveat: The OpenGL functions that require callbacks such as those used for NURBS and polygon tessellation cannot be supported here in a manner that would work with all environments. Many environments are not even compiled but rather are interpreted, and passing a pointer to a function is just not possible. The exception may be environments that produce true compiled code that is compatible with the C calling conventions (such as Delphi).

See the document for your environment for details on accessing external functions, as well as supplying C-callable routines from within the host environment.

Use and Operation of WaiteGL.OCX

The OpenGL OCX is named WaiteGL.OCX and is in this chapter's subdirectory on the CD. Using this control is very easy. Follow the directions in this chapter to register the control and install it into your environment. Then just place the control on a form and start calling its methods as if they were OpenGL functions and commands.

Each command is named just as it is in the OpenGL API, but with the leading *gl* dropped. By naming your own control *gl*, your code will look very much like C code that uses OpenGL. See the VB and Delphi examples that follow for an example of this.

This OCX fires two events that you can catch from your application. The first is SetupRC, which is called the first time the OCX tries to paint its client area. At this point, the pixel format and rendering context has already been created and set for the control. Here you can set up your lighting, background colors, and so on. The second event is Render, which is called every time the control needs to be painted. By placing your rendering code here, you effectively draw in the client area with OpenGL.

There are a few other caveats to bear in mind as you use the OCX.

■ Since you may wish to have more than one OpenGL control in your application, the OCX cannot assume that the rendering context for any specific control will always be current. Therefore, two methods—MakeCurrent and MakeNotCurrent—are provided. All your OpenGL calls must be placed within calls to these two functions; this includes within SetupRC and Render.

- Furthermore, you may always call the OpenGL API directly when you have made the rendering context for the OpenGL OCX current. You can do this for performance reasons, or in case new functions are added to later versions of OpenGL that aren't included in the OCX's method list. The source is also included, so if you have Visual C++ and the inclination, you can always make modifications in the control yourself.

- A 3-3-2 palette is created for this control and is realized every time the control fires the Render event. Trying to manipulate the palette yourself can produce unexpected results.

- Finally, the control window is double buffered, so you will always need to call the SwapBuffers method to see your image.

OpenGL Flags

It is impossible to make any use of the OpenGL functions and commands without access to the many special flags and state variables. Each of these flag's values is available via a method by the same name as the flag itself. The method name is in lowercase, however; having them match exactly leads to problems with the real defines in the header files. Although it would make sense for some of these state variables to be implemented as properties, for others it wouldn't. For consistency, then, the methods match the OpenGL API as closely as possible.

Although many functions have several variations, they are only implemented once as a method. This means functions such as

```
void glVertex2fv(const GLfloat *v  );
```

would be implemented as a method as

```
Vertex2(float x, float y)
```

A help file is included (WaiteGL.hlp) that contains all the methods defined for WaiteGL. They are organized by the three OpenGL libraries (gl, glu, and glaux), and for all the constant macro definitions. To use the help file, find the OpenGL function needed and then look for the WaiteGL OCX method for that function.

Now let's examine the specifics of setting up an OpenGL-enabled program in the two most popular 4GL environments. The next section discusses Visual Basic. If you are using Delphi 2.0 (the 32bit version), you can skip to the following section.

Installing and Using WaiteGL from VB 4.0

To make use of WaiteGL.ocx, it must first be registered as an OCX by the operating system (Windows NT or Windows 95). Copy the .ocx file into your system directory and run the supplied ocxreg.exe program. In the command line argument, specify the .ocx filename and either **install** or **uninstall**. For example:

```
ocxreg.exe WaiteGL.ocx install
```

You will find this program (with source) provided on the CD under the subdirectory for this chapter.

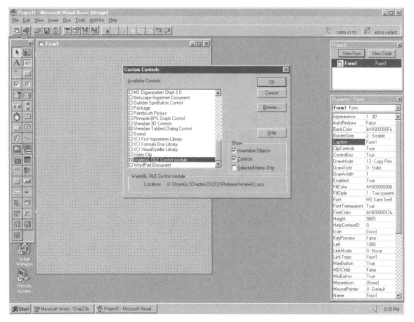

Figure 23-1 Installing the WaiteGL OCX for use in Visual Basic

Installing the Control

Once the control has been registered with the operating system, it must be installed into the Visual Basic tool palette. Select Tools from the main menu, then Custom Controls. Choose the Waite Group OpenGL OCX from the dialog as shown in Figure 23-1, and click OK. Now you can drag the OpenGL control onto your forms, and size and place it accordingly.

A Visual Basic Example

For our VB example, we placed our OpenGL control on a form and named it *gl*. We have also placed a timer on the form with a time interval of 200 milliseconds. See Figure 23-2. You may notice that the control does not paint or erase its client area. This is because the drawing code must be written in Basic and placed in the Render event handler.

As mentioned earlier, two events defined by the OCX must be supported in our code. One is the SetupRC event. You put code here that initializes the rendering context by setting up the initial viewing volume, setting the background, and perhaps drawing colors and any lighting definitions you may want. Listing 23-1 is the code for our rendering context setup. This code simply sets the background and drawing color along with the viewing volume.

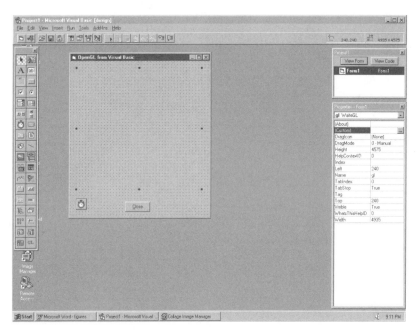

Figure 23-2 A VB form with the OpenGL OCX

Listing 23-1 Set up the rendering context from Visual Basic

```
Private Sub gl_SetupRC()
    Rem Make the rendering context current
    gl.MakeCurrent

    Rem Set the background color to black
    gl.ClearColor 0#, 0#, 0#, 1#

    Rem Establish the viewing volume
    gl.LoadIdentity
    gl.Ortho -100#, 100#, -100#, 100#, -100#, 100#

    Rem Set the drawing color, flush, and
    Rem make the rendering context not current
    gl.Color 0, 0, 255, 255
    gl.Flush
    gl.MakeNotCurrent
End Sub
```

Painting the OpenGL Window

The other event you must support is the Render event. This event is fired by the control whenever its window needs repainting. In this function you will place your code that accesses the OCX's methods to do the actual rendering. Listing 23-2 is the Visual Basic code that draws a wireframe teapot from the AUX library.

Note that the rendering context is first made current, then made not current after the drawing code. This is not strictly necessary if you have only one control and rendering context, but it ensures that no code changes are needed later if you add another control. After the rendering context is made not current, you must call SwapBuffers to bring the image to the foreground.

Listing 23-2 Visual Basic code to draw the AUX library teapot

```
Private Sub gl_Render()
    Rem Make the rendering context current
    gl.MakeCurrent

    Rem Clear the screen and draw the aux lib teapot
    gl.Clear (gl.glColorBufferBit)
    gl.auxWireTeapot (55#)

    Rem Flush the commands, make rendering context
    Rem not current, and then finally swap buffers
    gl.Flush
    gl.MakeNotCurrent

    gl.SwapBuffers
End Sub
```

Now for Some Action

The code above is all that is needed to display our OpenGL images. For this example, though, we have added some animation. We put a timer on the form shown in Figure 23-2, and set the interval to 200 milliseconds. Every time this timer fires, our function will make the rendering context for our OCX current, rotate the viewing matrix by 5°, and then clean up by making the rendering context not current. Finally, we tell the control to repaint, by calling the gl_Render function directly. See Listing 23-3.

Listing 23-3 Timer function that rotates the viewing volume by 5°

```
Private Sub Timer_Timer()
    Rem Make the rendering context current
    gl.MakeCurrent

    Rem Rotate 5 degrees
    gl.Rotate 5#, 0#, 1#, 0.5

    Rem Make rendering context not current, then
    Rem force a redraw
    gl.MakeNotCurrent
    gl_Render
End Sub
```

The completed Visual Basic program is shown running in Figure 23-3.

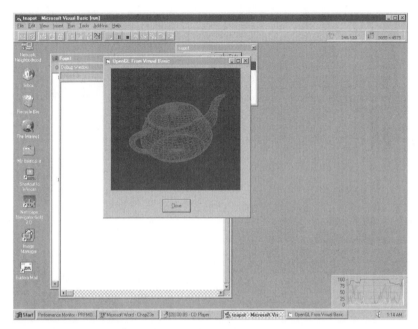

Figure 23-3 Output from the Visual Basic OpenGL program

Installing the OCX in Delphi 2.0

To make use of WaiteGL.ocx, it must first be registered as an OCX by the operating system (Windows NT or Windows 95). Copy the .ocx file into your system directory and run the supplied ocxreg.exe program. In the command line argument, specify the .ocx filename and either **install** or **uninstall**. For example:

```
ocxreg.exe WaiteGL.ocx install
```

You will find this program (with source) provided on the CD under the subdirectory for this chapter.

Installing the Control

Once the control has been registered with the operating system, it must be installed into the Delphi Tool palette. Select Component from the main menu, then Install. Click the OCX button, and the dialog shown in Figure 23-4 will display a list of registered OCX controls that can be installed.

Select the Waite Group OpenGL OXC and then click on OK. This installs the OCX into the Delphi tool palette for your use. Just drag the control onto your forms and you will have a window for OpenGL rendering.

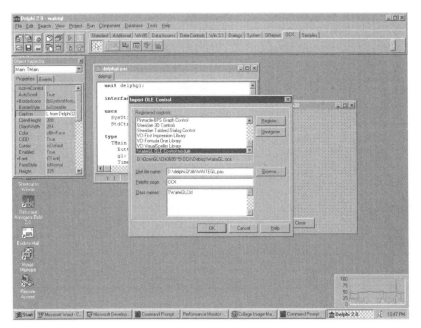

Figure 23-4 Delphi Install OCX dialog

A Delphi Example

For our Delphi example, we start with a new form and place our OpenGL OCX in the middle, taking up most of the client area. We'll also put a timer on the form to do some animation. Figure 23-5 shows the completed form. You may notice that the control does not paint or erase its client area. This is because the drawing code must be written in Pascal and placed in the OnRender event.

Our Object Inspector Events tab shown in Figure 23-6 shows two events that are unique to this control: OnRender and OnSetupRC.

Double-click on the OnSetupRC and the glSetupRC function is created. Your editor is opened to allow this function to be defined. The code in Listing 23-4 shows the setup, making the background color black and initializing an orthogonal viewing volume.

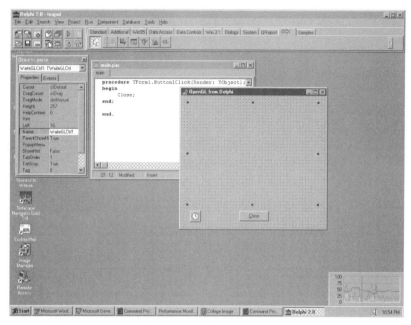

Figure 23-5 Delphi form with the OpenGL OCX

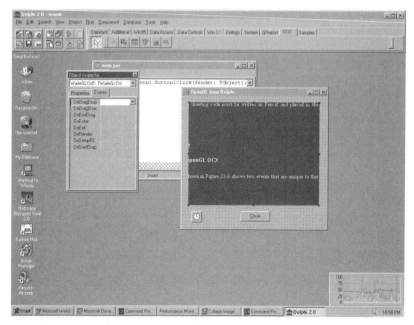

Figure 23-6 Object inspector showing available events for WaiteGL

Listing 23-4 Delphi code called in response to the SetupRC event from the OCX

```
procedure TMain.glSetupRC(Sender: TObject);
begin
     // Make the Rendering context current
     gl.MakeCurrent();

     // Set the clear color, and viewing volume
     gl.ClearColor(0.0, 0.0, 0.0, 1.0);
     gl.LoadIdentity();
     gl.Ortho(-100,100,-100,100,-100,100);

     // Flush the commands and make the rendering context
     // not current
     gl.Flush();
     gl.MakeNotCurrent();
end;
```

Painting the OpenGL Window

The glRender function is created in the same way, by double-clicking on the OnSetupRC event. The code for drawing the wireframe teapot is shown in Listing 23-5. Note that the rendering context is first made current, then made not current after the drawing code. This is not strictly necessary if you have only one control and rendering context, but it ensures that no code changes are needed later if you add another control. After the rendering context is made not current, you must call SwapBuffers to bring the image to the foreground.

Listing 23-5 Delphi code called in response to the Render event from the OCX

```
procedure TMain.glRender(Sender: TObject);
begin
     // Make the rendering context current
     gl.MakeCurrent();

     // Clear the background, and draw a teapot
     gl.Clear(gl.glColorBufferBit());
     gl.Color(0, 0, 255, 255);

     gl.auxWireTeapot(55.0);

     // Flush commands, free rendering context, and
     // swap buffers
     gl.Flush();
     gl.MakeNotCurrent();
     gl.SwapBuffers();
end;
```

Now for Some Action

The code above is all that is needed to display our OpenGL images. For this example, though, we have added some animation. Recall that we put a timer on the form in Figure 23-6, and set the interval to 200 milliseconds. Every time this timer fires, our function will make the rendering context for our OCX current, rotate the viewing matrix by 5°, and then clean up by making the rendering context not current. Finally, we tell the control to repaint, which we can do indirectly by calling the Delphi function Invalidate(). In Delphi, because all OCXs are windows, any command or message you can send a window can also easily be sent to an OCX. See Listing 23-6.

Listing 23-6 Timer code to produce the rotating teapot

```
procedure TMain.Timer1Timer(Sender: TObject);
begin
     // Make rendering context current, then
     // rotate the scene somewhat
     gl.MakeCurrent();
     gl.Rotate(5.0,0.0,1.0,0.5);
     gl.MakeNotCurrent();

     // Repaint the OCX
     gl.Invalidate();
end;
```

Figure 23-7 shows the output from our OpenGL Delphi program.

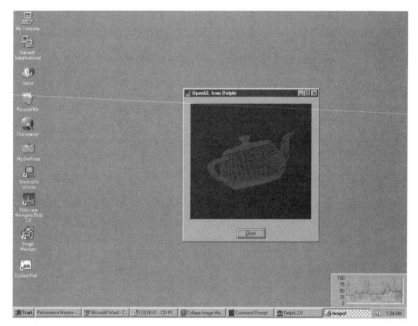

Figure 23-7 Output from Delphi OpenGL program

Some Notes About the Source

The WaiteGL OCX was written with Visual C++ and uses MFC version 4.0. This new version of Visual C++ makes OCX development a breeze and will likely spawn dozens of useful and reusable OLE custom controls. The purpose of this chapter is not to explain how to develop OCX controls. We wanted to present one that uses OpenGL, to let you do OpenGL graphics from within Visual Basic, Delphi, or any other environment that supports OCXs.

Nevertheless, the source code for this control is included on the CD in the subdirectory for this chapter. The code was originally generated by the Microsoft Control Wizard and is fully commented. In addition, the methods and flags are separated into four source files to make maintenance easier. The file ocxgl.cpp contains wrappers for all the gl library functions; similarly, ocxgl contains the glu library functions. The file ocxaux.cpp also contains wrappers for the AUX library wireframe and solid objects, such as the teapot. Finally, ocxflags.cpp contains the access functions that retrieve the OpenGL flags and other defines.

The main file of the project is WaiteGLCtl.cpp, which is the code responsible for setting up the rendering context and firing the setup and painting events. Also, any of the wiggle or OpenGL GDI-related functions are wrapped here. In addition, there are accessor functions that will return the device and rendering contexts directly, in case you need them for your own low-level code.

Note that the OCX uses the DLL versions of MFC. For your convenience, the redistributable portions are in the \REDIST subdirectory, as well.

Summary

In this chapter we have discussed the possibilities and challenges of using OpenGL from some popular visual development environments. Although direct low-level access to the API is certainly possible from any of these environments, a much easier means of access is provided in the form of an OCX control. Most of the sample programs from this book can easily be implemented in a 4GL using this OCX, and for your benefit some are provided in the supplementary examples.

24

THE FUTURE OF OPENGL AND WINDOWS

24

THE FUTURE OF OPENGL AND WINDOWS

This book is not just about OpenGL—more specifically, it's about OpenGL on Microsoft Windows. Let us look briefly at the current state of the art in OpenGL and graphics implementation, and sketch out a picture of likely developments in the near future.

OpenGL is essentially a software interface to 3D hardware. Although what we call a "generic" or "software-only" implementation is available for both Windows NT and Windows 95, 3D hardware for the PC is just beginning to come of age. Naturally, it makes sense for OpenGL to make use of 3D hardware (which is faster than 3D software) when it is available.

At the time this book was written, the 3D graphics acceleration market was immature. Prices of OpenGL-specific accelerator boards for the PC are beginning to come down, but the real driving force behind this market is PC-based games. Video games require the fastest hardware available and/or the most efficient coding. PCs make good gaming machines for a number of reasons. With the right peripherals, you get a high-quality color monitor that can produce higher resolution graphics than any TV set. You get sound, and even wave table synthesis for realistic instrument sounds. In addition to a joystick and a button or two, you also have a mouse and a whole keyboard, opening up new options for game input. Add to this the massive storage capabilities of CD-ROMs, plus the ability to store (and, let's admit it, copy) game programs on hard disks or floppies. Put it all together, and you have a very expensive yet supremely capable gaming machine.

Few people can justify buying a PC just to play games (unless, of course, they are *educational* games). But hey, let's face it—if you already have a PC for your home-based business or for telecommuting, you might as well have a little fun with it, right? When Microsoft Windows grew more dominant than DOS for business and productivity applications, many people installed Windows for just that purpose. Nonetheless, until the last year or so, game developers avoided Windows and kept right on writing games for DOS.

The reason for this can be summed up in one word: performance. Windows did make life easier for the applications developer because all graphics commands acquired similar identities regardless of the underlying graphics hardware. Want to draw a rectangle? Just call the rectangle function! You don't need to know how to convert row and column coordinates to a memory address, and there's no fussing with algorithms. All you needed for your graphics hardware was a Windows driver that would translate GDI calls into hardware instructions.

Unfortunately, this approach added many layers of code between the programmer's graphics instructions and the hardware that actually produced the graphics on the screen. This generated a graphics phenomenon commonly referred to as S-L-O-W. No sane games developer would consider writing Windows-hosted video games, and for a good long while, the most stunning examples of Windows-based games were Solitaire and Reversi.

Hardware vendors seeking to capitalize on the emerging markets in desktop publishing and Windows-based word processing started to bring out PC graphics cards that had hardware acceleration of many common Windows-based drawing commands. A flood of 2D accelerated graphics cards filled the market with speedy Windows-based workstations, which promised to make Windows-based games more practical. Developers have a hard time resisting a sexy new graphical environment that just plain looks cool in comparison to DOS's text-mode interface. Slowly, card games, strategy games, and even a few video games began to emerge into the marketplace.

By the time nearly everyone recognized that Windows ruled the desktop, most of the best games (particularly action games and vehicle simulators) were still being written for DOS. Developers simply could not achieve the frame rates and lightning-fast bitmap transfers under Windows that were possible under DOS.

Microsoft's first attempt to help game developers along was called the WinG API. It was really little more than just a few new functions that enabled very fast bitblts. The WinG API was a substantial improvement, but it still wasn't enough to woo the major players in the games market.

The release of Windows 95 proved to be a major turning point in this chronology. Microsoft desperately wanted to establish Windows 95 as the 32-bit successor to DOS for home and corporate users. History would have it that Windows NT actually got the major mind-share of corporate America, and that Windows 95 found a cozy place at home. But even before this became obvious, Microsoft wanted to make Windows 95 a premium gaming platform. For that, Microsoft would need to spruce up the multimedia capabilities of Windows 95 in a very big way.

To give game developers more direct access to hardware, Microsoft devised a set of APIs now known as DirectX. This includes Direct Draw for fast screen updates, Direct Sound for fast sound and MIDI streaming, Direct Play for networked multiplayer games, and Direct Input for better responsiveness to joysticks and other I/O devices. A new driver model rests atop a very thin hardware abstraction layer and gives Windows game developers unprecedented access to hardware—and thus unprecedented speed.

The latest component added to the Direct X family is Direct 3D. Today's video games are no longer flat, two-dimensional space games. They are highly complex flight simulators, and dungeon adventure games with texture-mapped monsters, walls, and corridors. Direct 3D is tightly integrated with Direct Draw and 3D accelerated hardware. If a feature does not exist in hardware, it is emulated in software. This lets developers code and test their applications and later seamlessly take advantage of extra performance benefits provided by new hardware down the road.

What does all this have to do with OpenGL? Quite simply, what's good for the goose is good for the gander! Within one to two years of the printing of this book, 3D accelerated graphics hardware will be practically ubiquitous. There are many historical parallels that support this prediction. For example, when CD-ROMs where first introduced they didn't play music CDs. Then someone had the bright idea that adding this capability would differentiate them from the rest of the market. Who wouldn't want to listen to music while at their workstation? Now, of course, you can't buy a new CD-ROM that doesn't play standard musical CDs.

The same was true of the original 2D graphics accelerators for Windows. Accelerated boards quickly became affordable; it was virtually free to get the extra speed boost. Finally, there's the example of fax/modems. Go ahead, try to find a modem (a new one, now) that won't also work as a fax board. The chip manufacturers put all the logic on one chip and mass-produced standard modems right out of existence.

Clearly, 3D on the PC is here to stay, and it is only going to get better and faster as time moves on. In early 1995, Microsoft purchased RenderMorphics, Ltd., creators of the Reality Lab 3D API. This is a high-performance 3D library for creating real-time 3D graphics on PC hardware. The Reality Labs API is faster than OpenGL, but its performance comes at the cost of some visual fidelity. In addition, none of OpenGL's special effects and capabilities are present in the Reality Labs API. But it's still perfectly well-suited for PC-based games in which speed is more important than absolute visual realism (for now!).

With the next release of the DirectX libraries, the Reality Labs API will be folded into Direct 3D. There will be two modes of operation for Direct3D: a retained mode, which is the original Reality Labs functionality; and an immediate mode, which is a lower-level API that operates closer to the hardware. The relationship between retained mode and immediate mode is similar to that between Open Inventor and OpenGL. The retained mode is a higher-level interface that simplifies scene creation and object manipulation, and is actually built using the immediate mode API.

The good news for OpenGL developers is that OpenGL will be able to take advantage of Direct 3D drivers that accelerate D3D immediate mode. Thus, the accelerated gaming graphics cards are also going to accelerate OpenGL performance. As PCs get even faster, as the competition among 3D graphics board vendors produces faster accelerators with even more features, the time will come when real-time OpenGL performance will be available on ordinary PCs. This time is approaching, and developers (maybe even you) will need to find other ways to distinguish their 3D products besides brute speed.

OpenGL will be an excellent choice for producing visually stunning effects and more realistic scenes and imagery. As fast 3D becomes a reality, your investment in OpenGL will not go to waste. For the very near term, it's likely that the DirectX API will continue to dominate for fast games and blood-splattering action on Windows. However, OpenGL is simply unchallenged when it comes to realistic cross-platform effects. Currently the hottest markets for OpenGL-based software are the entertainment industry (movie and commercial special effects), scientific and educational modeling, and simulation. In addition, many game developers are discovering that they can use OpenGL to create their title screens, background bitmaps, and textures, and even computer-generated animations (.avi or .mpg files).

Conclusion

When 2D graphics acceleration first became available, it was only for the few "power users" who really needed the extra boost in speed. Today, a Windows accelerated graphics card is standard fare. Games may still be the driving force behind 3D acceleration, but the development community is ready to take advantage of 3D acceleration "as long as it's there."

You can be sure that the size, complexity, and functionality of software will always grow to match or overcome capabilities of hardware. It's hard to imagine that color computers were once difficult to justify. Who remembers when the 386 was hailed as a "high-end" processor intended only for servers and scientific or engineering workstations? They said the same thing about the 486, the Pentium, and now the Pentium Pro. Anyone with a pulse and an IQ over 2 should be able to see a pattern here.

Soon everyday PC graphics cards will support both 3D and 2D acceleration under Windows. Just as color computers evolved from their "games" stereotyping, 3D gaming technology will also evolve into a real and valuable feature that we will learn to take for granted. The difference between hardware-accelerated 3D and software-only 3D is as dramatic as the difference between making music with your PC speaker and having a Sound Blaster. In the same way that sound cards are now becoming as commonplace as color monitors, 3D acceleration will become just another feature bullet on the sides of all those computer boxes in the electronics section of your local discount department store.

PERFORMANCE-TUNING OPENGL FOR WINDOWS

The object of this book is to explain OpenGL from a functional point of view. If you've read the entire book, you've covered the entire breadth of OpenGL from the standpoint of functions and commands. You've also studied some techniques, such as shadows, that don't map directly to a specific function or set of functions. With this information you have a solid foundation to carry you to new heights as you create applications that require 3D rendering.

But "there's more than one way to skin a cat!" Even if you've been programming for only a week, you know this is true—especially of software development. Any given problem can be solved in an almost infinite number of ways. Strategies—from large-scale approaches such as the choice of tools, to smaller details such as the use of specific algorithms—can often vary to wide degrees and still accomplish a given task. Your challenge as an accomplished software developer is to make optimal choices to yield cost-effective and high-performance solutions for your programming issues.

Now that you know how to program using OpenGL, we want to offer some tips and hints for writing the most optimal OpenGL code possible. These tips and hints are general recommendations and can be applied to your programs regardless of the platform you are using.

Display Lists

- Use display lists whenever you will render the same object more than once. Even on a software-only implementation, display lists can significantly improve the performance.

- Try to embed expensive matrix transformations and state changes in display lists—especially texture compositions. This includes the Rotate, Translate, and Scale functions, as well.

- Some systems/graphics boards can take an OpenGL display list directly (for instance, using DMA), so employing display lists will improve CPU→graphics board communication speed. However, operations such as glPushAttrib, glPopAttrib, glCallList, and glCallLists can slow this process down because those parts of the display list generally can't be DMA'd. It might be better to call a series of display lists rather than use nested lists.

Matrix Operations

- Use the native manipulation functions (glRotate, glTranslate, glScale) rather than composing and multiplying your own matrices. These functions are highly optimized, especially if rendering hardware is present.

- Use glLoadIdentity to clear a matrix stack rather than loading your own, for the same reason cited just above.

- Push and pop state variables (glPushAttrib/glPopAttrib), rather than querying and setting individual state variables.

Lighting Operations

- If you don't need smooth shading, use glShadeModel(GL_FLAT) instead.

- Provide your own unit-length normals instead of making OpenGL calculate them for you.

- Avoid using glScale when doing lighting calculations. It's better to scale your object manually before placing it in the scene.

- When possible, use glColorMaterial instead of glMaterial to vary material properties. This is only practical when only one set of material properties is changing.

Object Construction

- Use GL_TRIANGLES whenever possible. It is often faster to draw two or more triangles than it is to draw a single GL_POLYGON. If necessary, GL_QUADS is usually faster than GL_POLYGON and sometimes as fast or faster than GL_TRI-ANGLES in software only implementations.

- Stack similar primitives within a single pair of glBegin/glEnd statements.

- Use the vector form of the vertex and other commands to transfer as much data as possible in as few function calls as possible.

- When drawing or copying images, disable rasterization and per-fragment operations; otherwise, OpenGL will apply textures to pixel images.

- Use the stripped primitives (GL_QUAD_STRIPS, for instance) when tessellating flat surfaces; this drastically reduces the software computations involved in the rendering pipeline.

Miscellaneous Tips

- Do not make redundant mode changes, such as repeatedly setting the same color or enabling a state flag.

- Manually cull your scene. Try not to draw objects that you know will not appear in the scene (such as objects behind you). Do not attempt to test every object for visibility, but structure your code so that it's easy to eliminate some obvious candidates (see the tank simulator in Chapter 7).

- Under Windows, one of the biggest bottlenecks to performance is swapping buffers. When only a small portion of your scene is changing, use the glAddSwapHintRectWIN extension.

- Reduce the details of your drawings for better rendering speed. If you have a hardware accelerator, you can increase the details for better effects. Test for hardware acceleration by calling DescribePixelFormat. In version 1.1 and later, test for the presence of PFD_GENERIC_ACCELERATED in the dwFlags field of the PIXELFORMATDESCRIPTOR structure.

- Use a 16-bit depth buffer unless your application needs the extra precision. Not only does it save memory, but most of the low-end PC accelerators do not support acceleration when a 32-bit depth buffer is used.

B

FURTHER READING

This appendix lists sources of supplementary information on OpenGL programming. The books included here cover OpenGL programming issues specifically. You'll also find a few good books on Windows programming in general, and a couple on advanced 3D graphics programming concepts. In addition, we would be remiss if we neglected to provide you with a few hot Internet sites that are packed with OpenGL programming information, sample codes, and links to other sites of interest.

Books on Windows Programming

Windows 95 Win32 Programming API Bible
Richard J. Simon, with Michael Conker and Brian Barnes
Waite Group Press

Windows 95 Common Controls & Messages API Bible
Richard J. Simon
Waite Group Press

Windows 95 Multimedia & ODBC API Bible
Richard J. Simon
Waite Group Press

Programming Windows
Charles Petzold
Microsoft Press

32-Bit Windows Programming
Ben Ezzell
SAMS

Books and References on OpenGL

The OpenGL Programming Guide
Jackie Neider/OpenGL Architecture Review Board

OpenGL Reference Manual
OpenGL Architecture Review Board
Addison-Wesley

The Inventor Mentor
Josie Wernecke/Open Inventor Architecture Group
Addison-Wesley

The Inventor Toolmaker
Josie Wernecke
Addison-Wesley Publishing Company

3D Graphics Programming with Open GL
Clayton Walnum
QUE

Books and References on Graphics Programming (3D in Particular)

Computer Graphics: Principles and Practice
Foley, van Dam, Feiner, and Hughes
Addison-Wesley

OpenGL-Related Web and FTP Sites

Company	URL
Silicon Graphics	http://www.sgi.com/
Silicon Graphics	ftp://sgigate.sgi.com/
Silicon Graphics/OpenGL WWW Center	http://www.sgi.com/Technology/openGL/
Template Graphics	http://www.cts.com/~template/
Microsoft	http://www.microsoft.com/ntworkstation/opengl.htm
Viewpoint Datalabs	http://www.viewpoint.com/
3D Accelerator Information	http://www.cs.columbia.edu/~bm/3dcards/3d-cards1.html
Mark Kilgard's home page	http://reality.sgi.com/employees/mjk_asd/home.html
Silicon Graphics/Mark Kilgard	http://www.sgi.com/Technology/openGL/glut3.html

VRML Repositories

The VRML Repository	http://www.sdsc.edu/vrml/
Paragraph International	http://vrml.paragraph.com/
Silicon Graphics	http://webspace.sgi.com/Repository/
Vertex International	http://www.vrml.com:80/models/vertex/
The Geometry Center	http://www.geom.umn.edu/~daeron/bin/legitlist.cgi
Ziff-Davis	http://www.zdnet.com/zdi/vrml/
ORC	http://www.ocnus.com/models/models.html

C

OPENGL VERSION 1.1

In December 1995, during the writing of this book, the OpenGL Architecture Review Board ratified and approved version 1.1 of the OpenGL specification. With the release of Windows NT 4.0, Microsoft will become one of the first, if not *the* first vendor to ship a full implementation of the new OpenGL specification for a desktop operating system. In addition to compliance with the new specification, Microsoft has enhanced OpenGL's performance and added a few new features and capabilities, among them the ability to include OpenGL calls in enhanced metafiles, and improved printing support.

Some highlights of OpenGL version 1.1 include the following:

- New Vertex Array features to allow faster transfer of vertex positions, normals, colors and color indexes, texture coordinates, and edge flags.

- Allowing logical operations in RGBA color mode instead of just in color index mode.

- Many new and enhanced texturing features (these are probably the most significant additions).

OpenGL support for Windows 95 will follow within a few months of the shipment of NT 4.0, which isn't due to ship until after the manuscript for this book is finished. So that we could adequately cover the new specs and the Microsoft enhancements, we have included a special directory on the CD. This \OpenGL11 directory contains more complete documentation on the new 1.1 features, plus any new goodies thrown in by Microsoft. Several example programs are also provided.

D

GLOSSARY

Alpha A fourth color value added to provide a degree of transparency to the color of an object. An alpha value of 0.0 would mean complete transparency: 1.0 denotes no transparency (opaque).

Ambient light Light in a scene that doesn't come from any specific point source or direction. Ambient light illuminates all surfaces evenly and on all sides.

Anti-aliasing A rendering method used to smooth lines and curves. This technique averages the color of pixels adjacent to the line. It has the visual effect of softening the transition from the pixels on the line and those adjacent to the line, thus providing a smoother appearance.

Aspect ratio The ratio of the width of a window to the height of the window specifically, the width of the window in pixels divided by the height of the window in pixels.

AUX library A window system, independent utility library. Useful for quick and portable OpenGL demonstration programs.

Bézier curve A curve whose shape is defined by control points near the curve rather than by the precise set of points that define the curve itself.

Bitplane An array of bits mapped directly to screen pixels.

Buffer An area of memory used to store image information. This may be color, depth, or blending information. The red, green, blue, and alpha buffers are often collectively referred to as the *color buffers*.

Cartesian A coordinate system based on three directional axes placed at a 90° orientation to one another. These coordinates are labeled x, y, and z.

Clipping The elimination of a portion of a single primitive or group of primitives. The points that would be rendered outside the clipping region or volume are not drawn. The *clipping volume* is generally specified by the projection matrix.

Color index mode A color mode in which colors in a scene are selected from a fixed number of colors available in a palette. These entries are referenced by an index into the palette.

Convex Refers to the shape of a polygon. A convex polygon has no indentations; and no straight line can be drawn through the polygon that will intersect it more than twice (once entering, once leaving).

Culling Elimination of the front or back face of a primitive so that the face isn't drawn.

Display list A compiled list of OpenGL functions and commands. When called, a display list executes faster than would a manually called list of single commands.

Dithering A method used to simulate a wider range of color depth by placing different-colored pixels together in patterns that give the illusion of shading between the two colors.

Double buffered A drawing technique used by OpenGL. The image to be displayed is assembled in memory and then placed on the screen in a single update operation, as opposed to building the image primitive-by-primitive on the screen. Double buffering is a much faster and smoother update operation and can produce animations.

Extruded The process of taking a 2D image or shape and adding a third dimension uniformly across the surface. This can transform 2D fonts into 3D lettering.

Eye coordinates The coordinate system based on the position of the viewer. The viewer's position is placed along the positive z-axis, looking down the negative z-axis.

Frustum A pyramid-shaped viewing volume that creates a perspective view (near objects are large, far objects are small).

Immediate mode A graphics rendering mode in which commands and functions have an immediate effect on the state of the rendering engine.

Literal A value, not a variable name. A specific string or numeric constant embedded directly in source code.

Matrix A 2D array of numbers. Matrices may be operated on mathematically and are used to perform coordinate transformations.

Modelview matrix The OpenGL matrix that transforms primitives to eye coordinates from object coordinates.

Normal A directional vector that points perpendicularly to a plane or surface. When used, normals must be specified for each vertex in a primitive.

Normalize Refers to the reduction of a normal to a unit normal. A *unit normal* is a vector that has a length of exactly 1.0.

NURBS An acronym for Non-Uniform Rational B-Spline. This is a method of specifying parametric curves and surfaces.

Open Inventor A C++ class library and toolkit for building interactive 3D applications. Open Inventor is built on OpenGL.

Orthographic A drawing mode in which no perspective or foreshortening takes place. Also called *parallel projection,* the lengths and dimensions of all primitives are undistorted regardless of orientation or distance from the viewer.

Palette A set of colors available for drawing operations. For 8-bit Windows color modes, the palette contains 256 color entries, and all pixels in the scene may only be colored from this set.

Parametric curve A curve whose shape is determined by one (for a curve) or two (for a surface) parameters. These parameters are used in separate equations that yield the individual x, y, and z values of the points along the curve.

Perspective A drawing mode in which objects farther from the viewer appear smaller than nearby objects.

Pixel Condensed from the words *picture element.* This is the smallest visual division available on the computer screen. Pixels are arranged in rows and columns and are individually set to the appropriate color to render any given image.

Polygon A 2D shape drawn with any number of sides (must be at least three sides).

Primitive A 2D polygonal shape defined by OpenGL. All objects and scenes are composed of various combinations of primitives.

Projection The transformation of lines, points, and polygons from eye coordinates to clipping coordinates on the screen.

Quadrilateral A polygon with exactly four sides.

Rasterize The process of converting projected primitives and bitmaps into pixel fragments in the framebuffer.

Render The conversion of primitives in object coordinates to an image in the framebuffer. The *rendering pipeline* is the process by which OpenGL commands and statements become pixels on the screen.

Spline A general term used to describe any curve created by placing control points near the curve, which have a pulling effect on the curve's shape. This is similar to the reaction of a piece of flexible material when pressure is applied at various points along its length.

Stipple A binary bit pattern used to mask out pixel generation in the framebuffer. This is similar to a monochrome bitmap, but one-dimensional patterns are used for lines, and two-dimensional patterns are used for polygons.

Tessellation The process of breaking down a complex polygon or analytic surface into a mesh of convex polygons. This can also be applied to separate a complex curve into a series of less complex lines.

Texel Similar to pixel (picture element), a texel is a texture element. A texel represents a color from a texture that will be applied to a pixel fragment in the framebuffer.

Texture An image pattern of colors applied to the surface of a primitive.

Texture mapping The process of applying a texture image to a surface. The surface does not have to be planar (flat). Texture mapping is often used to wrap an image around a curved object or to produce patterned surfaces such as wood or marble.

Transformation The manipulation of a coordinate system. This can include rotation, translation, scaling (both uniform and nonuniform), and perspective division.

Translucence A degree of transparency of an object. In OpenGL, this is represented by an alpha value ranging from 1.0 (opaque) to 0.0 (transparent).

Vertex A single point in space. Except when used for point and line primitives, it also defines the point at which two edges of a polygon meet.

Viewport The area within a window that is used to display an OpenGL image. Usually, this encompasses the entire client area. Stretched viewports can produce enlarged or shrunken output within the physical window.

Viewing volume The area in 3D space that can be viewed in the window. Objects and points outside the viewing volume will be clipped (cannot be seen).

Wireframe The representation of a solid object by a mesh of lines rather than solid shaded polygons. Wireframe models are usually rendered faster and can be used to view both the front and back of an object at the same time.

INDEX

Books have a substantial influence on the destruction of the forests of the Earth. For example, it takes 17 trees to produce one ton of paper. A first printing of 30,000 copies of a typical 480-page book consumes 108,000 pounds of paper, which will require 918 trees!

Waite Group Press™ is against the clear-cutting of forests and supports reforestation of the Pacific Northwest of the United States and Canada, where most of this paper comes from. As a publisher with several hundred thousand books sold each year, we feel an obligation to give back to the planet. We will therefore support organizations that seek to preserve the forests of planet Earth.

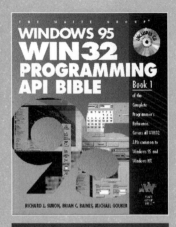

This is a legal agreement between you, the end user and purchaser, and The Waite Group®, Inc., and the authors of the programs contained in the disk. By opening the sealed disk package, you are agreeing to be bound by the terms of this Agreement. If you do not agree with the terms of this Agreement, promptly return the unopened disk package and the accompanying items (including the related book and other written material) to the place you obtained them for a refund.

SOFTWARE LICENSE

1. The Waite Group, Inc. grants you the right to use one copy of the enclosed software programs (the programs) on a single computer system (whether a single CPU, part of a licensed network, or a terminal connected to a single CPU). Each concurrent user of the program must have exclusive use of the related Waite Group, Inc. written materials.

2. The program, including the copyrights in each program, is owned by the respective author and the copyright in the entire work is owned by The Waite Group, Inc. and they are therefore protected under the copyright laws of the United States and other nations, under international treaties. You may make only one copy of the disk containing the programs exclusively for backup or archival purposes, or you may transfer the programs to one hard disk drive, using the original for backup or archival purposes. You may make no other copies of the programs, and you may make no copies of all or any part of the related Waite Group, Inc. written materials.

3. You may not rent or lease the programs, but you may transfer ownership of the programs and related written materials (including any and all updates and earlier versions) if you keep no copies of either, and if you make sure the transferee agrees to the terms of this license.

4. You may not decompile, reverse engineer, disassemble, copy, create a derivative work, or otherwise use the programs except as stated in this Agreement.

GOVERNING LAW

This Agreement is governed by the laws of the State of California.

LIMITED WARRANTY

The following warranties shall be effective for 90 days from the date of purchase: (i) The Waite Group, Inc. warrants the enclosed disk to be free of defects in materials and workmanship under normal use; and (ii) The Waite Group, Inc. warrants that the programs, unless modified by the purchaser, will substantially perform the functions described in the documentation provided by The Waite Group, Inc. when operated on the designated hardware and operating system. The Waite Group, Inc. does not warrant that the programs will meet purchaser's requirements or that operation of a program will be uninterrupted or error-free. The program warranty does not cover any program that has been altered or changed in any way by anyone other than The Waite Group, Inc. The Waite Group, Inc. is not responsible for problems caused by changes in the operating characteristics of computer hardware or computer operating systems that are made after the release of the programs, nor for problems in the interaction of the programs with each other or other software.

THESE WARRANTIES ARE EXCLUSIVE AND IN LIEU OF ALL OTHER WARRANTIES OF MERCHANTABILITY OR FITNESS FOR A PARTICULAR PURPOSE OR OF ANY OTHER WARRANTY, WHETHER EXPRESS OR IMPLIED.

EXCLUSIVE REMEDY

The Waite Group, Inc. will replace any defective disk without charge if the defective disk is returned to The Waite Group, Inc. within 90 days from date of purchase.

This is Purchaser's sole and exclusive remedy for any breach of warranty or claim for contract, tort, or damages.

LIMITATION OF LIABILITY

THE WAITE GROUP, INC. AND THE AUTHORS OF THE PROGRAMS SHALL NOT IN ANY CASE BE LIABLE FOR SPECIAL, INCIDENTAL, CONSEQUENTIAL, INDIRECT, OR OTHER SIMILAR DAMAGES ARISING FROM ANY BREACH OF THESE WARRANTIES EVEN IF THE WAITE GROUP, INC. OR ITS AGENT HAS BEEN ADVISED OF THE POSSIBILITY OF SUCH DAMAGES.

THE LIABILITY FOR DAMAGES OF THE WAITE GROUP, INC. AND THE AUTHORS OF THE PROGRAMS UNDER THIS AGREEMENT SHALL IN NO EVENT EXCEED THE PURCHASE PRICE PAID.

COMPLETE AGREEMENT

This Agreement constitutes the complete agreement between The Waite Group, Inc. and the authors of the programs, and you, the purchaser.

Some states do not allow the exclusion or limitation of implied warranties or liability for incidental or consequential damages, so the above exclusions or limitations may not apply to you. This limited warranty gives you specific legal rights; you may have others, which vary from state to state.

SATISFACTION REPORT CARD

Please fill out this card if you wish to know of future updates to *OpenGL SuperBible,* or to receive our catalog.

First Name: _____   **Last Name:** _____

Street Address: _____

City: _____   **State:** _____   **Zip:** _____

E-mail Address _____

Daytime Telephone: (_____) _____

Date product was acquired: Month _____ **Day** _____ **Year** _____ **Your Occupation:** _____

Overall, how would you rate *OpenGL SuperBible*?

☐ Excellent ☐ Very Good ☐ Good
☐ Fair ☐ Below Average ☐ Poor

What did you like MOST about this book? _____
_____
_____

What did you like LEAST about this book? _____
_____
_____

Please describe any problems you may have encountered with installing or using the disk: _____
_____

How did you use this book (problem-solver, tutorial, reference...)?
_____

What is your level of computer expertise?
☐ New ☐ Dabbler ☐ Hacker
☐ Power User ☐ Programmer ☐ Experienced Professional

What computer languages are you familiar with? _____
_____

Please describe your computer hardware:

Computer _____ Hard disk _____

5.25" disk drives _____ 3.5" disk drives _____

Video card _____ Monitor _____

Printer _____ Peripherals _____

Sound Board _____ CD ROM _____

Where did you buy this book?

☐ Bookstore (name): _____
☐ Discount store (name): _____
☐ Computer store (name): _____
☐ Catalog (name): _____
☐ Direct from WGP ☐ Other _____

What price did you pay for this book? _____

What influenced your purchase of this book?

☐ Recommendation ☐ Advertisement
☐ Magazine review ☐ Store display
☐ Mailing ☐ Book's format
☐ Reputation of Waite Group Press ☐ Other

How many computer books do you buy each year? _____

How many other Waite Group books do you own? _____

What is your favorite Waite Group book? _____
_____

Is there any program or subject you would like to see Waite Group Press cover in a similar approach? _____
_____

Additional comments? _____
_____
_____

Please send to: **Waite Group Press**
200 Tamal Plaza
Corte Madera, CA 94925

☐ **Check here for a free Waite Group catalog**

DATE DUE

BEFORE YOU OPEN THE DISK OR CD-ROM PACKAGE ON THE FACING PAGE, CAREFULLY READ THE LICENSE AGREEMENT.

Opening this package indicates that you agree to abide by the license agreement found in the back of this book. If you do not agree with it, promptly return the unopened disk package (including the related book) to the place you obtained them for a refund.